DATE DUE

DEMCO, INC. 38-2931

D1206936

First Sight

First Sight

ESP and Parapsychology in Everyday Life

James C. Carpenter

ROWMAN & LITTLEFIELD PUBLISHERS, INC.
Lanham • *Boulder* • *New York* • *Toronto* • *Plymouth, UK*

Every attempt was made to obtain permission from the publisher for the Rumi
quote as translated by Coleman Barks.

Published by Rowman & Littlefield Publishers, Inc.
A wholly owned subsidiary of The Rowman & Littlefield Publishing Group, Inc.
4501 Forbes Boulevard, Suite 200, Lanham, Maryland 20706
http://www.rowmanlittlefield.com

10 Thornbury, Plymouth PL6 7PP, United Kingdom

British Library Cataloguing in Publication Information Available

Library of Congress Cataloging-in-Publication Data

Carpenter, James (James C.)
  First sight : ESP and parapsychology in everyday life / James Carpenter.
      p. cm.
  Includes bibliographical references.
  ISBN 978-1-4422-1390-6 (cloth : alk. paper) — ISBN 978-1-4422-1392-0 (ebook)
  1. Extrasensory perception. 2. Parapsychology. I. Title.
  BF1321.C28 2012
  133.8—dc23

                                                                          2011034788

∞™ The paper used in this publication meets the minimum requirements of
American National Standard for Information Sciences—Permanence of Paper
for Printed Library Materials, ANSI/NISO Z39.48-1992.

Printed in the United States of America

To Jo

Contents

Contents

Preface

I was sent to college by *Sputnik*. That little, chirping ball had so alarmed Congress in 1957 that the next year it passed legislation that would pay the way to good colleges for thousands of bright kids. The aim was to build up our lagging corps of scientists and engineers to help win the Cold War. It also sent one boy from a small town in New Mexico to Duke to study extrasensory perception (ESP).

Not to say that I wasn't interested in outer space. Thanks to Ray Bradbury I knew well before *Sputnik* that it wouldn't be long before humans were exploring there. At eighteen in 1959, I thought I might become an engineer and help do that. But rockets weren't the only things that were bursting human possibilities wide open, it seemed to me. I had absorbed a couple of books by J. B. Rhine and his Duke colleagues about research that seemed to demonstrate mysterious and unknown capacities of the mind. The Soviets had sent up a spaceship, and Rhine's Hubert Pearce had somehow seen cards that were being laid out in a different building hundreds of yards away. All about equally amazing.

I had done a few little experiments of my own in a high-school kind of way, and I had gotten some results with a couple of kids that seemed surprisingly good. So, if not riding a rocket, I thought, I might plunge into the study of the mind's hidden places. If anybody asked then what I thought I might do later, I would say either outer space or inner space.

My mother, who had a number of curious experiences that seemed to be psychic, prepared me for my interest in inner space. I have vague, very early memories of going with her to some "séances" when my family lived in El Paso. I remember the lights were on, and a group of grown-ups sat in a circle and one woman did most of the talking. Kind of boring. But my mother's personal experiences were something else. Once when my dad was out of work and she was feeling pretty desperate, she collapsed in a chair and closed her eyes and proceeded to have a vivid vision (hallucination, I suppose we would say) of a kindly man who looked rather like Santa Claus in a business suit. He told her that the family would be all right. We would be moving to a town that was two towns divided by a river that had no water. And saying that nonsense (that somehow felt deeply reassuring to my mother), he vanished. She told the story to my dad, who had learned to take such things seriously with her. Then they both forgot about it, until some months later, after my dad had found a good job in Las Vegas, New Mexico, a place that neither of them had heard of before.

After moving there they discovered that the town's unique history (part Mexican Empire, part Anglo railroad town) had led it still to be two separate little municipalities, with their own school systems, town governments, etc. What separated them? The Gallinas River, almost always bone dry. There were other stories, too. She sometimes knew when something had happened to a family member back in East Texas. And there was no watch that she didn't mysteriously stop within a week. You get the idea.

Even at eighteen on the outskirts of civilization in a small town in northern New Mexico, I knew that parapsychology was controversial. But I had no idea just how controversial, and what deep fires of passion drive that controversy. It has taken many years to really grasp the force of that.

After I arrived at Duke, I met my roommate and found out how to find the dining halls and learned where the coeds lived, and then found my way to the parapsychology lab, where I quickly managed to meet Rhine himself. He was a white-haired, big bear of a man, with a gentle, thoughtful voice, and he seemed friendly enough about my arrival. Thus I began an adventure that I am still enjoying.

What to make of his work? I knew that many authorities asserted that his research was nonsense. However, many authorities also insisted that it was eternally correct that people of color should use separate public facilities and attend separate schools from those of whites. The South then was still in the grip of segregation. I was delighted later that first year to begin my participation in protesting that with sit-ins and picketing. I knew that authority shouldn't always be respected.

But I did respect truth and learning and science. My first textbook in psychology began with an introductory chapter that spelled out in the firmest way what the field was and wasn't. That behaviorist tome said that scientific clarity was paramount (I could buy that), but then it added that just about everything I was really interested in was outside the pale. No philosophical questions about human nature, no psychoanalytic theory, no mental health and illness—and especially and very definitely—no clairvoyance or mind reading or future telling or other aspects of the "paranormal." The paranormal probably didn't exist, I read, and even if it did it would be forever outside of psychology.

Why the big deal? Whatever it was, it was why Rhine's lab was not in the psychology department.

I was certainly not a True Believer in the occult, whatever that was. I was curious about Rhine's work, but also skeptical. As I spent more time with them, I came to know him and his colleagues as very earnest and self-critical people. But my psychology professors, with their hot-button hostility to parapsychology, also seemed like reasonable, serious people. Was there some fatal flaw in Rhine's work that just hadn't been quite pinned down? I searched for it. So much of the evidence was statistical. Was there a problem there? It's possible that I was not the most mathematically precocious student in my statistics courses, but I'm sure I cared the most. I needed to know how statistics worked, how they could be used to separate the true from the false. I couldn't find the problem there, and I learned that many eminent mathematicians could not either.

As it was being roundly dismissed by some, the parapsychological work was continuing on. It had spread beyond Duke to laboratories far and wide. Rhine's books had been very popular, the laboratory was famous around the world, and many other scientists took up the questions. Besides card reading at a distance, there was also mentally affecting the roll of dice (psychokinesis) and predicting the orders of decks of cards before they were shuffled (precognition). All these things were thought by then to represent some underlying process, denoted by the neutral Greek letter Ψ (psi). Much of the research was correlational by then, with psychological variables such as the belief that ESP was possible and emotional adjustment (both of which appeared to help people express it better). Many other laboratories reported confirming evidence. Some others didn't.

Meanwhile, I met more famous and unusual people hanging around the parapsychology lab than anywhere else at Duke. Where else could I rub shoulders with Burl Ives, share lunch with Arthur Koestler, chat with the president of Mexico, and then take the actor currently playing Tarzan for a beer at my favorite tavern? A stream of such personages stopped by as if to Mecca. They believed there was something important to it.

By the time I left Duke I had formed deep and lasting friendships with a handful of other people more or less my age who had come there to study, mostly during summers. Many went on to make their own research contributions: Rex Stanford, Chuck Honorton, Bob Morris, Dave Rogers, B. K. Kanthamani, John Palmer. I had already seen enough significant results clacked out of the mechanical calculators to know the thrill of finding new evidence for something astonishing, and I added a few results of my own.

While my fascination and respect deepened, I couldn't shake a certain confusion. There is an affront to common sense in parapsychology. So people sometimes know things at a distance or succeed in predicting something they have no way of knowing about or produce significant deviations from chance in the rolls of dice just by thinking 6 or 5 or 2. Suppose some of that is correlated with test scores on something or other.

What does that mean? Could I see around corners? I could not. Could I make things happen just by wishing? Not generally. Step out of the lab and open your eyes! Magic is for magic shows and children who haven't learned better. Isn't it?

What kind of ability is it that is only furtively present but generally absent? If something can only be seen when it is fished out of a tub of numbers with a statistical net, how real is it? I was just not as certain as the rest of my band of friends, such as Honorton and Stanford, who were heading straight for the further training and experience that would begin their careers in parapsychology. Instead, after Duke I went to Ohio State for graduate study in clinical psychology. My first year there I conducted a couple of successful ESP studies with conscripted OSU students and debated my history of psychology professor in a public forum on parapsychology (all my friends thought I certainly won—I knew lots more facts); but the background uncertainty wouldn't disappear. On one late-night trip on the West Virginia Turnpike to visit the woman who would become my wife, I set a long-term resolve. I would try very hard to learn whether or not the stuff of parapsychology (psi) is real, and if it is, how it works. This book is the outcome of that resolve.

Section I

A POINT OF VIEW

INTRODUCTION

First Sight is a model and a set of theoretical ideas about psi: the collection of controversial phenomena that are studied by parapsychologists. These phenomena primarily involve knowing things and affecting things in ways that go beyond the immediate boundaries of the organism.

Perhaps you know something of these matters from your own experience. Perhaps you remember a dream in which you seemed to have been alerted in an unusually accurate way to something that developed in your life later, well after the moments of dreaming. Perhaps you and a loved one sometimes anticipate each other's thoughts or know when each other will call on the phone or punch "send" with an e-mail. Or you may know of someone who has told you stories like the following. They happen in my life at times, and I encounter them not infrequently in my practice of psychotherapy. A couple of examples:

A few years ago, a ten-year-old girl I knew woke up screaming from a terrible dream. She and many of her friends were in a large, glassy mall. Suddenly, a huge passenger plane crashed into the roof and blew the building apart. The floor opened up, and they were beginning to tumble down into blackness just as a second plane crashed in. Her parents calmed her, but she stayed unusually shaken for a while. They reminded her that dreams are not real and that airplanes are very safe and stay up in the air where they belong. She went on to school. It was September 11, 2001. A couple of days later the girl's father called me, asking for psychological advice. His daughter was now flooded with anxiety, afraid to go to school where she

1

had learned about the attacks of 9-11, and afraid to go to sleep. She was alarmed and didn't know what to trust. "Damned dreams," her father said.

An acquaintance of mine, a successful software engineer, recently thought he would try his hand at being a "medium." I sat in a group in which a certain woman he did not know intended to test him out. She was interested in any information she might get about her deceased mother, but for the sake of good controls, she gave no information at all about herself or her family. He sat quietly for a moment, and then a distressed look came over his face.

"It's your mother," he said, "and I'm hearing one main thing but I hate to say it." After a little hesitation he went over to her in order to not embarrass her, and I could hear him whisper, "She killed herself. She's very sorry."

In fact, the mother had died that way, when her daughter was a girl, and when this was made known to everyone the group was stunned. Had a dead woman left her quiet grave and spoken secrets and feelings to a living man?

I could list many similar experiences I have had myself and heard about from people I trust. They are not every day for most people, but they are not that uncommon either, if you have an eye out for them. What can we make of these experiences in which the ordinary boundaries of reality are split apart and we are suddenly informed and affected by things that have no right to reach us? We can try to write them off, but a great deal of research on such experiences (telepathy, clairvoyance, precognition) strongly argues that they are real. We usually forget them because we don't know what else to do. They are unpredictable and strange. They are psychological lightning bolts.

Consider physical lightning bolts. For thousands of years they were just about all that people knew about electricity. They were unpredictable, awesome, terrifying, and beautiful. The ancients thought that when they erupted, the dormant sky had become suddenly and fiercely alive. Now we understand that lightning is one expression of electricity, and electricity is actually everywhere. Electric charge is a basic constituent of every atom. It helps make up the stuff of our bodies; it connects each bit of the synaptic chain. It tells your heart when to beat. As we came to understand electricity, we mastered it. Now you hold a domesticated lightning bolt in your hand when you use your cell phone. In a few moments you can use it to speak to someone in Beijing or Adelaide or Buenos Aires. The awesome anomaly is not anomalous at all, and we have tamed it.

The lightning bolts that we call paranormal experiences are also surprising and beautiful and disturbing. They shake the ground of solid reality. They seem different and anomalous. According to First Sight theory, they are not really anomalous either.

This book is about a radically new way of thinking about these things. It presents a revolutionary understanding of how each of us fits within the world and how we are put together within ourselves. A lot of evidence suggests that the theory is true. In light of this, much of what we normally assume will need to be changed.

First Sight theory proposes that, like electricity, psychic experience is actually going on all the time. Also like electricity, *it is almost always out of sight in its functioning*. Occasionally, it will be expressed in obvious ways, like lightning bolts, but normally it is unconscious. What is it for? According to the theory, it is the leading edge of the unconscious processes that the mind uses to construct all its experience and all its behavior. Because it traffics with things that have not reached the physical senses, it is our first line of engagement with the world, our first outpost of information. This is why the theory reconstrues what has been called second sight and calls it First Sight.

"Why the odd language?" you might ask. "Why talk about *constructing* experience and behavior? Isn't experience whatever simply occurs to us? Isn't my behavior just whatever I choose to do?"

CONSCIOUSNESS BEGINS UNCONSCIOUSLY

Scientific research now tells us that this is not as simple as we might think. We now know that there are preconscious processes that come before every bit of experience, every thought and feeling and decision. At a physiological level, brain activities precede conscious experience and lead to it. At a psychological level, past experience and subliminal perceptions and goals also precede conscious experience and lead to it. Our thoughts and actions don't come simply from ourselves, as we know ourselves consciously. They still come from us, and not anybody else, because they issue from our nervous systems and are structured by our unconscious memories and our nonconscious perceptions and our motivations. But consciousness begins unconsciously. According to First Sight theory, it also begins beyond the limits of our sensory systems, with apprehensions that are too far away or too hidden to be sensed and apprehensions of things that have not even happened yet.

It is hard to imagine any other way to really make sense of the lightning bolts of paranormal experience—and of all the scientific findings of parapsychology.

Parapsychologists have taken the paranormal lightning bolts into the laboratory where they can be studied in controlled conditions. They study the ability of people (and sometimes animals) to get information that is outside of sensory reach or that still lays in the future and the ability to affect physical events without touching them. This cluster of abilities is called psi, and psi is the subject matter of parapsychology. Although most people don't know much about it, this research has been going on in serious, reputable laboratories for over a century. Over thousands of studies, parapsychologists have accumulated solid evidence that these phenomena do occur. They have not always been easy to predict, but they are real.

The field has always aroused controversy, but skeptics who take the trouble to look deeply into the research tend to come away surprised at how solid and challenging it is. They scratch their heads and say, "There's something there but I don't know what it is." First Sight theory says what it is and how it fits in with the rest of our psychological functioning.

People are accustomed to the idea of psychic experiences, and according to surveys, a majority of people believe that they have had at least one themselves. However, experiences that seem shocking and anomalous are surprisingly easy to forget. They lack normal context, and we lose them. After a vivid paranormal experience one tends first to be surprised and moved, but then a sense of distance and unreality sets in. With nowhere to put it, no pocket to keep it in, we begin to wonder if we had been mistaken. The same is true of shocking anomalies that issue from the laboratory. When J. B. Rhine first announced his remarkable parapsychological findings in the 1930s and 1940s, a huge public and scientific response followed. But this has largely faded from public view. Not because the work was faulty—it was actually well done in terms of the best methods of the day, and led to more and better work. The anomalies didn't go away. But they remained anomalies, and anomalies that are never made meaningful slip away from consciousness.

The mind seems naturally to protect itself in this way from too much strangeness. Shakespeare understood this. After the wondrous experiences in *A Midsummer Night's Dream*, Demetrius, reflecting back, says to Helena: "These things seem small and indistinguishable / Like far-off mountains turned into clouds."

The point of view in this book removes the strangeness from parapsychology and makes it easier to think about. First Sight theory is revolutionary because, looked at through its lenses, the findings of parapsychology are not anomalous; they are meaningfully connected with all that we know about ourselves. As the book argues in detail, we can see that psi functions smoothly among all of our other mental functions—our memory, our perception, our motivation, and our creativity.

The theory is revolutionary because of what it says about the nature of consciousness: It is made partly (continuously, unconsciously) of psi.

And finally, First Sight is revolutionary because of what it implies about the eventual application of psi. This book is not a manual promising to make anyone psychic (although it should help one make more conscious use of ongoing psychic experience). It is more substantial than that. It presents a theory in terms of which we can come to construct a real understanding of psi. As with electricity, from understanding will follow application. One chapter in the book sketches some directions that this development may take.

This book will not summarize parapsychology, nor attempt to defend it from its critics. Several others have done these things.[1] While this book will not be a broad overview of this field of academic, scientific work, it will attempt to cover a sizable piece of the accumulated literature in order to assess how well the findings fit in with the theory that this book develops. In the process, two criticisms that are sometimes aimed at parapsychology *will* be addressed: the paucity of adequate theory and the alleged failure of experimental results to show meaningful consistency.

Many writers have cited the need for adequate theory in parapsychology in order to better explain accumulated findings, guide future work, and conceptually integrate parapsychology with other areas of mainstream science.[2] Others, such as Hyman (2010), have complained that parapsychological findings are "consistently inconsistent." This book offers a theory. And with the help of this theory it is easier to see that the findings of parapsychology are far more consistent and meaningful than is usually appreciated.

Besides offering an integration of parapsychology with other scientific work, there is another integration that is sorely needed: this is an integration of the "miraculous" parapsychological findings and our everyday life experiences in which such miracles very rarely seem to occur. The book offers a way to understand this discrepancy, too.

This discussion will focus primarily upon the results of formal experiments and much less upon the spontaneous experiences that people report. This does not imply that such informal experiences are meaningless or unimportant. To the contrary, they are the reason the scientific work has come to exist at all.[3] The problem with informal reports of spontaneous experiences (of accurate premonitions, or apparent thought transferences, or spiritual healings, or bizarre "poltergeist" disturbances, for example) is that each of them is a single anecdote, drawn out of uncontrolled situations. It is subject to the vagaries of informal observation and memory and impossible to evaluate against the possibility of coincidence. Even wildly improbable events can and sometimes do occur simply by chance. In a scientific experiment we can control variables, limit and standardize situations, take careful and reliably objective measurements, and evaluate results against the hypothesis of chance. The results of experiments can be additive, because the variables can be similar, the situations can be repeated, and the statistical results can be accumulated. Lashed to the mast of scientific method, we can avoid deceiving ourselves. As the social philosopher John Locke said, "Science is the great antidote to the poison of enthusiasm and superstition."

The reality of psi is a legitimate scientific question, and it is well debated in many other books and articles.[4] It will not be redebated here. This model is not intended to be proof of the reality of psi. It tentatively presumes that reality, and offers ways of thinking about psi that make it more sensible and more potentially congruent with the rest of our understanding of human nature. It is intended for those who think that the hypothesis of the reality of psi is worth consideration. If psi exists, how might it work?

It might go without saying that the theoretical ideas developed in this book did not arise out of thin air: some of their more important antecedents will be discussed in chapter 6.

A RADICAL DEPARTURE

The position developed here offers challenges to important assumptions that are held implicitly by scientists inside and outside of parapsychology and requires a central shift in perspective about these problems. These may not be readily apparent, but they can be made clearer by articulating just what these assumptions are and how this point of view departs from them.

First Sight is revolutionary because it turns so many things on their heads. Are you a being contained within your skin and confined to the present moment of experience? First Sight says that you are not. Are the paranormal lightning bolts and the parapsychological findings odd anomalies that don't fit in with normal experience? First Sight says that they are not, they are only a handful of visible expressions of processes that are going on all the time and that we unconsciously use with exquisite efficiency. Are we ultimately alone within our spheres of personal experience, with no real bridge to others? First Sight says that we are intimately entwined with others, and we swim in that unconscious sea each moment of our lives. Do your thoughts and feelings express only what you know about and remember? First Sight says they often show traces of things that haven't even happened yet. Does this make the world bizarre and disorienting? We have all been living with it comfortably from the moment of birth.

Outside of parapsychology, the mind and all psychobiological functioning are generally presumed to be primarily skin bound. Information is understood to arrive at an organism by way of the causal impingements of physical stimuli. Action is presumed to begin when skin touches object or when expressed ideas physically reach other nervous systems. These presumptions will be challenged and an alternative conception offered.

Within parapsychology, psi has been generally assumed to be an *ability*, sporadically active, that can sometimes be called into action by a challenge (as in a laboratory demonstration) or a need. After the moment of demonstration, the anomalous ability goes away. First Sight theory offers a very different conception.

PSI AND EXPERIENCE

Psi is essential to the construction of experience. Extrasensory perception is the leading edge of the mind's ability to move to the next experience. Psychokinesis is the leading edge of the mind's ability to move the next effect to its intention. These psi processes are continuously active but normally unconscious and implicit. Therefore, psi is the initial stage of the incipience of experience. This implies that all experience and the actualization of all intention begin at the psi level of functioning. Psi is not "second sight" but "first sight."

Psi is often thought of as anomalous and hidden. According to First Sight theory, if psi is hidden, it is hidden in plain sight and everywhere. What is the most ubiquitously present thing for every person? More frequently experienced than home, or work, or family? It is one's own thoughts. They are always present as long as one is conscious. Psi is hidden within each thought.

MODEL AND THEORY

The book presents both a *model* and a *theory*. By *model*, it is meant a kind of analogy. Scientific work is sometimes advanced by carrying an idea across from one area to another. An important aspect of this model can be summarized in the question: "What if extrasensory perception is like subliminal perception?"[5] Perhaps it is a ubiquitous, unconscious constituent in all experience. What would follow from imagining that? The central ideas of the model are given as two postulates.

A *theory* is an assertion about how things work. This theory is about how psi functions unconsciously, when and how it contributes to our experience and behavior.

The model and theory are specifically aimed at improving our understanding of psi and psi research. Some general premises about how best to understand the mind are included to make the whole thing sensible.

First Sight is not an attempt at an entire theory of personality. However, for those who might wish to try to understand its implications for that, it is probably best to think of it as fitting comfortably within, and extending, theories of personality that have an existential and phenomenological bent—theories that emphasize the personal reality of an individual self pursuing a personal life in relationship with other selves who are doing the same thing. It is especially congruent with perspectives that were developed in an earlier generation by Henry Murray (1938) and Andras Angyal (1941), and more recently by such theorists as George Kelly (1955), who spelled out how each person develops and lives out of a personal system of constructs about reality; Harold McCurdy (1965), who emphasized the reality of the personal world; and Seymour Epstein (1990), with his integrated understanding of the cognitive and experiential sides of persons. I will say more about Kelly and McCurdy in chapter 8.

Chapter 2 offers a summary statement of the major ideas involved in the First Sight model and theory of psi and the mind. There are two *Basic Postulates* in the model. Thirteen *Corollaries* elaborate these postulates and constitute the central ideas of the theory. Each corollary is named in a way that expresses the gist of the idea. Several of the corollaries can easily be elaborated further into operational language and testable hypotheses. Some of these hypotheses have already proven useful in helping to understand large amounts of published parapsychological findings.[6]

By way of introduction, we can say that we propose that organisms exist and transact continually in an extended, nonlocal universe, that the mind thinks unconsciously about all of these transactions along with other unconscious transactions, that this unconscious thinking produces consciousness and other goal-directed experience, that all such thought serves the need to predict and control a personal future, and that empirical elucidation of the rules of unconscious thinking must include an articulation of the patterns governing psi processes.

While I assume that at least many nonhuman organisms as well as humans can be characterized in these terms, I will focus primarily on human beings in this discussion.

PSI AND SCIENTIFIC PSYCHOLOGY

While the metatheoretical perspective of this point of view departs from that commonly assumed more than one might expect, the facts of parapsychology do not differ from those of general experimental psychology as much as many would expect.

This is a central thesis of this book, and it will be developed throughout. Many of the core findings of parapsychology will be discussed, but along with them I will also refer to considerable work in contemporary "normal" psychology. Research in cognitive psychology, social psychology, personality psychology, neuropsychology, and clinical psychology will all be drawn upon. We will see that this research helps us understand the findings of parapsychology. We will also see that comparing them makes it clear that parapsychology belongs to general psychology. It fits within it. It adds to it in very important ways. They should grow on from here together. The point of view in this book was developed in part to facilitate that incorporation and growth.

This book builds bridges: between psychology and parapsychology, between common sense and miracles, and between today's science of the mind and a larger science that must be created. It will help us to build still another bridge: one spanning the distance between what we now believe ourselves to be and much more that we unconsciously are and can consciously become.

NOTES

1. Broughton, 1991; Carter, 2007; Edge, Morris, Palmer, and Rush, 1986; Krippner and Friedman, 2010; Radin, 2009.

2. Carter, 2007; Flew, 1989; Hyman, 1996; Morris, 2000; Schouten, 2002; Schmeidler, 1988; Smythies, 2000.

3. There are current and competent sources in which one can find many examples of such natural, extralaboratory reports. For experiences implying direct knowledge of future events, see *The Power of Premonitions* by Larry Dossey (2009). For remarkable tales of acquiring knowledge of things so distant or hidden as to be inaccessible to the senses, see *The Stargate Chronicles* by the "remote viewer" Joe McMoneagle (2002), or for the similar stories of less celebrated persons, *The Gift*, by Sally Rhine Feather and Michael Schmicker (2005). A good history of events implying the direct action of intention upon physical events can be found in Pamela Heath's *The PK Zone* (2003). A spirited overview of these and other related kinds of "paranormal" experiences can be found in *A New Science of the Paranormal* by Lawrence LeShan (2009).

4. Carter, 2007; Krippner and Friedman, 2010.

5. The reader may be unfamiliar with the term *subliminal perception* (also referred to as perception without awareness, unconscious perception, and suboptimal perception). It refers to the fact that stimuli that are too brief or faint or unattended to be consciously perceived may still be seen to have an effect on subsequent cognitive and affective behaviors. Although quite controversial for a time, the phenomenon is so widely accepted by most psychologists today that it is used as a technique for testing many other ideas about cognitive/affective functioning (Greenwald, 1992).

6. Carpenter, 2004, 2005b, 2008.

1

A New Conception Guided by Two Analogies

Thus, the task is, not so much to see what no one has yet seen; but to think what nobody has yet thought, about that which everybody sees.

—Erwin Schrödinger

First Sight offers a new understanding of what psi is. It proposes that psi is a primary aspect of an organism's engagement with an extended universe of meaning that is carried out perpetually and almost entirely unconsciously. In the most basic terms, psi is the direct, unconscious expression of unconscious intention as it is engaged with things that are outside the sensory boundaries of the organism. If the expression is an effect upon the organism's own experience and behavior, and parts of reality distant from the organism are consulted in the process, we speak of this as *extrasensory perception*: the receptive or afferent side of psi. If the expression is an effect upon parts of reality outside the ordinary sensory boundaries of the organism, and no ordinary physical action upon those things is involved, we call it *psychokinesis*, the active or efferent psi domain. I will suggest some modified terms for these things in chapter 6.

The First Sight model is based upon a pair of related analogies. They can be expressed in the form of questions. What if ESP is like subliminal perception? What if psychokinesis is like unconsciously but psychologically meaningful expressive behaviors? These two things can be seen to imply each other. Subliminal perception (and ESP) can only be discerned by the inadvertent but meaningful behavior that it evokes. Inadvertent behavior can only be seen to be psychologically meaningful by virtue of the unconscious events (subliminal or extrasensory) that have evoked them. We will take these two guiding questions in turn.

11

ESP AND SUBLIMINAL PERCEPTION

Most people think of subliminal perception as a freakish and somewhat frightening way to manipulate people. First published in 1957, Vance Packard's book *The Hidden Persuaders* created a firestorm of interest in this sort of manipulation, and it has since gone through nine more editions.[1] However, in its common, moment-by-moment function, subliminal perception is actually a useful part of the history of every sensory perception.

Turn and look at something, anything. Perhaps you see a certain book on a shelf. Your eye moved to it, and you saw it. However, just before you formed a conscious perception of the book there was a very brief time, a few hundredths of a second, when photons bouncing off the book reached your nervous system before you became conscious of it. These preconscious photons also contributed to your visual experience, even though they were unconscious and you had no awareness of them. Why do we believe this? Because of experiments on subliminal perception. In such an experiment, the researcher controls the flow of light that reaches the retina and interrupts it by some sort of shield after that split second and before you are able to form an experience. Participants staring at a screen in such studies are aware only of a brief flicker of light, and perhaps not even that. No book.

And yet, these preconscious flickers have effects. Psychologists call them primes, because they facilitate the development of particular kinds of responses. If these flickers are of something emotionally disturbing or something happy, you will find yourself a few minutes down the road feeling a little more upset or happy, depending. Suppose the flicker is a picture of one person hitting another. You are not conscious of having seen anything, but if the experimenter then asks you to associate to the spoken word *beat* (or *beet*), you are more likely to think of a blow than a vegetable. This very early stage of a perception primes you to feel or think or understand in particular directions that are appropriate for the experience that is about to form.

This shows that even before you have had time to have any conscious awareness of anything, you are already beginning to respond to what you will become aware of shortly. Like a grossly detailed map, it does not show you the house you are headed for, but it directs you to the neighborhood. What is this good for? Surely it speeds up your ability to recognize what you are about to see and respond to the situation in an apt way. From an evolutionary angle, this extra speed could sometimes have important advantages. It probably helped some of your ancestors reach childbearing age and make your existence possible. It is true enough that advertisers can try to sway our purchases or our votes in certain directions using such preconscious primes, but in the common way we all use them, they are ubiquitous and helpful.

This whole subject of subliminal perception is so central to the First Sight model that it will be discussed further later on, in chapters 4 and 9.

For many decades the reality of subliminal perception was hotly debated among psychologists. The controversy was almost as heated as the controversy over parapsychology, and for some of the same reasons. It seems an insult to common sense to think that something so brief or faint that it is not consciously experienced can act as if it were a kind of experience by arousing meaningfully related responses. Much research was occupied with trying to demonstrate that subliminal perceptions were genuinely unconscious, or that they were not. One criterion used recently has been to set the stimulus at such a minimal level that the participant cannot accurately guess whether or not any sort of stimulation has even occurred. In recent years this controversy has died down, and many researchers have become so comfortable with the reality—and the power—of subliminal primes that they are widely used in research on such other questions as how opinions are formed, how moods affect actions, and how persons are perceived.

The point to emphasize here is that these subliminal primes are not available to conscious experience. It is really inappropriate and misleading to speak of them as perceptions at all. The problem came partly from the fact that consciousness is not simply all or nothing; it is a continuum. We can be partly aware of something. This is how the study of subliminality began, with perceptions that were somewhat clear but partly uncertain. When research progressed to the point that effects were being described with stimuli that were deeply subliminal, however, to call them perceptions at all became problematic. They are not conscious. Someone exposed to them does not know what they are (knowing is something we do consciously). We may not even know that anything has occurred. And yet they affect us, somewhat in the manner that a prime affects a pump.

WHAT IF EXTRASENSORY PERCEPTION IS LIKE SUBLIMINAL PERCEPTION?

If extrasensory perception is like subliminal perception, then it, too, works as an unconscious prime, affecting our experiences and behaviors but never being consciously available as such. The main difference is that in an extrasensory perception the intensity of the stimulus has dropped down to zero, as far as the sensory system of the person is concerned. Like a subliminal perception, it will not be conscious, not be known, and not in fact be any sort of perception at all. Might this be the case? Exploring this question was an important stimulus in developing the First Sight model. In fact, I believe that extrasensory perception is exactly like that. Just how this is so will be elaborated further in chapter 4.

PSYCHOKINESIS AND
UNCONSCIOUSLY EXPRESSIVE BEHAVIOR

Sigmund Freud made Western society familiar with the notion that the symptoms of various psychiatric disorders could be understood to be unwitting expressions of unconscious mental processes. He and his followers developed an elaborate theory of these unconscious processes, their origins, their dynamics, and their treatment through techniques of conscious uncovering. Partly due to the influence of a powerful pharmaceutical industry, this idea that symptoms have implicit meaning is perhaps less widespread today in favor of a model that understands people as isolated organisms with hypothetical brain diseases to be altered by medications. In everyday psychotherapeutic practice, however, uncovering unconscious meanings is a staple. In a single day an average therapist might find that a case of depression is an expression of the shame aroused by a loss, a teenager's falling grades speak for loyalty to a divorced and missing parent, and an anxiety before groups communicates a sense of guilt over some earlier failure. The shame, the loss, the loyalty, and the guilt are all unconscious. Making them conscious, seeing the connections, helps to unravel and relieve the symptoms.

It is not only in the realm of psychiatric dysfunction that such behavioral expressions of unconscious issues go on. They go on with everyone, all the time. Freud (1958b) himself moved in this direction, by writing about the "psychopathology of everyday life."

We needn't speak of psychopathology at all, however. Consciously inadvertent behaviors can regularly be seen to speak for meanings that are out of sight at the moment, if we wish to go to the trouble of untangling the connections. It isn't only painfully avoided meanings that may be implied by our behaviors. It may be anything that we simply don't have in mind at the moment, and it may be many things that are simply (by virtue of our constitution) never amenable to direct awareness at all. Mr. X is intent on what he is trying to communicate in his conversation with Ms. Y. As he speaks he takes a step toward the next room, then stands still again as he continues to talk. If he bothers to reflect on the meaning of the step, it will occur to him easily: he had decided a minute before to check on something going on in the next room. In the conversational moment his intention was temporarily forgotten, but he still expressed it inadvertently as his thinking and talking and listening flowed on. Reflect upon your own behavior and that of others around you, and I believe you will see a wealth of this going on continually and smoothly.

Sometimes unconscious behaviors and subliminal primes work hand in hand. The unconscious meaning prompting the behavior may not be just forgotten at the moment, it may have been apprehended subliminally and was never conscious at all. Consider the findings of Aarts et al. (2008) that were reported in the prestigious journal *Science*. Some of their participants were exposed to very brief presentations of words having to do with exertion. Half of the people were also consciously shown very positive scenes to observe while they were so primed, while half were not. Then all participants were asked to *exert* by squeezing on a hand grip. Those persons exposed unconsciously to the *exertion* primes gripped more quickly and aggressively than those who were not exposed. And those who were primed while looking at the positive scenes squeezed the hardest of all. As the authors conclude: "The mere activation of the idea of a behavioral act moves the human body without the person consciously deciding to take action."

Is this surprising and mysterious? It may seem so, but if these psychologists could capture this so easily in their laboratory it must be going on very frequently for everyone every day. Does it seem insulting to think that you are constantly being influenced by unconscious stimuli? Perhaps, but remember how wonderfully adaptive this is. It is not so much that the subliminal primes are controlling our behavior as that we are unconsciously using subliminal information to respond in a quick and optimal way to what will come to be seen as the demands of a situation. We use the primes implicitly in the service of our unconscious intentions.

WHAT IF PSYCHOKINESIS IS A KIND OF UNCONSCIOUSLY EXPRESSIVE BEHAVIOR?

If psychokinesis is unconsciously expressive behavior, then it also functions as an inadvertent statement of our unconscious intentions. The only difference from other unconsciously expressive behaviors is that it occurs outside of the physical boundaries of the organism. Instead of an odd act of clumsiness resulting in an accident and expressing an unconscious sense (perhaps) of guilt, a meaningful picture falls from the wall, expressing the same inner condition. Instead of gripping something extra forcefully to express an unconscious sense of pleasure in effort, a string of propitious random numbers spins out of an experimenter's random event generator, speaking for the same inner state. Is this a sensible way to think of the odd events (experimental and spontaneous) that we take to indicate psychokinesis? I believe that it is, and I will try to argue the case in more detail in chapter 7.

NOTE

1. Packard, 2007.

2

A Model and a Theory of Psi

Our normal waking consciousness, rational consciousness as we call it, is but one special type of consciousness, whilst all about it, parted from it by the filmiest of screens, there lie potential forms of consciousness entirely different.

—William James

The First Sight model consists of two assertions about human nature and the structure of the mind. The theory consists of thirteen corollaries that are elaborations of these assertions. I present these ideas in this chapter in a way that is purposefully formal, abstract, and concise. I will elaborate major ones more fully in later chapters. Testable implications can be found throughout this chapter, but particularly in the theoretical corollaries involving *intentionality*, *switching*, and *liminality*.

THE MODEL: BASIC PREMISES

1. Organisms are psychologically unbounded. They transact with reality in an unconscious way beyond their physical boundaries. They are unconsciously engaged psychologically with an extended universe of meaning of indefinite extent in space and time. This engagement is continuously ongoing and is referred to as psi. The efferent (active) aspect of these engagements is referred to as psychokinesis (PK). The afferent (receptive) aspect of the engagements is referred to as extrasensory perception (ESP). These two aspects of psi are always intimately conjoined in their unconscious functioning.

If the afferent engagement refers to some event in the future, it is called *precognition*, and if it refers to another person's experience, it is called *telepathy*. Direct access to the meanings of future events is necessarily prior to our potential access to those events in the present, and direct engagement with extrasomatic information necessarily precedes that information being able to reach the senses. For these reasons, psi may be referred to as First Sight—hence the name given to the model and theory.

2. All experience and all behavior[1] are constituted out of unconscious psychological processes carried out purposefully on multiple sources of information, including psi information, as mediated by unconscious intention and contextual appraisal. These processes are automatic in the sense that they are not volitionally conscious (one is not aware of choosing to do them), but they are not impersonal or mechanical. Inasmuch as it is capable of thinking at all, an organism thinks (makes discriminations and carries out cognitive/affective actions) unconsciously as well as consciously. Unconscious thought considers several sources of information, including nonlocal information (psi), sensation, memory, imagination, goals, and values. Consideration of the various sources of information occurs rapidly, holistically, and efficiently toward the end of bringing to consciousness the most useful thing for consciousness to consider at each moment. Unconscious intention is the primary guide that is used by unconscious thought in constructing experience and action.

While unconscious psychological processes, including psi, are not directly available to awareness, their activity is often expressed implicitly and inadvertently by various physiological, behavioral, and experiential responses. These implicit activities often achieve other personally desirable ends through situationally adaptive behaviors that may never result in an act of consciousness, such as making a certain consumer choice based partly upon an implicit memory. These activities also facilitate adaptive behaviors through physiological, emotional, and cognitive kinds of arousal that implicitly prepare the organism for an effective response to its situation. For example, subliminal information about something prior to awareness acts to prepare a person for a correct recognition of that thing a split second later as a conscious perception has time to form and the perception can be construed as the thing that it is. Similarly, an extrasensory evocation of a certain mood state or state of physical arousal helps to prepare a person for a quickly effective response to a danger as soon as that can be accurately perceived.

These implicitly adaptive responses are the means by which the existence and activity of unconscious psychological processes can be discerned. When a conscious perception and/or action are completed, these implicit aspects of response are generally unavailable to the consciousness of the person who is perceiving and acting. If perceptions and actions are frustrated and not completed, the implicit aspects may be more available to awareness.

THE THEORY: COROLLARIES

Personalness Corollary

A person's psychological transactions with the universe are best understood in terms of personal meaning rather than impersonal process. Even in regard to unconscious processing of reality, things are essentially what they mean to an individual in the context of the individual's concerns. These transactions extend beyond the physical boundaries of the person and cannot be adequately represented by reductionistic accounts in the impersonal language of chemistry and physics. Such accounts are useful within their frames of reference, but they are secondary to the psychological meaning of events and not primary to them.

The unconscious psychological processes that constitute consciousness are personal and unconsciously volitional. Personal proclivities, emotional preferences, personal memories, and personal goals are important aspects of these processes for each organism. More abstract factors such as beliefs, intentions, values, and attitudes that potentially may be articulated are also important considerations for these processes in the case of human beings. Unconscious thinking is automatic, but it is also done purposefully by an individual in the context of personal intentions.

Ubiquity Corollary

Meanings engaged distally by way of psi contribute actively and continuously to the array of sources for unconscious thought. Their distance from the sensory, potentially conscious boundaries of the organism may be along axes of space or time. These nonlocal meanings constantly contribute to the formation of experience and are used to guide other unconscious behaviors as well. Therefore, psi is a normal, continuously active, unconscious aspect of psychological functioning.

ESP contributes to the formation of experience by bringing distal meanings to the task of creating consciousness and guiding unconscious choices. Since its contribution is always available prior to any sensory information, it may be referred to as First Sight (as opposed to its traditional designation as second sight, which would imply that it is an unusual phenomenon, occurring to some persons in a secondary, supplementary way following the primary process of sensory perception).

PK contributes to the formation of experience by bringing intention to bear upon the physical processes of the nervous system. It contributes to the formation of intentional (conscious and unconscious) action by engaging the object of intention.

Integration Corollary

Other preconscious processes in addition to psi contribute to the formation of experience and action. These include motives and values held by the individual, memories, imaginary possibilities, and subliminal sensory information and other visceral activities. These different streams are processed together in the formation of experience and action in a rapid, holistic, efficient, unconscious manner to form integrated products of action and experience.

What is integrated we may call the unconscious psychological situation of the person at the moment. This understanding of the situation is different from the one we would expect from the physical sciences as normally understood. An ESP target in an ESP experiment, for example, is not in any sense physically present and active for the percipient in the experiment. If it were available for the senses it would be a poor ESP target. Since such a target exists as a part of the confluence of interpersonal meanings active at the moment (basically as an intention of the experimenter, interacting with the cooperative intention of the percipient), this implies that meanings and intentions regnant at the moment primarily constitute the situation. Representations of some of these meanings and intentions are immediately present for consciousness (as by a memory or a sensory sensation), while representations of others are not.

Processing of the different streams of potential information is assumed to follow similar patterns. Patterns found in regard to one stream of information will be generally expected to obtain in others as well, although it may also be that some patterns are unique to a given source. For example, many patterns observed with the contribution of memory material to experience will be expected to be obtained when studying the contribution of subliminal information, and patterns found with the contribution of extrasensory perception will be expected to be observed in the functioning of memory. Such "mapping" of patterns across these different domains of study should be heuristically useful.

Anticipation Corollary

The mind seeks to anticipate events.[2] In its pursuit of the construction of the meaning of experience, the mind uses preconscious processes in anticipatory ways that are not in themselves conscious but that may be inferred from other acts of consciousness or behavior. For example, an unconscious subliminal stimulus may lead an individual to interpret a later ambiguous situation in a direction that is congruent with the prior stimulus. It is as if the mind is using the subliminal stimulus to help to anticipate the meaning of the situation as it comes to develop. Another way of saying this is that the subliminal stimulus is contextual for and anticipatory about the ambiguous situation. In a similar way, a thematically congruent mood may be evoked by a subliminal stimulus, and this affective posture then serves as a prompt for the individual to behave in some way congruent with that mood when an appropriate situation becomes apparent. Memories, personal concerns, and extrasensory information all contribute to the formation of experience and behavior in similar ways, evoking an unconscious interest in certain lines of meaning, both cognitive and emotional.

Weighting and Signing Corollary

Along with switching, these are the most important new constructs in First Sight theory. They are used to explain how unconscious thought uses unconscious material in constructing consciousness and behavior. Implicit information (sensory and extrasensory) is first acted upon unconsciously by an action of weighting, in which all of the items in the vast array of potentially available information are sensed to be more or less important. The sense of importance of some piece of information is determined by its pertinence in terms of the needs and goals that are predominant at the time. The item that is weighted most heavily at any given moment will be focused upon by unconscious attention. These needs and goals may be relatively stable and chronic: for example, the need for air to breathe or the need to avoid danger or the wish to protect a loved one. They may also be transitory and situation specific, like the need to win in a competitive situation or the wish to avoid a particular obstacle while driving a car. The heavy weighting of an item does not automatically assure its direct participation in experience or action. After it is weighted, an item must be signed.

A heavily weighted item of potential information (one sensed to be important in the moment) is signed[3] either positively or negatively. If it is signed positively, it is included in the developing experience and/or action. If it is signed negatively, it is excluded. As elaborated below (Bidirectionality Corollary), signing is a function of unconscious intention.

Weighting and signing are generally applied hierarchically and sequentially in complex situations. Two concerns may present to a person, one of which is weighted more heavily than the other. Then that pair of concerns may itself appear in the context of some other concerns that are weighted more heavily still. For example, a person with a high need for achievement and also a strong wish to defend a primary relationship may first sense that one of two possible courses of action offers more opportunity for achievement, and it is more heavily weighted. Then the person may sense at the same time that a loved one is in danger, and this concern preempts the achievement concern. Then the course of thought or action that offers greater protection for the loved one is weighted more heavily than anything else that is unconsciously present at the moment. Then this apparently most pertinent element of meaning is signed either positively or negatively. In ordinary life outside the laboratory (in which a few variables are controlled and presented at a time), this complexity must be the rule rather than the exception.

These processes of weighting and signing are presumed to go on continuously at all levels of mental functioning, conscious and unconscious. Priorities are established (weighting), and then a point of focus is chosen (signing). The formation of a visual experience shows one employment of this process. Out of the huge array of potential visual experience that is available in the moment, some aspect is selected as most pertinent using cues of depth perception (say, someone approaching in a crowded room). The person coming closer and still closer is sensed as more immediately relevant than others (such a use of depth perception has obvious survival value, from an evolutionary perspective). Once depth perception and perception of motion help us understand what is most immediately pertinent, then focus is used to sharpen the visual experience of the person approaching and at the same moment suppress immediately surrounding visual information that would be distracting if experienced. The approaching individual (perhaps especially his face and hands) is signed positively and discriminated, while surrounding visual stimuli are signed negatively and excluded from awareness.

Summation Corollary

The content of conscious experience and the thrust of implicit experience such as emotional states and behavioral choices are constituted in a summative way by unconscious thought. Elements are weighted (assigned a degree of importance), signed (positively or negatively, for inclusion or exclusion), and then roughly averaged. The individual's values and goals and understanding of the current situation and its requirements are referred to in this weighting and signing of elements. This process of implicitly averaging (analogous to mathematical averaging) is carried out on the numerous sources of potential meaning, and a "best fit" is decided upon. The amount of potential information that can be processed holistically in this way is of indefinite extent. Sources of information that are close in time to the present moment, important to the concerns of the organism, and potentially verifiable in terms of sensory experience (current or remembered) will tend to be weighted most heavily, but a vast amount of less local meaning is continually apprehended as well.

Different streams of implicit meaning may reach some degree of summation and still not contribute additively to the final content of consciousness. For example, elements implying danger may summate sufficiently to arouse a mood of agitation in an individual, but this mood may not be apparent to the person himself or herself (although it might be discernable through a measure of galvanic skin response). Consciously, the individual might only be aware of focusing upon something else, such as some conceptual problem. Streams of implicit meaning may also summate sufficiently that they influence nonreflective behavioral choices (to drive more slowly or more quickly, to fly to a certain meeting or decline to do so), but they still never contribute additively to the content of consciousness to a degree that would permit an awareness of their participation in the choice.

Bidirectionality Corollary

This corollary elaborates the notion of signing, which is part of the process of summation. The organism makes use of each element of meaning available to unconscious thought in either of two ways. It may either "turn toward it" and appropriate it as such in the construction of experience, affect, or action, or it may "turn away from it" and exclude it from the construction of experience, affect, or action. In the first case we may say that the element is signed positively, and in the second case it is signed negatively.

If an element of potential experience is "turned toward" (signed positively) and appropriated into consciousness, it is said to be assimilated. For example, if one assimilates the memory content or subliminal exposure or the extrasensory meaning of an apple, the assimilation tends to be expressed in the conscious experience of the idea of an apple. If the element is "turned away from" (signed negatively) and excluded, it is said to be subject to contrast, and more generally, disassimilated. The conscious experience will not include the idea of an apple, and if many such conscious experiences and unconscious behaviors are compiled, the idea of *apple* will be found to be expressed less often than it should by chance alone.

The same thing applies to unconscious behaviors, although the term has not been used in this way before. If apple is assimilated, unconscious behaviors will tend to move toward the potential involvement with an apple. If it is disassimilated, such behaviors will tend away from that possibility. As these unconscious behaviors accrue over time, the encounter with an apple will become distinctly more likely or unlikely. Assimilation and disassimilation are the two modes of preconscious processing.

Thus, we may say that unconscious thought is bidirectional—meaning is either assimilated or disassimilated (avoided). It is important to remember that disassimilating something is not the same thing as ignoring it or making no use of it at all. Disassimilation is an active avoidance. These alternative modes of making use of implicit meanings apply to psi and also to other streams of potential information, such as subliminal stimulation, unattended physiological processes, and latent memories. The mind also treats these streams bidirectionally.

Intentionality Corollary

These two modes of utilization, assimilative and disassimilative (or additive and subtractive), are a function of unconscious intention in regard to an element of potential meaning. If the element is sensed to be useful and desirable in the context of the individual's situation in the moment, then the mode chosen will be the assimilative one. If the element is sensed to not be useful or desirable, the mode of contrast will be chosen.

If an element is assimilated, the resulting experience or action will be seen to reflect aspects of that meaning. For example, if a subliminal prime is a red apple, and it is assimilated, an elicited free association frequently will be found to express qualities of redness and/or roundness and/or suitability for eating, etc. The element will contribute additively. These positive references will be seen, across instances, to occur more frequently than in the case of other free associations not so subliminally stimulated.

If an element is disassimilated, or subjected to contrast, the opposite effect will be observed. The consequent experience or action will be found to not express those qualities. The element will contribute subtractively. In regard to a sensory subliminal stimulus, such references will be observed to occur less frequently than in the case of other free associations not subliminally stimulated by the pertinent material. (This is an important distinction that may be initially difficult to grasp. In a situation of disassimilation or contrast, the potential meaning is not simply ignored or left out of consideration, it is positively excluded and avoided to a degree that can be statistically discernable).

Assimilative use of psi-apprehended meanings in a psi experiment is called psi-hitting by parapsychologists. It is expressed by scores in ESP or PK tests that are significantly higher than the level expected by chance or by an increased likelihood of other emotional or behavioral expressions of the target. In a study on the formation of perceptions or judgments with sensory information, cognitive psychologists call it *positive priming*. It is expressed by associative or affective expressions of the primed material.

Disassimilative use of psi meaning in a parapsychology study is called psi-missing. This is expressed as scores that are lower than the level expected by chance or in the evocation of feelings or behaviors that are contrary to the implications of the material. Cognitive psychologists call the analogous suppression of sensory information *negative priming*.

Several important guides for this intentional choice can be listed, and others surely await elucidation. Most are drawn from research in cognitive, social, and personality psychology.[4] Several considerations pertain to qualities of the information being psychically prehended:

1. Because sensory information (either coming directly from physical events or from other persons) is a reliable source of experience, intention will habitually and normatively turn toward sensory information when it is available in preference to lingering with the innately implicit information of psi, or other purely unconscious potentiations of experience.

2. The degree to which a bit of potential meaning is congruent with other available cues and with the content of conscious experience that is already forming is one consideration. Material sensed to be congruent will tend to be assimilated, and material sensed to be incongruent will be disassimilated. For example, if one is engaged in a task of quickly naming colors, suboptimal primes involving color will tend to be assimilated while primes involving irrelevant meanings will tend to be disassimilated.[5]

3. Material that is associated with previously rewarding experiences and that is valued will often tend to be assimilated, as opposed to material associated with previously negative experiences.[6]

4. Material that is understood to be pertinent to an individual's general values and goals will tend to be assimilated, as opposed to material that is sensed to be irrelevant to those values and goals. For example, a person with a habitually high level of concern for his or her social presence in situations (an "extravert") will be more assimilative of unconscious cues regarding interpersonal attention and interest and less assimilative of less interpersonal cues; or a person whose racial attitudes are highly salient will be more responsive to unconscious cues involving racial grouping than will persons without such a high level of that concern.[7] Similarly, information that is congruent with a person's stable attitudes is more accessible to long-term memory recall than is information that is discrepant with such attitudes.[8]

5. More specifically, material that is of a sort that frequently has been found to be pertinent and useful before will tend to be assimilated as opposed to material that has not been found to be pertinent and useful. For example, a person for whom religion is very meaningful will be more prone to assimilate cues implying religion than more secular cues.[9]

6. Material that is of a sort for which the individual has a working frame of reference based upon prior experience will tend to be assimilated as opposed to material of a sort that is strange and outside of the individual's frame of reference. For example, English-speaking persons have been found to assimilate ESP targets in English and disassimilate targets in an unknown language.[10]
7. Material that is understood to be pertinent to the task at hand will tend to be assimilated as opposed to material that is sensed to be irrelevant to the task at hand. People will tend to assimilate unconscious cues that are mathematical when they are engaged in mathematical work, or verbal cues while writing an essay, or musical cues when composing a sonata.
8. Material that is sensed to come from a source that is understood to be reliable and important will tend to be assimilated as opposed to material that is sensed to come from some source seen as unreliable or irrelevant. For example, persons with different political attitudes toward certain candidates have been found to respond differently to unconscious cues associated with those candidates[11]; and persons who believe that ESP is a real source of potential information tend to assimilate ESP information while persons who do not believe that tend to disassimilate such information.[12]
9. Material that is sensed, via psi, to be relevant to some desirable outcome will tend to be assimilated, and material that is sensed to be associated with a less desirable outcome will tend to be disassimilated. Thus, psi information may provide a moderating context for assimilation/disassimilation of other psi processes. As one example, an ESP study by Stanford and Rust (1977) arranged a contingency unknown to participants such that their assimilation of targets resulted in a positive outcome for another person, while their disassimilation of the targets resulted in an unpleasant outcome for the other person. Results showed a statistically significant excess of outcomes in which persons were helped by successful assimilation. Such results suggest that a psi prehension of such contingencies provides a meaningful context that guides the unconscious approach to ESP targets.
10. Material that is sensed to be pertinent to highly critical issues in terms of an individual's needs will tend to be assimilated, even if it might be disassimilated for other reasons. For example, information about the life-or-death welfare of a loved one would be expected to be assimilated as opposed to information that lacks such critical importance, even in situations in which that source (ESP or memory, for example) would ordinarily be thought to be irrelevant.[13]
11. Material that is congruent with a person's emotional state at the moment will tend to be assimilated, while material that is not congruent

will tend to be disassimilated. For example, subliminal primes connoting unhappiness aroused greater activation of the amygdale (as measured by a functional magnetic resonance imaging [FMRI]) for depressed persons than for persons who were not depressed, while the amygdale response to subliminal primes involving happiness showed the opposite pattern.[14] Similarly, research participants in an ESP study who were in a more anxious state of mind tended to disassimilate (psi-miss) targets that were packaged together (out of sight) with potentially threatening, erotic material and tended to assimilate (hit) targets that were packaged with neutral material. Nonanxious participants showed the opposite pattern.[15]

12. The extent to which cognitive closure has already been attained is another consideration in determining what kinds of material will be assimilated or disassimilated. If the individual is already fairly clear about what is being experienced (or should be experienced) or intended, then only preconscious material that is highly congruent with the determined experience will be assimilated. The criteria for assimilation will be stricter and narrower than in the case in which cognitive closure is still unattained. In the case of relatively clear cognitive closure, a much broader range of other potential material will tend to be disassimilated. If I look at some stimulus array that I construe definitively as "a swarm of bees," my mind will automatically exclude from consideration preconscious information from any source that is contrary to the idea I have reached. On the other hand, if I think of it only vaguely as "a confusing cloud of shapes," unconscious processing will be open to sampling a broad range of unconscious material for potentially helpful information.[16] This is congruent with the maxim from remote viewing literature in parapsychology, that one must "say what you see and not what it looks like" if positive access to extrasensory information is desired,[17] because the mental act of deciding the meaning of a thing is cognitive closure. It is also congruent with the observation that participants whose utterances in a ganzfeld experiment were more cognitively elaborated were especially likely to miss the correct target.[18]

Switching Corollary

Over a period of time, the unconscious posture of assimilation or exclusion may be relatively constant in regard to a particular source of meaning, or it may switch from one to the other. This switching will occur at some frequency, sometimes more rapidly and sometimes more slowly. This constancy of posture is a function of the consistency and purity of unconscious intention, and this in turn is determined by the relative weight of the information over time and by other variables. These variables include situational factors that promote or diminish critical analysis and changes of approach in a task, certain moods and states of mind, and persistent individual differences in those conceptual styles, moods, and states of mind.

Something that is the most heavily weighted thing over time will evoke little switching. Something assigned less weight will be more subject to switching. Another way of expressing this is in terms of the concept of preconscious attention. The mind focuses unconscious attention on whatever most seems to fit the criteria of unconscious intention. Switching psi modes is presumed to reflect a change in unconscious attention in regard to the content. A heavily weighted item is given relatively consistent attention, and this is expressed as little switching of direction. Something with little weight, or with ambivalent weight, will be subject to more rapid switching.

Many things can influence the consistency of unconscious attention. These include characteristics of the material itself, the nature of the situation, the mood of the individual, and more lasting characteristics of the person.

1. Information that is highly central to the dominant concerns of the person will be expected to dominate unconscious attention and receive little switching. For example, danger to oneself or to some loved one is a universally dominant concern. Indications of such threat have been found to command attention in processing sensory information.[19] Threats that are understood to be severe and imminent evoke attention strongly and quickly[20] and hold it over time,[21] even though cognitive processing may be impeded. These things are expected to have similar effects on unconscious attention with extrasensory information. Sustained attention is expressed by slow directional switching.

2. Situations that facilitate critical, self-conscious analysis of performance and alertness to shifting situational concerns will tend to speed switching, and situations that promote a consistent direction of purpose and undistracted focus will tend to slow it.

3. As a consequence of this, shifts in situations with their contextual demands will tend to hasten shifts in unconscious direction of inclusion/exclusion.

4. Moods or states of disinterest, fatigue, fitful distraction, skeptical disengagement with a psi task, emotional distance, and shifting of intention from irritation or uncertainty will all tend to speed switching.

5. Moods or states that are unusually expansive, socially responsive or generally stimulus-bound will tend to produce rapid shifts of attention and lead to rapid switching.

6. States in which one is markedly self-conscious[22] or self-objectified[23] will be accompanied with more rapid switching.
7. Moods of strong motivation regarding the psi task, self-confidence, consistent purpose, and emotional security all tend to be associated with less switching.
8. Feeling that one is performing something with unusual "flow,"[24] or that one is "in the zone," will be accompanied by very little self-consciousness and self-objectivization and will tend to involve little switching.

Several more or less stable dimensions of difference among people are also expected to be pertinent to rapidity of psi switching in a psi task. Persons who are disposed to switch rapidly include those who:

1. tend to approach situations cognitively and analytically
2. lack consistent purpose and motivation
3. take a detached-observer posture toward most situations
4. are chronically ambivalent
5. are cognitively disorganized
6. are highly distractible

Persons who tend to switch slowly, conversely, tend to be persons who:

1. approach situations globally and holistically
2. are strongly and consistently purposive
3. engage themselves wholeheartedly in situations
4. are not overly self-doubting or uncertain
5. are well-integrated cognitively
6. are prone *to hold focus purposively and not become distracted*
7. are dissociative (when in certain states). Highly dissociative people often experience altered ways of being that are more complex and enduring than simple moods. They may experience what is called "alter personalities." For many such persons these subpersonalities are characterized by intentional approaches that are unusually single-minded and lacking in what cognitive psychologists call "cognitive flexibility" (the ability to shift cognitive sets based upon changing circumstances). As one such person once explained to me, her parts existed because each "has a job to do." With her, as with others I have known, when a given part is dominant, its single job is all that matters and things that would provoke a shift in tack or attention in most people are scarcely perceived. When a person is in such intentionally simplified alter states, such persons would be expected to show little switching. When shifting between inner states, they would be expected to show marked switching.

Extremity Corollary

This corollary defines the consequences of the rapidity of switching. If switching occurs relatively slowly over some period of activity (for example, in a psychological or parapsychological test), then there will be a relatively dense accumulation of either additive or subtractive references to the meaning in question across the time of observation. When looked at as a whole, a clear additive or subtractive reference to the potential meaning will be discernable across the elements of response (for example, calls in a forced-choice ESP test, bits counted in a PK trial, or ideas expressed in a free-association procedure).

If relatively slow switching continues to obtain across a number of blocks of performance (as in the case of several runs of ESP or PK testing, each made up of several guesses or bits of activity), then the level of reference seen in the blocks will be relatively extreme and clearly discernable. In an ESP test, the run scores will tend to be consistently divergent from the line of chance expectation. In parapsychology, an accumulation of highly chance-divergent scores has been referred to in several different terms, including *extreme scoring, large variance,* or *high scoring magnitude.*

If switching occurs rapidly over a period of activity (for example, several times within the span of an ESP test or free-association exercise), then additive and subtractive influences will tend to be expressed with roughly equivalent frequency, with the result that neither will be discernable as such. It will appear in this case as if the potential meaning had no influence at all in the formation of the experience or action. In terms of chance expectation, a score indicating degree of reference will be near the level expected by chance.

If relatively rapid switching is sustained over a number of blocks of effort (for example, across several runs of ESP responses), then the resultant set of scores will be seen to hover so closely to the level of chance expectation that the overall result is not reasonably attributable to chance. In parapsychology, this phenomenon has been referred to as small extremity, tight variance, or constricted scoring.

In terms of a parapsychological experiment, the accumulation of either chance-level or chance-divergent scores may be referred to as the degree of scoring extremity. Scoring extremity is assumed to express the rate of unconscious switching between the postures of assimilation and contrast in regard to the psi information within the periods of performance.

Scoring extremity is a characteristic either of performance that samples independent bits of response (as in the runs of forced-choice ESP calls) or of the more complex performance in tasks in which many subresponses are subjectively combined into single, general responses. For example, in a ganzfeld or remote viewing trial, a participant expresses a string of images, thoughts, and feelings. Someone then subjectively combines these elements into an overall impression that is then compared to the target. The degree of correspondence is expressed by the extent to which the summed impression can be seen to be associated with the correct target, as opposed to its degree of association with a field of decoys, or pseudotargets. A strong hit is the case in which the correct target is chosen in first place out of a field of several (often four or five) potential targets. A strong miss is the case in which it is chosen last. A chance-level score is the case in which it is picked in the middle of the set. A collection made up largely of highly chance-divergent scores (such as one, two, seven, and eight, when a field of eight potential targets is used) thus expresses extreme scoring, and it may be assumed to reflect relatively little switching across the different elements of performance (images, feelings, etc.) for each trial. Conversely, a collection of scores that hover closely to the chance line (three, four, or five among eight alternatives) expresses tight scoring, and this is assumed to represent rapid switching within the periods of performance such that one image might lead toward the target, then the next away from it, and so on.

Both slow switching and rapid switching are useful in everyday psychological functioning for different purposes. Slow switching is useful for making it highly likely that a given meaning will either be accessed or avoided in experience. Rapid switching is useful for rendering some potential meaning utterly irrelevant to ongoing experience, averting any distracting influence that might otherwise arise from the potential meaning.[25] Rapid switching is presumably adopted unconsciously in order to assure that the information involved plays no part at all in the formation of experience and action.

While rate of switching in a psi task is expected to affect the extremity of psi scores, in everyday life we might say that it affects the experiential psi density of experience. Persistent unconscious attention upon something will lead it to be densely represented (implicitly) in experience. Rapidly switching unconscious attention will lead its implicit referents to be dense or definitively excluded.

I listed various considerations in the discussion of the Switching Corollary that affect the rate of switching, such as meaningful versus meaningless information, situations favoring set shifting versus those inducing consistent focus, purposeful and cognitively organized persons versus ones who are indifferent or distractible, etc. These will all be important predictors of scoring extremity in psi tests. They will similarly affect the implicative psi density of everyday experience.

Inadvertency and Frustration Corollary

Psi engagements as such are intrinsically unconscious and not available to an individual's conscious experience. However, they do regularly contribute to the formation of conscious experience, and they do this by the arousal of anticipatory networks of ideas and feelings (assuming that they are heavily weighted, afforded slow switching, and approached with the intention of assimilation). Because of this arousal, their action can be glimpsed consciously only by observing thoughts, feelings, and behaviors that are inadvertent; that is, not intentional and not obviously caused by any current experiences.

When a perception is formed and securely construed, or an action is carried out and completed, the contribution of the preliminary unconscious processes that have led to these things will be invisible. Closure will have been achieved both cognitively and behaviorally, and this closure will dominate awareness to the exclusion of implicit constituents. However, if a perception or action is blocked or otherwise not completed and the intention guiding those things is thwarted, then implicit expressions of the unconscious anticipatory processes may be visible in the form of inadvertent aspects of experience (for example, dreams or slips of the tongue) or behavior that is unconsciously expressive or sometimes in a physical activity on the part of something beyond the individual's body.

Even as unconscious material available to the processes of unconscious thought, extrasensory "information" is only allusory, pointing to its potential content by virtue of the anticipatory cognitive and conative networks that are aroused by it. Since it has never yet reached consciousness and been construed as having the explicit content that is potential in it, it cannot provide more explicit information to unconscious thinking. This is in contrast to information that has been encoded consciously in verbally explicit form ("the new car is red"). Consciously encoded information is available for unconscious thought in its fully explicit form as an unconscious memory.

Individuals differ in the frequency at which they generate such consciously available inadvertencies and in the facility with which they correctly interpret them. Someone who generates many such experiences and has become skillful in interpreting them is thought of as relatively psychic.

Liminality Corollary

From the point of view of consciousness, we may think of such inadvertent and allusory experiences as liminal ones, in terms of the boundary between conscious and unconscious thought. In them, unconscious thought is not directly available to awareness (by its nature, it never is), but some of its implicit expressions are. Conscious experiences that are liminal include such things as dreams, moods, impulses, spontaneous internal imagery, preferences and aversions, acts of forgetting, hunches and vague impressions, jokes, judgments, and odd symptoms or errors (ranging from benign slips to psychotic symptoms). To one person observing another, nondeliberate, nonverbal but expressive behaviors may also be liminal in regard to the unconscious processes of the person being observed.

In addition to considerations pertinent to a specific source or item of information (as spelled out in the Intentionality Corollary), individuals differ in the extent to which they tend to make use of such liminal experiences. Some variables affecting this can be specified.

1. Habitual interest in aspects of experience that are liminal facilitates expression of psi processes. We may think of this as a person's *openness*. The more such interest or openness on the part of the person to the kinds of experiences that imply unconscious thought, the more they will make unconscious reference to psi material (and other streams of unconscious material), and the more they will be likely to consciously grasp elements of it. They will also be more likely to express these elements in their less conscious goal-directed behavior. On the contrary, a very practical, analytical, and concretely realistic orientation to life that systematically ignores liminal experience will tend to lead one to either disassimilate psi processes or subject them to rapid switching. There are a number of psychological constructs that to some extent imply this openness toward liminal experience. Openness to experience has been found to be a dominant factor in general personality batteries. It is most often measured by the NEO-PI test. On that inventory, the facets of openness to feelings, openness to fantasy, and openness to aesthetics are especially pertinent to liminal interest as it is conceived here. Besides openness itself, other relevant constructs include transliminality and intuitiveness. Several other, more general, constructs may partially reflect this dimension as well, such as competence, ego strength, and resilience.

2. The degree to which a person is engaged in creative work should be an important predictor of the extent to which they make use of liminal experience. Artists, creative scientists, and other creative persons habitually make reference to a level of experience that is not completely or easily verbalized in order to give form to some new meaning. Such persons are more likely to make use of psi prehensions along with other implicit sources of information in their creative efforts.

3. Highly dissociative people show an unusual tendency to compartmentalize areas of their experience and volition. They do not "smooth over" internal inconsistencies in emotional states, wishes, and memory streams into a single, socially presented persona, as most persons do. Rather, in different states they may display segregated memories or structures of intention or senses of identity that are unusually distinct from each other, and perhaps even strongly contradictory to one another. Such persons sometimes grow accustomed to noting and interpreting their own implicit expressions of meaning in order to keep track of what other parts of themselves are doing and feeling. Some such people I have known appear to comfortably make use of psi-implying information

along with other implicit, liminal material. This is an area that has not been explored scientifically very much, but it may be fruitful.

4. Persons high in what has been called "merger motivation"[26] may tend to be especially open to liminal information, particularly as it pertains to the experiences of other persons. Some parapsychological research[27] has begun to explore this question, but only further work can determine its reliability and generality.

5. Fearful (anxious, neurotic) people can be expected to narrowly restrict the range of the liminal material that they will assimilate. More emotionally secure and less anxious persons should generally tend to be more open and more prone to assimilating psi prehensions when they are otherwise pertinent to their intentions. Generally fearful people who are also dissociative (see number 3, this section) should tend to be exceptions to this rule when they are in more dissociated states.

In addition to relatively stable, dispositional attitudes toward liminal experience, a person's emotional state will be important in terms of their making reference or not to liminal experiences at a particular time. A more positive, open, secure state of mind will tend to facilitate reference to a broader spectrum of contextual, potentially liminal experience. On the other hand, a fearful, closed, negative state of mind will tend to narrow the focus of a person's unconscious processing and subject the liminal domain of experience to contrast and exclusion. This is why more fearful persons tend to score negatively in ESP tests[28] and why persons in good moods sample from a broader array of implicit, contextual sensory experience in forming perceptions than do persons in bad moods.[29]

Finally, liminality may be not so much a general disposition as a more specific openness or closedness to psi itself as a source of valid information. First Sight theory presumes that this is the cause of the predictive power of Schmeidler's "sheep-goat" dimension,[30] in which people sort themselves into two groups: those who reject the possibility of ESP influencing results in an experiment and those who do not reject that possibility (uncertain people are considered "sheep" by Schmeidler's criterion). Even people who are generally open toward liminal material may close themselves to psi if they believe it to be nonexistent or unreliable. There is more discussion of the sheep-goat effect in chapter 16.

NOTES

1. By *behavior* is meant all action that is explicitly or implicitly intentional. The body hitting things while falling down stairs is action, but it is not behavior in the sense intended here. See Macmurray, 1991, for one discussion of this distinction.

2. In this sense, all persons are lay scientists who devote considerable effort to construct predictive understandings of their personal worlds (see G. A. Kelly, 1955, 1979, for an elaborate theory of personality based upon this position).

3. The term *sign* is used here as it is in arithmetic.

4. Scientists in these various areas may object to the ways in which I reword and reframe some of their familiar constructs. I have found it necessary to do this in order to offer a single set of terms for some central ideas as opposed to the variety of terms that have developed in different research contexts, and also to be consistent with the nonreductionistic premises of unconscious thought and intention that distinguish the First Sight approach.

5. Ashby and Gott, 1988; Bless and Schwarz, 1998; Tversky and Kahneman, 1974.

6. William, 2003; Young and Claypool, 2010.

7. Fazio, Jackson, Dunton, and Williams, 1995.

8. Roberts, 1985.

9. Dijksterhuis, Preston, Wegner, and Aarts, 2008.

10. Kanthamani and Rao, 1974.

11. Weinberger and Westen, 2008.

12. Schmeidler and McConnell, 1958.

13. L. E. Rhine, 1964.

14. Suslow et al., 2010.

15. Carpenter, 1971.

16. Schwarz and Bless, 1992; Snodgrass, Bernat, and Shevrin, 2004.

17. McMoneagle, 2000.

18. Carpenter, 2005a.

19. Bar-Haim et al., 2007.

20. Paterson and Neufeld, 1987.

21. Buckner, Maner, and Schmidt, 2010.

22. Fenigstein, 1979.

23. Martin and Jackson, 2008; Quinn et al., 2011.

24. Csikszentmihalyi, 1991.

25. The switching and extremity corollaries primarily are intended to help understand when and how psi information may come to be definitely implied or disimplied in consciousness and action. In most tests of extrasensory perception, this definiteness of expression is operationally defined in terms of the extremity of scores. It should be noted that effects on scoring extremity (e.g., run-score variances) have been reported much less frequently in research papers than effects on simple directional scores (e.g., proportion of correct responses). For this reason, the pertinent research base is still relatively scanty. If more attention comes to be paid to the problem, it will be possible to build and test more elaborate hypotheses involving switching and extremity.

26. Siegel and Weinberger, 1998.

27. Carpenter, 2001, 2005a.

28. Palmer, 1978, 1982.

29. See Baumann and Kuhl, 2005; Gasper and Clore, 2002. This generalization refers to the formation of conscious experiences. Unconscious attention is another matter, and it is expected instead to show a special sensitization due to fearfulness, as discussed in chapter 16.

30. Schmeidler and McConnell, 1958.

Section II

ELABORATIONS OF THE MODEL AND THE THEORY

It has become accepted doctrine that we must attempt to study the whole man. Actually we cannot study even a whole tree or a whole guinea pig. But it is a whole tree and a whole guinea pig that have survived and evolved, and we must make the attempt.

—Gardner Murphy

3

A Model of the Mind and of the Place of Psi in Mental Functioning

The great value of psychical research is that it has begun to put perspective into the universe and to show us that neither we nor our world come to an end where we thought they did.

—G. N. M. Tyrrell

First Sight is a model with two major aspects: a model of psi and its functioning within the context of the mind, and a model of the mind and its place in the world. We define two basic assertions about the nature of psi and its place in mental functioning and then describe an approach to understanding the mind in which psi functioning can be seen to have a sensible place.

This is a psychological model, not a physical or neurobiological one. As important as those aspects of a person are, parapsychologists find that most of our more robust findings about psi are psychological in nature, and it is these findings that most need to be understood and extended. Therefore, the focus here is mainly upon the interface between parapsychology and general psychology, and not the various other fields of science.

PSI AND THE MIND

Basic Assertions about the Nature of the Mind

A basic premise of this model is that psi is an elemental, continuously active constituent of the development of all experience. The model assumes that all organisms are preconsciously engaged with reality beyond their physical, sensory boundaries. All such distal engagements are termed *psi*. Since extrasensory information (distal in time or space) is available to an organism before proximal, sensory information is, the development of experience may be thought of as beginning at the psi level of functioning. Thus, psi is First Sight as opposed to "second sight," in the colloquial phrase, which would imply that psychic cognizance is occasional and secondary to sensory experience. A second basic premise is that the mind thinks unconsciously as well as consciously and that processes of unconscious thought make active and continual reference to an indeterminately vast sea of potential meanings, including distal elements apprehended by psi in producing the contents of consciousness and other behavior.

Just as every perception is known to have a process of development that is largely preconscious,[1] all other modes of experience are assumed to have similar preconscious developmental histories.[2] The chain of preconscious development of a perceptual experience begins with the psi level of engagement with the extended world. These engagements are preconscious and anticipatory. They are the leading edge of the preconscious processes by which the mind assembles all its experience.

From the perspective of this model, psi processes are not unusual or exotic. They function as the initiating part of the mind's perpetual preconscious working toward the end of constructing its experience and framing its choices as well as implicitly directing less conscious behavioral choices. Psi processes are common and serve as the implicit foundation out of which all experience is formed. How may we conceive of the nature of the mind in a way that will make this understanding of psi functioning sensible?

HISTORICAL CONTEXT AND ALTERNATIVE VIEWS OF THE MIND

William James (1890) defined psychology as the study of mental processes. He said that the central problem for psychologists "is that thinking of some sort goes on." He spoke of the stream of consciousness, then immediately pointed out that it was actually more like a pulsing chain of mental events: thought, feeling, memory, thought, perception, feeling, etc. There is an essential problem here to which parapsychology can contribute in a basic way: how is it that a thought moves to the particular next thing and not some other? At any given moment there are presumably many contending possibilities, even excluding extrasensory events. This implies an even more general question: What causes a thought?

A Popular Model

In the conventional model of the Mind in the World, physical processes are the bedrock of reality.[3] Mental events are generated by physical (neurobiological) events. Organisms, including human beings, can be understood as biological machines with clear physical boundaries. Because the nervous system generates consciousness, the reality of mental events is secondary and derivative. As the biologist Karl Vogt famously said: "The brain secretes thought as the stomach secretes gastric juice, the liver bile, and the kidneys urine." More recently, the astronomer and popularizer of science Carl Sagan expressed the same idea in different words: "My fundamental premise about the brain is that its workings—what we sometimes call 'mind'—are a consequence of its anatomy and physiology, and nothing more" (Sagan, 1986). Since physical processes produce mental events, these events cannot also be elicited by happenings beyond the physical boundaries of the organism, except inasmuch as their effects somehow impinge upon the sensory system. The laws governing mental processes are mechanical and impersonal in nature. Implicit in this presumption of physiology generating mind is the deeper presumption of a reductionistic "hierarchy of the sciences," in which the constructs of physics are seen as reflecting the deepest substrate of reality. From this point of view, the answer to the question about why the particular next thought occurs must be found in the biophysical events that cause that thought to occur.

From the point of view of this model, psi either does not exist (the most intuitively sensible alternative), or else it is an occasional aberration that would require some additions or changes to our ways of understanding just how external events cause mental ones. For example, how the causal activity of an event at a distance might seemingly "magically" traverse space and give rise to a change in awareness in a nervous system would require some mechanism of action, analogous to an electromagnetic transmission or perhaps a quantum linkage. Since physical events cause mental ones, the rare and anomalous instances of distant influence would need to be explained by showing just how those physical events have their impact.

An Alternative Model

From another point of view, "mental" and "physical" are constructions placed upon reality, and neither is presumed to refer to processes more real or basic than the other. This general perspective has been developed for psychology by Kelly (1955) and elaborated more recently by Rychlak (1968); but it can be seen to have much in common with the philosophies of science of A. N. Whitehead and John Dewey. From this point of view, the notion of "organism" is itself a construction. In fact, when we look closely at any living being referred to with this construct, we see that it is not rigidly bounded, and at its edges it blurs into its surround such that the two are not entirely distinguishable. This blur applies to consciousness as well, at least in the case of human beings. All conscious processes occur in a context of unconscious or preconscious mental processes, which must be understood in terms of meaning rather than impersonal, biological mechanism. Mental processes are not mechanical in the sense that chemical processes are. Rather, they are primarily goal directed and personal, including those that are unconscious or "automatic."[4] Thus, First Sight adopts a kind of psychological determinism. Experiences and behaviors are caused by unconscious processes, but these processes are not impersonally mechanical. They are highly personal, always guided by one's particular unconscious intentions, goals, and aversions. What makes our experience? We do, but we do it unconsciously.

Assuming the reality of psi processes, our model states that at the edge of perception, an organism and its surround lack distinguishable identity. There is a transactional zone in which organism and surround, or self and other, *are* one another. Each organism is situated at its edges beyond the line of its sensory impingement with physical events, and it is responsive to meanings in the larger surround, which is of indefinite extent. From this perspective, the particular next thought occurs because it is chosen by an intentional self, using preconscious processes and consulting preconscious (including extrasensory) information.

Early Observations of Unconscious Processes

Interest in unconscious mental processes may be traced back at least to the earliest days of the field of psychology. At about the same time that James was defining the central problems of psychology, two other important lines of work were beginning that strongly suggested the reality of unconscious mental processes. Jastrow[5] noticed that subjects who believed that they were merely guessing could distinguish the difference between two weights correctly even when the differences were so slight that they were not consciously perceptible. Freud (1892 [1963]) found that with patients like Anna O., inscrutable physical symptoms could be explained and treated if they were seen as derivative of unconscious emotional conflicts. Alongside these observations, mainstream psychology developed a skeptical tradition in which unconscious processes are still viewed with strong suspicion by many.

The Current Scene

Despite this suspicion, Jastrow's and Freud's observations on the action of unconscious information on cognitive and affective/somatic functioning, respectively, led to much work on what has come to be called the "cold" and the "hot" unconscious. All of this work has grown considerably, and there is now much overlap.[6] Some scientists, such as Epstein (1994) and Shevrin (Shevrin et al., 1996), are now doing sophisticated research that is informed by both traditions at once. Out of all of this emerges a picture of the mind as being a zone of conscious self-awareness with a subliminal surround that precedes and conditions consciousness in many complex but systematic ways.[7] The findings of parapsychology are not incongruent with this picture but add to it the idea that an organism's engagement with this surround is not bounded by physical, sensory impingement but extends beyond that in space and in time.

Is it reasonable to suppose that an organism is not rigidly bounded but at its edges blurs into its surround, such that the two are not entirely distinguishable? This is obviously the case in a physical sense. The bagel on my plate at breakfast time is well on the way to becoming part of Jim Carpenter a couple of hours later. In the words of the children's rhyme: "It's a very odd thing, as odd as can be, that whatever Miss Gee eats, becomes part of Miss Gee." Or as Gardner Murphy asked (1956), at what point does the oxygen one breathes become part of oneself? In another example of blurry physical boundaries, consider the gecko, a lizard remarkable for its ability to walk upside down on ceilings. Recent research[8] has discovered that its defiance of gravity is permitted by the fact that the extremely fine hairs on its feet provide such a density of contact with a surface that it creates billions of weak molecular attractions called van der Waals forces. These forces act only at very small distances and hold together the molecules of objects. In other words, the same tiny forces that hold the gecko together and hold the ceiling together also hold the gecko to the ceiling. At this very fine level of contact, gecko and ceiling are energically merged. First Sight suggests that there is an analogous blur at the edge of our mental being. At the leading edge of perception and intention, organism and surround lack distinguishable identity. In this transactional zone, they are one another. Adding the dimension of time, it might be best to say that in this zone they become themselves out of each other. Each sentient being exists at its edges beyond the line of contact between physical events and the sensory-motor system and is responsive to meanings in that indefinitely larger surround.[9]

Were it not for the anomalies of parapsychology, we might not need to pose the idea that, by our nature, we extend beyond ourselves in apprehension and influence. Given the reality of those anomalies, this idea seems almost inescapable.

FIRST SIGHT THEORY AND THE CAUSE OF A THOUGHT

First Sight theory assumes that the behavior of persons is caused by their intentions, both conscious and unconscious. It is a teleological point of view, not an externally deterministic one. This runs counter to the assumptions of most psychologists. From the prevailing point of view, behavioral choices are caused by the situations around an organism. It may seem a subtle point, but it has huge implications in terms of where a scientist looks for the explanations for anything. Suppose we place food before a dozen hungry persons and observe that almost all of them eat it.

A traditionally behavioral point of view would say that the eating behavior is caused by (stimulated by) the food. For many contemporary scientists it may seem quaintly behavioristic to speak of the food causing the eating. There is a newer twist to the reductionist approach that now says that it is brains and the rest of the nervous systems of organisms that are responding to the food by eating. Brains are physical objects, made of chemicals, and they are obviously very important in behavioral activity. From this perspective, if we can see how the responses of brains stand behind the behavior of eating, then the eating will be explained physically, and no recourse will have to be made to any subjective idea like an intention.

Our teleologically oriented position would say that the hungry persons (unless deliberately fasting or too ill to eat) intend to eat and find the available food to be pertinent to their intention, so they respond to it accordingly. From this angle, the intentions still come first and use the brain and all the rest of the physical situation to find a successful outcome.

Obviously this is closer to a commonsense way of understanding things, but scientists have not wanted to resort to it because they have believed that reference to anything as subjective as intentions evokes the sort of "spiritistic" idea of human nature that science has tried to free itself from since the days of an oppressive medieval church. (They distrust anything that parapsychologists report for the same reason.) They also believe that according causal status to individual choice would run counter to a central aspiration of science: to construct an adequate account of reality that is as simple as possible. A world full of freely choosing agents would be difficult to reduce to a single, basically physical account. Besides, it can be argued, intention does not need to be considered a prior cause because much brain activity precedes the moment in which a person becomes aware of an intention and is able to announce it, and this brain activity apparently leads up to that moment. From this perspective, intentions are also caused by brains.[10]

First Sight theory responds that this preparatory brain activity is enacting unconscious intentions, and it is these unconscious intentions that are the most important determiners of behavior. Reductionists may become vexed at this point, but they must be reminded that when one examines behavior in light of unconscious thought (which may be objectively and appropriately measured), it is clear that this thought is intentional, motivated, and personally purposeful. We are not all the same at the level of unconscious thought, responding as predictably and identically as billiard balls to the forces impinging upon our sensory systems. Our personal intentions and goals idiosyncratically shape our responses to things, even when those responses are conducted with little or no conscious awareness. As the psychologist Drew Westen has said, "When conscious motives are activated, they guide behavior. When they are not—which is much of the time as people muddle through their lives—unconscious motives guide behavior." Considerable work in contemporary cognitive and social psychology is demonstrating the importance of these unconscious goals and intentions.[11] First Sight theory is in line with these developments.

A comprehensive understanding of the functioning of organisms that includes a causal understanding of intention can be developed. It will not necessarily be overwhelmingly burdened by countless independent agencies. The functioning of intention should itself prove to be "lawful" and patterned, and in fact it already seems to be so. General hypotheses can be framed that will be seen to apply across persons. Elucidation of these patterns should be a major scientific objective. Why go to the trouble? Because of the deepest commitment of science: to provide an account of reality that is true to its domains of study. The findings of parapsychology show that organisms engage the meanings of events in the world that extend far beyond the ordinary boundaries of those organisms and carry out those engagements in ways that are structured by personal intentions. These are some of the real events that science is committed to understand. First Sight theory (whether it proves to be true or not) is offered as a means by which to carry out that basic commitment.

NOTES

1. Gollwitzer, 1990; Solley and Murphy, 1960.

2. For prior conceptual and empirical work on the preconscious functioning of psi, see Schechter (1977) and Stanford (1978, 1991).

3. One popular understanding of James sees him as taking this position as well. In his *Principles* (1890) he rejected the idea of unconscious mental processes as they were popularly understood in his day, calling such ideas "whimsies." Below consciousness lies impersonal neurological process, as is the assumption for most scientists today. However, the whole body of James's work shows an abiding interest in unconscious mental processes (Kelly and Kelly, 2007; Weinberger, 2000).

4. Bargh, 1989.

5. Peirce and Jastrow, 1884.

6. Bornstein and Masling, 1998; Uleman and Bargh, 1989; Weinberger, Siegel, and Decamello, 2000.

7. Giving an adequate summary of this work would make this discussion far too long. Suffice it to say that many hundreds of studies on preconscious mental processes have been reported, and the field is very active today. Methods arousing

preconscious processes are so well accepted today by many researchers that they are used as techniques with which to study other questions. For example, the action of subliminal primes has proved useful for studying a variety of phenomena ranging from relationship schemas (Baldwin et al., 1993) to attachment theory (Mikulincer et al., 2001) to psychoanalytic theory (Silverman, 1976; Sohlberg, Billinghurst, and Nylen, 1998; Weinberger and Hardaway, 1990).

8. Autumn et al., 2002.

9. This is reminiscent of Heidegger's (1962) analogy of a human being as like an outrigger canoe, part of which is always away from itself.

10. Crick, 1995.

11. Bargh and Huang, 2009; Custers, 2009; Leander, Moore, and Chartrand, 2009; and Moscovitz and Gesundheit, 2009.

4

Psi and Consciousness

The brain may respond to external stimuli which, for one reason or another, are not consciously perceived. . . . The characteristics of conscious experience are what one would expect of a late stage in the transition from sensory to motor processes—relatively restricted, unambiguous, and determined by factors which do not themselves enter awareness. Conscious experience is, par excellence, a domain for representing a few end products of all that went before.

—Norman Dixon

The following discussion focuses more on the perceptive aspect of psi functioning (ESP) than on the active aspect (PK); however, the theoretical ideas may be applied to PK as well. We assume that ESP and PK are intimately connected functions. Psychokinesis is the *expression* of psi information. Extrasensory perception is the *impression* of psi information as it is reflected in the experience or behavior of a person or other organism. Much more psychological research has been carried out on ESP than on PK, so our discussion will focus here primarily upon the *impression* of psi. How does psi function in the formation of all experience? First we need to say a bit about why we think of experience as *forming* at all.

CONSCIOUSNESS BEGINS UNCONSCIOUSLY

We all assume intuitively that consciousness is simply given; it is whatever occurs to us. Actually, it has been known for a long time that each piece of experience has a developmental history that is unconscious. There is a physiological level to this development, as we know from research that shows that certain unconscious nervous-system events precede bits of consciousness and lead to them. There is a psychological side, too, in that unconscious long-term memories and goals and subliminal (or suboptimal) perceptions also stand behind single events of consciousness and condition their development. In psychology, this understanding dates at least to the Wurzburg school of the early twentieth century,[1] was important to gestalt psychologists such as Werner (1935, 1956), and was an essential premise in the New Look studies of the 1940s and 1950s.

PREHENSIONS, NOT PERCEPTIONS

It is worth reemphasizing one thing about truly subliminal perceptions: They are not conscious. In fact, it is not accurate to speak of them as perceptions at all, since perceptions are conscious experiences. What are they then? I find it helpful to borrow a term from Alfred North Whitehead and refer to them as *prehensions* (although I do not intend to imply all of the connotations he attached to the term). It is useful as a neutral term because of its Latin root, implying "to grasp." Prehensions get hold of things. Unconscious prehensions get hold of things unconsciously.

Then what about *extrasensory* perceptions (or prehensions)?

HISTORY OF A PERCEPTION
(OR A MEMORY OR FEELING OR IMAGE)

The following sequence, run backward, sketches a general series of events that appears to lead to every experience. Using the example of a visual perception and beginning at the end of the sequence:

D. I see X (an attributed understanding of an experience), and I think about it.
C. Just prior to that, I experience a collection of sensations that I attempt to construe.
B. Just prior to that, sensations register subliminally.
A. Just prior to that, an extrasensory anticipation of the event (and/or a psychokinetic elicitation of the event) initiates the perceptual process.

A great deal of the work of experimental psychology has focused on processes at step C, how perceptions occur and how they come to be understood. Psychologists studying subliminal perception, or "perception without awareness" (PWA), as it is preferred today,[2] added the preconscious step B to the cognitive account. The findings of parapsychologists add step A.

In the genesis of a perception, each step links to the next and orients it in a helpful way. Think of these as different parts of a person playing different roles all communicating quickly and efficiently: We might speak colloquially of an inner *Prophet*, an *Artist*, a *Scientist*, and a *Person of Ordinary Consciousness*. The *Prophet* knows something is coming, the *Artist* has a sense of something interesting, the *Scientist* sees a collection of facts and tries to form an understanding of it, and the *Person of Ordinary Consciousness* sees X—all in a fraction of a second. Each sends a rapid, helpful message on to the next.[3]

WHY CONSCIOUSNESS?

In regard to the guidance of the flow of consciousness, we ordinarily want consciousness to focus on the most useful thing at any given moment. This implicit motive guides the orienting information that is passed on from each perceptual stage to the next.

In seeking this "most useful" thing, we are pursuing a balance of several needs all the time, although different needs may be more salient at different times. Some of these needs are general, and many are shared with all animals. In the case of human beings, it is more adequate to think of these needs as "intentions" rather than blind "forces."

1. We want to continue to live, and to live happily and freely, so we also want to avoid potential danger, pain, and confinement.
2. We want to maintain harmonious and fruitful relations with our interpersonal network, so we also want to avoid conflict, shame, and guilt.
3. We want to maintain adequate control over our circumstances and a well-functioning predictive understanding of events, so we also want to avoid confusion, identity diffusion, the invalidation of core constructs,[4] and a loss of freedom to explore and investigate.

Many needs are more personal and particular to the individual and feature unconscious emotional reactions (as to events resembling former trauma or happiness), unconscious beliefs,[5] and habitual plans and values.

Rational consciousness is a marvelous, very powerful tool, responsible for human dominance of the planet. It is our "workspace."[6] Each of us is constantly selecting the most interesting issue to present to it from the myriad of potential concerns that exist in the present or the personally meaningful future.

One implication of the metaphor of inner "parts" or "roles" needs to be clarified. Starting with a single perception and moving backward, it might seem as if one event leads to one perception. Actually, this model assumes that at the A step, we are in touch with virtually everything, or at least so much that we currently have no way to assess its boundaries. *Step A must begin the winnowing process from virtually everything to one best thing.* This initial step of selection and deselection is the basic psi process. In everyday experience it is "bound" and functions entirely unconsciously, although it goes on constantly and must operate in what seems to the rational mind an unbelievably complex and intricate way. In making this selection, it must use two criteria: How important is the potential event? How likely is it to actually occur to me? These two criteria together might be said to constitute the event's *sensed relevance*. This is what in our theory is referred to as *weighting*.

With this mammoth task of selecting and deselecting in terms of sensed relevance, the psi function (the Prophet) has only one binary tool: in regard to ESP, it is to orient toward the thing or away from it to something else instead. In regard to PK, it is to impel the potential object of intention in the prointention direction, or in some contrary direction. As Freud said (1933), the unconscious mind has no sense of negation. It does not choose "this or not-this," it chooses "this or that." In the language of parapsychology, all psi-missing is some form of displacement. One thing is selected as "toward" and the rest as "away from." This act of choice takes place prior to the GSR or ERP deflections of presentiment studies, in which psychophysiological responses may be seen to anticipate future experiences,[7] or perhaps the GSR deflection signals the moment of decision about the future event in question (such as the later presentation of an emotional picture).

Focusing now exclusively on ESP and returning to the metaphor of inner roles, if the Prophet selects an event as "toward," the Artist is alerted. The Artist then senses that something interesting (or important, or ominous, or novel, or confusing or attractive) is coming, and preconscious attention is sharpened in the direction of the sensory events that are now beginning to impinge upon the peripheral nervous system. The Scientist is alerted that this particular collection of sensations (among the myriad that are present at any given moment) is especially salient and begins to focus upon it. Then the Person of Ordinary Consciousness arrives at his or her perception.[8]

UNCONSCIOUS THOUGHT

As already implied, an important assumption of this model is that the mind thinks unconsciously as well as consciously. Inasmuch as we understand thinking to be something that is necessarily conscious, we are using terms analogically here. Yet something like thinking must be going on in the dark processes that precede consciousness and action. This unconscious thought produces consciousness as well as all implicitly goal-relevant unconscious behavior. One way to understand the essential difference between the two kinds of thought is in terms of conscious attention, as Dijksterhuis (2006) has said. Conscious thought is thought with conscious attention. Unconscious thought is thought without such attention, or with it directed elsewhere. Indeed, much of the material processed by unconscious thought is inherently unavailable to conscious attention.

While the reality of unconscious thought has been hotly debated at times, a number of important theories have been offered about it recently.[9] Research done within the context of these and related theories has led to greater understanding of how unconscious thought works. One important characteristic of unconscious thought is its capacity to select elements in a given moment that are most important. This is what in First Sight theory is called *weighting*. This process depends upon another important characteristic of unconscious thought: its very great processing capacity (as opposed to conscious thought, which generally can process only one thing at a time). Its manner of processing information has also been found to be different from that used by conscious thought. Whereas conscious thought can follow precise rules in reaching decisions (as in solving a mathematical problem), unconscious thought cannot. Instead, it produces rough approximations of solutions to problems generated by a kind of holistic weighting and averaging across large domains of material.[10] These processes of weighting and holistically averaging across great domains of implicit meaning lead to all the contents of consciousness, including such things as decisions, perceptions, preferences, and feelings. They also lead to all unconscious but motivated behaviors, such as action tendencies and physiological reactions that are outside of awareness.

THE CONSTRUCTION OF CONSCIOUSNESS

Conscious experiences are either constituted by thoughts (ideas, images, feelings, memories) or sensory perceptions, which quickly give rise to thoughts or construals. All experiences have a preconscious phase that is quite brief.[11] What is known about the development of sensory experiences may serve as a model for the development of all experiences, including those that refer not to physical sensations but to feelings or ideas or conscious decisions to act.

When a preconsciously apprehended piece of sensory information is selected as salient (*weighted* heavily), this selection initiates an activation of preconscious affective responses and associated meanings. This activation does not by itself result in a conscious experience but in the arousal of an apprehensive network that potentiates experience. This network is not simply of a meaning but of presemantic effect and classes of meanings. This network poses a set of implicit questions that preconscious attention seeks to answer by consulting additional sensory information. With it the person poses tentative, general, preverbal hypotheses in terms of which to scan for confirmatory evidence. Thereby, the network guides the effort to construe. Through the anticipatory questions and the information we collect preconsciously, we construct our experience. All the preconscious sources of engagement and information, including psi, anticipate and implicitly structure the formation of experience.

At the very leading edge of the formation of a perception, before any sensory input is available, psi prehension arouses an anticipational nexus of meanings. These meanings pose, as it were, the set of questions that are to be answered by forthcoming sensory experience.

It is sensory experience that provides conscious perception. It provides the validating information to the anticipational questions. Psi is part of the preparatory process that helps the mind make the best use of its sensory experience. In the ordinary flow of developing awarenesses, the anticipational questions slip into oblivion before they can ever become issues to awareness, in favor of the actual developing experience.[12]

Suppose I notice a flicker of movement on my right, just at the edge of my visual field. I turn my head and see that my son has entered the room. This model proposes that before the flicker of light, a psi prehension suggested that something meaningful was forthcoming, and my awareness was alerted in a general direction and to a family of potential meanings. The flicker, as we know from work in PWA, itself arouses an anticipational network of potential meaning, beginning to question the movement and preparing me to understand it. When I turn and see my son, I have full visual information that I can quickly understand, and I have a simple awareness, a bit of knowing. All the rapid machinations of preknowing have vanished before I can glimpse them or know of their participation in my experience.

Including psi in our understanding of how consciousness forms requires a fundamental shift. It changes our idea of what role physical sensation plays. In the view most commonly held, consciousness is caused by stimulation. Physical events impinge upon the nervous system of a person and give rise to an awareness of some sort. According to First Sight, physical sensation comes along later in the process. First the person is engaged in the meaning of the situation (psi) in an anticipatory and allusive way, and then physical stimuli are used to sharpen the experience that develops. We might say that a major function of physical stimuli is to guide us about what to *not become aware of* by discriminating all that is less pertinent from the little that is most. Stimuli then go on to fill out the content of the experience. For First Sight, psi proposes and sensation responds.

PRECONSCIOUS EXPECTATION AND INADVERTENCY

What happens if this process is interrupted before the natural, rapid flow of events can develop and a perception is formed? Both parapsychologists and the psychologists studying PWA have been asking this question and have independently found many of the same answers. Basically, the orienting action of steps A and B can be glimpsed in the feelings, cognitions, and behavior of the person whose perception is being denied. Usually we can see these things more clearly in others than in ourselves, unless we are examining our own experience in retrospect with a certain detachment. When conscious perception is allowed to develop, this is what is available to awareness. That may be denied or prevented for different reasons, perhaps because the event never is allowed to impinge upon sensation (as in an ESP experiment) or because the impingement is interrupted too quickly for it to be grasped or is otherwise occluded (as in PWA). When conscious development is denied, one may see the anticipational arousal expressed inadvertently in the feelings or associations or behavior of the person, with the latter having no insight into the origin of those things. The expression must be inadvertent, because one cannot make a conscious choice in regard to something unless there is a conscious perception of it. Prior to the conscious perception, or in situations that prevent its forming, one is able to see no more than the effects of preconscious choices, experienced by consciousness as inadvertency.

In general, both psi prehension and subliminal prehension can be seen primarily in the interpretation of inadvertency. Ordinarily, the successful formation of a conscious experience occludes these preconscious processes and is oblivious to them. However, if conscious experience is prevented, we can glimpse the hints and whispers of implicit meaning. Analogously, the sky in the daytime, flooded with the sun's light, looks blue and empty, but at night without the sun, it can be seen filled with flickering starlight.

SEEING THE ACTION OF PRECONSCIOUS AROUSAL

Inadvertent psychological events are those that "just happen" as opposed to being experienced as things "I do." An image comes to mind, the memory of a song occurs of its own volition, a mood descends or arises, a silly mispronunciation intrudes into speech, one name is substituted for another, a shadow is misinterpreted as a snake, or in the depth of sleep a dream takes shape. In the context of an ESP experiment, the percipient utters free associations, the remote viewer scribbles and consults an inner flow of images, the card guesser impulsively throws a card on one pile among five, the subject being stared at by someone out of sight generates faint, unfelt neurophysiological responses being sent to a polygraph.

Although presumably active all the time, we rarely see the extrasensory and the subliminal-sensory levels of experience in action. I have an occasional experience in which I can see the subliminal at work in my own stream of consciousness. Since I have become a little hard of hearing, the volume necessary for my clearly hearing vocal speech is a bit louder than that for most people. Recently in a family conversation, I uttered some thought only to see my daughter roll her eyes in an expression that gently said, "He's doing it again." I had expressed a restatement of something that someone else in the conversation had said a short time before. Others had been conscious of the remark, but I had not. And it was clear to them that my thought had been stimulated by what had been said before, but I did not know that. My own words popped into my head as, I thought, a brand new idea. But they weren't. They had been subliminally prompted by the remark that others had heard consciously. This "popping up" is one kind of inadvertency. As with all such experiences of "popping up," it was not prompted by anything around me, as far as I could tell at the time.

Psychologists have studied inadvertent expressions of preconscious processes extensively. Poetzel (1917) found that images flashed briefly and not consciously seen were expressed metaphorically later in dreams. Cognitive psychologists found that subliminal or occluded stimuli affected later processes of learning, forgetting, affective response, and association if the later material was connected somehow to the unconscious stimuli.[13] Psychodynamic and social psychological researchers found that the emotional significance of subliminal material affected a person's later mood and spontaneous social behavior.[14] For example, a person exposed to an aggressive subliminal stimulus was more apt to be querulous when placed in a later contentious situation as compared to someone subliminally exposed to neutral messages. The same aggressive messages presented to full awareness had no such effect.[15] In a different finding, a subliminal prime associated with helpful groups has been shown to lead people to later be more helpful.[16]

In a parallel manner, parapsychologists found that people could indeed not see the material enclosed in opaque envelopes, but they could sometimes successfully guess them, and perhaps to a higher degree, could express a meaningful inadvertent response to the hidden content by their physiological responses or spontaneous imagery or affective responses to similar content exposed later. Many other examples could be listed of the various presensory and subliminal-sensory effects that have been studied. For instance, in a ganzfeld ESP study, the percipient relaxes in a shielded room that is isolated from target material that is being viewed by a sender who is elsewhere. The percipient allows the development of spontaneous feelings and images that are not consciously experienced as being caused by the target material (which is neither seen nor heard). However, later examination of the target material often suggests associative connections to the feelings and images that the percipient experienced, to the extent that the correct target material can be picked out of a field of decoys. In a typical PWA experiment, in which conscious recognition of a stimulus is prevented, the effects of the stimulus (seen perhaps as a meaningless flicker of light) may be observed by a variety of behaviors that the subject experiences as bearing no relation at all to the stimulus. For example, Banse (1999) showed that preconscious presentation of the names and faces of loved ones, compared to other persons, caused a shift in the emotional evaluation of meaningless Chinese characters; Verney et al. (2003) showed that a person's general level of cognitive ability could be assessed by the kind of pupilary response involuntarily given to masked stimuli; and Talbot et al. (1991) found that the number of cheddar crackers eaten in a bogus tasting task declined when subjects had been exposed subliminally to the words "Mommy is leaving me," designed to unconsciously arouse a depressive mood.

PSI AND OTHER PRECONSCIOUS PROCESSES

The model assumes that the mind democratically and unconsciously draws upon all available sources of information in arriving at an orientation to developing experience. That is, psi experiences are expected to be drawn upon, along with memories, subliminal stimuli, and elements of imagination in contributing to the formation of the ongoing flow of experience. It is in this sense that the First Sight approach is a model. A model in science is essentially an analogy, a presumption that things that are understood about one thing may be usefully carried over in attempting to understand something else. If psi contributes to the development of all of our experience, how does it do so? This model proposes that psi processes function in basically the same ways that other preconscious processes do and that patterns of functioning that have been found with, for example, subliminal perception, will obtain in regard to extrasensory perception as well. Such a presumption must be tested empirically to determine its value. It is worth noting that there are beginning efforts in this integrative direction in other areas of psychology that are studying preconscious processes, as, for example, in the work of McElroy, Seta, and Waring (2007) showing that preconscious processes involving self-esteem have impact upon the risk level of decisions.

SIMILAR ACTIONS OF PRECONSCIOUS PROCESSES USING SUBLIMINAL AND EXTRASENSORY INFORMATION

I first conceived of the First Sight model because of the many apparent similarities between extrasensory perception and subliminal perception. Similar conditions have been found to facilitate the expression of both subliminal and extrasensory information (this is elaborated further in chapter 7). Such common conditions include asking persons to draw responses as opposed to verbalizing them, providing sensory attenuation, inducing a state of hypnosis, eliciting free association, examining dreams, evoking a relaxed reverie, and providing a positive, encouraging environment.[17] Similar sorts of people have been seen to be more likely to show the effects: people with stronger tendencies toward dissociation or creativity or absorption, those positively disposed toward it, those who are more socially engaged, and those who are less anxious. The expressions of both kinds of stimuli tend to be fragmented and metaphorical, rather than literal and complete.[18] Finally, some studies have shown significant positive correlations when subjects were tested with both subliminal and ESP stimuli, suggesting that persons who are more likely to express one kind of influence will tend to express the other as well. Since the surveys of Nash and Schmeidler, continuing work in both perception without awareness (PWA) and psi processes has brought to light other commonalities between the two.

For example, both may more commonly be expressed by effects on emotion or on some aspect of psychophysiological functioning than by cognitive retrieval.[19] When effects on associative processes are assessed, familiar and well-learned material is often more sensitive to effects than unfamiliar material.[20]

There is evidence that the effectiveness of precognitive guessing and unconscious precognitive physiological responses tend to drop off sharply as the time between response period and target event increases.[21] In an analogous way, the effectiveness of subliminal primes tends to drop off logarithmically over time.[22] Thus it seems as if the mind's preconscious processes normally construct its experiences over very short time spans, reaching backward in using sensory primes and forward in precognition.

And finally, situations requiring careful assessment and judgment tend to make both kinds of effects vanish.[23] Putting all of this together, it appears that scientists in these different fields have been studying similar things without realizing it.

It is incumbent upon parapsychologists to join with other psychologists to elucidate those processes of unconscious thought that govern the movement of consciousness to the next thing (and that bring the next thing to consciousness). We may think of preconscious psychological processes as all of those processes that precede and condition conscious experience. If we come to understand the patterns governing the movement of consciousness to the next thing by way of these processes, we will also understand many of the working principles of parapsychology—and parapsychology will clearly be part of psychology. The focus need not be exclusively on the extrasensory. As the First Sight model proposes, we may find that the functions of preconscious processes as they govern preexperiential cognizance of events with weak or unattended sensory impingement will be found to be more or less the same as those that govern cognizance of events that have no sensory impingement. In the broad sense, the processes of psi and the other implicit psychological processes may be the same. In that case, defining the focus of our interest as "extrasensory" would be too narrow, like limiting the study of vision to the perception of blue things.

A PHENOMENOLOGICAL PERSPECTIVE

In a phenomenological approach, experience-as-such is taken as primary reality, and all of the myriads of constructions that we may invent and with which we interpret reality are taken as secondary and imposed. This is assumed to be true even if the constructions are so deeply presumed as to be experienced as "necessarily so" and even if the constructions are extremely powerful and useful, as are the constructions of physical science. Approaching reality with such conceptual innocence has some advantages in regard to our understanding of psi phenomena. Our preoccupation with the "extrasensory mystery" has led us to imagine that some special senses are required for dealing with reality not local to ourselves. This "mystery" is really created partly by the everyday fact of not being conscious of that extended reality but also by the physically reductionistic model of the human being as a "subjective" mind inside of a physical box, or body. This split is deeply presumed in Western culture and is even imbedded in the structure of our language.[24] A more adequate approach to the reality of human experience would be given by the existential-phenomenological position of Heidegger (1962), in which a human being is understood as "being in the world," or as the psychologist McCurdy (1965) put it, as the universe from a particular center. Boss (1979) similarly speaks of the person as a "world-luminating realm of openness." In this phenomenological approach, no split is assumed between the mind and the physical world, including one's own body. If the self is not presumed to be a bounded, subjective isolate inside a separate, objective reality, then the "mystery" vanishes.

A HYPOTHESIS OF FUNCTIONAL EQUIVALENCE

For one burdened with the metaphysical presupposition that an organism must have no interaction with its surround beyond its physical boundaries, the gap between a very faint stimulus and no stimulus at all is absolute and enormous. From a phenomenological perspective, the importance of this gap is an open question, and some evidence suggests that the gap may be very slight in many ways, or even nonexistent. This observation can seem astonishing or even outrageous. Imagine a cartographer surprised to step through a latitude without a scratch.

It may be that the mind uses its available extrasensory and subliminal-sensory and other implicit material in highly similar ways. We may call this a *hypothesis of functional equivalence*. It implies that psi information is not radically and qualitatively different from other implicit information, as far as the functioning of unconscious thought is concerned. It is drawn upon readily and used implicitly as sensed need requires.

This hypothesis will receive some indirect test in subsequent chapters, in which I examine how well patterns found in psi research fit with patterns reported in other areas of preconscious cognitive functioning, such as those involving memory, creativity, and subliminal perception, and with the preconscious effects of fear and extraversion.

NOTES

1. Gollwitzer, 1990.
2. Bornstein and Pittman, 1992.
3. Newell and Rosenbloom, 1981.
4. Allison, 1963; Carpenter, 2002; Darley and Gross, 1983; Stanford, 1966a.
5. Barrett, 1962; Heidegger, 1962.
6. Baars, 1997.
7. Bierman and Radin, 1997; Radin, 1997.
8. These terms are not chosen gratuitously, since it may be that more sustained, conscious focus on one of these levels of experience and preexperience tends toward different career choices. Perhaps more focus on everyday consciousness tends toward a life in one of the many practical modes (bankers, grocers, race car drivers), focus on freshly and adequately construing data tends toward scientific work, focus on incipient possibilities of meaning tends toward artistic pursuits, while focus on the preconscious leading edge of experience tends toward the life of a seer or psychic.
9. Brewer, 1988; Chaiken, 1980; Dijksterhuis, 2004, 2006; Epstein, 1994; Sloman, 1996; Smith and DeCoster, 1999.
10. For pertinent evidence, see e.g. Dijksterhuis, 2004; Levine et al., 1996; Wilson et al., 1993.
11. Schilder, 1942.
12. Note that in this model of the mind, preconscious processes are active and purposeful, posing hypotheses about reality and tentatively evaluating evidence. The mind even at this stage of functioning is not presumed to be mechanically passive, merely generating responses as the organism is stimulated.
13. Bornstein and Pittman, 1992; Dixon, 1981.
14. Chen and Bargh, 1997; Silverman, 1983; Silverman, Lachman, and Milich 1982.
15. Bargh, Chen, and Burrows, 1996.
16. Aarts et al., 2005.
17. Nash, 1986; Schmeidler, 1986, 1988.
18. Schmeidler, 1986.
19. Bem, 2003; Kunst-Wilson and Zajonc, 1980; Radin, 1997; Shevrin, 1988.
20. Bargh, 1992; Stanford, 1973.
21. Bierman and Radin, 1997; Honorton and Ferrari, 1989; Sondow, 1989.
22. Newell and Rosenbloom, 1981.
23. Allison, 1963; Carpenter, 2002; Darley and Gross, 1983; Stanford, 1966a.
24. Barrett, 1962; Heidegger, 1962.

5

The Vicissitudes of the Extrasensory: To Be Known or Not to Be Known

I've heard it said there's a window that opens
from one mind to another,
but if there's no wall, there's no need
for fitting the window, or the latch.

—Rumi, "Quatrain 511," *Night and Sleep*,
translated by Coleman Barks

THE UBIQUITY OF PSI IN THE CONSTRUCTION OF EXPERIENCE

Those apparent traces of psi phenomena that are available to most people in everyday life are so occasional and furtive as to make them seem to be exotic curiosities at best, or even transient illusions or misperceptions, hence the great argument over whether psi phenomena are real at all. I posit that the occasional psychic eruptions into everyday life are hints of a constant preconscious mental activity, one function of which is to prepare the mind for its incipient experiences and choices.

This model of psi as a seamlessly functioning part of normal preconscious processes normalizes parapsychology inasmuch as it suggests how psi phenomena function in everyday experience in an unconscious and implicit way. It also suggests the reason that we are not flooded with extrasensory awareness all the time.

THE ISSUE OF A FILTER OR BARRIER
BETWEEN PSI AND AWARENESS

We do not need to propose any sort of hypothetical barrier or filter to protect consciousness from psi processes any more than we need a barrier or
filter to protect consciousness from a subliminal or incidental stimulus, or
from a latent long-term memory. If I ask you to remember what you were
doing at 10 a.m. yesterday, you probably can, although you were not thinking of that a moment before. We do not posit some sort of internal filter
to account for why you are not always thinking about yesterday at 10 a.m.
Nor all of the other experiences you have had and can recall if you wish to
but do not generally have in mind.

The analogy is closer with a subliminal prime. We may be affected cognitively or emotionally by the prime, but *we can never* be aware of it as such.
Psi is the same.

The extrasensory exchange is intrinsically preconscious and not ever
available to awareness. The fact that it awakens an orienting nexus of potential meaning (both cognitive and affective) that quickly prepares us for
experience sometimes allows us to see its action by consulting this marginal
level of awareness. We gain this understanding by interpreting this marginal
experience, not by somehow having a direct experience of the extrasensory
engagement itself. Again, psi proposes and sensation responds.

In that marginal awareness, psi information is not transformed into
something fragmented or metaphorical, although it might appear to be;
it preconsciously alerts us to classes of potential meaning that help us to
interpret the sensory events to come, and these activated classes of meaning
can sometimes be glimpsed as such. When expressions of these activated
classes of meaning are later compared to the initiating stimulus in the full
light of consciousness, they may seem metaphorical or fragmented: a bear
may have aroused an image of some other kind of animal or some other
kind of danger, a line of windows in a building may have evoked an image
of a row on a checkerboard, or a scene of an automobile accident may have
stirred up an imageless sense of repulsion. These expressions occur when
the mind chooses to attempt an interpretation of preconscious experience
prior to obtaining clearly interpretable sensory information. The expressions will seem partial and allusory.

No barrier or filter mechanism is required to understand the relation
between psi and consciousness. Conscious awareness is the well-lit work-
shop within which each person constructs an understanding of reality
and negotiates within it. With conscious awareness, I can be sure of what
I know, remember what I have learned, communicate it to others, and
carry out disciplined processes of reasoning in order to reach more reliable
conclusions and make wiser decisions. Preconscious prehensions, includ-

ing extrasensory ones, are preparatory for that. They are constitutive of and subordinate to consciousness.

Psi processes are to conscious awareness as, in the language of Polanyi (1958), tool is to object. When I write a paper, the eye-hand skills of typing on a keyboard are largely implicit and out of awareness as I focus on the ideas I am trying to formulate. I need no filter or barrier to keep that typing knowledge away—it functions as a preconscious means to my intended goal. It is not the case that we "know" via psi and then somehow inhibit that "knowing" in favor of conscious awareness. Knowing is in the province of consciousness. Awareness requires sustained perceptual information or some memory of that. A better metaphor than "filter" would be to say that preconscious psi prehensions are not blocked from consciousness but rather serve as bridges to it.

Our unconscious psychological processes seek to construct reliable experience and to perform adaptive behaviors, all in accord with our basic needs and our intentions. Direct sensory experience of events and our sensory awareness of trusted others—the things they say and imply by what they do—are our most reliable sources of information for constructing experience and behavior. The mind will turn naturally and habitually toward them when they are available. This is why intense engagement with the purely implicit information of psi is normally short-lived. The mind moves automatically and quickly on to what it understands to be most reliable.

TENDING TO KNOW OR NOT KNOW, AND SWITCHING TENDENCIES

First Sight theory asserts that unconscious processes follow a dialectical logic;[1] that is, that meanings are naturally understood in the context of their potential opposites. Computers do not reason this way. They reason within a fixed set of premises, and those premises determine all their conclusions. Human reasoning uses premises that are always poised within a context of potential dialectical opposites, and this context shifts as our sense of the needs of the moment shifts. This reasoning-in-the-context-of-alternatives has important implications for how psi processes function.

WEIGHTING, SIGNING, AND SWITCHING

Three central constructs for First Sight theory are *weighting*, *signing*, and *switching*. To put it very briefly, *weighting* refers to a process of unconsciously determining a degree of importance to some element of potential experience. *Signing* means determining whether a heavily weighted thing will be incorporated positively or negatively in experience and action. *Switching* refers to a change in the direction of signing.

Signing

One basic dialectical issue pertaining to all unconscious thought, including psi processing, is the *signing* of elements of potential experience. The mind signs them positively or negatively, and this determines how they enter into the summary products of unconscious thought. Thus signed, these processes may lead the mind toward an understanding or some other expression of a meaning, or decisively away from it.[2] The tendency "toward" a potential meaning will lead to allusions toward that meaning and will tend to result in a psi-hitting event, if the proper inadvertencies are interpreted in the proper ways. The tendency "away from" that meaning will produce allusions away from that meaning and will be expressed as psi-missing.

It is worth noting that when something is signed negatively, it is the cognitive and affective and behavioral associates to that thing that are suppressed, not simply the thing itself. The thing itself is never known, since psi involves a preknowledge, evocative, allusory stage of the development of meaning. But the result is that whole "families" of meanings are suppressed. It is as if the mind is saying, in the words of the old insult: "To hell with you and the horse you rode in on."

Switching

Switching from one tendency to the other will result in a self-cancelling effect in a given period of effort. These tendencies "toward" and "away from" and the switching between them are all intrinsically unconscious phenomena, unavailable to awareness as such. The rapidity of switching of these tendencies will result in different densities of hitting and missing within a period of time and show itself in a psi test (or other test of implicit expressions of unconscious processes) as different degrees of scoring extremity. A situation in which the individual is inclined "toward" the event and in which little switching occurs will be expressed as a strong positive deviation from chance expectation, or strong psi-hitting. A situation with a predominant inclination "toward" but in which rapid switching occurs will result in only a negligible, overall positive deviation. Similar expectations arise in regard to a disposition "away from" the psychically apprehended event. An experimental condition in which individual participants vary in their orientation toward versus away from the target, but in which there is also a general elicitation of low tendential switching, will express itself in the form of scores that show large intersubject variance with little aggregate deviation.

HYPOTHESIS OF DIRECTIONAL INTENTION AND HYPOTHESIS OF INTENTIONAL STABILITY

Parapsychologists need to frame separate hypotheses about factors that make for directional tendencies and factors that determine the rapidity of tendential switching (presumed to be the mechanism for scoring extremity). I believe that these have often been confounded, and this has probably led to less reliability of results. For example, it appears likely that the tendency toward or away from an awareness is primarily determined by intention—particularly unconscious intention. We may call this a Hypothesis of Directional Intention. On the other hand, it seems likely that the rapidity of directional switching is probably a function of the relative consistency of (unconscious) intention.[3] This is the Hypothesis of Intentional Stability. A single-minded, consistent intention would express as relatively extreme scoring. Conflicted or alternating intentions would produce small deviations from chance.

More specific hypotheses about factors influencing directional intention and intentional stability were given in chapter 2, in the discussions about the *extremity corollary*, the *switching corollary*, and the *liminality corollary*.

PSI-MISSING

What is the function of psi-missing? This model suggests a particular interpretation of that vexing phenomenon. Since we are assuming that psi does function persistently and unconsciously, we must ask of what benefit might be the tendency to turn away from some potential event? The most obvious answer is that the winnowing function, described above, requires that all potential meanings but one be turned away from at the initial preconscious level in order to bring upon the stage of awareness the one most useful thing at that moment. If something elected to be an ESP target does not pass this test of "probably most useful" in a given instant, it will pass on only a sense of avoidance in favor of the other thing being selected instead. But what about the situation of a *persistent* avoidance of the meaning of some event? Why would we maintain a posture of avoiding a particular thing long enough to produce a significantly negative deviation in an ESP experiment? Why would it not only be deselected at a given moment, rather than systematically and positively selected against for a sustained period of time? From the point of view of the parapsychologist, these results have been seen as errors,[4] but this is probably too narrow a view. Imagine an early ancestor of yours walking through dense woods. On her right is a safe passage that she cannot clearly see; on her left is a dangerous predator crouching behind a bush. No sensory hint of the predator impinges upon her, but she psychically engages its presence. The best action, the one that leads her to live long enough to become your ancestor, is to very quickly become interested in something to her right and head that way. Suppose the psychic prehension instead alerted her to "some sort of trouble on the left?" It might lead her to pause for an instant and take too long a look at the dangerous bush. Immediate avoidance by simply preferring a dialectical alternative to the danger is the healthiest choice. If this dialectical counterpreference were encountered in an ESP test, it would be expressed as a psi-miss. In everyday life it would not be experienced at all but would pass on by as one of the countless experiences in which no extraordinary coincidence is noted at all—another of the many nonpsychic moments.[5]

ASSIMILATION AND CONTRAST

Psi is assumed to be bidirectional.[6] In regard to any potential experience, one's stance either may be toward the thing or away from it (a posture of approach or avoidance). A stance toward the thing will lead it to contribute additively to experience. A stance away from it will lead to a subtractive contribution to experience (the potential meaning will be decisively avoided in the forming experience).

The terms *assimilation* and *contrast*, drawn from general psychology, are useful in this context. Another term for additive participation of an element in an experience is *assimilation*. Subtractive participation is termed *contrast*. Assimilation and contrast are well studied in the formation of judgments[7] and in the gestalt study of percepts.[8] Events outside the focal boundary of an experience may be thought of as parts of its *context*. The model assumes that patterns of assimilation and contrast should often apply similarly whether the elements of context are subliminal, remembered, or extrasensory. It is known that elements of context sensed to be more similar to the experience that is forming, or to the intentions guiding it, are more likely to be assimilated into it.[9] On the contrary, elements sensed to be dissimilar or in some way contrary to the person's intentions in the task are disassimilated (or rendered into contrast and excluded from the experience). The more well defined an experience is, the more likely it is that contextual elements will not be assimilated and will be subject to contrast instead. This is because a more precise and highly defined experience implies a stricter criterion for "similar enough," leading to the exclusion of more potential elements. Conversely, a vaguely defined experience will evoke looser criteria and be less exclusive, leading to more liberal assimilation (for example, "a cloud of small things" is a highly indeterminate experience, whereas "a swarm of bees" is a well-defined one).[10] In an ESP experiment, assimilation will be expressed as psi-hitting scores and contrast as psi-missing scores.

As a consequence of the effect of the degree of determinacy of experience, a state of mind that is unfocused and receptive is more amenable to the assimilative expression of extrasensory prehensions. States that are highly focused and characterized by clear, cognitive work will make it likely that such prehensions will be subject to contrast and excluded from expression. If this latter situation involves an ESP test, the contrast will express as psi-missing. The same phenomenon can be seen in other activities that require sustained openness to unconscious material, such as artistic creation. As the oil painter David Leffel (2010) says, "If you think when you're doing it, you can't paint. You can't think and paint at the same time."

PSI-MISSING AND ANXIETY

This topic is treated in more detail in a later chapter. In this introductory context, though, it is fair to say that in general anxious people tend to psi-miss more than others do, at least in personally visible and otherwise challenging situations (for example, individual testing rather than group testing, unpleasant rather than positive target material, normal consciousness rather than states of unusual comfort and relaxation) in which vulnerability to anxiety would become a pertinent trait.[11] We also know that more anxious people find more events potentially dangerous, or anxiety arousing.[12] Hence, there are more things they are inclined to avoid, psychically and otherwise. A study I carried out some years ago[13] illustrates this point. Subjects carried out an ESP guessing task in which half their targets were placed with, and thereby were linked to, hidden material that was potentially emotionally arousing (erotic pictures) and the other half linked to blank cards. Subjects who were low in anxiety (in terms of scores on the Taylor Manifest Anxiety Scale) psi-hit on the targets linked to the more arousing stimuli (expressing an implicit interest in the more evocative material), while subjects who were high in anxiety psi-missed on that material, as if expressing a wish to avoid a potentially dangerous event (no subjects ever actually saw the evocative material, so this potentiality was never realized for any of them). Ballard (1980) in one study confirmed this tendency for more anxious females (but not males) to miss the targets linked to more evocative material. A second study did not permit a fair test of this relationship for females due to their unusually high group mean on trait anxiety, but a conceptually similar effect was found in that subjects of both sexes who showed larger declines in *state* anxiety after a relaxation procedure that preceded the ESP task showed a preference for the erotically charged targets; whereas those who failed to become less anxious avoided those targets by missing them. We might expect that the actual emotional state at the time of encountering the material would be more important than a general tendency to be anxious, so this result is not surprising.

Others have also reported a psi-missing tendency in regard to target material that was potentially anxiety arousing.[14] That psi-missing in these cases does not represent a mere absence of psi-response is underscored by the findings of Bem (2003) and Savva et al. (2004), in which fear-arousing material was found to elicit a greater *implicit* psi response than emotionally neutral material. The implicit response was relative preference within an emotionally matched pair of pictures for the one that was to be subliminally exposed later. Bem interprets this as an indication of "precognitive habituation" of the fear response. Analogous findings have been reported in the PWA literature with threatening subliminal stimuli; for example, Fox (1996), MacLeod and Rutherford (1992), and Mogg et al. (1994).

Anxiety generally leads to psi-missing, a point which will be developed in chapter 14. For now, I will only emphasize two things: first, the state of anxiety brings about a heightened focus on the issue of solving the fearful problem—of escaping something bad or otherwise dealing with it effectively. Attention is narrowed, and fewer things are available for potential assimilation. Second, if the material is itself seen as dangerous, avoiding it is likely to be sensed to be preferable to engaging with it. Attention will then tend to focus narrowly on some alternative to the feared thing.

We might pose as a general premise, then, that psi-missing, as an expression of a preconscious orientation away from a potential event, is as much an active event as psi-hitting, and it may be an adaptive strategy intended to minimize the probability of encountering something undesirable. Its being undesirable may simply reflect the fact that something else is considered more important at the moment, or it may reflect a prehension that the thing could be positively dangerous if encountered. Like psi-hitting, psi-missing is guided by (largely unconscious) intention: in this case, the intention to avoid something.[15] This is one of those situations in which conscious and unconscious intention may be at odds with each other. While they are often congruent and function in harmony with each other, this is not always so. In the psi-missing situation, the conscious intention to correctly come to know the material is contrary to the unconscious wish to avoid it, and the unconscious wish has its way.

THE SWITCHING OF THE TENDENCY TO HIT OR MISS

What is the function of a low rate of tendential switching (or relative tendential stability)? It is an indication that the event in question is sensed as being worthy of a definite response—a response seeking either awareness and engagement, or avoidance.

And of what value is rapid tendential switching? It is the creation of an effective psychological nonrelation to the event in question. Perhaps this is the treatment the mind gives to almost all potential meanings encountered in the indefinitely large surround. In terms of responses to an ESP target, it is expressed as scores clinging unnaturally closely to chance expectation. When directional tendency switches more rapidly than a period of guessing effort (for example, a forced-choice run, or a ganzfeld session), the associative bits leading toward and away from the target will tend to balance one another and produce overall a result clinging closely to chance expectation. From the point of view of this model, the chance-level score is as much an expression of psi functioning as is the score representing an extreme deviation from chance expectation. As bizarre as this idea may seem, this process might in fact represent an efficient psychological economy. In order to work well, consciousness must be singular and sustained. That would be impossible if we were not effectively oblivious to almost all potential meanings all the time. Similarly, the implicit behavioral responsiveness that the mind may make to preconscious information must be free to not respond to all but the few things at any moment that are sensed to be most salient.

In gestalt terms, the focus of preconscious attention and conscious awareness must be "figure," and everything else relegated to "ground." To borrow a theater analogy, the mind constructs not only the bright stage of awareness but also the unconscious background surrounding it, the darkened house lights, the unseen machinery backstage, the occluded noises, and distractions outside the theater.

Why would rapid tendential switching occur when one is consciously trying to "get" some extrasensory content? That is, why would chance-level scores be produced with some consistency in an ESP test (yielding an overall tightness of score variance)? Some hints can be gained by looking at patterns that have been reported.[16] Whittlesey's results might be particularly instructive. He administered a dose of LSD-25 to his subjects, thinking that a drug that might open the "doors of perception" might open doors to extrasensory perception as well. His subjects produced chance-level scores with such consistency that the overall tight variance was highly extrachance. In their psychedelic state, his subjects also complained that they found the ESP test profoundly trivial and meaningless. As they pursued their personal thoughts and visions, they also succeeded in removing the ESP targets far away from their experience, perhaps by an automatic bimodal balancing of responsive tendencies.

Looking over all the accumulated findings involving scoring extremity, it appears that large deviation scoring is associated with freshness, enthusiasm, a sustained, unreflective immersion in the task, more engaging target material, a task that is generally salient and involving for the subjects, and an absence of interruptions. Small deviation scoring is associated with fatigue, cognitive work, uninteresting target material, a nonengaging task, repetitive testing, self-reflective analysis of the experience, or by some situational change, such as a change in task.

Shifts in conscious attention during cognitive work and self-analysis seem to be particularly powerful in speeding switching and reducing the extremity of any reference to the extrasensory material. It might seem counterintuitive to suppose that shifts in *conscious attention* could affect access to *unconscious material*. However, this has been shown to be the case with subliminal sensory primes[17] and by the principle of functional equivalence; we would expect it to be so with extrasensory primes as well.

As already stated, inconsistent intention, conscious and unconscious, is hypothesized to be the cause of rapid switching and small deviations. This cluster of observations suggests that the degree of consistency of unconscious intention might be affected by variables such as: moods of unreflective absorption or playfulness versus moods of irritability or distractibility,[18] a mental set of suspended, free-floating attention versus a set of rational analysis, extrasensory information that is seen as vitally important and interesting versus unimportant or trivial, a general cognitive tendency (a trait) to intellectually analyze and break apart ongoing experience versus a capacity for fully engaged "flow," and situational constraints such as sustained versus interrupted conditions.[19]

These factors may be broken up into two main categories. On the one hand, irritation, uninteresting target material, and nonengaging and/or repetitive tasks are all situations in which one might easily imagine that the person has a wish to quit the task even while persisting in it, resulting in mixed or alternating intentions. The second cluster of factors includes distraction, rational analysis, obsessive doubt, and situational interruptions, and these would all seem to require the person to shift attention and move away from the sustained inner searching that is hypothesized to provide consistent intentional direction to some other focus of effort. In both cases there seems likely to be an internal conflict of intentions to know and not know, or some oscillation of such intentions.

The hypothesized rapid switching of direction with small-deviation performance at times of mixed motivation in regard to the extrasensory material would appear to be quite functional. This may represent all of the many times when some other task is more important than retrieving a bit of extrasensory information. For example, cognitive work might be required instead. At such times it is helpful to be free of distractions (as by extrasensory prehensions) so that the mind may attend effectively to the conscious matter at hand.

It may also be the case that rapid unconscious switching of potential directions of response is functional for the organism, in that it permits a rapid response if the information involved should suddenly seem more pertinent as the development of meaning takes shape. Then it could be quickly signed and used, positively or negatively. This might be analogous to the boxer who rocks rapidly from foot to foot before moving decisively toward or away from the opponent. This rocking permits a very quick response to the opponent's own movements, whereas being still would not. It is a sad boxer who is caught "flat-footed."

TENDENTIAL SWITCHING AND THE MAINTENANCE OF CONSCIOUS FOCUS

Extrasensory prehensions are unconscious, and we can only glimpse their effects by suspending cognitive work and consulting the vague material at the edges of experience. When rational, cognitive work is called for, attention to the preconscious material is best suspended. Since balanced hitting and missing tendencies produce an effective nonrelation to the material in question, this is a sensible mechanism for protecting the focus of conscious work. To attempt to use conscious work in an ESP test is therefore self-defeating, as White (1964) has reminded us from examining the introspective discoveries of earlier explorers in this area. I am suggesting here that it is self-defeating not primarily because it creates a tendency to psi-miss (it may not) but because it produces a tendency to highly internally balanced scoring, with little direct evidence of ESP at all.

In many situations, the cognitive work of rational analysis on clear mental contents is desirable. At such times, the mind protects its focus unconsciously by switching directional tendencies in regard to unwanted potential experiences, rapidly enough that there is no consistent, and thereby, distracting allusion toward or away from those realities. At such times, extrasensory engagement is "tightly bound" by cognitive functioning, and no evidence of ESP will be observed.

In general, a stable orientation toward or away from some potential meaning serves to assure that the behavior of the organism will reflect some response to the potential meaning (toward expressing and experiencing it, or in a counter direction), while rapidly shifting orientations will assure that no apparent response at all will be reflected in experience or behavior.

The mind strives to know what its experience is. In Jung's terms, the primary function of the psyche is to create consciousness and meaning.[20] When we can manage to perceive an experience clearly enough to be able to clearly construe it, we may carry out cognitive work. In fact, the act of construal of experience is itself a commencement of cognitive work. It is functional to do this work undeterred by extraneous concerns, including extrasensory ones. These are moments of cognitive closure and relative certainty. These conditions are necessary for analysis and judgment, and we generally experience it as satisfying to attain them and frustrating to have them elude us. They generally preclude access to the sort of material that might permit a sense of psychic cognizance as well as an awareness of the expression of subliminal stimulation.

TIMES OF UNCERTAINTY, CONFUSION, OR DISORIENTATION

When an experience cannot be tightly construed (interpreting the meaning of a shadow or mood or flash of light or strange sound or mind-tugging incipient memory), the mind consults allusions directed toward the potential meaning as guided by preconscious processes. If the ambiguity is sustained (perhaps a picture will not quickly come into focus), then one keeps guessing by consulting the allusions being suggested by preconscious thought as potential guides to meaning.[21] During such times, we preconsciously sustain a directional tendency in regard to the incipient meaning in order to generate helpful allusions toward the desired understanding. We will guess around the thing we are trying to see or to remember, and thereby close in on it, until with an "ah hah," we come to know what we have been trying to know.

There are states in which such ambiguity and uncertainty are sustained for relatively long periods of time. In describing the early delusional stage of schizophrenic breakdown, Jaspers writes:

> Patients feel uncanny and that there is something suspicious afoot. Everything gets a *new meaning*. The environment is somehow different—not to a gross degree . . . but there is some change which envelopes everything with a subtle, pervasive and strangely uncertain light. Something seems in the air which the patient cannot account for. . . . A patient noticed the waiter in the coffee-house; he skipped past him so quickly and uncannily. He noticed odd behavior in an acquaintance which made him feel strange; everything in the street was so different, something was bound to be happening. A passer-by gave such a penetrating glance, he could be a detective. Then there was a dog who seemed hypnotized, a kind of mechanical dog made of rubber. . . . In other cases patients have noticed transfigured faces, unusual beauty of landscape, brilliant golden hair, overpowering glory of the sunlight. Something must be going on, the world is changing, a new era is starting. Lights are bewitched and will not burn, something is behind it. . . . Gestures, ambiguous words provide "tacit intimations." All sorts of things are being conveyed to the patient. People imply quite different things in such harmless remarks as "the carnations are lovely" or "the blouse fits all right" and understand these meanings very well among themselves. . . . Patients resist any attempt to explain these things as coincidence. These "devilish incidents" are most certainly not coincidences . . . The fact that the soap is now on the table and was not there before is obviously an insult.[22]

During such times, what the person takes to be extrasensory experiences may virtually flood awareness. Simple events may be pregnant with secret meanings. The faces of others seem transparent as their unspoken thoughts seem to beam straight through. Stock market figures contain coded messages transmitted psychokinetically from somewhere in space, and the static on a radio is the whisper of an evil spirit. It is an occasional discomfiture to parapsychologists when such persons, understanding that they are experts in this field and expecting to be treated as someone with authority and wisdom, turn up at the laboratory door.

Is any genuine extrasensory knowledge displayed in the welter of delusion? Sometimes it seems possibly so, although the clinical setting is not conducive to the protocols of controlled research, and such research as has been done has produced mixed results.[23] Such sustained confusion and sense of ineffable, implicit meaning do appear to result in the person consulting inadvertencies and trying to wrest meaning from them. The need for meaning, for *an explanation*, can be agonizingly strong. If the person can then reach some delusional interpretation of his or her situation, it may feel like a great relief ("Ah! It's the FBI!"). Often, with sensitive clinical examination, the odd constructions of such a person can be seen to contain a grain of truth, perhaps gleaned subliminally or extrasensorily. As Laing (1961) has said, delusions may be "realizations gone wrong."[24]

There are briefer, more benign conditions in which cognitive certainty is delayed to an unusual extent. In the dissociated states of highly dissociative people, there may be prolonged periods of disorientation in which an adult may behave and seem to think in the manner of a confused little child. During a few such periods in my clinical practice, I have observed what seemed to be striking instances of accurate ESP. Brain damage may also be linked to periods of disorientation, confusion, and cognitive uncertainty that are prolonged. Perhaps it is of interest that some famous "psychics," including ones who have done well in a controlled laboratory study, experienced brain and other nervous system damage that seemed to initiate or heighten their psychic experiences,[25] while Schmeidler (1952) has reported strong psi-hitting among patients suffering from brain concussion, particularly those whose adaptation to their injury seemed to feature passive acceptance.

Finally, it is also possible for a well-functioning person to deliberately adopt a mental set of suspended cognitive closure, of "free-floating" attention. This is the "evenly suspended attention" that Freud (1958a [1912]) recommended to practicing analysts as they listened to the free associations of their clients. Coupled with a strong wish to know the unknown material, it is also the set recommended by a number of highly successful ESP performers, based upon their introspections.[26] Adopted deliberately, perhaps honed by practice and inward disciplines such as meditation, it appears to permit relatively reliable access to images and feelings that inadvertently express connotations of nonsensory material. Laboratory evidence that this is so is given by the findings of Bem (personal communication) of superior ESP performance on the part of experienced meditators and of Palmer et al. (1979) of extreme psi scoring in a sensory-attenuation situation on the part of meditators who reported achieving relatively free and spontaneous imagery and a deep loss of awareness of their bodies.

PSI-CONDUCIVE STATES

I suggest that states of mind in which there is a prolongation of cognitive openness or uncertainty, with a relative absence of a clearly interpreted focus of experience, will permit little intentional conflict and cognitive work of the sort that is hypothesized to trigger tendential switching. Therefore, an unconscious posture of "toward" or "away from" some important extrasensory reality will tend to be maintained with some stability and result in access to inadvertencies that strongly imply or disimply the thing in question. In an ESP test, there will be extreme scoring, with strong deviations from chance expectation. If the unconscious intention to engage the particular important thing is positive, then strong hitting would be expected. However, if unconscious intention is negative (as it might be in the terrified persons experiencing psychotic breakdown), a great deal of distortion away from the actual realities would be expected—or as in an ESP test, strong psi-missing.

Persons wishing to be more expressive of psi phenomena are advised, then, to approach their task by sustaining an open, nonanalytical frame of mind while also maintaining a commitment to the goal of psi expression. Cognitive analysis, self-criticism, and doubt would all be expected to trigger unconscious switching of directional tendencies and lead any psi expression to be less discernible. These conclusions are very similar to those reached by phenomenological studies of successful demonstrations of ESP[27] and psychokinesis.[28] More will be said about this subject in chapter 17, discussing the more psychic person.

NOTES

1. Jung, 1960a, p. 539; Kelly, 1955; Rychlak, 1968, 1973.

2. For other helpful discussions of the importance of dialectical thinking in these parapsychological processes, see Ballard, 1991, and Rao, 1965a, 1965b, pp. 116–28.

3. These theoretical ideas about switching of psi-hitting and psi-missing modes of scoring (or, more generally, assimilation or contrast in regard to extrasensory prehensions), may seem strange and arbitrary to many readers. They developed out of work on run-score variance effects in ESP testing (e.g., Rogers and Carpenter,

1966), and the specific model for explaining variance effects was first proposed in Carpenter (1977, 1983). In this work, the size of deviations of scores around chance, irrespective of direction, was seen to be a somewhat lawful and predictable expression of psi in its own right. Particularly intriguing theoretically was the case of small deviations—scores that were too consistently close to chance to be explained by chance!

4. Rhine, 1952.

5. This interpretation of psi-missing is congruent with that of Stanford (1974, 1977, 1991), who has argued that psi cognizance may lead toward conscious awareness or not and that often its more important expression is the facilitation of behavioral tendencies *without* any accompanying awareness. In his model of "psi-mediated instrumental response," missing may represent a highly adaptive response to some undesirable potential event.

6. Rao, 1962, 1964.

7. DeCoster and Claypool, 2004.

8. Kohler, 1947.

9. Bodner and Masson, 2001; Jaskowski and Skalska, 2003; Schwarz and Bless, 1992.

10. DeCoster and Claypool, 2004; Suls and Wheeler, 2007.

11. Palmer, 1977.

12. Hollander and Simeon, 2003.

13. Carpenter, 1971.

14. Johnson and Nordbeck, 1972; Johnson, 1977.

15. This may cast a new light on the clinical phenomena of repression and denial. Freud early in his theorizing proposed that the unconscious censor prohibited certain meanings from entering awareness because the experience of knowing them would be somehow too upsetting. We now know from cognitive research that to "know" anything requires a memory of it, and that we remember, basically, whatever we think about (Ebbinghaus, 1885 [1964]; Erdelyi, 1990). If something is not thought about, even though it is initially experienced, it is quickly forgotten and then not known. Perhaps in general terms, in repression the mind decides first to not become engaged with something, and not becoming engaged leads to not knowing. Avoiding the unpleasant awareness may not be the motivator of repression, but its by-product. In terms of the parapsychology study, it may not be the case that the wish to avoid awareness leads to behavioral avoidance of associates to the target, but rather that the desire to avoid the target leads to the behavioral avoidance of it, and with that, avoidance of the occasion to come to know it. We choose to know A, not to not-know B. Freud thought that we want to not-know and therefore avoid. Perhaps we want to avoid and miss the opportunity to know. If an event is not either remembered or sensed, it cannot be experienced and construed. As stated above, this latter fact is also why we are not flooded with conscious information of all the extrasensory engagements available to us.

16. Carpenter, 1966, 1967, 1968, 1977, 1991; Carpenter and Carpenter, 1967; Palmer, 1972; Rogers, 1966, 1967; Stanford, 1966a, 1966b, 1967, 1968; Whittlesey, 1960.

17. Sumner et al., 2006.

18. Carpenter, 1991.

19. Carpenter, 1977.

20. Jung, 1960b, p. 323; Rychlak, 1968.

21. Systematizing such a consulting process in the face of protracted uncertainty may result in some procedure of divination (von Franz, 1980).

22. Jaspers, 1964, pp. 98–100.

23. See Greyson, 1977, for a review and the latest published study.

24. For further discussions of psi in the context of mental illness, see Carpenter (2002), Ehrenwald (1955, 1970), and Eisenbud (1970).

25. McMoneagle, 1997; Mitchell, 1876; Puharich, 1973.

26. White, 1964.

27. White, 1964.

28. Batcheldor, 1984.

6

Some Implicit Assumptions That Need to Be Changed

If you do not change direction, you may end up where you are heading.

—Attributed to Lao Tzu

This understanding of psi has new, basic implications for what scientific research on psi means and how it should be conducted. There are many such new implications, but this chapter will highlight a few that are particularly important. The reader should consider them thoughtfully in order to appreciate how different an approach is involved in First Sight. Of course, some may not agree that all of these changes are necessary or desirable, but they are all central to the perspective that is developed in this book.

Three things that are commonly assumed, implicitly as much as explicitly, are that psi is a collection of anomalous experiences, that psi is some kind of ability, and that psi stimuli somehow cause psi responses. From the First Sight perspective, these are not helpful assumptions, and some alternative ways of construing things are preferred. To sum up in advance, psi is not a kind of experience, nor is it a collection of abilities, nor are psi responses caused by psi stimuli.

A. PSI IS NOT ABOUT ANOMOLOUS EXPERIENCE

Psi as Anomalous Experience

A major assumption that is held almost universally by parapsychologists as well as their critics is that psi is a matter of unusual *conscious experiences*. Events suggesting the action of nonlocal events upon a person are thought of as a kind of *knowing*. Events implying the direct effect of intention upon the physical world are seen as a kind of *doing*. The language that has been used to describe the basic categories of the subject matter has implied this. Being affected by future events is called pre*cognition*. If the effect is from some distant thing, it is called clair*voyance* (clear *vision*). If it is an effect of another person's thoughts or feelings, it is tele*pathy* (far *feeling*). Responding viscerally to some distant or future thing is called pre*sentiment* (*feeling* or *emotion*). All of these together are referred to as extrasensory *perception*. *Cognition, vision, emotion, feeling,* and *perception* are all terms that refer to experiences in which something is consciously known. Similarly, when sheer intention is found to have some apparent effect upon a distant physical process, this is thought of as a kind of *action*, which means something that is consciously done. However, *parapsychologists do not actually study consciously knowing or consciously doing*, even though many of them may assume that somehow they do.

It is true that the kinds of connections that parapsychologists find and study may be considered anomalous, in the sense that ordinary biochemical models do not readily account for them. But they are not anomalous *experiences* and do not involve conscious knowing or doing. Then what are they?

Psi Events Are Implicit Indicators of Unconscious Connections

Consider the operations that parapsychologists use to generate their basic measurements (all assure that there is no sensory means for the participant to actually know anything about a target, nor any physical way to affect it). One of the first was card guessing. A guess is not a form of knowing. What is available to consciousness in guessing is one's intention, plus perhaps a flow of more or less random internal chatter that is picked from and nominated as a guess. If we know something, we do not need to guess about it. Take the ganzfeld studies on telepathy. The participant sits alone in a quiet room and generates free associations. The sender is not being heard, seen, or felt. All that is available to the participant is an internal flow of personal feelings, thoughts, and images. Consider the remote viewing subject. He or she similarly sits alone and consults an inner parade of images, scribbling drawings and snatches of words. Why are any of these things considered to be expressions of psi? Because they can often be seen to *imply* or *allude to* the target material. They are not direct experiences of the target, but they may allude to it too strongly to be reasonably attributed to mere chance.

Then Why Do We Use Terms That Imply Consciousness?

The choice of such terms has been more implicit than deliberate, but I think it probably stems mainly from a wish to emphasize the odd, anomalous aspect of the connections observed by using paradoxical language. We are said to be dealing with vision that is blind, perception that does not know, action that is passively detached. There is something appealing and challenging about such language. Like psi connections themselves, it arrests us and demands that we confront a puzzle. However, it is easy to slip into taking this paradoxical language more literally. At that point, without knowing it we have become mystified by our own rhetorical device. And this mystification can have negative consequences.

Mystifying Language and Implicit Misunderstanding

Many people know next to nothing about parapsychology and feel little innate sympathy for its questions. If they pay attention to its findings at all they are apt to take the terms of parapsychologists literally and find them shocking and nonsensical. Imagine a skeptically inclined scientist in some other field who reads a statistically significant study demonstrating precognition. It is as if the author is proposing this conclusion: *People can know the future, and we just haven't noticed this before now.* Our scientist considers this proposition highly unlikely, whatever the statistical analysis of a particular data set. He or she is apt to assume, as Chuck Honorton used to joke, that ESP stands for "Error Some Place."

Closer attention to the operations used by the parapsychologist to gather data, however, will show that no one in the study gained conscious knowledge of the future, and the experimenters were not trying to gather measurements that suggest that they did. Therefore, no one in the study experienced reality in any way that radically departed from that typical of our skeptical scientist, and no one is really claiming that they did. If the study examined visceral responses to an emotional stimulus that participants generated shortly before they were shown the stimulus, the data actually represent an unconscious response suggesting a reference to something in the future. Nothing about the future is *consciously known* by the participant. If the study asked participants to generate strings of guesses about an order of symbols and then used some random means later to generate the targets, the data only show that internally imagining symbols and then impulsively picking some and not others can show a real relation to an order of symbols that will be determined in the future.

Parapsychologists would be better served in reporting such studies by couching their experimental hypotheses in language that makes it clear from the outset that what is proposed is that *inadvertent behaviors of a person can implicitly reflect future events.* The study was not about pre *cognition* at all. It was about implicit, unconscious response to nonlocal (future) events.

This may still seem unlikely to our skeptical scientist on other grounds. It seems odd to think that future events can have an influence on earlier behaviors. But it does not present the same affront to common sense. Most educated people understand that behavior and experience often reflect unconscious processes. As I walk across the room I do not consciously make each muscle move. All of the coordinated movement happens unconsciously, and I am quite comfortable with that fact. It is odd to think that some of those unconscious processes may reflect events that haven't happened yet. But the skeptic is not being asked to believe that a few research participants, or gifted "psychics," differ so radically from his or her own everyday experience as to consciously know things that people patently do not know.

Some might object that, while this way of thinking about psi events might describe the "weak phenomena" observed in the laboratory, they do not fairly describe the more dramatic events encountered spontaneously sometimes in "real life." Closer examination, however, will show that this is not so.

For example, the psychiatrist Elizabeth Mayer (2007) reported an experience in which the location of a lost harp was pinpointed by a douser in another state using a map and a pendulum. The event was startling enough that Mayer said that it permanently changed her view of reality. Fair enough. But did the douser *know* where the harp was? What the douser actually did was to hold a pendulum over a map and observe the spot over which its movement became stabilized. He took this inadvertent action of the pendulum (presumably influenced by unconscious trembling motions of his hand) as implying an answer to the question about which he was trying to help. He had been dousing like this for a long time and was used to being able to assume that such pendulum activity might refer accurately to a sought location. His act is amazing and wonderful, but it is not an act of *knowing* in the sense of a conscious experience of the harp in a particular place. It is the generation of inadvertent behavior with a certain intention in mind and then interpreting that behavior based upon many other experiences with similar behaviors.[1] If we were to examine other dramatic stories of psi-in-real-life we would similarly find that they also involve the generation of inadvertent behaviors and experiences and then understanding those behaviors as referring implicitly to things beyond the ordinary sensory boundaries of the person.

Of course, our skeptical scientist may still be skeptical. Can dousing behaviors really allude to the answer to a question about the location of some lost thing thousands of miles away? This is a fair question, and the data should be examined to find the answer. But the scientist can imagine holding a string with a pendulum attached and dangling it over a map. He or she is not being asked to imagine an experience of knowing or doing something in a way that is alien to all accumulated experience. And he or she has become accustomed to the reality of unconscious influences on perception and behavior, as with subliminal perception and implicit memory. There are still problems of not understanding a mechanism by which a more distantly connected accurate allusion could take place. But this kind of ignorance is the familiar business of science. It only calls us to work.

Impasses Are Often Due to Implicit Misunderstandings

I know from my work as a family and marital psychotherapist that impasses—grinding, repetitive, insoluble conflicts—may be due to hidden, implicit misunderstandings that neither party can clearly see. If one asks the two parties to the conflict the nature of the problem, each one will usually be able to answer with crystal clarity. The outsider hearing this, however, will usually be confronted with a fascinating fact: *The ideas about the nature of the problem are not the same.* Both people believe that they know what the problem is, and both assume that the other one sees it the same way. But they almost never do. If they did, the problem would long ago have ceased being an insoluble impasse.

There has been such an impasse for many decades now between the proponents and the deniers of psi research. Both sides have their ideas about the causes of the impasse. Proponents argue that the deniers are really poor scientists because they are unwilling to look at facts. Deniers argue that the proponents are either frauds or fools pretending to be scientists because they are making claims that cannot possibly be true. The argument long ago became tiresome, something like listening to a bickering, chronically unhappy couple. Listen closely and I think we will hear the skeptic saying something like this: "You are claiming to have proven that people can know and do things in ways that I have never personally experienced. I don't think so!" The parapsychologist is saying: "I have facts here that have been very carefully gathered and interpreted, and you are too bullheaded to accept them!"

I believe that some portion of this impasse comes from an implicit misunderstanding about what is being claimed by the parapsychologists. Language that implies that psi events are conscious experiences of knowing or doing has created confusion and deepened distrust.

The First Sight model makes it explicit that psi events are not about such conscious experiences.

B. PSI IS NOT AN ABILITY

In order to understand what psi is from a First Sight perspective, I will first sketch the historical development of basic models for what psi is in order to frame a context.

Psi as the Action of Spirit Agencies or Forces

The ancient literatures and folklores of many cultures have numerous references to experiences and behaviors of people and even animals that seem to imply an unusual, "miraculous" ability to know of something at a distance or in the future, or to have an impact on physical events by sheer intention or prayer. In many societies these phenomena apparently were taken for granted and functioned smoothly in the worldview shared by their members. Deities and spirits of various sorts were generally assumed to be responsible for these events, and many techniques were developed to attempt to influence these agents to provide useful information and good events and withhold false ideas and bad events. Seers and priests with special ability and training to access these agents were often sought and valued. Early scientific thinking was itself so riddled with magical and spiritistic ideas that there was virtually no standpoint from which to question the validity of psychic claims or make any deeper kind of sense out of them.[2]

On the border of modern science, but still operating largely within this model, the spiritualist movement of the nineteenth century attempted to study the alleged abilities of specially gifted mediums to gather information and evoke physical actions from spirits of deceased persons. When the Society for Psychical Research was founded in England in 1882, new techniques of controlled observation and careful record keeping ushered in a kind of systematic observation, but what most of the researchers believed they were studying was the actions of these invisible, discarnate entities in an attempt to ascertain their real existence. Current research on mediumship[3] still operates within this framework, although consideration is generally given to the alternate possibility of the phenomena being an expression of some sort of special ability of the medium.

Another movement on the borders of modern science of the day was mesmerism. Anton Mesmer was a highly charismatic and persuasive man who created a sensation in his lifetime by developing procedures by which he could induce a kind of "sleep" in patients and allegedly cure virtually every sort of infirmity. He attracted many disciples and imitators, all of whom shared his belief that there exists an invisible, energetic fluid that is the source of all life and indeed of all nature and that can be manipulated toward the end of improved health by "magnetic" movements of appropriate materials. (When sheer persuasive suggestion was later found to produce similar effects, the less mysterious idea of hypnosis was created and studied.) Rather than spirits and deities, "mesmeric fluid" was held to be the agent responsible for extraordinary physical effects and access to anomalous information.[4] The latter aspect was highlighted especially by the early claims of the mesmerist Puységur, who developed the idea of the hypnotic trance that was accompanied by a "state of lucidity," in which distant things could be seen at will. He called this "traveling clairvoyance."[5] A contemporary version of this idea is "remote viewing,"[6] although this is now thought of as expressing a special ability or skill rather than the action of an energetic fluid.[7]

The idea of a supersubtle fluid that pervades all of nature and that can be manipulated by physical means appealed to many in an age that was just discovering the marvelous hidden realm of electromagnetic energy. This basic model still finds adherents in many contemporary "New Age" circles, with their ideas of a pervasive "energy" that can be manipulated by the actions and intentions of a gifted practitioner.

The early efforts to study the claims of spiritualists and mesmerists in a controlled and roughly scientific way first of all tried to ascertain which if any claims were genuinely anomalous and were not simply the results of fraud or coincidence or observational error. There was much of this to sift through. Of the apparently genuine residuum, other sorts of questions could be asked.

When psi events are construed as the actions of any of these external agencies—deities or spirits or supersubtle fluid or energy—one presumes that scientific work should tell us more about the nature of these agencies and how they can be reliably manipulated or at least understood. One could ask, for example, if different circumstances of death might influence the urgency with which spirits wished to communicate; or was one sort of material better than another for magnetizing the mesmeric fluid?

Psi as a Special Ability or Skill

Psychical researchers soon hit upon another possible interpretation for some of the mental phenomena of mediumship: *telepathy*, the ability of one mind to communicate directly with another. This was not necessarily exclusive of the idea of a communicating spirit, since something like telepathy would presumably be necessary for such spirit communication to occur. But it might also occur between two living minds. The idea of *telepathic ability* was conceived.[8] The question then became: How could this mysterious, latent power of the mind be called up into action? What characterized the rare and especially gifted persons (the "mediums" or "sensitives") who could more reliably call up this power to influence the minds of others or be open to their influences?

The advent of parapsychology as an experimental science is generally attributed to the publication of J. B. Rhine's monograph *Extrasensory Perception* in 1934. Rhine had moved away from the conception of psi as the action of discarnate spirits and mesmeric fluid to see just what could be found with living persons in ordinary experimental conditions. He, his wife, Louisa, and their colleagues had begun their work at Duke University in 1927 by testing students for their telepathic abilities. In the basic paradigm, one person would look at a card that showed some symbol while another person would try to guess what symbol it was. A scientific laboratory for the study of these questions was born. Since a fixed set of symbols was being used repeatedly and the order of symbols could be made random, statistical methods could be used for assessing how strong a person's telepathic ability was. Perhaps to everyone's surprise, a number of students were found who could "beat chance" with some regularity, some of them spectacularly so. Apparently some people "had telepathic ability." Then soon in their work the Duke group discovered that persons who were doing well in tests of telepathy sometimes did just as well when no one was looking at the cards at all, but they simply sat shuffled in their packs. In homage to the earlier French work on lucidity, Rhine called this a "clairvoyant ability."

The Duke group's little family of abilities multiplied further when they discovered that it was sometimes possible to guess the orders of cards before they were shuffled—"precognitive ability." But there was a difficulty of interpretation here: was the subject guessing the future, or was he or she influencing the shuffle somehow by the stated intention to find a certain order? Refinements of methods were developed, including willing the falls of mechanically thrown dice and guessing future outcomes that seemed far beyond any possible effect of willing. By these means both precognition and "psychokinesis" (the influence of sheer intention upon the physical world) were established as separate abilities.[9]

This is how things have stood since. Although efforts have been made to find a way to think of all these abilities together (as by calling them all "psi" abilities) or to find new labels in order to temporarily escape the controversies that have accumulated around the earlier terms, the idea that parapsychological research is the study of this collection of abilities has remained at the core of the field.

Psi as a Set of Abilities to Generate Anomalous Experiences

Parapsychologists would generally agree that their branch of science is devoted to a set of abilities that involve the production of extraordinary, anomalous experiences—for example, the ability to know the thoughts of another person. The First Sight model would not agree with the basic characterization. It would assert that psi is not a set of abilities and that it does not have to do with anomalous experiences. Let us examine these two radical departures in turn.

The Study of Abilities

The dictionary defines *ability* as "the quality or state of being able to perform—either a natural aptitude or an acquired proficiency." Rhine moved research from the study of the actions of external agencies to the study of certain capacities of living persons. His emphasis on the notion of ability was natural and progressive at the time and opened up a host of questions that were familiar to psychologists and suggested that familiar methods could be used to study them.[10] Psychologists were (and still are) keen on the study of abilities. For example, while Rhine was developing the study of ESP, two of his respected Duke colleagues at the time, Karl Zener and William McDougall, were busy in their work trying to learn more about how skills may be acquired versus how they may be inherited aptitudes. Could abilities thought of as inherited also be learned? Could abilities understood to be learned also be inherited? Zener showed that perceptual abilities can be influenced by Pavlovian conditioning (learned),[11] and McDougall (1929) tried to show that sometimes learned skills such as maze running can become heritable.

If scientists were to move to the individual living person as a possible source of psychic phenomena, the shift to the construct of "ability" was a natural one. Remember the field started with odd and unruly observations and is still popularly characterized by them: a medium produces information she has no way of knowing about; a douser finds a lost object from another state using only a map and a pendulum;[12] a cancer researcher, using nothing but intention, seems to be able to influence the rate at which plants grow;[13] one of America's most beloved authors claims that his dreams sometimes tell the future.[14] Such events are unusual, but according to recent polls, most Americans believe that they are real, and a large portion believe that they have personally experienced them. Still, if such events are real, they clearly seem to be relatively rare. Why do they occur, when, and to whom do they occur? It seemed reasonable to suppose that something like an ability or a group of abilities might be involved.

Some people can ride a bicycle, and others cannot. Some can discriminate red from green, while others can't. We think of color vision as a sheer ability, a biological given. Riding a bicycle is an acquired ability, part talent and part training. And even among those who can ride a bicycle, not all can do it equally well. Some are clumsy riders, while others are champion cyclists. What sort of ability might lead to paranormal events? Is it biologically given? Is it learned? Is it a matter of degree?

Not all situations can call an ability into play. In a room without bicycles, the ability to ride them could not be directly tested. A picture with no red or green cannot be used to discriminate those who can tell the difference from those who cannot. This is how the psi abilities came to be seen—as skills, innate or acquired, that may be prompted into action by need or by an experimental demand in some appropriate situation. Perhaps it is pertinent that the founder of experimental research in this field, J. B. Rhine, was an expert marksman—the finest in the U.S. Army in his day. Perhaps it was natural for him to think of psi as the ability to hit a target.

Research on Psi "Abilities"

This implicit assumption, that psi is an ability, has led to a certain way of thinking about the meaning of research on psi. It has become so deeply assumed by parapsychologists that they are scarcely aware that they are holding it. From this point of view, a study is an attempt to call up and demonstrate a rare ability. Since the ability is rare, the stage must be set carefully to find it and evoke it. Persons with the right ability (the "gifted subjects") and the appropriate "psi-conducive" conditions must all be provided for the rare demonstration to occur. Somewhat like those experiments in physics in which elaborate situations are provided to try to produce very rare and transient subatomic particles, the rare psi event is ardently courted but may still be fickle and withhold its presence. Some researchers have gone so far as to personify these presumed qualities of psi, calling it a trickster or saying that it is innately elusive and nonreplicable by its nature.

This unarticulated assumption of psi as an ability has even held sway in those studies that have assumed that psi may function unconsciously, without deliberate intention (see the discussions on Stanford's Psi-Mediated Instrumental Response Theory in chapter 8). In those studies it is assumed that the psi ability may be called up unconsciously as a function of need, but it is still implicitly assumed to be a rare and transient thing, called into action temporarily and disappearing thereafter.

Once Again, Psi Is Not an Ability

In First Sight theory, several almost universal, implicit assumptions about psi are changed. Psi is not an ability; ESP is not knowledge; PK is not action. Perhaps the most important one is the new assumption that psi is not an ability. Instead, it is a universal characteristic of living organisms, a basic feature of their being in the world. It is the fact that we are all unconsciously and perpetually engaged in a universe of meaning that extends far beyond our physical boundaries in space and time. It is not an ability, better in some than in others, called up sometimes and not other times. It is always going on for all of us. It is less like riding a bicycle or discriminating red from green and more like being perpetually engaged as physical bodies with the reality of gravity, or as social beings with an interpersonal world of others. It is an unconscious and ubiquitous but still largely unmapped aspect of our nature. This basic definition will be spelled out more fully in the next three chapters.

A Different Function for Psi Research

If psi is not an ability, then research will not be understood as an attempt to coax it into action and measure it. Instead, it will be an effort to design situations in which the ongoing psi activity can be discerned in the context of everyday actions and experiences where it always is. A study will not be designed to try to catch psi; it will try to reveal it.

In fact, a shift in research perspective toward this point of view has been going on in this field recently, although its full implications have not been spelled out. The time is ripe for First Sight theory. A new generation of studies has begun to demonstrate the unconscious expression of nonlocal information and influence in the course of ordinary experiences and behaviors. Radin (2004) and others have shown that one's subtle electrodermal responses to emotional pictures include an element that *precedes* the exposure to the stimulus alongside the larger, well-understood responses that follow it. Carpenter (2002) has demonstrated that spontaneous social behavior in a group is a function not only of the unfolding stimulation that group members are providing for each other in the room but also reflects the content of a distant ESP target being chosen randomly for them by a computer in another city. Palmer (2006a) has shown that in the course of efforts to discern subtle order in strings of numbers, people are showing an influence not only of the numbers that they are seeing but also of the numbers that they will be seeing shortly in the future. Bem (2005) has shown that people who are expressing emotional evaluations of pictures are showing not only the influence of the picture facing them but also the influence of their future exposures to either that picture or a different one.

In each of these cases, the psychic feature of the experiment may have been mentioned to the participants, but they are not being asked to "show ESP or PK." They are simply responding to pictures physiologically, or trying to discern the patterns hidden in a situation, or developing a social encounter with a group of friends, or making evaluations about how much they like or dislike something. In other words, they are doing entirely ordinary things on entirely conscious and immediate grounds, so far as they know. But in the process of doing these things they are also implicitly using and expressing an ongoing engagement with reality that is unconscious and beyond their immediate sensory boundaries.

No rare ability has been coaxed and caught. An ongoing implicit process has been revealed. The experimenters have managed to design and control the situation in such a way that these ordinarily invisible elements of psychic participation in everyday experience can be exposed. First Sight theory provides a way of thinking about this fact that psi is not an occasional ability but is instead an unconscious feature of each person's ongoing engagement with reality.

C. PSI RESPONSES ARE NOT CAUSED BY PSI STIMULI

Where Do Experience and Behavior Come From?

It is virtually a truism for psychologists that experience and behaviors are caused by stimuli interacting with the nervous system of the organism. These stimuli are sensory impingements upon the nervous system from the "outer world" surrounding it. If there is such a thing as a "psi response," then this must also be caused by some sort of "psi stimulus." This assumption that stimulus-causes-response is so habitually held that it is contextual and unconscious for most psychological work. As a working assumption, it has proven to be enormously useful. It may seem odd and troublesome to consider changing it, but the approach represented by this book cannot be understood unless we do.

The Beginnings of Experimental Psychology

In the nineteenth century, the burgeoning new science of neurophysiology began to be concerned with how humans experience the world and how they behave. Thus, an even newer science of physiological psychology was born. The century began with Kant's dictum that psychology could not be experimental. As Descartes had thought, mind and body were separate and parallel. Each somehow influenced the other, but one could not be reduced to the other. The province of the mind was consciousness, and it could be studied qualitatively but not quantitatively. Events would prove all of this wrong.[15]

The functioning of sensory and motor nerves, the nature of specific nerve energies, and the physiology of sensation all came to be better understood thanks to the work of scientists such as Sir Charles Bell (1948), Johannes Müller (1826), and E. H. Weber (1834 [1978]). Sensation (a primary aspect of experience) could in fact be quantified and understood as a physiological process. But what about human behavior? Surely that is still a function of human intention, and not to be reduced to the mechanics of physiology? This assumption yielded, too. Even Descartes had noted that some of the movements of humans might be automatic and involuntary. A little later the concept of *reflex* was born—behavior that does not depend upon reason but upon sheer electrical stimulation of nerves. The first wet battery ever invented used a frog's leg, and Luigi Galvani discovered with it that muscle movements not only did not require intention, they did not require a living organism! Later it became clear through the work of such scientists as Broca (1861) and Fritsch and Hitzig (1870 [1960]) that the in vivo location for such electrical stimulation is the brain. The broad outlines of a new science of experience and behavior, purely naturalistic and biological, had been forged and would be rapidly filled out.

Already a century before, Jullien Offroy de La Mettrie (1748 [1996]) had boldly proposed that the human being should be understood as a kind of reflex machine. Even such a tender-minded psychologist as William James paid tribute to the "automata" model of human nature in his *Principles* (1890) and demonstrated it with the illustration given here as figure 6.1, showing a child as a reflex machine, approaching a burning flame.

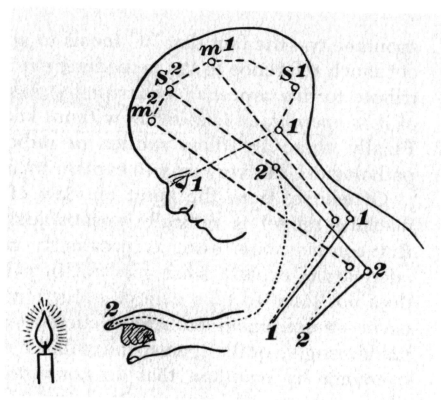

Figure 6.1.   Model of a boy as a set of reflex arcs.

I believe that to understand psi, we must take a position contrary to this biologically reductionistic one. For First Sight, psi "responses" are not caused by stimuli because no physical stimulus exists for the sensory system at the point at which psi interactions between self and the world occur. In many cases the pertinent events have not even happened yet. Even if they have occurred, or if the matrix of conditions that make them more or less probable have occurred, this is beyond the ken of the sensory system of the organism. Then with what does the mind interact? It seems to be that the mind interacts with meanings, however we may ultimately come to understand that. And it is not simply propelled into action by them. It seeks them and engages them intentionally.

TO SUM UP THE DIFFERENCES

In the First Sight model, psi is no longer understood in the way that it has been. Psi is not an ability, and it is not an anomalous experience (because

it is not an experience at all). It is an active process of unconscious engagement, mediated by unconscious intentions, with events that lie outside of
the ordinary sensory boundaries of the organism. Because psi is not an ability, research will not most profitably try to call it up by a challenge to demonstrate. Instead, research should try to arrange the situation such that the
implicit psi engagements can be revealed in their ongoing activity. Because
psi is not a conscious experience, it is probably best to not instruct participants to know things or do things by way of psi, because such instructions
are self-contradictory and confusing. It is true that research participants are
usually good sports and can generally tolerate our paradoxical instructions.
(See this hidden card. Affect these dice being rolled in another room.) In
any case such instructions do not usually seem to be particularly helpful in
producing results.

Even more important, such language adds to the problem of the acceptance and respect of parapsychological work by mainstream science.
Parapsychologists should describe to others and to themselves their experimental operations as they are—as assessments of implicit, inadvertent
expressions of unconscious intention acting upon nonlocal events—and
not as if they were some odd kind of conscious knowing or doing. They are
not a kind of conscious knowing or doing, and being careful to not imply
that they are will avoid unnecessary confusion and misunderstanding with
other scientists who will already find our assertions about time and space
to be troubling enough without also seeming to violate their prescientific
sense of everyday reality.

SOME NEW TERMS FOR PARAPSYCHOLOGISTS

From time to time parapsychologists have offered to rename their basic
constructs. Sometimes they have wanted to escape certain implications of
the old terms and emphasize others. Sometimes they probably wanted to
make a fresh start for the reception of parapsychological research by other
scientists, free of the controversy that has accumulated around the old constructs. ESP has been renamed as Anomalous Cognition (or Anomalous
Perception), Psi-Gamma, Nonlocal Awareness and Afferent Delta, among
other things. Psychokinesis has been relabeled Anomalous Perturbation,
Mind-Matter-Interaction (MMI), Psi-Kappa, Nonlocal Influence, Distant
Mental Influence, and Efferent Delta. If the PK effect is on another organism's physiological processes, it has been called Distant Mental Influence
on Living Systems (DMILS).

In fact, none of these changes in terminology have achieved widespread
usage (with the possible exception of DMILS), and none have escaped for
long the critical eye of skeptics, who know a rose by any other name smells
the same—not too sweetly for them.

So I face the prospect of renaming these things with mixed feelings. There is no point to add to a pile of discarded words; but there are real problems with the old terms if the perspective of First Sight is taken seriously.

The major problem is that the terms imply some things that are really basically incorrect, from the point of view of this model. The term *extrasensory perception* and all its subdivisions and flavors (*telepathy, clairvoyance, remote viewing, precognition, retrocognition, clairaudience, psychometry, anomalous cognition, nonlocal awareness*) all in their roots carry implications of conscious knowledge (perceiving, feeling, seeing, viewing, cognizing, hearing, measuring, being aware). As argued in the first section of this chapter, all of this is incorrect since psi functions only unconsciously and implicitly and can no more be known as such than can a deeply subliminal stimulus or an utterly forgotten prior experience. Yet these things, like psi prehensions, can implicitly influence the products of experience and behavioral decisions.

There is a similar problem with *psychokinesis* and its variants. The word *kinesis*, in biology, refers to the action of a cell in response to some stimulus, while the term *psyche* is used by psychology as a synonym for the conscious mind. Hence, *psychokinesis* implies some action caused by a conscious wish or thought. From the First Sight perspective, psychokinesis is not any kind of conscious doing. It is unconscious doing—still intentional and personal—but not consciously deliberate. The older and mostly neglected term *telekinesis* is actually preferable, since its roots only imply action at a distance, without the implications of consciousness, although it might suffer from having no connection to human intention at all. It might as well refer to cell phones or remote-control drones, even though it isn't used that way in practice.

Recently another problem has arisen, in that many have begun describing parapsychology as part of a larger *Science of Personal Unconsciousness*. From a First Sight perspective, parapsychologists are not primarily concerned with acts of consciousness, but rather with acts that are unconscious. We might say that the field belongs with a larger *Science of Personal Consciousness*.

So, here goes with an effort at renaming to find more consistency with this model. The effort is guided by the need to remove the implications of conscious experience and mechanical causation. I will rely upon the term *prehension* in place of all those words and parts of words that imply conscious perception, feeling, willing, and so on. *Prehension* should be understood to be a kind of grasping that can be both conscious and unconscious, and also both receptive and active. It implies that the mind is taking initiative in the matter and not merely being caused to respond by a mechanical stimulus.

I also follow the lead of Jan Ehrenwald (1970), who achieved a more objective description of our basic categories by speaking of ESP and precognition as *efferent psi* and psychokinesis as *afferent psi*.

To what larger field of study does parapsychology belong? To the study of *Personal Unconscious Psychological Processes* (PUPPs). (This acronym might accidentally be somewhat propitious: our unconscious psychological processes do serve us with all the devotion of a loyal canine and are as lacking in conscious cognitive deliberation.) Other PUPPs include our memories, our creative impulses, our long-term goals, our subliminal perceptions, and our characteristic moods (as the phenomenologists would say, our attunements).

The term *Psi* can stand as it is, if it is taken to mean our ongoing unconscious engagement with an extended personal world.

I nominate the following other changes:

Extrasensory perception is called *Efferent Extrasomatic Prehension* (EESP). Prehensions may be conscious or unconscious, and in this case they are understood to be unconscious. *Efferent* indicates that the action is receptive, into the forming experience and behavior of the organism. *Extrasomatic* implies that the action is nonlocal; beyond the ordinary boundaries of the body. *Prehension* means "to engage, to take hold of" both actively and receptively. And it may be either conscious or unconscious. In this case, it is understood to be unconscious.

Precognition (and *presentiment*) is called *Efferent Antecedent Extrasomatic Prehension* (EA-ESP). *Antecedent* indicates that the prehension of the event is prior to its occurrence.

When we are referring to an inadvertent expression of psi about the future that appears in guessing behavior or inadvertent behavioral choices, then that operation can be specified. For example, EA-ESP expressed by card guessing, or EA-ESP expressed by avoidance of accidents. Similarly, when the expression is a physiological one, this can also be specified. For example: EA-ESP via electrodermal response, EA-ESP via amygdale arousal, EA-ESP via heart-rate variability, etc.

Psychokinesis is called *Afferent Extrasomatic Prehension* (A-ESP). *Afferent* indicates that an action is proceeding from within outward, toward influence beyond the body. The other parts of the term bear the same implications as with EESP.

If we wished, this could be elaborated in terms of temporal direction. If we are intending to affect future events, we could say *Afferent Antecedent Extrasomatic Prehension* (AA-ESP), as in intending that a medical treatment should prove beneficial or that a random event generator should come to behave in certain ways. If we would like to influence past events (what has been called *retro-PK*), this could be called *Afferent Consequent Extrasomatic Prehension* (AC-ESP).

This is it. PUPPs, psi, EESP, A-ESP, and EA-ESP, and their elaborations (along with the previously defined terms: *weighting*, *signing*, and *switching*). With this small lexicon I believe we can more accurately describe the operations with which we acquire our indications of psi and speak meaningfully about the workings of psi and other unconscious mental processes. In doing so we can avoid the troublesome implications of the old terms and suggest the coherence with which these things apparently tend to work together.

Of course, there is some awkwardness and oddness to the terms. This always seems to be so when new terminology is nominated. The acronyms do not lack all virtue. I do like PUPPs. The familiar ESP is retained, and EESP could be an exclamation of surprise, appropriate for some nonlocal event. EA-ESP would tend to be pronounced as "ee-esp," which would at least be different from A-ESP

Still, such musings are irrelevant if the terms do not seem helpful enough to adopt. Time will tell. In fact, I will not refer to them much in the remainder of this book. This is because I attempt to cover a great deal of ground there involving the findings of past research and that work used the conventional terms. It would be too confusing to try to discuss that work and change the basic terminology at the same time.

In future work, these terms might seem useful if researchers find it important to conduct programs of research within the First Sight model, or some other model like it, in which it is explicit that psi functions are not directly, consciously experienced and not forced upon a passive mind by mechanical stimuli.

NOTES

1. Mayer herself inadvertently perpetuated the long-standing mystification about such experiences by calling this an instance of "extraordinary knowing."
2. Beloff, 1977.
3. Schwartz and Simon, 2003.
4. Ellenberger, 1970, chapters 2 and 3.
5. Dingwall, 1968.
6. Targ, 1993.
7. Although the term *remote viewing* has come to be used synonymously with clairvoyance, this is incorrect. The term really refers to a technical protocol developed following the ideas of Ingo Swann for staging trials about unknown information and generating responses that are intended to refer to it. See McMoneagle (2000) and Swann (2000).
8. Gauld, 1968.
9. Rhine, 1977.
10. Mauskopf and McVaugh, 1980.
11. Bevan and Zener, 1952.
12. Mayer, 2007.
13. Grad, 1961.
14. Mark Twain, in Calkins, 1982.
15. See Boring, 1950.

7

Psychokinesis: First Sight and First Act

How does it come that even inanimate objects are capable of behaving as if they were acquainted with my thoughts?

—Carl Jung

FIRST SIGHT AND FIRST ACT

First Sight theory asserts that the afferent aspect of psi, psychokinesis (PK or A-ESP), is essentially unconscious and ongoing continuously, just as ESP is. Through psychokinesis the mind begins the process of actualizing its intentions. It anticipates action and takes the first step toward initiating it. Thus, psi is not only *first sight*, it is also *first act*.

The primary and most basic function of PK is in affecting the nervous system processes that carry out actions. Thus, it is the effective link between mind and body, between intention and matter. In its normal functioning, it is almost entirely contained within this sphere.

PK also is engaged preactively beyond the boundaries of the physical organism, just as ESP is engaged preperceptively beyond those boundaries. Unconscious intentions continuously engage (prehend) processes beyond the body, and these engagements potentially participate in action just as the preperceptive engagements of psi always potentially contribute to experience. In its most common form, this psi activity works in preparation for taking physical action upon those processes. Thus, if I reach for a cup, my intention is affecting not only my bodily processes in taking action (my brain, my nervous system, my muscles), it is also potentially acting upon the cup itself in preparation for my grasping it. As with ESP, this incipient activity is almost always invisible in everyday experience.

This assertion of continuous, potential, extrabodily activity is conjectural at this point, based upon assuming a parallel sort of function between the afferent and efferent sides of psi. As stated before, much less psychological research has been done on PK than ESP, so there is less to draw upon in testing this or any model. Still, what there is will be referred to in later chapters.

While ostensible ESP experiences are rare, experiences suggesting PK are reported less often still. No valid comparisons of their rate of occurrence exist, but Louisa Rhine (1963) noted that PK reports were considerably less frequent in her large case collection. Still, they do appear to occur, and research demonstrating the sheer reality of PK in the laboratory is strong, as judged by a meta-analysis of Radin and Nelson (1989). If PK occurs in the laboratory, it must figure into everyday life as well. A First Sight model of PK poses interesting questions for empirical research.

PK IS UNCONSCIOUS, INTENTIONAL, AND BIMODAL

Psychokinesis is unconscious. It is guided ultimately by the same thing that guides extrasensory perception: unconscious intentions. These may be congruent with conscious intentions or contrary to them or completely unrelated to them, concerned with other issues entirely.

Like ESP, PK is bimodal. It may act in congruence with my developing action, or contrary to it. If I reach for the cup, the cup may move toward me (the assimilative side of PK) or away from me (the disassimilative side). Or, as in the case of ESP, the two tendencies may alternate so rapidly that they cancel one another out, in which case there would be no resultant tendency of movement at all on the part of the cup. This rapid switching of tendencies, as with ESP, expresses an inconsistency of unconscious intention, generally because of being held in abeyance by more regnant intentions on other matters.

WEIGHTING AND SIGNING IN PK

Just as with ESP, the object of my intention is first *weighted* unconsciously, in terms of its degree of pertinence to my personal hierarchy of unconscious intentions in the moment. If it is highly pertinent for my most regnant unconscious intention, it is weighted heavily. If it is weighted heavily, then it is *signed* either positively (as being congruent with my uppermost unconscious intention and my unfolding understanding of the situation) or negatively (as incongruent with those things). If it is unconsciously judged to be congruent with my intention and situation, the action tendency will be signed positively, and the physical process (within the body or outside the body) will be set in motion toward the expression of my intended act. If it is judged to be incongruent with my dominant unconscious intention, the action tendency will be signed negatively and the physical process will be set in motion in some way contrary to my conscious wish. For example, within the body we see this with the alcoholic, who remembers that he must stop drinking as he opens a fresh bottle. Despite his conscious wish, his dominant unconscious intention to drink preempts the moment and suppresses the behavioral alternative of pushing the bottle away. Outside the body, we see it with the poltergeist agent who is terrified of being hurt by flying objects and wishes them to stop at the same moment that something hits her in the head from behind (an event I have witnessed myself, as well as heard described by others whose objectivity I trust).

All situations are actually vastly complex, with many interacting physical processes active at once. Unconscious thought makes weighting and signing decisions very rapidly and holistically within this complex surround.

PK IS LIKE UNCONSCIOUSLY EXPRESSIVE BEHAVIOR

Psychoanalysis has made us all familiar with the idea of unconsciously meaningful behavioral slips. It may be a slip of the tongue, an errant word that inadvertently expresses something that we might be wishing to hide. In an intimate moment, a woman may utter the name of a former lover instead of her current date. Once a nervous suitor of my daughter was telling me about his research in genetic engineering. "Why," he exclaimed proudly, "we are making whole new orgasms! I mean organisms!"

Other behavior can similarly slip and express hidden concerns. Once a patient described to me how he was driving home in a distracted state of mind, absorbed in radio music, when he noticed that he had taken a wrong turn some blocks back. Where was he? In front his town's mortuary. Then he realized that for some days he had been trying to not think about a serious illness in his family.

Our model asserts that something very similar is going on when unconscious intentions reach beyond one's own bodily actions and engage the world beyond the body. If we look thoughtfully at the behaviors of things around us, at times they may also seem to inadvertently express unconscious intentions. When this occurs, we call it a *PK experience*. As with behavioral slips, such events are not experienced as consciously, deliberately done. They "just happen," "have a will of their own," and feel ego-alien or even threatening. If we see them as meaningful at all, it is by recognizing a possible inadvertent meaning. Even when we attribute such meaning, we never feel sure of being its author. It generally seems more to bring information *in to us,* as if from somewhere else.[1] Even the information feels dubious. It seems to be as likely that it is a "mere coincidence" (and of course, it may be).

As in the case of ESP, the ordinary action of PK is invisible, even when it is weighted heavily, because psi processes (including PK) are unconscious and their actions cannot be consciously experienced as being done deliberately. Thus, a PK event, even when it accords with a conscious intention, is always experienced as autonomous, not consciously controlled. We are denied an experience of agency. In the action of picking up a cup, the proposed participation of PK in bridging my intention with my musculature is innately unconscious. All that I experience is behaving as I wish and picking up the cup. Should the unconscious intention bypass my body and be expressed by an apparently autonomous bounce of the cup, it would not feel like my action. It would seem to come "from somewhere else."

PK ordinarily participates in an anticipatory way in actions, just as ESP ordinarily participates in an anticipatory way in perceptions and unconscious behavioral choices. It is the first step toward fulfilling my intention, the initial stage of the incipience of action. When action is allowed to proceed undeterred toward its goal, PK functions primarily within the confines of one's own body, and its participation in the situation is invisible.

INTENDED BUT PREVENTED

The frustration of intention is important for the action of psi to become visible. We see expressions of ESP when a perception is intended but prevented. Then we can grasp the anticipatory allusions to the perception that might-have-been as the possibility was suggested by extrasensory prehension. Occasionally these allusory experiences grip our attention strongly enough that they emerge as conscious experiences in their own right. We call these "ESP experiences." Similarly, we occasionally see expressions of PK when an action is intended but prevented. Then we see the anticipatory participations of physical processes beyond the person. These would have been part of the intended action had it developed.

To reiterate the case of ESP: When a conscious experience is fully formed, a psi prehension is invisibly present within the experience if the prehension was congruent with the experience as it formed, and it is invisibly rejected by the experience if it was incongruent. It is the same with PK: When an action proceeds smoothly to a conclusion (I walk across the room), the psi prehension is invisibly present if it was congruent with the act (an unconscious wish to be in the new place), and it is invisibly suppressed by the act if it was incongruent (a wish to be somewhere else instead).

PK IS NOT ACTION AND CAN ONLY BE DISCERNED WHEN ACTION IS BLOCKED

All of this implies that PK is not action as normally understood, just as ESP is not knowledge. Action is consciously intentional behavior. PK is the initial part of the mind's unconscious preparation for action. Processes within and beyond the body are engaged in an anticipatory way by means of PK. The unconscious mind evokes the implicit participation of these processes in enacting our intentions.

The effects of PK upon extrabodily processes can only be discerned when unconscious intention is strong and unequivocal and the processes are sensed to be highly pertinent, but action is prevented. Then the implicit participation of "external" processes can be seen. The rolls of dice may express the faces we want, even though we are prevented by the nature of the situation from physically manipulating them. The rapid decisions of a random event generator may likewise express our wishing for *ones* or *zeros* (or run counter to that conscious wish), even though we have no tangible, direct way of influencing that process. On a larger scale, the behavior of a table in a séance room or some object in the vicinity of a poltergeist agent may express the unconscious intentions of the people involved, even though no one is able to physically interact with the table or object. Blocking the development of an action is similar to blocking the development of a perception, as in a subliminal perception experiment or an ESP study. When the normal course of events is interrupted and the physical expression of an intention is blocked, the anticipatory participation of PK in the situation may be discerned.

PK AND ESP AS ASPECTS OF A COMPLEX WHOLE

A psi prehension is a kind of grasping, in both the receptive and active connotations of that term—both *seizing* and *understanding*. By an act of abstraction we may separate the afferent and efferent aspects of a psi prehension, but in reality (our model assumes) they are always going on together.

Psi is the beginning of our experience, our behavior, our action. Psi is implied in our behavior, and it is also implied in the action of the events around us. Unconscious intention continuously prehends aspects of reality beyond the physical boundaries of the person, and these prehensions always have both active and perceptive aspects.

We wish to know our situation and affect it in optimal ways. These two aspects of intention are always active at once. The line between ESP and PK is not only blurry but also it is artificial and potentially misleading. It is useful if we wish to focus upon one of the aspects of intention while not considering the other. In ongoing experience they are always united, at least implicitly.

Even omitting psi, in its normal functioning, all cognitive processing is tied to action, at least potentially. As the psychologist L. L. Thurstone has said, "Consciousness is unfinished action." In ongoing life, cognitive processing often leads to action and action then loops back as feedback to consciousness.

ESP and PK are terms that arose out of a perspective in which these things were seen as separate abilities. First Sight does not understand them as abilities but instead as aspects of an ongoing, unconscious engagement of all living beings with an extended reality. PK is not the ability to move things at a distance. It is an ongoing unconscious process of engagement with things within the body and external to the body, in as much as they involve my effecting my intentions.

Experience and action are intimately and complexly conjoined for all of us almost all of the time. Both are shaped by unconscious mental processes that are guided by unconscious intention in the context of a rapidly developing sense of what matters in the situation. This complex integration is as true of matters beyond the body and the sensory system as within it.

ESP and PK are constructs for different aspects of a whole, complex process. I intend to pick up a cup and then pick it up, and I have a conscious awareness of the cup as I perform the action. My perception is a part of my action, and they inform one another and flow together seamlessly. At a preconscious and presensory level, my PK initiates my extrasensory engagement with the meaning of the cup as it initiates my behavior. My extrasensory prehension of the cup informs my developing visual and then kinesthetic experience of the cup, and these bits of awareness guide my intention, the signing of my PK, and my developing act. A complex weave of feedback involving both unconscious anticipations of experience and unconscious anticipations of action is ongoing. These unconscious anticipations are normally invisible unless they are interrupted.

Although these things are conjoined and interacting, they can be teased apart to some extent by experimenters who design studies that focus on measuring one thing while holding others constant (or allow them to vary "randomly" across enough instances that statistical conclusions are obtained). For this reason, we can have studies that meaningfully examine ESP or PK or subliminal perception or memory, in isolation, as if that thing is all that is going on. These are actually never the only things that are going on, but our experimental design allows us to sustain a focus upon one to the exclusion of all the rest.

EXPERIENCES IMPLYING PK ALSO IMPLY ESP

In a laboratory experiment, participants are handed lists of random targets that no one else has read (in an attempt to make the psi of the experimenter less of a factor) and are asked to influence the output of a random number generator in such a way that a light seems to "walk" in either a clockwise or counterclockwise direction around a small circle of bulbs. If the bulbs respond in the way that is typical of such tests, for a time they will tend to obey the wishes of the participants more often than chance would predict, and then if testing goes on too long they may be likely to drop to chance or even below. If the bulbs are indeed expressing the intentions of the participants to some extent, it is not because the participants know clearly what is happening. Like average sixteen-year-olds learning to drive, they have little knowledge of what is going on "under the hood." It may be that the radiation emitted from a small piece of strontium-90 is triggering a tiny electronic switch by which it is determined that a bulb either to the right or to the left of the last one will light up next.[2] Such a mechanism is really understood only by physicists and electronic engineers, not the typical research participant nor their psychologist experimenters! In whatever way unconscious intention is grasping the bulb-lighting outcome, it is not with any sort of analysis and comprehension and step-by-step guidance. It is with the sort of summary, holistic apprehension that we have said is characteristic of ESP.

The same considerations apply in cases of real-life PK. Suppose a woman hears a loud bang in another room, and upon investigating finds that a small chair that had belonged to her mother had split in two—in an empty room, all by itself! Then a little while later the woman gets a phone call telling her of her mother's death in another state at about the time that the chair was split. Such death-announcing events are among the more frequent things that people take to represent possible PK.[3] Assuming that the woman is the one whose imminent grief is being expressed by the event, then at the moment it happened the death itself could only have been prehended by psi, unconsciously and distantly. If we wish to imagine that the dying woman is the one responsible, then the chair in her daughter's home is equally distant and could not be prehended by her in a normal, sensory way. Or could it be the discarnate spirit of the mother already dead? However the destruction of the chair might be guided by such a spirit, it is not by ordinary sensory perception, since with death that has ceased to function. And by what process did the chair split? Whatever it is, it is as unknown to the mother and daughter as the radioactivity and circuitry in the laboratory experiment. When sensory information and deliberate action are not allowed into a situation in which some physical event nonetheless is apparently expressing human intention, then we are left with only the implicit, holistic anticipations of information that we have defined as ESP to inform the expression.

While every study of ESP and PK can be understood logically to imply the action of the other, at least one study set out to combine them explicitly, at least from the point of view of the experimenter. Stanford and some of his students[4] administered a standard PK test to their participants. Then each one was led to a different room to carry out a motor procedure designed to be unpleasant and boring. Meanwhile, a random event generator was left running. If a certain criterion level of events defined by the experimenters as a hit occurred during the second period, the participants were released from that task and asked instead to do something that the experimenters thought would be innately interesting for this group of males—rate the attractiveness of erotic pictures. The participants beat chance significantly, and many more of them were released to the pleasant task than would be expected if PK were not influencing the result. The authors argue that success at this required somehow knowing of the second random number generator (RNG) by way of ESP, followed by influencing it with PK.

Even here the issue of whose agency is involved in this effect cannot be determined with certainty. Presumably it was the participant, but the experimenters' kindheartedness or wish to get a good result would be good reasons for them to participate psychokinetically and implicitly as well.

THE INTERPERSONAL COMPLEXITY OF PSI

Bringing in the uncertainty about which person might best be understood as responsible for a psi event reminds us again of an important fact that scientific analysis might make it easy to forget. We are all interpersonal beings, born into interpersonal worlds and making our way there as long as we live (and perhaps even beyond?). Science analyzes things into consitutent parts and then tries to establish regularities of function in terms of those parts. For that reason we tend to think in terms of one person, or organism, at a time. But we live in active engagement with others, and this is an inescapable dimension of our reality. Even hermits alone on mountaintops exist in an internal dialogue of voices. It is unwise to forget that our analyses, while necessary, are always artificial and partial. A scientist who does forget this is in danger of committing the crime attributed to science by William Wordsworth, who said that science must "murder to dissect."

Not only are ESP and PK woven together, but surely part of what our unconscious intentions are privy to is the unconscious intentions of one another. And surely part of that outer world that we can affect includes the experiences and behavior of other beings. In fact, a lot of evidence has accrued that this is the case.[5] How does PK work when two or more people intend different things, which is certainly often the case? What becomes of ESP when we wish to deceive each other? We understand next to nothing about all this, and have barely begun to imagine how we might scientifically pose the questions (although some interesting starts have been made). Even a relatively straightforward scientific experiment becomes much more complex when we apply the psi hypothesis to the situation. How might the intentions of the experimenter contribute directly and inadvertently to results? How might participants in drug trials be expressing implicit prehensions about the treatment they are receiving in blind conditions? How might the responses of participants be unwittingly expressing reference to previous responses of other participants, or even affecting those other responses? Does such complexity make research impossible?

Surely it does not, or empirical research would not have proven to be as powerfully useful as it has. Situations are almost always quite complex, even omitting the dimension of psi. We make progress by taking one thing at a time, using large samples when possible and replicating on new samples. In the process all of the other things going on can be temporarily ignored as we try to establish relationships among a few things. Patterns can emerge against the background of all the other variables varying more or less at random. But then we must avoid the arrogance of the scientist who falls into believing that all that is known is all that there is. At the psi level of engagement, we become ourselves out of one another. Understanding this better will not deaden the world for us as Wordsworth feared, but further reveal its vitality.

NOTES

1. L. E. Rhine, 1963.
2. Schmidt, 1970a.
3. Myers, 1891–1892; L. E. Rhine, 1963.
4. Stanford, Zenhausern, Taylor, and Dwyer, 1975.
5. Braud, 2003.

8

Precursors of the Model

Every man is a quotation from all his ancestors.

—Ralph Waldo Emerson

This model is the result of many years of my own reflection on the mystery of psi as well as pondering the thoughts of others. I was struck by the parallels between the discovery of new personal meaning in clinical psychological work and discovering sensorily unavailable meaning in the parapsychology experiment,[1] as well as parallels between research in subliminal perception and in extrasensory perception. My own first experimental explorations in the direction of this model showed both these influences. In one pair of experiments,[2] highly emotional extrasensory stimuli were treated as if they were subliminal primes in forced-choice guessing tasks, and extrasensory success was examined as a function of the "primes" and certain subject variables having to do with attitude and affective style—all in the manner of subliminal perception studies of the period. In another study that began in 1986 and was carried on for many years,[3] a quasi-psychotherapeutic group was used as a receptive medium for the influence of a randomly selected ESP target. This design was inspired by PWA studies that showed the behavioral/emotional influences of subliminal primes in spontaneous interpersonal behavior and by the personal experience of many cases of psychotherapy in which the important discovery of personal meaning and the apparent intrusion of extrasensory information went hand in hand.

SOME NONPARAPSYCHOLOGICAL INFLUENCES

Alongside these influences, I was helped to think as I have about parapsychological questions by some nonparapsychologists. The major ones that I recognize are Sigmund Freud, George Kelly, Harold McCurdy, and Medard Boss. In each case, it was some of their more general attitudes that were especially helpful rather than their particular conclusions.

Freud had an interest in the possibility of telepathy, but it was far from the focus of his theoretical work (I have more to say about his interest in telepathy in chapter 18). What I have found most helpful from Freud are two basic assumptions.[4] The first is *psychological determinism.* For him, no human behavior was accidental. Even the bizarre, physiological symptoms of hysteria were caused by meaningful forces; but for Freud they were forces *within the self* rather than physical forces *acting upon the self.* Before Freud, something as odd as a hysterical blindness or as commonplace as a slip of the tongue would either be attributed to some external, nonpsychological cause (like a brain dysfunction) or written off as meaningless, mere happenstance. Freud insisted that a multitude of such phenomena are indeed caused, but that they are *caused psychologically.* To explain how they were caused, he used his second major assumption: that of *personal and dynamic unconscious processes.* The mind works unconsciously as well as consciously for Freud, and the very personal and meaningful processes there constantly influence what people experience and do. Many psychologists today also use the assumption of unconscious mental processes (and by implication, psychological determinism), while most of them would disavow other particulars of Freudian theory. It seems obvious that his bold use of these assumptions paved the way for many other theories, including First Sight.

George Kelly developed a theory of personality and psychological treatment that he called Personal Construct Psychology (1955, 1979). One thing that I have found useful in developing my own ideas is his assumption of *constructive alternativism.* This is a thoroughly pragmatic approach that assumes that there is an infinite number of possible ways to construe anything and that the most important criterion to use in choosing among them is their usefulness. He applied this assumption both to the constructions of individuals in their personal lives and to those of scientists trying to develop a formal understanding of nature. If some construction is dysfunctional, then discard it and try something else. Whether it is a paranoid individual too apt to construe strangers as enemies or a research psychologist trying too hard to be strictly behavioral and reductionistic, much can be gained by claiming the freedom to try new constructions and test them for their usefulness. Kelly also emphasized that constructs could be perfectly useful within certain domains of experience (he called these "ranges of convenience"), but not helpful elsewhere. Constructs about elementary physical forces are useful for describing the actions of billiard balls and constructs about legal precedents are useful for describing behaviors brought into criminal court, but neither set of constructs is particularly useful in the other's natural domain, and we should be under no obligation to try to force them to fit. This is not to say that Kelly believed that constructs *must not* be applied outside their ranges of convenience, only that it might not be useful to do so. Constructs are invented by people, not owned by departments of reality. Thus, Kelly would never say that a certain kind of event *belongs to physics* or *belongs to psychology*.

Applied to the phenomena of parapsychology, Kelly's pragmatic approach allows a theorist to not worry overmuch about conventional prescriptions and proscriptions about how things must work or how they must be construed.

Another important implication of Kelly's work, for me, is his insistence that persons cannot be usefully understood entirely "from the outside," using constructs that belong to the scientist without referring to those that belong to the persons in question. Each person is his or her own scientist, for Kelly, inventing contructs with which to try to predict and understand the world and the self, testing them, revising them, testing them again. A scientific understanding must have room in it for the understandings of those who are being understood. This is a major departure from the functionalist, positivist path that experimental psychology has taken. This includes cognitive psychology, which attempts to understand how people think, feel, and react. This disharmony with prevailing method has left Kelly's work tangential, and at another level, probably inscrutable and offensive for most experimental psychologists. He thought that a science of clinical psychology and psychotherapy could not possibly do without such a reference to an individual's own system of experience and understanding. I think the same is true of parapsychology, where we see a direct engagement of meaning with physical process at an unconscious level of functioning. Meaning is not something that can be easily dealt with by natural science, with its analysis of impersonal processes. Yet it appears to be meaning itself that is prehended by ESP and expressed physically by psychokinesis.

Medard Boss (1979) brought the basic attitudes of Husserl's phenomenology and Heidegger's metaphysics into psychological and psychiatric theory. He rejected the reductionistic and mechanistic tendencies of contemporary psychiatry in favor of a phenomenological understanding of the human being (*dasein*). A person may not be adequately understood as a kind of object in the sense emphasized by natural science. Rather, a person is himself/herself the whole of existence from a particular center of experience and concern. Nor is a person alone—persons exist innately in relationship with others. Boss often used the concept of *light* as being the character of existence. An existence is a being-in-the-light. The lit space may be large and healthy or shrunken and pathological. He also stressed the importance of moods and "attunements." An angry man, for example, is alert to angry, dangerous, and aggressive things. A depressed woman is attuned to sorrows, losses, and shadows. He thought that dreams were an especially illuminating area of experience, and he took the existence of dream life literally in a phenomenological sense (1958, 1977). He only alluded in passing to extrasensory implications of dream life, but the possibility was clearly not incredible to him.

Boss argued that one can usefully step away from the Cartesian assumption of a split between mind and body to a singular understanding of human being by focusing upon experience as it is given, rather than upon preconceptions placed upon experience. From this perspective, the direct interaction of a person and the extended world (as by psi) no longer looks like a miracle and does not need to be "explained" by labored accounts of how a physical stimulus might be imagined to impinge upon a nonphysical mind. If in experience these things are found to be related, then no dreadful mystery about them needs to be assumed or solved.

Harold McCurdy took an approach much like Boss's into the context of American psychology and developed a theory of personality that was no less phenomenological, but perhaps more easily assimilated by his contemporaries (1961, 1965). Like Boss, he eschewed what he called "mechanomorphism," the tendency to view persons as machines, which science has seemingly pursued relentlessly since the time of Descartes. Each self is the center of a personal world, for McCurdy. He borrowed Alfred North Whitehead's term *prehension* to describe the relations, conscious and unconscious, that a self has with the objects of its world—including those objects that are themselves other selves-in-worlds. If the self relates to those others as objects only (and not selves-in worlds), then the relationships become barren and merely manipulative. A scientific psychologist who views persons the same way suffers the same dehumanizing fate.

McCurdy was more explicit than Boss about the reality of psi. He considered it a particularly direct and illuminating way in which selves and objects can relate.

HELPFUL PARAPSYCHOLOGICAL PRECEDENTS

There are also several major congruencies that I have come to appreciate between the work of other parapsychologists and the First Sight model. I will cite the major ones of which I am aware.

THE WORK OF MYERS, RHINE, SCHMEIDLER, AND RAO

One of the great founders of psychical research, F. W. H. Myers, bequeathed to all subsequent researchers a conception of unconscious mental functioning that was almost equal in scope to that developed more elaborately by Sigmund Freud, but it has not been nearly as well known. His lifework culminated in an encyclopedic two-volume study (1961 [1903]), which covered almost the whole spectrum of states of consciousness: normal, pathological, and paranormal. Myers assembled broad ranges of data, building up a concept of the subliminal self, which provided a platform for a scientifically respectable hypothesis about the experiential survival of a person after physical death. He carefully and methodically derived supporting evidence for such a subliminal stratum from information about sleep and dreams, hysteria, psychosis, genius, automatism, and hypnosis, along with the current state of evidence for thought transference and clairvoyance. He coined the term *telepathy*. He developed a distinctive concept of unconscious mental functioning that William James (1903) referred to as "evolutive." He emphasized the capacity of the subliminal self to reach beyond consciousness in positive and transformative ways. This was distinguished from the "dissolutive" concepts that were emerging then from neuropsychiatry, in which expressions of unconscious activity were thought of as indicating degeneration and disease.

Myers thought that the subliminal self constituted an unconscious, but organized, agency. He thought it was active at all times, but only under special circumstances could it break through into consciousness. Hypnotic phenomena, for example, represented an evocation of the subliminal self through suggestion. More esoteric phenomena such as phantasms of the living and dead suggested that the subliminal self could establish independent relations with space as well as with other minds. He drew attention to the similarities of various states that encouraged the expression of unconscious material, such as mediumistic trances, hypnosis, and reverie. He was a grand theorist, taking a variety of apparently discontinuous phenomena and showing how they represented a single, continuous agency.

The importance of his model of unconscious functioning for understanding psi processes has been reexamined recently in the light of current thinking in psychology and neurology, as well as a century of new observations of paranormal processes, and is revealed as fresh and heuristically vital.[5]

J. B. Rhine is generally credited with founding the science of parapsychology, as distinguished from the naturalistic studies of psychical research. He brought parapsychology out of the séance room and into the academic scientific laboratory. He pioneered its methods, coined much of its terminology, collected and oversaw the collection of mountains of scientific data, and fought valiantly for respect for his new field (1934 [1973], 1957).[6] He also laid down a number of particular assertions that constitute much of the ground of this theory.

He insisted that psi abilities have been demonstrated to be real, and he asserted that they were distributed throughout the general population of persons and probably throughout the animal kingdom as well, not just limited to a few startling individuals. He called special attention to the

importance of psi-missing (1952) and declared that this negative performance was a meaningful expression of psi. He asserted that psi functioning is essentially unconscious (1957, 1958), yet still dirigible. He also laid
out a general program for work that assumed that psi functioning would
ultimately be understandable within the general terms of a broadened,
normal science of psychology and biology (1953, 1957, 1979). All of the
subsequent scientific efforts to understand psi, including First Sight, are
built upon this foundation.

Gertrude Schmeidler, throughout her very productive career, demonstrated the fruitfulness of considering parapsychological phenomena as essentially continuous with the rest of normal psychological functioning. She
declared that parapsychology had been working with an implicit theory for
over a century,[7] and it was this: *Psi is a psychological function.* One example
of her conscious application of this premise is her "sheep-goat" effect. She
asked people if they believed that ESP was impossible or not, and showed,
after the fashion of "New Look" theory, that the subject's attitude was as
important in determining the quality of extrasensory perception as it had
been found to be with normal sensory perception.[8] In her survey of findings
assessing the extent to which paranormal processes followed the same patterns as normal psychological processes,[9] her discussions of cognitive and
perceptual patterns are especially germane to the point of view developed
here. In particular, she emphasized the functional similarity of extrasensory
perception and subliminal perception (1986).

K. R. Rao (1962, 1991) elaborated Rhine's constructs of psi-hitting and
psi-missing and developed a broad conception of psi process as inherently
and preconsciously bidirectional. He showed in many datasets that both
directional processes were active at the same time and that they could be
meaningfully discriminated and predicted. He and his students also contributed conceptually and empirically to studies elucidating the interaction
of memory and psi processes and explored the importance of extraversion,
neuroticism, and other personality variables on a person's direction of
performance.[10]

THE THEORIES OF REX STANFORD

Perhaps the strongest parallel between the current model and previous work
is with the Psi-Mediated Instrumental Response (PMIR) theory of Rex Stanford (1974a, 1974b, 1977, 1991). There are important similarities between
Stanford's model and First Sight, so it is worth pointing out in some detail
just where these ways of thinking about psi merge and where they differ.

Stanford's model, introduced in 1974, was bold and innovative. He was
hoping to bridge an important conceptual gap between psi phenomena as

they were understood in the laboratory and spontaneous experiences suggesting psi abilities as they occurred naturally. He wanted a set of terms and predictions that could apply to both domains.

Before Stanford first articulated his theory, some reports had appeared in which quasi-experimental methods of measurement and analysis were applied to situations that might be understood as expressing psi abilities functioning unconsciously. For example, W. Edward Cox (1956) had demonstrated that people spontaneously chose to ride trains less frequently on days when train wrecks would occur than on control days with no accidents. Thus he showed what appeared to be unconscious precognition spontaneously at work in a protective way. Stanford himself (1970) showed that hidden ESP targets could be used unconsciously to assist persons taking a memory test, and Martin Johnson (1971, 1973) reported that university students could spontaneously and unconsciously be helped on tests by hidden correct answers that were taped to their answer sheets. And Douglas Dean (1962) demonstrated that people being monitored physiologically by a plethysmograph produced different kinds of reactions when a distant agent was looking at names of persons important to them as compared to times when random names were looked at. All of these things demonstrated that psi could work in a nondeliberate way, but Stanford wanted a systematic theory, not just a patchwork of observations implying a pattern.

Stanford noted that in the laboratory people were generally asked to try to consciously use psi ability, whereas spontaneous occurrences suggested that the abilities could be unconsciously called into play in times of need (and so did observations, such as those involving train wrecks, memory tests, and unconscious physiological response). How can we account for the instances in which psi abilities might unconsciously mediate responses? He laid his ideas out systematically in the form of a theory reminiscent in structure of the theories of motivation and learning of Clark Hull or Neal Miller.

He grounded his model in a set of assumptions, which stated (as worded in 1977):

1. In the presence of a particular need the organism uses psi (ESP), as well as sensory means, to scan its environment for objects and events relevant to that need and for information crucially related to such objects or events.
2. When extrasensory information is thus obtained about need-relevant objects or events . . . a disposition toward psi-mediated instrumental response (PMIR) arises.
3. Preparation for or production of PMIR often involves such changes as motivational or emotional arousal, attention-focusing responses, and other preparation for response.

4. All else being equal, the strength of the disposition toward PMIR is
   directly and positively related to: (a) the importance or strength of
   the need(s) in question; (b) the degree of need-relevance of the need-
   relevant object or event; and (c) the closeness in time of the potential
   encounter with the need-relevant object or event.

Other propositions filled this picture out by asserting that such PMIR's
may be totally unconscious; that they act by facilitating otherwise readily
available responses including behavior, thoughts, and feelings; that they
may be blocked by certain situational and psychological factors, such as
behavioral rigidity and intense preoccupation with something else; and
that people will sometimes misuse PMIR (turn it in a negative direction) as
an expression of self-defeating tendencies caused by such things as motivational conflicts or poor self-concept.

Of course the central idea of PMIR (that people can unconsciously use
psi abilities to serve their needs) was not new. Many earlier statements of
it can be found. For example, Thouless and Wiesner (1946) (in the paper
in which they introduced the overarching construct of "psi phenomena"),
wrote: "Even when there is no resultant conscious process we must postu-
late a projection of part of the external universe on to the behavioral system of the organism when (as in psi-determined responses) there is more
than chance correspondence between the behavior of the organism and
some part of its environment." Stanford's major contribution was that he
articulated this assumption sharply and elaborated it with a set of related
propositions to form a coherent theoretical statement and then went on to
show how its implications could be meaningfully tested. He showed that
the distinction between laboratory and naturalistic phenomena was artificial, and he offered guidance for research.

Stanford revised his model over time, in response to developments in
the research literature and to improve it conceptually. In the early version
of his model, Stanford relied on two core constructs: *scanning* and *need*:
psi is a mechanism used by an organism to scan its environment for need-
relevant objects and events and for useful information about those things.
When important information is obtained by scanning, the probabilities of
behaviors already in the repertoire of the organism change in such a way
as to make the fulfillment of its needs more likely. This model stimulated
a number of research studies, particularly in the areas of the nondeliberate
use of ESP.[11]

In an important revision of his theory, Stanford (1978) dropped the
assumption of psi scanning. He came to think that it presumed far too
much computing capacity of the human brain and was less necessary since
experimental evidence suggested that psi functioned in a goal-directed way
(for example, psi somehow reached a "best answer" and did not apparently

need to process all of the steps that might logically seem to be involved in a given solution[12]). He also dropped the idea that psi involves an exchange of information at all and minimized the importance of need.

In place of need-driven scanning and information acquisition, he proposed a Conformance Behavior Model. Instead of picturing an organism scanning for information and altering its behavior, he said that it is in the nature of things that if relatively random systems are in conjunction with "disposed systems," then the relatively random systems will alter the probabilities of their events in order to better conform to the structure of the disposed systems.

This is intentionally abstract and is meant to apply to many different kinds of systems. They can be organisms with needs or extrapersonal events with different probabilities of occurrence (a random event generator is less disposed than a highly reliable electrical switch).

One interesting implication of the *conformance* position is that it gives a way of thinking of ESP and PK at once, in the same terms. Every psi event is actually both, as viewed from different angles. From the point of view of the more fixed system, a psi event is PK, an influence upon the action of the other, more random system. From the point of view of the more random system, on the other hand, the same event is ESP—a reception of information from elsewhere. When at least one of those systems is a sentient being, this approach seems sensible.

By the time of the last formal statement of his theory, Stanford (1991) implicitly retreated a bit from this highly general emphasis by focusing on humans again. A person may be thought of as a system, too. How may a person-system be more or less disposed? In this restatement, he said it was the strength of a person's *inclinations*. Stanford, again following learning theory, defined an inclination as an innate or acquired need. Such inclinations affect how a person references sensory information. For example, a familiar face will stand out among a background of unfamiliar ones because of the extent to which it is embedded in learned associations. In a similar way, inclinations also influence how people use extrasensory information.

Many potentially researchable hypotheses can arise from these ideas. Spell out ways in which inclinations may be stronger and weaker, and this may give a useful way to predict when psi-mediated responses are more or less likely to occur.

In general, Stanford advanced scientific work by offering an explicit set of testable propositions about how psi abilities may be called into play without conscious intention, and he showed that psi in the laboratory and psi in personal experience could be understood in the same terms. He took the more implicit assumptions of workers like Cox (people may use ESP unconsciously to avoid disaster) and Dean (people may display a physiological ESP response that is not available to consciousness) and showed that they could become building blocks for a theory. Such a formal statement of propositions is stimulating for research that can apply both to laboratory studies and to more naturalistic studies of spontaneous experiences.

The First Sight model holds that psi is a level of engagement with reality that is unconsciously going on all the time. Stanford implies this as well (as did Myers before him), inasmuch as either scanning or "conforming" must be somehow available all the time. First Sight makes this explicit and goes further by stating that the normal function of psi is to contribute actively to the construction of all action and all experience, whether apparently "psychic" or not—this is what psi is "for" in its most commonplace employment. Psi is not an occasional, anomalous event. It is a foundational component in all experience.

First Sight theory accepts and builds on PMIR by sharing the assumptions that psi engagements may be expressed physiologically and behaviorally and never become conscious as such, and that needs and intentions are important in determining how psi is expressed. It extends beyond these assumptions in many ways. For one thing, it shows that psi is ongoing not just when these expressions are present but also when they are not. It also goes further by asserting that expressions of psi are *always* essentially implicit and inadvertent from the perspective of consciousness and that "psi experiences" and tests of "conscious psi" are really misdescribed. It shares with PMIR the assumption that psi in the laboratory and psi in "real life" can be understood in identical terms, and it goes beyond that to assert that psi is also active in those countless instances in which no obvious expression of it is found in either place.

The models differ in terms of the role they imagine for psi in human functioning. PMIR helps us understand that psi abilities may be used even at moments when one is not consciously intending to use them. First Sight shows how psi can be seen as acting all the time, functioning as a ubiquitous substrate in all human experience and volition. First Sight *theory* goes on to specify some of the rules that govern when a psi impression is used positively and when it is excluded and when these tendencies are applied consistently and when inconsistently, and how all of this fits into the whole matrix of unconscious processes. It applies the hypothesis of functional equivalence across many domains of functioning, and offers a different understanding of the meaning of psi-missing and scoring extremity. I will say more about this later when discussing the relation between psi and memory in chapter 12, when Stanford's use of an essentially physical model of the action of an ESP target (as a *weak signal*), is contrasted to the view of First Sight Theory in which a target consists purely of meaning and the concept of stimulus strength or weakness does not apply.

While PMIR offers some hypotheses about variables that should facilitate the positive expression of psi, First Sight Theory offers many others, some of which are drawn from what is known of other preconscious processes, and it also offers a number of hypotheses pertaining to when psi expression is expected to be negative and when it should be weak or strong.

The importance of psi in the construction of all experience and action is a central point. As was noted in chapter 2, PMIR still stands within the tradition of thinking of psi as a kind of occasional response to a particular demand or need. For First Sight, psi *is not an ability called forth on demand but a perpetual level of engagement with reality that is expressed in various ways and that may be revealed by appropriate methods at any time.*

The models have different starting points and differ in the metatheoretical context in which they are imbedded. The Conformance Model and the scanning idea that preceded it both work within the implicit assumption of a mind (or nervous system) that is separate from some "outer" event and must be imagined to be connected to that event in some way to be able to know of it or to affect it. As stated earlier, First Sight is embedded within the sort of existential/phenomenological position developed by Heidegger in philosophy and Boss in medicine and psychology. From this perspective, human being is natively "in the world," not separated from it inside an insular "mind," peeping at it through sensory or extrasensory windows. The understanding of an insular mind and an exterior world is the product of a dualistic intellectual construction of the sort bequeathed to us by Descartes. They are not given realities, in spite of how comfortable they seem for us in light of the conceptual tradition we have inherited and within which we must think.[13]

Both the early version of PMIR and First Sight are teleological positions, and both depart in that sense from the mainstream paradigm of science.[14] First Sight, however, is more existential and personal in its perspective. This contrast is particularly marked between First Sight and the Conformance concept. In Conformance, it is systems that affect one another, the more random deferring somehow to the more fixed. Stanford leaves behind the language of persons doing things for purposes, except inasmuch as a purpose is one way in which one kind of system (a person) can be more fixed and less random. Here Stanford is proposing something very general about how nature works. First Sight articulates an understanding of what organisms, including persons, *do*. It stays within the perspective of the motivated business of living, and it offers a conception keyed to the interests and experiences of the organism. Stanford follows the guiding presumption of reductionistic psychology that an account of reality must ultimately subordinate purposive action to impersonal causes.

Thus First Sight also understands ESP and PK to be different aspects of a complex whole process, but it is not required to imagine that abstract "systems" somehow conform to one another. Intention is the key operating factor in First Sight, not sheer fixedness. Nonintentional physical systems do not exercise PK, do they? We do not expect that a clock built only to move forward sitting next to a random device moving forward and backward will impart its forward-moving tendency to the random system. Intention is an aspect of a living, sentient being, and these are the beings that are involved in psi.

First Sight holds that an organism is not only natively in a broadened world in a perceptual sense, but it is also engaged with it actively, in pursuit of its concerns. ESP is not impressed upon an organism by the action of a distant stimulus; it is taken and used by an active agent. In First Sight, purpose is causal, not merely caused.

NOTES

1. Carpenter, 1988.
2. Carpenter, 1971.
3. Carpenter, 2002.
4. Munroe, 1955.
5. Kelly et al., 2007.
6. Pratt et al., 1966.
7. Schmeidler, 1988.
8. Schmeidler, 1945; Schmeidler and McConnell, 1958.
9. Schmeidler, 1988.
10. Kanthamani and Rao, 1973; Rao, 1978.
11. Schechter, 1977.
12. Kennedy, 1978.
13. Barrett, 1962.
14. See Edge, 1978. Rychlak (1968) has in a more general way shown the need to introduce a teleological conception of causation into any psychology that aspires to adequately account for human behavior.

9

A Reiteration of Essential Points

My own brain is to me the most unaccountable of machinery . . . always buzz-
ing, humming, soaring, roaring, diving, and then buried in mud. And why?
What's this passion for?

—Virginia Woolf

At the risk of some redundancy, it seems worthwhile to summarize major points of this model in order to provide focus for the chapters to follow.

PSI IS UNCONSCIOUS ENGAGEMENT
THAT IS ALWAYS GOING ON

The model holds that psi processes are an ordinary and continuous part of the psychological functioning of all organisms. In fact, they are the leading edge of the formation of all experience and all volition. Preconscious psychological processes that are intrinsically unconscious precede and condition the development of all experience. Cognitive psychologists speak of these as providing the *context* of consciousness.[1] These processes typically function very rapidly and transiently. Studies of perception without awareness demonstrate that unattended stimuli serve to arouse nexus of meaning and feeling that serve to channel the development of perceptual experience. The model assumes that the development of all other forms of experience in addition to perceptual, as well as all volitional action, are similarly preceded by preconscious orienting processes. Psi processes initiate these series of activity. Prior to the action of a subliminal stimulus, an extrasensory prehension of its general nature and significance serves to orient the mind toward the development of the meaning to come. Prior to the commencement of any deliberate action, psychokinetic influence acts to begin the physical processes in the body that will enact the decision and may begin to exert some influence on the object of intention beyond the body as well.

ORGANISMS TRANSACT BEYOND
THEIR PHYSICAL BOUNDARIES

For this conception to be sensible, we will need to assume that each organism exists, by its nature, beyond its own physical boundaries, in some sort of commerce with the larger surround of space and time. A phenomenological/existential model of the nature of conscious being is used. One implication of this is that the problem of the connection between body and mind is not solved; rather, the split between them is not assumed to begin with. Another implication is that it is assumed that even preconscious processes are best understood in terms of personal meaning and choice rather than impersonal biological mechanism.

Psi information is not kept from awareness by some sort of screen, and it is not rendered into analogical form by any secondary, disguising process. Its intrinsic ambiguity is a function of the fact that with it alone there is no sensory information available, and sensory information is required to clarify the impression into a perception that can be construed. Anything that comes to consciousness must go through four steps: 1. An unconscious surround; 2. an impression; 3. conscious material; and 4. construal or understanding. This is true whether the experience is a matter of memory, immediate sensory experience, feeling, or cognition. First there is an unconscious, orienting surround, then a vague semiconscious impression, then conscious material upon which one can focus (stimulus, memory, feeling, or idea), then an interpretation or construal of that material. At the point of construal we have some idea of what it is that we are seeing, hearing, remembering, thinking, feeling, or beginning to do. Without the conscious material to construe, no conscious experience can be grasped.

The initial psi stage of the process involves an access to potential knowledge that is indefinite in extent. We cannot know its boundaries, or anything else about it directly, since it is thoroughly unconscious.

PSI IS IMPLICITLY USEFUL, BUT ONLY
GLIMPSED IN INADVERTENCIES

Psi in its normal, everyday functioning is presumed to be continuous, extremely efficient, and invisible to conscious awareness. Like the effects of subliminal stimulations, extrasensory prehensions can be inferred by examining nondeliberate expressions of the orienting nexus of meaning and feeling that they arouse. Both subliminal and extrasensory prehensions can be seen most clearly in such inadvertent behaviors as dreams, slips of the tongue and other errors, associational processes, expressions of feeling and meaning in projective tests, the flow of spontaneous social behavior, shifts in mood, and the development of spontaneous imagery. The actual psi processes themselves are intrinsically unconscious. They are neither knowing nor acting, as we ordinarily use the terms, since these phenomena belong to the province of consciousness. Rather, they serve as bridges toward the efficient development of these phenomena. If the development of a conscious experience is impeded by the removal of the thing from the sensory field before it can be consciously known, then only the inadvertent expressions of the anticipatory arousal can be seen.

PSI IS BIDIRECTIONAL AND MORE OR LESS EXTREMELY EXPRESSED

Psi functioning is presumed to be bimodal. In terms of extrasensory perception, the mind either elects to orient toward the object of potential awareness or away from it. The mind is presumed to preconsciously orient toward or away from as befits the needs of the organism. The primary determinant of the direction of orientation is conscious and unconscious intention.

These bimodal tendencies may be relatively stable in regard to some meaning, or may be relatively unstable, switching rapidly. In an ESP test, a stable orientation toward the potential meaning is expressed as psi-hitting, and a stable orientation away from it is expressed as psi-missing. A relatively stable tendency is shown by a large deviation from chance expectation, while a rapid switching of tendencies produces small deviations from chance expectation. Switching directional tendencies is presumed to be a function of mixed or shifting intentions in regard to the potential meaning. This is referred to as the Hypothesis of Intentional Stability. In ordinary experience beyond the laboratory, a stable tendency toward knowing the potential meaning facilitates our rapid and accurate experience of it. On the other hand, a stable orientation away from the meaning will facilitate the development of some alternative experience and behavior instead. Since (as we assume) the mind always strives to experience the one most useful thing at any given moment in terms of a shifting fabric of needs and intentions, the movement away from many potential experiences is functional, permitting focus and freedom from distraction. A stable orientation away from some meaning also may serve to avoid preconsciously apprehended danger in an efficient behavioral manner. In general, a stable orientation serves to assure that the behavior of the organism will reflect some response to the potential meaning, while rapidly shifting orientations will act to assure that no apparent response at all will be reflected in behavior.

When anticipational networks have been aroused by some extrasensory or suboptimal-sensory information, and validating sensory experience is *not forthcoming*, then the mind ordinarily adjusts to this situation by turning away from the original concern in favor of something else that may be more importantly incipient to an experience-to-come. The turning away is affected by movement to a rapidly shifting pattern of intention, which acts to "bind" the concern safely out of awareness. If ESP testing is kept up in relation to such a "bound" concern, consistent chance-level performance will result. In the preconscious part of our mind we wish to form and understand meaningful experience, and we will ordinarily move on to where it is actually developing. ESP testing sustained past this point may be in accord with conscious intention, but it will probably run counter to the unconscious intention of moving on efficiently to actual experience.

Cognitive closure, or a situation in which one is committed to some construction of experience, is presumed to trigger unconscious tendential switching in regard to alternative meanings or potential experiences. At such a moment, I know what I am concerned with experiencing, and I am engaged with understanding it or working with it. In favor of this concern, other potential issues are held in abeyance.

On the other hand, brief or prolonged states in which closure is delayed and uncertainty is sustained are presumed to facilitate the consulting of inadvertency, a sustained concern with the unknown meaning and a relatively stable psi-hitting or psi-missing orientation. States of sustained uncertainty and absence of clear cognitive work have been found to be psi conducive as well as conducive to the expression of subliminal stimulation. Persons who are more prone than most to psi-expressive behavior are likely to be able to sustain cognitive uncertainty, or for some reason, to be relatively unable to achieve clear closure (as in the case of persons with certain brain or nervous system injuries). Relatively more "psychic" persons are also expected to be generally positively oriented to express such extrasensory meanings, to be relatively free of anxiety and self-defeating tendencies, and to be relatively skilled in the interpretation of their own inadvertent psychological expressions, as in understanding their dream life or personal imagery.

THE MEANING OF SCORES IN TESTS OF PSI

A participant's score on an ESP test is not presumed to reflect primarily some stable individual characteristic. Rather, in terms of the First Sight model, such a number reflects a momentary preconscious posture of a certain sort toward the target and other aspects of the task.

A correct guess is presumed to indicate the action of an unconscious intention to approach the potential experience and possibly to become aware of it. The guesser is preconsciously judging the extrasensory content to be sufficiently congruent with the demands of the task and one's desires involving it, that the content is assimilated into the response (impulse, image, association, or whatever) and is then used to guide a correct choice. When scoring is significantly positive across a period of effort, it suggests a consistent unconscious intention to approach.

A miss reflects an unconscious intention to avoid the incipient material. The material is being judged to be sufficiently incongruent with one's wishes in the situation (for whatever reason) that it evokes a contrast response that has led toward a choice in some alternative direction. Significant missing across a period of effort indicates the action of a consistent unconscious intention to avoid the potential experience and knowledge of it.

A chance-level score across a period of effort is not taken as an absence of psi process, but rather it is seen as implying an implication of switching of intention and direction of approach such that neither an additive nor a subtractive reference to the material is evident overall.

Considering aggregate performance across runs, when no overall directional trend is present in a subject's performance but the scores show an extrachance extremity of scoring (large variance), this is taken to express the action of a persistent, unconscious sense that the potential experience is salient across runs of guessing effort but also to express the switching of intention to approach or avoid across runs. That is, the direction of intention is stable within runs but switches between runs.

When significantly consistent chance-level performance is observed across a participant's runs (small variance), it expresses a consistent intention both within and across runs for the participant not to be distracted by the potential experience by moving either toward or away from it.

To sum up, different possible performances have these meanings:

- When significant hitting is observed in a participant's performance, it indicates the action of a consistent unconscious intention to approach the potential experience and possibly to come to be aware of it.
- When significant missing is observed in a participant's performance, it indicates the action of a consistent unconscious intention to avoid the potential experience and knowledge of it.
- When no overall directional trend is present in a participant's performance but the scores show an extrachance extremity of scoring (large variance), this expresses the action of an unconscious sense that the potential experience is salient (it is heavily weighted) but that the

intention to approach or avoid it is switching across runs of guessing effort.

- When significantly consistent chance-level performance is observed in a participant's performance (small variance), it expresses the intention to not be distracted by the potential experience (it has low weight) by moving predominantly neither toward nor away from it.

Since psi, in its normal, unconscious functioning, is presumed to work alongside other preconscious psychological processes, an important issue to be considered is how they might be expected to interact and to examine pertinent evidence about this that has been reported. This is the concern of the next section.

NOTE

1. Baars, 1997, pp. 115–29.

Section III

PSI AND OTHER PRECONSCIOUS PROCESSES

Freed from desire, you can see the hidden mystery.
By having desire, you can only see what is visibly real.
Yet mystery and reality
emerge from the same source.
This source is called darkness.
Darkness born from darkness.
The beginning of all understanding.

—Lao Tsu, translated by J. H. McDonald

THE COMMINGLING OF PSI AND
OTHER PRECONSCIOUS PROCESSES

This model implies that in its preconscious functioning the mind democratically draws from all its potential sources to solve its problems of finding the most adaptive response to a situation or bringing the most important issue to the stage of consciousness. This was referred to above as the hypothesis of functional equivalence. It appears that there are many streams of potential reference that are available for the formation of consciousness, and these intermingle, cooperate, and compete as a function of unconscious "laws" or patterns of functioning. They involve many factors, including unconscious attitudes and motives, the content of the material contributed by the source, the task at hand, and the extent to which, at a given moment, the content of consciousness is certain or ambiguous. Psi prehensions are expected to be used along with all other material available, such as that from ongoing sensations or from memory or from the imaginative resources of the creative process. However, it is only when uncertainty is sustained for a time and the solution is not readily at hand that we would expect to see the traces of the psi process. If something is clearly seen or readily remembered, or some problem is easily solved, the issue will be quickly closed, and we will see only the clear working of consciousness. Therefore, it is when something is uncertainly remembered, or unclearly perceived, or when some creative production is not quite within reach that preconscious processes, including psi, may be visible.[1] In such cases, this model predicts that extrasensory information will be combined with information from other sources, frequently additively but sometimes subtractively.

In general terms, I propose that the extrasensory information combines additively with sensory information when it is preconsciously understood to be contextually useful in the interpretation of the sensory information. When it is preconsciously judged to be irrelevant to the sensory material, or otherwise contrary to the task of most fruitfully understanding it, the effect of the extrasensory material will initially be subtractive (for example, it will tend to be expressed by some sort of behavioral reference less often than chance would expect), and subsequently, through the mechanism of rapid directional switching, it will come to have no apparent behavioral reference at all. What is judged to be useful may be a matter of categorical relevancy or will bear on other matters of intentions and goals. In this context, it is helpful to refer to the social psychological literature on the formation of judgments of other persons. Sometimes subliminal primes have been found to have the effect of biasing responses in the direction of their content (called *assimilation*), but sometimes they show the opposite biasing effect (called *contrast*). Schwarz and Bless (1992) proposed an *inclusion-exclusion* model, proposing that the influence of a prime depends on the ease with which it can be incorporated in a target impression. A prime that can be easily included with the target becomes assimilated, biasing the impression toward its suggestion. A prime that cannot be included may be expected to have the opposite effect, causing contrast and biasing the result away from the prime. For example, if the faint target that one is trying to see is a picture of an apple, the word *eat* as a prime may facilitate the perception. However, if the prime is the word *frangible*, which has no relevance for the meaning of *apple*, it would have no effect upon the perception, except perhaps to make any idea of frangibility even less likely to occur than it otherwise would. I assume that this principle of inclusion/exclusion is a general one, effecting psi-hitting and psi-missing as well as subliminal and unattended sensory material. This subliminal contrast effect and psi-missing appear to be similar processes.

Because psi prehensions always potentially initiate the process of the development of perceptual experience, they should in one sense be the weakest source of influence. They pose the initial questions in the light of which preconscious information is examined; but as soon as some information from the sources ordinarily more relevant to personal intentions (memory, sensation, desire) appear to contradict their implications, they will retreat obediently into the shadows of contrast, and from thence into the "bound" state of directional balance, where they will not disturb the further development of meaning. Thus, the mind protects the "theater of consciousness"[2] from the infinite surround of things that might distract it.

Psi events, when they can be seen to occur, appear to pop up "out of nowhere" as far as consciousness is concerned. Something more than what is immediately at hand is somehow being registered in experience or choices that are being made. This is what makes such events seem exceptional and mysterious. There are three other areas of mental life that are more widely accepted and better studied than psi events that also arise rather mysteriously from somewhere beyond what is immediately given in awareness. These are responses to subliminal or unattended stimuli, memories, and creative ideas and impulses.

We do frequently respond to stimuli of which we are not consciously aware, as psychological research has made clear. And we all have memories that arise from situations that sometimes are long past—as a child might ask: "Where do they come from?" Creative ideas and impulses arise in awareness that often seem surprisingly beyond what is obviously present. We may wonder why such moments of creation occur when they do and why some people are more given to them than others.

First Sight theory asserts that all of these phenomena are guided by preconscious processes and that these are the same preconscious processes that guide the expression (or inhibition) of psi. Theory also asserts that the needs and goals of the individual are important factors in how these processes work and that they help guide the more mysterious expression of psi as well as the slightly less mysterious expressions of subliminal response, memory, and creativity. And finally, theory asserts that all of these things work together meaningfully and harmoniously in unconscious thought and that each of us uses these unconscious processes holistically to interpret our experiences and choose our actions. The next few chapters focus on these aspects of experience, their relation to unconscious processes, and their coordinated action with psi. In each domain, research that has accumulated on their relation to psi will be discussed and interpreted in light of First Sight theory.

In this section and also in the next, much reference will be made to research studies, and I will have to discuss some fine points of experimental design and interpretation. Some of this detail may be less interesting to some readers than the more general sections. If you wish to skim over the nitty-gritty, you can still follow the central ideas by reading the beginnings and endings of the chapters.

NOTES

1. In the context of normal, sensory psychology, this is congruent with the Zeigarnik (1927 [1967]) effect, in which it was shown that the failure to cognitively complete a task led to prolonged motivation that in turn led to an enhancement of memory of the uncompleted problem (Lewin, 1935; Martin, Tesser, and McIntosh, 1993; Rothermund, 2003).

2. Baars, 1997.

10

Psi and Ambiguous or Unconscious Sensory Information

If the grace of God miraculously operates, it probably operates through the subliminal door.

—William James

When sensory information is clear and unambiguous, conscious perceptions spring quickly to mind, and the influence of psi processes are not expected to be visible. However, when sensory information is so attenuated that it is difficult to perceive, one must struggle some to understand it, "guessing around" the cues until a perception is formed. If the stimulation is so attenuated or unnoticed that it is subliminal and in no way conscious, then even the effort to construe ambiguous cues does not obtain, and any effects of the stimulation may be experienced only as inadvertency, or misattributed to something else. It is in this situation of subliminal, or "suboptimal priming,"[1] that an interaction between suboptimal-sensory and extrasensory processes may be sought and seen.

First Sight theory lays out several expectations, and I will argue that the research we have generally confirms them. First, we expect that effects frequently will be additive when they are acting together. This is supported by the fact that subliminal stimuli themselves often have been found to show additive effects.[2] We will expect that subliminal information will often affect how people utilize extrasensory information, and conversely, that extrasensory information will affect one's response to subliminal material. First Sight theory also predicts that similar patterns will be observed between the ways people unconsciously use psi information and the ways they unconsciously use subliminal information. And finally, I will argue that an apparent inconsistency in the findings on psi and subliminal perception can be accounted for nicely by First Sight theory.

EXTRASENSORY PERCEPTION AND SUBLIMINAL PERCEPTION AS CORRELATED CAPACITIES

One direct form of this hypothesis is that people who show a tendency in a given situation to assimilate extrasensory information should also tend to assimilate subliminal information as well—at least in cases in which the information is so thoroughly subliminal that it is not available for conscious processing at all. Conversely, people who disassimilate one should also disassimilate the other. The two tendencies should positively correlate.

A number of studies have been done in which scores have been obtained from both extrasensory and subliminal-sensory paradigms on the same participants. Schmeidler (1986, 1988) has carried out an analysis of twenty-four reported experimental series of this type, dividing them into two groups: weak subliminal or suboptimal stimulation (well below the conscious threshold) and strong stimulation (near the threshold). She expected, and found, that of the twenty-two series with weak stimulation, seventeen showed a positive relation between subliminal and ESP scores. Nine of those were statistically significant. There were no significant relationships in the opposite direction. The two series with stronger subliminal stimulation produced significant negative relationships. Schmeidler concluded from this that truly subliminal stimulation functions in a way very similar to ESP, but that stronger stimuli are processed differently. This finding fits the assumption of First Sight theory. Information that is somewhat vague permits the opportunity to consciously work at the task of making it out and solving the puzzle of its content. Such conscious work should tend to make implicit information irrelevant and distracting and lead to its exclusion. Persons who are good at such conscious work should also be good at excluding implicit information, including psi. Persons who do not do well at this (those who "subliminally miss" with vague stimuli) are presumably not expending the same mental work and are cognitively free to access implicit information positively—hence the negative correlation that was often found with marginally subliminal information. On the other hand, information that is deeply subliminal (the usual criterion is that the exposure be so brief and otherwise attenuated that even its sheer occurrence cannot be reliably guessed) permits no more conscious work on the stimulus than is possible with an ESP target. The same tendencies to access one positively or negatively should be found with the other—and they are.

SIMILAR PROCESSING FOR SUBLIMINAL AND EXTRASENSORY INFORMATION

In another series of studies, a high-scoring special subject was found to process information similarly in subliminal and extrasensory responding, relying on cues of visual similarity in both cases.[3] These findings support the idea that when persons are producing responses based upon preconscious prehensions, extrasensory and subliminal-sensory information is accessed (or not) in generally similar ways—in this case, by attending to the visual features of imagery.

In general, persons who are relatively prone to successfully consult pure inadvertency when uncertain may demonstrate this tendency whether the inadvertencies imply extrasensory or subliminal material, while persons who are prone to focus more exclusively on more tangible sources of information may be more successful when such information is at hand, like the subjects in Schmeidler's review who were better at interpreting marginally subliminal, somewhat conscious, stimulations (they tended to score negatively on ESP targets). In terms of the First Sight model, one would say that a person's tendency to make positive use of preconscious information for whatever reason will be expressed with extrasensory and subliminal-sensory information alike; whereas a tendency to avoid such material, and express it subtractively, will tend to be shown with both as well. For more discussion on this point, see the discussion of openness in chapter 13.

PSI-MISSING AND SUBLIMINAL-MISSING

Psi-missing is expected to occur whenever a variety of considerations make the extrasensory information seem irrelevant or contrary to unconscious intention in the process of forming a behavior or perception. First Sight theory suggests that the same thing should be observed in the case of deeply subliminal information. A few reports suggest that this is the case, although few psychologists have reflected very much about the observation.

Kunst-Wilson and Zajonc (1980) introduced a phenomenon that has gone on to be widely studied, particularly by social psychologists: the Mere Exposure Effect. In a nutshell, this describes the fact that merely being exposed to something leads one to come to like it more (or dislike it less). Perhaps surprisingly, this effect occurs even when the exposures are subliminal. In fact, meta-analysis has shown that it is strongest when the exposures are deeply subliminal.[4] In this paradigm, participants are subliminally exposed several times to certain stimuli, and then later they are shown the stimuli along with other control pictures of equal general likability that were not exposed and asked to rate how much they like them both. The previously exposed pictures

tend to be liked better, demonstrating an implicit, subliminal effect on preference. In many of these studies, participants were also asked to guess the
content of the subliminal exposures. A chance level of guessing is expected
and hoped for, since this shows that the exposures did not permit conscious
awareness. However, in many of the studies, this task produced *below chance
scores*. First Sight theory would explain this by noting that the attempt to
guess the content of a flicker of light might be expected to call up both mental
work and some anxiety on the part of participants who had no idea how to
do what was asked. Both mental work and anxiety would be expected to produce psi-missing if this were a psi test, and subliminal-missing in this case.
In fact, this has often been noted.[5]

PARALLEL EFFECTS OF OTHER VARIABLES

It is also pertinent that many other variables affect in similar ways the success in expressing both subliminal and extrasensory information . As mentioned in chapter 5, openness, creativity, and dissociativeness all appear to
benefit both kinds of implicit influence. Also, both have been found to be
facilitated by similar conditions, including hypnosis, relaxed reverie, and
sensory attenuation.

SUBLIMINAL EFFECTS ON A PSI TASK

When extrasensory and subliminal-sensory information are both controlled
in an experiment, the First Sight model predicts that they should interact
meaningfully with one another in influencing behavior. John Palmer and
his colleagues have carried out a relevant series of studies in which they
attempted to affect the mood of the percipient with a subliminal stimulus
and thereby influence the effort at guessing an extrasensory target (the correct element among several in a visual field). The studies were exploratory,
and the results sometimes surprised them. An attempt to control high and
low scoring by accompanying targets with subliminal primes intended to
be either reassuring or threatening resulted instead in overall tight variance
of scores,[6] a finding that was successfully replicated.[7] A subsequent attempt
to heighten the reassurance effect with a combination of incidental and
subliminal cues resulted in overall psi-missing.[8] The next study[9] examined
the effect of a reassuring prime (a suggestion of merger), which was sometimes presented immediately before another subliminal prime involving a
threatening face. The condition considered most propitious for psi-hitting
(subliminal merger/no threat) did yield psi-hitting in the first series in
which the participants were tested, but not the second. None of these stud-

ies used manipulation checks for mood, so one cannot say whether or not the subliminal primes had the desired effects upon the subjects' state.

Carpenter and Simmonds-Moore (2009a) manipulated participants' moods with subliminal primes and did demonstrate with an independent check that the manipulation was successful. Half the participants were exposed to a prime intended to induce a state of relative well-being and openness, and the other half were exposed to primes intended to have the opposite effect. The degree of emotional well-being was affected as predicted, as assessed by an implicit measure of mood. The subliminal manipulation also affected the participants' responses to extrasensory targets. The positive mood essentially had the effect of potentiating the influence of several other variables expected to predict the direction of scoring: Openness to feelings and fantasies, freedom from anxiety, belief in ESP, and a tolerance of interpersonal merger all predicted positive scoring, and the influence of all of them was significantly stronger in the more positive mood. This pattern was confirmed in a second study.[10] These studies give clear support to the idea that subliminal affective primes and extrasensory cognitive primes interact in meaningful ways.

All of these findings together suggest that the effects of affectively charged subliminal stimuli do enter into the preconscious processing that leads to the ESP response. More research on these combined effects is clearly needed. In regard to the Palmer studies, the repetitive presentation of subliminal faces may evoke a vigilant state in which the ESP test feels irrelevant or distracting, resulting in tendential switching and small variance. It may also be that primes intended to evoke a mood of safety had the opposite effect in some cases, resulting in psi-missing. This possibility is suggested by the finding of Sohlberg and her colleagues,[11] in which they report a tendency of subjects to experience a change in mood in a negative direction when a stimulus ordinarily found to elicit a positive mood was subliminally exposed too many times. This sort of negative "overdosage" might have affected Palmer's findings because the stimulus intended to be reassuring was presented many times over. This negative effect may have been less marked in the first series of the study in which psi-hitting was observed, as in that condition fewer exposures had accumulated. Only five exposures were used in the studies by Carpenter and Simmonds-Moore, a number that research has found to be in the optimal range.

PSI EFFECTS ON A SUBLIMINAL TASK

Another approach to studying the patterns of interaction of subliminal and extrasensory information was taken by Kreitler and Kreitler (1972), who exposed their subjects to letters projected on a screen at an intensity and duration that had been found in pretesting to permit correct identification 40 percent of the time. They were told that the letter identification was the sole task, and no extrasensory element was mentioned. In half the cases, however, an agent added an "extrasensory stimulus" to the situation by telepathically trying to transmit the correct letter to the subject as they were viewing the exposure, while the other half looked at an irrelevant picture. The extrasensory "transmission" was effective in boosting the rate of identification, as shown by a significant difference between the conditions. Another series involved an examination of the influence of both subliminal and extrasensory material upon the perception of ambiguous optical illusions. There was no overall evidence of an extrasensory influence; however, an interaction was observed in this study, in that when the ESP "prime" was contrary to that of the subliminal exposure surrounding the supraliminal figure presented to the subject (the optical illusion), the subjects' judgments showed more influence of the ESP information than in the case in which no subliminal information was present. When the extrasensory "prime" competed with a subliminal prime, the extrasensory information predominated, and it was also expressed more strongly than when no competing subliminal information was present. The authors interpret this rather odd finding as suggesting that extrasensory information may be especially salient when it contradicts other low-intensity (for example, subliminal) stimulation. Other interpretations that the authors make of these and two other series appear to be vitiated by problems of design.[12] These findings suggest that psi may interact with subliminal information sometimes in an additive way and sometimes in a competing manner (that is, sometimes with assimilation, and sometimes with contrast).

PSI EFFECTS MODELED AFTER SUBLIMINAL EFFECTS

Some researchers have followed the model of an established subliminal effect drawn from nonparapsychological study and applied it to extrasensory information, expecting that similar patterns might be found. Some researchers have taken the model of the "mere exposure effect,"[13] in which a great deal of research has shown that simple exposure for something tends to lead to an enhanced liking for that thing. As already noted, Bornstein's meta-analysis (1989) demonstrated that this effect is stronger if the exposure is subliminal than if it is fully conscious, suggesting that the effect works primarily on an unconscious level. Demonstration of it also has been found to be more reliable if the stimuli are simple and emotionally neutral and if some period of time is allowed to elapse between the exposure and the ratings of liking of the material.

Moulton (2000) carried out a standard mere exposure (ME) study using simple line drawings, but with a parapsychological wrinkle. Instead of subliminal exposure of the drawings, he used a "telepathic transmission." Assistants employed as senders looked at some drawings but not others and attempted to "send" them to the experimental participants when they were relaxing in a sensory-attenuation situation. Later ratings of the material showed that the drawings that had been "telepathically exposed" by the attention of the senders (and/or the intention of the experimenter) were liked more than other control drawings that no one had intended to send.

Similarly, Bem (2003, 2011) has shown in several studies that participants who were subliminally exposed *later* to pictures liked that material better when they rated it *before* the exposures as compared to material that would not later be exposed. That is, Bem's participants showed a *precognitive* ME. The subliminal exposures did influence people to like the exposed material more, but the familiar effect was time reversed. At the time of the judgments, the exposures only existed in the future, as precognitive ESP targets. Yet they showed the same effect as normal subliminal exposures.

Another line of subliminal research has shown that participants exposed unconsciously to appropriate subliminal primes show a heightened tendency to act out congruent behaviors that are unwittingly associated with the primes. Carpenter (2002) followed this model by having a computer randomly select pictorial material while an unstructured quasi-psychotherapy group was meeting in another city. The group knew that selected material would serve as an ESP target, but of course they did not know its content. The idea was that the group would "try" implicitly to express the target through the nature of the interaction that developed spontaneously during the one-hour meetings. During the meetings themselves, which were typically very engaging, the members virtually always forgot about the issue of the target. At the end of each session, the group members were shown the target picture along with three randomly selected decoys, without anyone present knowing which was which. They rated each of the pictures in terms of its congruence with the session that had just transpired in its degree of similarity in content and mood. The group met for several years, for a total of 386 sessions. Overall, the group's similarity ratings showed that they were able to pick out the target picture to a statistically significant degree. The ESP target was in fact expressed in the spontaneous process of the unstructured session—the topics that people thought of bringing up, the feelings that came to be expressed, and the themes that were acted out.

SUBLIMINAL AND EXTRASENSORY
PROCESSING SHOW REAL SIMILARITIES

The Hypothesis of Functional Equivalence in regard to subliminal and extrasensory unconscious processing has received empirical support from several different directions. When subliminal stimulations are extremely short and faint (and "deeply" subliminal), those who respond in an assimilative way to them tend to do the same with extrasensory targets, while those who disassimilate the subliminal material tend to show psi-missing in regard to extrasensory material. That is, the use of one is positively correlated with the use of the other. Congruent with this, one very highly scoring ESP participant showed similar patterns of "near-misses" on both subliminal and extrasensory material (for example, if he miscalled a face card, it tended to be by calling another face card).

When sensory material is only marginally subliminal, however, it has shown a *negative* relationship with ESP performance. This contradictory finding, noted by Schmeidler, has seemed puzzling but can be explained by First Sight theory. Since vague and almost-perceptible information calls up cognitive effort, theory would expect ESP information to be excluded when perception is successful but more likely included when the perceptual work is not successful. Thus the negative relationship is sensible in this case.

Many other variables influence both kinds of response in similar ways, including situations that facilitate or impede them and the types of personality that are prone to use them or reject them both.

Subliminal effects have been found to influence a person's use of extrasensory material. This suggests that at the level of unconscious processing, the mind is drawing upon both kinds of information at once and combining them in reaching a response. In particular, the moods aroused by subliminal stimuli appear to either open up or shut down the salience of extrasensory information, so that it can then be influenced differently by characteristics of the participant.

Likewise, psi information has been found to influence the ways in which people respond to subliminal primes. When a subliminal prime was "boosted" by a similar extrasensory prime, the response was enhanced, suggesting that the influences can combine additively. However, when they contradict one another, the two sources of information can compete, one suppressing the other. A host of new research questions about unconscious psychological processes has been opened up by these intriguing findings.

Finally, effects that have been well established with subliminal stimuli can be demonstrated when the information is extrasensory instead of faintly sensory. The mind does appear to use extrasensory information frequently in the same ways it uses subliminal sensory information; for example, by changing its emotional interest in something or by taking cues to inadvertent behavioral expressions from it.

NOTES

1. Murphy and Zajonc, 1993.
2. Bargh and Tota, 1988; Fulcher and Hammerl, 2002; Jaskowski and Skalska, 2003; Murphy, Monahan, and Zajonc, 1995.
3. Kanthamani and Kelly, 1974; Kelly, Kanthamani, Child, and Young, 1975.
4. Bornstein, 1989.
5. Bonnano and Stillings, 1986; Ionescu, 1991; Mandler, Nakamura, and Van Sandt, 1987; Merikle and Reingold, 1991.
6. Palmer and Johnson, 1991.
7. Palmer, 1992.
8. Palmer, 1998b.
9. Palmer, 1994.
10. Carpenter and Simmonds-Moore, 2009b.
11. Sohlberg, Billinghurst, and Nylen, 1998; Sohlberg, Samuelberg, Siden, and Thorn, 1998.
12. Child, 1977.
13. Zajonc, 1968.

11

Psi and Memory: Are the Processes Similar?

Memory is a central part of the brain's attempt to make sense of experience, and to tell coherent stories about it. . . . Yet our stories are built from many different ingredients: snippets of what actually happened, thoughts about what might have happened, and beliefs that guide us as we attempt to remember. Our memories are the fragile but powerful products of what we recall from the past, believe about the present, and imagine about the future.

—Daniel Schacter

Important preconscious processes contribute to the act of remembering, and cognitive psychologists such as Daniel Schacter (1997), whose quote is given above, have studied these extensively.[1] A memory is hardly a simple photographic reproduction of some event. As Schacter says, many other implicit contributions figure into it. Psi prehensions must be added to this list of contributions.

The First Sight model asserts that the preconscious processes of memory and psi processes interact with one another and that they will show similar patterns of functioning. Thus when we examine research about memory and psi, we will expect to find that the functioning of one will be like the functioning of the other, and that both streams of potential meaning will affect the ways in which the other contributes to experience and behavior. Their similarity of functioning is the subject of this chapter, and their influence upon each other is discussed in the next.

During a roughly twenty-year period beginning in 1967, the problem of the relation between memory and ESP was a relatively active research topic for the small field of parapsychology, with over forty studies accumulating. There were many different operations used for both memory and ESP, and several different kinds of questions were asked. The work developed idiosyncratically within parapsychology and unfortunately made little reference to the burgeoning field of memory research in mainstream cognitive psychology. The various results reported appeared contradictory, at least if viewed superficially, and this, along with the loss of interest in forced-choice ESP test methods (upon which the studies mostly relied), may have led to a decline of activity in this area.

BACKGROUND

Psi/Memory Theory

Theories of psi proposed by Roll (1966) and Irwin (1979b) have emphasized the importance of memory traces as vehicles for psi expression. Roll's ideas were influenced by H. H. Price (1949 [1967]), who stressed that memory traces are essential for all experience, including psychic. By this concept, ESP has no medium of its own for carrying information. A psychic stimulus evokes a memory trace, and this bit of memory is what carries the psychic information to consciousness. An implication of this idea is that the more strongly an item is placed within the associative network, the more likely it can carry ESP information.

This chapter explores the relation between ESP and memory by reviewing most of the experimental literature on the topic and by offering some possible syntheses of that literature in terms of the First Sight model of psi.

Similar Function of Memory and Psi in the First Sight Model

This model hypothesizes that ESP mingles with other preconscious processes in shaping experience. Psi is not assumed to function uniquely in the human psyche, like an unpredictable "wildcard" with magical properties. To the contrary, the model assumes that both memory and ESP (and other preconscious functions) all work together smoothly and continuously, and they should show many similar patterns of functioning. It also assumes that remembered material and extrasensory material should be drawn upon conjointly in anticipating and shaping experience, although their mutual influence may sometimes be additive and sometimes subtractive as a function of different conditions.

The questions that have been studied in past reports will be grouped in three general categories.

1. Are ESP and memory similar processes? If so, they should be positively correlated when tested in the same or similar situations and should follow similar internal patterns of functioning.

2. Can ESP "stimuli" influence memory retrieval? Testing this involves adding some element of ESP to a memory task.
3. Does remembered information influence the attempt to retrieve ESP information? Testing this involves examining the effect of some variable of memory in the context of an ESP task.

In examining these questions it will be important to remember that "memory" is not a simple concept, so these are not simple questions. In fact, it comprises many different processes and operations in different research contexts. We experience and use these processes differently, and different neurophysiological activities are involved in them. Prior work in parapsychology has often not appreciated this complexity, and this has contributed to inconsistency in findings.

ARE ESP AND MEMORY SIMILAR PROCESSES?

If one or more of the major types of memory and extrasensory perception are similar processes, then they should be positively correlated within the performance of given participants tested in similar situations. They should also show similar patterns of functioning in terms of other variables.

Are ESP and Memory Correlated Capacities?

The first report on this question described three series that attempted to confirm a serendipitous observation of a positive correlation between participants' scores on memory and ESP tests. The effect was significantly confirmed.[2] Attempts at replication by other investigators gave mixed results. Two studies produced significantly positive confirmations,[3] and two yielded significant negative relationships.[4] Several other studies yielded nonsignificant trends in both directions. A review at the time[5] noted that this mixed picture was provocative and seemed potentially important, but the researchers themselves had offered little conceptual clarity.

Some clarification of the mixed findings that had accumulated by the late 1970s was suggested in a subsequent review by H. J. Irwin (1979a), who noted that researchers had not made reference to the important distinction between primary (or short-term) and secondary (long-term) memory. Primary memory (now usually referred to as working memory) is a relatively conscious, effortful matter in which one is actively holding some item in mind through rehearsal and then attempting to reproduce it. Think of holding a phone number in mind long enough to dial it, or trying to keep count of the number of plural nouns in this text as you read along. Long-term memory is a less effortful process of calling up or otherwise responding to some item of information previously learned. One important operational difference that has been used in many studies in assessing the two types is the use of some interpolated task between memorization and recall in tests of secondary memory, while tests of primary memory are given immediately after learning without an interpolated distraction. Including such a distracting task makes it impossible for a participant to continue to hold something in working memory. To recall something successfully will then require that one call it up out of the latent storehouse of long-term memories.

When the studies that had been reported were broken down in terms of this distinction, tests of secondary memory (like Feather's original studies) tended to confirm the positive correlation, while tests of primary memory tended to show negative relationships. Some other studies used designs that Irwin thought gave room for participants to rely on either memory strategy, depending upon their personal proclivities; these studies tended to give mixed or null relationships. While Irwin was not sure how best to interpret this pattern of results, we may say in retrospect that they are consistent with the expectations that would be drawn from First Sight theory.

Expectations of First Sight Model

The model assumes that psi prehensions are available for positive influence of inadvertent preconscious processes, and hence for possible assimilation into the formation of experience, if the unconscious posture toward the event is predominantly "toward" and if any switching of directional tendency is relatively slow. A "toward" posture requires that the content of the prehension seems pertinent to the person's needs and interests in the moment and seems relatively congruent with the primary nature of the experience as it is developing. Little switching assures that this sense of positive pertinence is relatively unitary or stable. An open, "free-floating," relatively undefined state of mind facilitates these conditions, whereas cognitive work on clear, conscious content inhibits them. There are at least two reasons for this. For one thing, the better defined an experience is, the less likely it is that elements of context will be sensed as pertinent and assimilated. For another thing, it is now known that working memory is more than conscious—it also affects preconscious processes by channeling them toward things associated with whatever is being held in mind and away from other things (Hassin, Bargh, Engell, and McColloch, 2009; Magnussen, 2009). Assimilation of psi-based material is highly similar then to the activity of retrieving or responding to elements from secondary memory; whereas the consciously effortful process of retaining and reproducing primary memory should act to exclude the extrasensory.

We may distinguish among four different situations and state the theory's expectations in regard to each. All of them presume that the information to be accessed by ESP is different from the information that is being recalled.

- In *primary (short-term) memory*, active cognitive effort is required for successful recall of material. Hence, anyone carrying it out successfully should be excluding extraneous implicit contextual elements (including extrasensory) at the same time. However, if someone is doing poorly at the task, they are presumably being less successful or using less concentration and might be expected to be more amenable to extraneous influence in their responses. Hence a negative relation is expected between the two tasks in a given situation.
- In *secondary (long-term) memory*, reproduction or recognition of material previously learned requires a more passive inner searching of experience, associations, images, etc. In the context of an ill-defined ultimate experience, this posture facilitates a broadly inclusive sampling of contextual elements, making assimilation of potentially pertinent material (from whatever source) more likely. Someone carrying it out successfully must be rather passively and openly searching a broad range of inner associations, images, and sensations looking for some sense of fit, and this is the same sort of posture most likely to facilitate the expression of extrasensory prehensions. Hence, in a given situation, the two tasks should be positively correlated.
- However, if some information is very securely learned, other considerations enter in. In the extreme case, highly rehearsed memorization is called *overlearned*. An example is one's own name. In this case, the item to be recalled is so well learned that any cue toward it calls the information up immediately, with no searching required. In this case, the task to remember leads to immediate cognitive closure. Cognitive closure is assumed by the model to elicit the exclusion of extraneous information by either contrast or by rapid switching of directional tendencies. In this case then, being tested successfully with such material should be *exclusive* of the expression of psi prehensions, and high memory scores should be accompanied by negative ESP scores. While in the unusual instances in which one may be amnestic about such material, a posture of inner searching might be expected. Hence, a negative correlation is expected.
- In the opposite extreme, material to which one was never conscious of being exposed has never been consciously rehearsed at all, and it is termed *incidental memory*. This type of unrehearsed, secondary memory is generally assessed by noting inadvertent responses to information to which one has been exposed incidentally (like recalling the items in

a room through which one recently passed without paying particular attention). In this case, trying to consciously recognize the information is experienced as mere guessing, similar to the experience of taking an ESP test. Because success at this task requires a posture that is the same as that assumed to facilitate extrasensory expressions, a positive correlation between the two is expected.

Summing up then, the model leads us to expect that tests of primary memory should be correlated negatively with measures of extrasensory perception. Tests of secondary memory should generally be positively correlated with extrasensory perception, but how well learned the material is (or strength of association) is an additional consideration. Positive correlations are most strongly expected when material is rather poorly learned (as in incidental memory, in the extreme case), whereas material that is overlearned should show a negative relationship.

Reported Patterns of Correlation

By way of further support for this hypothesis, and of Irwin's observation, two subsequent reports[6] both used designs testing primary memory without an interpolated task, and both yielded significant negative relationships. Blackmore (1980), in one of her methodologically sound studies of memory and ESP,[7] found a significant positive correlation between ESP scores and scores on a test of secondary memory. A study by Stanford (1970) looked for a relationship between ESP and incidental memory, and it reported a significant positive relationship, as this model would predict. Three apparently unflawed studies by Blackmore (1980) also tested the relationship between implicit memory and ESP scores. One yielded a suggestively significant ($p < 0.1$) effect in a positive direction, and the other two found insignificant negative trends.

All the studies just cited examined the relation between independent tests of ESP and memory given in the same situation. A different line of work examined the correlation of ESP and memory not only in the same situation but also in the same response,[8] and our model would expect that the same pattern of results should hold there as well. These were dual-aspect tests, in which participants were given lists of paired associates to memorize and then tested on their recall with a response sheet that also required a binary choice in the manner of responding, the latter aspect serving as an ESP test. For example, a list of trigrams (such as FAM or QEN) were each paired with meaningful words and memorized. Then in the memory test, the trigrams alone were presented, with the participant asked to write the associated word. The additional aspect was provided by two possibilities of writing the response, as, for example, in one of two adjoining spaces next to the trigram. The choice of space, participants were told, would serve as an ESP test, as one of the spaces had been picked randomly as a target. One additional variable was sometimes controlled in these studies: association strength. Some of the trigram-word pairs had high association strength (for example, SOS—help) and some had low association strength (for example, JUQ—tree).

The experimenters expected that ESP and memory would be positively correlated within the trial; that is, that memory responses that were correct would tend to be paired with ESP responses that were also correct, and vice versa. Their expectations were born out in a generally consistent way across several series. Palmer (2006b) calculated tests for overall significance from their series and found that recall-correct trials were associated with significant psi-hitting, and recall-incorrect trials were associated with significant psi-missing, and the two differed significantly from each other. These series all used a distraction task of several minutes between memorization and recall and also provided additional distraction with each trial by the requirement of the ESP response in terms of a placement decision. This makes it appear likely that secondary memory was primarily being sampled.

An important additional finding was that in studies in which association strength was controlled, the effect was contributed entirely by the pairs with low association strength. Again, as the model would predict, when something is not too securely learned (has lower association strength), the pertinence of the ESP target appears to be enhanced, and it is more likely to be positively expressed in the response.

This effect of a within-trial correlation of memory and ESP was significantly confirmed in one of two series reported by O'Brien (1976). Instead of controlling association strength, O'Brien controlled degree of normative usage in his word lists. He found that the correlation was evident only with the more rarely used words. Emmerich (1976) also reported a conceptual replication, in that he asked participants to give both a primary and secondary associate to each cue word (they had previously studied a list of jokes from which the cue words were drawn) and also elicited an ESP response in terms of the choice of writing the associates in one of two spaces. He found that memory and ESP correlated significantly and positively when considering the secondary associates, but not the primary associates, as he predicted. This showed again that less securely learned material, evoking less immediate responding, was more likely to carry ESP information. A failure to confirm the effect in a design closely modeled after that of Kanthamani and Rao was reported by Lieberman (1975). Harary (1976) also failed to confirm the effect in a study that departed from all the others in using group testing, suggesting that the heightened meaningfulness provided by individual testing may be important for the expression of the effect. Gambale (1976) and Gambale, Margolis, and Cruci (1976) also failed to confirm the effect, although they used a design that would have permitted participants to make their ESP responses after and separately from their memory responses if they chose, and this would seem likely to bring in the problem highlighted by Irwin (1979a) in mixing primary and secondary memory.

Summing up this last line of work, it appears that there is considerable evidence that secondary memory and ESP are positively correlated within the response, particularly when memory is not very strong, and that expression of the effect may be heightened by experimental designs that preclude the use of primary memory and by heightening the meaningfulness of the experimental situation by individual attention.

The Importance of ESP Priming in the Context of Secondary Memory

It may be an important matter whether or not participants are informed that they are taking a test of ESP. If they are told, we may say that this extrasensory aspect of potential experience is being primed by the information. Such contextual priming has been found to be important in the processing of subliminal or implicit cues,[9] and the logic of our model leads us to expect a similar pattern with ESP. This issue may be examined in a series of studies of the relationship between memory and ESP scores in which ESP items (with unfamiliar content) were imbedded in the context of academic examinations. Students were asked to indicate with each response whether they were completely certain of the correct answer or not. The initial study found a positive correlation between scores on the real items for which answers were not certain, and the scores on the ESP items.[10]

This confirms the relationship described above, in that ESP and secondary memory were positively correlated as long as recall was not so certain as to be immediate. A number of attempts to replicate this effect were reported with mixed results. Rammohan (1990) reviewed this literature, and although she did not carry out a meta-analysis, she detected a strong trend in which the positive relationship was found in studies in which students were alerted to the presence of the nonacademic, ESP questions, but negative relationships tended to be found when the ESP aspect of the situation was not revealed. The three significant positive relationships reported were all designs in which the ESP aspect of the situation was revealed, while the one significant reversal was in a study in which that was not revealed. Rammohan then carried out two more series to test this hypothesis, one in which the information was revealed and one in which it was not. In both series she found significant relationships in the directions she predicted.

This pattern appears sensible in light of the First Sight model. If ESP is not understood to be pertinent (and perhaps particularly in the anxiety-arousing context of an academic examination), preconscious contextual material sensed to be irrelevant to the task at hand would be expected to be subjected to contrast and expressed subtractively in responses by those who are remembering their more difficult (uncertain) academic material effectively. High memory scores accompanied low ESP scores. On the other hand, those who sense that they are remembering poorly might well cast about for inner "hints" about right answers, and preconsciously cast a broader net, assimilating more contextual material. Thus, their poor memory scores would accompany good ESP scores. Such a situation would produce a negative correlation. However, if extrasensory material is made more salient for everyone by the information that some items will be testing for it, then this information should serve as a prime leading that type of prehension to be sensed to be pertinent and likely to be assimilated additively. Given that ESP prehensions are understood to be important in the situation, those recalling uncertain but previously seen information effectively would be expected to be responding equally well to extrasensory prehensions, while those remembering poorly should be equally poor with ESP—hence a positive relationship should be obtained. It would be interesting to replicate Rammohan's finding by comparing academic test performance to another testing situation that is more playful, in which the results hold no personal consequences. We might predict that in the latter case, not knowing about the extrasensory element might not arouse such a strict contrast response in those remembering well.

SIMILAR PATTERNS OF FUNCTIONING

Use of Association

When attempting to recall something about which one is not certain, one searches inwardly, holding open a certain anticipatory "space" in which images, thoughts, associations, and feelings are scrutinized for a sense of correctness or pertinence. One consults the internal associative flow of images and feelings, looking for a doorway to the lost item. Actually, both memory studies and parapsychological ones suggest that such associative scanning is a matter of degree and is subject to individual differences. One line of ESP research elicited measures of strength of association among a set of target and response words and used this set in both memory and ESP tests. The investigators were particularly interested in responses that were incorrect. Some participants, in their wrong memory answers, tended to use instead some close associate to the correct response, as if their memories were not exactly right but were searching the correct neighborhood. Other participants showed no such tendency to rely on close associates when their memories were in error. Then the investigators examined the ESP performance of these two groups of participants. In several studies it was found that those who responded incorrectly with close associates on the memory test tended to do likewise on their ESP tests when incorrect responses there were examined. Likewise, participants who did not respond with close associates in one situation did not do so in the other.[11] Partial confirmation was also reported in a further study.[12] Palmer (2006b) has pointed out that a possible artifact may have inflated some of these results (although not all), but if the effect is found to be reliable, it may be taken as one indication of similar processing of ESP prehensions and long-term memory.

Effect of Anxiety and Attitude

Although not studied together in the same situations, additional evidence of similar functional processing can be found in the similar effects of anxiety and attitude upon both memory and ESP.

In a review of several studies, Palmer (1978) found a relatively consistent tendency for various measures of trait anxiety to bear a negative relationship with ESP scoring, particularly in the context of individual participant-experimenter interaction. This trend has continued since.[13] Anxiety has also been found to degrade the efficiency of recall. Two mechanisms by which this has been thought to occur are by a narrowing of the band of associative encoding and recall[14] and by the interference of extraneous, intrusive thoughts.[15] In regard to narrowing the band of association, it is known that highly anxious persons are overly responsive to the aspects of situations that might connote danger and are less than normally responsive to other aspects of experience, which degrades attentional resources.[16] The First Sight model proposes that the same processes that degrade attentional resources and memory recall also inhibit the accurate response to ESP prehensions.

Attitude toward the test and toward the material being accessed have also been found to affect both ESP scores and memory efficiency. In both cases, positive attitudes have been associated with positive access to the material, and negative attitudes have been associated with poorer access to the material. Although not always a significant predictor, attitude toward the possibility of ESP in the test situation has been a relatively robust correlate of ESP performance.[17] Attitude toward the target material has also been found to be important, with higher scoring often reported with material that is more important to the participant.[18] In the area of memory, a meta-analysis of several decades of work[19] concludes that a more positive attitude toward memory content does predict better memory performance, particularly when delayed recall is being tested. As with the correlation of memory and ESP, it appears that it is in regard to long-term memory that similarity of processing with ESP can be seen.

NOTES

1. Schacter, 1997.
2. Feather, 1967.
3. Kanthamani and Rao, 1974; Rao, 1978.
4. K. Parker, 1976; Rao, Morrison, and Davis, 1977.
5. Palmer, 1978.
6. Kreiman, 1978; Weiner and Haight, 1980.
7. See Berger, 1989, for a summary of methodological problems in her reports.
8. Kanthamani and Rao, 1974, 1975.
9. Blair, 2002.
10. Rao and O'Brien, 1977.
11. Rao, 1978; Rao, Morrison, and Davis, 1977; Rao, Morrison, Davis, and Freeman, 1977.
12. Rao, Kanthamani, and Palmer, 1990.
13. Carpenter, 2005a; Sargent and Harley, 1981.
14. Mueller, 1979.
15. Sarason, 1984.
16. Fox, Russo, and Georgiou, 2005.
17. Palmer, 1977, 1978; Schmeidler, 1988; Schmeidler and McConnell, 1958.
18. DaSilva, Pilato, and Hiraoka, 2003; Kanthamani and Rao, 1975.
19. Roberts, 1950.

12

Psi and Memory: How Do They Affect One Another?

It's a poor sort of memory that only works backwards.

—Lewis Carroll

DOES ESP AFFECT MEMORY?

Assumptions and Questions

The First Sight model predicts that extrasensory prehensions commingle with memory "traces" at a preconscious level and should often be discernable either additively or subtractively in the experience of remembering. By the logic of our model, this is in a sense an untestable proposition, since we are assuming that extrasensory prehensions are always available and no control condition can be devised in which they are not. It is an empirical question how such prehensions might be used in the effort to remember, and what things might influence such usage. What happens when an experimenter inserts an ESP "source" into a memory task? Our theory suggests that several considerations are probably important, among them:

1. Whether the information "primed" by ESP (for example, a sending agent) is congruent with what was learned or contrary to it. If it is congruent it should work additively and improve memory performance. If it is contrary it should compete with memory and weaken it.
2. Whether or not the participant is told about the ESP dimension of the situation. If the ESP aspect of the experiment is explicit, it should make it more salient and more likely to be positively expressed.

3. How well-learned the memory material is to begin with. Well-learned material would be expected to lead to quick closure and exclusion of the ESP information, and poorly learned material should lead to prolonged openness and more inclusion of the psi information.
4. How important and desirable correct remembering and ESP guessing are to the participant in that situation. The more important either is to the intentions of the participant the more likely it is that correct material of that sort will be expressed.

In all the reports discussed in this section, participants were given memory tests in which certain questions were also "loaded" by having ESP targets associated with them as well, sometimes congruent with the material to be remembered, and sometimes contrary to it.

MEMORY "PRIMED" BY ESP

One line of work was begun by Johnson (1973) on the contribution of ESP to performance in academic examinations, a "real-life" test of memory. In his three series, he attached sealed envelopes to the response sheets of essay tests in his psychology courses. In all series he deceived the students about the unusual envelopes, explaining them as something that would speed up test scoring. In two series, the envelopes contained typed information that was correct, applying to half the test questions (chosen randomly). No information was provided pertinent to the other questions. In the third series, half the questions contained misleading information associated with half the questions, and no information pertinent to the others. He found that the students performed better when they were "primed" by correct information relative to no information and performed more poorly when they were "primed" by incorrect information.

Some findings supportive of the effect of correct ESP targets "boosting" the efficiency of memory of the appropriate items have been provided by Braud (1975) and Schechter (1977), although the evidential value of these studies is weakened by the inadequately random assignment of targets to participants (Stanford, 1991). Stanford also demonstrated lessened performance on memory items paired with misleading ESP targets (1970). In this complex study, ESP targets were assigned to multiple-choice memory items, sometimes congruent with information that had been viewed previously and sometimes incongruent. His participants showed significantly poorer memory performance when the ESP targets were incorrect in terms of memory.

The Moderating Effect of Strength of Memory

Kreiman (1978) reported a similar intrusion of ESP targets into memory performance in a test situation in which grades were not at stake. His participants were students in a parapsychology course, and he knew them to be highly interested in the topic of ESP. They were given a short time to memorize a list of words and then tested on their recall. Twenty of the fifty words were randomly picked for each participant to be ESP targets as well as memory items, and this list of ESP targets was given to them in a sealed, opaque envelope. Thus, like Johnson's (1973) situation with memory-correct ESP targets, Kreiman was simply "priming" twenty of the fifty memory items by tagging them as ESP targets as well. Thinking that the psi intrusion should be greatest when memory is poorer, he divided each participant's response list in half, under the assumption that participants would first write down the words they recalled most securely. He predicted lowered performance (therefore, psi-missing) on the ESP-linked items in the first halves when memory should be stronger and heightened performance (psi-hitting) in the second halves when memory would tend to be weaker. Participants knew that some items would represent an ESP test as well as a memory test, but not which were which, and they were not told of his plan to split their responses. His predictions were confirmed. Although memory scores declined across the run of fifty trials, the ESP performance improved.

Some nonsignificant trends toward confirming this effect were reported by Weiner and Haight (1980) (who used precognitive ESP targets with no physical "prime" in the form of a hidden target list) and Schmeidler (1980, 1981). However, Schmeidler also found that when she carried out a study with participants that were most like Kreiman's (believers in ESP who found the test interesting) the effect was confirmed significantly. She later refined the hypothesis further and found that when she tested ESP believers who were in a good mood and restricted the psi-hitting prediction to the bottom quarter of their response lists, the prediction was confirmed significantly in two of her three series, and in all three series pooled. The one nonsignificant trend was produced by a series in which the ESP aspect of the test was not revealed to the participants, suggesting again that alerting participants to the importance of ESP information may facilitate its expression. Lieberman (1976), using a different design, also confirmed the expectation that ESP hitting should be better when memory is weaker and negative when memory is stronger, but only when his subjects were tested individually (the effect reversed to a nonsignificant degree when groups were tested). We might speculate that the individual testing situation heightened the participants' interest in the task, making their motivation more comparable to Kreiman's and Schmeidler's more highly engaged participants.

A study by Berman (1979) adds cross-cultural validity to the proposition that in a moment of uncertain memory, the mind unconsciously broadens its search and calls additively upon psi information, whereas when memory is clear, the doors to ESP are closed. He was teaching science to rural Swazi students, and he incorporated an ESP test into a science test for 184 of them. Following each space for a response to a science question, he placed another space in which the student was to mark either a star or a bar as an ESP response. On items following correctly answered science questions, the ESP scores were below chance, and on items following incorrect answers the ESP responses were highly above chance. The difference between them was significant.

Implications about the Interaction of Memory and Psi

While more work in this area needs to be done, this collection of findings suggests several things. First, information intended by an experimenter (or teacher) to serve as ESP targets can be inadvertently expressed in participants' responses to a memory test. When memory is strong, the expression is likely to be subtractive, as if the unneeded psi information is being subjected to contrast and avoided. When memory is relatively poor, the expression is likely to be additive, as if in the context of uncertainty, the *participant consults the ESP* prehensions with more positive, unconscious interest. Additional priming may make the intrusion more likely, whether priming the source by attaching odd and somehow important envelopes to answer sheets or by alerting participants to the presence of a test of ESP that is somehow part of the situation. The latter factor seems to most influence participants who are personally and positively engaged by that possibility. However, such priming apparently is not always necessary, as shown by the results of Stanford (1970).

DOES MEMORY AFFECT PSI?

Expectations of First Sight Theory

How might memory enter as a variable into a person's attempt to express and recognize some information that has been apprehended extrasensorily? The First Sight model holds that previously learned information must mingle somehow with extrasensory prehensions, at least when the learned material is sensed to be pertinent to the ESP task. In tests of ESP that are not also memory tests, the material used for targets will always have some degree of familiarity to participants, depending upon each person's history of exposure to the material and personal use of it. Material that is familiar enough to feel relevant to the task at hand should be eligible for assimilation. However, ideas so well learned that they predictably evoke fixed associations and patterns of response should be associated with rapid cognitive closure and cause ESP prehensions to be turned away. Some work pertinent to this question was reviewed in the last section, in which the same items on a test served as responses to both remembered material and ESP targets. One generalization that can be drawn from that is that some exposure may be helpful to ESP hitting, but material that is so well learned as to be immediately and accurately retrieved is more likely to be associated with psi-missing.

Findings

The meaningfulness of target material and its availability to memory have been found to affect results. Some studies suggest that some prior exposure to material to be used as ESP targets, as opposed to no exposure at all, can be helpful to psi-hitting. Kanthamani (1965) found that English-speaking participants who were unfamiliar with Hindi scored positively in ESP tests using English targets and negatively with Hindi targets (the test involved blindly matching sealed cards, so no linguistic understanding was involved in the response with either type of target). In a later study she found[1] that meaningful three-letter syllables (for example, UFO) evoked psi-hitting as targets, and nonsense syllables (for example, KEQ) evoked psi-missing. Nash and Nash (1968) tested participants with personally meaningful words and with digits picked by the experimenter and found better performance on the words. In some cases, targets that were more meaningful to the participants (and in that sense, better known to them) evoked psi-hitting relative to arbitrarily provided targets. Dean (1962) found that participants reacted physiologically to names of friends when they were used as targets but did not react to names of persons known to the experimenter or to names drawn randomly from a phone book. Rao (1962) compared targets chosen by participants to ESP cards and found hitting with the personal targets and missing with the arbitrary symbols. However, this pattern of preference has sometimes been found in reverse. Skibinsky's (1950) participants were tested with symbols and with names of intimates, and they scored significantly negatively (and more extremely) with the names and at chance with the symbols, and Rao (1963, 1964) found that chosen or otherwise more meaningful targets sometimes seemed to induce missing rather than hitting, depending upon other variables. Their responses were made by consciously guessing target content.

Our model suggests that some of these targets (for example, Skibinsky's names of intimates) may have been too meaningful to evoke positive scoring as targets, inasmuch as they may have evoked instead a clear set of conscious meanings that served to exclude extrasensory material. In this case, more meaningful material would be expected to unconsciously evoke greater weighting and more extreme scoring (as it did for Skibinsky), but scoring that is sometimes in a negative direction.

Evidence for a different but perhaps related negative effect has come from a series of studies initiated by Stanford (1967) on response bias.

Stanford reasoned that when participants demonstrate an associative bias, such that some target alternative comes much more readily to mind than others, ESP guesses that conform with that bias are less likely to be correct than calls that use the response alternatives that are biased against. He drew an analogy to signal-detection theory (the weak ESP signal is drowned out by the "louder noise" of the strong associative habit) and related this to the common experience of noticing some unusual element in a familiar situation. He carried out analyses of data from some high-scoring participants in past research and found evidence for the hypothesis. For example, the remarkably scoring Pavel Stepanek, who called the colors green and white, called green more frequently than white. Although his scoring was highly significant on both types of call, it was much higher on the less frequent white calls. Stanford went on to produce some data of his own in several studies to support the hypothesis,[2] and others have confirmed it as well.[3] However, some studies have found no effect.[4] No meta-analysis has been reported, but the negative effect of strong response tendencies has been found often enough that it would seem to represent a frequent if not invariable phenomenon. Pertinent evidence is also provided by several earlier studies that introduced new test material into a series of ESP tests that had been ongoing using small sets of forced-choice material that had become very familiar. In most cases, the fresh material (which had not accrued any associative habits) quickly and significantly produced improved scoring.[5]

Putting these two lines of work together, we have evidence that psi-hitting in an ESP test is made more likely by some associative familiarity or meaningfulness to the participant, but if it is so entrenched that it evokes a responsive rigidity, it is likely to be associated with negative scoring (this is discussed more fully below, when I deal with the issue of competing interpretations of results).

One study by Stanford (1973) demonstrated both these effects at once in an interesting way. He gave his participants a word-association test, using cue words that had strong norms for a primary (most frequent) and secondary (next most frequent) associate. He randomly assigned an ESP target to each trial, either the primary or secondary associate (trials were only scored for ESP if one of the two was given). He predicted that some degree of associative strength would facilitate ESP, and he expected this to be demonstrated by superior hitting when the target was the primary associate. The results bore out this expectation. However, he also expected a response-bias effect. He predicted that the opposite trend, greater hitting on secondaries than on primaries, would be found with participants who gave a preponderance of primary responses (those who had a strong response bias for primaries). This prediction was confirmed.

CONCLUSIONS

In sum, the studies reported on the effect of degree of prior learning on ESP performance do conform in large measure to the expectations that arise from the First Sight model. Some degree of familiarity with target material facilitates a sense of pertinence to the task at hand and makes psi-hitting more likely. An extreme degree of familiarity, accompanied by highly pre-dictable cognitive associates and behavioral responses, leads to such rapid closure that psi-missing is likely. The First Sight model suggests that with cognitive closure, the target material is subjected to the process of contrast and held decisively outside of the response, as evidenced by deviations significantly below chance in that situation. The meaningfulness of target material, inasmuch as this reflects personal familiarity and pertinence, may often predict hitting, but actually the model predicts[6] more generally that scoring with particularly meaningful material should generally be more extreme and in a positive direction only if other factors make the content seem desirable or useful in the context of the task. Most of the research reviewed has not reported scoring extremity, however, so this expectation could not be evaluated.

CODA: WHAT IS THE MEANING OF EXPERIMENTAL FINDINGS ON MEMORY AND PSI?

Reconstruing Findings

None of the studies reviewed in this section and others were carried out with the First Sight model in mind. It had not been described in the litera-ture when they were carried out. Is it reasonable, then, to turn to findings that were collected with other ends in mind to the service of this model?

Viewed pragmatically, all experimental findings are neutral as to interpre-tation. They are raw pieces of fact awaiting construal. Still, some researchers might fairly object to their own construals being dismissed in favor of those of a latter-day reviewer.

Many findings, in fact, have been presented in this literature almost bare of interpretation. When Feather (1967) reported a positive correla-tion between memory scores and ESP scores, and when Johnson (1973) described finding that ESP "primes" that were correct in terms of memory information acted to boost test scores of material that students had tried to remember, no interpretations of just why ESP and memory should bear these sorts of relations with one another were offered at all. Many other findings have been as naked or almost as naked of construal. Sometimes interpretations have been tentatively suggested but not developed or further tested, as when Rao, Morrison, and Davis (1977) reported a finding contrary to previous ones in that their participants' ESP scores correlated negatively with memory scores, instead of positively, as they had found before and expected again. They indicated that the poor attentiveness that may be evoked by group testing might have been responsible somehow, but they did not spell out just why this would have such an effect. No confirmations of this hypothesis have been reported.

When Irwin (1979a) offered an important clarification of the mixed results reported in terms of the direction of relationship between ESP and memory by distinguishing between procedures testing working memory from those testing long-term memory (as described above), he still could offer no interpretation as to why memory and ESP should be related in these ways. He briefly considered, and then rejected, an interpretation based on some speculations about the meaning of ESP scores, and then suggested that real understanding of the relationships would have to await greater understanding of what ESP scores measure. The First Sight model does offer one cogent interpretation of what ESP scores measure, and it may prove Irwin right by also offering an explanation of the pattern of different relationships that he found.

Reconstruing Inconsistency

Irwin noted that there was one group of studies that used similar procedures and found mixed and often null results in terms of the relation between ESP and memory scores. This was a set of studies reported by Rao and his colleagues.[7] As described previously, Irwin suggested that the inconsistency could be attributed to the fact that the learning period that immediately preceded testing was unusually long with a relatively large number of items, so participants could be free to follow individual proclivities in terms of using either working memory or long-term memory in responding to the test. In Rao (1978), this inconsistency of results was shown clearly by two groups of participants who were tested identically, with one showing a null relationship and the other a strong positive one. Rao noted that the two sets were analyzed separately, one by human checking followed by computer scoring and the other by computer scoring only, and he speculated that this different scoring procedure might somehow have influenced the results. He also noted another difference between the groups but attributed little significance to it. The first group that produced the null relationship was given a lecture on parapsychological research and then immediately given the procedure of memorization followed by testing. The second group had an intervening period between the lecture and testing in which most participants viewed a biofeedback demonstration while a few others watched a film. These participants showed the positive relationship between ESP and memory.

The First Sight model would suggest that these activities (in particular the biofeedback demonstration) encouraged a less cognitive, more inwardly exploring kind of set,[8] which would tend to prime the use of both long-term memory and access to ESP information. In addition, the use of any intervening procedure at all would, as Irwin argued, make working memory less accessible at all. On the other hand, a lecture on research followed immediately by testing would tend instead to prime a more cognitive, self-critical set that our model would consider to be conducive to the employment of working memory for at least some participants and to provide no intervening task to make working memory unavailable. Compare the utility of these two explanations. The First Sight understanding is a way of accounting for this effect as well as all of the differential memory relationships described by Irwin and reported subsequently. Different manners of checking results, on the other hand, apply to only very few studies and have not been found to show any consistent effects, and in any case just why scoring procedure should affect the relationship between memory and ESP performance is not specified at all.

Comparative Construals

More sophisticated interpretations have been presented in some reports on ESP and memory, and it is important to remember that these should be considered alongside of those offered here. Sometimes one construal may fare better than another. As one example, consider in more detail the innovative research of Stanford (1973) mentioned above, in which a word-association protocol was used as an ESP test. One of his series used cue words that were known to have strong primary and secondary associates. These two classes of responses were used as ESP targets, assigned randomly. Whenever a participant gave a response that was one or the other, it could be scored in terms of the ESP target (primary or secondary) associated with that trial. Stanford was testing two hypotheses with this series. One was a prediction from Roll's (1966) theory, which held that ESP must always be expressed by the arousal of memory traces (since the ESP "stimulus" is not available sensorially, there is no straightforward sensory channel by which it can come to awareness, so to become conscious at all it must be by way of stimulating memory material). An implication of this position is that information that is more well remembered (represented here normatively by the primary associates) should be a more sensitive carrier of ESP information than information that is less well remembered (the secondary associates). Thus, he expected an overall tendency for higher ESP scoring when the targets were primary associates. At the same time, Stanford expected that another tendency would tend to push scoring in the opposite direction: the response-bias effect.

As noted above, Stanford had pulled together a number of observations[9] to reveal a rather general pattern: whenever a strong tendency for a certain class of response exists, correct ESP information is most likely to be expressed whenever the person's response *deviates* from the bias. He called this the *response-bias* effect. Since in general there is in the population a bias toward responding to the words he was using with primary rather than secondary associations (as determined by the norms that established the primary and secondary categories for the words), this effect should act to produce higher scoring on the secondary responses. Stanford tested both of these expectations at once in an ingenious way. He looked for confirmation of the memory-trace hypothesis by comparing the rates of scoring overall when participants were giving primary versus secondary responses. He predicted that scoring should be higher overall on the primary responses, and this is the result he obtained. To test the response-bias hypothesis, he predicted that participants who demonstrated, *as individuals*, a strong preponderance of primary to secondary responses should have better scoring on their secondary responses than on their primary responses, since they were particularly biased toward the primary associates. As a secondary test of the response-bias effect, he also predicted that longer average reaction time in responding should be associated with better scoring on primaries than on secondaries, with shorter average reaction time showing the opposite pattern, since brief reaction time is known to be associated with sampling from the top of the associative hierarchy. He found both of the expected relationships.

What about the persons who did not show a strong preference for responding with primaries? As expected by the memory-trace hypothesis, they scored better when giving primary associates.

To sum up, across all his data, Stanford found confirmation for the memory-trace hypothesis: scoring was higher when responding with more highly associated words. For those individuals who exhibited a strong personal response bias in favor of the normative primaries, however, the pattern was reversed, and he found evidence for the response-bias effect. They scored better when they deviated from their bias and responded with less strongly associated words.

How should these findings be best construed? In order to make a comparison, I must make an assumption not explicitly justified by Stanford's report. He gave no means for scoring by different groups in his study but reported only correlational analyses. I will assume that the better scoring for certain classes of responses relative to the lower scoring for other classes (for example, primaries better than secondaries, overall) represents a psi-hitting tendency for one and a psi-missing tendency for the other. I assume this because Stanford does not report significantly high scoring for his data overall, and it is conventional in parapsychological reports to note such overall tendencies when they are found. Therefore, "better" scoring in one case versus "poorer" scoring in another must represent a tendency to hit in one and miss in the other, rather than hit very highly in one and produce chance scores in the other. Both the memory-trace and the response-bias hypothesis generate predictions of hitting versus chance-level scoring, and they offer no predictions about psi-missing. The First Sight theory predicts both.

The memory-trace hypothesis comes from the assumption that stronger memory traces should be more ready vehicles for expressing ESP information. Relative to them, weaker memory traces should simply be less effective vehicles and thus less likely to show a tendency to give correct information. The theory is mute in terms of responses that show a positive tendency to express counterfactual information. The case with the response-bias hypothesis is a bit more complicated. Stanford has construed the response-bias effect (1966b, 1973) in terms of signal-detection theory.[10]

Use of this theory with ESP requires us to assume that extrasensory information presents to the organism as an occasional weak signal occurring within a noisy background (like a personally significant phrase uttered by someone nearby at a party in which many conversations are going on simultaneously). To have a strong bias for certain classes of response means that a hearer will, in terms of the example given, tend to "hear" certain things quite frequently and therefore will tend to tendentiously misinterpret what is heard in accord with his or her bias. There will be a high rate of "false alarms" in favor of the bias. If a signal is relatively weak relative to the contextual noise, this tendency to mishear in favor of the bias will override the tendency to hear what the signal actually is, reducing the accuracy of the response. If there is no strong bias in responding, there will be fewer "false alarms" and the weak signal will have a greater opportunity to rise to awareness and be correctly perceived. Thus, low-bias listeners should be better able to discern the weak ESP signal accurately and show psi-hitting in their responses. High-bias listeners should be responding so strongly in terms of their bias that the information coming from the ESP "signal" should be unable to rise to consciousness, and the responses should show only a chance level of association. Again, there is no prediction that is generated of negative scoring in any situation. This "weak-signal" model is intuitively appealing if one makes the conventional assumption that experiences are caused by stimuli. If a stimulus causes a perception in the way that a hammer drives a nail, then weak stimuli should have less clear-cut effects than strong stimuli.

If the Stanford (1973) study had been framed in terms of First Sight theory, a different sort of reasoning would have been used. ESP information is not an occasional signal but a constant presence, each bit of which

is either approached or avoided in regard to the formation of every experience. Preconscious information is accessed not by virtue of its force as a
physical stimulus but by its *meaning* as appraised in light of the intentions
and contextual assessments of the organism. The perceiver is an agent, not
merely a recipient of biochemical forces. Thus, the ESP target is always an
active constituent in every ESP response (in this case, in the choice of every
associate). All things being equal, more meaningful material will tend to
be approached more frequently and less meaningful information will tend
to be avoided because more meaningful material tends to be unconsciously
presumed by the participant to be more likely to be important and personally salient.

Thus in general, more meaningful material should evoke a tendency to
psi-hit and less meaningful material should evoke a tendency to psi-miss,
and primary associates (being generally more meaningful) should tend
to express hits and secondary associates should tend to express misses.
However, another important determiner of approaching or avoiding the
extrasensory material is the presumption that extrasensory information, as
a general source, is likely to be useful or not in the particular situation. If
one has a strong bias for certain classes of response, irrespective of subtle-
ties in the available information, then at a moment when the motivation to
express the bias is dominant the extrasensory domain will be eschewed in
general in favor of the pressing motivation to express responses congruent
with the bias.

To eschew this whole domain, in this model, is not to be simply oblivious to it but rather to subject it to contrast and demonstrate a tendency
to produce responses that definitely avoid it (express it less frequently
than chance would predict). Thus, when a high-bias person is generating
a probias response (in this case, a primary association), the extrasensory
domain *as a source* will be subjected to contrast and this will be expressed
as a negative reference to that material, or a psi-missing score. However,
when the same person is producing an association that is not driven by
the bias, he or she would be expected to be freer to sample from a broad
domain of alternatives, and a positive reference to the part of the situation
that is represented by the ESP target would be expected. This is because
this person is willingly participating in an ESP study and presumably has a
general motivation to succeed in that commitment by expressing the target
correctly. This would be expressed as a tendency to hit the target in the non-
bias responses. Thus, if my assumption about the group means is correct,
Stanford's results would be predicted by First Sight theory more precisely
than by either the memory-trace or the response-bias/signal-detection lines
of reasoning in that tendencies to miss are as much accounted for as tendencies to hit.

The General Applicability of First Sight Theory

In addition to making specific comparisons between the explanations offered with a specific study and explanations drawn from the First Sight model, we should also take note of the general utility of the model. Many of the various proposals may serviceably account for their particular sets of results, but none of them has the general capacity to account for almost all of these findings in the way that the First Sight model does. Checker differences or testing situations that may vary in terms of aroused interest or interactions with experimenter gender or a great many other proposed variables may be cogent possible interpretations of certain studies, but none of these ideas pertain to most studies and they have not been found to have general explanatory power. The First Sight model accounts for a great many findings involving ESP and memory and makes them understandable in a common set of terms.

There are also many cases in which particular hypotheses appear to be largely supported, but the confirmations are also found alongside contrary results that seem inscrutable. The First Sight model offers higher-order explanations that subsume the apparent contradictions. As just one example, recall the several studies that found higher ESP performance with more meaningful material[11] and the contrary results of Skibinsky (1950), who found negative and significantly extreme scoring with his more meaningful targets. The First Sight model offers a much more integrative set of interpretations, and it embraces and incorporates the general finding and accounts for Skibinsky's negative scoring as well. It also offers a meaningful interpretation of the extreme scoring, for which Skibinsky did not attempt to account at all.

SUMMARY OF FINDINGS ON ESP AND MEMORY

In our research literature, the idea that ESP and memory might be related processes arose serendipitously in an unpredicted correlation observed in a pilot study that had other objectives.[12] Attempts to confirm the relationship led to interesting but conflicting results, and efforts to conceptualize the matter began trying to catch up.

The First Sight model holds that psi prehensions are continually ongoing, and in their ordinary, everyday functioning serve unconsciously to anticipate and guide the development of all of our experience. As the mind constructs its experience toward the end of usefully construing it, it unconsciously consults incoming information from whatever source in the light of implicit questions that were posed by earlier sources in the process. These preconscious processes have been studied for a long time, at least since the Wurzburg school of the early twentieth century.[13] This model asserts that the earliest source of guiding questions comes from our nonlocal engagement with reality that we term psi. All of this preconscious processing happens very quickly as conscious experience flows along. Psi in its most common expression is thus assumed to be quite a normal process, quickly deployed and quickly abandoned, and normally invisible to conscious experience.

As we attempt to know what we are trying to remember (or what we are perceiving or creating or feeling or intending) the anticipatory questions of any one stage call up ideas from our personal associative network of images, words, feelings, values, and motives for what help they might offer. Thus in this model, psi questions, and memory attempts to answer, all in the light of other input that might be developing in the moment.

At this preconscious stage of experience then, psi and memory must work hand in glove. The general expectation that arises from this model is that before experience has been construed, while it is still uncertain and moving toward meaning, both psi and memory should be seen to be contributing their parts, harmoniously and efficiently. Thus, they should be found to correlate positively (if one is contributing effectively, the other should be also), and their contributions should be generally additive, *until the point that some step in the assertion of meaning has made one or the other seem less pertinent to what is developing*. Then they will diverge, and one will contribute positively to the experience (be assimilated) while the other will contribute negatively (be subject to contrast).[14] The various results just reviewed all appear to conform to this basic expectation.

Moving beyond the purely parapsychological literature, I believe that there will be an ongoing need for the cognitive psychologists who study memory to take account of psi processes if they are to fully understand the operative processes in their domain and a need for parapsychologists to keep up with the active, fruitful field of memory studies. First Sight theory is essentially harmonious with theories in cognitive psychology that try to account for the structure and accessibility of latent memories. The most popular models accounting for how primes call up memories, such as those by Collins and Loftus (1975), use a concept of spreading activation throughout a semantic network of memories organized in hierarchical nodes. Guided by the hypothesis of functional equivalence, First Sight would lead us to expect that this structural model of latent mental contents should apply to psi material as well as to memory. After all, while psi presumably has access to virtually everything, the unconscious mind will normally choose to traffic with what is personally meaningful, as a function of what is personally remembered. Thus, the expression of psi should be dependent upon the structure of memory, as William Roll (1966) emphasized some time ago; and the expression of memory should be enriched by the infusion of psi. Consciously integrative work between these disciplines will be fruitful.

NOTES

1. Kanthamani and Rao, 1975.
2. Stanford 1967, 1970, 1973.
3. Glidden, 1974; Morris, 1971; Palmer and Johnson, 1991; Sargent, 1982.
4. Shrager, 1978.
5. Cadoret, 1952; Hallett, 1952; Pratt and Woodruff, 1939; Thouless, 1949.
6. Carpenter, 2005b.
7. Rao, 1978; Rao, Morrison, and Davis, 1977.
8. Carpenter, 2004.
9. Stanford, 1967.
10. Swets et al., 1964.
11. Kanthamani, 1965.
12. Feather, 1967.
13. Gollwitzer, 1990.
14. Can memory contribute negatively to developing experience in a way analogous to psi-missing? Studies on repression and motivated forgetting suggest that it can (e.g., Anderson and Green, 2001; Brewin and Andrews, 2000; Singer, 1995).

13

Psi and Creativity

You must give birth to your images. They are the future waiting to be born.

—Ranier Marie Rilke

WHAT IS CREATIVITY, AND WHY
MIGHT IT BE RELATED TO PSI?

The human act of creation, the production of some extraordinary poem or symphony or play or scientific theory, seems as mysterious and awesome as the furtive flashes of preknowing or distant seeing that we term psi. Human in their expression, both seem somehow extrahuman in their source. Logical consciousness can marvel at them and study them, but it cannot produce them at will. The First Sight model holds that they emerge from similar preconscious processes and are expressed by the same principles of operation.

Several writers have pointed out many similarities that appear to exist between psi processes and creativity. F. W. H. Myers (1961 [1903])[1] held cases of "genius" alongside observations of spontaneous psychic experiences and concluded that both represented an intrusion into conscious life of material from an unconscious strata, involving both an openness to such material and a desire to express it, a view echoed later by Gardner Murphy (1963) and Carl Jung (1960c). It seems reasonable that psi and creativity should be related. A relatively large number of research studies have been carried out on the question. However, the actual results obtained have seemed so mixed and confusing that one reviewer[2] remarked wryly that it would require that someone have a great deal of creativity to be able to make sense of them. In this chapter we will see how much clarity can be brought to this confusion by First Sight theory.

Just what is creativity, and what things characterize creative people? These are intently studied questions in psychology, particularly in recent decades. From the 1970s through the mid 1990s over ten thousand creativity references were added to the research literature of psychology.[3]

In its essence, creativity means the ability to bring something new into existence. It may be a new combination of obviously available things, or it may appear more radically new than that, as if "out of nowhere." In practice, though, we usually mean something more than sheer novelty in defining some human act as creative. We require it to be a new thing that is also somehow successful or apt in its own context (a fine painting, a heuristic theory, a timely invention). We often want it to be in some sense beautiful or satisfying. And we also understand that its experiential origin is somehow mysterious, a thing not simply deduced from obvious givens but emerging from some extrarational source not identical with logical calculation.

What are the essential features of the creative process? One classic account by Wallas (1926) and Hutchinson (1931) argued that it involved four stages: preparation, incubation, illumination, and verification. One must be deeply steeped in the issues in the context of which one would do something creative (preparation). Then some nonlogical, unconscious process must go on in which this background information is altered and combined (incubation). At some point, the new thing must spring to consciousness (illumination). Finally, the inspired new thing must be worked out in the light of day, articulated, polished, tested, and made useful (verification). Kelly (1955) proposed a similar pattern in his two-stage theory that he called "loosening and tightening." First, an individual's ways of construing things must loosen and embrace many new potential kinds of connections, and then they must tighten up so as to yield some new understanding or product that is inventive and also effectively expressed and serviceable.

The questions of what sorts of persons are more creative and what characteristics make them so have received much attention. Virtually all personality theorists have addressed the issue, from Freud to Skinner. To summarize the burgeoning literature on what creative persons are like, several extensive reviews have been published.[4]

A relatively large body of research has been carried out on the question of the relation between psi and creativity.

EXPECTATIONS FROM FIRST SIGHT THEORY

Several of the characteristics repeatedly stressed about the qualities of creative persons bear a close resemblance to some that the First Sight model holds to be important in the expression of psi phenomena. For example, Barron and Harrington (1981) concluded that the robust correlates of creative achievement included aesthetic sensitivity, openness and broad interests, intuition, and creative self-concept. Aesthetically sensitive, open, and intuitive people are all keenly attuned to a personal world of nonrational experience, including what we have referred to as *liminal* experience. Persons with a creative self-concept are personally committed to reaching beyond everyday facts and assumptions in problem-transforming and self-transforming ways. The accounts of many eminently creative persons demonstrate the generality of this process of grappling with a flow of irrational material from some nonconscious source and wresting meaning and beauty out of it. The interested reader is referred to accounts by Annie Dillard (1974), Peter Ilich Tchaikovsky (1906), and Maurice Sendak (1988), which are illustrative. Some, like the writer N. Scott Momaday,[5] attribute an explicitly paranormal dimension to the process. All of this is reminiscent of the assumption from the First Sight model that persons who are more attuned to inadvertent, liminal experience and are more committed to understanding it creatively and usefully should be more able to express extrasensory information correctly.

What do creative people do when they compose a sonata or write a play or sculpt a figure—or construct a scientific theory? Whatever else they do, they must take seriously and consult fruitfully an inner stream of images, thoughts, and feelings, without ever knowing precisely what those things mean and exactly where they will lead. They must suspend cognitive work while they are doing this. And if they are successfully creative people, they must do these things successfully; that is, with enough stamina and skill and judgment to produce something original, beautiful, and useful. It seems a natural assumption that such persons might successfully access the inner life for psychic allusions as well, when that suits their intentions.

In terms of the First Sight theory, the Integration Corollary posits that preconscious processes involving sensory and remembered material (such as used in creative acts) should function similarly to and in harmony with the processing of psi information. The concept of intentionality suggests that in terms of preconscious process, one generally finds what one seeks and values, something characteristic of creativity as well as psi. The importance of switching in psi suggests that a capacity to hold a persistent, disciplined interest over time in something is essential for a notable expression of some discovery concerning it. This is another characteristic that seems likely to characterize both psychic and creative production. Finally, our model holds that one must be able to correctly understand *inadvertency* for extrasensory information to come to consciousness, and the illuminations of the creative person similarly require that one usefully interpret the often ragged and unruly expressions of creative thoughts, feelings, and images, while suspending too much cognitive closure. In general then, our theory predicts a relationship between a capacity to work creatively and ESP performance (both extreme scores and hitting scores, although analyses have generally been carried out only in terms of hitting).

PSI ABILITY IN CREATIVE PEOPLE

In general, this theory holds that an unconscious wish to realize the meaning of extrasensory material, coupled with an invariant attention to inadvertent phenomena, should make the expression of such material more likely. Creative persons who are engaged in a psi task would be expected to display these things. Several factors would seem to be at work. First, demonstrably creative persons tend to be highly motivated and successful at producing effective performances when called upon to do so. Because of that, we may assume that their conscious motivation to perform is generally matched as well by an unconscious intention to do well (not all potentially creative persons have this happy harmony of intention). This unconscious wish to succeed should result in a tendency to construct allusions toward the potential meaning at the psi level. Another requirement of successful artistic work is that one suspends rational analysis at times and consults an inner field of sensed preferences, impulses, and incipient understandings. How does the poet find the next image or the cellist sense the right emotional interpretation of a solo, or the actor's body find the right posture for a character? They must "feel their way," suspending clear decisions and cognitive analysis long enough for an implicit sense to emerge and declare itself. This sustained openness to the "felt sense"[6] and suspension of premature cognitive closure should allow an individual to attend to the implicit information in such inadvertent experiences as flowing ideas, aesthetic feelings, sudden leaps of association, even anomalous errors and synchronicities. Finally, commitment to generating a usefully articulated creative product is necessary for creative work to be successful and recognized. While cognitive work must be set aside at one point, it must be employed skillfully at another. Sheer access to incipient, liminal material may permit a flow of original ideas, but without a disciplined commitment to crafting a completed work, such a flow would be fitful and fruitless. Access to psi information would be expected to require a similar commitment; otherwise preconscious attention to one psychic source or piece of information could be quickly replaced by competing attention to another source or piece, resulting in no discernable information at all. And there seem to be skills that can be learned in better interpreting psi inadvertencies (see chapter 19). Disciplined thinking is needed for this sort of work as much as in the crafting of a painting or a poem.

What do the facts say? Are creative people especially prone to psychic experiences? Apparently based upon their own experience many believe that they are: Walter Prince (1928 [1963]) described psychic experiences reported by many eminently creative individuals, including Mark Twain, Robert Browning, Robert Schumann, Johann Wolfgang von Goethe, and Emanuel Swedenborg. Many other such reports could be adduced. Congruent with this, several studies have reported that more creative persons (variously defined) are more apt to believe in the reality of psychic experiences and to think that they have experienced them themselves than their less creative counterparts.[7] For example, one study on this question was reported by Davis et al. (1974), who found sizable correlations in the 0.5 range between scores on belief in paranormal phenomena and measures both of attitudes, values, and motivations associated with creative persons and with expert ratings of the quality of the participants' creative products. In fact, a tendency of interest and belief regarding unusual and paranormal experience has been found to be one of the stronger attitudinal associates of the "creative personality," according to Barron (1969, p. 77) and Torrance (1962).

Scientists generally prefer evidence that is more objective than personal self-reports when dealing with something as dubious as psi (unless specified otherwise, all of the research results discussed below refer to actual ESP scoring in controlled tests, not to self-reports of psychic experience). What does the empirical work say? Do more creative people have better scores on tests of ESP? Several studies have reported generally positive but somewhat mixed results. It seems likely that some of the unreliability in results has to do with operations used for assessing creativity. There are hundreds of measures of creativity in use,[8] many of which have minimal or no intercorrelation.[9] Cognitive measures thought to be relevant to creativity generally have little validity in terms of a person's capacity to produce demonstrably creative works.[10] Whatever the different measures may be said to mean, they mean different things from each other. To clarify the results that have been reported about psi performance and creativity, I will discuss them in terms of the criteria that have been used in the studies to define creativity.

DEMONSTRABLE CREATIVITY

Significantly positive findings have been reported several times on ESP performance (hitting) in more creative persons, when the latter are defined in terms of what many researchers have considered the most valid way: persons who are successfully engaged in a creative pursuit[11] and on ESP performance in persons who were objectively assessed to have produced creative work.[12] Sometimes these select groups have been tested alone and sometimes in comparison to others who are not successfully creative. When comparisons have been made in these studies, above-chance scoring has been observed with the (actually) creative persons, and most often chance-level scoring on their general-population controls; although below-chance scoring in the latter has been reported as well. Some studies have shown significant differences between the groups, and others have not; but the general effect depends primarily upon the positive scoring of the creative participants. Some studies, notably Dalton (1997b), with her artistic population drawn largely from the Edinburgh artistic community, and Schlitz and Honorton (1992), with their Juilliard students, demonstrated positive scoring in their creative participants that was dramatically high.

Several partial confirmations of the effect of high scoring on the part of artistic participants have been reported. Moss, Paulson, Chang, and Levitt (1970) found that four of their eight artist participant-sender pairs scored significantly high, although the others did not. The ones who did had also been hypnotized and given suggestions of high performance, while the chance scorers had not received that hypnotic treatment. The artistic participants of McDonough, Don, and Warren (1994) scored significantly high when their free-response performance was measured by objective judges, but not when it was self-rated. Gelade and Harvie (1975) found significantly more hits in agent-perceiver pairs in which both were artists than in other pairs in which either participant was not an artist. I could find no reports of significantly negative scoring on the part of creative participants, although one study reported only a nonsignificant trend in the expected direction.[13] Holt's artistic participants showed positive scoring in terms of first-rank free-response ratings (40 percent first rank hits in a situation in which chance expectation was 25 percent), but her statistical test was weakened by another effect in her data: a significant tendency on the part of these participants to score *extremely* as well as highly, which reduced her linear effect to nonsignificance. This effect of significantly extreme scoring (negative as well as positive) on the part of artists has been replicated by Carpenter (2006). Null results in terms of hitting were reported by Jackson, Franzoi, and Schmeidler (1977) in a study that used a less-demanding criterion for actual creativity (being a music major).

One study assessed the creative quality of the participants' efforts in the context of the ESP test itself. Moon (1973) collected drawings from his participants (all of whom were advanced arts majors) and asked trained judges to assess their quality. The participants whose drawings were rated as higher in quality did produce significantly high ESP scoring, but the scoring of the less-competent artists in the sample was also positive (although less strongly so), and the difference between the groups was not significant.

Moon did not test to see how representative this small sample of work was to his participants' overall level of ability.

In general, it appears that demonstrably creative people show a fairly robust tendency to score highly (or sometimes extremely) on tests of ESP.

SELF-ASSESSED CREATIVITY

Perhaps the index that comes next most closely to the criterion of actually demonstrating effective creative work is the simple one of asking participants whether or not they consider themselves to be particularly creative people. Several studies have reported positive relationships, although some others have not. Bierman (1995) found that persons who identified themselves as having serious artistic interests scored significantly highly in an experiment carried out on the Internet. Two studies from the University of Edinburgh reported finding that the *level* of self-assessed creative interest produced significant scoring discriminations in their two groups of participants who were already selected for their artistic interests.[14] Rather than a relationship with hitting, Rebman, Radin, and Stevens (1996) found significantly more extreme psi scoring among self-described more creative participants than their less creative counterparts. This relationship was particularly strong in sessions that were associated with low geomagnetic activity. They replicated these effects in another sample. One failure to confirm this effect has been reported: Sondow (1986a) found no relationship between self-assessed creativity and hitting, and she did not analyze for scoring extremity.

A more formal index of self-assessed creative interest can be obtained with the Torrance Personal-Social Motivation Inventory.[15] Honorton (1967) administered ESP tests to a group of high school students and found a significant discrimination between two groups that he formed by splitting the scores, apparently near the empirical median (although this was not specified). His whole sample scored significantly negatively, and all of this deviation was contributed by the low-creative group, with the more creatively interested participants scoring near chance. A correlational analysis would presumably have shown a simple linear relationship. Honorton, Carlson, and Tietze (1968), with a different group of schoolchildren, found another significant linear relationship between Torrance interest scores and ESP scores in a drawing test, and also reported that the strength of the discrimination was improved significantly by focusing on participants whose drawings were more expansive (and presumably more playful and uninhibited, and hence more actually creative in that situation), as well as on the group predicted to have an optimal level of anxiety (mid-range).

Nicola Holt used a different instrument for measuring self-rated artistic interest, the Amended Creative Activities Checklist (ACAC).[16] In a small study with a selected sample of visual artists,[17] she found that those expressing higher interests in music and performing arts showed *less* inadvertent response to negative stimuli to which they would later be subliminally exposed as compared to participants who expressed less artistic interest. She interpreted this as implying less avoidance of negativity on the part of those with more creative interest. This is sensible if we take a larger view of the skills and attitudes involved in being a visual artist, from the point of view of First Sight theory. Visual artists tend to be committed to working creatively with visual material of all sorts in a creative way and should be generally more responsive than others to such material. The more creative ones would be expected to show less aversion than others to material that happens to be negatively toned. In a larger study, Holt (2007) collected free-response ESP responses from another group of participants who were self-identified as having creative interests. She collected her responses throughout the day at self-selected optimal times and expected a simple positive correlation between hitting and creative interest. Instead, she found a nonsignificant reversal of her expectation and also a null relationship with scoring extremity.

Overall, it seems that asking persons if they consider themselves to be creative and collecting a more delineated measure of this self-assessment appear to be promising in terms of identifying persons who will score either relatively highly or extremely in ESP tests. The fact that results have shown less consistency compared to those with demonstrated creativity may be due in part to the lower validity of self-reports.

PERSONALITY MEASURES DESIGNED AS PREDICTORS OF CREATIVITY

Some psychologists who have studied the topic of creativity have developed personality tests intended to predict creative behavior. Some of these have been carried into parapsychological studies in the hope that they might predict extrasensory ability as well.

Harrison Gough has developed tests intended to predict creativity, one of them made up of items from the Adjective Check List.[18] Holt (2007) examined a creativity factor comprised of the Gough scale plus indications of a greater interest in science than in art and found no relationship with hitting in her free-response ESP study; but she did find a positive association with scoring extremity. Schmeidler (1963, 1964b) used a similar test of creative attitudes combined with a test of divergent thinking and found a significant negative relationship with scoring; however, examination of her tables makes it appear that the attitude test was a negligible contributor to the relationship.

Preference patterns for abstract figures have been used to construct non-verbal personality tests for predicting creativity.[19] Pang and Frost (1967) used the Barron-Welsh Art Scale as an index of creativity and found a significant positive relationship with ESP hitting. However, the relationship was contributed entirely by his male sample; the scale bore no relationship with ESP for his female participants. However, Sondow (1986a), in her ganzfeld study with only female participants, did report a significant relationship between the Art Scale and hitting. A similar measure using the Welsh Figure Preference Test[20] was used by McGuire, Percy, and Carpenter (1974), and it entered significantly into a regression equation that was predictive of ESP hitting, but no report was made of its independent relationship, and no validation of the regression solution has been attempted.

This collection of findings makes it appear that personality measures predictive of creativity may also be useful in predicting extrasensory scoring, but they have been so little used that further study would be necessary before drawing any definite conclusions.

MEASURES OF ATTITUDES AND TRAITS RELATED TO BOTH CREATIVITY AND PSI PERFORMANCE: OPENNESS

Perhaps things that are predictive of creativity are also predictive of ESP performance. This is another way that the two things should be related, according to First Sight theory. Several researchers have identified patterns of attitudes and personality traits that are correlated with creative achievement in various fields of endeavor. A meta-analysis by Feist (1988) found that the largest relationships with creativity were with the traits of openness, conscientiousness, self-acceptance, hostility, and impulsivity. In turn, these correlates are sometimes used as indices of creativity. Parapsychologists have used them sometimes as well in the hope of finding useful predictors of ESP performance. Openness has been studied far more than the other traits.

Schmeidler (1988) reviewed twenty-four studies that demonstrated a strong trend for openness (defined in various ways, ranging from Rorschach scales to inadvertent behavioral indices) to be positively predictive of ESP hitting. An earlier review by Palmer (1978) citing some of the same material concurred with the general trend.

Subsequent to the studies cited in these reviews, openness as measured by the NEO-PI,[21] including its six subscales (or the shorter NEO-FFI), has been the single most studied measure of openness for psychologists. It has been found to significantly predict actual creative work of high quality,[22] as well as other traits thought to contribute to creativity, such as cognitive fluency.[23]

Several parapsychological studies have used it as well. Morris et al. (1993) found a nonsignificant positive trend with ESP hitting for the overall scale and a significant relationship with Openness to Actions. Examining physiological responsiveness rather than ESP guessing, Broughton (2004) found a strongly significant relationship between openness and response to emotionally arousing (positive and negative) versus nonarousing pictures that would be presented shortly in the future. Holt (2006), using a related design, similarly found a suggestively significant (p < 0.10) relationship between openness and precognitive responsiveness to emotional stimuli, but again no relationship with emotionally neutral stimuli. Carpenter and Simmonds-Moore (2009b) predicted that three of the facets of openness as measured by the NEO-PI (openness to fantasy, feelings, and aesthetics) should predict participants' implicit response (in terms of enhanced liking) to positively toned ESP targets and found significant evidence for this, which they then replicated in a second study. Using a measure highly correlated with the NEO-PI Openness scale, Luke, Roe, and Davison (2008) reported a significant positive correlation with a different unintentional psi task that carried affective consequences for success and failure. Houtkooper et al. (1999) found that openness acted as a significant moderator for a negative relationship between ESP scores and geophysical sferics (low-frequency electromagnetic waves emitted from thunderstorms). The ESP scoring of more open people was more affected by the sferic activity. Using a different measure of openness, Osis and Bokert (1976) found that meditators whose openness scores increased after meditation scored significantly better at ESP than those whose scores decreased. One study reported a null relationship between NEO-PI openness and an unintentional psi test.[24]

While it has not been generally explored, it may be that openness will more reliably relate to the extremity of ESP response rather than to direction. This is because more open people would be expected to be more likely to weigh ESP information heavily in an ESP experiment than less open people, who would tend to find the extrasensory domain of dubious value. The studies just mentioned, that showed a positive relationship between openness and psi-hitting, may have succeeded in presenting conditions that encouraged the material to be positively signed as well (leading to positive as well as internally consistent scoring). This is suggested by the study of Howat (1994) using the implicit psi response of electrodermal arousal in response to being stared at by someone viewing a person on closed-circuit television. She found that more open people responded extremely, but in both directions (some becoming more aroused and others more calmed) in response to being viewed. Their arousal responses were consistent enough across several view and control epochs to produce extreme scores. The direction of their response was predicted by other variables.

Another instrument intended to measure a construct much like openness is the Intuition (versus Sensation) scale of the Meyers-Briggs Type Inventory, which is intended to operationalize Jung's concept of the intuitive function. According to Jung (1960a), more intuitive people are oriented more to the possibilities implied by experience than they are to surface facts in themselves, and he believed that they should demonstrate greater creativity. The Meyers-Briggs measure of this dimension of Jung's (intuition versus sensation, or I-S) has been found to correlate substantially with various measures of creativity,[25] and it correlates highly with NEO-PI openness.[26] Unfortunately, the other Meyers-Briggs dimensions also correlate with creative interests and behavior as well, notably Feeling (as opposed to Thinking, or T-F) and Perceiving (as opposed to Judging, or J-P), although a best-measure estimate of creativity determined by Gough and his colleagues[27] used all four MBTI dimensions, including the one involving extraversion versus introversion.

Given this lack of discriminative purity, it is perhaps not surprising that studies of ESP performance using the Meyers-Briggs scales have not shown a clear superiority on the part of the intuition dimension, although various combinations of scales, some using the I-S dimension and some not, have been found to be useful. Using dichotomous classifications (typing persons as simply "intuitive" versus "sensing" or "feeling" versus "thinking," etc.) rather than continuous scores, Honorton (1997) found that participants in the ganzfeld did best when they were both Perceiving and Feeling types, omitting reference to Intuition. This may well have been largely because almost all of his participants were Intuitive types (something that is frequently true when participants in ESP research are volunteers who are taking part because of their interest in the subject). In this case, the dichotomy could not have had much discriminatory power. In the study mentioned above, Broughton (2004) found that the MBTI Intuition scale successfully predicted a presentiment response to arousing pictures, but not quite as well as the Openness scale of the NEO-FFI did. Since the two scales were surely correlated, it appears that the latter was the superior predictor in this study (although no regression analysis was reported).

Because of the tendency of the I-S, T-F, and J-P dimensions to correlate with each other, Palmer (1997, 1998a) blended them into a composite measure that he called NFP, assuming that scores on intuition, feeling, and perceiving should all correlate and all bear some relation with ESP performance. He found in three separate databases a significant positive relationship between this composite measure and ESP performance in the ganzfeld in terms of the extremity of performance: persons higher on NFP produced more extreme scores, hitting and missing, than persons lower in NFP.

L. Braud and colleagues developed an eighty-eight-item exploratory scale to measure openness. The item construction was apparently based on face validity and was intended to yield three summary scores emphasizing openness to unusual experiences, openness in regard to various social and political issues, and openness to the self, including three subscales indicating facing even undesirable inner states ("undefensiveness"), general interest in the self, and willingness to self-disclose to others. No relationships between these measures and more standard scores for openness were ever reported. Across four studies,[28] the most promising subscale was the third one involving self-openness that was at least marginally significantly related to psi scoring in three of the four data sets. Less defensive, more inwardly oriented, and more disclosing subjects tended to score more highly in the tests of ESP. This relationship was partially confirmed by Bellis and Morris (1980), who found that two of the three subscales of the self-openness cluster showed some relationship with psi-hitting in their participants: the relationship with nondefensiveness was significant, and the one with self-disclosure was marginally significant. The other two parts of Braud's scale were again unrelated to scoring in their sample. No analyses in terms of scoring extremity were reported.

Two other well-standardized scales bear a strong conceptual and empirical relationship with openness, but in a negative direction. The Personal Need for Structure Scale[29] is intended to measure an individual's need for highly structured situations and problems and discomfort with ambiguity and open-ended exploration, and it has been found to be inversely related to artistic interests, flexibility, and measures of openness. As one would expect, given the findings just discussed with openness, it has also been found to be significantly *negatively* related to implicit ESP response in two studies (Carpenter and Simmonds-Moore, 2009b). A similar measure is the Need for Closure Scale, and it also has been found to relate negatively to ESP response.[30]

In summary, a relatively strong case can be made for the importance of openness (a strong personality antecedent of creativity) for extrasensory response. This has tended to hold across several different laboratories, experimental situations, and related measures. Most often the relation has been a positive one with ESP hitting, but positive relations with ESP extremity of scoring has been found as well. It may be that the more basic relationship is with extremity of scoring, but that in situations that are conducive to the positive scoring of more open people, this is generally expressed as a relationship with strong positive scoring.

MEASURES OF DIVERGENT THINKING

A number of investigators have developed measures of a person's ability to produce unusual and original productions when called upon to do so, based upon the belief that this is an important element in creative aptitude. Guilford and his colleagues developed measures of several intellectual skills such as fluency, originality, and flexibility and referred to them collectively as "divergent thinking." One of the more commonly used single instruments is his Alternate Uses test,[31] in which participants are asked to provide a number of possible uses for such things as paper clips or bricks, and the quality of the responses is rated. Other instruments developed to measure similar constructs include the Torrance Tests of Creative Thinking[32] and several tests of Wallach and Kogan (1965). Parapsychologists have paired several of these measures with ESP tests hoping to find positive correlations between this aspect of creative ability and ESP scoring. Results have been mixed.

Braud and Loewenstern (1982), in a study using a number of procedures designed to be creativity enhancing (discussed further below), found a significant positive relationship between alternate uses and ESP scores. Honorton (1967) combined alternate uses scores with a measure of creative motivation and found a significant positive relationship with ESP performance, but it is not clear whether or not the alternate uses test was a significant discriminator by itself. Levine and Stowell (1963) likewise found a predicted but only suggestively significant positive relationship with ESP for this measure when only their participants who believed that ESP was possible ("sheep") were considered. Disbelievers ("goats") showed the opposite pattern, as the experimenters predicted. Two studies by Schmeidler (1963, 1964b) produced significant negative relationships between alternate uses (combined with a measure of creative attitudes) and ESP. It appears from her tables that alternate uses carried the bulk of this negative relationship. Barron and Mordkoff (1968) found largely nonsignificant results in their study of time-linked physiological arousal in pairs of separated twins, although two of the highly creative pairs in terms of divergent thinking did show some evidence for such coordinated arousal. Overall they considered their results equivocal. Perez-Navarro and colleagues (2009b) found a null relation between ESP in the ganzfeld and their measures of alternate uses.

Using the figural scales of the Torrance Tests for Creative Thinking (TTCT), Schlitz and Honorton did not find a significant relation with ESP in their small, highly creative sample of Juilliard students when all cases were considered; however, when two outliers were removed, a significant positive relationship did emerge. Relationships were stronger with flexibility and elaboration. Roe, McKenzie, and Ali (2001) also reported relationships between figural Torrance scores (notably fluency, flexibility, and elaboration) and ESP that would have been significant if they stood alone, but not when corrected for multiple analysis (despite the earlier Schlitz and Honorton finding, they did not limit their prediction to the figural scales—had they made the specific predictions, the relationships surely would have been significant). The verbal scales bore no relation to ESP performance. Dalton used the Torrance verbal scales with all of her artistic participants and found no relationship with ESP for most of the subgroups of participants; however, her musicians did show a significant positive discrimination. Holt (2007) reported a null relation between ESP hitting and figural divergent thinking, although she found a significant negative relation between this measure and scoring extremity.

More research will need to be done before it will be clear just what relation to ESP performance can be expected with the various measures of divergent thinking. Two suggestions arise from these studies that deserve further test. First, the positive results found have tended to come from testing situations in which motivation was apparently high and creative activity was made salient. Subjects who did not believe that ESP was possible[33] or who were tested by skeptical, hostile experimenters[34] demonstrated reversals of the predicted relationship. Second, figural creativity, particularly flexibility and elaboration, may be a more reliable correlate with ESP scoring than the various measures of verbal divergent thinking. This pattern, if it proves to be true, would be congruent with First Sight theory. Such verbal test scores are highly correlated with other measures of verbal intelligence and represent a tendency to use analytical thinking in solving tasks. For that reason, First Sight theory would predict that persons scoring high on them might tend toward chance-level scoring and show negative overall deviations as often as positive.

Divergent thinking would even be expected to have a *negative relation* with ESP scoring *extremity*, as opposed to hitting. This is because persons high in divergent thinking of any kind would be expected to tend to rapid sequences of changing approaches to solving some problem. First Sight theory holds that instability of intention should produce rapid switching and chance-level scoring, while stability of intention permits a sustained directional tendency and extreme psi scores. This hypothesis receives some confirmation in Holt's (2007) finding that her divergent thinking measure correlated significantly negatively with scoring extremity.

Failure to find a clear relationship between divergent thinking and extrasensory perception is probably not a failure to demonstrate a relationship between psi and actual creativity. We should remember that these scores also do not show a reliable relation with creative production itself.[35] They correlate most effectively with each other, but numerous attempts to relate them to criteria such as artistic eminence or quality of creative work have produced meager and often conflicting results.

First Sight Theory may have something to offer in elucidating this failure to demonstrate clear linear relationships between divergent thinking and both creative production and extrasensory performance. Producing a genuinely creative production requires a capacity to generate original possibilities, but it also requires more than that. Sustained focus and disciplined attention are also necessary. Just as Kelly (1955) asserted that creativity requires construct tightening as well as construct loosening, many psychologists and creative persons themselves have asserted that sheer originality in itself counts for little in the business of successful creative work. Persons who score very highly on tests of divergent thinking may be athletic in their capacity for originality, and may even enjoy demonstrating that competitively, but unless their bursts of originality can be followed by sustained focus it will come to naught. If a person is motivated primarily by the intention to be original, one direction of work will be quickly replaced by another. In terms of First Sight theory, their intentions regarding their forming thoughts will quickly and repetitively switch. Such switching will create a series of alternations in what the mind considers for assimilation and disassimilation. On an ESP test, this will result in a tendency to produce chance-level scores, or low extremity. In creative work, it will result in the repetitive preconscious abandonment of developing elements of any given line of creative work, which will in turn result in a series of fitful little projects or promises of projects that are of little consequence.

First Sight theory, then, predicts that there must be important moderating variables to consider before the relation between divergent thinking skills and either ESP or creative work can be determined. One must also be interested in and capable of a sustained intention to produce a good product. Sometimes one holds to the structure of a craft, sometimes simply to an invariant wish to know.[36]

In general, this model holds that an unconscious wish to realize the meaning of extrasensory material, coupled with an invariant attention to inadvertent phenomena, should make the expression of such material more likely. Creative persons who are engaged in a psi task would be expected to display these things. At least two factors may be at work. First, demonstrably creative persons tend to be highly motivated and successful at producing effective performances when called upon to do so. Because of that, we may assume that their conscious motivation to perform is generally matched by an unconscious intention to do well (not all potentially creative persons have this happy harmony of intention). This unconscious wish to succeed should result in a tendency to construct allusions toward the potential meaning at the psi level. Another requirement of successful artistic work is that one suspends rational analysis at times and consults an inner field of sensed preferences, impulses, and incipient understandings. How does the poet find the next image, or the cellist sense the right emotional interpretation of a solo, or the actor's body find the right posture for a character? They must "feel their way," suspending clear decisions and cognitive analysis long enough for an implicit sense to emerge and declare itself. This sustained openness to the "felt sense"[37] and suspension of premature cognitive closure should allow a relatively stable directional tendency at the psi level of engagement and show itself as extreme scoring deviations, generally positive if psi expression fits the individual's intention at the moment.

THE CONTRIBUTION OF PSI TO CREATIVE ACTS

The First Sight model predicts that extrasensory factors participate with other preconscious processes in the construction of creative acts. I could locate no studies in which there was an attempt to influence the outcome of some creative act by serious artists, such as writing a poem or interpreting a piece of music, by some extrasensory intention. This rather obvious question cries out to be explored.

There are a number of studies, however, that examine responses that are somewhat like a creative act. The free association task of the ganzfeld study elicits an uncensored flow of ideas, and it has generally produced significant evidence of psi influence (usually high scoring, but sometimes extreme scoring as well), although null and even negative results have been reported.[38] Other studies have examined more restrictive forms of free association.[39] Ganzfeld studies are discussed further below.

Dreaming may be thought of as a generically "creative" act in which almost everyone engages; and dreams have often been found to express extrasensory intrusion.[40] Other creativelike activities that have been shown to express such intrusion includes producing hypnotic dreams,[41] freely drawing,[42] engaging in spontaneous social interaction in a congenial, unstructured group,[43] moving a Ouija board planchette,[44] free playing on the part of children,[45] and making up stories in response to cards from the Thematic Apperception Test.[46] Such "creative-expression" tasks have often shown either relatively high or relatively extreme ESP scoring, although null performance has been reported as well. The effect has often been moderated by other variables. For example, the effectiveness of drawn responses has been found to depend upon how expansive the drawings are and whether or not an agent is involved in the test,[47] spontaneous group interaction was more psi expressive when sessions were rated as less emotionally intense,[48] and Ouija board movements showed psi-hitting more effectively when the participants reported that they felt externally caused. Apparently, providing a situation or task that permits creative expression is one step toward evoking either extreme or positive scoring, but the manner in which the individual responds to the task is also critically important.

THE EFFECT OF MORE CREATIVE
APPROACHES TO THE PSI TASK

A number of other studies have examined aspects of participants' performance when they are being tested for ESP in terms of qualities that we may assume reflect the degree of creativeness being expressed, or else they have attempted to induce sets or mind states that are relatively creative before the ESP test is carried out. In ganzfeld studies, postsession reports have often found that participants who experienced a state with more "altered" imagery, body experience, and mood during their sessions scored more strongly than others reporting less of these qualities.[49] Stanford and colleagues[50] have examined actual session transcripts and found that the variability of the length of time making up discrete blocks of speech, or utterances, related positively to hitting. They interpreted this variability as reflecting the fluidity or spontaneity of the response. Another approach to the analysis of session transcripts was taken by Carpenter (2001, 2005a), who analyzed data from several laboratories and found that when persons expressed a more active involvement in their own imagery and more emotional openness toward it, they scored highly. On the other hand, those whose imagery showed signs of intellectualization and cognitive analysis scored below chance. Using a measure of creativity modeled after R. Holt's (1970) Rorschach score (involving primary process material and tolerance for irrational content), he found that more creative sets of utterances were associated with hitting when the high creativity scores were not accompanied by many signs of anxiety. When high anxiety was present along with high creativity, scores were negative. In these same data it was also found (unreported relationships) that scores on the measures of intellectualization and cognitive analysis were associated with scores that tended to depart very little in either direction from chance expectation (tight variance), whereas profiles indicating emotional openness successfully predicted more extreme deviation scores.

In still other ganzfeld studies, Sondow (1979) found that asking participants to free associate to the various target alternatives after they had gone through the ganzfeld session improved their hitting rate relative to other participants who did not carry out the free association; and she[51] also found that participants who reported making a slight effort in producing their material scored more positively than those who described their imagery as occurring to them in a completely uncontrolled way. Free association is a technique that would be expected to facilitate consulting the implications of imagery in a creative way, and making a bit of effort in generating the material would seem likely to show that the participant was creatively engaged in the task and not simply being a passive self-observer.

In a related study Braud, Shafer, and Mulgrew (1983) asked participants to project meanings onto a looping audiotape of the word *cogitate* and found that those who drew upon larger numbers of independent associations showed more positive intrusion of the ESP targets. A greater number of associations seem plausibly related to the aggressiveness and facility with which the participants searched their inner material. In the behavior of an unstructured group, as mentioned above, Carpenter (2002) found significant evidence of implicit behavioral reference to the ESP target when sessions were relatively lighthearted and spontaneous, with free-ranging thoughts and feelings, and found psi-missing when the group was extremely serious and focused on difficult emotional material. Palmer (1994) found that participants scored most highly when they reported having "felt drawn" to their choices, as opposed to when they chose them more rationally. However, this failed to replicate in a different ESP test.[52]

Even forced-choice ESP guessing tends to show more positive evidence of psi influence when the task is carried out more "creatively," in the sense of being more spontaneous or being freer of rigid, intellectualized patterns.[53] Finally, some reports have indicated that very high ESP performance may be found when persons with special facility for creatively consulting inner inadvertencies (such as professional artists or trained meditators) are themselves observed to be approaching their task in measurably more creative ways,[54] as compared to their peers who are not so creatively carrying out the psi task.

THE INDUCTION OF MORE CREATIVE
APPROACHES TO THE PSI TASK

A few studies have attempted to induce mental sets in participants that we might think of as more creative, but unfortunately the one that worked most elaborately toward this end did not use a comparison condition with which to test the effect of the manipulation. Anderson (1966) carried out a series of three studies with elementary school children in which a very playful, gamelike atmosphere was created around ESP guessing tests. The first two involved two classes over extended periods of time, and the third engaged the attention and energy of an entire school. The tests were carried out when the space program in the United States was in its fledgling stages, and all the tests involved trying to guess correctly in order to successfully do such things as launching a satellite, achieving orbit, and communicating from space. In the most elaborate of these, the tests were carried out by the principal using the school intercom to urge the students on to contribute their part to the space effort. Quite a pitch of excitement and interest seems to have been achieved; and overall high scoring was as well. Without a control condition, we can best evaluate the results by comparing them to other school classroom tests of ESP, which often showed significant effects of moderating variables such as the mutuality of teacher-pupil liking[55] but not overall significant scoring.

Pilkington (1984) built upon the inspiration provided by Anderson's study by having her second-grade participants produce fantasy material that they then used to rate targets that an agent was trying to "send" to them as compared to control targets. She did use a control condition (a relaxation exercise prior to the fantasy production) and compared that to an active, gamelike condition in which participants were engaged in fantasies about the characters E.T. and Elliott from the popular film *E.T.: The Extra-Terrestrial*. E.T. was imagined to have returned to his home planet, and he and Elliott were trying to communicate across the huge distance with telepathy. Her fantasy-induced group did perform above chance and considerably better than the control group, but with Ns of only six children in each group, meaningful statistical analysis was not possible. Her design is appealing though, and it awaits a larger test.

Stanford (1966a) reported another manipulation of set that we might think of as influencing creativity, or at least flexibility and spontaneity. With some participants he used a "closed deck" in which all targets were represented an equal number of times. He told them this fact and instructed them to keep careful count of their calls so that they could be certain of calling the symbols equally within the run, implying that this might help their performance. With another group he used an "open deck" in which targets were placed randomly, and often in unequal numbers. These participants were asked to be spontaneous in their responses and pay no attention to how frequently they might be using different symbols. The more spontaneous set did not produce higher scoring, but as Stanford predicted, it did yield more extreme scores, while the restrictive set produced scores that hovered closely to the chance line to a significant degree.

William Braud and Lendell Braud and their colleagues developed a straightforward means of evoking more and less creative sets (they called them "non-analytic" versus "analytic") in their participants, and demonstrated an effect on psi performance. In an ESP study,[56] all of their participants engaged in a relaxation exercise, and then half of them spent twenty three minutes carrying out tasks designed to induce an analytical mode of thought (such as solving math problems, counting the letters in words, reading passages in things like constitutional law and linguistic philosophy, and so on) while the other half passively listened to a gentle array of natural sounds (birds, crickets, wind, surf, rain), and slow, contemplative music. The group induced to be more cognitively free scored significantly more highly than those induced to be analytical. They followed this up with three studies in which the same sets were induced before participants carried out a PK test.[57] Again, the results showed significantly better psi performance in the group in which a more creative state of mind was evoked.

A study by Kreitler and Kreitler (1982) attempted to evoke a creative set in a somewhat similar way by arousing in one group of their thirteen- and fourteen-year-old participants what they called "personal-subjective meaning." They did this by conducting a friendly, playful, individual exercise for eight minutes in which they asked some of the students to communicate, as if to some other person, various aspects of some persons and things that were important to them, and to do that in metaphorical, symbolic ways. Free-ranging expression of ideas and feelings was encouraged. Many entered into this enthusiastically, inventing images, dancing, singing, or shouting. Then they were instructed to relax and sensitively report all bodily experiences of emotion of which they could be currently aware and then to fill out a sentence-completion blank that permitted a range of affective responses. The control groups were asked to fill out a rather impersonal sentence-completion blank in silence or simply to wait alone for an equivalent period of time. While the participants were doing these things, without their knowing it an agent was attempting to convey an emotion of anger to some of the participants using a psychodramatic enactment of some angry scene. For other participants, no agent was involved. The ESP response was measured from implicit references to angry themes (and other emotional themes) in the language used in the postsession introspections and sentence-completion blank. There was a highly significant difference between the groups that had been prepared differently: those in whom "personal-subjective meaning" had been induced produced many more references to anger and relatively fewer to other emotions. But perhaps the induction simply made participants angry? We are assured that this is not the case by a significant effect of the agent variable. When no agent was present, the excess of anger-implying responses was not present either. It only occurred with students for whom the unknown agent was "sending" the emotional message. And it was the creatively prepared students who showed this differential response. A secondary effect showed that not all of the participants were equally affected by the inductions. Prior to the ESP measure, the experimenter rated each child's response to the induction in terms of how fully they seemed to enter into it. The ESP effect was carried entirely by those who entered more fully and creatively into the spirit of the induction.

A nonstatistical study on psychokinesis also showed the importance of playfulness on the positive expression of psi.[58] Iris Owen and a group of friends devoted themselves to the task of trying to recreate the anomalous phenomena of nineteenth-century séance rooms with the device of a purely fictional "ghost," a character invented by the group. They hoped to demonstrate that these things might be expressions of the psychokinetic abilities of the living persons in the group and not necessarily the actions of a deceased person. The group met for a year and engaged in quiet but implicitly connected meditation in hope that an experience of an apparition of their "spirit" (Philip) might be generated. It was not. Then Owen hit upon the work of Kenneth Batcheldor (1979, 1984), who reported many dramatic, spontaneous physical effects (movements of objects, anomalous rappings, anomalous gusts of wind, etc.) in sitter groups. One of Batcheldor's recommendations was to create an active, partylike atmosphere, with joking, singing, and other things that people do when they wish to enjoy a moment in a creative, fun-filled way. Owen's group adopted this approach, changing the sessions to spontaneous and active times, with dancing, laughing, singing, and joking, not unlike the children studied by the Kreitlers. They were quickly rewarded, not with a visual apparition, but with a host of poltergeistlike noises and movements, including the complete levitation of a table that was not physically being supported in any way and a long series of intelligent responses from "Philip" to questions, issuing in the form of raps, in walls, ceiling, floor, and table. These phenomena continued unabated for many months whenever the group met to call them up, and a number of precautions made it seem apparent that the effects were anomalous and not being produced in any normal way.

SUMMARY ABOUT PSI AND CREATIVITY

The general trend of these findings supports the idea that psi processes and creativity are indeed related. A wide range of different but conceptually related findings supports this general contention, and while there are some failures to replicate particular relationships, I could not locate any reports of significant reversals of the expected effects. Psi information may well be expressed in many creative efforts, and psi tasks seem to be especially likely to express the intrusion of extrasensory material when the participants are more creative persons or at least are engaging in the current task in more creative ways.

Generally the greater psi effect is shown as hitting but sometimes as extreme scoring in both directions (although extremity of scoring has been much less frequently analyzed). The more general effect of creative inner searching may be a tendency toward greater scoring extremity, which tends to be expressed as high scoring if other conditions are propitious for the intentional pertinence of the psi task and the target content. Some illustrations of how such differences in condition might work can be taken from the last section. The participants of Anderson (1966), Owen and Sparrow (1976), and the Kreitlers (1982) were involved in psi tasks that were highly engaging and fun. They showed significant hitting in response to their creative involvement. Stanford's (1966a) participants carried out a rather impersonal guessing exercise with little room for personal engagement. In this case the more creative set produced extreme scores rather than uniformly high ones, as if some participants found the task meaningful and interesting and others did not—a result that would not be surprising in this situation.

This is congruent with the report of Howat (1994) mentioned above, which showed more open people performing more extremely than less open people. Her more open participants responded to being viewed unawares both by becoming more physiologically aroused *and* by becoming calmer, rather than one or the other. Whether they became more aroused or more calm was affected by other variables, primarily their vulnerability to anxiety, as measured by the neuroticism factor of the NEO-PI (see also chapter 12). It seems as if greater openness let these people be more unconsciously responsive to the extrasensory situation, while their level of emotional vulnerability determined the direction of their response.

The moral seems to be this: more open people and more creative approaches are likely to lead to increased responsiveness to nonlocal, extrasensory concerns as the First Sight model predicts, but the direction of response may often hinge more upon other variables. This is an area ripe for further research.

NOTES

1. See also Kelly et al., 2007.
2. Palmer, 1978.
3. Feist and Runco, 1993; Sternberg and Lubart, 1999.
4. Barron and Harrington, 1981; Dellas and Gaier, 1970; Eysenck, 1995; Freeman, Butcher, and Christie, 1971; MacKinnon, 1978; Simonton, 1999; Stein, 1968.
5. Bruchac, 1987.
6. Gendlin, 1997.
7. Barron, 1969; Holt, Delanoy, and Roe, 2004; Joesting and Joesting, 1969; Moon, 1975; Torrance, 1972.
8. Houtz and Krug, 1995.
9. Barron, 1995; Treffinger, 1985.
10. MacKinnon, 1965, 1978; Nicholls, 1972.
11. Dalton, 1997b; Holt, 2006; Moon, 1973; Morris, Cunningham, McAlpine, and Taylor, 1993; Morris, Summers, and Yim, 2003; Moss, 1969; Moss and Gengerelli, 1968; Schlitz and Honorton, 1992.
12. Anderson, 1966; Moriarty and Murphy, 1967.
13. Holt, 2007.
14. Morris, Cunningham, McAlpine, and Taylor, 1993; Morris, Dalton, Delanoy, and Watt, 1995.
15. Torrance, 1972.
16. Griffin and McDermott, 1998.
17. Holt, 2006.
18. Gough, 1993; Gough and Heilbrun, 1980.
19. Barron and Welsh, 1952; Welsh, 1981, 1987.
20. Welsh, 1981.
21. Costa and McCrae, 1985.
22. Dollinger and Clancy, 1993; Soldz and Vaillant, 1999.
23. Rawlings et al., 1998.
24. Watt and Ravenscroft, 2000.
25. Myers and Myers, 1980; Wiggins, 1989.

26. Furnam, Moutafi, and Crump, 2003; McCrae and Costa, 1989.
27. Thorne and Gough, 1991.
28. Braud, 1976, 1980.
29. Kruglanski, 1989; Neuberg and Newsom, 1993.
30. Perez-Navarro, Lawrence, and Hume, 2009a.
31. Guilford, Christensen, Merrifield, and Wilson, 1978.
32. Torrance, 1976.
33. Levine and Stowell, 1963.
34. Schmeidler, 1963.
35. Hocevar and Bachelor, 1989.
36. One method of wresting genuine production out of a welter of creative possibility is given in this quotation from Igor Stravinsky: "Will I then have to lose myself in this abyss of freedom? To what shall I cling in order to escape the dizziness that seizes me before the virtuality of this infinitude? However, I shall not succumb. I shall overcome my terror and shall be reassured by the thought that I have the seven notes of the scale and its chromatic intervals at my disposal, that strong and weak accents are within my reach, and that in all of these I possess strong and concrete elements which offer me a field of experience just as vast as the upsetting and dizzy infinitude that has just frightened me. It is into this field that I shall sink my roots. . . ." (Stravinsky, 1942; quoted in Barron et al. 1997, p. 194).
37. Gendlin, 1997.
38. Bem and Honorton, 1994; Milton and Wiseman, 1999; Palmer, 2003.
39. Stanford, 1973; Stanford and Schroeter, 1978.
40. Child, 1985; Dunne, 1927; Kanthamani and Broughton, 1992; Kanthamani and Khilji, 1990; Sherwood and Roe, 2003.
41. Honorton, 1969, 1972; Honorton and Stump, 1969; Krippner, 1968.
42. Bevan, 1947; Humphrey, 1946; Shrager, 1978; Targ, 2004.
43. Carpenter, 2002.
44. Palmer, 2001; Sargent, 1977.
45. Anderson, 1966; Anderson and Gregory, 1959; Tornatore, 1984.
46. Barron and Mordkoff, 1968; Kreitler and Kreitler, 1972.
47. Palmer, 1978, p. 166.
48. Carpenter, 2002.
49. Harley and Sargent, 1980; Palmer, Khamashta, and Israelson, 1979; Parker, 1975; Sargent, Bartlett, and Moss, 1981.
50. Stanford, Frank, Kass, and Skoll, 1989.
51. Sondow, 1986.
52. Palmer, 1995.
53. Cadoret, 1952; Ross, Murphy, and Schmeidler, 1952; Scherer, 1948; Stanford, 1966a, 1966b, 1968; Tart, 1976.
54. Carpenter, 2001, 2005a; Watt, 1996.
55. Anderson and White, 1957.
56. Braud and Braud, 1975.
57. Andrew, 1975; Braud, Smith, Andrew and Willis, 1976.
58. Owen and Sparrow, 1976.

Section IV

FIRST SIGHT AND OTHER RESEARCH FINDINGS

Individuals differ. Phenomenologically, we can say that we differ in our ways of being-in-the-world. Our personalities are not all the same, and our individual constellations of needs and goals and personal histories of experience are all essentially unique to each person, no matter how much people may also resemble each other. Drawing upon these individual constellations of meaning, each of us implicitly structures what and how we experience and what courses of action we choose. We do this both consciously and preconsciously. First Sight theory proposes that individuals use psi inputs in shaping experiences and actions in much the same way that more immediately accessible inputs are used, although in the case of psi, the use is almost always implicit and unconscious. Any gain in understanding how we use either the sensory or the extrasensory domain should be of help in understanding how we use the other.

Psychologists have been interested in defining and studying broad ways in which persons differ from one another in their basic approaches to life. Parapsychologists have applied some of these same dimensions of difference to research on psi. Two important areas are fearfulness and outgoingness. It would be a mistake to confound these two things, to assume that they are two ends of the same dimension. They are not. Some fearful people are quick to engage others, and some quiet and retiring people are relatively free of fear. These things are really best understood as separate domains of approach to life (they emerge as independent factors when character traits are analyzed statistically), and psychologists have studied them that way.

In the next two chapters we will examine the issues of fearfulness (or anxiety or neuroticism) and extraversion. Both have been studied extensively in general, and both have been of interest to parapsychologists as

187

well. We will not attempt to give an overall summary of what is known in these fields—many books by experts would be required for that. Rather, we will focus upon what parapsychologists have found in their research about how these matters are involved in our expression and use of psi information, and we will see how First Sight theory can be of help in understanding those findings.

In the small field of parapsychology, these two areas have been relatively widely studied. Many strong and apparently meaningful results have been reported, but apparent inconsistencies in findings have also occurred. Can First Sight theory clarify these inconsistencies and draw a picture of psi functioning that is more coherent and sensible than we have thought before? It can. The next two chapters spell out how this is so. The chapter to follow will discuss some other areas of research in less detail. Research on the belief in psi, hypnosis, and the importance of caring about the information to be retrieved, among other things, will all be placed in the context of First Sight theory to see how well its expectations fare in those areas.

14

Fear and Psi

Of all base passions, fear is the most accursed.

—William Shakespeare

THE POWER OF FEAR

Fear is a powerful emotional force and an important factor in ordinary perception and action. First Sight theory predicts that it should be important in extrasensory perception and psychokinetic action as well, in generally similar ways. The fearfulness of the perceiver, the fearsomeness of the thing to be perceived, and the stressfulness of the situation in which one is perceiving should all be influences that the perceiver consults implicitly when determining how to use psi information in constructing experience and guiding behavior. Parapsychologists have studied these matters. General psychologists have as well in regard to the use of information that is available to the senses. We may ask to what extent the findings of both conform to the expectations that would be drawn from First Sight theory.

Threat (a characteristic of a situation) and fearfulness (a characteristic or state of a person) are generally important in forming perceptions and actions, but their influences are rather complex. The issue of fear and its effect on perception and action is one in which the work of cognitive psychology blurs into that of clinical psychology. We often avoid things that are threatening, but sometimes we seek them out instead. We may avoid thinking of threatening things, but sometimes we think of them persistently or even obsessively. We may even tend to not perceive threatening things

189

when they are present, and then we speak of defense mechanisms such as denial or repression. Or, we may fail to experience how threatening we know something to be and then we speak of dissociation. On the other hand, one may be especially quick to perceive threats, and then we consider the person vigilant, or even paranoid.

For research to be adequate to the subject here, it must take this complexity into account. The situational context, the kind of perceptual response, the strength of the fear or threat, and the goals and needs (both immediate and long term) of the perceiver must all be considered.

Fearfulness and threat are important concerns for clinical psychologists as well as cognitive psychologists because of their commitment to help persons with various anxiety disorders, including post-traumatic stress disorder (PTSD), social anxiety disorder, and the various phobias, to name a few. A disabling degree of fearfulness of one sort or another characterizes persons who suffer from these conditions. Theories aimed at understanding these disorders often assert that persons who have them process information and act upon it differently than persons without them. We might speak of "clinical parapsychology" when we extend these questions about fear and anxiety to processing and acting upon psi information.[1]

EXPECTATIONS OF FIRST SIGHT THEORY

Our theory attempts to help understand and predict how an individual will engage and use meanings that are apprehended beyond his or her immediate sensory boundaries. We are presuming that at each moment the mind has access to a vast array of potential experiences, both within the sensory boundary and beyond it. Theory and research must help us understand the principles that guide unconscious thought in selecting certain items for consideration in constructing action and consciousness. How will these meanings be signed and then assimilated or avoided in ongoing experience and action? In the case of psychokinesis, how will they be expressed in the activity of extrapersonal physical events? In general, First Sight theory proposes that the mind gives priority to information that meets its needs in constructing experience and action.

How do fear and threat enter into the calculus of inclusion and exclusion? Clearly recognizing and avoiding danger are pressing needs for all organisms. At the same time, for many persons avoiding unpleasant or disabling states of anxiety are also pressing needs at times.

Our theory asserts that individuals differ to some extent from one another in terms of the needs and motives that are most important to them and that these personal needs and motives (and associated goals) affect unconscious thought processes as well as conscious ones. More specifically in the case of fear, we would predict that meanings that represent real potential danger (either generic or more idiosyncratically understood) should be especially pertinent and should generally receive priority from preconscious attention. In terms of preconscious prompts to action, we would expect that behavior aimed toward avoiding some danger would be facilitated. However, whether this vigilant prehension is assimilated into consciousness or not is a more complicated issue. We expect that it would tend to be assimilated if the following three things are all true: if it is not sensed to be too contrary to some ongoing committed engagement, if the mind senses that conscious awareness of the danger would be of help in dealing with it, and if the state of anxiety that might be aroused by the awareness is not felt to be in itself too disabling or painful (in which case conscious awareness would not be sensed to be helpful). When awareness is sensed to be too disabling or unpleasant, then awareness of the danger will probably be unconsciously avoided. Of course, behavioral avoidance of the dangerous thing and avoidance of awareness of the issue can and often do occur at the same moment.

Our theory also suggests that in order to understand how psi information is processed we can look for clues at what is known about how the mind handles other preconscious information (the Functional Equivalence Corollary). How do we deal with marginal sensory information when fear is a factor? Since First Sight theory assumes that the processing of psi information should generally parallel the processing of implicit sensory information, we look in the next sections at theories about how anxiety affects preconscious processing and then at studies that exposed people to fear-related information subliminally and assessed the consequences of that.

THEORIES ABOUT FEARFULNESS AND PRECONSCIOUS PROCESSING OF SENSORY STIMULI

Many different theories have been proposed about the role of anxiety in the processing of preconscious and conscious information. For example, Beck[2] has argued that anxious individuals use cognitive schemas that are biased toward threat and therefore display a bias toward responding to threat at both preconscious and conscious levels. Other theorists have emphasized different patterns at different stages of information processing. The point of view of J. M. G. Williams and colleagues at the University of Wales (1997) harmonizes especially well with the approach of First Sight theory. They argue that during early, preconscious stages of processing, anxious persons should be especially responsive to threatening information, but at later stages of processing they should be less apt to become actually conscious of threat in order to avoid developing a state of conscious anxiety.

RESEARCH ON ANXIETY AND PRECONSCIOUS PROCESSING OF SENSORY INFORMATION

Many studies have been carried out on the effects of threat in preconscious (sensory) information processing for more and less anxious individuals. At first glance, the findings of these studies seem rather mixed and confusing. Bar-Haim and colleagues (2007) have carried out a helpful meta-analysis that clarifies these findings and helps to articulate what might be expected with extrasensory processing.

Two major research protocols have been used to study these questions, and it is worthwhile to describe them here. The first method assesses how quickly an individual becomes consciously aware of some item of information that has threatening connotations. The second measures something at an earlier stage in information processing: how quickly preconscious attention is oriented toward some threatening item of information (even before awareness forms). In the arena of preconscious processing, attention precedes awareness.

The technique used for assessing the rapidity of forming awareness is called the *emotional Stroop technique*. This is a modified version of a widely used technique in cognitive psychology, the Stroop interference paradigm, named after the psychologist John R. Stroop (1935). In the basic paradigm the percipient is asked to quickly name the color of some stimulus that appears on a screen. Sometimes the content of the stimulus will match the color, and sometimes it will contradict it. For example, the perceiver may be expecting to see either the color red or green. What appears on the screen is one of two words: *red* and *green*, in one color or the other. The perceiver is asked to ignore the *content* of the word and respond only to the *color* of the image. If the word *red* appears in red, the task and the distracting content are matched. If the word *red* appears in green, then they are discrepant. A basic finding is that responding is faster if the color to be named and the content of the word are congruent. For example, if you are asked to name the color that the word blue is highlighted in, you would say red. It turns out that we are slightly slower at naming the highlight color when it clashes with the word than when the colors and the words match because we can't decide not to read the words when we see them—it happens automatically—and this interferes with trying to name the ink. Even though we consciously ignore the content of the word, the discrepancy between the task and the distracter acts to slow our response to some extent.

In the emotional Stroop procedure, the experimenter can assess interference that is caused, not by cognitive discrepancy, but by emotional threat. In this case the content of the word (or the quality of a picture) is either threatening or benign. If the person is relatively faster to name red or green if the content of the word is threatening (for example, *cancer*) than if the word is neutral (for example, *plate*), then we might describe the person as relatively "vigilant," alerted to faster awareness by the element of threat. On the other hand, if the person is relatively slower to name the color if it is associated with the threatening content, we may say that he or she is displaying "defensiveness." For the vigilant person the element of threat is preconsciously raising the sensed importance of the item and helping it come to consciousness more quickly. For the defensive person the opposite is true: the element of threat is provoking a preconscious avoidance of the item and helping it evade conscious awareness for a longer time.

Defensiveness has been of more general interest. Threat-related bias is thought to be demonstrated when color naming takes longer with a threatening stimulus than with a neutral one.[3] A variation of the procedure might have the threatening or neutral content delivered before the presentation of the color, sometimes subliminally. For example, a smiling or an angry face might be flashed so briefly that it cannot be consciously perceived, and then a colored object is shown and the perceiver tries to rapidly name it. A relatively defensive person will be slower in identifying the color when the angry face has preceded it.

The emotional Stroop paradigm was initially the most widely used one for studying the effects of threat on perceptual processing. However, researchers soon realized that the technique could not distinguish between a delay in focusing attention and one caused by some reluctance (conscious or unconscious) to either become aware of the content or to express it. Attention might be focusing on the threatening item very quickly, but color naming could still be delayed if there was a preconscious wish to not consciously know the threat or to confess the knowledge to the experimenter.

An alternative paradigm that was developed was called the *dot-probe paradigm*.[4] In this technique, two things are flashed briefly on a screen at the same time. One of them is threatening, and the other is neutral. Then a small object (called the *probe*) appears on the screen in the location that had just been occupied by one of the objects. The percipient's task is to indicate as quickly as possible when the second object has appeared. Since the probe is a mere dot and not a symbol with any meaningful connotations, no conceptual work is involved. Only the location of something appearing has to be identified. The response will be a little bit faster in the spot to which attention has already been drawn. If the person is prone to attend more to a brief stimulus that is threatening than to one that is not, then responses to the probes that appear in the location that had just been occupied by the threatening thing will be faster than those that appear in the other location. Because the probe itself is always emotionally neutral, any raw attentional bias toward or away from threat can be seen and separated from a possible reluctance or difficulty with knowing or expressing some threatening thing. A variant of this technique, called the *emotional spatial cuing paradigm*, has also been developed to study more specialized questions, but those details need not concern us here.[5]

It is important to note that both the emotional Stroop and the dot-probe paradigm can use initial stimuli that are either fully conscious or subliminal. The element of threat or nonthreat can be shown so briefly or faintly that it is never available to consciousness. When this is the case, we can learn something about how the mind is unconsciously attending to unconscious material. Since this is where psi information always resides, it is the studies using unconscious, subliminal threats that are of most interest here.

Bar-Haim's meta-analysis was based upon 172 studies that yielded 323 effects. Each study compared anxious and nonanxious percipients. Sometimes the anxious groups were clinical populations (phobics or persons with performance anxiety, for example), and sometimes they were defined by scores on self-report anxiety questionnaires.

In sheer aggregate, these effects seem quite mixed. However, when a finer-grained analysis is made, the patterns across studies become clear and sensible. In the emotional Stroop paradigm (when the cognitive decision of identifying a color is required), anxious people tend to respond *more slowly* when the contextual element is threatening than when it is neutral or pleasant. Control groups that are not so anxious do not show this difference. The effect is much stronger when the initial emotional stimulus is fully conscious than when it is subliminal, although it is present in the subliminal situation as well. This suggests that the decision making of anxious people is slowed down by previous exposure to something threatening when they have been required to become aware of it, but it is less affected (although still hampered) when the exposure is purely unconscious. The responses of nonanxious people are not compromised in this way by exposure to threatening material.

In the dot-probe paradigm (where the sheer placement of preconscious attention is assessed), anxious people are *faster* when responding to probes associated with threats than they are to probes associated with nonthreats. Nonanxious persons tend to respond in the opposite direction, more quickly to probes associated with nonthreats. These patterns are *stronger when the emotional stimuli are subliminal*. This implies that theorists like Beck are right when they assert that anxious people are especially oriented to the threatening aspects of experience and are especially quick to attend to them. People who are not anxious, on the other hand, tend to deploy their attention very rapidly away from negative things and toward things that are pleasant or neutral (this was especially true when the emotional stimuli were words rather than pictures). All of this occurs at a preconscious level of mental functioning. However, we must remember that this does not imply that more anxious people are also quicker to *respond* to threats.

As the emotional Stroop results show, they are actually slower, particularly if the threatening thing has become available to awareness and the person must grapple with the issues of knowing what is being seen and responding to it consciously.

To put it in a nutshell, when emotionally threatening sensory information is presented along with neutral information outside of awareness to an anxious person, he or she preconsciously deploys attention differently than a person who is not anxious. Anxious people tend to orient immediately to the threatening information and away from alternative information that is not threatening. People who are not anxious tend to do the opposite: they orient unconscious attention toward the pleasant or neutral information and away from the negative information. This applies to most real-life situations in which a multitude of information is potentially available subliminally. Anxious people focus quickly on any implicit signs of danger, while emotionally secure people attend quickly away from those things and toward pleasant and neutral things instead. This deployment of attention happens extremely rapidly, before a conscious experience of anything is formed in the mind.

When more and less anxious people have to go on to do some cognitive work (say, decide what is being seen, or make a signal as soon as a certain class of thing appears) in the context of an unconscious threat, they again behave differently. In this case the work is slowed down for the more anxious people relative to those who are not anxious. In a real-life situation, if some threat is present or even if it is only implicitly sensed, anxious people are a bit more impaired in their thinking, deciding, and acting than people who are not anxious. They appear to be expressing an internal conflict. On the one hand they are trying to correctly identify something, but at the same time they seem to be trying to avoid awareness of whatever might be threatening. In terms of First Sight theory, they are trying to "move toward" the thing and "move away from it" at the same time.

These are the principle findings of research on the effect of the anxiety of the percipient upon processing of emotional information that is sensory and subliminal. They square with the expectations of First Sight theory. Anxious people (as defined either by psychiatric classification or self-report) are especially concerned with information that has connotations of possible threat. Clinically, many of them have histories of traumas that have left the indelible knowledge that certain situations can be dangerous indeed, and these people are concerned with avoiding such things in the future.

Remember the distinction in First Sight theory between *weighting* and *signing*? Preconscious thought will weight threatening things particularly heavily in anxious people because of the sensed importance of those things, and it will express that weighting by quickly orienting attention toward those things in preference to less dangerous alternatives. When this significant information is signed, different considerations enter in. The more anxious person wishes to avoid any engagement with the threatening thing and at the same time to avoid the disorganizing distress that accompanies a state of anxiety. The information will be signed negatively, and unconscious avoidance behavior will be initiated. At the same moment, unconscious thought will suppress any awareness of the threat and use alternative information instead to form the contents of consciousness. Of course, if the threat persists and unconscious behavioral avoidance does not succeed in removing it from the situation, the information comes to be more likely to enter consciousness anyway. Even then, various distortions may accompany the awareness.

OTHER ASPECTS OF THREAT IN
RELATION TO PROCESSING INFORMATION

Up to now, we have only been considering the effect of threat in terms of the information that is being preconsciously accessed. But there are many other possible sources of threat in any situation, and these also have been found to influence information processing and the response to whatever is being processed.

There are many thousands of studies of different sorts that attest to the fact that a state of high anxiety tends to degrade an individual's efforts, unless those efforts have to do with directly addressing some perceived threat (particularly by getting away from it). The judgment, memory, efficiency, and morale of persons with high anxiety levels all tend to show impairment as compared with persons who are not anxious, particularly in the face of some threat or stress.[6] These impairments may be so severe as to qualify a highly anxious person for one of the anxiety disorders that have been defined by psychiatry. All of this leads us to expect that psi engagements of anxious persons should follow similar patterns: if a person is too anxious, deliberate efforts to express psi information or to exert psychokinetic effects will probably suffer in some way, unless the psi expression directly helps to relieve a threat.

I examine in this chapter the parapsychological literature that has accumulated that deals in some way with the issue of fear and danger as they relate to psi. Please remember that very few of the studies that are covered were carried out with First Sight theory in mind. Most were done before it was conceived. Still, just as with studies on memory or creativity or subliminal perception, it is legitimate to examine prior findings with an eye to assessing how well they accord with the expectations that would be drawn from theory. It is also justified in regard to this body of literature, because looked at en masse, it seems to be contradictory and confusing. It will be helpful if First Sight theory brings to it some order and clarity.

In order to examine the parapsychological literature that deals with anxiety, we will first draw a distinction between psi protocols that assess the sheer placing of unconscious attention and those that require some sort of cognitive response. Then we will need to assess how threatening the target information is, or how threatening other aspects of the situation are. And finally, we will need to see if the studies examining the effect of threat also used some classification of participations as being more or less prone to anxiety or perhaps even directly assessed their anxiety in the experimental situation. Many studies have not looked at such differences between participants.

We will expect that anxious persons will deploy unconscious attention preferentially to threatening extrasensory information and that nonanxious persons will not and will prefer instead to attend to neutral or positive things. This should be observed in studies in which the extrasensory or psychokinetic response is purely implicit or unconscious and does not involve conscious identification of the information.

When cognitive responses of some sort to extrasensory information are being assessed, we will expect that the response to threatening psi information, or to any psi information in threatening situations, will show some impairment for anxious persons relative to nonanxious persons. The strongest experimental designs with which to test these expectations will be ones that either use some valid (often implicit) measure of actual anxiety in the moment or that examine both the degree of the percipient's vulnerability to anxiety and the degree of threat in the situation. Many studies varied one of these things but not the other. In these cases we will expect findings that are less consistent.

In one situation, conscious identification that is attempted is very simple and rudimentary—an unarticulated feeling. In most cases, however, a more differentiated kind of cognitive work is involved, such as the identification of one out of a set of forced-choice targets or the production of fantasy material intended to be associated with a target.

In a few studies we can be fairly certain that some participants were in a state of anxiety during the test because some direct means (self-report or behavioral) has been used to identify that fact. In other cases, we will only know who is relatively prone to experiencing anxiety in general because of responses to self-report inventories. In these studies, it will be especially important to see how threatening the target material or the testing situation is, since being prone to anxiety should not lead to an actual state of anxiety unless something in the situation is calling for it at the moment.

In addition to the state of anxiety of the percipient, we also need to consider the impact of the degree of threat in the percipient's situation at the moment. This may often be the most powerful factor in determining an extrasensory response, even when the threat itself is not within sensory contact!

If parapsychologists had been seriously guided by the kinds of experiences that people report when they believe that they have had a "psychic experience," as some have advised,[7] one particular kind of event would have been studied in great depth: feelings of danger to oneself or to some loved one. Experiences of that particular sort are perhaps the most common kind to be found in the collections that have been made.[8] The same thing can be said for dream experiences seen as precognitive: fully half of them involve death, and the two next most common categories are accidents and injuries.[9] It seems a great irony that these prehension-of-danger responses have hardly been studied at all in the laboratory. In fact, almost the only studies of this sort that could be found involve the feeling of being stared at, and these have for the most part not been discussed as involving threat!

Finally, some studies will not examine the effect of anxiety as such, but rather some *psychological defenses against anxiety.* Sigmund Freud and other psychodynamic theorists have been creative in their descriptions of ways that people can respond inwardly to the potential threat of a state of anxiety. Three of them have especially drawn the attention of parapsychologists—vigilance, repression/distortion, and dissociation. First Sight theory will have expectations about each of these defensive postures.

Because the number of studies to be reviewed is fairly large, and because they differ on several dimensions that may be important, they will be discussed here in three general sections. The last large section will be further divided into several subsections:

- Studies examining unconscious psi responses
- Studies requiring a minimal level of conscious identification
- Studies examining conscious psi responses, involving some degree of cognitive effort
- Standard individual-testing procedures
- Group testing
- Testing in highly relaxed situations
- Use of threatening target material
- Studies that varied both anxiety proneness and threat of target
- Studies on defensiveness against anxiety rather than anxiety itself

STUDIES ASSESSING AN IMPLICIT, UNCONSCIOUS PSI RESPONSE TO THREATENING INFORMATION

There are three different sets of studies that have examined this question. One has assessed precognitive physiological responses to some negative event that will soon happen in the future, and these responses are compared to those that precede a pleasant or neutral event. These have been called studies on "presentiment" or "prestimulus response." The second group is similar in that it has assessed physiological responses to an extrasensory meaning, but the event is in the present rather than the future. Only one kind of generally aversive situation has been studied this way—the person is either being stared at or not being stared at by some other person without knowing when this is happening. In the third group of studies it is not a person's unconscious physiological response to an extrasensory meaning that is measured. Instead, these studies assess a response to either a future or a current negative extrasensory event by seeing how it implicitly affects some other psychological process, such as how much one experiences liking something when it is presented to full awareness. The expectations drawn from First Sight theory will be given with each group, and then the empirical results will be described.

PRESENTIMENT STUDIES

Theoretical Expectations

First Sight theory presumes that one is perpetually engaged unconsciously with an extended universe of potential meanings, including those that will develop in the individual's future experience. Ones that are closely impending should be particularly pertinent, and ones that will be aversive should be the most pertinent of all. This heightened pertinence should be expressed by fixing unconscious attention upon the event to come, as if preparing to deal with it. Persons who especially find the given event more aversive should be especially apt to show this anticipatory response of fixated attention. How might such unconscious attention be expressed? By an *anticipatory* arousal of the same sorts of response that are known to attend an event when it occurs in the full light of present consciousness. People have many well-studied physiological responses to danger and stress: changes in autonomic activity, heart rate, brain-wave patterns, eye fixation and dilation, and others are all reliably observed.[10] Changes in these things in response to an aversive event that is shortly to occur in the future can all be taken as evidence that unconscious attention has seized upon it in an extrasensory fashion and is guiding an anticipatory response to it. Theory predicts that such danger-related anticipatory responses should be especially likely when the events to come are more aversive and when the individual is more prone to find them unpleasant.

Research Findings

Dean Radin (1997) initiated this fascinating line of research. His procedure was elegantly simple and well conceived. A participant is seated in front of a computer monitor and hooked up to leads that will capture a continuous reading of electrodermal activity (EDA), which is commonly used to measure physiological responses to stressful events (a person's skin becomes more electrically conductive when he or she is alarmed to even a slight degree). The participant is led to understand that a series of pictures will appear on the monitor at some certain interval, and they should simply wait and see them when they are shown. Some of the pictures will be emotionally disturbing (scenes of violence, accidents, or erotic activity), and some will be emotionally neutral. A computer then controls the random selection of the appearance of the preselected set of pictures.

In each of three studies, Radin found that when the pictures were presented to consciousness and being viewed, the EDA readings showed the familiar response pattern: a spiking and gradual decline of activity when the picture was disturbing that was not found when the picture was emotionally neutral. However, the readings just *before* the computer's random decision was made and the picture appeared also showed an *anticipatory response* (or "presponse") of the same sort that was smaller in magnitude but still sufficient to statistically discriminate between the disturbing and the neutral pictures. Thus, the participants not only showed the familiar sort of arousal to viewing something disturbing but also showed an anticipatory response (unconscious to them) over the three-second period *before* it appeared.

This initial finding of an anticipatory EDA effect was then replicated by a Dutch colleague of Radin's, Dick Bierman,[11] and this was followed by more replications by the same authors.[12] Radin then followed with three more studies[13] that not only showed the discrimination between the preselected disturbing and neutral pictures but also demonstrated that an even finer discrimination could be achieved by asking the participants themselves to rate how emotionally disturbing they found the pictures to be. The more the picture was personally seen as arousing, the stronger was the anticipatory response.

Other replications of this EDA effect followed the initial reports, by Norfolk (1999), Parkhomtchouk and colleagues (2002), Spottiswoode and May (2003), Wildey (2001), and Alvarez (2010). Spottiswoode and May changed the stimulus from emotionally disturbing and neutral pictures to the sounding of an unpleasant auditory alarm versus periods of silence and found the same difference in anticipatory response. Both Radin (1998) and Spottiswoode and May (2003) also added an important measure of individual difference: Both found that participants who were more emotionally reactive to the startle when it occurred were the ones who most strongly anticipated it by a presentiment response. Thus a behavioral measure of individual emotional reactivity to the pictures was added to the self-report assessment of the same thing used by Radin (2004a). This dimension of emotional reactivity will come up again later when we consider research that has used other, conceptually congruent measures that are intended to predict more generally an individual's vulnerability to having a fearful response to events.

Other conceptual replications of the presentiment effect have assessed other aspects of physiological response to alarm or emotional upset: brain activity as measured by functional magnetic resonance (fMRI),[14] heart-rate variability,[15] pupilary dilation and spontaneous eye movements,[16] changes in slow cortical potentials,[17] heart rate,[18] and EEG activity.[19] Some of these studies used as stimuli upsetting versus neutral pictures, some used unpleasant noises versus pleasant tones, some used glaring flashes of light versus calm darkness. All of them found clear, statistically significant evidence for a prestimulus response to the more emotionally upsetting stimuli as compared to neutral stimuli—a difference that would be anomalous without the psi hypothesis.

One other difference between participants has appeared to be important in some studies: gender. Females have sometimes shown stronger presentiment effects than males. This may be especially so in regard to emotional pictures. This makes psychological sense, because females have been found to have stronger aversion to the sorts of negative pictures generally used in these studies than males do. Most used the standardized pictures of the International Affective Picture Series (IAPS).[20] The norms for those pictures showed that males rated every one of them as less negative and less arousing than females did. Also, an fMRI study has shown that males have significantly fewer brain regions than women that register response to pictures thought of as disturbing.[21] Thus, this effect of gender seems to be another case in which the individual for whom a given stimulus is more disturbing is the one more likely to fix attention upon it prior to its occurrence and express that with an anticipatory emotional response. Broughton (2004) found an insignificant trend in the predicted direction between presentiment response and a measure of neuroticism, although it is noteworthy that he compared responses, not to emotionally negative and neutral (or positive) pictures, but rather to more arousing (positive and negative) pictures to less arousing ones. His failure to find an overall presentiment effect and the lack of a clear correlation with anxiety proneness would certainly seem more likely in these circumstances. He did not report an analysis in terms of gender.

Through 2009 there have been twenty-three studies on this presentiment effect with human subjects, and the results have been impressively consistent. Eighteen of the studies have been statistically significant, and only one showed an insignificant trend in the opposite direction. Two studies using animals have also been confirmatory, one marginally significant[22] and the other strongly so.[23]

Agreement with Theory

We expected that such studies should find that the fixation of unconscious intention upon an impending negative event would be expressed
by an anticipatory physiological arousal of the same sort that occurs when
the organism is responding to such an event in present awareness. We expected that such a "presponse" would be strongest when the event is more
aversive, and it should occur most reliably to persons who are especially
vulnerable to such a stress response. These expectations have been strongly
confirmed by this body of research.

STUDIES ON AN EXTRASENSORY,
PHYSIOLOGICAL RESPONSE TO ONGOING THREAT

Studies in this section are almost entirely on one threat-related situation,
but not completely. A few other studies have examined physiological
responses to the distress or alarm of another person in the experimental
situation—the sender, when the situation is one of a sender and a receiver.
The great bulk of research, however, has been carried out on one situation:
being stared at.

Expectations of Theory

Danger or distress for oneself or some other person who is emotionally
important should be salient issues for the participant in a psi study. If the
other person in distress is of strong personal significance, the effect would
be expected to be stronger than if the relationship is an indifferent one.[24]

In regard to the situation most at issue here, being secretly watched is
something that most people find at least slightly threatening under most
circumstances. The biologist Rupert Sheldrake (2003) argues that this
probably has an evolutionary basis in the relation between predator and
prey. Being watched surreptitiously can be dangerous! The fear of being
watched is more acute for some persons than others. If severe enough, it is
one of the central diagnostic features of social anxiety disorder or paranoid
schizophrenia. In a civilized and free society, being killed by a predator is
not such a constant issue, but being evaluated is, and being "peeped at" in
a sexualized manner is especially threatening for many persons. In societies
that are less free, surveillance can be a relentless and demoralizing concern.
Of course, sometimes being watched can have the opposite connotations
if there is a strong context of love and caretaking, as a child with a parent.
But in general, discovering that one is being watched is at least initially
unpleasant and unnerving in most circumstances. Much scientific evidence
supports this general perception. For example, being watched (not by inti-

mates in intimate situations) decreases cognitive efficiency,[25] increases feelings of shame and physiological stress response,[26] increases perfectionistic concerns,[27] and diminishes creativity;[28] and in apes it increases agitated behavior.[29]

Since being surreptitiously observed is something that most people experience as being at least mildly dangerous, First Sight theory would predict a percipient will fix unconscious attention upon an extrasensory prehension of being observed contemporaneously just as he or she fixes attention upon unpleasant events (such as gruesome photos or blasts of noise) that are impending in one's personal future. Since we are assumed to live unconsciously in an extended universe in space and time beyond immediate organismic boundaries, both the near future and the currently unknown will be of similar interest and will be drawn upon equally. And we expect that the mind will express the fixation of attention by initiating the same sorts of stress responses that it uses to respond to dangers when fully aware, both in order to begin to deal with a possible danger and to inform consciousness that some sort of danger might be ongoing. Unconscious electrodermal activity, for example, should tend to increase during periods in which one is being secretly observed. As in the case of dangers-to-come, it should be persons for whom being observed is especially aversive that will most reliably show such a stress response, or it should be situations that do not clearly obviate a sense of danger (such as protective viewing by an intimate other) that will most reliably evoke it.

THE FINDINGS OF RESEARCH

An Agent in Distress

Only four studies have reported findings about an unconscious, extrasensory, physiological response to a condition of danger or distress to another party in the experiment, and three of these are only described in a short report. Two studies involved a momentary condition of distress for a sender who was not intimately connected to the participant. Tart (1963) acted as both experimenter and agent in a situation in which participants thought that they were trying to identify moments in which they were being shown very dim, subliminal impressions (actually none were shown). They were connected to equipment that monitored their electrical skin conductance as the session proceeded. Tart, in another room, was hooked to a device that could deliver an uncomfortable shock. Each session was divided into three periods. In one period, the control, no current was sent. In the other two conditions an electrical charge was generated, but half of the time it was sent to Tart and half the time it was diverted to an electronic resistor, sparing Tart his punishment. Analysis of the data did not show that electrical activity was higher for the shock versus the two nonshock conditions as Tart expected. It was higher for both conditions in which a charge was delivered versus the control condition. The participants unconsciously expressed an emotional response to the generation of the charge but showed no response to Tart's being shocked or not (their clairvoyant responsiveness was present, but their telepathic empathy was lacking). In another study done before the days of research ethics boards, Rice et al. (1966) suddenly fired a gun behind the back of an agent in one room while the participant was being monitored for galvanic skin response in another. There was no personal relationship between the agent and the participant, and the latter's GSR showed no response to his moments of alarm. Rice's other two studies, however, involved agents who were closely related to the participant, and an unconscious response was demonstrated. In one study daughters served as agents and mothers as percipients. Again, a gun was fired behind some of the daughters and not others. The GSR records showed that those whose daughters experienced the alarming event experienced greater arousal than those whose daughters were undisturbed. Rice's final study used husbands as agents and wives as percipients. Some of the husbands were required to immerse their feet in painfully cold water, and others were not. The GSR responses of the wives again showed higher arousal in the distress versus the control condition.

Being Stared at Unawares

A much more substantive and well-reported body of work has accumulated around the situation of being looked at remotely. This line of work was begun by William Braud and colleagues at the Institute of Transpersonal Psychology in California.[30] They were hoping to improve on research that had attempted to test the folk belief that people can often intuitively "know" when they are being stared at (this line of work will be discussed below, when we examine research in which the response has had more of a cognitive component). They took continuous electrodermal recordings of their participants ("starees") during the session, which was broken up into twenty blocks of time. During ten of the blocks, the participant's image was observed via video camera by an experimental assistant ("starer") in another room, and during the other ten blocks the participant was not observed. The stare/no stare conditions were randomly assigned, and no sensory cue of the observation or lack of it was available to the staree. Braud added one other element: he compared normal, unselected participants with others who had undergone about twenty hours of intensive "connectedness training." This training involved reading materials and viewing films that presented concepts about the possibility and desirability of experiential merger between two people. Group exercises involved staring in another person's eyes for long periods while trying to develop a sense of attunement of feelings and thoughts and becoming comfortable with this. Later group and individual discussions focused on the intellectual objections and emotional resistances that arose during such exercises. All of these participants reported that they grew in their sense of attunement with one another and came to enjoy and value this.

Who was doing the staring with these two groups? For the unselected participants it was an assistant whom they did not know. For the ones trained in merger, it was a fellow trainee in the course, with whom they had learned to tolerate and enjoy an unusual degree of closeness. Braud's unselected participants showed the response that one would expect given the assumption that being stared at secretly by a stranger is a bit threatening: their electrodermal activity increased when they were being stared at as compared to periods in which they were not being observed. However, the connectedness-trained participants did the opposite: When they were being viewed, their EDA decreased, showing that they became slightly calmer. They responded as if being calmed by the attention of a trusted intimate.

Several studies followed up on this result, but only with participants who were not specially trained in connectedness. Schlitz and LaBerge (1994) reported two replications and found in both a significant tendency for EDA to be higher when being monitored than when not. A further study followed by Radin, Taylor, and Braud (1995), which also significantly replicated the effect. Failure to replicate the effect was reported in two studies by the skeptical experimenter Richard Wiseman and a colleague.[31] A third of their studies did significantly replicate, but the authors noted that some flaws in randomization might have compromised this result. That the experimenter can be an important variable in these studies was demonstrated by a later report by Wiseman in collaboration with another experimenter who had previously been successful in demonstrating this effect, Marilyn Schlitz.[32] Each experimenter served as starer with half of the participants who were otherwise drawn from the same pool, and they were tested in exactly the same situation in the same ways. Schlitz's participants again significantly demonstrated the effect, and Wiseman's again did not. Schlitz and Wiseman collaborated in two additional studies designed to replicate this differential effect of experimenter.[33] One produced null results, and the other significantly demonstrated the effect again.

Several reports followed the initial one on this staring effect, and by 1997 a meta-analysis of eleven studies showed a highly significant overall effect of staring on raising the electrodermal activity of persons being viewed.[34] A later meta-analysis[35] included additional studies and made the conservative assumption that studies that showed participants becoming calmer when being viewed would be treated as contributing counter results even though (as in the initial study by Braud, Shafer, and Andrews with intimate viewers) the effects were anticipated and were conceptually congruent with the understanding of EDA as measuring an extrasensory response to relative calming versus threat. The overall effect size as thus measured was smaller but still significant across studies and could not be accounted for by methodological problems. Later studies have not altered this general picture. The effect appears to be genuine.

These meta-analyses show that a general effect of increased arousal in response to being stared at unawares is a real and reliable phenomenon, but they also necessarily blur over the effects of other variables that affect when and to whom the effect is most likely to occur. Not many studies looked at such additional variables, but those that did found results that are sensible in terms of First Sight theory. For example, Howat (1994) found that people who were more prone to be anxious (higher N scores on the NEO-PI) showed the effect to a marginally more significant degree than participants less prone to be anxious. She also found that persons who were more perceptually defensive (slower to note the presence of a threatening subliminal stimulus) responded with less arousal to the extrasensory act of being stared at than did people who were perceptually vigilant (faster to respond to the subliminal threat). Juniper and Edlmann (1998) conducted another study that found meaningful moderators of the staring/arousal effect. They found that one of their starers (a male) evoked significantly more electrodermal arousal in the participants than the other (a female) did. But this difference was contributed entirely by the female participants. In a great deal of psychological research, women are found to be generally more physiologically responsive to threatening stimuli than men, and this study found that it was the female participants who were most responsive to being stared at by the male starer. When stared at by the female, on the other hand, they showed no particular arousal at all.

Agreement with Theory

We expected that some current, ongoing situation of relative threat to oneself or to someone else of personal importance should tend to seize unconscious intention and that this would be expressed by an increase in the same sort of physiological arousal that we generate when consciously threatened. Two studies showed a rise in EDA by persons whose family members were being distressed relative to control participants whose family members were undisturbed. Although the data are scanty, the results are in the expected direction and deserve further study. In regard to the paradigm that was much better studied, being covertly watched by a stranger is at least mildly threatening for most people, so we expected that an extrasensory response should be discernable when this is happening. By virtue of the meta-analyses, we may conclude that there is strong evidence that this is true: being viewed unawares by a stranger can evoke a subtle, unconscious physiological response as if to a potential threat, and this is expressed in increased electrodermal activity. Being viewed in a caring way by a trusted intimate seems likely to have the opposite effect of calming, although this has not been so often tested.

What can be made of the anomalous results of Wiseman-as-experimenter? This does not seem so mysterious when we remember the assumption of First Sight theory to the effect that one is continuously engaged unconsciously with one's entire situation. It is the pertinent aspects of a situation that should be most referred to in weighting various elements of it and constructing an unconscious response to it. When one is a participant in a psychological experiment, the intentions and motivations of the experimenter are an important part of the situation in which one has agreed to play a role. If the experimenter wishes to not get results, this is also part of the situation to which one is responding. Which is the greater threat? To be stared at on a computer monitor without any real consequences forthcoming, or to displease the person who is, for the moment, running the show? Of course, speculations like these are not really explanations until they are themselves tested in research. It will be intriguing research to do, as the findings of Wiseman and Schlitz (1997, 1999) and Schlitz et al. (2005) imply.

STUDIES ON IMPLICIT PSYCHOLOGICAL EXPRESSIONS OF EXTRASENSORY FEAR RESPONSE

Expectations of Theory

Physiological responses like heart rate changes and electrodermal activity are not the only implicit responses to unconscious fear-related information. There are psychological effects, too. Once again, First Sight theory predicts that if some fearsome thing is impending in the near future or is ongoing but beyond sensory contact, the unconscious mind will focus attention upon that fact and will respond accordingly. This response will be discernable by examining inadvertent expressions of the fixation of attention, such as changes in emotional assessment of the thing when it is consciously seen (it may be disliked less), or in the speed of responding to some conceptually related thing (it may be perceived more quickly), or in the likelihood of spontaneously emitting allusions to the thing if the situation permits such free responding. For example, persons whose telepathic agents had viewed ugly pictures of spiders might be more likely to produce imagery that is dangerous, or spiderlike, or weblike in subsequent dreams or free associations. And it is persons who are especially prone to respond with anxious vulnerability to the stimulus when it is conscious that are most expected to show such implicit responses.

As in other areas, we expect a close parallel to patterns found with sub-liminal stimulation. Several examples of analogous subliminal processes can be cited. For example, Shevrin (2001) found that subliminal exposure to aversive events can produce classical conditioned learning. Gray et al. (2009) showed that subliminal presentations of frightening material in-duced a heightened tendency to quickly perceive angry rather than neutral faces (but only for people who were high in vulnerability to anxiety). Di-jksterhuis and Smith (2002) found that subliminal exposure to negative words caused a kind of emotional habituation—their participants rated them less negatively after the unconscious exposures.

Findings of Research: Implicit Avoidance of Frightening Material

Daryl Bem (2011) presented participants with a series of simple prefer-ence choices, but he used their choices to cause them to be shown, in the immediate future, either a neutral or a frightening, aversive picture. He assumed that their precognitive prehension of the implicit consequences of their choices would lead them to make the decisions that minimally exposed them to the frightening material. All participants were shown pairs of emotional pictures drawn from the International Affective Picture Series. The pairs were matched for general appeal, so people would tend to like one as much as the other. Still, they were asked to make a choice as to which one they preferred a bit more than the other. Immediately after their choice, the computer running the session made a random decision as to whether the picture chosen would be linked to either the frightening or the neutral picture. Then they were shown the picture that their choice had just implied. He found that, in fact, people did succeed in successfully avoiding the fearful exposures to a statistically significant degree. He then divided his participants into two groups depending upon their responses to a short questionnaire assessing their boredom proneness (or stimulus seeking). He thought that the easily bored, stimulus-seeking participants would be especially oriented to move on to events in the immediate future. As he expected, it was this group of participants who showed the effect sig-nificantly more strongly.

Findings of Research: Precognitive Habituation

Bem (2003, 2011) has also initiated a clever series of studies on what he calls "precognitive habituation." In them he has shown that precog-nitive ESP targets can influence judgments of preference. It is part of a larger series (including the study just mentioned, on avoidance of fearful experience) in which he has attempted to show that events that are to be experienced shortly in the future can have implicit effects upon psychological processes that are similar to the effects seen when the same kind of material is presented prior to the response. Part of his work has involved exposing participants to material that is negatively arousing, and it is this aspect of his research that is of interest here. In his first study, Bem wanted to demonstrate a kind of "precognitive habituation," analogous to the subliminal habituation of Dijksterhuis and Smith (2002). It is well known that repeated exposure to something tends to result in a diminished emotional response to it. For example, frightening pictures that are repetitively seen (either supraliminally or subliminally) will come to be seen as less upsetting.

Bem reversed this effect in time by showing his participants pairs of pictures that were matched for how intensely unpleasant they were for people in general. He asked them to pick which of each pair they liked a bit better. After their choice was made, his computer randomly picked one of the pair as the ESP target and exposed this picture subliminally several times. He expected that the one that would be shown shortly in the future would be picked as a bit more likable (less intensely unlikable) than its partner. His results bore him out. He also included a two-item measure of "emotional reactivity" that asked people how attuned they were to their own reactions to frightening or gruesome things and how intensely upsetting they found such things to be. When he summed responses to these two items, this score was shown to mediate the ESP effect: persons who were highly emotionally reactive demonstrated precognitive habituation, others did not.

Bem then went on to successfully replicate this effect in two other studies and found again that it was the emotionally reactive participants who were demonstrating it. He also found that many more women than men showed the effect, but since many more women than men also scored as highly emotionally reactive, the two things are confounded. Some other analyses showed that it is emotional reactivity, and not gender per se, that is the important issue. He then carried out a study in which the postchoice exposures were fully conscious and not subliminal. The effect occurred again, but only if participants were instructed to keep their eyes open during the displays! (Many women in particular were tending to keep their eyes closed during the most unpleasant pictures.) Then he asked a skeptical colleague at another university to replicate the study and found that the skepticism of the experimenter did not interfere with the effect in this case. It was confirmed very significantly—again, only by the more emotionally reactive participants.

Four other studies in the Bem paradigm on precognitive habituation of negative emotion have been reported. Savva, Child, and Smith (2004) did not assess emotional reactivity using a questionnaire, but instead they tested a population of persons known to have phobias to spiders as compared to others who were not phobic. They exposed them all to matched pairs of spider pictures, asked for a preference, and then randomly picked one of the pictures for subliminal exposures. The spider phobics demonstrated habituation to the future exposures; the others did not.

Batthyany et al. (2009) conducted a precognitive habituation study but added a couple of wrinkles. They used words as well as pictures as stimuli and included another participant trait variable in addition to emotional reactivity—"affect regulation" (high scorers report being able to recover adaptively to high levels of emotion, whereas low scorers become dysfunctional or "fall apart" when highly upset). This variable would seem to be similar to the Vulnerability facet of NEO-PI Neuroticism. They also replicated Bem's basic finding of habituation, but it was again only to intensely negative stimuli. And they found again that the effect was only present for those who were emotionally reactive. Participants high in affect regulation also showed the effect, whereas low scorers on that dimension did not. The habituation effect was found most strongly for persons who were high on both dimensions; that is, persons who react intensely to negative stimuli and also report being able to adapt to that emotional state effectively. Since habituation is one way of responding adaptively to the repeated exposure of something intensely negative, this finding is sensible.

Carpenter and Simmonds-Moore (2009b) carried out a similar study on a general population of participants but used a much less intensely negative set of photographs than Bem or Batthyany. Rather than using Bem's emotional reactivity questions, they collected scores on Neuroticism as measured on the NEO-PI. They found no overall habituation effect using the mildly negative targets and no mediating effect of neuroticism.

Parker and Sjöden (2010) used a similar design to that of Bem, but the relationship found between emotional reactivity and habituation was not significant, although in the right direction. They also had another way of separating the reactivity of the participants that would be expected to have even more validity, however. They tested the same participants in a subliminal habituation task using the same negative and neutral materials used in the ESP test. They found that those participants who showed habituation to negative material in the subliminal situation also showed it in the extrasensory one as well. Those who showed no subliminal habituation also showed no extrasensory habituation.

One other study on an implicit psi response to future exposures also used spider phobics, but it did not test for precognitive habituation.[36] The researchers adapted the emotional Stroop paradigm, discussed earlier in this chapter, by exposing their participants to spider stimuli after rather than before they performed a reaction-time task using spider-related words. They found no evidence for an ESP-based interference on reaction times.

Summing up the work reported on extrasensory (precognitive or contemporaneous) habituation, there seems to be a solid trend toward replicating the phenomenon, particularly when the emotional vulnerability of the percipient is taken into account and when it is known for certain that the negative material is actually strongly aversive for them. The extrasensory version of an emotional Stroop paradigm may not be as useful for parapsychology, but only further research could determine that for sure.

Findings of Research: Imagery Experienced in Dreams

It has been known for a long time that material to which a participant is exposed subliminally often tends to be referred to later in the participant's dreams.[37] First Sight theory would expect a similar kind of reference to occur for psi information. Since dream imagery is generally understood to be autonomously generated and outside of conscious control, research involving dreamed material is best treated as another example of implicit psychological effects as opposed to the somewhat "dreamlike" imaginings that are generated in waking free-response studies. These latter are still conscious productions, guided and censored by conscious concerns, and they will be treated in a later section. We expect that emotionally upsetting material should be particularly arresting for unconscious attention and that this should be expressed in research findings using dreaming experience.

Four studies have examined the question. Krippner and Zeichner (1974) reported a study carried out in a dream laboratory in which dreamers hoped to produce dreams that made accurate reference to art prints that were being viewed by senders during the periods of dreaming (rapid eye movement) sleep. Their results were successful. When the prints were rated as to how emotionally negative they were, the successful ESP effect was found to occur only using the more negative pictures.

Dalton, Steinkamp, and Sherwood (1999) carried out a similar study, only the dreams were generated by their participants at home rather than in a laboratory. Target video clips were shown in the laboratory on the designated nights. Overall, dreams succeeded in expressing target-relevant imagery and mood sufficiently that target clips could be distinguished objectively from decoys. Again, the effect was carried entirely by the target clips that were rated as being more negative and potentially upsetting. Sherwood et al. (2000) repeated the procedure with a new group of participants and found the same results. As before, it was the emotionally negative clips that were responded to in the dreamers' imagery.

There were only three participants in this study, and no measures of emotional reactivity were taken from them. However, two of them were female, and inspection of the figures given in the report make it clear that the two females contributed all of the significant hitting performance on the negative targets (the significant habituation). With such small numbers there is little one can conclude, of course, except to say that the pattern is consistent with that reported by Bem: females, who tend to be more highly emotionally reactive to negative stimuli, again displayed the effect more strongly than the male. Unfortunately, the other studies on dreams also did not examine differences in participants in their proneness to emotional reactivity and reported no sex differences, so the importance of these things in the domain of dreaming psi cannot really be assessed as yet.

One final study by Sherwood's group[38] did not find overall psi hitting. Of the three participants, one scored significantly well, one significantly below chance, and one at chance. The one who scored significantly above chance showed the same positive correlation with ratings of how upsetting the targets were that had been found before. The one who scored significantly below chance showed the opposite correlation. The preponderance of his missing performance was with the highly negative targets. First Sight theory would interpret this result as indicating that the negative targets are having the firmest hold on unconscious attention as before, but that since some other factor appeared to turn this individual away from expression of the targets, his negative scoring showed itself most strongly with them. A hypothesis for future studies would be that in cases in which overall significant hitting is not observed, a correlation between target negativity and scoring extremity would be expected. A final study by this group[39] used only emotionally neutral targets, so no effects of target emotionality were possible. Scoring overall was nonsignificantly below chance.

Agreement with Theory

We expected that fear-inspiring stimuli should be seized upon by unconscious intention and that this can be expressed by implicit psychological responses, just as it is by physiological responses. And we expected that it should be persons who find such fearful stimuli especially important who most strongly show such effects. These expectations have been tested primarily by the paradigm of precognitive habituation developed by Bem and carried on by others, and to a lesser extent by examination of dream content when the dreamer wished to express some prehension of ESP information. Consistent support has been found for the expectations. Reactions to stimuli that will be exposed in the near future become habituated particularly if the stimuli are intensely unpleasant and if the participants are highly emotionally reactive. Dreams convey extrasensory information primarily if the information is negatively charged. However, since only four studies have examined the dream effect, more research is desirable to see how robust it is.

OVERVIEW OF THEORY AND FACT IN REGARD TO THREAT AND UNCONSCIOUS PSI EXPRESSION

Three bodies of research have been reviewed in this section: those involving physiological response to an alarming event that will soon befall the participant (presentiment studies), those examining unconscious, physiological responses to being stared at by a distant other person, and those assessing kinds of unconscious psychological responses to threats that could only be apprehended by psi. In all of these cases we interpret the unconscious response as indicating the fixing of unconscious attention upon some threat that is beyond the sensory ken. Since no cognitive work is involved, we expected a linear, positive relationship between threat and response. We expected that the responses should be most robust when the degree of threat is greatest and when the person involved is one who is most apt to be emotionally responsive to the threat involved. In general, these expectations have all been confirmed by the bulk of findings.

A Distinction between the Next Two Sets of Studies

The next two sets of studies involve some degree of consciousness for the psi response. In the first set, the conscious identification that is attempted is very simple and rudimentary—whether a feeling is either present or not. In the second set, however, a more differentiated kind of cognitive work is involved, such as the identification of one out of a set of forced-choice targets or the production of fantasy material intended to be associated with a target. We will expect that a state of anxiety in the percipient will interfere with this kind of work and will tend to produce psi-missing, and that freedom from anxiety (assuming proper motivation on other grounds) will allow psi-hitting.

Among the studies in the second set we can be fairly certain that some participants were in a state of anxiety during the test because some direct means (self-report or behavioral) had been used to identify that fact. In other cases, we will only know who is relatively *prone* to experiencing anxiety in general because of responses to self-report inventories. In these studies, it will be especially important to see how threatening the target material or the testing situation is, since being prone to anxiety should not lead to an actual state of anxiety unless something in the situation is calling for it at the moment.

Finally, some studies will not examine the effect of anxiety as such, but rather some *psychological defenses against anxiety*. Sigmund Freud and other psychodynamic theorists have been creative in their descriptions of ways that people can respond inwardly to the potential threat of a state of anxiety. Three of these defensive postures have especially drawn the attention of parapsychologists—vigilance, repression/distortion, and dissociation. First Sight theory will have expectations about each of these defensive stances.

In general, our theory asserts that when successful response to an ESP or PK task requires conscious, cognitive work, it should be rendered less effective by a state of anxiety. This is in contrast to the research just covered in the last section, in which it was expected (and found) that fear-arousing stimuli *facilitated* an extrasensory response, when that was measured by implicit means that presumably express the sheer fixation of unconscious intention. Just as in the case of subliminal stimulation, unconscious attention is expected to be facilitated by threat, but cognitive work should be hampered.

The first set to be considered is one that we might think of as intermediate between those assessing an implicit response and those requiring some cognitive work—studies in which the participant is merely trying to identify the *feeling* that something is going on or not.

Studies Requiring a Minimal Cognitive Response to Threat

The studies in this section all ask a participant to report the presence of a feeling. Is this cognitive work? There are important implications to the question. If it is cognitive work, we would expect that it should be subject to the same sort of interference by a threat that Bar-Haim et al. (2007) found to accompany conceptual work on subliminal material. On the other hand, if it is not cognitive work, we would expect it to be facilitated by something threatening or otherwise emotionally arousing. This is a class of response that seems to be intermediate between these two things.

It is important to note that there are important differences between feelings and thoughts. Feelings are momentary, evanescent, not subject to memory, and in a real sense, not ever repeatable. One can struggle to add articulation to them, but they cannot be evaluated and manipulated in the way that thoughts can.[40] They are more readily accessible than conscious judgments.[41] They belong to what William James (1890) called the "fringe" of consciousness. They have implications suggestive of meanings, but they are not yet meanings.[42] They are also examples of what, in an earlier section, we referred to as "inadvertencies." We may attend to them or not, but we do not consciously make them or manipulate them. Thinking, on the other hand, is subject to many operations of evaluation and manipulation, memorization and recall.

We noted above that it has probably been a serious deficiency that parapsychologists have done so little sophisticated work on an extrasensory response to threat, given the apparent predominance of such experiences in life outside the laboratory. This is not to say that parapsychologists have not been interested in the psychic response to threatening material.

They have, but they have tried to assess it almost entirely by methods that require the percipient to produce some cognitive information about the target. It would seem that they have been perpetuating an error first made but then largely corrected by psychologists studying perceptual defense and subliminal perception: confounding awareness and recognition, which are two very different processes.[43] Simple awareness of the presence of something (such as a faint smudge of light not bright enough to be discerned as a picture) may be facilitated by the element of threat, while the subsequent recognition of the picture's content (as it is made brighter) can be delayed by the same threat.

In noting the presence of a feeling, the cognitive discrimination required is very minimal. It requires, essentially, only that the participant is able to gain some awareness of the kind of physiological responses that were studied in the presentiment and staring studies. In fact, these are staring studies, but instead of measuring physiological reactions, they ask the individuals being looked at if they do, at a given moment, have a feeling of being stared at or not. For the reasons just stated, even though such feeling reports involve a degree of consciousness, First Sight theory expects that they should behave more like visceral responses than like cognitive work. They should be facilitated by the element of threat.

All of the studies in this set involve a single thing: the *feeling* of being stared at. While research on being stared at was also covered in the last section, those studies all involved an unconscious, physiological response. In this section we examine studies on a person's ability to express a conscious report indicating a feeling of awareness. It is an interesting question as to whether or not there will be a similar effect. Does a feeling about being stared at tell the truth sometimes, even when the one who is staring is not within sensory contact?

Studies on the Feeling of Being Stared At

There are two old folk beliefs in this domain. Many people believe that they can somehow *sense* when they are being stared at and say that they often turn around and find that it is true. Some other people also believe that they somehow have the power to affect others with their stares and can frequently "make them" turn and look around. Many surveys have found that these beliefs are quite prevalent.[44] Are they true?

Expectations of Theory

Almost no cognitive work is required for an individual to *sense* that they are being stared at by someone out of sight. All is needed is that one have a vague feeling for the kind of arousal that was captured by the polygraphs of Radin, Braud, Bierman, and others discussed above. Nothing is being learned or identified or categorized; only a vague unease or aversion, or even a less delineated "feeling of something," is being sensed. For this reason, the subtle anxiety that might be aroused by the event should not generally have the power to disrupt performance. After all, many subtle, implicit decisions are made in most people's daily lives to avoid this or that on the basis only of such unexamined feelings, and our theory suggests that all of them are probably informed in part by psi information. And as Sheldrake (2003) has argued, such aversive behaviors surely have had considerable evolutionary value by avoiding potential dangers, so people might generally be expected to intend to be able to perform them. However, if the task involves too much cognitive work (perhaps the *identity* of someone staring is being guessed) or if the situation involves too much additional threat (perhaps the testing environment is hostile to the ability) then anxiety might be expected to interfere and turn the performance in a psi-missing direction.

Finally, if information is available about the motivations of those involved (starers and starees), more discriminating predictions can be made. Threat may be an issue in some cases and not in others. Some people may wish to be looked at, such as the socially isolated people studied by Braud et al. (1993), and in certain contexts many people wish to seem attractive or interesting.[45] Also, the intentions of starers may be flattering or benign and not in the least sinister. In such situations, being stared at would still be expected to be important to the one trying to feel the fact, since positive attention is something most people prize. Fear does not need to be the only thing that makes it salient. Prehension of these intentions probably unconsciously attends the sheer prehension of being stared at, but whether or not this strand of potential information will be incorporated or rejected in a final feeling is a complex question depending upon the person's predisposition, motives, and other competing elements of the situation. In many cases we might expect that the issue of threat is not raised at all, whereas with persons very disinclined to be looked at, or those being looked at in some way that is critical or predatory, the issue of threat would be highly pertinent.

The Findings of Research

The first scientific report on the issue came from one of the patriarchs of Anglo-American psychology, Edward Titchener (1898), and he set out to disprove this unfortunate superstition. He asked a number of people to make guesses while someone else was either staring at them or not, and collected their responses, which basically set the model for all research to follow. He reported no data but assured his readers that he was satisfied that there was nothing to the myth, and he gave a sensible lecture on the dangers of misinterpreting coincidences. This old article was quite influential and is still quoted as being authoritative today.

The first detailed empirical test of the question was carried out by Coover (1913), who also concluded that he found no evidence that people could detect being stared at to a statistically significant degree, although a later and more sophisticated analysis by Colwell et al. (2000) found that his data actually supported the hypothesis.

The next study by a psychologist named J. J. Poortman (1959) was reported in Dutch in 1939, but it appeared in English translation twenty years later. He asked a woman known to have an especially commanding stare to assist him by staring or not at him behind his back while he tried to identify the stared-at feeling. He also concluded that he found no evidence for the ability, but he inadvertently continued what was almost becoming a tradition when a more appropriate reanalysis of his data later again discovered that he had indeed found such evidence and had been significantly more often right than wrong. It began to look like an effect that no one wished to find but might be cursed with anyway.

The next study brought an improvement in method by having the starer look through a one-way mirror from another room.[46] Results again were significantly positive. The study that came next[47] introduced another safeguard by having the starer observe from a distant room using closed-circuit television (CCTV). This work found significantly positive results also.

Many studies have been reported since, and they fall mostly into two classes. A large number have been done by Rupert Sheldrake or his colleagues and follow the Coover procedure of having the starer behind the staree in the same room.[48] Many are done in very informal situations such as elementary school classrooms. While he has used various experimental safeguards such as blindfolding guessers on some occasions, Sheldrake's primary concern has been making his experiments accessible and widely known and discussed. His accumulated results are astronomically significant.[49]

Still, a number of his critics have identified important possible contaminating factors. One of them, which is especially important, involves the possibility of participants implicitly learning and anticipating a pattern in the sequence of stare and no-stare trials when feedback is given and the sequences are not properly randomized. Another is the danger of subliminal cues from the starer when the two parties are in close proximity. Because of this, the second class of studies has primarily come from other researchers and has used improved randomization, frequently no feedback at all, and physical separation, mainly CCTV, which makes sensory cues impossible. When these best studies have been examined with meta-analysis, the accumulated result is still highly significant.[50] The finding seems conclusive enough: People can often sense when they are being stared at, even though they have no sensory means for doing so.

What of the differences between participants in terms of anxiety and related dimensions? These investigators have scarcely examined the question. I could find only one study that pertains to it. Jonathan Jones[51] administered a schizotypy inventory to his participants and expected that those high on the dimension would be more sensitive to being stared at than low scorers. His high schizotypes did show the effect, while his low schizotypes did not. It is known that schizotypal people (who tend to have odd experiences and are often socially withdrawn in ways that are suggestive of signs of schizophrenia) are more anxious than the general population, so this finding is at least consistent with the expectation that being stared at should be especially salient and threatening for persons who are highly anxious.

Agreement with Theory

The fact that people are able to sense a subtle difference between times when they are being stared at and times when they are not is consistent with First Sight theory, which held that such a preconceptual response should be heightened by the sense of threat that might be expected to accompany the situation. Since almost none of the studies controlled or assessed the motives of the starers or the individual differences of the starees, very little can be said about the other theoretical expectations. While one study does suggest that more anxious persons will be especially sensitive to the implications of threat, the effect of individual motives and sensitivities have scarcely been studied. This research will be interesting when it is done.

STUDIES ASSESSING THE AFFECTS OF ANXIETY (OR NEUROTICISM) ON CONSCIOUS PSI PERFORMANCE

The reports to be examined in this section vary widely, and I will discuss them in subgroupings. All involved the attempt to consciously identify something by way of ESP (or to consciously affect some outcome, in the case of a few PK studies). All of them also involve in some fashion the issues of threat or anxiety, or vulnerability to threat and anxiety.

THE EFFECT OF A STATE OF ANXIETY ON CONSCIOUS PSI PERFORMANCE

Expectations of Theory

The studies reviewed here are all ones in which there is reason to believe that the percipient is in an anxious state at the time of testing. This has been ascertained either by self-report assessments or by some behavioral indication of anxiety or by the use of a situation designed to produce anxiety. A state of anxiety is assumed by First Sight theory to create a conflict for persons trying to engage in any cognitive task, including the cognitive task of identifying an ESP target or influencing a psychokinetic outcome. An inverse relationship between psi performance and anxiety is therefore expected.

Research Findings on Participants Known to Be in an Anxious State

The first set of studies in this group placed percipients in a situation that the experimenters believed should make almost all of them anxious. Rao, Kanthamani, and Sailaja (1971) tested persons who were being interviewed for either a job or admission to a prestigious graduate program that would almost certainly result in procurement of a good job. This involved an Indian population, in a setting in which good jobs are difficult to obtain, but once gained usually assure a lifetime of relative security, so the stakes were high in the interview. All participants understood that the interview evaluation was critical for their acceptance. In two studies groups of applicants, upon arriving for their interview, were surprised with the announcement that they would first be required to take a test of their intuitive ability, with the implication that their performance on the test would show something important about their suitability. They were then given an ESP test, with the interview following (the interviewer tried to be nonthreatening and friendly in that process). After the interview, they were told that their evaluation was over, but they were asked to take another ESP test, only for the sake of accumulating more data. The experimenters expected that scoring would be below chance before the interview and improve after it. Their expectations were significantly confirmed in both studies, with scoring that was significantly negative before the interview and above chance after the interview, with a significant difference between them.

Sailaja and Rao (1973) then reported two variations on the design . A study in which separate groups were used (one tested before the interview and one after) also significantly replicated the effect. In the next study, the experimenters tried to make the effect go away. They reasoned that it was the shock of being surprised by the test in this evaluative context that made it especially aversive. In the last study, participants were warned ahead of time that they would be taking an ESP test before their interview. In this situation, the significantly negative scoring and the significant difference both disappeared as they predicted.

Schmeidler, Mitchell, and Sondow (1975) administered a brief projective test (the Hand Test) at the time of conducting a test of psychokinesis—an attempt to influence the temperature of a remote and shielded thermistor. One score on the test is known to be a good indicator of the individual's current state of anxiety.[52] Scores on this state-anxiety variable correlated significantly negatively with performance on the PK test.

Stanford and Schroeter (1978) gave their participants a choice as to how fully reclined their reclining chair should be as they participated in their ESP experiment, which involved listening to verbal materials through earphones. The most reclined were taken to be the least anxious.[53] The most anxious (most upright) group did score significantly negatively, as predicted, with a marginally significant difference from the less anxious.

Carpenter (1991) asked 383 percipients to rate their moods at the times they carried out a self-administered test of precognition. One factor on the mood scale assessed one's current state of anxiety. This measure of state anxiety was significantly negatively correlated with precognition scores.

Braud and Braud (1974) measured the muscle tension of their participants (known to correlate highly with states of anxiety) and found that it significantly predicted performance in a free-response ESP task in a negative direction.

The State Anxiety scale of Spielberger was used by Broughton and Perlstrom (1986, 1992) in three studies on psychokinesis in competitive situations. Significant negative correlations were found in all cases between state-anxiety and performance when the participants believed that they were competing against another player. The difference was significant in only one of the studies when participants believed that they were working cooperatively with someone else, and not significant in the other two in the cooperative condition. Crandall (1998) attempted a replication, but in this case state anxiety did not correlate with PK success.

Carpenter (2001, 2005a) carried out a projective analysis on ganzfeld mentation protocols using data from previously reported studies that had been provided from several different laboratories. One of the scales rated implicit expressions of anxiety in the verbalizations of the participants (responses such as "I see a scared rabbit running away," "I think I see a package that might be a bomb," and "I'm a little nervous right now" would give points for anxiety). This measure was taken as an implicit assessment of how anxious the person was (perhaps unconsciously) at the time of the testing. It was based on similar ones using various projective tests such as the Rorschach and the Hand Test (just mentioned) whose measures of anxiety have demonstrated validity. In one collection of 364 transcripts these anxiety scores correlated significantly negatively with ESP success. The relationship was replicated successfully in a second sample of 220 additional sessions (although interestingly not with a subsample of professional artists in various fields, who were apparently not affected by their unconscious anxiety in the ordinary way).

Palmer, Ader, and Mikova (1981) tested two series of participants in conditions that varied the amount of feedback given of performance and also asked for ratings of current comfort versus anxiety. No strong effects were found for feedback, but the expected negative relationship with state anxiety was found in both studies.

Carpenter (2002) reported a long-running experiment in which the unstructured weekly sessions of a group of friends were used as media for acquiring extrasensory information. The design was modeled after studies that had shown that that subliminal stimulation can have behavioral consequences. Briefly, this leaderless, quasi-therapy group met at a designated time with a dual purpose: first, to engage one another in helpful and meaningful ways, and second, to express the content of an ESP target through the course spontaneously taken by their session. As the group met, a distant computer randomly selected a picture. After the session ended, the target picture, along with three decoys, was presented to the group. Each picture was then rated by all members in terms of how closely associated it was with the content and mood of the session. Before this rating was done, however, the participants also rated some qualities of how the session had affected them emotionally. One item asked how anxious the session left them feeling. Overall, the group (using averaged target ratings) succeeded in identifying the correct target significantly often, providing evidence that the targets were inadvertently expressed by the course of the sessions. Averaged scores on anxiety were negatively correlated with the ESP performance at a marginal level of significance ($p = 0.07$).

Roe, Davey, and Stevens (2003) reported a study in which both ESP and PK were tested at the same time. In half the trials the participants were told correctly which psi activity was involved, and in the other half they were misled (ESP trials were disguised as PK trials and vice versa). None of the categories of the task produced significant psi scoring, and they were not significantly correlated with one another. However, two of them (True ESP and Disguised PK) were correlated negatively with state anxiety at a marginal level of significance.

Altogether, sixteen experiments on state anxiety and psi have been reviewed here that reported nineteen relationships, and in seventeen of them the predicted negative relationship has been found, at least to a marginally significant degree. There was one simple failure to replicate[54] and one deliberately manipulated nonrelation that was predicted by the experimenters.[55] This is a strong effect in the behavioral sciences. It seems safe to conclude that being in a state of anxiety at the time of testing tends to result in performance on a conscious-response psi task that is below chance, while being free of such anxiety tends to produce the opposite result. The results of Broughton and Perlstrom suggest that being tested in a way that lets the participant think that he or she can "lean" cooperatively in the task on the joint efforts of another person may tend to obviate the relationship, but further research on the question will let us be more certain about this.

Agreement with Theory

First Sight theory asserts that being in a state of anxiety should interfere with the cognitive work of trying to identify the content of an ESP target or determine the specific outcome of a PK trial. A state of fear leads one to be unconsciously preoccupied with the wish to escape the fearful situation, whatever one's conscious intention, and should tend to be expressed by moving away from actual targets toward other alternatives. Being free from anxiety is expected to allow a person to carry out those cognitive tasks relatively successfully when that is the intention. This body of findings, with its overall preponderance of negative correlations, strongly supports this contention.

THE EFFECT OF A TENDENCY TO BE ANXIOUS ON CONSCIOUS PSI PERFORMANCE

Expectations of Theory

A fairly large number of investigators have asked their participants to fill out self-report questionnaires assessing their general proneness to become distressed and anxious, or more generally, to respond to situations in "neurotic" ways that are largely characterized by anxiety. These tests of anxiety or neuroticism do not ask the person to identify the state they are in at the moment but to characterize the emotional states they are likely to be in frequently.

Persons who score highly on such tests are not always anxious. Usually enough stress has to be present in the situation in order to call this trait out into expression. Parapsychologists have often not seemed to take much account of this fact. In the understandable wish to find some simple and reliable correlate with psi performance, many studies have been carried out without explicit attention to the importance of the degree of stressfulness of the situation. Perhaps for that reason, results have been mixed. The studies I will discuss here will be broken down into three subgroupings in terms of the amount of stress that might be generally expected in the situation. First, there is the individual testing situation, in which one is seated alone with a parapsychologist who is administering a test asking one to perform a skill that most people have no idea about how to perform. Yet, the test is being carried out in all seriousness, and the experimenter at least seems to think that the results will be measuring something about an "ability" of the participant. Feedback of performance is typically given at the time.

This situation may be assumed to be somewhat stressful for many people. Because of this, in studies using such individual testing there is a relatively high expectation that trait anxiety or neuroticism will be called up and expressed, so that high scorers on anxiety questionnaires should often tend to actually be in a state of some anxiety while taking the psi test and low scorers should often tend to not be anxious. In a relatively stressful situation, the test will tend to predict the state, and the state should affect performance, as it did in the group of studies just surveyed in which actual state anxiety was being assessed or manipulated.

Many parapsychological studies have been carried out in groups.[56] Participants sit together, frequently in familiar classroom situations. Performance is usually anonymous (participants identified only with codes), with feedback on performance either not given or received later in writing. Most people will not find this situation particularly stressful. Therefore, we expect mixed and largely null results in this situation. While at times something may make the situation relatively stressful, generally this should not be so. In some cases, the anonymity and safety of the setting might even lead to a reversal of the normal expectation, in which people who tend often to be anxious might respond to their temporary safety with relief and perform especially well.

There are still other studies in which some effort has gone to make the experimental situation not stressful at all. Such studies have provided sensory isolation, soothing sounds, suggestions of relaxation and well-being, meditation or hypnosis—all in the attempt to ease the participant as much as possible into a secure and comfortable state of mind. In these situations also, we will expect that trait anxiety or neuroticism will tend to not be a pertinent variable, and that relationships with performance will tend to be null, or occasionally even reverse.

Findings of Research: Studies Using Individual Testing without Relaxation

Betty Humphrey (1945) reported the first study of this sort. She used a popular personality test of the day, the Bernreuter Inventory, to measure anxiety and other tendencies. The relationship between ESP performance and the anxiety dimension was the strongest that she found and was independently significant ($p = 0.029$, 2-tail). She went on to find further significant confirmation for the negative relationship (highly anxious people scored below chance, low anxious ones above chance) in two other studies.[57] Several other researchers followed this lead. All used standard measures of anxiety proneness or neuroticism. Additional significant confirmations of the negative relationship have been reported in eight articles involving thirteen studies.[58] Marginally significant results ($p < 0.10 > 0.05$) were found in two studies.[59] Null results were reported in seven studies.[60]

One reversal of the effect was found, but it was only in one of two conditions in the experiment. Haight, Kanthamani, and Kennedy (1978) tested high and low anxiety prone participants individually in two conditions. In one they gave feedback as to success, in the other they did not. In the no-feedback condition, the high-anxiety group significantly outperformed the low-anxiety group. There was an insignificant trend in the opposite direction in the feedback condition.

All together, eighteen studies have found the negative relationship at a significant or nearly significant level, seven found no relationship, and one found a reversal of the relationship in one condition. While no formal meta-analysis is being done here, the trend is clear and relatively strong across the set as a whole. The standard individual testing situation (perhaps particularly with feedback as to performance) will tend to induce highly trait-anxious participants to score more poorly than their less anxious peers.

Findings of Research: Group Testing Studies

Humphrey, along with her Duke colleague Burke Smith, also initiated this line of work.[61] They reported three studies and found a significant negative relationship in one of them, along with insignificant trends in a negative direction in the other two. Since their work, two other significant negative relationship have been reported with group testing,[62] although it might be noted that one of the two involved a testing procedure that was presented to the participants as especially challenging (responding to targets in one language, while the targets themselves were translations in a different language that was unknown to all the participants). Seven experiments finding null relationships have been reported.[63] Two studies reported a significant reversal of the effect, with highly anxious people scoring more highly.[64]

With three significant negative relationships, two significant positive relationships, and ten studies showing null relationships, this group of findings offers little support for the idea that more anxious people will reliably perform more poorly than less anxious people on ESP tests when tested in groups. Since some significant relationships have been reported, it seems likely that other variables may make the group-testing situation more stressful, while others will make it facilitative for people who otherwise are often anxious. However, these other variables have not been studied.

Research Findings When Participants Are Tested Individually but in Highly Relaxed Conditions

Eisenberg and Donderi (1979), who used a free-response situation in which the receivers were induced to become deeply relaxed by instructions modeled after those used in hypnosis and relaxation therapy, reported the first study of this sort. They found no relationship between performance and a measure of neuroticism. Another study tested participants singly but alone in their homes, carried out at their leisure, with responses sent in later by mail.[65] She also reported no relationship between performance and neuroticism. Seven studies involved the ganzfeld situation, in which participants are isolated and induced to become deeply relaxed. Six of them reported null relationships with anxiety proneness.[66] One other ganzfeld study correlated ESP performance with the six facet scales of the NEO-PI Neuroticism factor and found a significant correlation with one of them, Vulnerability (a propensity to become upset and dysfunctional under stress). While this finding may be worth following up, this single relationship was not predicted in advance, and its significance would disappear if corrected for multiple analyses.

Thus it is fair to say that all nine of the studies that examined the effect of anxiety proneness when participants were induced to become very comfortable found no relationship with ESP performance. The trait appears not to be salient in this circumstance, as would be expected.

Findings of Studies on Anxiety-Proneness That Compared More and Less Stressful Conditions

There are only three studies in this category. Honorton (1965) attempted to stress one group of subjects by instructing them that the task they were about to undertake was probably impossible for most as it was too complex. His second group was told that the same task was easy. Highly anxiety-prone participants scored significantly poorly in the "impossible" group, while the other group was slightly above chance. An attempt to replicate the effect with a second pair of groups yielded null results. In an individual testing situation, Sargent (1978) found that when he tested his participants in the usual way, the anxiety prone performed significantly more poorly, whereas when the same participants were hypnotized and given suggestions to relax and do well, the relationship vanished. Mischo and Weis (1973) carried out a PK experiment. Half of the participants were tested in conditions designed to be especially frustrating and stressful, and half in a relaxed control condition. Scores on anxiety proneness showed a significant negative relationship with scoring in the stressful condition, but not the control condition.

These findings are all consistent with those already discussed. In more stressful circumstances, the trait of anxiety becomes more salient and tends to affect psi performance. In circumstances that are not stressful, it has no reliable effect.

Agreement with Theory for Studies on Anxiety Proneness and Conscious Psi Response

Theory predicted that being more prone to a state of anxiety should have a negative effect on efforts to consciously identify or influence psi targets to the extent that circumstances in the testing situation make that tendency salient. More stressful situations should call it forth more than less stressful situations, and threatening target material should call it forth more than target material that is not threatening. The studies just reviewed conform to the expectation about situational stress with few exceptions.

People who are most likely to be in a state of anxiety during the test do tend to find their efforts hampered, producing below-chance scoring when they are aiming to be correct. A state of anxiety is assumed by theory to create an unconscious situation in which extrasensory information will tend to be subjected to contrast and excluded from awareness, even while it is being unconsciously attended to! This is because of the more important competing wish to avoid the situation of threat and protect consciousness from it. Even though the individual may be consciously wishing to respond correctly to the target, the unconscious concern is preemptive. Persons who are not anxiety prone tend not to be vulnerable to the degrees of stress that these studies have usually provided, and they typically perform better, as one would expect given the secure state they are likely in. It may be that especially secure and comfortable circumstances will sometimes even reverse the normal effect and permit the anxiety prone to experience relief and do particularly well (as suggested by Palmer, Ader, and Mikova), but more research would be needed to establish the circumstances in which that might reliably occur.

Findings of Studies That Varied the Fearfulness of Targets

The studies reported in this section all required participants to identify the content of targets either through making forced choices, as with traditional Zener cards, or asking them to generate imagery that could later be used to pick an actual target out a field of decoys. All of the studies also examined how threatening or upsetting the targets were. Thus, while they did not examine the state of anxiety of the participants, nor their proneness to such states, they did examine performance, using targets that, if seen consciously, would be more or less fear inducing.

Martin Johnson (1965) reported the first study of this sort. He asked his participants before the ESP test to rate a series of pictures in terms of how they associated each of them to his or her past personal experience. Some were picked as upsetting, some as neutral, and a few for each were associated to very negative or traumatic experiences. Johnson made up individual randomized sets of ESP targets out of these pictures, including equal numbers of upsetting and neutral targets, and including as many traumatic targets as possible. Responding was by blind matching, sorting a set of concealed response cards into piles that were each associated with a concealed target card (thus the potentially upsetting pictures were never seen during the testing). When he analyzed performance, he found psi-hitting on neutral targets and psi-missing with unpleasant and traumatic targets, with a significant difference between them.

Dalkvist and Westerlund, with a similar procedure, found the same results, and also found that the degree to which the target was rated as unpleasant correlated significantly in a negative direction with scoring. Four more significant replications of this effect have been reported. Three used standard, nonrelaxed testing conditions,[67] and one used the ganzfeld.[68] Null results have been reported by Eisenberg in a study in which participants were induced to relax, and by Sondow, Braud, and Barker (1981) in a ganzfeld study.

Palmer and Johnson (1991) used a different, but related, procedure. Their ESP targets were always intended to be emotionally neutral (the letter a, b, c, and d—however, they later realized that their college-student participants could easily have associated them to academic grades), but they were tested in two conditions that were intended to give the targets connotations of more or less threat. In one, just before their ESP test they were subliminally flashed a picture of a scowling male face. In the other condition a smiling face was flashed instead (recall the studies that have shown that emotional subliminal primes affected the emotional quality experienced with neutral images a short time later). Throughout the procedure, participants were required to keep their eyes fixed in eyepieces and chins in a chin rest while they stared at a small screen (many found this awkward and uncomfortable). The experimenters expected higher scoring with the friendly face, but did not find it. Instead they found significantly small scoring extremity (tight variance) in both conditions. In First Sight theory this result would be interpreted as a withdrawal of unconscious attention from the psi information that the task was trying to access, but the investigators thought of it as an indication of a state of discomfort, perhaps with the very idea of being subliminally stimulated or with the physical discomfort that their procedure involved. Of course, an uncomfortable state might be expressed by an unconscious withdrawal of attention, so the two interpretations are not contradictory. In any case, Palmer (1992) attempted to replicate the small-extremity effect (this time using simple figural targets) and did, to a marginally significant degree. It was especially strong with participants who complained that the test was difficult to carry out.

Altogether, five studies using standard, nonrelaxed testing situations have reported significant differences in performance between threatening and neutral targets. No reversals and no null results have been reported. Among the three studies that induced deep relaxation in their participants, one showed the negative effect of threatening targets, and two did not. Although these numbers are not large, they appear to support the hypothesis that threatening target material will tend to turn ESP scoring in a negative direction as long as the participants are not induced to feel very secure and relaxed. When they are so induced, the effect of the negative targets seems to be less reliable.

In the two studies that attempted to *prime* targets either with threatening or neutral connotations, scoring differences were not found, but an overall effect of small scoring extremity was induced. This suggests that if a testing situation is too uncomfortable or emotionally off-putting in some way, this may tend to evoke a general avoidance of extrasensory information, obscuring any response to more subtle aspects of the target situation.

Findings of Studies of Conscious ESP or PK Response that Varied Both the Anxiety Proneness of the Participant and the Threat Level of Targets

These studies all used target differences that, at the time of testing, were not consciously accessible to the participants but which the experimenters believed would be more or less anxiety arousing had they been seen consciously. They were thus all modeled after classical studies on perceptual defense using subliminal stimuli. In many of these, the threat level of the subliminal exposures had been found to interact with the anxiety proneness of the percipients in meaningful ways.[69]

I reported the first study of this type.[70] Participants responded to a test of anxiety proneness and carried out a blind-matching test using emotionally threatening (erotic) versus neutral targets. The participants were middle-school children who never saw the disturbing material and never knew of its involvement in the study but who might be expected to find it particularly anxiety provoking (this was in an earlier, more innocent time). When participants were divided into groups in terms of their anxiety scores, a significant interaction was found with type of target. Highly anxious people scored below chance on the threatening targets and above chance on the neutral ones, while low anxious participants did the reverse.

Two attempts to replicate this effect were carried out by Ballard (1980) using adult participants (who might have been expected to not find his mildly erotic material particularly disturbing had they known of it—which they did not). Before the ESP test, Ballard administered a relaxation exercise to his participants and asked them to rate their state of anxiety before and after the exercise. In his first study he found the predicted relationship for females but not for males, which is reminiscent of the gender differences in emotional response to pictures that was discussed earlier. In his second study his test of trait anxiety was compromised because the great majority of his participants (females particularly) scored as highly anxious. Therefore, he could not test for the effect of gender in the second study. Looking at *state anxiety* scores instead, he found that those (males and females) who declined in anxiety more as a result of their relaxation exercise performed better on the erotically associated targets than did those whose anxiety declined less or not at all. Thus, those who were *not* successfully induced to relax performed more poorly on the arousal-linked targets than did the participants who did manage to become less anxious.

Johnson and Nordbeck (1972) found that their highly anxiety-prone participants performed significantly more poorly on threat-related targets than on targets with pleasant associations, while the nonanxious did the opposite.

Johnson and Houtkooper (1988) asked their participants to respond to a scale measuring the degree to which they had suffered a history of emotional trauma, and also to fill out a scale of anxiety proneness. The participants then sorted pictures as to their degree of association to personal trauma experiences. The experimenters then took pictures that were highly associated with trauma and others that were neutral, and they paired them with some trials in an ESP study. They analyzed results in terms of performance on the trauma-associated targets (the pictures were not visibly present at the time of the ESP test). The anxiety proneness scale predicted scoring on those targets in the expected negative way—but only for those participants with higher scores on traumatization. The less traumatized people (whose negative pictures presumably had much less upsetting connotations for them) scored equally well on the two kinds of targets.

De Graaf and Houtkooper (2004) reported a similar study. They did not use a measure of anxiety, but they did ask their participants to fill out a questionnaire to indicate the degree to which they had experienced trauma. They then asked participants to sort pictures into groups that they found neutral, pleasant, unpleasant, or trauma related. These pictures were then associated with certain trials in a forced-choice ESP test (again, the association was only extrasensory as determined by the experimenters, not visibly present). Results were analyzed both in terms of direct hits and *displacements* (cases in which the call for a target matches the targets *around* the one being aimed for, before it or after it). They assumed that such displaced scores might indicate the operation of unconscious emotional defenses in the percipient (this is analogous, say, to someone saying that they are in a bad mood because of the weather, only to realize upon reflection that they were really responding to some bad news that they wished to not think or talk about). Trauma scores did not significantly predict the responses to the actual targets associated with unpleasant versus neutral/positive material. Rather, they strongly predicted *displaced hitting* (calls aimed at trials before and after the unpleasant target tended to match it significantly often). The more traumatized people displaced; the others did not.

Agreement with Theory for Studies Using Threatening Targets

First Sight theory predicts that upsetting target material should arouse the kind of unconscious conflict over response that has been studied in regard to subliminal material in the perceptual defense literature. Any move in the direction of consciously knowing a threatening thing (especially for anxious people) will be unconsciously avoided—even if it is only the subtle approach of placing a concealed card upon a concealed target. The mind will tend to wish to not approach such a thing, even while one consciously is attempting to cooperate with the experimenter and show some cognizance of it. Material that is not threatening will not tend to evoke such avoidance. Sometimes one's response may express a fixation of attention in one way while simultaneously avoiding a potential awareness in another, as shown in the displacement findings of de Graaf and Houtkooper. If people are encouraged to become unusually comfortable, or if they do not actually find the "negative" target aversive personally (like the adult males of Ballard with mildly erotic material), these interference effects should become less reliable or vanish altogether. These studies as a group show a trend toward confirming these expectations. In their way they are congruent with the findings that were discussed above, in regard to threat when unconscious, physiological extrasensory response is assessed—except here, the threat impedes conscious work, even while it seizes unconscious attention.

STUDIES INVOLVING PSYCHOLOGICAL DEFENSES AGAINST ANXIETY

Psychodynamic theories of the personality all hearken back to the seminal work of Sigmund Freud (1926), who posited that anxiety is a driving force in forming one's personality and is an engine that powers all forms of psychopathology. Anxiety is a problem for us, according to Freud, and we are motivated to not be overcome by it. One *defends* against it, he said. His daughter Anna (1937), developing his theory further, defined a specific list of *defense mechanisms* that people use to various degrees when the anxiety they must manage internally becomes too great. This list includes *repression* (simply becoming unaware of some emotional problem), *denial* (perceiving it not to be a problem), *projection* (seeing it as a problem for someone else), and so on. The various forms of pathology (and relative freedom from pathology) are all determined, she said, by the characteristic *defenses* that the mind uses to deal with anxiety. While the particulars of this theory have continued to develop over time and are now of great interest primarily to psychoanalysts, the general idea of psychological defense against anxiety has become part of the culture and has been applied in different forms by psychologists who are not strictly psychoanalytic in their thinking. It has also been carried into the studies of a few parapsychologists.

   In this context, there are three primary ways the idea of defense has been applied. First, those defenses that limit or distort awareness (repression, denial, distortion, projection) of threatening material in general have been assumed to work psychically as well. If one tends to avoid an accurate and fully conscious experience of something threatening in everyday life, then that person will probably avoid an accurate and conscious awareness of threatening things that are available only by ESP as well. That is, they should act like the anxious people who have just been surveyed have acted, although—and here is why this must be studied separately—they may not appear to be anxious or represent themselves on tests as being anxious. In fact, the more successfully their defenses are operating, the less anxious they will appear to be! Their defensiveness must be assessed somehow independently of their awareness and their more obvious indications of anxiety.

Another response to anxiety that has been of interest has been called *vigilance*. This is the proactive, "go right at it" approach to anxiety. Vigilant people are extra quick and extra clear in their awareness of threatening things.

There is another defense against anxiety that does not stem from the Freudian tradition, and many theorists believe that it is not adequately covered by the constructs of the psychoanalysts. This is *dissociation*, which involves a splitting of consciousness into somewhat self-contained parts. The idea comes to us mostly from Pierre Janet and his turn-of-the-century school of psychiatry,[71] although it has come back into important usage in psychiatry and clinical psychology in work with the effects of trauma.[72] Janet considered it the most basic defense against anxiety, particularly when it is overwhelming. People who use dissociative splitting of consciousness are often (but not always) quite debilitated psychiatrically, with chronic depression, suicidality, and a host of other problems. However, such splitting sometimes seems to enable the person to be in the presence of something very upsetting without having any awareness of a problem. When a person is markedly dissociative, the very self may be split into different parts that are aware of somewhat different domains in the personal world.

Many apparently gifted psychics have raised the issue of dissociation and psi from the days of mediums in séance rooms to the present, because such persons often appear to be unusually dissociative.[73] And looked at from the other angle, a high proportion of people with marked dissociative experiences (and often trauma histories) report an unusually high frequency of ostensible psychic experiences.[74]

While such marked dissociation has sometimes seemed to be associated with dramatic instances of apparent psychic cognizance, it is the milder forms of dissociation that have been studied in the laboratory. These milder degrees of dissociation are usually measured by questionnaires that ask people how often they have experiences of odd lapses of memory, finding themselves in some place and not remembering how they got there, feelings of being "beside oneself," losing track of time, feeling some loss or change in identity, etc.

Expectations of Theory in Regard to Psychological Defenses

First Sight theory humbly borrows from psychoanalytic and other theories of the unconscious to the effect that ways of managing threat intra-
psychically in general should apply as well when a threat is present only
by way of ESP. If a person tends to repress and deny difficulties, and have
delayed or distorted awareness of them, this same tendency should be seen
in regard to extrasensory information. If he or she is vigilantly alert and
responsive to such things, this also should carry over to the unconscious
treatment of psi information. And if someone is dissociative, it may be that
the extrasensory presence of danger will have no deterring effect on psi
awareness, or may even heighten it.

Findings of Research

Studies in this section fall into three clusters: those using the Defense
Mechanism Test (DMT),[75] those using a procedure developed by Watt
(1991), and a few studies using different ways of assessing dissociation.

The Defense Mechanism Test is a tachistoscopic procedure that exposes an
individual to very brief exposures of a set of pictures—initially far too brief
for anything to be seen except a flicker of light. The length of exposure is gradually increased in a series of steps, while the person makes guesses as to what
is in the picture. Scoring assesses how many tries, and how many increases
in clarity, are needed before a person is able to fully and accurately describe
what is being seen. In some of the pictures there is a threatening element.

The rationale of the test follows Freudian theory, in which the dynamics
of defense mechanisms involves three things: a threat or danger, anxiety
about that, and efforts to defend against the state of anxiety. The test provides a pictorial threat, assumes that anxiety is aroused, and looks for signs
that various defenses are being used at a preconscious level (which is where
defenses are presumed to generally operate). The test not only assesses how
long it takes the person to clearly see but also it takes note of the various
kinds of distortions that may occur in the perception along the way. For
example, repression might be indicated if the picture is almost fully described but the threatening figure is left out, or denial might be indicated
if the threatening figure is misdescribed as someone generous and kind.
Other defensive operations, such as isolation of affect, reaction formation,
reversal of gender, etc., are also assessed.

The test is ingenious and has proven validity; for example, more defensive people tend to be accident prone and to respond ineffectively to stress.
It has proven to be particularly useful in screening applicants for training
as fighter pilots,[76] the purpose for which it was initially constructed, and it
has been used for that purpose by several countries. It has also been used

by parapsychologists, who have hoped that its measure of preconscious defensiveness could identify persons most likely to miss when they attempt to identify ESP targets. Unfortunately, scoring the test is laborious and somewhat subjective, in spite of an elaborate manual of scoring rules.[77] This fact has caused some problems for parapsychologists.

Martin Johnson is the Swedish psychologist responsible for bringing the test to bear upon parapsychological problems, but actually the first report to appear using it bore my name.[78] Johnson administered the test to a group of schoolchildren and scored their responses. I and two others gave the same children a series of different ESP tests without knowing their defensiveness scores. Their ESP scores were combined for an overall estimate of performance, and a strong negative correlation with defensiveness was found—the more defensive participants scored below chance and less defensive above. Replications soon appeared by Johnson and Kanthamani (1967), Johnson (1974), and Miller and York (1976).

Despite its laborious nature, the test became somewhat popular, and a few years later a meta-analysis by Haraldsson and Houtkooper (1992) of the sixteen studies reported up to that point showed a track record of many significant studies and a highly significant cumulative effect. Use of the test seemed to be making real inroads into understanding the unconscious psychodynamics of psi processes.

A chill entered into the next report by the same authors, however.[79] They reported the results of ten more studies carried out in Iceland using the DMT with ESP tests. Again, they found a significant overall effect, but it was significantly smaller than before. They looked at possible factors that might contribute to such a decline in effect size, but found none, except for the fact that the effect was strongest when participants were students in the humanities as opposed to other fields. This decline in effect size from the one reported in 1992 led the authors to contribute an ironic new term to parapsychology: the MAD effect (Meta-Analysis Demolition effect) for the apparent power of a successful meta-analysis to destroy an effect. Actually, the effect did not seem to be destroyed, but it did seem to have diminished mysteriously.

Still another problem appeared ten years later upon the report of another study, this time from a German laboratory.[80] In hope of making DMT scoring more efficient and reliable, subjective scoring of the test was replaced with an automated procedure using only the most objective scoring rules of the DMT Manual as weighted by the results of a regression analysis that took earlier human ratings as the criterion to match. Using these automated ratings, no relationship between defensiveness and ESP scoring appeared in the new data, even though ESP scoring was high overall and other predicted relationships (with religiosity and psychoticism) were replicated.

The investigator then turned back to the ten studies that had been reported in 1992 and replaced the subjective scores with new automated ones. Those relationships with ESP disappeared as well. Whatever the true relationship with defensiveness and ESP might be, the automated scoring was not capturing it. Its appearance depended upon the laborious and somewhat subjective hand-scoring procedure. And in the previous studies, this had all been done by Martin Johnson. DMT scoring and ESP testing had always been done double-blind, by independent investigators who did not know each other's results, so there was no implication of possible cheating or inadvertent influence on participants or on the subjective DMT ratings. But could there be an extrasensory "Martin Johnson Effect," such that some of the subtle scoring decisions made might have been influenced unwittingly by Johnson's own psi? This is the kind of problem that only parapsychologists would worry about. However, they must consider it if they are to take all the rest of their own work seriously.

To make matters worse, another trained rater coded the same protocols that Johnson had in the ten experiments from the 1992 report and could not completely reproduce Johnson's scores! And the new scores did not successfully predict ESP. For one thing, rating rules themselves had changed over time with developments in the rating manual. Johnson was ill and not available to participate and help clear up the confusion.

It should be noted here that a great deal of accumulated research on other projective techniques such as the Rorschach and the Thematic Apperception Test has shown that purely objective, automated scoring procedures are virtually never completely satisfactory. Rating such instruments requires understanding the meanings of the words given in responses by participants, including sometimes their subtle implications, and we have yet to develop computer programs that can do that with the same validity as human raters. Yet there are still mysteries that remain about the status of the accumulated body of ESP/DMT work, much of which was rated by Johnson. He is now deceased, so the mysteries will probably never be resolved.

It still seems likely that a defensiveness/ESP relationship may be real—if defensiveness scores are obtained by trained human raters—but that it may be a rather weak one across different situations. It is also likely that other factors moderate the strength of the relationship. The open-mindedness of the participants toward the ESP test (humanities students) is likely to be one such factor, as it has appeared to moderate other effects as well. The interpersonal context of the experiment, including the attitudes and feelings of the experimenters, are probably important also (remember Wiseman and Schlitz). Trying to confirm an effect is emotionally a rather different thing than adventurously trying to find one in the first place. However, these are complex and subtle issues, and they have only begun to be studied.[81]

Finally, researchers have not looked at the amount of stress present in the test for ESP, and they should, given the findings surveyed earlier in this chapter. Even highly defensive participants should not express their defensiveness if there is not enough stress in the situation to make partici- pants anxious at all and call it forth. The importance of this is suggested by the fact that the most significant confirmation of the effect in the ten studies of Haraldsson and Houtkooper (1992) used an ESP test in which participants were competing against others (which would be expected to heighten stress and anxiety), while at least one failure to replicate[82] tested ESP in the ganzfeld, in which participants were induced to become highly secure and relaxed. The stressfulness of the ESP test should be included as a moderating variable in future tests of defensiveness and psi. Up to now, the investigators have sometimes been in the odd position of taking a measure of response-to-stress (the DMT with its threatening figures) and comparing it to ESP performances done in situations that are lacking in stress.

Partly because of the complexity of the DMT, Caroline Watt wondered if a simpler, more objective procedure could be developed that might capture at least some of the same meaning and also show some power to predict ESP performance. Her method is similar to the DMT inasmuch as she uses subliminal exposures, but it assesses, not the point at which someone can become aware of the content of something, but the point at which its sheer presence can be noticed (that is, she assesses "awareness threshold" rather than "recognition threshold"). Her test (called Pan- dora's Box) involves presenting a slide at very dim illumination—so dim at first that its mere presence on a screen cannot be discerned. Then the experimenter gradually increases illumination until the person reports the first awareness of a slight haze of light. Watt set an illumination ceiling on the procedure, such that *no presentation could ever* become recognizable as to its content. Some of the slides exposed contain unpleasant scenes, and others are neutral.

Some people show an average tendency to become aware of the pres- ence of the unpleasant slides first, and they are termed *vigilant*. Some see the light of the neutral ones first, and they are termed *defensive*. And some show no real difference at all. They were omitted from ESP testing, at least in her initial report.

Watt's ESP test uses the same apparatus, with the same instructions: "Tell me when you see a light." This time all the participant's slides are blank. During each trial of the task, an agent in another room views either an unpleasant or a neutral slide. An average difference score is calculated on the participant's tendency to report awareness of light more quickly when the slide being seen by the agent is unpleasant or neutral. This is what Watt calls her measure of "unconscious psi." On each trial, after awareness of light is reported, the participant is then asked to guess whether the agent is seeing something unpleasant or not. The extent to which they get this right is their score on "conscious psi." Both ESP scores can then be correlated with her measure of vigilance/defensiveness.

In her first report, Watt (1991) found a correlation in the predicted direction between defensiveness and scores on conscious ESP (vigilant people scoring more highly than defensive ones), but with a very small N, it was only marginally significant. The correlation for unconscious ESP was also in the predicted direction, but smaller. Three confirmatory results with the conscious ESP task were reported by Watt (1993) and Watt and Morris (1995). Watt and Ravenscroft (1999) reported a failure to replicate, although they appear to have used less extreme groups in their defensive/ vigilant categorization. None of the studies after the first one used an agent but instead displayed the target slides to an empty space. It should also be mentioned that Watt's studies suffer from a problem mentioned above in regard to DMT, in that her defensiveness measure assesses a response to different levels of stress (the unpleasant and neutral slides) but then compares that to ESP performance that is not systematically varied in terms of stress. Research using her measure would be more instructive if she took extremely defensive and vigilant persons and then studied their ESP performance in more and less stressful circumstances, or compared performance on more and less threatening targets. An exception to this is the study by Watt's student Howat (1994) that was mentioned above in relation to the effect of being stared at. Howat found that more vigilant people taking Pandora's Box responded to being stared at (a threatening situation) with an increase in arousal relative to nonstare periods, whereas more defensive people responded by becoming calmer.

Watt's technique is intuitively appealing and appears to have promise for a way of predicting how people will respond to an ESP task, particularly when that task (as in Howat's study) is more appropriate.

Agreement with Theory of Findings on Defensiveness and Psi

First Sight theory assumes that the unconscious processing of psi information and the processing of subliminal information should follow similar patterns. Factors that lead one to tend to sign threatening information in positive or negative directions (assimilate it in responses or avoid it) in a subliminal situation should also affect the similar use of extrasensory information. The fact that people who are relatively defensive perceptually also tend to psi-miss, while more vigilant ones tend to psi-hit, is certainly in general accord with the theory. However, the theory also suggests that the hypotheses tested should have been somewhat more discriminating than they have been. These investigators examined perceptual defensiveness against threatening material, but then for the most part tested ESP with material that was not threatening and in situations that were also not designed to raise the issue of threat. That is, they measured perceptual defensiveness by arousing threat but tested ESP without arousing threat. As in studies on anxiety proneness, it appears likely that results will be more reliable when the degree of threat in the ESP test, either in target material or in the experimental situation, is varied and assessed.

DISSOCIATION, ANXIETY, AND ESP

Findings Examining the Effect of Dissociation upon ESP Performance

Only three reports bear on this issue, but I am including them because from a theoretical point of view, the joint effects of anxiety and dissociation should prove to be important in how people make access to ESP information, so any clues that have accumulated seem worth mentioning.

Contemporary psychological thinking on the meaning of dissociation tends to stress the power of a dissociative style of experience to protect a person from the otherwise debilitating effects of anxiety and stress in an emergency, while also being linked generally to much psychiatric vulnerability. Indeed, dissociative persons often seem to embody unusual degrees of courage, productivity, and happiness, in spite of histories of trauma and/ or neglect and current situations of danger.[83] A dramatic example of such dissociation came to me in a conversation with a very dissociative friend (and apparently a very successful psychic) who was describing for me "one of the most beautiful experiences of my life." She spoke of wandering about in the night under a huge and beautiful sky full of stars and other lights. After awhile it became clear to me that she was describing wandering in the night as a very young child during a firebombing of Tokyo by American airplanes, during which she had lost her mother.

Dissociation appears to have the power to allow a person to survive and even in some ways thrive following experiences of acute abandonment and panic. There is even experimental demonstration that dissociation strongly tends to accompany panic.[84]

John Palmer (1994) developed an ESP test that he hoped would come close to assessing a kind of sheer awareness of an ESP target without requiring very much in the way of conscious work about it. In some ways, he was continuing his earlier work that was discussed in regard to the effect of threatening targets,[85] but he was using a procedure that he thought would be more physically comfortable and less generally threatening. In his "caret test" he presented the participant with a random array of carets (< >) facing in four different directions: left, right, up, and down. He presented participants with a tachistoscope for one-tenth of a second, long enough for a vague impression of the content for most people. Then Palmer asked them to say which direction of caret they most strongly noticed at the moment that the array was exposed. At the same time, an agent in another room was viewing one direction of caret, which constituted the ESP target. An ESP hit then would be obtained by picking the caret facing the same direction as the one being viewed by the agent. Palmer added a wrinkle that he hoped would increase the level of threat for some trials and decrease it for others. On some trials, the agent viewed the target superimposed upon a message that was hoped to be reassuring ("Ashley and I are one"—Ashley was the name of the agent). On other trials the target was superimposed on a line drawing of a monster. This figure was intended to introduce an element of extrasensory threat.

Participants also filled out a questionnaire measuring dissociative tendencies ("trait dissociation"), and they responded to a question after the test indicating how dissociative their responding was (how "drawn" they felt to certain responses).

Palmer found in his initial study a provocative but unpredicted finding involving anxiety proneness, dissociativeness, and ESP performance. First he noticed that people with stronger dissociative tendencies scored in highly extreme ways (means departing both directions from chance) in the threatening condition, so he was interested in finding if some other variable might separate them into high and low scoring groups. He turned to the anxiety measure. He found that, for high-trait-dissociative participants, their degree of anxiety proneness correlated positively with their ESP performance. People who were highly trait dissociative and also prone to be more anxious scored highly when the monster added the element of extrasensory threat. Highly trait-dissociative people who were not anxious scored poorly in that condition (behaving more as most people might be expected to behave).

Palmer also found that when he divided his participants who *responded* more dissociatively to the test (said they often felt "drawn to" certain parts of the array) versus those who said they thought their responding was mainly random, he found higher scoring for those who felt "more drawn."

Palmer then carried out another study almost identical to the first to test these findings. In his second study he found the effect of trait anxiety and trait dissociation again, but at only a marginal level of significance. When the two studies are combined, the overall effect is a strong one. He also found, overall, significantly higher scoring for the more dissociative responders ("felt drawn") than the less dissociative responders ("just random").

In his next study of this series, Palmer (2011) primarily followed up on the last finding, the effect of the extent to which people said they were responding dissociatively in the ESP task. He did not vary the anxiety of the participants nor the threat of the target situation. His ESP test this time involved the movements of a planchette about a board circled with letters of the alphabet, modeled after the Ouija board. Participants carried out this task while alone in a darkened room, as a sender looked at a word in another room. They were asked to speak aloud (for recording) when the marker seemed to stop at one letter or another. After their thirty-minute session they rated how frequently, if at all, the movements of the board seemed to them to reflect an "outside force." Then they were shown the target word along with four decoys and rated each word for its degree of similarity to the behavior of the planchette. This was their ESP score.

Palmer made up a new, exploratory test that he intended to measure an aspect of dissociative tendencies using experiences that are reported by people who suffer from temporal lobe epilepsy, but his main interest was in how dissociatively people felt they responded (how much the planchette seemed to move itself). He broke these ratings into three groups with roughly equal numbers of participants. These were: (a) no movements perceived as autonomous; (b) some autonomous, up to 40 percent; and (c) over 40 percent of the movements perceived as autonomous. Analysis of his results showed that the middle group scored well over chance on the task, and the extreme groups below. His new measure of dissociative tendency did not relate to ESP scoring nor to his dissociative-response measure.

Palmer also carried out the third study in this set (Palmer and Lieberman, 1975), although he did not use the term *dissociation* at that time. The studies just cited looked at one aspect of dissociation: feeling that one's decisions do not quite come from oneself. This study looked at another aspect: that one's experiential self is not quite connected to one's physical self. Participants were induced to relax, and half were also asked to try to "leave their bodies" to travel to the distant ESP targets and then try to report them. Those who later reported that they were able to experience the dissociative sense of leaving their bodies scored significantly better with their free responses than those who did not dissociate in that way.

Agreement with Theory for Studies on Dissociation

Palmer's first finding, involving at once trait anxiety, trait dissociativeness, and threat of targets, is the one that is most pertinent to this discussion. This finding, which was replicated and seems to be likely reliable, implies that when people who are prone to dissociation are also likely to be anxious, and then find themselves in a situation that extrasensory information tells them is especially stressful, will tend to make positive access to other extrasensory information as well. However, in such a stressful situation, if dissociative people are not anxious they will tend to unconsciously decline to incorporate that other extrasensory information and respond to it by excluding it from awareness.

This relationship sounds complex, but it would make psychological sense if we remember that dissociative tendencies are understood to often result from experiences of emotional trauma. In fact, people who have "earned their dissociation the hard way" through traumatic experiences would be likely to be the ones who are both dissociative and frequently anxious. It would be a sensible survival mechanism for such persons to be more vigilant than most at an extrasensory level, more unconsciously alert to signs of possible danger, and use extrasensory information more vigilantly when they find such signs. This pattern is reminiscent of the self-report of the remarkable remote-viewer Joe McMoneagle, who has said that he grew up in a dangerous environment and used psi abilities to survive there. He believes he then carried these abilities over to a very successful career as an intelligence officer placed in many dangerous combat situations in Vietnam before he settled into the safer means of gathering intelligence through accurate use of extrasensory information.[86]

In regard to the assessment of dissociative responding, it appears that such a self-report at the time of testing, given a procedure that permits some degree of "automaticity" in response, can be a sensitive indicator telling us who is actually experiencing the procedure in a dissociative way and thus is most likely to transform any anxiety involved into a successful acquisition of extrasensory information.

Then why did the people who reported the very highest level of dissociation in Palmer's study score poorly on the test involving an alphabet board? We can only speculate, but it may be important to note that this study involved people who had participated in other research at his laboratory, and many were quite invested in their identities as having psychic abilities, mental healing powers, etc. To say that one's Ouija board planchette is moving almost half the time or more *by itself* is an extreme position to take for someone who is not psychiatrically dissociative. In this case, it might well represent a strong commitment to seem psychic. If so, then it is relevant that in a number of studies on the effect of open-mindedness toward psi, experimenters have tended to find that while ratings of belief in the reality of psi show generally positive relationships with performance, strong assertions on the part of the participant that he or she is personally psychic and will certainly do well in a test are more often associated with below-chance actual performance. Such a high degree of ego involvement in an outcome might be expected to raise the level of stress and unconscious anxiety and result in an unconscious avoidance of the extrasensory information. Of course, it is speculative to account for Palmer's finding in this way and these ideas would need to be confirmed in further research.

From the point of view of this discussion, it is unfortunate that Palmer's ouija board study did not examine dissociation in the context of different levels of anxiety and threat. Research that examines the complex interaction of all these things seems most likely to be instructive.

At any rate, the study of dissociation, anxiety, and psi has barely begun, and no firm conclusions can be drawn from this handful of findings. Such as they are, though, they are at least roughly consistent with the expectations of First Sight theory, which would assert that if an individual has a tendency to manage anxiety and threat in a dissociative manner, then these maneuvers of unconscious thought should be brought to bear on the treatment of extrasensory information. If someone can respond dissociatively to threat, then it seems likely that they will be able to make positive use of extrasensory information at the same time, if it is their intention to do so.

OVERVIEW OF THE RELATION OF FEAR AND PSI

Researchers live in the dense woods of their methods and findings, but most people do not. When we withdraw from the thicket, what are the main things to conclude about fear and psi and their relation to First Sight theory?

First, the theory expects that fear should affect the use the mind unconsciously makes of extrasensory information in ways that are generally similar to how it affects unconscious usage of subliminal, sensory information. A wide range of evidence suggests that this is generally true.

A cluster of well-studied physiological responses expresses an active state of anxiety. These may be consciously experienced, but very often they are subtle and unconscious. Besides arousing these physiological responses, a state of anxiety also reliably hampers the effort to bring preconscious information quickly, completely, and accurately to conscious awareness. There is good evidence that this is equally true for sensory and extrasensory information.

Unconscious attention orients rapidly to threat. Attention to both extrasensory and preconscious sensory information should be more likely if the thing involved is potentially dangerous.

The ability to bring preconscious information to consciousness and work with it cognitively in any way is impeded if the individual is in a state of anxiety. This is equally true with preconscious information that is sensory and preconscious information that is extrasensory.

Unconscious attention to an extrasensory threat arouses an anticipatory threat response, and this is expressed by appropriate physiological and psychological activity. Examples of such physiological activity include an increase in electrodermal activity and in heart rate and heart rate variability. Examples of such psychological effects include a priming response to the recognition of emotionally similar material and an appropriate change of mood state. One sees these sorts of unconscious physiological and psychological responses to subliminal information that is potentially threatening, and evidence is strong that the same sorts of effects tend to occur in regard to information that is extrasensory and threatening.

One way that a state of anxiety (perhaps subtle and unconscious) can be aroused is if the information in question is threatening. Since threatening information is likely to induce anxiety, the presence of threatening information will tend to be attended to rapidly by unconscious attention (and expressed physiologically and by unconscious psychological processes) but avoided in conscious awareness. This is true whether the information is extrasensory or is subliminal/sensory.

With both sensory and extrasensory preconscious information, this impeding effect will be most reliable with people who are generally more prone to becoming anxious or who find the particular information to be particularly upsetting for them. This is because it is these people who will most reliably react to the threatening information with anxiety.

Anxiety is not only aroused by anxiety-arousing (threatening) things that one is trying consciously to perceive and respond to in some task. It may also be a function of many other things, including other aspects of the situation or a personal state of arousal that the individual is bringing into the situation. Anxiety from any source will have the same effects on preconscious processing as anxiety due to the quality of information in a task. Evidence is good that this is true whether the mind is preconsciously processing sensory or extrasensory information.

Specific ways of responding preconsciously to threat when one is actually or potentially anxious have been described in regard to sensory information—ways such as vigilance, repression, or dissociation. If a person tends to rely upon such a pattern with regard to preconscious sensory information, he or she will tend to rely upon it with preconscious extrasensory information as well. More evidence about this is available in some areas than others, but the general trend of findings suggests that this is true.

Our emotional state—whether fear or emotional security—is an important factor that we consult unconsciously when we make use of preconscious information. Apparently, we apply this contextual factor similarly to things that are just beyond the fringe of consciousness whether they are within our sensory ken or beyond it.

NOTES

1. We can hope for the time when our engagement with psi information is generally understood to be an integral part of our psychological functioning. Then all of the "paras" can be decently buried and will no longer burden our language.

2. Beck 1976; Beck and Clark, 1997.

3. MacLeod, 1991.

4. MacLeod et al., 1986.

5. Stormark, Nordby, and Hugdahl, 1995.

6. For a pertinent theory and research overview, see Eysenck et al., 2007.

7. Rhine, 1967.

8. Gurney, Myers, and Podmore, 1886; Rhine, 1953, 1964, 1967.

9. Van de Castle, 1977.

10. Andreassi, 1989.

11. Bierman and Radin, 1997.

12. Bierman, 2000a; Bierman and Radin, 1998.

13. Radin, 2004a.

14. Bierman and Scholte, 2002.

15. McCraty, Atkinson, and Bradley, 2004a.

16. Radin and Borges, 2009.

17. McCraty et al., 2004b; Radin and Lobach, 2007.

18. Tressoldi et al., 2009.

19. Hinterberger et al., 2007.

20. Lang and Greenwald, 1993.

21. Canli et al., 2002.

22. Wildey, 2001.

23. Alvarez, 2010.

24. Broughton, 2002.

25. Conty et al., 2010.

26. Gilbert and McGuire, 1998.

27. Saboonchi and Lundh, 1999.

28. Amabile et al., 1990.

29. Kaminski et al., 2004.

30. Braud, Shafer, and Andrews, 1993.

31. Wiseman and Smith, 1994; Wiseman et al., 1995.

32. Wiseman and Schlitz, 1997.

33. Schlitz et al., 2005; Wiseman and Schlitz, 1999.

34. Schlitz and Braud, 1997.

35. Schmidt et al., 2004.

36. Savva and French, 2002.

37. Fisher, 1988; Poetzl, 1917.

38. Roe, Sherwood, Luke, and Farrell, 2002.

39. Sherwood, Roe, Simmonds, and Biles, 2002.

40. Robinson and Clore, 2002.

41. Zajonc, 2008.

42. James, 1962, p. 177.

43. Dixon, 1981, pp. 139–44.

44. Sheldrake, 2003.

45. Sheldrake, 2005.

46. Peterson, 1978.

47. Williams, 1983.

48. Sheldrake 1998, 1999, 2000, 2001a, 2001b, 2002, 2003.

49. Sheldrake, 2005.

50. Radin, 2005; Schmidt et al., 2004.

51. Unpublished thesis, reported by Sheldrake, 2005.

52. Hoover, 1978; Walter et al., 1998.

53. This implicit index of anxiety has established validity. See, for example, Nakamura and Wright, 1965.

54. Crandall, 1998.

55. Sailaja and Rao, 1973.

56. The author is indebted to Palmer (1978), who noted that neuroticism scales tend to predict negative scoring better in individual testing than in group testing situations. Here we add additional studies to his survey and provide a theoretical rationale for the pattern.

57. Smith and Humphrey, 1946; Nicol and Humphrey, 1953.

58. Houtkooper, 2003; Kahn, 1952; Kanthamani and Rao, 1971, 1973; Nash, 1963; Rao, 1965b; Sargent and Harley, 1981; Watt, 1991.

59. Ballard et al., 1983; Roe, Davey and Stevens, 2003.

60. Ballard et al., 1983; Green, 1966; Haraldsson et al., 2002; Houtkooper et al., 1999; Nash and Nash, 1967; Nicol and Humphrey, 1953; Roe, Henderson, and Matthews, 2008.

61. Smith and Humphrey, 1946.

62. Kanthamani and Broughton, 1992; Rao, 1965b.

63. Aström, 1965; Johnson and Houtkooper, 1988; Kanthamani and Broughton, 1994; Krishna and Rao, 1981; McGuire, Percy, and Carpenter, 1974; Randall, 1974; Weiner, 1986.

64. Freeman and Nielsen, 1964; Haight et al., 1978.

65. Steinkamp, 2005.

66. Sargent, 1980; Parra and Villanueva, 2003; Rogo and Sargent, 1982; Broughton and Alexander, 1997; Morris et al., 1993; Haraldsson and Gissurarson, 1985.

67. Ballard, Cohee, and Eldridge, 1983; Johnson, 1971; Johnson and Nordbeck, 1972.

68. Dalton, 1997b.

69. Blum, 1955; Henley and Dixon, 1976.

70. Carpenter, 1971.

71. Janet, 1889, 1907; Putnam, 1999.

72. Putnam, 1989.

73. Murphy, 1966; Richards, 1991.

74. Ross and Joshi, 1992.

75. Kragh and Smith, 1970.

76. Kragh 1960a, 1960b, 1962.

77. Kragh and Neuman, 1982.

78. Carpenter, 1965.

79. Haraldsson and Houtkooper, 1995.

80. Haraldsson et al., 2002.

81. Watt and Ramakers, 2003.

82. Haraldsson and Gissurarson, 1985.

83. Bucci, 2007.

84. Bryant and Panasetis, 2005.

85. Palmer and Johnson, 1991; Palmer 1992.

86. McMoneagle, 1997, 2002.

15

Extroversion and Psi

Society is no comfort to one not sociable.

—William Shakespeare

EXTRAVERSION AND PSI PERFORMANCE
HAVE BEEN FOUND TO BE RELATED

This chapter begins with an observed fact and then moves on to examine how well First Sight theory can accommodate it. A positive relationship has been found many times between extraversion and scores on ESP tests. This may be the most consistently replicated finding in parapsychology, even though it has received little theoretical attention. The lack of attention might be because many, perhaps most, parapsychologists are more introverted than extraverted, and they believe that they have had their own shares of psychic experiences and known other introverts to report them, too. An edge for extraverts may seem confusing or a little unpleasant. But a relationship has been frequently found and demands to be understood. Can First Sight theory account for this relationship and its variants? An argument that it can will be presented and compared to other hypotheses that have been proposed.

Remember that First Sight theory asserts that psi engagements are ubiquitous and continuous for all organisms. They are not the exclusive property of extraverts or any other subclass of being. Theory also proposes that it is unconscious intention that determines the signing of elements of psychic and other preconscious bits of meaning, and thereby the direction of scoring in ESP tests. If First Sight theory is to explain a relationship between scoring and extraversion, it must be in terms of the sorts of unconscious intentions that extraverts and introverts are likely to have in the context of tests of extrasensory perception.

EXTRAVERSION AND PSI

In 1945, Betty Humphrey, a psychologist with the Duke University Parapsychology Laboratory, published a paper in which fifty-five persons were tested individually for their ability to correctly guess concealed cards, and they were also given a standard questionnaire of the day: the Bernreuter Personality Inventory.[1] One dimension of the test was called Introversion, and two others (Dominance and Gregariousness) have been found subsequently to be highly associated with general measures of extraversion-introversion. Correlations showed that more extraverted persons on these scales tended strongly to score more positively than the introverts. Humphrey's study was exploratory: she did not explicitly predict this relationship, although she followed it up a few years later,[2] found the relationships again, and reported that they were statistically significant. Her research began a sizable series of investigations that have explored this connection. Reviewers[3] have noted that a clear preponderance of the studies that have looked into it have found that individuals who score more highly on various measures of extraversion also tend to score positively on tests of extrasensory perception, while introverts tend to score below chance. While most relationships found have been positive, a few have been reversed, with introverts scoring more highly than extraverts. Some of these reversals have been predicted and are actually helpful in shedding more light on the meaning of the connection between these things. This will be discussed further below.

Still, the predominant pattern has been to find extraverts scoring positively and introverts negatively. Honorton, Ferrari, and Bem (1998) conducted a meta-analysis of sixty studies reported by seventeen different investigators. They found a highly significant overall effect ($p = 0.000004$, 2-tail). The effect was not limited to a few experimenters and was unrelated to ratings of study quality. Since that meta-analysis was compiled, three other reports have appeared that reported new, significant confirmations of the positive relationship.[4] Three reports[5] found no relationship in ganzfeld studies. No significant reversals of the relationship were reported. While not invariant, the trend found by the meta-analysis has tended to hold up over time, perhaps with less consistency in ganzfeld studies (this is discussed further below).

Leaving the laboratory for a moment, it would seem that even if parapsychologists had no theoretical reasons to expect extraverts to express ESP more positively, the naturalistic reports of extralaboratory work should have prepared them for the fact. If one surveys the famous psychics and mediums whose apparent psychic abilities stimulated the development of the science to begin with, it is clear that they have tended overwhelmingly to be socially active, charming, assertive, and attention-seeking people. D. D. Home, generally acknowledged as perhaps the greatest psychic in history, was so expansive in his ambitions for attention and acclaim that he crossed oceans and dared many barriers of convention to secure it.[6] The same may be said for the flamboyant Eusapia Palladino.[7] Whatever one might conclude about the genuineness of her apparent gifts, her extraversion could not be doubted. Many of the other famous female mediums of the nineteenth century are more complex cases. Mrs. Leonard, for example,[8] was seen as rather quiet and proper in many situations, but when in trance and guided by her "spirits" she could be quite assertive and even bawdy. Zingrone[9] has reminded us that in the Victorian society in which these phenomena flourished, women were generally constrained to fit the requirements of a demure and submissive role. These mediums were as a group assertive and expansive woman who found a kind of situation in which these traits could be expressed and enjoyed and simultaneously disowned. Gifted mediums (or psychics) have been found to be just as extraverted in more recent times. Schmeidler (1982) tested a small group of them and found marked extraversion to characterize each one.

Their own star subjects in the laboratory also should have alerted parapsychologists to the importance of extraversion. In his monograph in which the new methods and findings of parapsychology were first revealed, J. B. Rhine (1934 [1973]) noted that the little group of highly scoring students he had discovered were all friendly, sociable people. His superstar, Hubert Pearce, was described as particularly so: "[He was] . . . very sociable and approachable and much interested in people."[10] Notable extraversion can also be seen in more recent star subjects, such as Billy Delmore,[11] whom I remember charming audiences and partygoers with the charisma of a successful politician, and Joe McMoneagle (2002), who apparently enjoys performing extremely challenging psi feats for huge television audiences in Japan when he is not successfully demonstrating remote viewing abilities in other settings. Delmore's and McMoneagle's extrachance performances have been obtained repeatedly under well-controlled laboratory conditions, so their genuineness need not be debated.

Among the laboratory stars, perhaps only one exception to the rule of extraversion stands out. This is Pavel Stepanek, the subject of Milan Ryzl.[12] If not the highest-scoring person in a single performance, he was perhaps the most enduring. He was tested routinely and repetitively in a task in which he tried to identify the uppermost color (green or white) of a card enclosed in a sealed envelope. He sustained psi-hitting performance at this for over four years, accumulating 42,598 trials with a 59.7 percent scoring rate (chance was 50 percent). This includes only published results, although the authors[13] assure us that the rate would be even higher if all work done were included. Stepanek was a quiet, shy man, certainly an introvert. His remarkable performance may have a lot to do with the unusual circumstances of his testing. His ability was trained over a long period of time in private hypnotic sessions with Ryzl, and testing was almost always carried out with Ryzl present. Visitors had to be introduced gradually and carefully for his performance to rebound to high levels. Stepanek and Ryzl had the kind of intensely private relationship and calm, orderly, repetitive testing situation that would appear to be comfortable for an introvert and probably stifling for an extravert.

In general, the positive relationship between ESP performance and extraversion appears to be a real, if not invariant, association. To understand it better we need to move beyond the colloquial use of these terms and see what psychologists mean when they speak of extraverts and introverts, and we need to know what makes these groups of people different from each other.

EXTRAVERSION AND INTROVERSION

Webster defines *extraversion* as "the act, state, or habit of being predominantly concerned with and obtaining gratification from what is outside the self." The term is associated with an opposite tendency, *introversion*, defined as "the state of or tendency toward being wholly or predominantly concerned with and interested in one's own mental life." In popular usage the terms are usually used to describe persons who tend to be friendly, cheerful, and assertive and enjoy being with others as opposed to quieter and more reflective types who often prefer to be alone or to relate to others one-on-one, and when in groups tend to be more retiring and reserved. The distinction, in one form or another, is a perennial one in Western thinking about human nature. Claudius Galen, in the second century AD, believing that mental functioning was colored by the balance of bodily humors, contrasted sanguine people, who are sociable and happy, with phlegmatic ones, who are reserved and thoughtful.[14] Friedrich Nietzsche (1956) contrasted *dionysian* persons who were adventurous and expressive with *apollonian* ones who were inward and thoughtful.

The constructs were carried into psychology in slightly different terms by Heymans (1929) and then brought to broader clinical and popular usage by Carl Jung (1960a). Jung proposed that there were two basic *attitudes* that people may use to organize their psyches: the attitude of the extravert is outward, toward the external world of people and things, while the attitude of the introvert is inward, toward the inner life of feelings, memories, and imagination. (Jung himself was a decided introvert, as indicated by the title of his autobiography, *Memories, Dreams, Reflections,* in which there were thousands of searching, inward observations but not a single mention of World War II.) This dichotomy of *attitudes* was part of a complex and highly subjective typological system for Jung that also included four *functions*: thinking and feeling are the *perceiving* pair of functions, and sensing and intuiting are the *judging* pair of functions. Jung implied that one's primary attitude of extraversion or introversion was probably determined both by temperament and by choice, although the choice is probably made early in life and is largely preverbal. Since Jung was a psychiatrist and intended for his theory to help explain emotional disorder, he was interested in the pathological extremes these basic attitudes could take. He believed that extreme extraverts are vulnerable to hysteria, a condition in which internal emotional conflicts are experienced as external, medical disorders, with no insight into the personal origins of the symptoms (features of this syndrome are now divided between the more modern labels of dissociative disorder and somatization disorder). Extreme introverts were prone to psychasthenia, a condition of chronic exhaustion and withdrawal in which external realities feel overwhelming.

For purposes of research, these Jungian dimensions in their nonpathological forms have been assessed by self-report questionnaires. By far the most frequently used has been the Meyers-Briggs Type Indicator,[15] although several other instruments have appeared in the literature as well.[16]

Outside of Jungian theory, psychologists who have studied extraversion have relied upon factor analysis to resolve the underlying correlational structure of questionnaire responses.[17] Most of the parapsychological research has used these self-description instruments (Jungian or not). As with most questionnaires measuring personality traits, scores tend to follow a bell-shaped distribution, so that while a few persons are represented as extreme types, most express more subtle tendencies in one direction or the other. Sometimes nonquestionnaire, more directly behavioral ways of assessing this dimension have been used as well, such as the ratings of peers or teachers—from the point of view of First Sight theory, this may be the most promising approach.

Although this dimension of personality has been assessed by many different methods developed in different ways, it is striking that across this large literature the various measures tend to correlate with each other quite well—perhaps better than for any other human trait. This is certainly in contrast to the poor agreement among various measures of creativity discussed earlier. Western culture apparently finds this dimension intuitively sensible and meaningful.

This does not imply that the construct is unitary. There is general agreement that the dimension is a complex one, with many constituent parts.

The makers of the NEO-PI,[18] the currently most widely used instrument measuring it, have acknowledged this complexity in building their test. Their extraversion score is the summary of the subscores of six "facets" of extraversion:

- *Warmth* refers to a tendency to be affectionate and friendly. A sample item is: "I really like most people I meet."
- *Gregariousness* means enjoying the company of others, particularly in large groups. An item: "I like to have a lot of people around me."
- *Assertiveness.* People high on this facet tend to be interpersonally dominant. They endorse such items as: "People look to me to make decisions."
- *Activity.* Such people are rapid tempo, vigorous, energetic, and impulsive in their actions. They say: "I often feel as if I'm bursting with energy."
- *Excitement Seeking.* These people crave excitement. They "love the excitement of roller coasters" and reject the statement, "I avoid movies that are shocking or scary."
- *Positive Emotions.* This refers to a general tendency to be happy and joyful. Such a person says: "I laugh easily" and "I am high spirited."

THE CORE OF EXTRAVERSION

Given this cluster of related qualities, is there any core trait that binds them all together and serves as the central "cause" of the disposition? Different approaches have been taken to answering this question. Jung[19] defined it as basically a matter of unconscious interest, a direct approach that is congruent with First Sight theory. Eysenck (1967, 1970) took a reductionistic tack and hypothesized a difference in nervous system functioning that might account for it. Very briefly, he proposed that people differ biologically on two related dimensions. One is the level of chronic cortical activity or arousal. The other is the capacity to inhibit cortical arousal. The ratio of these two things in an individual is the critical matter. If a person has a tendency toward a high level of arousal and also a poor ability to inhibit it, he or she spends a lot of time in a state of high internal arousal. Such persons are introverts. If someone has a low level of chronic arousal and a strong ability to inhibit it, he or she is normally unaroused and is considered an extravert.[20] Others who are more balanced on these matters fall in between the extreme types. Eysenck assumed that these differences are heritable. Since research has shown that about one-third of the variance in this trait is attributable to genetic factors,[21] this is a reasonable assumption, at least to some extent.

It may seem odd to say that extraverts, who are generally more energetic and active than introverts, are chronically unaroused. Eysenck explains this by saying that because extraverts are lacking in internal arousal they are more motivated to seek it outside themselves. They seek it by mixing more with other people and pursue it with more energy.

Some evidence has confirmed Eysenck's hypothesis about chronic cortical arousal. For example, extraverts tend to have less aroused patterns of EEG activity in quiet situations,[22] they are less responsive to stimuli according to galvanic skin readings and other indications of sympathetic nervous system arousal, and are slower to be aware of extraneous stimuli.[23] Many less obvious predictions have been supported too, such as a tendency of introverts to sustain longer the swirling illusion that follows staring at a rotating spiral.[24] This is presumably because extraverts are able to inhibit this internal stimulation more rapidly. Extraverts have also been found to experience periods of time as being shorter than introverts do, especially in quiet, monotonous situations, because lacking internal stimulation, they bore more quickly.[25]

Because extraverts are motivated to seek stimulation outwardly, by implication for Eysenck the "excitement-seeking" aspect of the trait is the most central one and acts to pull the other qualities along with it. For example, a cortically subaroused extravert seeks excitement with other people and so is more gregarious and finds the excitement they afford to be pleasurable, so is also friendlier. An introvert, more absorbed with chronic internal stimulation, spends more time with personal thoughts and feelings, has less energy for other people, and finds extra stimulation more tiring than pleasurable.

Other researchers have sought the "core" of extraversion not in biology but in the patterns of correlations and factors produced by the tests that measure it. While some have argued that *sociability* is the core trait of extraversion,[26] others have produced theoretical and empirical evidence that it is really something called *reward sensitivity*; that is, a tendency to respond in a motivated way to challenges and opportunities for reward.[27] The conflict between these views seems to have been resolved by further research that has shown that reward sensitivity in general is not the central concern for extraverts but is rather a tendency to find *positive social attention* very rewarding and a strong motivation to seek such attention.[28] Desiring the positive attention of groups and of strangers is an especially strong discriminator between the two types. Extraverts desire this; introverts do not so much and might even find it aversive. To sum up the matter in terms of goals and interests (as First Sight theory would do) extraverts find positive social attention to be more rewarding than introverts do and are more motivated to seek it, especially in front of strangers and groups. When they are in situations that offer little such potential attention they become quickly bored and yearn for more stimulating opportunities. Desiring such attention when with others, they behave energetically and competitively and warmly to evoke it and are perceived as dominant and friendly. When they win such attention they find it very enjoyable and are happy and cheerful. Introverts, on the other hand, are not so strongly motivated to receive this sort of interpersonal reward, are relatively more occupied with their own concerns, and so are generally less attention seeking, energetic, competitive, and buoyant. They are also more patient with relative isolation and time-consuming tasks and tend to find group situations distracting and tiring.

Returning to the facets of extraversion defined by the NEO-PI, from the social-reward point of view the central ones would seem to be *assertiveness* and *gregariousness.* Extraverts want to win approval, power, and other indications of social success and seek the company of others in hope of gaining these rewards. Introverts either care less about such success or are pessimistic about their chances of earning it. In the first case they are content with less consistent attention, and in the second case they tend to endure some degree of chronic loneliness and distress.

Could all of this go along with differences in cortical arousal, as Eysenck has said? Of course. The more socially motivated extravert experiences little arousal unless the opportunity to pursue the relevant goals are available, whereas the introvert can find less social situations interesting and engaging enough. Just because introverts are more cortically aroused does not mean that this is entirely the "root cause" of the trait. The meaningfulness of an activity in the moment influences cortical arousal, and at the same time cortical arousal influences the experience of the situation. As Jung said, this difference in motivation, interest, and arousal appears to be partly due to constitutional factors and partly a matter of long-engrained patterns of choice.

Some patterns of differing performance between extraverts and introverts appear to be readily explained by referring to differences in social reward motivation. For example, while some research has shown that extraverts become frustrated and quit complex tasks before introverts do,[29] other studies show that extraverts outperform introverts on other demanding tasks that have a stronger social component, such as sales[30]; and a meta-analysis[31] has found that the dimension has no reliable relationship at all with the kind of cumulative learning expressed in academic success. In a different approach to this issue of achievement, McKeachie et al. (1966) compared students' performance in classes in which teachers used language implying teamwork and affiliation with other classes in which teachers used language that stressed achievement but not affiliation. Male students who were high in their implicitly measured need for affiliation did better than those low in need affiliation in the classes in which affiliation issues were cued, but they did more poorly in the other classes. Komarraju et al. (2009) found that their measure of intrinsic motivation predicted academic performance significantly, but extrinsic (social reward) motivation did not. They also found that extraverts were much more extrinsically motivated than introverts were, who tended more toward intrinsic motivation. Opportunities for social reward have been found to be important in the pertinence of extraversion in other, nonacademic situations as well. Extraverts have been found to use their social skills to better facilitate a sense of cohesiveness in work teams, but only when the teams meet face to face and not when they carry out equally demanding work in a video, virtual environment.[32] Similarly, scores on extraversion predict behavioral differences very nicely when the individuals' performances are explicitly attributed to them, and the prediction is especially powerful when the ones assessing the performance are of higher status; but scores do not predict so powerfully when the evaluators are of lower status and do not predict performance at all when results are anonymous.[33]

A larger social context (more than one or two other people) makes extraversion more salient in performance.[34] The gender composition of the social situation has also been found to be important in terms of how great the reward potential is. Reasoning that potential reward should be greater when one is with another person of the opposite sex, Campbell et al. (2003) found that extraversion scores predicted behavior when the participant had an evaluator of the opposite sex but not when the evaluator was of the same sex.

The implication of these studies and others like them is that extraversion/introversion will become an important predictor of performance in situations that contain an opportunity to earn immediate interpersonal reward and in which the potential interpersonal reward is highly valued. In situations that do not offer such opportunity and importance, the trait is not expressed or may even show a reversed effect.

EXTRAVERSION AND ESP

Why should extraverts tend to perform better on tests of ESP than introverts do? What ideas have been proposed?

Eysenck (1967) hypothesized that the higher level of chronic internal activation of introverts somehow makes it more difficult for them to acquire extrasensory information. He made two assumptions in his rationale without explicitly stating them: one is that persons differ in their ability to access extrasensory information (and that ESP tests measure this stable trait of extrasensory ability); the other is that the expression of this ability trait should be moderated by the same sorts of things that moderate the ability to learn and remember and express other skills. Extraversion has been found to be such a moderator. Eysenck cited the Yerkes-Dodson Law that is familiar to all students of introductory psychology. This law states that for any task there is some optimal level of arousal for performing it well. Too little arousal and the organism is insufficiently motivated to work optimally. Too much arousal and the organism is overwhelmed and again performs poorly. There is a "sweet spot" of arousal level for any skill that must be found for it to be optimally expressed. Extraverts tend to perform better in ESP tests, he reasoned, because most testing situations are suf-ficiently but not excessively stimulating for them, whereas introverts are liable to find the same situations overstimulating and then underperform. But just why does optimal stimulation open the extrasensory doors, and excessive stimulation close them? Eysenck does not specifically address this question. He simply makes the analogy to other skills. If the ESP "ability" functions like memory, as he implies, by retrieving internal information, then it appears that he is proposing a kind of signal-detection idea, similar to that proposed by Stanford (1978) and discussed earlier. Extraverts, with relatively low arousal and little internal noise, should be better able to discern the weak extrasensory signal, given that stimulation is high enough that they are willing to expend the effort. Introverts, with a higher level of arousal and internal noise, should have greater difficulty discerning the weak signal.

However, it is important to remember that Eysenck does not expect that the association would be invariant across situations. It might be that some kinds of situations and tasks should favor the performance of introverts rather than extraverts. These would be ones in which external stimulation is very low. As noted earlier, a disadvantage of this signal-detection hypoth-esis is that it can account for positive and chance-level performance, but it is mute as to psi-missing.

Why is ESP ability a trait, according to Eysenck? Because extraversion is. He seems to be proposing that extrasensory ability is almost one of the ac-companying features of extraversion, such as the capacity to inhibit distract-ing stimuli and the motivation for external arousal. A disadvantage of the trait assumption is that consistent performance on the part of an individual across time in tests of ESP or PK has been much more the exception than the rule. Yet correlational patterns with other variables are often relatively robust. If tests of ESP and PK measured traits, then the old truism of psy-chometrics would hold true: validity can be no greater than reliability (the strength of relationship of a trait with another variable can be no greater than the consistent measurement of the trait itself). Yet with ESP and PK, validity often does appear to be higher than reliability—that is, persons are not very consistent over time in their scores on ESP or PK, but these scores may show fairly robust relationships with other variables, such as extraver-sion. This becomes sensible if we discard the assumption that ESP and PK are traits and instead consider them to be transient responses to situations against a backdrop of consistent access to potential information to be used however the organism finds optimal in the moment. Remember that this is the primary assumption of the First Sight model.

John Palmer (1978, 1997, 1998a) has taken a different tack in explaining the extraversion-ESP relationship. In a model summarizing and generalizing from previous findings, Palmer has argued that the direction of scoring in ESP tests is a function of the percipient's comfort. When comfortable, people can access the information more easily and express it positively. When uncomfortable and anxious, psi information is avoided and scoring turns in a negative direction. Extraverts tend to be comfortable and happy when in group situations, and introverts tend to be uncomfortable and anxious. In testing involving the presence of others, particularly groups and strangers, the extraverts would be expected to outperform the introverts. Palmer offers this as an empirical generalization without attempting to offer a mechanism for why it should be so. His idea is not necessarily independent of that of Eysenck, who also expects that extraverts should be happier and less anxious in social situations. Palmer adds the idea that anxiety should turn scoring in a negative direction, so by implication he is not depending upon a simple signal-detection model. We have already seen that anxiety does tend to turn extrasensory performance in a negative direction. Support for the importance of happinesss versus anxiety in the context of extraversion/introversion would be obtained by examining situations in which extraverts had in fact been found to outperform introverts and finding independent indications that the extraverts had indeed been happier and the introverts more anxious.

It may be worth noting here that introverts are not all alike when it comes to anxiety in social situations. Some researchers have addressed this problem by distinguishing two distinct types of people who score at the introverted end of the scale. Different names are given for this distinction, but they point to more or less the same thing. Eysenck says that some are "stable introverts (phlegmatics)" because they also score low on his neuroticism factor, while those who score high in neuroticism are "unstable introverts (melancholics)." Stable introverts are calm, thoughtful, and passive, while unstable introverts are anxious, pessimistic, and avoidant.[35] Henjum (1982) distinguishes "Type A Introverts," who are self-actualizing, confident, and independent, from "Type B's," who are shy and have poor self-concepts. Singer and Bonanno (1990) point out that "Thinking Introverts" are reflective, independent, and have a more highly differentiated consciousness than most people, while "Social Introverts" are anxious, shy, and lacking in self-awareness. Clearly, persons who receive high scores on introversion scales (low scores on extraversion) may be very different from one another in their quality of adjustment and their response to social situations. Some tend to be autonomous and self-confident and engaged with personal concerns such as self-understanding and meeting internally set goals, and not so much motivated by social approval. These people do not tend to be anxious in social situations but simply find them less compelling. Another group may care as much about social approval as extraverts do but they believe themselves to be socially inadequate and likely to fail more than succeed in social situations, so the prospect of being with others (especially strangers) arouses fears of failure and shame. To the extent that anxiety does account for the negative extrasensory performance of introverts, the tendency should be found more strongly in the latter group. This seems to be an important question to explore with further research.

Schmeidler (1982, 1988) has proposed that comfort and anxiety might not mediate the relationship between extraversion and ESP scores so much as the greater dissociativeness and openness of extraverts. She makes a parallel between Eysenck's idea of inhibition and the concept of dissociation. Extraverts are better able to forget (inhibit) internal concerns and memories and are therefore more able to enter into each moment fresh and unencumbered by inner noise. Being more (nonpathologically) dissociated, they are more open to new experiences. She then draws upon the research discussed above in the discussion of psi and creativity that has shown that more open people tend to perform better at tests of ESP. Her idea is a sensible one, and does fit with some of the characteristics associated with extraversion versus introversion. However, the major test currently used to measure extraversion and openness, the NEO-PI, has been constructed in such a way that the two dimensions are uncorrelated factors. Schmeidler's idea could be tested by using that instrument. One would predict that openness would predict extrasensory performance more successfully than extraversion.

First Sight theory suggests an explanation that is not necessarily contrary to those of Eysenck, Palmer, and Schmeidler, but it incorporates them tentatively and puts them in a larger framework. It also offers a more delineated account of what forms the relationship should take and just why it should happen that way. First, the theory proposes that ESP (and PK) tests do not measure an ability trait but a response to a situation in the moment. Everyone swims in an extrasensory sea but accesses it and responds to it differently depending upon unconscious intention, and this is an individual and often highly variable matter. The direction of extrasensory response (assimilation or contrast) is held to be a function of unconscious intention, and the extremity of response is a function of the consistency with which such unconscious intention is maintained over time. Thus the theory asks: What are likely to be the unconscious intentions of extraverts and introverts? Expectations can be stated in terms of the facets of extraversion.

Following the research of Ashton et al. (2002) and others, it appears that extraverts and introverts differ primarily in how strongly they are motivated to earn the reward of positive social attention, so this may be assumed to be a primary determiner of unconscious intention in situations that are appropriate to call the issue up. In social situations and in relatively challenging social situations in particular, extraverts should be motivated to rise to the challenge of a test and should sense unconsciously that making a positive expression of the target material meets their goals. In less social and less challenging situations there is much less approval to win, and extraverts might be expected to turn away unconsciously from the target material in favor of competing unconscious sources of information. Introverts, on the other hand, are less strongly motivated to earn positive social attention and tend to find such situations uncompelling or unpleasant. Without the goal of earning such a reward, and sometimes with the goal of avoiding the whole situation, they would be expected to unconsciously intend to avoid the target material and express that by negative scoring deviations.

What about testing in situations that offer very little by way of potential positive attention for success? The salience of the dimension of extraversion-introversion would tend to vanish, and other more individual concerns would become more important for determining the direction of scoring. In such situations, however an individual scored, it generally should not be as a function of their scores on extraversion but a matter of other concerns and interests. No correlation with extraversion would be expected, unless the situation was pertinent in some other way to the characteristic interests of the two groups.

This expectation can be tested by examining the extraversion-ESP relationship in situations that differ in terms of the potential for social reward. As it happens, the meta-analysis of Honorton et al. (1998) provides just that. They divided studies that had been carried out in groups from those that used individual ESP testing with an experimenter (their analysis focused on forced-choice studies, since very few free-response studies used a group situation). In the typical group-testing situation,[36] a class or lecture group would sit en masse and fill out questionnaires and a paper-pencil test of guessing at lists of randomly chosen ESP targets. Response sheets are typically coded anonymously rather than identified by name to protect confidentiality, and percipients are typically assured that results will only be reported in terms of group statistics rather than individual performance for the same reason. No individual interaction with an experimenter or sender is provided, and no individual attention is given to performance. In many studies, percipients do not even learn privately how well or poorly they have done. In short, the situation is a very anonymous one, providing no opportunity for individual visibility and interpersonal reward. Individual testing, on the other hand, is an immediate social situation, typically with a stranger, in which feedback about performance is almost always given immediately with much opportunity for recognition and praise (or implicit disappointment) from the experimenter. If a sender is involved, this person is usually met by the percipient as well. Opportunity for social reward is ample.

Extraversion should be a salient trait in the individual testing situation, and not very salient in group testing. The results of Honorton's meta-analysis confirm the expectation. In the twenty-one studies using individual testing, the relationship between ESP and extraversion is positive and strongly significant ($z = 4.54$, $p = 0.000006$). In the twenty-four studies that used group testing there was no relationship. The difference between the two summary correlations is also quite significant ($z = 3.47$, $p = 0.00052$, 2-tailed).[37]

Another way in which situations may differ in their personal reward potential is in terms of the amount of competition involved. Extraverts are known to be more drawn to competitive activities than introverts are,[38] which has been interpreted as evidence that competition is more salient to the interests of extraverts. Crandall (1998) asked his participants to play a game in which virtual greyhounds could be made to advance on a track by influencing a random-event generator with psychokinesis. Half were tested in a competitive condition and half in what he called a "relaxed" condition, in which no competition was involved, participants were tested alone, and success was rewarded with cash. Extraversion scores correlated positively and significantly with PK performance in the competitive condition, but the relationship was nonsignificant in the relaxed condition. Also congruent with this pattern is the finding of Green (1965), who carried out an ESP test with respondents to a test in a popular magazine in which the article promised recognition and an award for high performance. Extraversion was not measured directly, but Green found that first-borns who were not also only children performed much better than everyone else, and this group is known to have high scores on the Dominance facet of extraversion.[39]

Finally, it is consistent with the importance of social reward that a group of seven of the highest individual performances ever recorded in tests of extrasensory perception up to the time of the report (1964) were all situations in which the percipients were given an unusual degree of challenge and expectation for success.[40] All of them appeared to be socially oriented people who found the challenge highly motivating. The author concluded that effective percipients were likely to be "responsive to the stimulation of audience attention. . . . natural public performers."[41]

EXTRAVERSION AND THE GANZFELD

There is one individual testing protocol that has been frequently used by parapsychologists that we would expect to be rather equivocal in terms of its salience for the trait of extraversion. This is ganzfeld testing. The ganzfeld situation is one in which a person is immersed in an undifferentiated visual field, and often a gentle auditory field of random noise as well. For parapsychologists it has been intended to submerge the percipient in a distraction-free environment where he or she might better discern subtle extrasensory promptings (inspired by a weak-signal idea of how ESP works).

The ganzfeld situation was first used by psychologists in the 1930s to study the internal determiners of visual perception.[42] The experiential evocativeness of the ganzfeld situation was first noticed by psychologists who adopted it, along with other varieties of sensory deprivation procedures, because of its capacity to induce hypnogogic experiences in participants.[43] A relatively short time in the ganzfeld will induce in many persons a flow of imagery that is dreamlike, along with altered bodily experiences. For this reason the ganzfeld also appealed to parapsychologists who had been finding extrasensory effects in other altered states, such as dreaming sleep[44] and hypnosis,[45] under the assumption that it might similarly "reduce the noise" of waking consciousness and allow more access to preconscious and potentially extrasensory material. Charles Honorton,[46] William and Lendell Braud,[47] and Adrian Parker (1975) all began using it more or less simultaneously.

In a typical ganzfeld ESP study, the *receiver* is placed in a reclining position on a comfortable chair or mattress in a soundproofed room and fitted with earphones that pipe in random "white noise" that sounds rather like the gentle whooshing emitted by a radio tuned between stations. Meanwhile, the eyes are covered with halves of table tennis balls gently taped in place, while a reddish light is placed overhead. When the eyes are open, this creates an even, pinkish glow in an undifferentiated visual field (a *ganz-feld*). In order to further reduce internal, somatic "noise," the percipient also typically undergoes a mildly hypnotic progressive physical relaxation procedure prior to the beginning of the extrasensory test. While the percipient (or *receiver*) is undergoing this distraction-free relaxation, most studies ask a *sender*, who is in a different room, to concentrate on target material (often a picture or a short video clip) in hope of influencing the spontaneous imagery of the receiver. The receiver is asked to provide an ongoing report of experience as it occurs, which is recorded (this is called the "mentation report"). A percipient might say, for example: "Now I am flying through clouds. The clouds are becoming little dots, and now they are becoming very far away. And now there is just a swirling silence . . . Oh, there's my grandmother . . .," etc.

After the session is over the percipient is shown the target material along with several instances of dummy, nontarget material of the same sort and asked to try to guess which was the actual target based on its degree of association with the experience that they have just had. If they can pick the correct target, they are said to have a "hit."

The power of the ganzfeld to induce reliable extrasensory performance will be discussed more in the next chapter. In the present context, the important point is that it has been used several times to assess the relation between extraversion and ESP performance. In ganzfeld studies overall a strongly significant positive relation has been found, according to the meta-analysis of Honorton et al. (1998). However, they also wondered if the extraversion or introversion of the *experimenter* might have an effect on how strongly this relationship occurs in the ganzfeld situation. Perhaps extraverted experimenters would evoke the correlation more strongly.

In fact, they were found to do so, but this sample of studies was small (eight experimenters, two extraverts and six introverts), and most of these involved a rather small number of participants. The difference did not reach statistical significance. In a moment we will examine a test of this question using a larger body of data. But first we must ask why the personality of the experimenter should matter in this way.

The ganzfeld is an equivocal situation in terms of the salience of extraversion because, while it is an individual testing situation, with personal experimenter-participant interaction, it is one specifically designed to permit the kind of internal, undistracted exploration of private experience that should be more interesting to introverts than to extraverts—extraverts seek rewarding positive attention in a social context. Here the percipient is urged and facilitated to leave all such distractions behind and embark on an inward journey in which he or she may privately encounter extrasensory information. And this is done alone, typically for a half-hour, without external stimulation. This procedure might be expected to be boring for extraverts but engrossing for their introverted brethren. At the same time, there is an obvious social aspect to the situation as well. An experimenter describes what is to happen and settles the recipient into his or her role and usually listens in another room as experience is reported. Then the experimenter will assist in the process of judging the target and decoys and will respond somehow to the outcome once it is known (the experimenter is always blind as to which material is the correct target during judging, just as the recipient is).

In other words, the ganzfeld might be appealing for both extraverts and introverts, but for different reasons. How the experimenter handles these social and more solitary aspects of the situation should be important in whether the experience is approached mainly as an inward journey (as introverts would prefer) or an opportunity for a marvelous kind of success to be applauded (as extraverts would find meaningful).

The Extraversion of the Experimenter: Defining the Social Situation in Ganzfeld Studies

It has not been lost on psychologists in general that a psychological experiment is a social situation, and the interpersonal manner of the experimenter may often be an important variable in the kinds of results that are obtained. Rosenthal (1966) and his colleagues have shown that the responses of subjects in experiments can be influenced inadvertently by characteristics of the experimenters and various qualities of the interaction. For example, Friedman (1967) found that how long experimenters spent with subjects, and how many times they glanced at them, significantly affected how the subjects perceived the interpersonal material they were asked to judge. Jones and Cooper (1971) replicated the general finding. Li-Pang Tang (2001) has shown that the amount of interest experimenters show in the subjects alters how the latter's personalities relate to their problem-solving behavior. And Richardson (1982) has shown that whether the subject is tested by an experimenter of the same or the opposite sex changes how the extraversion of the subjects affects their learning of new material (extraverts perform better in the opposite-sex situation than in the same-sex one, presumably because they find it more stimulating and potentially more rewarding). Finally, Etaugh (1969) showed that persons being tested by extraverts learned more effectively than those tested by introverts, particularly if the experimenters were allowed to deliver verbal reinforcements.

Ganzfeld ESP studies are not typically tightly scripted in terms of how the experimenter is to relate to the participant. In general, there is an effort to orient participants thoroughly to what will happen, make them comfortable, and encourage success and a positive experience. But extraverted experimenters would be expected to do this in a more engaging, energetic, talkative, and stimulating way than introverted ones would. They should offer more social reward, and by their own manner imply a context in which such reward could be pursued and amply received. This should model extraverted behavior for the extraverted participants and provide them good stimulation, while perhaps being somewhat intimidating or mildly overwhelming to the introverts. Introverted experimenters would not behave as energetically and would not overstimulate the introverted participants nor evoke the extraverted tendencies of the extraverts. One quite extraverted ganzfeld experimenter, Carl Sargent (1980), describes how engaging he made the situation for his participants: "Whilst our studio is large, the walls are covered in plush, heavy drapes and varied stereo music facilities are available to us so that subjects can listen to music of their own choosing before and after sessions. It is rare, in our experience for a subject to leave the laboratory within 45 minutes of completing his or her session; they wish to remain and discuss our work with us. Perhaps the most telling point in favor of an assertion that our subjects greatly enjoyed the experiment is that their friends frequently contacted us saying 'X told me about your experiment and how enjoyable it was—can I take part in it?'"[48]

More introverted experimenters have not described such responses from their participants.

In order to test more adequately the possibility that the extraversion-ESP relationship should be more robustly positive with extraverted experimenters, I collected findings from other ganzfeld experiments that also reported extraversion measurements on participants and that were conducted by five experimenters known to be clearly extraverted or introverted (the only studies in which I could make that determination) and added these to the ones examined by Honorton et al. for a more complete meta-analysis. These studies generally used more participants than the samples of the eight experimenters originally examined, so their weighted contributions to a meta-analysis are greater.[49] All together the six extraverted experimenters tested 276 percipients in the ganzfeld. The average weighted correlation between extraversion and ESP in their studies was 0.294, and this is highly significant ($z = 4.62$, $p = 0.000002$). The six introverted experimenters tested 170 participants and found a slightly negative relationship: average weighted r is -0.11. This trend is marginally significant with a 1-tail test ($z = -1.41$, $p = 0.08$). The difference between these two correlations is itself quite significant.

One other study using extraverted experimenters would have added to this conclusion, but it could not be included because the positive correlation between extraversion and ganzfeld performance was only described as "highly significant."[50]

It seems likely that extraverted experimenters do in fact tend to engage in different interpersonal behaviors and express different attitudes in the experiment than introverted ones do and that these behaviors and attitudes create a context in which the extraversion of the participant is more salient—more potentially rewarding for the extraverts and more off-putting for the introverts. Introverted experimenters do not create such an extraversion-facilitating environment, and may even evoke heightened comfort and engagement in their introverted participants and less of those things in the others.[51] More direct study of these different experimental styles in the ganzfeld would be interesting.

Sex: Another Way to Heighten Potential Social Reward in the Ganzfeld

First Sight theory holds that the unconscious motivation of the percipient should affect the direction of their scoring in an ESP test. There is general agreement among scientists studying extraversion that the importance of social reward is greater for extraverts than for introverts, and we have seen that when the potential for social reward in a situation is greater, and the reward involved is seen as greater, extraverts will express this heightened motivation in higher levels of performance while introverts will find the pressure uncomfortable and perform more poorly.

The social milieu of the experiment is an important consideration here. The involvement of a person of the opposite sex in the situation may be assumed to offer social rewards that are generally greater than that present in a same-sex situation. Indeed, Campbell et al. (2003) showed that when participants were paired with persons of the opposite sex extraversion strongly predicted how motivated and successful their performance was, but in same-sex situations the trait was not important. The central relationship in a ganzfeld study is the one between the sender and the receiver. It is presumed to be an intimate connection—if the trial is successful a remarkable extrasensory contact between the people will have been demonstrated. If social reward matters more to extraverts than to introverts and is less stressful for them, then in mixed-sex sender-receiver pairs the trait should have an effect on scoring that is greater than in same-sex pairs. As it happens, Charles Honorton provided other researchers all the data from ganzfeld studies collected using an automated testing procedure at his Psychophysical Research Laboratory prior to its closing. Extraversion scores and specification of sender and receiver gender are available for 330 sessions. I analyzed these data and found the correlation that Honorton et al. (1998) reported before. However, when the data are divided into same-sex and opposite-sex sender-receiver pairs, the correlation is only found to be significant in the opposite-sex situation ($r = 0.181$, $p = 0.01$) with an insignificant trend in the same direction in the same-sex pairs. Heightened social reward in the form of an opposite-sex partner in the experiment did appear to facilitate the effect of extraversion upon ESP performance.

One study is particularly pertinent to understanding how the interpersonal environment of the ganzfeld experiment affects the expression of the participant's degree of extraversion. Carpenter (2006) carried out eighty ganzfeld sessions. Percipients filled out self-assessment materials prior to their sessions, including the Meyers-Briggs, yielding an extraversion score. Most receivers brought a friend along with them to serve as sender. Then they were run in one of two different conditions. In the standard condition, participants were greeted cordially and then went through the normal ganzfeld experience, including progressive relaxation, the sender in a nearby room, judging of potential target material assisted by an experimenter in a third room speaking through earphones, etc. Percipients in a socially enhanced condition were treated differently in some ways that were designed to reduce their anxiety and increase their openness to the situation and hopefully to the extrasensory targets as well. Some implicit cues of emotional connection were arranged differently: in the standard condition, some pictures on the laboratory wall showed experimenters professionally testing subjects and the percipients were exposed subliminally to a random series of letters while fixating on a video monitor. In the enhanced condition the pictures on the walls showed mothers holding or otherwise being warmly engaged with their children, and instead of random letters the percipients were subliminally exposed to the words "Mommy and I are one," a message that has been used in other research for its capacity to increase openness, lessen anxiety and heighten performance.[52] Instead of being shown their separate rooms and oriented separately as in the standard condition, in the enhanced condition all parties were oriented together as to their various roles, senders sitting in the receiver's seat and vice versa, along with several expressions to the effect: "We are in this together." Prior to the sending-receiving period in the enhanced condition, all parties gathered closely for a minute of silent meditation in which all were asked to experience their closeness and prepare to enjoy the interesting experience they were about to share. In the standard condition this "sharing period" was omitted. In the enhanced condition, the last instructions to the receiver given over the earphones before the mentation period were these: "You may feel like the boundaries between you and the world are blurred, and that you are merging with your environment. Your friend (name of sender), I and you are all part of a group working together." This section was omitted in the standard instructions.

In the enhanced condition the experimenters attempted to lessen anxiety and heighten a sense of interpersonal closeness. Such a situation should heighten the experience of the experiment as a social situation and diminish the aspect of solitary exploration—hence heightening the importance of the trait of extraversion. The results bore out these expectations. In the enhanced condition extraverts significantly outperformed introverts in the ESP task ($r = 0.32$, $p = 0.025$). In the standard condition there was a slight reversal, with introverts tending to perform a little better ($r = -0.14$, $p = 0.2$). The difference between the two correlations is significant ($\chi^2 = 3.86$, $p = 0.05$), demonstrating that the conditions did affect the expression of the extraversion trait on ESP performance differently.

The two conditions had other intended effects also, which helped make the observed difference in ESP performance more understandable. All of the mentation reports were transcribed and scored by a projective rating system developed by Carpenter (2003, 2005a), by which trained and reliable judges first break up the transcript into "idea units" (blocks of text with a single meaning) and then code each one of them on thirty-two different scales. These scales are intended to measure various qualities of response, including verbal quantity (numbers of words, numbers of idea units); kinds of utterances (for example, images, memories, remarks); and emotional state (for example, anger and hostility). An example of a statement coded for anxiety is "I see a crowd that looks like it could turn ugly." One for hostility is "There are two snakes fighting over something." Other scales codify such things as the degree and quality of personal involvement in the imagery experience, while still others are analogous to the "determinants" of Rorschach inkblot scoring (for example, mention of color, movement, and shading). This set of scales has been found to predict ESP scoring in several hundred ganzfeld protocols drawn from several different laboratories around the world. They have also been found to differentiate the protocols of introverts and extraverts. For example, extraverts normally simply talk somewhat more and produce more words and idea units per protocol, as well as more *remarks* (a category for a statement that does not describe ongoing experience as such but is rather a comment given to the experimenter or the receiver, such as "You know, this is as good as you said it would be," "Try harder, Susan!," and "These earphones aren't too comfortable, are they?"). *Remarks* are taken to indicate that the percipient is treating the experiment as if it were a social situation eliciting conversation with the other parties involved.

Testing of these implicit indicators showed that the experimental conditions had their desired effects. Receivers were expected to be more talkative in the socially enhanced condition (more words and idea units), act more as if the experiment was a social situation (more remarks), and experience less emotional discomfort (less anxiety and hostility). In fact, all of these differences were found: Words and sum of idea units were marginally significantly higher in the enhanced condition ($t = 1.33$, $p = 0.09$, and $t = 1.59$, $p = 0.06$, respectively), while remarks were significantly more plentiful ($t = 2.95$, $p = 0.002$). Anxiety ($t = -1.97$, $p = 0.03$) and hostility scores ($t = -2.93$, $p = 0.003$) were significantly lower.

A study by Szczygielski and Schmeidler (1974) bears mentioning here, even though it is not a ganzfeld study because it tried to establish conditions that would not only nullify the advantages of extraverts but also even reverse them. The experimenter, described as highly introverted, met with his subjects privately in their homes for testing. All of them were personal friends or acquaintances, and the experimenter noted that all found the situation relaxed and comfortable. He tested for extraversion-introversion both with a self-report questionnaire and with a behavioral method that uses the fact that extraverts have been found to underestimate the passage of time while introverts do not. This technique was laborious and time consuming. It involved asking the percipient to sit for a period of time (fifteen seconds) and then asking them to reproduce another span of time of the same length without counting or using anything other than the sheer subjective sense of time passing. Then the subject's estimate was used as the baseline for the next estimation trial. This process was repeated ten times. The final estimate gave a score for introversion (extraverts have significantly shorter final estimates). He combined the two extraversion measures (which were positively correlated) into a single variable and correlated this with the results of an ESP test conducted at the same sitting. The experimenter expected a negative relationship between extraversion and ESP scoring, and he found that to a significant degree. He made sure that the situation was optimally comfortable and relaxed for introverted participants and used a tedious testing procedure that was intended to frustrate extraverts.

These findings of Carpenter and Szczygielski are not unexpected, in that all of the major theorists on extraversion have said that differences in the trait should only be expressed behaviorally in some kinds of situations but not in others, and some studies in other areas have demonstrated that experimental conditions can be arranged so as to induce introverts to behave more as extraverts normally do and vice versa.[53] After all, almost all introverts can be socially talkative and extraverts can be quietly reflective if they wish to, they only differ in their degree of readiness to respond in these ways across situations. They differ, as First Sight theory would have it, only in terms of their typical intentions to respond in those ways and to seek the outcomes that they value and associate with those responses.

IN SUM: HOW TO EQUALIZE INTROVERTS AND EXTRAVERTS

We have seen three ways in which experimental situations can make social-reward possibilities more or less equally desirable for introverts and extraverts. One is by virtually removing those possibilities for all participants, as in the group testing situation. Another is by using an introverted experimenter to implicitly frame the experimental situation in such a way as to deemphasize the importance of social reward and emphasize instead more inward concerns. A third way is asking experimenters to deliberately frame the social situation in such a way that social rewards appeal equally to both types, as in the study of Szczygielski and Schmeidler (1974). A fourth is to reduce the amount of important social reward that is available in the situation, as in using same-sex sender-receiver pairs in ganzfeld sessions. In each of these cases, we see that when the value of social reward is reduced, the effect decreases. When the value is heightened for participants, the expression of the trait in terms of ESP performance increases.

If the situation is also made especially difficult for extraverts, it can even be made to reverse.

ESP AND THE FACETS OF EXTRAVERSION

The findings discussed so far can all be understood in terms of the motivational difference that appears to be most central in determining people's locations on scales of extraversion-introversion: their desire for positive social reward, particularly in the context of groups and strangers. However, as noted above, extraversion is actually a complex trait, with several major facets. The same numerical scores may hide important differences between people in regard to these facets. One individual may be very gregarious and only moderately dominant, while another is very dominant and only moderately gregarious, and a third is consistently very cheerful but only moderately dominant and gregarious. Yet all three could have identical extraversion scores. To say that these people have equivalent desires for social reward may be somewhat correct, but it also glosses over other differences in motivation that should be important in certain kinds of situations.

Further research could profitably focus on the different facets of extraversion, as measured by the NEO-PI or by other means. First Sight theory would predict that more differentiated predictions as to the probable unconscious interest of the participants could be made. For example, persons particularly high and low in Sociability should call upon ESP information differently in situations in which performance had special interpersonal significance, while persons high and low in Activity Level should respond differentially in situations in which ESP cognizance was assessed in highly active ways.

Research in other domains has shown that predictions using facet scales reveal more powerful relationships than ones using only the general factor.[54] Unfortunately, parapsychologists have not frequently used this approach, although some findings suggest that it would be useful.

In several series, Carpenter (1991) tested 575 participants in an unusually private and retiring way. Each person on four occasions found quiet times to sit alone and fill out a sheet of ESP guesses immediately followed by checking off the items on a mood-adjective checklist to describe his or her current state of mind. Feedback was only received a few weeks later in the mail, and in many cases it was never given at all. This was a solitary and anonymous situation, which should provide virtually no potential for social reward. Would anything about extraversion-introversion be pertinent for scoring? While no measure of extraversion was obtained, some factors of the mood items had clear implications for being in a more-or-less extraverted *mood.* One factor had items connoting interpersonal warmth (for example, friendly, warm-hearted), another had connotations of sociability (for example, talkative, witty), and a third had implications of dominance (for example, forceful, masterful, decisive). As it had in prior research, it turned out that the items of the third factor did show a strongly significant relationship with scoring. Persons in the more dominant mood scored above chance, and those in the contrasting mood scored below. The other two factors showed no relationship. This seems sensible in that the purely social dimensions of extraversion had no pertinence in this solitary situation. However, a sense of strength and dominance was apparently still relevant and was expressed by more successfully mastering the unusual challenge of the ESP test and reaching outside the bounds of isolation. A general factor of extraversion would surely have obscured facts like these to some extent, while they may be more adequately revealed by more discriminating analyses that separate facets of extraversion.

A more direct test of the importance of a different facet of extraversion comes from the work of Daryl Bem (2011). In one study he administered to his participants a two-item test of the "excitement-seeking" facet of extraversion (he called it "stimulus seeking" or boredom proneness), and then gave them an ESP test in which they tried to identify which of two curtains "hid" a picture. As soon as the guess was registered, a random function picked one of the curtains as the target, and another picture was presented for another guess. If a guess was correct, a picture was shown as feedback. Participants had been warned in the announcement for the experiment that some of the pictures to be used would feature explicit erotic content and that some might wish to not participate for that reason. Bem wanted to see if guessing would be more accurate when the feedback picture was erotic than when it was not erotic. It was, significantly so. However, this effect was contributed only by participants who were high on excitement seeking. We might presume that they had greater interest in the exciting targets and expressed that by better guessing.

Another study also featured erotic target material, but in this case (and in all the rest of Bem's studies discussed here), the ESP test was an *implicit* one, not calling for a guess at a target but rather assessing the unconscious contribution of ESP information to an everyday psychological act—making a preference choice between two things. Bem wanted to demonstrate a kind of precognitive diminishment of arousal, or as he called it, "retroactive habituation." Other studies[55] have demonstrated that subliminally exposing a person to some unpleasant picture a few times leads to that thing's being *disliked less* than similarly unpleasant things that have not been preexposed. Bem reasoned that the same sort of diminishment of arousal surely applies to erotic stimuli that are generally known to become less interesting when seen repetitively. He time-reversed the usual order of his study by showing participants pairs of erotic pictures and asking them to choose which they preferred. Then his computer randomly picked one of the two and flashed it subliminally several times. Bem's hypothesis was that the picture that was to be shown shortly in the future would tend to be liked less than the matched control picture that would not later be seen. His results showed that he was right. He also asked people to provide responses to a variant of excitement seeking particularly aimed at one's interest in sexual matters—he called it "erotic stimulus-seeking." Participants that were high in this interest contributed all of the ESP effect. Luke et al. (2008) reported a similar effect of erotic stimulus-seeking at a marginal level of significance.

Bem went on to show that this excitement-seeking dimension of extraversion was an important moderator in some other ESP effects. In one study he wanted to induce in participants a kind of "precognitive boredom." It is known that exposing someone too frequently to some stimulus leads him or her eventually to dislike it. His exposures were time-reversed—that is, they came after the person made a decision about liking something rather than before, as if they were reaching forward in time to note whether they would be unpleasantly saturated with the thing in the near future and dislike it on that account. Participants were shown matched pairs of pictures and asked which they preferred. If they chose the picture that was then randomly selected as the target, they were shown ten repetitions of the picture. Bem predicted that participants would choose the target less often than chance would predict in order to precognitively avoid the unpleasant repetitions. They successfully did so as a group. However, he also collected responses to the two-item excitement-seeking scale. Because persons high in excitement seeking are also known to be relatively quick to become bored, he expected that these participants would be especially effective in avoiding the boring consequences. They were, significantly so.

Bem also reported two other studies in which persons high in excitement seeking seemed more motivated to reach forward and respond to something in the future than their less boredom-prone peers. One of these studies was intended to demonstrate a capacity to precognitively avoid negative stimuli. The participants were shown pairs of pictures that were matched in terms of how generally likable they had been rated by others, and they were asked to choose which of the two they liked better. The computer then made a random decision that one was the target. A liking choice to the target picture resulted in the subliminal exposure three times of a pleasant picture. A miss was followed by the subliminal exposure of a highly unpleasant picture. Overall, the participants demonstrated implicit psi-hitting by preferring the target picture significantly more often than the nontarget (and significantly avoiding the unpleasant subliminal exposures). When participants were divided as to being high or low on excitement seeking, the effect was again found to have been contributed only by the higher group.

The next study examined "retroactive facilitation of recall." In a standard learning study, being exposed to something and rehearsing it repetitively aids in committing the thing to memory. Bem conducted his practice sessions *after* his memory test rather than before. He exposed a list of words to his participants, removed it, and then asked them to list all the words that they could from the list they had just seen. His computer then randomly selected some of the words as ESP targets, and these were given to the participants for a series of practice exercises. His psi hypothesis was that the practice-to-come would facilitate the learning, and he found clear evidence that this was so—but only for the participants that were high in excitement seeking.

Interestingly, two of Bem's other studies *did not show* an effect of excitement seeking. In these studies he set out to demonstrate a kind of "retroactive priming." In a standard priming study, some stimulus that is either pleasant or unpleasant (the prime) is exposed subliminally, and this is followed by the supraliminal exposure of something else that is also either pleasant or unpleasant. The participant's task is to quickly identify whether the consciously seen thing is pleasant or unpleasant. The standard finding is that the identification is a bit faster if the target and the prime are congruent (both pleasant or both unpleasant) than if they are incongruent. That is, the pleasantness or unpleasantness of the prior subliminal exposure has *primed* the person to more quickly perceive something that belongs to the same general category. Bem again reversed the usual order and showed his pleasant or unpleasant target words to his participants *before* they were shown the subliminal prime, rather than before. Just as in a standard experiment, he found that when prime and target were congruent, response time was significantly shorter than when they were incongruent. He followed this up with a confirmatory study that found the same thing. However, in these studies, excitement seeking did not matter—both groups showed the extrasensory priming effect equally.

This different result actually seems to make sense psychologically, although Bem did not stress the point. In the two studies involving erotic material, excitement seekers responded in ways that express their greater interest in sexually exciting material, in one case by arranging psychically to be able to see it and in the other by becoming psychically palled by too much exposure to it. In the study on the avoidance of negative stimuli, the participants who performed more poorly were required to more frequently experience something unpleasant repetitively. Excitement seekers showed their extra interest in avoiding such experiences by responding psychically in ways that let them successfully be avoided. In the retroactive learning study all participants were required to engage in repetitive practice exercises on certain randomly selected words—the kind of work that excitement seekers find especially boring and unpleasant. Their special sensitivity to this sort of work seemed to heighten its importance to them and enhance their response to it, as shown by their better memory performance on the material that would be worked on. By contrast, in the priming studies participants had no opportunity to respond to more exciting things or to avoid more boring things or to express their special distaste for repetitive work. It seems sensible, then, that this excitement-seeking facet of extraversion has no pertinence in the priming studies.

EXTRAVERSION AND IMPLICIT PSI RESPONSE

What about situations in which no explicit effort is being made to produce a psi response? As we saw in chapter 1, studies that attempt to reveal ongoing implicit psi processes are especially congruent with the basic assumptions of First Sight theory. But when there is not explicit psi performance at stake, and no potential social reward for doing well at psi, should the extraversion of the participant be pertinent at all? The answer is yes, if other aspects of the complex trait of extraversion are called into play by the experimental situation.

Three lines of work are pertinent to this question because they all showed a mediating effect of extraversion on extrasensory response when no conscious expression of ESP is involved at all (in the third one the possibility had not even occurred to the experimenter). In the last two series the researchers observed *differential* relationships of ESP response with extraversion—correlated in one direction in one condition, and in the other direction in another. Since all of this research discussed in this section used implicit assessments of extrasensory response, there was never any kind of deliberate attempt to "hit" the ESP target. Although some of this work has been discussed already, it is the implicit character of the response that I am emphasizing here.

The first line of work is by Daryl Bem (2011) and was covered in the last section. The reader may wish to refer to it again. Recall that he focused on the facet of extraversion that is called "excitement seeking" in the NEO-PI and measured it with simple two-item questionnaires. In several lines of work he found that persons who are high on this aspect of extraversion implicitly use psi information in ways that others don't, and the ways they use it make sense in terms of their particular interests and intentions. In some studies they expressed their tendency to become bored with repeated exposures to things by responding in ways that implied boredom (habitu-ation) apparently due to *future* exposures to those things. In another study this group showed an implicit use of psi information to *avoid* potential boredom by making preference choices that permitted them to escape subsequently boring repetitive exposures to things. Then in another study the excitement seekers showed a capacity to achieve high performance (and social reward), but they thought it was for performance in a memory task, not an ESP task. They were able to access future rehearsals with sets of words as if it had been practiced in the past and improved their memory scores thereby.

To sum up Bem's findings, he showed that persons who are extraverted in the high excitement-seeking sense reached forward in time and responded to events that would shortly occur in the future in the same way that they would have responded to those things if they had already been experienced and were only available in memory. They became erotically satiated and bored in advance, profited from rehearsals in advance, and succeeded in avoiding an unpleasant situation by implicitly responding to cues in ad-vance. The more introverted, low-excitement seekers did not make this sort of implicit use of future material.

Braud, Shafer, and Andrews (1993), in a series of studies that were also discussed in the last chapter, monitored the spontaneous electrodermal responsiveness of participants continually while they sat alone in a room and were being viewed by a video camera that sent a signal to a monitor in a different room. At random times the monitor was turned on and off while a viewer watched. The "staree" was blind as to these time periods. The experimenters were interested in seeing whether the subtle, largely sub-conscious variations in electrodermal activity (a measure of physiological arousal) might reveal an extrasensory response to being viewed by another person, and they planned to see this by comparing the average levels of arousal during the two kinds of periods. If response went down during the staring periods relative to the control periods when the monitor was turned off, the "staree" was responding to being viewed by becoming a bit calmer. If it went up, he or she was becoming a bit more aroused. The first study in the series involved no personality assessments. All parties (starers and starees) received extensive training in "connectedness" in which group meditation and guided imagery were used to heighten tolerance for and appreciation of a deep sense of connectedness, merger, and "oneness" with others. (Braud is a decided introvert himself and a teacher of meditation.) Starers, when staring deliberately, held the intention to lovingly increase the degree of comfort and relaxation of the person they were watching. It was expected that these starees who were also trained and oriented to con-nectedness might react to being viewed (even without their knowledge) by a subtle decrease of arousal compared to control periods in which they were not being viewed. In fact, they did so, to a significant degree.

In the next study Braud again used persons trained in connectedness as starers, but he was interested in finding a naturally occurring individual difference that might influence the response of untrained starees. He administered a measure of social avoidance and distress (SAD) to these participants on the assumption that persons high on this dimension might be especially in need of intimate connection and so be especially responsive to the calming effect of being viewed with such relaxation intentions. It is important to note in this context that the SAD scale[56] is a good measure of the aspect of introversion that was mentioned above as indicating poor social adjustment (Eysenck's "unstable introvert" and Singer's "social introvert"). Low scores on the SAD scale indicate only a low amount of social anxiety; they do not necessarily imply strong affiliativeness or extraversion. Low scores might as easily represent socially comfortable introverts.

In the third study these SAD measurements were collected again, along with the introversion-extraversion scale of the Meyers-Briggs (the two were correlated at a moderate level, showing that they were measuring similar but not identical things). Reasoning in terms of First Sight theory, what unconscious intentions might be expected to be pertinent for these groups of participants in this situation? First, the socially anxious people should wish to find information that would help to lower their discomfort, as Braud thought they should, while the nonanxious persons would not find this information so pertinent to their needs and might be expected to show no reaction to being viewed. Meyers-Briggs introverts, with their general preference for intimate connections and, for some, their higher social anxiety, would also be expected to find the extrasensory intimacy to be pertinent to their needs and respond to it by becoming calmer. Extraverts, on the other hand, with their general tendency to seek stimulation by contact with others and to find the promise of such contact to be potentially rewarding, might be expected to respond with heightened interest and excitement to being viewed. Their level of arousal might be expected to increase. In fact, these were the patterns Braud found. There was a clear linear relationship between SAD and relaxation. Starees whose SAD scores were higher relaxed more. Persons with very low SAD scores showed no decrease in arousal relative to control periods; that is, this mixed group of extraverts and secure introverts showed no particular response to the staring condition at all. Data in the third study replicated this effect of SAD scores on extrasensory response. When SAD scores increased from zero to high levels, relative degree of relaxation also increased from zero to high levels. Using the introversion-extraversion scale, the results were somewhat similar but also showed a reversal of the relationship for extraverts. Like high SAD scorers, introverts showed a strong relaxation response to being viewed. Extraverts, however, did not merely show an absence of response. They became significantly *more aroused* when they were being looked at.

To sum up, introverts and socially anxious people became calmer when being viewed without their knowledge, people who were not socially anxious showed no response, and extraverts became more alert and engaged. Such results make it clear that any real understanding of the extraversion-ESP relationship must move away from a simple expectation that extraverts should perform "better" and introverts "worse." There was no better or worse in this series of studies, but there was a clear response to an extrasensory situation of subtle, intimate contact and a response of more arousal for some and less arousal for others, in nice accordance with their self-reported patterns of interest and intention.

Klintman (1984) is a cognitive psychologist who did not set out to measure an ESP response, but he found one in his data anyway. Puzzled by the finding, he repeated the study and found it again. He used a behavioral measure of extraversion: how long the mental image of a rotating spiral persists for an individual after the spiral itself is removed. As Eysenck predicted, the image disappears more quickly for extraverts, presumably as a result of their greater ability to suppress cortical excitation. Klintman was studying the effect of extraversion on the speed with which one can identify a visual stimulus after it is presented. The stimuli were given in sequence, and in some cases a stimulus was repeated (occurred twice in succession), and in some cases stimuli were different. Klintman hypothesized that extraverts would be quicker in identifying a stimulus when it was different from the one preceding it, and introverts would be quicker when the stimuli were the same. He used the reaction time to the preceding stimulus as a baseline for assessing the time of the following one.

When he analyzed his results he found the effect he had predicted, but he also found something he had not expected. The reaction time of the preceding stimulus was also longer or shorter depending upon what kind of stimulus *was about to follow it.* In other words, he found an anticipatory or precognitive effect, alongside the normal, real-time effect. He also found that extraversion had the same mediating relationship with the precognitive effect that it had on the normal one: times were shorter for extraverts when the stimulus *to come* was different, and longer for extraverts when the stimulus to come was a repeat. Introverts showed the opposite pattern.

Klintman did not attempt to interpret this anomalous finding but simply recognized that it was an apparent instance of implicit precognition. The interpretation offered by First Sight theory is straightforward. A piece of information in the immediate future is precognitively available to all of the study participants, but it would be expected to hold a different kind of interest for introverts and extraverts. Extraverts tend to be change-seeking, stimulus-seeking people, relatively quick to become bored and impatient and usually looking for something new to become engaged with. A changing stimulus would be of particular interest to them. Introverts, on the other hand, are calmer and more retiring people, who prefer stable situations in which they can either pursue their internal interests or avoid challenges that might be upsetting. They are more oriented to sameness than to change. As we saw in the chapter on subliminal perception and ESP, subliminal primes tend to arouse a stronger response in persons for whom they are particularly interesting. First Sight theory assumes that extrasensory information and subliminal primes will tend to arouse responses similarly.

This is not to say that Klintman construed his results this way. He was working within a framework inherited from research on learning and, like Eysenck, preferred constructs implying a closer possible reduction to the psychophysiological level of analysis. And he did not make any reference to the literature on subliminal perception. It is First Sight theory that is offering an integrative perspective in which psi phenomena, learning, and subliminal perception may all be understood to be working together and construed in similar terms. And it is First Sight theory that places an emphasis upon intention and interest as causal in their own right and not as epiphenomena to be glossed over in favor of impersonal mechanisms of action.

In general, this work by Bem, Braud, and Klintman combine together to suggest that psi effects that are measured implicitly may be especially reliable indicators of the effects of extraversion—and of other individual differences that imply different unconscious intentions. If this proves to be true, it is congruent with the expectations of First Sight. Such findings show how extrasensory responsiveness is occurring all the time and being expressed continuously in ordinary behavior. Learning things, preferring one thing to another, avoiding unpleasant events, feeling a bit more vigilant or a bit more secure—these are examples of simple things that people are doing all the time. No extrasensory guesses are required to show the psychic engagement with an extended surround. If the situation is properly arranged in the laboratory, this engagement can be seen silently at work.

EXTRAVERSION, ESP, AND FIRST SIGHT THEORY

According to First Sight theory, the direction of unconscious intention is the primary determiner of the signing of psi information and thence the direction (above or below chance) of extrasensory performance. If one examines the nature of an experimental situation in terms of the unconscious intentions that are likely to obtain differently for introverts and extraverts, then the hypothesized intentions seem to work well in predicting the direction of extrasensory performance. Many of the typical ESP testing situations favor the motivations of extraverts more than introverts, and they tend to show higher performance for the extraverts. Pertinent alterations in the experimental conditions lead to altered relationships between extraversion and ESP performance in ways that are sensible.

What about the contending hypotheses mentioned earlier, of Eysenck, Palmer, and Schmeidler? Do they account for findings as adequately?

Eysenck's ideas about chronic cortical arousal may indeed be pertinent for extrasensory response, but his reasoning for why this might be so is hampered by his use of a weak-signal model for ESP that cannot account for psi-missing. The situations in which introverts (and occasionally, extraverts) score below chance cannot be explained in these terms.

Palmer proposed that emotional comfort might be the deeper cause of the relationship, since in many testing situations extraverts might be expected to be more comfortable. Some of the patterns discussed above could also be congruent with this idea. For example, in anonymous group testing situations introverts should tend to be as comfortable as extraverts, and in that condition their extrasensory performance has been found to be no worse.

Schmeidler proposed the rather similar idea that it might not be comfort as much as openness and dissociability that mediate the extraversion-ESP relationship. No direct tests of this hypothesis have been reported.

Even if emotional comfort or openness, or any other variables, were found to mediate the relationship of extraversion with ESP scoring, it would not necessarily contradict First Sight theory. The strength of this point of view is that it does not pose a simple hypothesis about extraversion and ESP. Rather, it asserts that extraversion has various implications for the likely patterns of unconscious intention for persons in different kinds of situations. The theory has an overarching flexibility that matches the complexity of a human trait such as extraversion. When extraverts wish to be more comfortable, it assumes that promoting comfort might be an important consideration. When extraversion interacts with the reward-value of a situation or how boring or stimulating it is or how important or unimportant some class of outcome is for the person, these are the things that would be expected to relate to unconscious intentions in that situation.

This sheds light on the question of why extraversion has proven to be such a robust moderator of psi effects. Its complexity (remember the six facets) can carry the relationship differently in different circumstances. And these different circumstances are all pertinent to the situations in which we try to assess psi performance.

There is a general moral to draw about using any trait construct in parapsychology. To use First Sight heuristically and most effectively, it is important to understand the implications of a trait in some depth and complexity and then to use that understanding to pose hypotheses that are both person and situation specific. Used this way, our clumsy constructs can come to more closely approximate the true complexity and subtlety of human experience. Then they can be more useful in anticipating how a person will use the psi level of engagement with reality.

NOTES

1. Humphrey, 1945.
2. Humphrey, 1951.
3. Irwin and Watt, 2007; Palmer, 1977, 1982; Schmeidler, 1994.
4. Honorton, Ferrari, and Bem, 1998; Parra and Villanueva, 2003; Roe et al., 2008.
5. Goulding, 2005; Roe et al., 2004; Roem, Sherwood, and Holt, 2005.
6. Lamont, 2006.
7. Braude, 1996; Carrington, 2005.
8. Gauld, 1984.
9. Zingrone et al., 1998.
10. Rhine, 1934 (1973), p. 72.
11. Kanthamani and Kelly, 1974.
12. Ryzl and Ryzlova, 1962; Ryzl and Pratt, 1963.
13. Ryzl and Beloff, 1965.
14. Kagan, 1994.
15. Myers, 1961 [1903].
16. Budd, 1993; Gray and Wheelwright, 1945; Kier et al., 1998; Loomis, 1982.
17. Cattell, 1957; Costa and McCrae, 2009; Eysenck, 1970; Guilford and Guilford, 1939.
18. Costa and McCrae, 1985.
19. 1960a, pp. 337–80.
20. Eysenck, 1957.
21. Eysenck, 1956; Pincombe et al., 2007.
22. Rajamanickam and Gnanaguru, 1981.
23. Coles et al., 1971; Gange et al., 1979; Geen, 1984.
24. Holland, 1962.
25. Barnett and Klitzing, 2006; Zakay et al., 1984.
26. McCrae and Costa, 1987.
27. Lucas et al., 2000.
28. Ashton et al., 2002.
29. Cooper and Taylor, 1999.
30. Dellas and Gaier, 1983.
31. Trapmann et al., 2007.
32. MacDonnell et al., 2009.
33. Fleeson, 2007.
34. Fleeson, 2001.
35. Eysenck and Eysenck, 1975.

36. Nash, 1966; Thalbourne and Jungkuntz, 1983.

37. Honorton et al. do not emphasize this finding very strongly in their report because they also reach the conclusion that the ESP/extraversion relationship as found in forced-choice testing may be generally invalid because much of it used designs in which extraversion was assessed after the ESP results were known, and most of the positive relationship found came from studies of this sort. They reasoned that knowing ESP results may have influenced the self-assessments of extraversion and led to a spurious relationship. They pointed out that free-response studies did not generally use this order of testing, so they considered the relationship to be valid with those cases. However, Palmer and Carpenter (1998), analyzing the same data set, found that in the forced-choice studies this variable of testing order was strongly confounded with the individual versus group testing breakdown (most group tests assessed extraversion before ESP, and vice versa). When the two breakdowns are combined and compared in multiple regression, the variable of group versus individual testing emerges as the stronger and only independently significant predictor. Thus, the apparent effect of testing order appears to be a spurious artifact caused by its association with the testing situation. It also seemed to Palmer and Carpenter that personality questionnaires measuring extraversion are not likely to be vulnerable to perturbations as slight as receiving scores on ESP tests. Empirical evidence supporting this skepticism was obtained by Krishna and Rao (1991), who tested the power of ESP test feedback to influence subsequent self-assessed extraversion scores and found none.

38. Colley et al., 1985; Daino, 1985.

39. Beck, Burnet, and Vosper, 2006.

40. Rhine, 1964.

41. Rhine, 1964, p. 49.

42. Avant, 1965; Metzger, 1930.

43. Bexton, Heron, and Scott, 1954; Murphy and Myers, 1962.

44. Child, 1985.

45. Stanford, 1992.

46. Honorton and Harper, 1974.

47. Braud, Wood, and Braud, 1975.

48. Sargent, 1980, pp. 22–23.

49. Alexander and Broughton, 2001 [my analysis]; Carpenter, 2006; Sargent, 1980, 1981; Sargent, Bartlett, and Moss, 1982; Sargent and Harley, 1981; Sargent and Matthews, 1981; Sargent et al., 1981 [all Sargent relationships were averaged]; Parra and Villanueva, 2003.

50. Rogo and Sargent, 1982.

51. See Thorne, 1987, for analogous results showing differential effects of extraverted and introverted interviewers on the verbal behavior of interviewees who are extraverted and introverted.

52. Silverman et al., 1982.

53. Thorne, 1987; Wright and Mischel, 1987.

54. Mershon and Gorsuch, 1988; Paunonen and Ashton, 2001.

55. Dijksterhuis and Smith, 2002.

56. Watson and Friend, 1969.

16

Other Individual and Situational Factors

What consciousness is willing to tolerate and what it is willing to exert itself upon determines substantially its own content.

—Matthew Hugh Erdelyi (1988)

Previous chapters have assessed the model in terms of findings reported in the areas of perception without awareness, memory, creativity, and extraversion. This chapter more briefly examines some other more strongly confirmed findings in the parapsychological literature and casts each of them in terms of the First Sight model.

THE SHEEP-GOAT EFFECT

Participants in ESP experiments who affirm their belief in the reality of the sort of extrasensory ability that the test is purporting to measure have often been found to score above chance, while disbelievers have tended to score significantly below chance. Using Schmeidler's[1] basic definition: that "goats" believe that ESP is not possible under the conditions of the experiment and "sheep" are all others, it appears that this criterion assesses whether or not the person understands psi to be a reliable source of information. If a person discredits psi as a source, the unconscious mind will tend to misuse its offerings by signing them negatively and systematically negating them. The effect of sheep scoring above chance in ESP tests and goats scoring below is relatively robust, and it has been found in many studies using several variations on the measure.[2]

It is pertinent here to recall the social psychological literature on assimilation and contrast of subliminal primes in the perception of other persons,[3] and presumably in many other sorts of judgments as well. As stated earlier, a prime is assimilated when it apparently is judged preconsciously to be relevant to a target, and it then biases perception of the target in the direction of the prime. A subliminal prime shows the phenomenon of contrast when it is preconsciously judged to be irrelevant to the target, and this is expressed by a lowered probability that the prime will be expressed in the perception (analogous to psi-missing). It has also been found that contrast effects may be a result of more conscious processing, in which subjects are aware that they may be influenced by a prime (perhaps a supraliminal, semantic term), and try to correct for this bias by avoiding the use of the prime (often overcorrecting in the process). On a conscious level, persons may form "naive theories" in which they believe themselves to be biased by some information, and then they will tend to decline to use that information and use alternatives to it instead.[4]

In the ESP experiment, "sheep," who are comfortable with the idea that emerging ideas and images may express ESP target material, would be expected to consult that imagery directly and use it trustingly (in First Sight terms, they sign the information positively); goats, on the other hand, should consider such inner material to be only a source of error and tend to "overcorrect" by signing it negatively and calling in directions different than their naive impressions. This might happen both at preconscious and more conscious levels of processing.[5]

Some studies demonstrate that if previously learned information comes to be thought of as invalid, the unconscious mind will reverse its ordinary effect when generating implicit effects. This is pertinent, because we expect that the unconscious mind will consult long-term memory information and psi information in similar ways. In one example of this research, Peters and Gawronski (2011) first taught their participants that certain target faces were generally good people (for example, "Mike gives to charity") and some were bad ("Susan steals at work"). Then participants were told that in regard to some of the target persons the information had been true and with some it was false. Participants then generated implicit responses (unconsciously) to all of the faces exposed subliminally. When the information was considered valid, the unconscious mind used it positively ("good" people were sensed to be good, "bad" people were sensed to be bad). When the information was believed to be invalid the effect reversed (target persons who had been paired with "good" statements evoked implicit responses indicating that they were sensed to be "bad" and vice versa). Thus a conscious attribution of validity or invalidity affected the unconscious process of emotional response.

A further indication that the power of the sheep-goat distinction lies in its implication about the validity of psi information comes from an interesting study by Lovitts (1998). She showed that the effect of the validity-attribution implied by the sheep-goat question can be reversed as expressed by ESP performance. Her participants were exposed to subliminal stimuli that actually contained no discrete target information at all (jumbled parts of all targets), while participants were asked to generate guesses. These guesses were scored against randomly selected ESP targets that were not exposed at all. Some participants were told that they were taking an ESP test, and others were told that it was a test of subliminal perception that, if they did well, would disprove the idea that ESP exists. When they thought they were taking an ESP test, sheep and goats scored in the usual way—believers positively, disbelievers negatively. In the other condition, when participants believed that good performance would show that ESP is not real, the effect was reversed—disbelievers performed above chance, and believers below.

Apparently another way of assessing the validity that a person attributes to psi can be gained from a questionnaire that asks about attitudes to luck. Luke and his colleagues[6] found predicted relations between performance on ESP tests and degrees to which people believed that luck was a real thing or that providence was available to help or that mere chance could not account for meaningful coincidences. In one study they also found an effect of the standard sheep-goat question but did not report an analysis showing to what degree these two attributions overlapped with each other. These findings appear to be congruent with reports of positive relationships reported between religious orientations and psi performance.[7] Persons who cultivate an active belief in God and practice prayer surely tend to believe that nonphysical communication is a valid possibility.

Whatever the best explanation for the effect, it is a relatively robust one. Reviews of all available literature through the early 1980s[8] showed a strong preponderance of relationships to be in the predicted direction (many significant), and no strong reversals. Belief that ESP is possible has also been found to relate positively to scores on PK tasks.[9] The trend seems somewhat stronger for studies using Schmeidler's original criterion (specific to the experimental situation), but basically the same pattern was found when sheep-goat was defined as belief in ESP in general. A later meta-analysis that covered even more reports reached the same conclusion.[10] Apparently believing in the validity of the psi source (or in luck, or providence, or "something more than coincidence") tends to let one access psi information positively, while discrediting these things has the opposite effect.

One report suggests that the question itself serves as a situation-specific prime in the moment and is not best thought of as representing a stable trait. In one series of studies I carried out,[11] participants were self-tested at home for four sessions spread out over two or three weeks. At the first session they responded to Schmeidler's sheep-goat question, but not again. When people were grouped according to that first response, sheep scored much more positively than goats in the first session, only barely significantly so in the second, and the two groups showed no difference in the last two sessions. If this pattern is found to be reliable, it would make sense. Attitudes toward the reality of ESP are not pressing, regnant concerns for most people, and they are probably not very constant over time. However, raising the issue in a given situation makes it salient then, and the position one takes then can be expected to be influential.

Belief in Personal Psi Ability

It is a different matter if someone is asked, not if they believe that ESP is possible in general, but whether or not they personally expect to perform well on a test of ESP or PK. These two kinds of belief have sometimes been combined or blurred together, and this is probably unfortunate. Such a self-attribution, in a situation in which the unconsciousness of psi makes any real control impossible for most persons, would be expected to generate anxiety, at least unconsciously. Our theory leads us to expect that such anxiety would tend to turn scoring in a negative direction. In fact, a negative relation between this belief in *personal* ability and actual performance was reported in two studies, one involving ESP,[12] and one with PK.[13] Null results have been reported in other studies,[14] so the reliability of the effect is not clear.

The Psi-Facilitating Effect of Hypnosis

While flaws in design make some matters of interpretation uncertain,[15] many studies have shown above-chance scoring in subjects who are hypnotized and chance or below-chance scoring in control groups. Hypnosis, particularly in persons inclined to be especially responsive to it, would seem to be a good situation for securing a positive unconscious intention to score well when the hypnotist suggests it and it is generally acceptable to the subject. Hypnosis should also tend to produce a manner of effort characterized by an absence of cognitive analysis and planning, selective inattention, and heightened access to memory and fantasy as opposed to ongoing realities and an absence of the kind of reality testing that ordinarily characterizes waking consciousness. These are all characteristics described by Hilgard (1965) as typifying the hypnotic state. The positive intention would be expected to make an inclination toward psi-hitting generally likely, and the manner of effort would be likely to assure a tendency toward relatively large scoring deviations while providing access to an inner stream of inadvertent material of the sort that expresses preconscious activity. This is the combination most likely to result in strong overall positive scoring.

DREAMS AS VEHICLES FOR PSI

The dreaming state of awareness is noted both for its lack of reflectiveness and for the absence of conscious, rational processing.[16] Thus a shifting of intentions and cognitive tack, with consequent shifting of directional tendency, would be unlikely to occur. Like the hypnosis situation, both these things, a proknowing orientation with little directional switching together with the particularly inadvertent material of the dream, would be expected to lead to strongly positive performance. Spontaneous experiences suggestive of psi come more often from dreams than from waking consciousness (Rhine, 1962b). Confirming this, a review by Child (1985) has shown that dreaming sleep has been found to be especially propitious in conveying ESP information about target material that the dreamer desires to perceive. Going to the trouble of participating in an ESP dream study would seem to make it likely that a person intends, at both a conscious and unconscious level, to come to positively grasp the target information.

THE GANZFELD AS A PSI-CONDUCIVE SITUATION

The ganzfeld protocol's combination of mild sensory deprivation, the provision of an undifferentiated visual and auditory field, and relaxation provides to some degree the same combination of ideal conditions just described for hypnosis and dreaming, and it has often been reported to show positive scoring.[17] First Sight would predict that these factors would be especially propitious for participants whose manner of verbalizing suggests a positive implicit approach to the situation and an absence of anxiety and cognitive analysis. This is the pattern that has been found.[18]

THE IMPORTANCE OF CARING ABOUT THE INFORMATION

We know from collections of reports of spontaneous psychic experiences that most involve personally important information. Information about beloved other persons is particularly common.[19] While reporting bias may account for some of this trend, it is congruent with several experimental findings demonstrating that caring about the information, or about aspects of the situation intimately associated with the information, affects the expression of psi.

Dean (1962) found that when a distant agent viewed names of friends of the percipient, unconscious physiological response was aroused, while viewing names of friends of the agent did not have that effect. Rao (1962), Nash and Nash (1968), Kanthamani and Rao (1975), and Skibinsky (1950) all found more significant expression of psi in forced-choice guessing with targets that were personally meaningful to the subjects than with targets that were less meaningful. Similarly, Rogers (1966, 1967) found that people produced more extreme scoring when they self-tested at times in which the test felt meaningful to them than at times when it did not feel meaningful.

The personal importance of the agent in a telepathic situation also matters, judging from the results of Honorton et al. (1990) and Broughton and Alexander (1997), who found that participants who worked with "emotionally close" agents (close friends, family members or loved ones) produced better results in the ganzfeld than did those whose agents were strangers. This relationship was confirmed in new sample of ganzfeld data by Carpenter (2006). Stuart (1946) had earlier reported a similar finding using a different free-response protocol. I could find no reports of negative relationships so the finding may be a general one.

Several studies suggest that sexual interest enhances ESP response to information with sexual implications. Stanford and colleagues[20] set up contingencies for their undergraduate male subjects such that successful psi performance permitted the relatively pleasant outcome of a second task involving rating pictures of females, while poor performance earned a rather onerous task performed in isolation. For subjects whose motivation was primed by being tested by an attractive female, performance was significantly high, earning a majority of subjects the more interesting outcome. In the same vein, a gifted psychic (a young, single male) was found to perform with particular accuracy on "readings" given to strangers, when the latter were female and the content areas had to do with "physical description" and "love life."[21] Carpenter (1971) found that college males who believed that ESP was possible scored above chance with targets that were "primed" with hidden erotic stimuli (and were presumably more interesting on an extrasensory level) as compared to below-chance performance on targets paired with neutral stimuli. And Luke, Delanoy, and Sherwood found that participants who reported themselves to be "erotically reactive" scored better than "unreactive" ones in an ESP test in which good results led to the opportunity to view erotic images.

Similarly, the quality of the emotional connection between the experimenter and the participant affects results. Anderson and White (1956, 1957) and Nash (1960) found that in many cases when the experimenter-and-subject relationship (they were also teacher and pupil) was characterized by mutual liking, scoring tended to be higher than in the other sorts of relationships.

The First Sight model predicts that an unconscious intention to know about something will produce positive signing of the information when some pertinent event about that thing is impending. Something or someone of central emotional importance to the person will be expected to be associated with a relatively invariant intention to know, hence producing a stable directional orientation or a relatively large deviation in response from chance expectation, along with an assimilation of the information.

It would seem that it is what we most care about that we most learn about, in the arena of presensory prehensions as well as in sensory experience. Perhaps, again it might be fruitful to consider that paranormal phenomena are rather like creative ones. In that case, these words attributed to Amadeus Mozart are pertinent: "Neither a lofty degree of intelligence nor imagination nor both together go to the making of genius. Love, love, love, that is the soul of genius."

NOTES

1. Schmeidler, 1945; Schmeidler and McConnell, 1958.
2. Lawrence, 1998.
3. Fazio, Powell, and Herr, 1983; Higgins, 1996; Srull and Wyer, 1980; for a meta-analytic review, see DeCoster and Claypool, 2004.
4. Wegener and Petty, 1995.
5. A similar use of naïve theory may explain a phenomenon that is typically found in the forced-choice guessing patterns of participants in ESP tests, or by persons asked to produce a string of responses "randomly"—the tendency to avoid repeating the same call sequentially to a nonrandom degree. The last number one has generated comes readily to mind in the course of both tasks, and the participant may think something like "I am thinking this because I just called it, so it cannot be due to ESP (or cannot be truly random)," and then systematically rejecting that option in favor of some other that is brought to mind.
6. Luke, Delanoy, and Sherwood, 2008; Luke, Roe, and Davison, 2008.
7. Haraldsson, 1993; Nash, 1958.
8. Palmer, 1978; 1982.
9. Rubin and Honorton, 1971; Watkins, Watkins, and Wells, 1973.
10. Lawrence, 1998.
11. Carpenter, 1991.
12. Nash, 1958.
13. Watkins, Watkins, and Wells, 1973.
14. Palmer, 1978, 1982.
15. Schechter, 1984, Stanford and Stein, 1994.
16. Boss, 1977.
17. Bem and Honorton, 1994; Storm, Tressoldi, and Di Risio, 2010.
18. Carpenter, 2001.
19. Feather and Schmicker, 2005; Gurney, Myers, and Podmore, 1886; Rhine, 1962a, 1962b; Schwarz, 1971; Stevenson, 1970.
20. Stanford, Stio et al., 1976.
21. Roll, Morris, Damgaard, Klein, and Roll, 1973.

17

Two Vexing Problems: Experimenter Effects and Decline Effects

If people could do this, don't you think we would have noticed by now?

—William Howell (in response to a
student's question about parapsychology)

You are to note that it hit for the most part though not always.

—Sir Francis Bacon (on how to assess superstitious claims)

Parapsychologists seem to want other scientists to believe some outrageous things. "We have evidence," they say, "that people can see through walls, foretell the future, read each other's minds, and make objects move around with nothing but their thoughts." Small wonder that other scientists want plenty of evidence before they will even bother being interested.

I believe that some of this problem comes from the fact that our terms actually misrepresent our findings, as I argued in chapter 6. We don't actually find that people consciously know what is beyond walls or in the future or in other's heads, only that people's experiences and behaviors can make inadvertent but real *reference* to such things and that those implicit references can sometimes be interpreted as alluding to some piece of reality. For this reason, I proposed that we speak of *efferent extrasomatic prehension* (EESP) instead of extrasensory perception (ESP), and *afferent extrasomatic prehension* (A-ESP) instead of psychokinesis (PK), and so on.

But still, it is astonishing enough to assert that any kind of real reference, conscious or implied, can be made to things that are not within the organism's ordinary physical boundaries. Skeptical scientists need proof. This includes the honest skeptical parts within each parapsychologist. None of us want to fool ourselves or fool others.

In responsibility to these skeptical voices, we carry out experiments. Follow the rules of scientific procedure and let nature render her verdicts. But here a complication comes in. When does the finding of an experiment provide definitive proof? In fact, no individual study ever does. We want the results of a given study to be replicable. We want to be able to carry out the study again with new people and find the same result. We want the findings to be repeatable by anyone, and not dependent upon a charmed few, who may be actually making some kind of mistake without knowing it or may be failing to follow the honest rules of research. And we want a claimed effect to hold up over time. We want to be like physics, especially the physics of an earlier day. The relationships of pressure and volume and temperature specified by Boyle's Law hold up over and over, whoever is conducting the experiment and however many times the experiment is run.

It is a complication of parapsychology that results are not so tidy. For one thing, who the experimenter is does seem to matter, and repeating the demonstration of some effect does seem to change the effect itself, at least in some cases. To the skeptical scientist impatient to get on with other work and root out nonsense for the good of us all, this can seem like strong circumstantial evidence that the effects must not be real in the first place. But is this so?

From the perspective of First Sight, experimenters *should matter* in demonstrating psi effects, and repeating attempts to demonstrate something *should alter* the demonstration in many cases. These are things that we would expect. They are part of how psi works. This chapter discusses this perspective.

THE EXPERIMENTER EFFECT

Different experimenters frequently get different results when they carry out what otherwise appear to be the same psi experiment. This has been a vexing problem. Others, including Gardner Murphy (a leading light in psychology for decades), have thought it probably indicated a centrally important aspect of real psi processes that should be accepted and studied head on.

Is selling a car a real phenomenon? I cannot imagine someone arguing that it is not. Yet do all salespersons do it equally well? Of course not. Selling is an interpersonal skill, or set of skills, and considerable work has been expended in trying to understand it. The same thing would seem to apply to being a successful psi experimenter. We might wish the world were simpler, that buying a car or performing in a psi experiment were utterly one-person matters, dependent only upon the buyer in the first case and the research participant in the second. But it is not so. Both processes are dependent upon the interpersonal context in the moment. A serious scientist must accept that and work with it.

First Sight theory proposes that the primary determinant of the expression of psi processes is the unconscious intention of the person involved and that a person's interpersonal context is a very important arena of meaning that is being continually accessed nonlocally via psi. We are not alone in a universe of mere things. We are alive in a world brimming with the lives of others, their concerns, their intentions, their experiences. This living surround is in fact the dominant focus of people's attention, conscious and unconscious, most of the time. One illustration of this fact comes from the classic study by Roger G. Barker and Herbert F. Wright, called *Midwest and its Children* (1971). These authors defined behavior objects as the points around which behavior occurs and estimated that in the town they studied, with its population of about seven hundred, there were about 1,200,000 behavior objects, if objects are considered in gross and not in detail (for example, trees, not branches and twigs). They carried out a painstaking study of the behavior of three children (ages seven and eight) in one twenty-four-hour period and noted what things engaged them. They discovered that it was the human environment that was predominantly important in their transactions, although many more nonhuman than human things were there for them to deal with. From their figures we can see that over 80 percent of the behavior objects were human (as persons or as artifacts), and over 85 percent of their transactions came under human influence. Probably these figures would be even higher today, with our more urbanized and densely humanized modern lives.

It has been pointed out that like beavers and wolves, humans are pack animals. We come to our being in families of one sort or another, and it is in an interpersonal world that we build and conduct our lives. First Sight acknowledges this fact and assumes that this interpersonal world is of predominant interest at an unconscious and nonlocal level of functioning as well. There is not only a psychology of psi—there is also an important *social psychology* of psi.

One implication to be drawn from this is that the interpersonal context of an experiment is a predominant feature of how a participant will respond to it. Should we assume that the participant is privy to the intricate goings-on of a random event generator powered by radioactive decay and not to the intentions of the experimenter who is conducting the procedure? To do so would seem foolish.

The experimenter is obviously a dominant influence in an experiment. He or she defines the task, spells out what is to be done and how to do it, and collects the data of interest. The participant cooperates, more or less.

We might hope that results robust enough to persist across any potential experimenter might emerge, but probably this is a naïve and false assumption as well. Even the behavior of rodents in simple learning trials has been found to be sensitive to differences among experimenters. This is the famous "Rosenthal Effect."[1] In human situations it has been shown to be amply communicable in nonverbal, implicit, generally unintended ways.[2] Rosenthal himself (1980) has pointed out that it is surely an important aspect of parapsychological research as well.

From a First Sight perspective, we might hypothesize three ways in which an experimenter might be an important factor in the results of an experiment.

1. The intentions of the experimenter might be adopted by the participant during the period of the experiment.
2. The interpersonal manner of the experimenter might affect the participants psychologically in ways that are known to be important to expressing psi effects; for example, their creativity or their openness or their anxiety.
3. The intentions of the experimenter may directly affect, on an unconscious psi level, the operations being used to assess psi effects in the experiment; for example, the productions of a random event generator or the selection procedure by which participants are sorted into experimental and control groups.

We will examine each of these possibilities in turn.

The Participant Adopts the Intentions of the Experimenter

Evidence that this sometimes happens can be gleaned from examination of some cases of extremely successful psi performance.

One of the most successful psi experimenters was J. B. Rhine, the man who introduced the study of psi to the university laboratory. During the years in which he was actively involved as an experimenter himself (before he turned to developing and administering a program), he elicited remarkably high performances from an unusually large number of individuals. The observations of Gardner Murphy (1949) on Rhine and his methods may be especially telling. As he wrote:

My mind goes back to the year 1934, in which I first visited Rhine at Duke University, and saw the rugged force of the demands which he made upon his co-workers and subjects. In the light of his glowing intensity, it became possible to begin to understand the accounts given in his book of the way in which he had driven some of his subjects in the demand to get extrasensory phenomena. It may well have been this intensity which produced the results—including some of the best-authenticated long distance results which we have in this entire field.

Elsewhere Murphy (1948) had more to say about Rhine himself:

Everyone who knew J. B. Rhine during the early days of the Duke work knew that a great deal depended upon the combination of flexibility and terrific determination which characterized him—attributes often thought to be mutually exclusive. An iron will and an irresistible determination to get a real performance out of his good subjects was combined with great gentleness and charm in dealing with each person as a person.

We might define this as the *charisma* of the experimenter, a combination of iron will and interpersonal grace and charm. Such persons can found and lead movements, as Rhine himself did for many people for a while.

Another kind of charisma on a very small scale is that enjoyed by a hypnotist with a very suggestible hypnotic subject. This was the situation of Milan Ryzl with his subject Pavel Stepanek,[3] who became one of the star ESP performers of all time in that his above-chance scoring persisted over several years instead of suffering the kind of rapid decline that has been the general fate of other stars. Whatever else one might say about their relationship, it seems clear that Ryzl strongly intended that Stepanek do well at ESP, and Stepanek agreeably and hypnotically complied with this wish.

There are other experimenters who have earned reputations among their peers as being highly psi conducive, and I think it is safe to say that they all could be described as somewhat charismatic, with a combination of intense determination toward certain objectives and sense of adventure, along with charm and personable flexibility. Such people would sell lots of cars or win many votes if they were inclined toward sales or politics. They include Margaret Anderson, Whately Carington, Carl Sargent, Chuck Honorton, Marilyn Schlitz, Dean Radin, and Kathy Dalton. We would say, from a First Sight perspective, that such relatively charismatic persons have the skill to insert their intentions as powerful primes into their experiments, and other people tend to be influenced by them, taking those intentions as their own in the context of the study.

For experimenters who are not so interpersonally persuasive, psi research can be a frustrating business. After all, in everyday life psi functions invisibly, not visibly, with most psi prehensions never reaching definitive expression. With no strong intention to make it different, no need to heighten the unconscious salience of the target, the landscape of the experiment will be as barren of apparent expressions of psi as is the rest of life. Even with more charismatic people, conducting successful research can be exhausting as well as thrilling, and lead to burnout. I quote from J. B. Rhine (1948):

> Anyone who has taken part in a successful psi experiment knows that the pitch of interest developed is something out of the ordinary. Nobody could maintain it indefinitely, and it is not to be put on and taken off with a laboratory coat. Once the experimenter's high level of motivation has run its course, once he satisfies his intellectual curiosity and is thoroughly convinced of the occurrence of the psi phenomenon in question, he comes down to a more relaxed plane of living. As one looks back to his own days of most productive work with psi tests, he recalls a sense of adventure, of suspense, of concentration on the problem that one can acquire only through a very genuine and quite profound personal interest in knowing what the experiment will reveal. But once he is well satisfied, he cannot hope to recover the same spirit again over the same problem, not genuinely. (p. 74)

The Experimenters Induce More Psi-Conducive States in Their Participants

As profoundly interpersonal beings, we influence others and are influenced by them in many ways other than sheer response to their intentions. As the one primarily defining the atmosphere of the experiment, the experimenter can also powerfully influence the moods and attitudes of participants. Some of those moods and attitudes are probably helpful in freeing the expression of psi, and this may be involved in making some experimenters more successful than others. From the perspective of First Sight it seems likely that some persons are better than others at stimulating a creative spark in participants, just as some teachers of creative writing or musical composition inspire more wonderful work than others. In a similar way, people differ in how interesting they can make something seem or how secure or anxious they make others feel.

This has not been studied systematically very much, but anecdotes about successful experimenters are certainly consistent with this. Margaret Anderson was known to have an unusual ability to stir up a wonderful pitch of happy, playful enthusiasm in a group of children. William Braud is understood to have a deeply calming and reassuring effect upon people by his sheer presence. Carl Sargent made his participants want to stay behind after the study and talk with him for hours. Gertrude Schmeidler made every participant in her studies feel important, intelligent, and virtually incapable of producing results that would not be deeply interesting. J. B. Rhine invoked the sense in people that they were embarking upon a remarkable voyage of discovery in which they themselves had the parts of Magellan and Columbus (his wife, L. E. Rhine, in retrospect[4] called this trait "necessary spirit"—the capacity to convey a sense of transcendent mission).

Empirical studies on these general qualities would be difficult to carry out. Schmeidler and Maher (1981) made at least one beginning. They first collected ratings of experimenters by their peers in terms of how "psi conducive" they had proven to be. Five relatively extreme cases on each end of the continuum were matched for age, sex, and general similarly of physical characteristics, and videotapes of each of them giving a presentation (sound omitted) were played to classes of undergraduates who then rated the two groups on various characteristics. Significant differences in perceptions emerged. Members of the psi-conducive group were seen as more flexible, enthusiastic, free, friendly, likeable, playful, and warm. The psi-inhibiting experimenters were rated as more rigid, cold, overconfident, irritable, tense, egotistic, and unfriendly.

Perhaps the sheer belief or disbelief on the part of the experimenter that he or she is studying something real is a factor. From a First Sight perspective we would certainly expect it to have some influence in the situation. A number of studies have attempted to study this question, with different methods and different results. Three studies used the same experimenters who played different roles with their participants.[5] In one role they were described as generally successful as psi experimenters and indicated belief in psi and an expectation of positive results. In the other role they were said to tend to produce negative results and expressed the opposite positions. These manipulations affected how the participants rated their experimenters (how professional they were, how likely they were to help or hinder success, etc.), but there were no significant effects upon actual psi performance. Another pair of studies by Layton and Turnbull (1975) produced mixed results in an interesting way. In their first study they each played different roles with their participants, in one group saying that they believed in psi and were enthusiastic about this particular test because it was likely to succeed and be important evidence. With the other group they said the opposite. Their manipulations were successful in this case. Participants scored significantly above or below chance according to the expectancy they were given. They then conducted an exact replication with another group of participants. Their results this time showed no effect of the manipulation at all.

But how exact can a replication be? I happen to know a hidden drama involved in this work, the sort of thing that never becomes part of the research report. Layton and Turnbull were graduate students in social psychology at the University of North Carolina, and they designed their study as part of their work in a course I taught on experimental parapsychology. By the end of that course they were excited to have discovered this strange area of work, surprised that it was so extensive and yet never discussed, and eager to contribute to our understanding of psi. They carried out the first study under the direction of my coinstructor, David Rogers, and me with no input from the professors in their major area. When they presented the results of their first study to their advisors and announced their intention to seek publication, they encountered a sternly negative attitude that they naively had not expected. They were made to understand that such work is not productive, and publishing it could be a death knell to their budding academic careers. Still, they wished to publish. All right, their professors said, but first they had to conduct an exact replication (and hope for negative results)! They did not consult Rogers or me about their second study, and I expect they were dissuaded from doing so. They got the negative results that their professors let me know that they hoped for. Then their students could argue in their report that the initial findings had probably been a fluke. So if the concerns and interests of the experimenter are part of the situation to which participants respond, as our theory proposes, what were the psi primes to which the participants were responding? They could not have been exactly the same in the two studies.

Three other investigators have used groups of experimenters who naturally either believed or disbelieved in psi and compared the results of participants tested by them.[6] In all cases, the experimenters who believed that they were investigating something real evoked significantly better performance from their participants. Finally, three studies reported by Marilyn Schlitz (who believes in psi) and Michael Wiseman (who does not) are pertinent here.[7] In all cases they worked together in the same laboratory at the same time using the same procedures but ran different experimental participants. In two studies Schlitz's participants scored significantly well while Wiseman's performed at chance. In the third study no differences were found.

Some other studies have looked not at what experimenters believe about psi but at how well they treat their participants, and while these are not as pertinent in this context, I will mention them. Honorton, Ramsey, and Cabibbo (1975) treated some of their participants very warmly and supportively and others very curtly and distantly. The persons nicely treated performed significantly better at their ESP task. Crandall (1985) similarly treated some participants in a warm and friendly way and expressed enthusiasm about psi research, while with others he tried to be cold, hostile, and indifferent to the research. The ESP effect he normally found was found again in the group treated warmly and enthusiastically, but not in the other. Schneider's team[8] used perhaps a less drastic difference in approach, treating some participants personally (allowing personal conversation, expressing personal interest in opinions, etc.) and some impersonally, with no room for personal discussion. This manipulation did not affect the implicit ESP performance of the groups.

To sum up, the actual beliefs of experimenters do seem to function as important primes for participants in psi experiments. These experimenter intentions appear to be unconsciously contextual for the participants, influencing how salient the extrasensory targets and the other variables involved in the study are for them. When experimenter attitudes are only pretended, they may influence conscious ratings but seem to not matter as much as the implicit real attitudes that are presumably part of the unconscious situation that is being prehended. This should not surprise the parapsychologist.

The Experimenter Directly Influences the Psi Result

The experimenter is a human being as much as his or her participants and is frequently strongly motivated to achieve certain kinds of results in the study. If participants can influence random event generators and the behavior of other organisms (including human beings), what prevents the experimenters from doing the same thing, even if not deliberately? Well— nothing.

This complication of psi research has provided headaches for parapsychologists, but it has not much bothered skeptics of the field. They tend to believe that no form of psi can be valid and are not concerned about the intricacies of one person's psi versus another's.

Here we are discussing how our theory helps give an account of experimenter effects that will let them seem a meaningful aspect of how we expect psi to function, rather than an indirect indication that the phenomena are not real. For that reason, we only need to say that yes, another way that experimenters can be expected to be an important variable in psi results is by way of their own psi interactions with the behavior of randomizers and the experiences of participants.

Still, this does make things seem very messy for experimenters who want to be able to isolate variables. John Palmer (1989a; 1989b) has pondered these questions perhaps more deeply than anyone else. I think we need to conclude with him that this is an issue that should be kept in mind in designing all research and that assessments of the conscious and unconscious motives and needs of all the players in the study should be made to whatever extent is possible so that we can come to discern whose needs are prepotent and at what times. From a First Sight point of view, we would say that all the needs of all the parties in the experimental situation are involved all the time but that we are all well practiced at an unconscious level at sorting out what counts most at any given moment. Most people can slip into being sometimes the leader and sometimes the follower, depending. This is true irrespective of psi, and according to our model, should be just as true with interactions that are extrasomatic. Sometimes, in a more passive state, one's intentions may be rather diminished in general. At such times we may unconsciously elect to respond to the more sharply felt intentions of someone else in the situation. If this is so, it is not strange or maladaptive. When one is idly daydreaming and someone else bursts into the room with the news that the house is on fire, there is no doubt whose intentions at that moment will seize the stage of cognitive processing.

Remember that this sort of holistic sorting out is assumed to be a basic function of unconscious thought. As the participant samples her revery for imagery or the random generator counts out a plus or a minus, some balance of all the swirl of intentions is being expressed. We will better articulate the hidden patterns that guide this process as our science develops.

THE DECLINE EFFECT

The decline effect has been described as perhaps the most consistent finding in parapsychology.[9] It means that scoring drops off over time. While it has often been reported, it has rarely been desired by the experimenter and seldom planned for in experiments designed to produce it. It has almost always been reported after the fact, as an interesting if unfortunate side effect, and perhaps as evidence of the perversity of psi.

From a First Sight perspective, psi is always going on, but its functioning is almost always invisible. Normally it does not produce extreme enough intrusions into experience or behavior to allow obvious discernment, either in everyday life or in the findings of experiments. Times when it does so intrude are the exceptions to be explained, and a drop off to the normal invisibility of functioning should hardly be surprising. However, from the point of view of the skeptics among us (and within each of us), psi might not exist at all, and performance that drops off to chance might seem like a sign that strong signs of ESP and PK are flukes that vanish because the inexorable laws of chance have been given time to assert themselves. We must see which explanation seems to fit more facts.

Three major types of declines have been reported: episodic declines (declines within a period of experimental work, like a run of twenty-five ESP guesses), long-term declines of high-scoring subjects,[10] and declines of demonstrated relationships.[11]

Episodic Declines

R. H. Thouless (1972) first applied this term to the pattern of results reported by many experimenters in which psi performance would tend to be strong at the beginning of an experimental session and then fall off as effort continued, followed by rebounding in a new period. He found it in his own work as well.[12] It was first reported by Ina Jephson in 1928. She asked 240 people to work in pairs, with one person drawing a playing card without looking at it while another person tried to guess its identity. The one with the card then looked at it and recorded the trial. She asked them all to work in sessions of five trials, thinking that much more could hurt performance due to fatigue or boredom, and to complete five such sessions. Altogether her participants produced two thousand "divinations." The odds of a correct call are one in fifty-two, since there are fifty-two cards in a deck. However, participants also got credit for partial hits on suit, color, and number (the statistical analysis of Jephson's data was done with methods made up for her by none other than R. A. Fisher, one of the fathers of the then-new mathematics of statistics).

Her overall results were too strong to be due to chance. However, within each session of five trials she noted a U-shaped curve that was itself statistically significant. Scoring began well above chance, dropped off considerably, and then rebounded in the last trial.

Many other workers have reported such episodic declines, sometimes with the dip up at the end and sometimes not.[13] They were also reported in early PK research,[14] and have been reported since.[15] This within-session decline has even been reported to occur in PK tests when aggressive fish[16] and cockroaches[17] were the participants whose well-being stood to be effected by the behavior of a random event generator; and in an ESP test with kittens.[18]

Within-session declines of scoring *extremity* have also been reported.[19] Since most reports of scoring declines have been drops from psi-hitting to chance performance (in one case from psi-missing to chance performance),[20] the decline of scoring extremity may be the more general phenomenon.

First Sight theory suggests three things that could contribute to declines in scoring and scoring extremity with a period of testing effort. First, we would expect a loss of unconsciously perceived pertinence of the extrasensory information as actual sensory experience continues to be denied. Second, as effort persists in what is, from the point of view of sensory experience, an innately impossible task, it is likely that the participant slips into an increasingly critical, self-conscious approach and a rapidly shifting exploration with various internal cues as he or she searches for something pertinent to base responses upon (see the Switching Corollary, chapter 2). Third, in the case of strongly successful initial performance, there is likely to be a build-up of anxiety over success.

Loss of Unconscious Pertinence

In regard to the first matter, at the beginning of a fresh effort at the challenging task it is more likely that conditions are such that high scoring is favored (positive, consistent intention), and then psi-hitting performance is observed. However, as effort continues and no sensory experience is forthcoming, our model predicts that the mind will obey its ordinary pattern of moving away from the extrasensory "prime" toward other sources of incipient experience. Initially, this may tend toward a switch in direction to a tendency to misidentify or significantly miss the target. Before long, however, when extrasensory information remains steadfastly extrasensory (as in ESP experiments) it would seem highly functional to move away from extrasensory information altogether in favor of other sources of information that are more pertinent to actual developing experience. Unconscious thought would then tend to assign less importance to the extrasensory, weight it less, and move to chance-level scoring.

This is congruent with findings in both PWA and parapsychology. As mentioned above, Sohlberg, Billinghurst, and Nylen (1998) have reported that an "overdosage" of too many subliminal exposures of a stimulus normally evocative of a good mood gives a reverse effect of a bad mood. Bem (2005), in his "precognitive boredom effect," has found that a relatively large number of exposures of an emotionally neutral stimulus lead toward a precognitive aversion in regard to that target. Smaller numbers of exposures had no effect at all.

Apparently the mind tends to preconsciously choose to move away from any stimulus that is presented too often without the development of any accompanying sensory material. This is the contrast effect mentioned in an earlier chapter as a basic mechanism for psi-missing. Tease it too much, with no experience forthcoming, and the mind will lose interest and turn away. It may then be the case that if testing effort is kept up even past this point, one will preconsciously wish to avoid the material still more decisively by having no consistent direction of interest at all. In order that the now-abandoned material not be distracting by any sort of referential tendency, a rapidly shifting pattern of intention will come into play, which will be expressed as chance-level performance. If effort is still maintained, the mind's "binding" action will be expressed by a chance level of performance so consistent across runs that it is extrachance! This is the decline from significantly large extremity scores to significantly small ones that has been observed several times.[21]

Drift into Self-Critical Analysis, Cognitive Effort, and Shifting Tacks as Testing Progresses

In an initial effort to carry out a psi task there is a sense of freshness and spontaneity. With no previous recent efforts, there is no build-up of uncertainty and partial failure to contextualize the task. However, as work goes on, and there continues to be no reliable sense of control over the phenomenon (even if scoring is high), it is likely that one will become more self-conscious[22] and begin more cognitive work trying to see patterns of success and failure, noting feelings and images that flit by, exploring one vaguely formed hypothesis after another as to how some more control might be gained, etc. All such cognitive work is likely to produce more unconscious switching of direction in regard to the psi prime (as discussed in chapter 2) and hence performance that clings more tightly to chance expectation.

Build-Up of Anxiety over Success

This would be expected to occur particularly in cases in which there is ongoing feedback of ESP or PK performance, and the participant comes to realize that he or she is doing very well. It is very common for people to report feelings of anxiety, sometimes bordering on panic, at this point. This usually feels surprising. It seems to be the case that for many people there are innate fears of being too psychic.[23] It also seems likely that, unless in a state of "flow,"[24] our participant is realizing that this high level of performance is intrinsically out of control. A fear of failing would be a natural development for many people at this moment. Anxiety is assumed by our theory to constrict the range within which the mind draws preconscious information in forming experience and behavior. This would tend to exclude psi information rather than continue to include it and lead to a drop in performance below chance.

Some indirect evidence that these ideas are correct can be gained by looking at the only two studies that I could find that contradict the normal pattern and describe within-session *inclines* in scoring extremity from near chance to above chance levels. One involved participants in the ganzfeld.[25] When the free associations from their participants' sessions were divided in half, it was found that the material from the second halves showed strong psi-hitting, while that from the first halves was at chance. The second study looked at dreams.[26] Dreams from the second halves of the night showed strong psi-missing in relation to the target, but those from the first halves were at chance. Ignoring the direction of scoring, it is worth noting that both dreaming and the rather dreamlike experience of the ganzfeld should not tend to increases in self-consciousness, fear of failure, and cognitive work as they proceed in the same way that performing in a fully alert state will tend to do. Instead, a deeper immersion in the flow of the experience might be expected for many participants. The fact that one is *not* self-conscious in dreams is one of the distinguishing characteristics of that kind of experience.[27] And people whose verbalizations imply a relative freedom from self-consciousness in ganzfeld sessions have been found to be especially likely to do well.[28]

High-Scoring Subject Declines

It has been the fate of virtually all high-scoring participants in psi research to eventually lose the ability to perform strongly above chance.[29] Perhaps Bill Delmore, Joe McMoneagle, and the star participant of Martin and Stribic (1940) stand alone among participants with extended testing who never reached a point where high performance was lost. Delmore has long gone untested, but McMoneagle appears to still be performing at an extraordinary level as of this writing, although his work in formal studies has ceased. The person who achieved the longest run of high ability in continuous laboratory testing was Pavel Stepanek, the hypnotically trained Czech tested by Milan Ryzl. His remarkable performance extended over a ten-year period.[30] The list of other extraordinary performers who did eventually fall to chance is a long one.[31]

First Sight theory would propose that the eventual declines of even the stars can be accounted for by a slow build-up of the same things that make for the much more rapid episodic declines in unselected participants that I have just discussed. Surely over a long period of continuous work undeveloped extrasensory primes come to seem to the unconscious mind as less pertinent in their own right than other issues of life that are of normally greater concern for all of us. Cognitive work should eventually replace fresh spontaneity as even something as adventurous as psi become repetitively boring. As controversy heightens and scrutiny increases, a fear of failure should build up in even the boldest or most implacable performers. These psi performers are called "stars," the same word we use for those who produce remarkable artistic or athletic achievements. Which of them can repeat their remarkable feats consistently, indefinitely? Few or none. Being a psi star does not appear to be very different.

The exceptions may be instructive and should be studied carefully. Delmore was unusual in his relentless, hyperactive pursuit of new approaches to doing everything.[32] Stepanek was honed to a remarkably persistent focus of intention by his long hypnotic development. By my own observation, McMoneagle is a perpetual soldier and adventurer, whether in uniform or out, and is distinctive in the persistence and appetite with which he seeks challenges and refuses to be dismissed. Unconscious intention determines the direction and intensity of psi expression. There are different ways to maintain a persistent pitch of unconscious intention over even a long time, and these three men seem to embody three of those ways.

Declines of Demonstrated Relationships

When Rhine began his ESP studies at Duke, he tested many volunteers from his staff and the Duke student body and found that, while most people did not display significant talent, a considerable number did. He estimated in his first report that perhaps one person in ten might be expected to score significantly. This proved to be far too optimistic. As testing proceeded at Duke and elsewhere, strong scorers continued to emerge, but in a smaller proportion.

Similarly, when Rhine's work was taken up by other laboratories, there were a good number of early confirmations of his basic findings. Then disconfirmations appeared too. Over time, it seemed safe to expect that reconfirmation would continue to occur, but not invariantly.

The same thing has been said to be the case for some of the demonstrated relationships between psi phenomena and other variables. For a number of years one that seemed highly reliable was a negative relationship between ESP scoring and a measure of unconscious perceptual defensiveness, the Defense Mechanism Test.[33] However, failures to confirm the basic relationship became increasingly common, and in recent reports evidence for the effect appears to have vanished.[34]

Another example is the report of successful psi-hitting in the ganzfeld test situation. Initial reports made it appear that reliably high scoring could be repeated robustly simply by asking participants to carry out their testing in this condition of mild sensory deprivation.[35] But then over time failures to confirm and even a few reversals of performance were reported, which led to a series of contending meta-analyses of later work that reached different conclusions. The authors of the most negative one[36] concluded that the effect was not really reliable at all. Others pointed out that this negative analysis suffered from the odd omission of significant results during the period they sampled, as well as inappropriate statistical analyses. Later meta-analyses[37] have concluded the effect is real, but probably smaller than had been believed before.

What should we make of such apparent declines of the strength of relationships? It seems best to take each of these three in turn. Rhine's basic early finding of strong scoring with a fairly high proportion of people who tried the test probably benefited from a number of psychological considerations that have been discussed earlier. Rhine's own charisma as an experimenter and leader of a new branch of science was at its peak, and many who have looked back on that period have remarked upon his enormous personal magnetism then. Excitement and interest were at a high pitch. Our factors of the direction and consistency of intention were surely running strongly in favor of good performance. This would have to wane, due to the factors that have been discussed above under *episodic declines*.

The Defense Mechanism Test is a very complex projective instrument, measuring over 130 separate variables all thought to relate to the general concept of defensiveness. Many of these require the subjective judgment of highly trained raters. The early reports mostly used data that were analyzed by one person: Martin Johnson. While the consistency of the relationship between psi and defensiveness did decline some over time using Johnson-scored data, the worst failures involved protocols that were not scored by him but by an automated system that attempted to approximate subjective scoring (with limited validity). It is an unsolved mystery what the "true" relationship of human-scored DMT defensiveness to ESP performance is independent of Johnson, and the time-consuming nature of the procedure makes it seem unlikely that the mystery will be solved any time soon.

The ganzfeld debate has raised many interesting issues about the pitfalls and appropriate use of meta-analysis.[38] One of the most important is the question of just what is actually being compared when many studies that can all be said to assess the same thing in some general sense are combined. Every study is different, too. When do the differences matter? As time went on and more studies were carried out on psi in the ganzfeld, experimenters came to vary the procedure in many ways, testing new ideas. When more recent studies were divided into those that basically followed the original ganzfeld protocol and those that departed from that in significant ways, it was found that the replication rate of the former group was significantly better and more closely approximated the early findings.[39]

This brings up a vexing problem for those who would replicate findings. Experimenters are motivated by the quest to learn new things. They show an understandable wish to change approaches. Otherwise they will become increasingly bored, and such boredom has been proposed as a major factor in making replication more difficult.[40]

The dwindling over time of experimental relationships is not limited to parapsychology. It seems to be quite widespread. Jonah Lehrer (2010) has proposed that "the truth wears off," in a discussion of the fact that many findings in fields as disparate as pharmacology, biology, psychology, and physics often show a pattern of declining effect size. He attributes this mostly to an inadvertent selection bias, which leads many investigators to report only strongly significant findings and motivates many scientific journals to publish findings that are different and new. By this account, many relationships that are really spurious (occur just by chance) find their way into publication. This explanation is a bit more difficult to apply to parapsychology, which has had a tradition of publishing all work that is decently done, including failures to replicate.

Some parapsychologists have argued that the decline of experimental relationships is based upon some characteristic of the structure of observations and probability itself, typically basing their ideas on some extrapolation from quantum mechanics. For example, Biermann (2000b) believes that the effect of multiple observers will necessarily lead to the erosion of demonstrated relationships, and von Lucadou[41] argues that inasmuch as a replicated psi phenomenon implies a transfer of information it is prohibited by QM and will tend to destroy the correlation itself.

Others have pointed out that in fact declines of effects over time are often not found in parapsychology,[42] so the idea that they generally obtain is highly conjectural. One group has even called this sort of decline effect a "myth."[43] Clearly they have not been systematically, prospectively studied but only described after the fact when there is much room for subjectivity in assembling findings to form a pattern.

Skeptical View of Declines in Parapsychology

If phenomena appear to decline, it may be taken as a kind of circumstantial evidence that the relationship might not have ever been real. If the declines have no sensible pattern and cannot otherwise be explained, this may be a reasonable idea.

It is difficult to dismiss the findings of parapsychology so easily, though. Episodic declines appear to be systematic phenomena in their own right. We do not conclude that ice does not really exist because it changes its state to liquid. Could the high scoring of the "stars" of parapsychology be flukes, given the eventual decline of almost all of them? Their performance before it declined is in many cases simply too strong and too prolonged to make this a reasonable explanation. Does the decline in a relationship effect size mean that it was never real in the first place? Not if the earlier work was well done, was not selected arbitrarily out of a batch of nonsignificant data, and showed strong and meaningful relationships.

But the most important reason that we are not driven to a skeptical conclusion regarding these things is that they are all psychologically meaningful and follow patterns that we find characteristic of psi in all its manifestations. We know that ice is real despite its melting because we understand why it melts. First Sight theory provides this sort of meaningful interpretation in regard to the decline in psi effects.

NOTES

1. Rosenthal, 1966.
2. Rosenthal, 1967.
3. Ryzl and Beloff, 1965; Ryzl and Pratt, 1963.
4. White, 2002.
5. Watt and Baker, 2002; Watt and Brady, 2002.
6. Parker, 1975a; Taddonio, 1976; Watt and Ramakers, 2003.
7. Schlitz, Wiseman, Radin, and Watt, 2005; Wiseman and Schlitz, 1997; 1999.
8. Schneider, Binder, and Walach, 2000.
9. Palmer, 1978.
10. Banham, 1966; Brugmans, 1922; Pratt, 1973; Rhine, 1934 [1973].
11. Bierman, 2000b.
12. Thouless, 1949–1952; 1951.
13. Dean and Taetzsch, 1963; Humphrey, 1945; Lowry, 1981; Osis, 1956; Parker and Beloff, 1970; Roll and Klein, 1972; Schmeidler, 1968; Van Busschbach, 1959.
14. Pratt, 1946; Rhine and Humphrey, 1945; Thouless, 1945; 1951.

15. Andre, 1972; Dunne, Dobyns, Jahn, and Thompson, 1994; Forwald, 1954; Heseltine and Kirk, 1980; Honorton, Barker, and Sondow, 1983; Lowry, 1981, Tart and Boisen, 1972.

16. Braud, 1976.

17. Schmidt, 1970b.

18. Osis, 1952.

19. Carpenter, 1966, 1968, 1969; Carpenter and Carpenter, 1967; Rogers and Carpenter, 1966; Sailaja and Rao, 1973.

20. Schmeidler, 1964b.

21. Carpenter, 1969.

22. Fenigstein, 1979.

23. Eisenbud, 1963; Tart, 1984; Tart and LaBore, 1986.

24. Csikszentmihalyi, 1988, 1990.

25. Sargent, Bartlett, and Moss, 1981.

26. Harley, 1989.

27. Boss, 1958, 1977.

28. Carpenter, 2005a.

29. Palmer, 1978.

30. Pratt, 1973.

31. Banham, 1966; Brugmans, 1922; Eisenbud, 1967; Rhine, 1934 [1973]; Rose, 1955.

32. Ed Kelly, personal communication.

33. Haraldsson, Houtkooper, and Hoeltje, 1987; Johnson and Haraldsson, 1984: Johnson and Kanthamani, 1967.

34. Haraldsson et al., 2002.

35. Braud, Wood, and Braud, 1975; Parker and Wiklund, 1987; Terry and Honorton, 1967.

36. Milton and Wiseman, 1999.

37. Storm, Tressoldi, and Di Risio, 2010.

38. Rosenthal, 1986.

39. Bem, Palmer, and Broughton, 2001.

40. Tart, 2007.

41. von Lucadou, 1995; von Lucadou et al., 2007.

42. Utts, 1996.

43. Walach et al., 2002.

Section V

FIRST SIGHT BEYOND THE LABORATORY

Even scientists live their lives outside of the laboratory. As important as measuring and analyzing are, we must all venture beyond them to live. It is a basic premise of the First Sight model that psi is ongoing continually in unconscious psychological processing. It is not merely brought into play in the laboratory for the convenience of scientists. Still, because our most reliable information about psi comes from the laboratory, discussion so far has focused on findings there.

Psi prehensions, and their inadvertent expressions, should be just as readily observable in natural situations. And the patterns and forces that are found to be at work in the laboratory should be expressed spontaneously in the larger world.

If parapsychology is to be ultimately relevant for human concerns, it should have implications for life as all people live it. Does it make any difference on a practical level whether or not psi processes are ongoing and whether or not we understand them? It potentially makes enormous differences. Most of this is waiting to be explored, but some beginnings have been made.

18

Ordinary Nonpsychic Experience

We have normality. I repeat, we have normality. Anything you still can't cope with is therefore your own problem.

—Douglas Adams

Even if the model has some utility for accounting for psychic experiences, these events are still odd or perhaps even dangerous aberrations from the point of view of everyday experience for most people. Is the model helpful in accounting for this discrepancy between normal experience and the constructs of parapsychology? Can the model make those parapsychological constructs seem more palatable?

THE APPARENT INCONGRUITY OF
EVIDENCE FOR ESP WITH THE ABSENCE
OF PSYCHIC KNOWLEDGE IN EVERYDAY LIFE

When first confronted with what appears to be evidence for the reality of ESP, common sense is offended. Everyday experience tells us that we cannot see around corners or read next week's newspaper. As a professor of mine once quipped: "If people could do that, don't you think someone would have noticed by now?" We are all initially skeptical when very reliable assumptions appear to be violated. It seems as if we are being asked to choose between an understanding of human nature as we know it from our experience and another version endowed with magical powers of knowledge and action. This model implies that we are not forced into such a choice. It suggests that the apparent, predominant absence of paranormal phenomena

307

and their occasional, unbidden intrusions are all part of a sensible whole. A person is not endowed with magical powers of knowing, because, according to this model, ESP is not knowledge at all. It is the mind's capacity to unconsciously anticipate knowledge at a point prior to any actual sensory experience. In everyday experience, consciousness is occupied by knowledge that is the result of all of the active preconscious processes, including psi, and which is often validated and given closure by interpretable sensory experience. The preconscious processes themselves are not available to awareness. This is not belied by the fact that accurate *guesses* may often be made about events not sensorily available (or only subliminally available). For example, Emanuel Swedenborg's famous vision of a fire three hundred miles distant from him,[1] as remarkably accurate as it was, was not *knowing*, in the sense that knowledge was available to those near the fire. It was an accurate interpretation of fantasy images provoked by extrasensory prehensions experienced in a state of reverie. As another example, the skilled remote viewer is not assumed by this model to *know* the location of a sought missing person. Rather, the place of the missing person, which the viewer desires to know, arouses an anticipational network of preconscious feelings and meanings that serve to orient his attention. If someone were about to simply tell him what he wants to know, this anticipation would merely make him slightly quicker and more efficient in understanding what he is about to be told. He would never consciously know of having anticipated it. However, if this information is not available to the viewer, this anticipational arousal must "hover" on the edge of awareness, without cognitive closure, because no validating sensory information is available. The skilled and practiced viewer tolerates this suspended uncertainty, consults the inadvertent feelings and images issuing from the "hovering" anticipational activation, and draws out a collection of allusive chunks of content containing measurable truth.

In everyday life, we do not ordinarily search out the possible connection between inadvertent psychological phenomena and distant realities; nor are situations generally conducive to doing so. Many truth-implying experiences probably flow by uninterpreted and unremembered. We pass most of our hours sensibly intending to understand what is close at hand for us, in good critical touch with reality and in states of mind other than those most suited to glimpsing the activity of preconscious processes. Those processes are not inactive at such moments, but they are invisible.

More than this, our theory suggests that at times when we are occupied with immediate and practical concerns our minds will weight most heavily information that is unconsciously understood to be most reliable, most available for validation. This is sensory experience. It may be immediate and personal sensory experience, as in my experience of flowing traffic as I drive. It may be remembered sensory experience, as I recall a previous accident at a certain curve in the road. Or it may be sensory experience of someone else's apparent experience, as when I read the facial expression of someone I am with as indicating that I should turn around and see what is behind me. At such times purely implicit experience that does not in itself lead immediately to any validation will be automatically weighted lightly and turned away from by unconscious attention. If allusions to it appear at all in experience or behavior, they will most likely be negative ones and will not be interpreted as referring to anything. We will experience the vast realm of extrasomatic transaction as utterly absent. In fact, this is our normal experience as we go through our days sensibly occupied with our affairs.

Thus, by this model, the general absence of psi experience and the occasional occurrence of psi experience may be understood in the same terms, all as sensible parts of normal functioning. This reasoning may not be compelling to someone who has never felt the need to seriously confront the possible reality of psi phenomena, but it may at least encourage an open-minded attitude about the possibility.

THE FEAR OF PSI

Besides thinking of psi as unusual and improbable, many people also find the possibility of psi experiences a frightening idea. There are probably many sources of this concern. One would appear to be the popular association of psychic claims with mental illness, another is our fears of being influenced or controlled by extrapersonal forces, and a third comes from the moral proscription against delving into such questions by major religious traditions. This model may offer some help in regard to each of these matters.

Psi and Mental Illness

Experiences that people construe as psychic, or "subjective paranormal experiences,"[2] are popularly associated with madness, and indeed, they may characterize psychotic breakdowns of either a manic or schizophrenic sort[3] as well as less malignant conditions, such as schizotypal personality disorder and (in my own clinical experience at least) with dissociative identity disorder. Many people are fearful of apparently paranormal experiences for this reason, and many who believe they may have had such experiences are fearful that others will think that they are insane. In my role as a clinical psychologist, I have often found that it is reassuring to authoritatively tell such persons that they are perfectly sane, when I am sure that they are. Assuming that the premises of this model are correct, it might be even more reassuring to inform them that psi is not only normal, it is probably universal among human beings, although its normal mode of functioning is almost entirely preconscious. It might be most reassuring if we could say that there is absolutely no connection in reality between genuine psi and psychosis, but reality may be more complex than our constructs would have it.

The First Sight model suggests that persons who are suffering from prolonged confusion or disorientation might in fact be open to experiencing a plethora of preconscious processes, including psi, but their ability to interpret the experiences accurately and use them constructively would be severely compromised. However, persons who appear to be able to exercise some control over their psi productions and make constructive use of them present a very different picture. Their openness to preconscious material represents a positive adaptation, not a breakdown of functioning. In this way, they are like the artists and other creative persons described by Kris (1952), who have the capacity of "regression in the service of the ego." Like persons who have developed their sensibilities in art or music or cultivated their powers of memory or attention to detail, many such persons seem to have gone to the trouble of developing the skill to make use of cues that are probably available to all of us—cues that are useless and quickly forgotten without the requisite skill in using them.

Fear of Extrapersonal Influence

This fear arises not only in regard to extrasensory phenomena but also with the idea of subliminal influence. To say that some activity is unconscious or preconscious seems mystifying and gives us the sense that the activity might be done somehow by something separate from our conscious intentions. If such influences occur, perhaps we all are really slaves to impersonal, physical processes that control us.

However, these "influences" are actually our own (preconscious) activity in which we engage in pursuing the construction and meaning of our experience. They are not done *to us*, but are done *by us*. Acts can be intentional and unconscious at the same time. This is one reason I have grounded this model in an existential context; that is to say, I have attempted to look at it in terms of life as it is actually lived altogether, as opposed to seeing it in the context of some abstraction about some aspect of life. Existentially, we are active, whole beings; we press forward with our lives. We are not simply the products of mechanical processes impinging upon us, but we *use* those processes for our doing and becoming. Some important aspects of this using are not conscious. The fact that part of my using is unconscious does not mean that this part is being done by someone or something else. It is still being done by me. When I walk from one place to another, I am not conscious of all the myriad of muscular actions that make the walking work. They are unconscious constituents to my action of walking. However unconscious, they are still being done by me; they are part of my walking and are serving my intention of getting to the new place. Now adding reference to the observations of parapsychology, we may say that at the outermost edge of all of our pressing forward, we use psi processes, which is to say, we make use of the fact that we exist always a little beyond ourselves in space and ahead of ourselves in time (actually, we can make use of bigger spans ahead and beyond if that meets our needs, but ordinarily a little ahead and beyond is most useful for us).

Scientists frequently contribute inadvertently to this fear of being impersonally driven. Since many scientists presume (preconsciously) that the best account of something is one that is impersonal and does not refer to any sort of intention, they often gravitate to ways of thinking about unconscious processes that imply that the processes are purely physical actions, such as chemical reactions. This may feel comfortable to the scientist since it seems to be accounting for something on a basic level. It also adds to the mystifying sense that somehow we might all be robots, in spite of our experience of intention and consciousness. Even more oddly, given the findings of parapsychology, we might be robots driven by distant influences! However, if a scientific account of the person is to be adequate to its subject, it must take account of the existential fact that life-as-lived is much more a *project* than a *process*. Impersonal processes such as chemical reactions are certainly constituent parts of the project of life, but they are not the whole story. To proceed as if they are is mystifying and is a failure to avoid the reductionistic fallacy.[4] For psychology to be adequate to its subject matter, our model suggests that it must take account of the fact that preconscious processes are used by each individual in the pursuit of meaningful experience, not inflicted upon him or her. Conveying this sort of understanding to the general public should help dispel the fantasies and fears of external control.

Still, in some people these fears may be extreme. I have met many such people in my clinical work. They may feel that they are transparent to others and cannot stop their thoughts from being known against their wishes, or cannot stop experiencing the thoughts of others. Or they may feel controlled by malign "voodoo" aimed at them psychically by some other person. Such people are suffering from serious psychological dysfunction, and their fears have escaped the bounds of reality.

What parapsychologists have learned runs counter to these nightmare terrors. Our intentions, including intentions of self-defense and privacy, work at an unconscious as well as a conscious level of functioning. Research shows that we use that defensiveness to become less aware of frightening unconscious material than might otherwise be the case, not more. If one feels passively overwhelmed by frightening things this is because his or her functioning in general is radically compromised. Then one experiences the terror that accompanies that kind of breakdown. Can we be influenced by the intentions of others? Research suggests that this is so only if this influence meets our own needs. This is suggested by the slightly apprehensive feelings that we can notice when being stared at by others, as studied by Sheldrake (2003); and by the slight relaxation experienced by isolated people who were viewed by someone with loving and calming intentions, as observed by Braud (2003).

Moral Proscriptions against the Paranormal

The Holy Bible and the Koran, along with many other texts of the monotheistic faiths, contain numerous references to paranormal phenomena such as prophecies, blessings, curses, and miracles. Sometimes these are seen as sacred events and are viewed with great reverence. At other times they are seen as evil and condemned severely. Similarly, great texts of Eastern wisdom, such as the Yoga Sutras of Patanjali[5] speak of the various sidhis, or paranormal powers, that accompany the highest levels of spiritual development, but they caution that they must not be sought for their own sake but should be experienced only within the context of utter compassion and reverence for the Supreme. Perhaps a common theme for all of these traditions of spiritual life is that paranormal abilities may be real, but if they are sought for their own sake and developed toward the end of personal power and aggrandizement over others, they are destructive and should be avoided. In that way they are like any other form of power, which can always corrupt the powerful. If held in the context of loving reverence for all creation and for the transcendent powers behind creation, paranormal abilities may lead in the positive directions of healing, enlightenment, and self-transcendence. Certainly notable *paranormal experiences* seem to generally have such effects on a personal level.[6]

The First Sight model has no theological commitments, but it does stress a conception of human nature in which each person is not contained within personal, physical boundaries but is ontologically and epistemologically extended beyond that into intimate commerce with all the rest of reality, including all other persons. To pursue paranormal experiences selfishly, over and against the interests of others, would therefore be self-contradictory, and by the logic of the model, probably doomed to failure. If the model is basically correct, it implies that as we learn more about the functioning of psi processes, we will in turn learn more about our profound interconnectedness and the inseparability of our interests from those of all beings. Seeking such knowledge seems to be in tune with the great traditions of wisdom and faith, not contrary to them.

NOTES

1. Sigstedt, 1952.
2. Neppe, 1983.
3. American Psychiatric Association, 2004.
4. Rychlak, 2003.
5. Satchidananda, 1990.
6. Kennedy, Kanthamani, and Palmer, 1994; Kennedy and Kanthamani, 1995; Milton, 1992; White, 1997.

19

The More Psychic Person

Purity of heart is to will one thing.

—Soren Kierkegaard

In terms of paranormal cognizance or influence, the everyday lives of most people are long, quiet spans of well-bounded normality, punctuated perhaps by extremely rare, anomalous physical events or occasional lightning flashes of unusual knowledge. However, some people are different. Some individuals report a great many incidents of apparently genuine paranormal knowledge or physical effects, and some of them have also demonstrated these things in well-controlled laboratory conditions.

In this chapter we are especially interested in those persons who show some *control* over the expression of psi and some *skill* in understanding and using these expressions. There are other persons for whom apparent psi experiences are something that *befall them*, often against their wishes. Sometimes people are flooded with unbidden, unwanted, even terrifying flashes of apparent psi reference, perhaps in the context of a radical breakdown of adjustment. Others seem to be the centers of storms of bizarre and uncontrollable "poltergeist" or RSPK (*percent spontaneous psychokinesis*) events, and these things, too, seem to be more likely in dysfunctional interpersonal situations. We must set these cases aside for the moment and focus upon persons who have demonstrated psi phenomena that are wanted and subject to some degree of control.

Laboratory validation is especially important when trying to identify persons who are unusually given to psi experiences in this more controlled way. Persons with delusions involving psilike ideas and frauds posing as "psychics" are more numerous than the genuine article, and it is important to not be led astray at the outset if we are attempting serious study.

What distinguishes the genuine article from the rest of us is a question that deserves the fullest study. This effort has only begun. The First Sight model and theory propose some characteristics that should matter, and these expectations can be held up against what we have learned about more powerful psi performers to see how well they fit.

Unconscious intention is the key variable for our model in directing us beyond our bodily boundaries to interact meaningfully with information and events there. There are several important features of this intention that are required to make a psi prehension more visible.

The direction of the intention must be positive, in favor of using the prehension. Psi itself must be understood to be a valid and useful source of information and influence. The information itself (in ESP—or EESP) and the events themselves (in PK—or A-ESP) must be unconsciously understood to be meaningful and important in the moment.

For psi to seem to be a real and helpful source of meaning and influence, it would be very helpful to be raised in a milieu that believed these things to be true. Cultures vary in their normative beliefs in this matter, and those that are friendlier to it would be expected to contain a higher proportion of persons who make active reference to psi. In even our own largely materialistic culture that mostly dismisses the reality of psi, there are subcultures, religious groups, and families that view it more positively. Our unconscious intentions take shape over time and are deeply influenced by those who were most important in raising us. If we were raised by persons who thought psi to be real, we will be more likely to make use of it at an unconscious level.

Anxiety must be low enough to be manageable, whether the anxiety is about psi itself, the information involved, other aspects of the situation at the moment, or some more general state. The person must be able to sustain a high level of performance at something and enjoy it. Self-doubt, shame, guilt, poor self-esteem, and a wish to not be too exceptional must not be so great as to interfere with doing something extraordinary that others can witness.

The person must be able to sustain a consistency of intention, not only at a conscious level but also at an unconscious one. He or she must not be too analytical or confused or distractible or conflicted or diffident. Only consistent unconscious intention will produce successful demonstrations of psi (or virtually any other objective, in fact). First Sight agrees with Kierkegaard when he said: "It seems essential, in relationships and all tasks, that we concentrate only on what is most significant and important."

Consistent unconscious intention may sometimes arise simply from the great importance of some concern, as that aroused by impending harm to a loved one. But this distinguishes psychic moments, not psychic persons. There are various paths to the goal of a personal capacity for consistent unconscious intention. The development of an integrated and harmonious inner life through such means as meditation, depth psychotherapy, or contemplative prayer should be helpful for many.

Arranging one's life in such a way that provides a circle of supportive and like-minded others is also helpful. We are intensely interpersonal, socially contextual creatures. Too much time with others whose intentions basically conflict with one's own must diminish the intentional purity of even the strongest among us.

It might seem paradoxical, but a different path to consistent unconscious intention is a dissociative state. I know from my clinical work that this permits an unusual single-mindedness of intention at both a conscious and unconscious level of functioning. Highly dissociative *people* can sometimes seem disorganized and self-contradictory when we know them over time, across the shifting ascendancy of different "parts" of themselves.[1]

But while firmly in one part and not another, we can see in the dissociative person a remarkable singularity of purpose that is not granted to less dissociative persons who are more likely to shift intentions as situations develop (just try to reason out alternatives with a very self-destructive part of a very dissociative person). Similar dissociationlike states of unreflective single-mindedness may arise in some cases of neurological impairment, such as epilepsy, or in the headlong enthusiasm of persons diagnosed as bipolar.

I have just listed some factors that First Sight theory assumes are required to make positive reference to extrasomatic prehensions, and do so with sufficient extremity to permit somehow expressing an inadvertent allusion to them. In addition to that, one must develop skills at negotiating inadvertencies sufficiently well to interpret them when they occur (in EESP) or encourage their physical expression (in A-ESP).

In the first place, one must respect inadvertencies as sometimes being meaningful and instructive. Then it is necessary to develop experience at exploring the ineffable margins of experience and drawing useful meaning out. Artists of all stripes do this, as do some scientists and psychotherapists and creative people in other walks of life.

These features include a kind of consistent and devoted intention, outgoingness and freedom from anxiety, a high level of general effectiveness, strong motivation, creativity, and the cultivation of skills in interpreting marginal, inadvertent experience.

INTENTION

Persons who are prone to having many psychic experiences and who have some degree of control over their production would be expected to have a general intention to gain knowledge (or have influence) in this way, and this intention should be relatively congruent at both a conscious and unconscious level and be consistent over time. This intentional pattern probably begins at an early age. In some cases,[2] the ability seems to have been prized by important adults. Many apparently gifted psychics such as Alex Tanous,[3] Helene Smith,[4] and Daniel Home[5] all had a family tradition of close relatives who appeared to have psychic experiences. This is popularly taken as indicating a hereditary factor in psychic ability, but it may also indicate family environments in which psychic matters were of strong interest. In the childhoods of some other individuals such as Gerard Croiset,[6] Ted Serios,[7] and Eileen Garrett,[8] psychic awareness seems to have relieved the problems of a difficult early environment, or as with McMoneagle,[9] had even been an important survival skill in dangerous circumstances. Having a relatively strong intention to gain paranormal knowledge should tend to orient preconscious response positively, resulting in the evocation of anticipatory material of a procontent sort, and the consistency of the positive intention should lead to a stable tendency to produce discernable referents to the content.

ADVENTUROUSNESS, OUTGOINGNESS, AND RELATIVE FREEDOM FROM ANXIETY

Persons who are characteristically timid, avoidant, and fearful would be expected to carry a preconscious attitude of avoidance toward many potential experiences. On the contrary, persons who boldly tend to seek out new experiences and meet life cheerfully and optimistically should tend to be more positively responsive at a preconscious level to important extrasensory information. A person whose life is largely constrained by illness[10] or societal constraints, and is thereby frustratingly unadventurous, may find that paranormal experience offers an important compensatory freedom.[11]

A HIGH GENERAL LEVEL OF EFFECTIVENESS (OR A RELATIVE ABSENCE OF GENERAL SELF-DEFEATING TENDENCIES)

Persons who are generally effective are presumed to have motivations to succeed that are consistent at different levels of awareness and are relatively invariant over time. On the contrary, persons who are self-defeating may be understood to have unconscious motivation to fail, in spite of a conscious wish to be successful.[12] Persons who have unusual facility in producing psychic information would be expected to display a general tendency to be successful across situations. This appears to be true of a number of gifted individuals, for example, Bill Delmore[13] and Pat Price,[14] and it seems consistent with biographical material about several others.

MOTIVATION TO RISE TO
CHALLENGES IN TESTING SITUATIONS

Related to the last point, a general tendency to be stimulated by challenges and to wish to succeed at them should be related to expressing psi information and psychokinetic effects positively and strongly when the ability to do that is being tested. First Sight theory holds that unconscious intention is the basic determiner of such positive expression, and the purity and consistency of this intention is expected to determine how strongly or densely accurate the expression is. Persons who are motivated to succeed in an ESP or PK testing situation would be expected to tend to succeed. One implication of this is that persons who are more extraverted (also see chapter 13) should tend to be more successful than introverts, at least in testing situations involving rising to challenges in front of an audience. This is because extraverts are known to be characterized by such social reward sensitivity.[15]

CREATIVITY AND A CAPACITY TO
DELAY COGNITIVE CLOSURE

This model suggests that cognitive closure (a condition in which one knows clearly the content of one's experience) serves to "bind" preconscious prehensions and leave them securely outside of awareness. Delaying such closure permits one to consult inadvertent material such as inner imagery, stray associations, and novel impulses—all of which may convey the influence of extrasensory prehension. Creative persons are characterized in part by a capacity to sustain a condition of fruitful uncertainty, a need to find a new solution, and an ability to eschew premature closure of experience while the new, creative thing finds form.[16] William Stafford (1998, p. 4) says about writing a poem, "I wait deliciously. And the thing that occurs depends partly upon how much I hunger." Thus, in a general sense, effectively psychic persons might be expected to be relatively creative, at least in the general sense of McCurdy: ". . . the power to see the world in new ways, to utilize fruitfully the abilities which one has, to expand and reorganize one's life, to transcend one's previous limitations."[17]

THE CULTIVATION OF SKILLS IN
INTERPRETING INADVERTENCY

First Sight leads to the expectation that persons who are particularly facile at generating accurate extrasensory information have developed some experiential skills at attending to marginal experience, questioning it patiently but hungrily, and understanding the structure of their own preconscious associative network.[18] Persons who practice the "inward" disciplines of prayer or meditation might be expected to have developed such skills. For example, Amanda Jones (1910), a well-known psychic of the nineteenth century, believed that ". . . the development of what may be called spiritual illumination seems to me a not unlikely result of those inner communings characteristic of Quaker worship." Similarly, those who have learned how to produce creative works of art or science, or those who have developed great insight into their own dream life,[19] may also be particularly well equipped. There may be experiential skills that are peculiar to many persons who cultivate extrasensory information, such as the capacity to attend to mental imagery.[20]

Different individuals who work persistently at extrasensory perception often report finding subjective cues that guide them in discriminating more veridical information. Some describe a subjective sense of "rightness" that accompanies information that is more reliably expressive of the extrasensory. Mary Craig Sinclair, for example, as recounted in the book by her husband Upton (1930), learned to distinguish between a "guess" (almost always misleading) and a "hunch" (almost always truth telling). I will discuss her at greater length in the next chapter.

One particular technique apparently used by several relatively psychic persons I have known might be called "serial divination," by which I mean a process of imagining associations to some inadvertency (say a bit of dream content), and following that by treating those associations as material to question by further imagining associations to those, and so on, all the while avoiding jumping to some conclusion that seems too "logical." Then, finally one reaches a sense of unanticipated rightness. Interestingly, this is not unlike the associative procedure taught in psychoanalytic psychotherapy, when one is seeking not extrasensory information but a leap in self-understanding.

PLAYFULNESS, EMOTIONAL ENERGY, AND A DARING SENSE THAT ASTONISHING THINGS ARE POSSIBLE

People who demonstrate controlled PK (or A-ESP) effects probably profit from all the things just discussed in regard to ESP (or EESP), but some other matters also seem to be important in this case.

The effects vary enormously, and some that have been observed with good experimental controls include the noncontact bending of metal objects, rolls of dice, outputs of random number generators, temperature alterations in thermisters, production of anomalous noises, deflections in magnetometers, changes in the rate of hemolysis of blood cells, bending of laser beams, changes in weight of things sitting alone on scales, levitation of tables, alteration of the growing rate of seedlings, and production of "thoughtographs," or odd photographic, effects including detailed pictures appearing on unexposed film.

Something that is often mentioned in regard to such demonstrations is an interpersonal atmosphere that is energetic, playful, expansive, daring, and fun. A playful belief that the odd events desired can occur and probably will seems to help.

The people involved are often (but not always) described as extraverted, dominant, charming, charismatic, and sometimes flirtatious. These persons function best both socially and psychically in cheerful, active settings that are partylike and sometimes border on controlled chaos. This poses quite a challenge to experimenters who would observe their effects while maintaining careful control over crucial aspects of the situation.

Some of the persons who have performed best under well-controlled conditions have also been found to stoop to cheating at other times, so ironclad controls are essential if we wish to believe that any given effect is genuinely paranormal and not some kind of magician's trick. A well-controlled situation can become a stilted one, not at all partylike, and this seems sometimes to truly diminish the likelihood of PK events. Fortunately, many observations of statistically significant and sometimes dramatic PK effects have been reported when controls were very good, so we can have confidence that they are possible.

Another characteristic of persons who are strong PK performers is the capacity for an intense emotional state. This is often a cheerful, playful kind of emotion, but strong anger may be helpful as well.[21] A very angry state of mind can permit a highly focused, unequivocal, and energetic state of intention.

Finally, playfully acting out a temporary suspension of ordinary disbelief and skepticism is an important feature of the kind of party atmosphere that PK performers tend to facilitate. "Let's act as if it will happen!" they say.[22] Thus, they deliberately evoke strong and unequivocal intention in themselves and others in the situation.

First Sight theory holds that PK effects should tend to occur when unconscious intention about some event is strong and unequivocal and normal action (such as bending a piece of metal with a hammer or holding a flame next to a thermister) is prevented. Most people sometimes go to parties and understand that the dull limitations of everyday life can be transcended there. Talk flows more freely about more things and sometimes with more depth, physical fun that is often neglected can go on, flirting happens. Dancing, game playing, joking, substance imbibing, showing off—these are all ways that people create fun and temporarily expand their possibilities of action, engagement, and self-expression. At a good party, intentions become unequivocal; self-analysis and self-doubt can be forgotten for a time. Strong feelings can be indulged and developed. One can let go and engage.

And in regard to anger, it is noteworthy that many athletes develop the skill of getting angrily "pumped" before a contest. Their motivation can become very intense and single-minded, and obstacles to their goal can seem to disappear.

All of these ingredients appear to characterize those persons who are especially good at demonstrating PK (A-ESP) effects, and many of the moments when they express them. The same things seem often, if less universally, to characterize the high performers at ESP as well—but then it is good to remember that they are frequently the same people!

PSI IS NOT A TRAIT

Some characteristics of persons were just listed that are expected to be associated with a greater capacity to express psychic, nonlocal information in either their own experience and behavior or in physical events around them or both. It should not be concluded from this that being psychic is a trait. A trait is a personal characteristic that is expected to be expressed with some fair degree of consistency over time and across situations. Scoring on tests of ESP and PK manifestly does not tend to show such self-consistency, and in First Sight theory this approach has been renounced. If someone claims to be generally psychic, our first response should be skepticism.

However, some persons do tend to perform well with some consistency during *some spans of time* and across *certain kinds of situations*. Tests of psi, after all, measure a response to particular situations, including those nonlocal aspects of the situation that are serving as ESP targets or random devices measuring PK influence. It would be maladaptive if this sort of response were too consistent.

From the perspective of First Sight theory, psi is no more a trait than is, say, "seeing blue things" or "feeling persecuted." These things are necessarily variable across situations, depending upon the amount of blueness in the visual situation or the presence and intensity of personally directed malice in the moment, as well as one's intentions regarding responding to these things. If someone claims to be invariant on these things we would consider them to be visually impaired in some way or given to paranoia. Nor is psi a *skill* except in a very general sense. It is a basic aspect of being-in-the-world common to almost all living beings (some individuals may be specially impaired, but we have no evidence of that as yet) comparable to the skills of seeing or of sensing emotionally. What does discriminate individuals in the expression of psi is their unconscious intentions to use the capacity, and their tendencies to hold different intentions about this may vary as a function of certain other traits or general tendencies.

Some traits have just been listed that probably do have some fair degree of consistency over time: intention to use psi, adventurousness, freedom from anxiety, general effectiveness, social reward sensitivity, playfulness, charisma, dominance, creativity, and pertinent skill development with patient hard work. Persons characterized by these things are expected to be more likely to positively express psi (knowledge or action) in appropriate situations.

NOTES

1. See, for example, Putnam, 1989.
2. See, for example, Tanous and Ardman, 1976.
3. Tanous and Ardman, 1976.
4. Flournoy, 1900.
5. Burton, 1944.
6. Tenhaeff, 1953.
7. Eisenbud, 1967.
8. Garrett, 2002.
9. McMoneagle, 2002.
10. Mollie Fancher and Caryll Houselander in Smith, 1969.
11. Zingrone, 1994.
12. Engel and Ferguson, 1990.
13. Edward Kelly, personal communication.
14. Targ and Puthoff, 1977.
15. Denissen and Penke, 2008; Lucas et al., 2000.
16. Fellini, 1997; Kelly, 1979; Perls, 1970.
17. McCurdy, 1961, p. 562.
18. Vaughn, 1973.
19. Boss, 1958.
20. Watt, 1996.
21. Heath, 2011.
22. Batcheldor, 1984.

20

First Sight and Personal Exploration of Psi

Of a great metaphysician / he looked at his own Soul with a Telescope
What seemed all irregular, he saw & shewed to be beautiful Constellations & he
added to the Consciousness hidden worlds within worlds.

—Samuel Taylor Coleridge

Bits and pieces—these are the skills of a psychic.

—Joe McMoneagle

As Coleridge reminds us, not everyone explores in a laboratory, but many more of us wish to explore things in our own lives. We each do a kind of personal study of whatever matters to us. The conclusions we draw and the behaviors we choose are not unlike the scientists' experiments.[1] We implicitly pose some question and then see how life answers us. Such personal, existential study lacks some of the certainty that we can gain in the laboratory, but in one way or another we all engage in it as best we can.

If psi interests us we may want to explore it ourselves. Like Coleridge, we turn our telescope of observation inward. Is psi real? Can we see it in ourselves? How should we proceed to find out? Can First Sight theory guide us? Can it be done safely, without falling into self-deception or something still unhealthier? In this chapter we will look at the work of a few other personal explorers.

MARY CRAIG SINCLAIR

Another poet like Coleridge, who also proved herself as an extraordinary ESP subject, was Mary Craig Sinclair, the wife of the novelist Upton (in the

325

rest of this discussion I will refer to her as MCS, rather than Sinclair, to distinguish her from her better-known husband). Together they wrote a book about her personal explorations with psi called *Mental Radio*.[2] The book carried an appreciative preface by Albert Einstein and aroused a tremendous amount of popular interest at the time it was published.

MCS had experiences that she thought of as psychic throughout her life. This may imply that she was starting with some extra talent, but it may also simply mean that she was raised in a family that had an interest in such things and implicitly encouraged her to construe her experience in those terms. Still, a new science of parapsychology was in the air in the 1920s, and she wanted to conduct some research to learn if it was real or not.

Her experimental method was informal but highly disciplined. Typically, she would ask someone apart from her to produce a drawing of something at random, and then seal it in an envelope. When she felt ready, she would recline, relax, clear her mind of inner chatter and distraction, and hold the envelope next to her solar plexus. She would firmly set the intention to "see" the hidden picture and wait patiently for images to occur. Then she would draw her impressions and write any words that seemed important in describing her experience. Only then would she open the envelope and compare the drawings. She was assiduous in her record keeping of all trials, including ones that did not seem particularly impressive. There were variations in her procedure—sometimes the agent was in another town, and sometimes there was no agent at all but only a book that she had not seen and that no one in the household had yet read—but her part of the exercise was consistent. Over a three-year period she accumulated 260 trials, a very large portion of which showed remarkable correspondence with the targets. While statistical analysis was not as developed then as it is now, a control analysis matching responses randomly with other responses produced a very low rate of similarities. A more formal analysis would certainly show that the results were wildly significant. A few examples of targets and her responses are shown in figures 20.1, 20.2, 20.3, and 20.4.

MCS wrote very tellingly about the circumstances and state of mind that she found necessary for the exercise of telepathy and clairvoyance. In doing this, she made up a three-part model of her mental functioning as a way to think about different classes of her experience: the conscious mind (logical and social thought), the subconscious mind (which is the source of trains of association and most stray thoughts and images), and the *deep mind*, which is independent of the other two and a source of genuine extrasensory prehensions. In her words:

> You want a message from the person who is sending you a message; you do not want a train of subconscious day dreams. The subconscious answers questions, and its answers are always false; its answers come quietly like a thief in

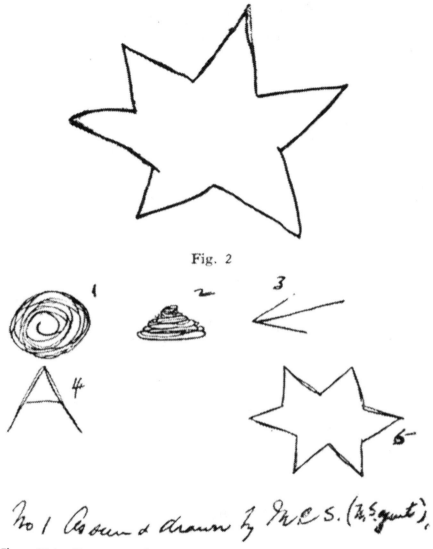

Fig. 2

Figure 20.1.   Star target and response. Sinclair, Upton, *Mental Radio: How Does It Work?* London: T. Werner Laurie, 1930.

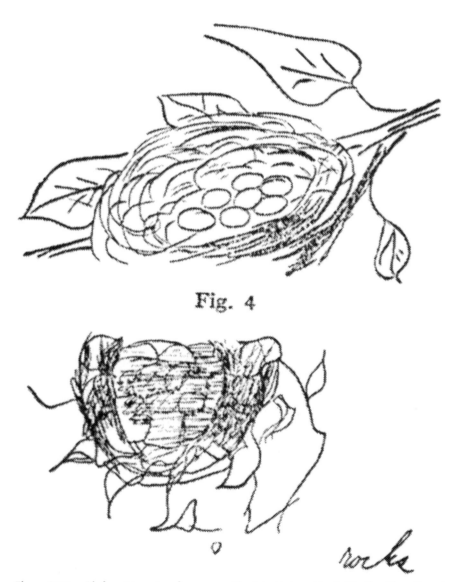

Fig. 4

Figure 20.2. Bird nest target and response. Sinclair, Upton, *Mental Radio: How Does It Work?* London: T. Werner Laurie, 1930.

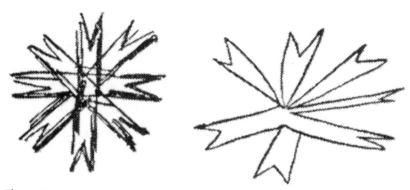

Figure 20.3.   Cross design target and response. Sinclair, Upton, *Mental Radio: How Does It Work?* London: T. Werner Laurie, 1930.

Fig. 9

*May be elephant's
snout — but any way
it is some kind of
a running animal*

Figure 20.4.   Target drawing of dog chasing toy and response. Sinclair, Upton, *Mental Radio: How Does It Work?* London: T. Werner Laurie, 1930.

the night. But the "other" mind, the "deep" mind, answers questions too, and these answers come with gladness and conviction. . . . These two minds seem different from each other. One lies and rambles; the other sings and is truthful.

She emphasized that avoiding jumping to conclusions—in our terms reaching cognitive closure—was something that must be avoided. She emphasized the importance of *not* allowing any thoughts about the meaning of what she was "seeing" in her mind's eye to intrude into the process until after her data gathering was over. She resolutely resisted such closure because she found that it always misled her. I quote her again, along with the pair of pictures she refers to:

> This error of allowing the conscious or the subconscious mind to finish the object [is] one to be most careful about. As one experiments, he [sic] realizes more and more that these two minds, the conscious and the subconscious, are really one, subconsciousness being only a disorderly store-house of memories. The third, or "deep mind" is apparently the one which gives us our psychic phenomena. Again I say, I do not know what this "deep mind" is; I use the words merely to have a name for that "other thing" which brings the message. The conscious mind, combined with the subconscious, not only wants to finish the picture, but decides sometimes to eliminate a detail which does not belong to what it has guessed should be there. For example, I will discuss the drawings which have been given as Figures 35, 35a, in this book. I "visioned" what looked like a figure 5, except that at the top where there should be a small vertical line projecting toward the right, there was a flare of very long lines converging at one end. I consciously decided that the long lines were an exaggeration and multiplication of what should properly be at the top of a five, and that I should not accept them. Here was conscious mind making a false decision. But by obeying the rules I had laid down in advance, I was saved from this error of consciousness. I closed my eyes, gave a call for the true picture, and the lines appeared again, so I included them in my drawing. When I opened the envelope and looked at the picture inside, it was an oil derrick. So the flare of long lines was the real thing, while the figure 5 was the interloper at least, so I now consciously decided. I thought that the figure 5 and the flare of lines were entirely separate mental images, one following the other so rapidly that they appeared to belong together.

These images are given in figure 20.5.

Many times her drawings bore a striking similarity to the target, but her interpretation of it was wrong. For example, Upton intended the target drawing 4a to represent a bird's nest with eggs, whereas she interpreted her response as a rock well with vines growing down. She interpreted the next drawing partly correctly and partly incorrectly, even though the physical resemblance was striking. Upton intended his drawing as a puppy chasing a toy, and she thought of hers as a running elephant.

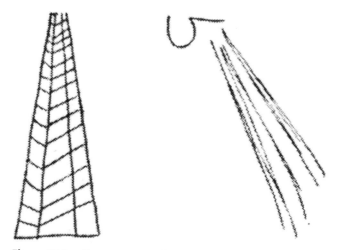

Figure 20.5. Tower target and response. Sinclair, Upton, *Mental Radio: How Does It Work?* London: T. Werner Laurie, 1930.

However, it was not only physical similarities of shapes, lines, and angles that carried the information. Sometimes there were also striking allusions in terms of moods she felt, or odors she sensed, or meanings that could be seen as related to the meaning of the object, as in the idea and *sense* of danger when the target drawing involved a lit match (a traumatic early experience for her involved the family home burning down, and her ESP often seemed especially responsive to any elements of fire in the target).

As another example, related to the levels of mind, MCS learned to distinguish between a "hunch" and a "guess." Her hunches tended strongly to be correct. She described always keeping in her mind the question as to whether some idea was right. Sometimes an answer came as if from some other, independent place: "Yes it is." This constituted a hunch. This is reminiscent of Bill Delmore, another psychic who was very successful in the laboratory. Delmore learned that when an unusually clear visual image occurred to him, it was usually correct. These visualizations for him also seemed to come from some independent source and served as his kind of "hunch."[3]

MCS's work showed great determination and persistence and a strong will to maintain a clear focus of intention during her explorations. And she always demanded of herself an ironclad objectivity to protect her from an illusion about connections that were really only coincidental. If you want to begin your own explorations of psi, you could do no better than to emulate if you can this single-minded resolve. Then follow her other advice (get your own copy of the book). I will end this section by quoting more from her at length, since her words are so clear and direct. This is only a sampling of her instruction (pp. 112–16).

> You have to inhibit the impulse to think things about the object, to examine it, or appraise it, or to allow memory-trains to attach themselves to it. The average person has never heard of such a form of concentration, and so has to learn how to do it. Simultaneously, he must learn to relax, for strangely enough, a part of concentration is complete relaxation. . . .
>
> All I can say is this: when I practice this art which I have learned, with my mind concentrated on one simple thing, it is a relaxation as restful, as seemingly "complete" as when I am in that state called normal sleep. The attention is not allowed to be on the sensations of the body, or on anything but the one thing it is deliberately "concentrated" on. Undivided concentration, then, means, for purposes of this experiment, a state of complete relaxation, under specified control. To concentrate in this undivided way you first give yourself a "suggestion" to the effect that you will relax your mind and your body, making the body insensitive and the mind a blank, and yet reserving the power to "break" the concentration in a short time. By making the body insensitive I mean simply to relax completely your mental hold of, or awareness of, all bodily sensation. After giving yourself this suggestion a few times, you proceed to relax both body and mind. Relax all mental interest in everything in the environment; inhibit all thoughts which try to wander into consciousness from the subconsciousness, or from wherever else thoughts come. This is clearly a more thorough affair than "just relaxing." Also, there is something else to it: the power of supervising the condition. You succeed presently in establishing a blank state presented to consciousness when you are ready to become conscious. For example, you want a message from the person who is sending you a message; you do not want a train of subconscious "day dreams. . . ."
>
> The next step, after having turned off the light and closed your eyes and relaxed mind and body full length on the couch, is to reach for the top drawing of the pile on the table [the targets that were prepared by someone else ahead of time]. Hold it in your hand over your solar plexus. Hold it easily, without clutching it. Now, completely relaxed, hold your mind a blank again. Hold it so for a few moments, then give the mental order to the unconscious mind to tell you what is on the paper you hold in your hand. Keep the eyes closed and the body relaxed, and give the order silently, and with as little mental exertion as possible. However, it is necessary to give it clearly and positively, that is, with concentration on it. Say to the unconscious mind, "I want the picture which is on this card, or paper, presented to my consciousness." Say this with your mind concentrated on what you are saying. Repeat, as if talking directly to another self: "I want to see what is on this card." Then relax into blankness again and hold blankness a few moments, then try gently, without straining, to see whatever forms may appear on the void into which you look with closed eyes. Do not try to conjure up something to see; just wait expectantly and let something come. My experience is that fragments of forms appear first. For example, a curved line, or a straight one, or two lines of a triangle. But sometimes the complete object appears; swiftly, lightly, dimly drawn, as on a moving pic-

ture film. These mental visions appear and disappear with lightning rapidity, never standing still unless quickly fixed by a deliberate effort of consciousness. They are never in heavy lines, but as if sketched delicately, in a slightly deeper shade of gray than that of the mental canvas.

JOE MCMONEAGLE

Joe McMoneagle is widely acknowledged to be the star remote viewer of the formerly secret Stargate Project, carried out by the U.S. Army Intelligence Agency and the Stanford Research Institute (SRI). He has carried out many hundreds of trials in well-controlled conditions and sustained significantly high—often startlingly high—performance throughout. Much of his other remote-viewing work has involved describing distant and unknown targets and cannot be precisely evaluated statistically. But it includes remarkable successes at such things as finding a downed American aircraft, describing a new Soviet submarine that was then unknown in the West, and identifying the location of a kidnapped air force general. Since his service days he has continued to accumulate remarkable stories of remote information, including many cases of finding missing persons on a live Japanese television show dedicated to his exploits.

Like Mary Craig Sinclair, McMoneagle grew up thinking of psi as real and believed that he had his share of extrasensory experiences. In his case, though, he considered it a survival skill in a rough and dangerous world. The first danger was from surgery as a baby (about which he had confusing and terrifying memories before discovering their origin), the second was from his own mother who was very controlling and often viciously punitive in her fearful wish to control Joe's rambunctiousness in their very poor and dangerous neighborhood. The third danger was that neighborhood itself, as he got old enough to adventure in it beyond his mother's control.[4] As a young man he entered the military and found himself working in an intelligence unit behind enemy lines in Vietnam. In that setting, he believes his "survival skill" served him well.

Another thing McMoneagle has in common with Mary Craig Sinclair is that, despite his apparent proclivity to use extrasensory information, he came to rely heavily upon a highly disciplined training program that spanned many years before he believed he had any really secure understanding of how ESP worked for him. His training was not self-developed but was imposed by researchers at SRI. He has gone on to insist that the *protocol* of remote viewing, which includes a research team in which no one involved with the viewer knows the target location, is essential for genuine development. There are at least two dangers that arise if persons around the viewer know the material. First, there will be inevitable if inadvertent cuing about the information, so the viewer and everyone else can become hopelessly self-deceived, believing that something is psychic when it is not. This can lead some persons to a dangerous loss of their sense of reality that can come from spending too much time wandering the inner world looking for what might seem like correspondences to outer things but really are not. Second, information that is known (especially if "hints" are explicitly known) will interfere with the process of viewing, which must be utterly free of any tendencies toward cognitive interpretation. McMoneagle calls this "front-loading," burdening the viewer with logical cues that will inevitably lead *away* from the actual remote information.

In several books, McMoneagle chronicles his experiences as a remote viewer and offers advice about how to develop this talent.[5] Anyone wanting to learn from his experience should study this material, especially his *Remote Viewing Secrets* (2000). Still, I can offer here some highlights of things he believes are important. Besides the adherence to a disciplined protocol, he lists the following steps for initial preparation:

- *Practice the skill of processing information in complex and stressful environments.* This implies that one hone the skill of attending to implicit, nonverbal processes while busy doing something else at the same time (like composing a piece of music while negotiating a busy freeway).
- *Be open to the possibility of psi.*
- *Become tough enough to tolerate public scrutiny, ridicule, and failure.* Remote viewing won't always work, so failure is inevitable. Many people loathe such things as remote viewing, and you will be subject to hostility if you are not discrete about it.
- *Develop artistic skills.*
- *As much as possible, make yourself good at providing imaginative (outside the box) answers to problems.* Remote viewing information is not logical, and you have to be able to surprise yourself.
- *Learn to relax and reduce physical stress responses when you want to.* Otherwise you will not be able to hear the subtle, inner implications of psi.
- *Learn to pay attention to inner feelings, images, and other subtle internal processes.*
- *Tolerate an altered view of the world.* You will have to tolerate a sense of how time and space work that is abnormal in terms of everyday experience.
- *Be willing to accept challenges and try new things.* There are no clear rules for remote viewing, and each person has to be willing to do his or her own adventure of discovery.
- *Go through a disciplined process of training, such as what he describes.* McMoneagle thinks of remote viewing as a kind of martial art. A lot of practice and training are required.

A great deal of this training has to do with a disciplined process of consulting fragmentary inner experience and writing it down as it is, with no interpretation at all for a long while. He expects this fragmentary material to be made up of feelings, pictures, and words (more pictures for most men, more words for most women). Like Sinclair, McMoneagle insists that the material be consulted in the raw, not construed, and laid down as bits of nonsense only to be compared later with the actual thing.

Try this, and you will find that it is hard to do. The mind reflexively interprets experience, even the barest fragments of light or shadow or mood. It will look like a snowman or feel like a certain song. Like the meditator practicing detachment, move away from these interpretations and then move away again and again. Stay with the fragments and do not interpret them. If you work at this, you will get a little better. Then see if you are hitting targets. Tolerate lots of failure and you may get better at that, too. If you seem to be successful, don't be too elated or full of yourself. This can be dangerous since you are about to fail again and you will make a fool of yourself. Keep at it with an attitude of humility. Do you still want to try this?

McMoneagle gives many helpful examples of this kind of fragmentary perception without too much thought:

> If you believe that you are actually seeing a target, you may assume that you can take your time in looking it over. Nothing could be further from the truth.
>
> In actuality, when remote viewers open to a target . . . they are doing something akin to a quick taste. As in using our sense of taste, it is a sensation that strikes home very quickly. . . . If, for instance, when you are blindfolded and someone puts a small bit of strawberry on your tongue, as soon as you rub it across your palate you know it's strawberry—not much processing going on there. But, if someone puts a small piece of something else on your tongue, which has been soaked in strawberry syrup, you are in trouble when it comes to identifying what it might be. Remote viewing is much the same way. . . . When a viewer tastes the target, it is only for a few nanoseconds and then contact is broken. The rest of the exercise is internalized processing, or determining when strawberry is important and when it is not. It is definitely not a full-scale model or pictogram laid out in total wonderment before our mind's eye.

McMoneagle says that such bits of information come in many forms: a vague sense of movement, a flash of a shape, the hint of an odor, a feeling that raises goose bumps. Then how can such things ever be understood to point to certain things? How does one get to be the way McMoneagle apparently is—often able to not only gather fragments that imply but also understand what they are about? Ah, the training! This cannot be simply taught, as by the words in this chapter, but must be personally developed through much disciplined trial and error. Part of the training consists in learning the habitual language of your own unconscious. Does your nose itch just before you smell smoke? Do you get a cool feeling before you realize that there is something to be afraid of? Learn your personal patterns. They will carry over to your remote viewing work.

And after all the training, McMoneagle also believes that people differ in terms of talent (wherever that comes from) and this will always be a limiting factor. Still another indispensable ingredient, he thinks, is to have a like-minded, disciplined group within which to work (and after work, often to play). This group of colleagues must share an intense, singular intention that the work will be well done and that it *will succeed.*[6]

DEVELOPING PK (A-ESP): BATCHELDOR AND OWEN

If PK is more to your taste than ESP, then you will get useful guidance from the experience of Kenneth Batcheldor and Iris Owen.

Batcheldor believed that the many vivid experiences reported from the séance rooms of the nineteenth century surely had some core of reality, even after the froth of deception and enthusiasm was cleaned away. However, by his day in the mid-twentieth century, they seemed to have largely disappeared. He carried out some experiments with friends who emulated earlier circles by sitting together in dim light and attempting to call upon "spirits" who might be expected to express themselves by making noises (raps in wooden tables, floors, and walls were common) or moving physical objects, such as a table around which all sat with their hands touching the top. Perhaps to his initial surprise, he got good results, very reminiscent of the old reports. Apparently anomalous noises and movements developed and often seemed intelligently responsive to the questions and interests of the group.

Batcheldor (1979, 1984) proposed three factors that might determine the success or failure of such efforts.

1. *The first is belief.* Belief that such PK (or spirit-driven) events can occur is essential for their occurrence. Belief *in the moment* is much more important than a more long-standing rational opinion. He noted that even characteristically skeptical people, if they are swept up in the adventure and drama of the moment, can seem to become effective agents for such events.
2. *The second is ownership resistance (or its absence).* Batcheldor thought that there is something innately frightening about PK at a nonrational, unconscious level. To feel that one might be the source of it is scary, no matter how much we might imagine otherwise. A good way to overcome this is to work in groups in which no one is sure who, if anyone, is the source of the effects.

3. *The third is witness inhibition.* When some participants in the situation hang back diffidently or skeptically, casting a wary eye on the proceedings, this inhibits the phenomena. This could be because the witnesses themselves are exerting a negative-PK effect so that they will not be disturbed by something that they sense would only make them uncomfortable. And it could be because such uninvolved observers act as inhibiting influences upon those who would more positively contribute, like the sober chaperones at a party of teenagers. The cure for this, he thought, is to induce a cheerful, active atmosphere in which all in the room must participate happily (or excuse themselves).

Batcheldor developed a group-sitter situation that he hoped would optimize a sense of enthusiastic belief and minimize ownership resistance and witness inhibition. Everyone played as cheerfully as children with the idea that spirits might be real and interested in participating in their activities; thusly, they heightened belief, at least in the moment. They maintained semidarkness or darkness in which no one could see who (for example) might be cheating and physically moving the table. Such cheating wasn't taken as a problem since Batcheldor thought it could "prime the pump" by enhancing a sense of belief. And the darkness and group nature of the meeting made it impossible to know which individual if any was responsible for any events, diminishing ownership resistance. And a happy, partylike atmosphere was created, with singing, dancing, and joke telling along with the spirit conversing, which itself was carried on in a very light-hearted way. Batcheldor reported a plethora of old-style séance PK events under these conditions, including many things that he believed could not have been carried out by normal means by any in the group.

The Batcheldor approach has been picked up by other groups with some apparent success. One group that found it especially helpful was one from Toronto that had been meeting for a year under the direction of Iris Owen.[7] We have already discussed their work in chapter 13. Like Batcheldor, they had wanted to recreate séance-room phenomena of earlier times, but their focus had been upon creating a shared vision of a spirit—a "phantasm." Owen believed that they were working with psi phenomena of group members though, and wanted to rule out any possible interpretation of their results as being due to the spirit of some deceased person. To show this the group consciously made up a fictional "ghost" named Philip to focus their efforts upon. They developed an elaborate and poignant biography for him and met in weekly meditation sessions hoping to produce a shared vision. The group developed nicely in the sense that members became very close and trusting with one another, but nothing paranormal developed.

When they learned of Batcheldor's approach they applied it, except for always meeting in full light. They set out to create sessions that were silly and fun, with singing and laughing and much joking talk to each other and to "Philip," urging him to express himself with table movements and noises. They never got their phantasm, but they did soon get lots of movements, blasts of air, changes of temperature, table levitation, and noises. The noises (usually clearly not made by anyone in the group) functioned as a means for "Philip" to answer questions and otherwise communicate "his" reactions to things. For example, he would often make an especially loud and unpleasant noise whenever his estranged and cruel wife was mentioned. "Philip" developed quite a lively personality. A psychologist commenting on their material speculated that important emotional issues in group members were being expressed and vicariously worked through by the phenomena. However that may be, the meetings continued on very productively for many months and, upon the time of their report, were still ongoing. The group had never been intended to have a therapeutic purpose, but it came to in fact. Deep personal changes were made by several in the group, which they attributed to their remarkable experiences there.

PSI EXPLORING

So if you wish to explore psi in a personal way, here are some examples of exploration that can give you hints on how to proceed. It is interesting to note that all of them, in different ways, stress some of the things that are stressed by First Sight theory. It is important to develop openness to psi, a working belief that it is real and valid. You should strongly want to succeed at expressing psi and develop ways to make that intention seep into the unconscious levels of your functioning. You should do things to diminish your anxiety and heighten your experience of playful creativeness. Be disciplined and objective and protect yourself from self-deception. Have a scientific attitude, seeking truth more than self-gratification.

There is one other important feature that Sinclair, McMoneagle, Batcheldor, and Owen had in common. They worked in groups. They did not try to do their exploring alone. The Sinclairs had a solid team of two. McMoneagle has always worked in a strong team of collaborators. Batcheldor and Owen worked with warm friends. And all these participants, while delighted with the adventure, were also committed to scientific objectivity and held each other to that. I made my own entry into personal exploration of psi in the context of a group, in the research project that I describe in chapter 22. I had been an experimenter upon other persons for a long time but had always refrained from exploring psi very much myself in a personal way. Now I can see that reluctance was largely due to fear. My success at it during one white-hot period blew my mind and changed my belief in psi from an intellectual idea to a changed sense of the world. Other personal explorers describe similar reactions. I needed the group I worked with—its support and energy, its objectivity and balance.

There can be a dark appeal to psi for people who are too isolated and alienated. If that is your condition, remedy it first and then try exploring psi. Otherwise there is a danger that you may deceive yourself and deepen your alienation in an unhealthy way. First Sight implies this, too. Psi is a subsidiary function in normal life, assisting us unconsciously in forming experience and behavior and carrying out actions. It is not a substitute for experience, action, and relationship. Explore psi if you wish, but first honor your life by living it fully.

NOTES

1. Kelly, 1955.
2. Sinclair, 1930.
3. Kanthamani and Kelly, 1974.
4. McMoneagle, 2002.
5. McMoneagle, 1997, 2000, 2002.
6. McMoneagle, personal communication.
7. Owen and Sparrow, 1976.

21

First Sight in the Consulting Room

But if the phenomenon of telepathy is only an activity of the unconscious mind, then no fresh problem lies before us. The laws of unconscious mental life may then be taken for granted as applying to telepathy.

—Sigmund Freud

A little over a week before the terrorist attacks on New York City and Washington, D.C., in 2001 I was speaking in a psychotherapy session with a middle-aged man who was in an agitated state of mind. The first day I met this man he said that he considered himself to be somewhat psychic and had sometimes been called The Prophet, since all his life he has given people prophecies that they are unhappy about. He was angry this particular day at various people and felt called to rise from his chair and lecture vigorously to me and the world in general about the foolish arrogance of America and our illusion of safety. Many people hate us, he said, much more than we imagine, and our smug isolation would soon be shattered. According to my notes, he said, "Our oceans won't protect us. Remember the World Trade Center bombing in '93? That was just a shot across the bow. Believe me, a shot across the bow. It was the tip of an iceberg. Things will come down in a fiery ruin!" I wondered at the meaning of this speech, which went on a few minutes longer in the same vein, and chalked it up mostly to his anger at some family members. It wasn't until his next session, when I reviewed my notes, that I was struck by the strange portent in his words. This white, middle-class American man had no ties to political organizations or international terrorism. He certainly had no knowledge of any impending attack on the United States. Nor did he think he was making a specific prediction. The reference to the World Trade Center simply leapt to his mind in the course of his invective. This striking coincidence is among a few I observed with this patient.

FIRST SIGHT AND PSCHOTHERAPY

According to First Sight theory, psi information is likely to be more heavily weighted if it is highly relevant to a person's unconscious goals and intentions. When it is heavily weighted it should be potentially observable because of physiological arousal that it evokes and because of a tendency to generate inadvertent expressions such as dreams, moods, accidents, etc., that either imply or disimply its meaning in a strong way. If moving toward the implied meaning is unconsciously desirable to the individual in terms of the needs and cognitive commitments of the moment, then the information will tend to be positively implied by the inadvertent experiences and behaviors that arise. Theory also reminds us that these implicative inadvertencies should be most likely to occur to people who are positively oriented to producing them—people who are open, creative, and, at the moment at least, not too fearful.

There are several reasons we might expect that intensive, experientially, and psychodynamically oriented psychotherapy could be fertile ground for producing psi-expressive experiences and behaviors.

Focus on Important Goals

Psychotherapy is a unique situation. We carry to it our most pressing concerns in hopes that they can be addressed usefully. The participants are highly motivated and seek only the most centrally important and pertinent information that can be found. As opposed to the countless situations that are more role-bound and socially defined, this one seeks only the most personally useful truths. Because of the personal importance of the material being dealt with, many themes and issues should tend to be heavily weighted at an unconscious level and receive attention that is directionally consistent.

Commitment to New Understanding

In intensive therapy the parties share a commitment to learn important new things about the patient's feelings, conflicts, life patterns, and other core aspects of the self. They maintain this commitment even though the process may be emotionally difficult or incidental to other ongoing roles and tasks. Because of this, there should generally be an unconscious inclination to use psi engagements in a positive, assimilative way. Such an inclination would be expressed as inadvertencies that positively imply pertinent extrasensory content.

Shared Involvement

If the psychotherapy is intensive and psychodynamically oriented, then the relationship with the therapist is accepted as an important part of the process of learning more about oneself and growing into greater freedom and less suffering. Both parties care and both are involved, even though it is the experiences and situations of the patient that get almost exclusive attention. The coparticipation of both parties (and more than two, in group and family therapy) provides a rich atmosphere for the development of shared meanings at both a conscious and unconscious level. There are periods in many treatments during which the patient's emotional attachment to the therapist becomes very strong and positive—what Freud called the positive transference. Freud used the term *transference* to emphasize that such a patient-therapist emotional connection carries over central, unresolved issues from the patient's emotional history and presents them in the present where they can be worked on afresh. When there is such strong positive transference, First Sight theory would predict that psi information about the therapist should become especially available to the patient (and perhaps vice versa, sometimes), since the therapist has become such a focus for important concerns.

Valuing and Being Alert to Implications of Unconscious Thought Processes

In almost all situations we naturally focus on the literal side of things: what people say and do, what problems there are to solve and how to solve them. A therapist who believes that "making the unconscious conscious" is important for a patient's growth will value the inadvertent experiences and behaviors that bespeak unconscious contents. He or she will also remain alert to the fringes of experience and often wonder about the possible implications of things rather than just stop with their literal meanings. As in the *New Yorker* cartoons, just "being late" or "having a mood" or "forgetting a word" may not simply be taken literally but are fair game for conjecture about unconscious implications. Since our theory says that it is in such inadvertencies that psi involvement is most likely to be glimpsed, this peculiar kind of valuing should make unconscious material more likely to be positively expressed than in many other situations. Alertness to them and their implications should make them easier to spot and understand.

Opportunity for Consistent Observation

Therapists are not only alert to things with unconscious implications; they are also in a privileged position to simply get to see a person's various self-expressions with unusual consistency and persistence. Perhaps sadly, most of our relationships in modern life, even the very important ones, often feature scattered moments of involvement punctuated by long periods of separateness and focus on other things. In therapy there is regular contact, usually weekly and sometimes more often, and an intense focus that is sustained over time on central concerns. Since we expect that psi engagements will most often be seen in the form of inadvertent behaviors and experiences that are not usually easy to decipher for the person involved, having a consistent observer provides an unusual opportunity to notice psi implications when they pop up.

Diminished Threat

As we have seen in chapter 12, a state of fear tends to constrict the range within which the mind will unconsciously assimilate psi information. While most of us strive to make our lives as free of anxiety as possible, it is an inevitable and continuous part of life. In therapy we try to create an unusually safe environment. If it were not safe enough, the work of therapy would become impossible. The fear we live with makes it much harder to see through our own unconscious processes, whether they involve psi or not. If it were not so hard to make some useful sense out of our nightmares or obsessions or addictions or gyrating moods, we would not need the help of therapy. In the safety of the therapy relationship the meanings hidden within these things can begin to be discernable. Some of these hidden meanings may involve psi.

For all of these reasons—the importance of the concerns, the commitment to understanding, the mutuality, the attention to implications, the consistent observation, and the relative freedom from fear—First Sight theory would predict that, at least for more open and creative patients, psi events might often be observed. We will review observations that have been reported by therapists of psi-implying events in psychotherapy and see to what extent they conform to these expectations.

PSYCHOTHERAPY AND PARAPSYCHOLOGY

For all of my adult life I have been both a psychotherapist and a parapsychologist. Before I began to conceive of the First Sight model these two departments of my life seemed to be largely separate from each other, except for two things. First, I noticed that the intimate setting of intensive psychotherapy did seem to provide a stage in which apparently psychic events could be seen at play sometimes. Second, I came to realize that both parapsychology and psychotherapy, at least as I pursued them, implied one similar core concern. This is the effort to approach an apparent absence of meaning and somehow wrest meaning out of it. The psychotherapist faces a person's fears or compulsions or anomalous patterns of self-destructive behavior—things that may often seem inscrutable to the patient—and attempts to find the implicit emotional meaning within them.[1] The parapsychologist sets some ESP target or random event generator firmly outside of a person's ken and then tries to see if he or she is meaningfully interacting with those things anyway. And third, over the years I encountered many instances in which these two kinds of meaning-discovery seemed to occur together in meaningful ways. The most important insight in a patient's treatment might arrive in the form of a dream that he or she has about me—a dream that contains some things about me that *the patient has no normal means of knowing*. Or an anomalous hunch of my own, coming apparently out of nowhere, might tip me off to some secret of the patient that hides the core of the misery. The apparent unconscious reference to the tragedies of 9/11, with which I began this chapter, illustrates this point. This woman's stream of thought seemed to contain both a vivid extrasensory allusion and (I came to learn) a reference to personal emotions and almost-forgotten traumas that were deeply important. In many instances like this, the extrasensory knowledge and the potentially healing knowledge arrived together in one package.

PSYCHOTHERAPY AND PARAPSYCHOLOGY ARE HISTORICALLY CONNECTED

Probably no major textbook in the field of psychotherapy today makes explicit reference to parapsychology. Even so, the enterprises of psychotherapy and psychical research are joined at their roots. The founders of both[2] were similarly intrigued by the phenomena of hysteria and dissociation. Patients in the clinic might demonstrate odd amnesias and numbnesses and behaviors that the patient had no sense of causing. The medium in the séance room might exhibit a strange "fainting" or "seizure" and scribble notes or voice utterances for which she disavowed any authorship, attributing these things instead to the intentions of invisible spirits.

Both groups of founders were also intrigued by hypnosis, which seemed capable of creating a kind of temporary dissociation and could be used in both settings—to treat the hysterical symptoms and guide the mediumistic experiences. And finally, both developed conceptions of a large and powerful unconscious mind that lay behind conscious experience and relied on similar methods of accessing that unconscious and studying its workings. As I pointed out in chapter 6, Freud presumed a principle of psychological determinism that acted out of an unconscious level of the mind. First Sight theory has borrowed these assumptions. These ideas have also been at least tacitly adopted by all post-Freudian approaches to psychotherapy that do not simply rely upon training the patient to think or act differently or upon applying pharmaceuticals. These ideas are also implied in Myers's thought.

F.W.H. Myers and Freud and the other founders of psychotherapy and psychical research knew and appreciated each others' work, even though they surely kept a certain distance and mutual skepticism as well. Both may have seemed somewhat scandalous to the other—psychical research for its openness to the idea of a surviving spirit, Freud for his emphasis on sexuality. While there were similarities between their ideas, there were also important differences. Freud's unconscious mind was a purely personal, skin-bound affair, in keeping with the presumptions of physical science, whereas the unconscious mind of Myers was supposed to transcend the boundaries of the individual to interact with other minds and even spirits of the dead.

THERAPISTS CONNECT THINGS

All psychotherapists who work within Freud's tradition of an unconscious mind and all its later variants work partly by drawing connections between things within a patient's experience to try to help illuminate how unconscious processes may contribute to current suffering. They try to "make the unconscious conscious."

Psychoanalysts, following Freud's lead, try to track the operations of the patient's unconscious mind in several ways in order to uncover its issues and conflicts. They wonder how the patient's symptoms may be unconscious expressions rather than just ways of suffering. They pay attention to dreams, to slips of the tongue and other inadvertent "mistakes," to the productions of free association, to the layers of meaning in jokes, to the developing emotional themes of the relationship with the analyst (the transference), to the physical responses of the patient that seem to be emotionally expressive. And they also attend to the similar preconscious behaviors of the analyst as they seem to pertain to the patient. It is through paying attention to such shadowy aspects of behavior, where conscious intention plays little part, that the analyst attempts to hear the whisperings of the unconscious at work behind the scenes. All of these areas appeared to be fertile ground for ESP information as well. As stated above, we expect such inadvertencies to express unconscious psi engagements.

A very simple example of how one works to make the unconscious conscious can be seen in many therapy sessions in which a patient will speak of one thing, change the subject and speak of a different thing, and then a third thing, all while noticing no important thread connecting them. It is easy for a therapist to seem like a genius just by noticing what implications this handful of things seems to have in common and how these relate to issues that have been talked over previously. For example, consider a patient who begins a session by complaining of worsening gastrointestinal symptoms that seem to be accompanied with a collapse of energy each afternoon. He says that his depression may be "acting up" and he might need a change of medication for this condition, which he tends to think of biomedically. Then after a silence he changes the subject and begins to discuss his wife's recent, rather serious illness and his concern about her. After talking about this a while, he changes the subject again and mentions that he had seen for the first time in many months a woman with whom he had an affair some years before—an affair that had been devastating to his wife and nearly led to their divorce but which both had tried to put into the past and firmly out of their minds. He only saw the woman for a moment from a distance, and it surprised him but didn't seem to arouse much feeling. Then after another few minutes he changes the subject still again and mentions a friend he has been thinking about who is estranged from her husband and had recently been unable to attend meetings of a board they are on. I ask if he thinks that seeing the woman from his past might have awakened more guilt than he had consciously felt, especially in the context of his wife's current illness—and that all this might have a certain resonance with the marital drama that his board friend was undergoing. Could this guilt be adding to his symptoms? He is silent for a moment, and then this very tough "man's man" begins to weep silently. The session nears its end, and he is consciously feeling the guilt that he had been keeping away from his awareness. At the same time his stomach feels more at peace, and his depressed lethargy has lightened.

Psychodynamically oriented therapists can relate such stories from the course of most days' work. Here the connections are simply among a series of topics in the course of an hour that feel unrelated to the patient but are easy for an outsider to see as probably connected. *Psychotherapists make connections.*

Connections may involve other things as well: between changes of topic with a scene from a dream, between a new symptom and something familiar but oddly forgotten, between an unusual mood and an unusual metaphor chosen to stand for something else. As Freud noticed, and First Sight theory endorses, much of our mental functioning is unconscious and expressed only implicitly by behaviors that feel inadvertent to the self but may be clearly meaningful to another person.

This story just related has nothing about it that we would think of as psychic. This man knows that he is depressed, has an aching stomach, and that his wife is ill. When he tries, he can remember that he had an affair, and he is perfectly aware that a friend is experiencing marital distress—he is only unaware of all of the emotional significance of these things as they resonate together for him at an unconscious level of functioning. The only connections being made are within the patient, between experiences of his own that he did not consciously understand were connected.

But what if the connections involved other people or distant events beyond the sensory ken? What if it had been his wife who had seen the other woman and had resolved to not mention the fact so that he did not know about it? Or what if someone important in my own life, about whom the patient knows nothing, happened to be experiencing great current marital distress of a sort that strongly resembles what he and his wife suffered earlier? We think of such things as mere coincidences. But might they also be meaningfully related to his sudden increase in symptoms? Some bold therapists have been struck by this possibility and explored it.

PSYCHOTHERAPY AS SCIENCE

A psychotherapy session is not a laboratory experiment, but it is does permit instructive observations that are systematic and penetrating—a kind of naturalistic science.[3] Since a single person is observed carefully over time, it permits a kind of loose test of scientific hypotheses and is a good setting for generating hypotheses that can be tested in a more controlled way in the laboratory. Eisenbud (1970) especially has pursued a strategy of naturalistic research in the context of his psychoanalytic sessions, and he believes that the emotionally intensive and intimate situation there is not only uniquely favorable for generating paranormal connections among the experiences of different persons but is also uniquely equipped for observing them, given the depth of knowledge which the analyst develops about the patient and the intimacy and frequency of his opportunity to observe.

PSI AND PSYCHOANALYSIS

Most of the observations suggesting the action of psi in psychotherapy have come from psychoanalysts. To set the context, consider how a psychoanalytic session is conducted. Typically, a patient attends several sessions a week during which he or she lies on a couch with the analyst out of sight behind. Then the patient does almost all of the talking, obeying the "first rule" of psychoanalysis—to try to say whatever comes to mind without censoring. Thought leads to thought, feeling leads to feeling, association to association. The analyst meanwhile is attending to the stream of associations, sometimes concentrating on trying to understand connections and sometimes in a posture of "free-floating attention," in which his or her own thoughts are allowed to drift in and contribute to the incipient understanding that is sought. While the patient tries to free associate, we might say that the analyst tries to "constructively associate." He or she looks for connections between the things being said, or between dreams and symptoms, or between feelings and issues that have been raised before.

The analyst has followed the "second basic rule" by having finished a personal analysis, so while the personal associations that come up will certainly express the analyst's own emotional issues, he or she can understand them as such and not be in danger of distorting the process by unconsciously turning it to meet personal unconscious needs. Sometimes the analyst will offer interpretations of the material or broader issues of the developing emotional relationship (the transference), but mostly he or she sits in silent attention. At times ideas flow freely and much becomes clearer, and at other times associations grind to a stubborn halt and the time becomes frustratingly empty. These periods of "resistance" are seen as especially important to the analyst. Interpreting them successfully and resolving them provides the greatest gains the treatment can offer since they hold within them the core of the unconscious conflicts that cause the suffering to begin with.

By normal social standards this is an odd situation in many ways. It is highly one-directional, with one person doing almost all the talking with little response from the other. It is remarkably, persistently attentive, and inasmuch as all material is welcomed, however strange or socially undesirable, it is deeply permissive. When one spends so much talking to another attentive but largely silent person, feelings and fantasies about that listener begin to develop. This is called the transference relationship, and in some way it will be a reenactment of the interpersonal dilemma that has come to dominate the patient's unconscious life. Feelings of love and/or anger toward the analyst develop and demonstrate the character of the inner issues. Meanwhile, some feelings also develop in the analyst toward the patient—the "countertransference." These express the analyst's own issues but also have a lot to say about the patient as well. A well-analyzed analyst works at telling which is which.

Consider the position of the analyst—listening away persistently for many hours to the dreams and associations and reports of symptoms and noting the nonverbal indications of feelings in the patient and attending also in a free-floating way to his or her own inner material. What if striking correspondences begin to pop up between the unspoken concerns of the analyst and the dreams of the patient, or between the material from the last patient's session and the meandering associations of this one, or between a dream of the analyst and some surprising news that the patient reports from his or her own experience? And what if all of these seem to indicate some kind of knowledge well beyond any that has been normally acquired? Are these correspondences meaningful? Do they simply mean that the analyst is overinterpreting coincidences and may need a vacation—or treatment for some incipient illness of his own?

These are not unimportant concerns for an analyst who knows a lot about delusional thinking and its morbid implications and has been taught by Freud to fear the infantile wish for omnipotence that is supposed to lie within the unconscious of all of us and would like nothing better than to believe that mere thought can control things.

What if this analyst hears so much of this that he or she forms a considered opinion that it is more than misunderstood coincidence and wishes to mention it to the patient or report it at a conference with other therapists? Might it encourage something morbidly infantile in the patient? Might it lead to derision and suspicion from colleagues at the conference? A few have tried talking to both patients and colleagues about such connections.

FREUD AND PSI

Freud himself (1933) reported a few astute observations suggesting the possibility of telepathy and speculated about the mechanisms involved in the expression of such material. Two of his stories involved "prophecies" told to his patients by an astrologer and a fortuneteller. Neither came strictly true, but both inadvertently referred to important unconscious issues of the patients that the seer could not have known about and that the patients themselves understood only dimly at the time. Because of this, Freud thought that perhaps the telepathic experience (of the soothsayers) was triggered by unconscious material that was on the verge of becoming conscious in the patient: issues of considerable emotional force that the patient was struggling with knowing or repressing.

In another story that Freud related, a patient's associations seemed to imply a telepathic response to something going on for Freud that the patient knew nothing about. The patient had gained little from analysis and had agreed to a stopping date. The end of World War I had come, and Freud was for the first time able once again to accept new patients from other countries, something he was pleased about. The first of these, a physician from England, wrote that he would arrive shortly. Just at that time the current patient began to produce a series of associations that, following the logic of psychoanalytic interpretation, seemed unmistakably to imply some kind of jealousy toward a rival for Freud's interest. This seemed to Freud exactly the kind of material that would be produced if such a patient had heard that a more interesting rival was coming on the scene and then had pushed that knowledge out of awareness. It so struck Freud that he wrote that if other analysts reported such observations, it would "put an end to any remaining doubts of the reality of thought transference." In spite of these penetrating observations, Freud generally expressed neutrality toward the subject. Perhaps he followed the advice of his disciple and biographer, Ernest Jones

(1926), who warned him not to become associated with something that was even more controversial than psychoanalysis.[4]

OTHER ACCOUNTS OF PSI IN PSYCHOANALYSIS

Several other psychoanalysts with an interest in parapsychology have watched their sessions with an eye to possible evidence of paranormally acquired information on the part of their patients or themselves. Perhaps because of their more wholehearted interest, they have had much more to report than did Freud.

István Hollós (1933) watched his analytic sessions for twenty years, noticing such correspondences and keeping extensive and careful notes for twelve years with over one hundred patients before reporting his observations and tentative conclusions. We will look more below at the patterns he and others have noted. His report aroused a firestorm of controversy and derision within the psychoanalytic community.[5]

Jan Eherenwald (1942, 1948, 1955, 1970) and Jule Eisenbud (1946, 1969, 1970) have also mapped this territory of psi-implying correspondences in psychoanalysis. Like Hollós, they kept track of striking allusions in the dreams of their patients to events in their own lives that the patient had no way of knowing about, and also noticed dreams of their own that appeared to anticipate events in the lives of their patients or to alert them to issues in their treatment that they had not consciously known to be present. At a preconscious level, the ESP material in the dreams seemed to be serving the interests of the treatment by imparting important information and maintaining the transference relationship, much as other dream material could be seen to be doing. How could one guard against overinterpreting a mere coincidence? All the therapists who have collected such material have been aware of this problem, and all have tried to develop criteria to guard against it. Ehrenwald, for example, described "psi tracer elements," or striking, highly particular aspects of correspondence, all of which he thought should be satisfied before a given dream or other production should be considered probably paranormal.

A number of other psychoanalysts have offered collections, large and small, of ostensible psi-implying material observed in the process of psychotherapy and offered many ideas about patterns worth exploring further. Perhaps the more important are Fodor (1942, 1949), Jung (1963, 1998), Meerloo (1949, 1964), Nelson (1964, 1965, 1975, 1988), Servadio (1935, 1955), and Ullman (1949, 1959, 1975). A helpful overview of much of this material through the early 1950s is given in Devereux (1953). Several nonanalytic therapists have added to the collections of observations, too: notably Mintz (1983), Orloff (1997), and Schwarz (1965, 1967).

These therapists offer many examples of connections observed in psychotherapy that imply the action of psi (what Eisenbud has called "psi-conditioned behaviors"). Most can be broken down into a few major categories. I will call each of them a kind of "almost knowing" rather than "knowing" since, true to First Sight, I am not claiming that anyone gains explicit knowledge via psi but only inadvertently expresses implicit references to it. In the context of psychodynamic psychotherapy this sort of language seems less strange than it otherwise might, since trying to understand the underlying meaning of implicit references of all kinds is a big part of the work of treatment.

WHEN THE PATIENT SEEMS TO ALMOST KNOW THINGS NOT NORMALLY AVAILABLE

The story with which I began this chapter, about a woman whose verbal outpouring seemed to imply a kind of prescience about the attacks of 9/11, is one example of an event that may occur in therapy that makes the therapist wonder about a possible psi meaning. I could tell several others involving that same fateful day that so gripped the emotions of Americans and many others around the world.

Another example came from a therapist friend of mine who told me of a dream that a patient of his suffered through the night of September 9, 2001. She was in a building working when suddenly the floor collapsed. She fell not just to the floor below, but further and further down until she awoke terrified. After awhile she went back to sleep, only to have the same dream and awaken sobbing with fear. Then a third time she went to sleep and wakened from the same nightmare. Finally, only a sleeping pill and her husband's comfort could ease her into a sleep that lasted the rest of the night. She had never had such a night before. A couple of days later she remembered the dream in the light of the collapse of the World Trade Center and asked her therapist if it could have any meaning.

WHEN THE PATIENT SEEMS TO ALMOST KNOW THINGS ABOUT THE THERAPIST

Another friend told me this story about an experience with a regressed schizophrenic patient with whom he had developed a fairly long therapeutic relationship in a hospital setting. There had been some real progress in their work in that they had come to have meaningful conversations, often touching upon deeply disturbing and long-buried experiences. Then one morning the man acted as if my friend simply didn't exist. He had abruptly regressed to much earlier behavior by becoming mute, staring off into space, and rubbing his feet against the floor repetitively. Eventually the therapist left, utterly frustrated. He came back later that afternoon to try again. This time the patient spoke a little. He said he knew that my friend was dead. Why did he believe this? Because in a dream the patient had seen him driving along mountain roads for a long time until he suddenly decided that he would die. Then the patient stopped speaking again. In fact it was the last time that they would speak because my friend the weekend before had driven through a mountainous area to another city where he had agreed to take another job. He had come to his patient that day with the uncomfortable mission of telling him that they would soon have to terminate therapy because he would be leaving.

Here is an example with several pieces from my own experience. It displays many of the features that others have noticed. A male patient who had been involved in intensive treatment for over two years e-mailed me the following dream prior to our session. "I'm at the White House. I park a car which then seems to be chained in, but I can get out anytime by opening the car door. Somebody, maybe me, is watching TV. The president and others retire for the night. Then I'm in my office. There's a guy from the White House outside the window and he seems to be intruding. I give him the finger. He breaks the window and seems to knock someone's head off. I get scared and run into a room in the White House. There's a friendly guy with a gun, maybe I'll be okay."

In another dream the same night he was ". . . in my house. Then I see a store window with mannequins wearing tuxedos. As if moved there by some huge earthquake. I can't get out. Then the house shakes again. Seems very serious." At this point in his treatment, this patient had a strong positive transference to me, which had opened him to great fears of rejection and abandonment. He had been emotionally abandoned by all the parental figures in his childhood and had felt pressed into a position of premature autonomy at a very young age. He had difficulty in forming satisfying relationships, partly because of the fear and anger that emotional closeness would invariably bring him. When these issues arose, he also always felt confinement and a wish to escape (being "chained in" and unable to "get out"). The dreams certainly seemed to be pertinent to these themes and were familiar material in that sense.

Unknown to this patient, however, during this time I had been wrestling with whether or not to take on the presidency of a board. I knew the job would involve considerable time and work, and I was concerned about how this would compromise my busy practice, particularly with patients like this one, who were working with considerable intensity. I was currently wrestling with that decision, and the same evening that he had his dreams I had attended a banquet of that organization. The event symbolized for me the first step toward a new role as president. I rarely wear a tuxedo, but one was required for that event, and the day before I had bought one. I remember thinking as I tried on several suits that I looked rather absurdly like a mannequin. The points of correspondence between the patient's dreams and my situation at the time are obvious, but what about the other elements: the intrusion, the danger, the anger, the earthquake? Psychodynamically, considerable understanding is gained if we allow the premise that the dreams unwittingly referred to me. My accepting commitments that would lessen my ability to attend closely to this patient's treatment would in fact be important concerns for him if he had consciously known of the danger. His reactions of fear and anger would certainly come up like clockwork. It would be a shift of the ground he stood on with me: an "earthquake." The friendly man with a gun might refer to the fact that I was concerned as well and was determined that my new obligations would not weaken my investment in my patients' treatments. Of course, all of this could be an interesting but meaningless coincidence. However, of hundreds of dreams I had collected from this individual, no other reference was ever made to a president or the White House or a tuxedo. More striking to me, it is also one among scores of dreams and associations from him that seemed to suggest paranormal information about me. They usually seemed to occur at times in which something I was involved in was drawing my interest away from our work, and he was still insecure about my attachment and commitment. The transference issue was loud and clear. The apparently paranormal element only seemed to underscore the importance of the issue and the vigilance he needed to maintain because of his concern.

Some months later, when I was still seeing this patient, I was preparing a presentation in which I was going to make reference to this story. He knew nothing about my doing this, but he provided an amusing postscript for it. To sum up what might be the salient aspects of the situation from his point of view: His therapist was writing a paper that he knew nothing about to take to a conference in Portugal, about which he was also ignorant. The paper partly involved material about him in which his ability to have good relationships was described as limited, all without his being told specifically of it (I had a general sort of permission to use such material in papers as long as he was not identified). The morning after I finished this paper and sent it off, the same patient e-mailed this dream to me: "You reappear in a dream: as a critic. You say to me that I have an 'andalusian attitude toward friendship,' maybe also something about this not being conscious. . . . As for transference, I feel something of an irritation toward you, maybe it is father stuff, nice of you in the dream to offer an exotic and unintelligible criticism!!!" (He later went on to make great strides in relationships.)

When I asked about his associations to the unintelligible criticism with the odd phrase "andalusian attitude," he came up with very little, then said that perhaps it was associated with flamenco and might imply that I thought his relationships were too casual. But why pick a region of the Iberian Peninsula that abuts Portugal as an indicator of "too casual"? It made no sense to him, but certainly it might suggest some implicit knowledge of my impending trip to Portugal where the offending paper would be delivered.

This patient's treatment continued for a couple more years, during which his concern about my interest in him diminished as he felt secure in that regard and went on to work on other issues. The psi-implying references to me in his dreams virtually disappeared during this period. That he was still capable of them was illustrated by a dream that occurred later during a time in which he was considering reinvolving himself in his religious heritage in order to find more spiritual meaning in life. In his dream I appear again, and I make some startling statement to him about the fact that I believe in God and pray regularly. In fact, I am careful to never bring my own religious opinions into therapy because I believe that such matters are highly personal and patients must be free of any possible influence from me in this regard. However, that being said, the afternoon before his dream I had made a very unusual, perhaps unique, admission to a different patient that in fact I did pray regularly. (This was in response to a direct and heartfelt question based on things the woman had heard about me from someone else who knew me personally.) Thus, when his need to know something about me arose again, a psi-inspired dream responded to aid his quest.

WHEN THE PATIENT SEEMS TO ALMOST KNOW SOMETHING PERTINENT ABOUT THE THERAPIST THAT THE THERAPIST WISHES TO BE SECRET

A pattern that has been mentioned by several writers is that the patient may be especially likely to convey apparently paranormal information about the therapist regarding matters about which the latter feels somewhat secretive, troubled, or guilty. This may be especially likely if the therapist's emotional issues dovetail somehow with those of the patient. It is telling that so many mention this pattern but few give any examples of it!

One example that I can give involved an artistic client of mine who considered herself somewhat psychic and was neither troubled nor overly excited about it. She did try to use her intuitive ability, however, and one way was to attempt to anticipate what my state would be when she arrived for her therapy session. She had a long drive, and at a certain point in the trip, would often consult her imagery for some tip. One particular day she arrived, saying, "I know you have done something really bad or stupid, and you won't be worth much today." In fact, I had arrived at the office that morning to find a very angry note taped to my door. Because of a scheduling error I had failed to meet an earlier patient at her appointed time. This very unstable person was furious, and her note implied that suicide would be a good revenge. I had spent the half hour before this next client frantically trying to locate the one I had stood up. I finally managed to talk with her, and just as my next session was to begin, I got some reassurance about her safety until we could talk again in a few hours. I was still rattled, though, when this next client appeared and announced her prediction. In her imagery she had seen my face looking forward calmly, then turning upward, where over my head a huge egg was splitting open and spilled its contents onto me. I had "egg on my face" in a big way, and she read her imagery to mean that I had somehow embarrassed myself and would be preoccupied.

Montague Ullman recounts another incident involving potentially embarrassing material.[6] He was in the process of building a house, the cost of which was alarming him. A chromium soap dish had been accidentally shipped to him, and Ullman, who described his mood as "belligerent dishonesty," neglected to return the rather expensive item. A workman had noticed the dish and teased him about it, to which Ullman responded with a "sheepish smirk." One day the incident, with its charge of embarrassment, came to mind in the course of conversation with a neighbor. On the same day, a patient brought in this dream: ". . . someone gave me, or I took, a chromium soap dish. I held it in my hand and I offered it to him. He took it. . . . Then I sort of smirked and said knowingly, 'well you're building a house.' He blushed, he smirked. . . ."

Both Ullman's client and my client in these anecdotes shared some characteristics. Both were becoming intensely involved in the treatment, and both were distrustful, isolated people. Both had strong reasons in their personal histories to distrust situations that called for dependency and closeness, but both longed to be able to use the treatment toward the end of becoming able to have deep relationships. If there was any unreliability, or even temporary inaccessibility, about their therapist they were strongly motivated to know about it, and seemed to "home in" at an extrasensory level to seek the knowledge. This is congruent with the assertion of First Sight theory that highly important psi information is especially likely to be assimilated.

WHEN THE THERAPIST ALMOST KNOWS
SOMETHING PERTINENT ABOUT THE PATIENT

My personal need for psychic vigilance may have been expressed by this next dream of my own. It involved a patient I was to see for a session the next day. I quote from the notes I made in my journal early the next morning before any sessions began: "S. T. (the patient's college-age daughter) climbs up and sits in my lap. W. T. (her mother, my patient) is in the room. She entwines her legs around mine arrogantly and suggestively. I'm confused, don't know why she is doing this, and make her get down. She is very hostile toward her mother, and insolent toward me. Struck with her long legs, and with her arrogance toward her mother and me." I was left not with a sense of an erotic theme (although, of course, dreams can burgeon with them), but with an unpleasant feeling about an insolent attack on generational boundaries. I reflected a bit on what might be the countertransference implications of the dream, and I couldn't come up with much. I had seen this girl at a distance only once some years before, and I could find little emotional reaction in myself to her as a person. I was mystified about her dream appearance. I knew that my patient (the mother) was troubled at the time by her relationships with all her children, who were caught up in different ways in a raging battle that was going on between their parents over an impending divorce.

Mid-morning, my patient phoned me saying that her daughter (S. T.) was in town and was upset, and she wanted to bring her to the afternoon's session. I agreed. When they appeared, the quiet, rather gawky young teenager I had seen before had been replaced by an attractive, dramatically dressed (and long-legged) young woman. Almost before we sat down, the daughter launched into what had clearly been her agenda for the meeting: a furious denunciation of her mother. She wasn't happy about her mother's psychotherapy either, which she partially blamed for the parents' divorce. I had come to know the spouses fairly well, and I knew that there was a lot of distortion in what the daughter was saying, but she was clearly echoing her father's views. I was surprised by her feelings, since she and her mother had always been very close before. Apparently she had come to ally with her previously distant and busy father, who I learned was leaning heavily on his children in his own distress and desire to influence the situation. As my dream had suggested, it seemed clear that there was an oedipal crossing of generational lines being carried out in a very angry spirit by a daughter who had always admired her father but was never able to capture his attention for long. The quality of her position in the session was rather shocking and assaultive, and I was struck at the time that I was perhaps a bit more prepared for this event by my dream and my reflections on it.

Sometimes the therapist's apparent ESP may be expressed not in a dream but in a spontaneous utterance, almost like a slip of the tongue. The renowned analyst Theodore Reik was well known for emphasizing the importance of intuitive listening on the part of the therapist. A story of his concerns a female patient who had never recovered from the unhappy ending of a long-past love affair. Their treatment was moving slowly, and his attempts to analyze the resistance had not yielded much movement. In this particular session, after a long silence the patient mentioned a visit to her dentist for a tooth extraction. Another long silence. She then looked at Reik's bookcase and remarked, "There's a book standing on its head." Reik says that then, "Without the slightest hesitation and in a reproachful voice I said, 'But why did you never tell me that you had an abortion?' I had said it without an inkling of what I would say, but something in my head had said it." The surprised patient revealed that she had had an abortion (considered a terrible crime at that time) and that her physician lover had performed it. She had vowed unending silence to protect him, and this had been blocking her treatment. How did Reik make this striking guess? Of course, there may have been some chain of unconscious inferences. After all, he did know the patient well. But he said the remark surprised him too: "I did not think of any psychoanalytic theory. I just said what had spoken in me and against all logic, and I was correct."[7]

Experiences that appear to involve psi may appear in group therapy as well. Elizabeth Mintz (1983), a creative psychotherapist who pioneered methods of working in groups using very long, "marathon" sessions, recounts the following story. In these sessions, the therapist or other members frequently role-played important figures from a patient's past in order to work through important, unfinished emotional business.

A man Mintz called Jack had managed occasional sexual affairs in his life, but never a lasting relationship. He had been placed in a succession of foster homes since age seven and could remember little of his life before then. His childhood experiences had been so negative and depriving that Mintz was impressed that he was able to function in society at all. He was participating in a three-day marathon therapy group, and Mintz asked him to speak of his early experiences. He courteously said he could still remember almost nothing. Mintz then noticed that her own speech was showing an odd impediment of a sort she had only noticed once before when she had been exhausted with a bad cold. "My voice caught in my throat and became at once shrill and guttural, almost like a grunt." A member remarked that she sounded funny, and her cotherapist asked her in a whisper whether she was all right. She felt okay, but the odd speech continued, and then she realized that she wished to say, "I'm going to send you off. I don't want you. I'll kill you!" Jack had no conscious memory of his mother, so Mintz knew nothing about her and did not offer to role-play her. However, Jack asked her to, and she reluctantly agreed. To Mintz's astonishment, Jack then asked, "Mom, did you ever want to kill me?" Mintz became totally unable to speak. Only odd noises like pig grunts came out, but at the same time she thought, "His mother put him in a foster home because she was afraid she'd kill him." Jack then glared and said, "Mom, you are a pig. You make me sick. I'm going to vomit you out." Jack then left the group, went to the bathroom, and came back looking relieved. In processing this later, Jack remembered more about his mother, who would beat him while she was so angry that she couldn't talk but instead grunted like a pig. In this case as in many others, the odd, anomalously acquired information was conveying material of the deepest possible importance at that therapeutic moment.

WHAT KINDS OF MATERIAL ARE ESPECIALLY LIKELY TO BE ALMOST KNOWN?

I can sum up many observations by many therapists with this generalization, which was essentially anticipated by Freud: *Material is especially likely to intrude into therapy in a psi-conditioned way when it is connected with something important for one or both of the parties and for some reason is difficult to reveal or to face at all.*

There may be something that the patient needs more awareness about, but defensiveness has prevented it. Such material may seem to be a direct message from the unconscious, with the unconscious wish that the therapist will understand it and use it helpfully. In this sense, an extrasensory dream or association or spontaneous utterance functions exactly as does any other expression of the unconscious, only perhaps with special insistence. The psychic element, if taken seriously, may serve to alert the therapist that something really serious is being expressed.

The experience may imply countertransference issues about which the therapist needs to be more aware. At such times apparently extrasensory information of the patient about the therapist (or vice versa) seems to serve as a helpful alert.

When the material involves important emotional issues that dovetail for both parties at the same time, it may be especially likely to arise.[8] This might be expected to be especially true in situations in which the congruence involves therapist issues about which the patient has no sensory knowledge (for minor examples, remember Ullman's soap dish, and the big egg on my face).

WHAT KINDS OF PEOPLE ARE ESPECIALLY LIKELY TO BRING IN SUCH MATERIAL?

Several patterns have been noted, and I can say that all of them ring true with my experience.

- *The patient is in a strongly positive transference relationship with the therapist.* Such persons are especially likely to bring in experiences that seem to pertain to the therapist. Ehrenwald (1948) thought that this is because such a transference is a regressive duplication of the early condition of symbiotic closeness of mother and child, in which possibly telepathic connections often may be observed.[9] First Sight theory would say more simply that assimilation of psi material is more likely when the information involved is highly personally important. If the therapist is very important, then information about the therapist is important.

- *The patient is artistic or otherwise creative.* Such people are especially likely to show psi-implying events. This is congruent with the experimental results discussed in chapter 13.
- People who are quite dissociative may be likely to show them, at least when in certain "parts."[10] We should note here that highly dissociative people, perhaps because of their lack of integrated insight into their own behavior, may also be prone to construe events as expressing psi when there seems to be little objective reason for doing so.[11]
- People whose lives have been severely disrupted by a great loss or a severe injury or trauma, for whom "everything has fallen apart," are especially given to such experiences.
- People who are quite withdrawn may bring in such experiences, and they usually have to do with possible losses in the therapeutic relationship.
- We should also mention a negative category here. Sometimes patients who are psychotic and claim to be psychic may show flashes of possible extrasensory material, but much more often their ideas seem to be merely delusional.[12]

WHAT SORTS OF THERAPISTS EVOKE THESE EXPERIENCES?

Jule Eisenbud has remarked that early in his study of psi in psychotherapy, he blithely assumed that once their attention had been drawn to it, other psychoanalysts would also notice instances of probable psi in their sessions and become interested in learning more about it. He was disabused of this notion. As he said: "I now believe differently. I have come to believe that few psychiatrists or analysts possess what I call . . . psychically sensitive dispositions and do not, consequently, create—and thus have the occasion to observe—psi-conditioned experiences in their interactions with patients."[13] Instead of interest and shared observations, he tended to experience many years of suspicion that was only partly tempered by the high regard his colleagues almost always had for him personally and clinically.

My own experience coincides with Eisenbud's. When I have mentioned my many fascinating observations of apparent psi-implying material in psychotherapy, some colleagues have responded enthusiastically with stories of their own, but more have drawn a blank—and perhaps avoided me somewhat thereafter.

Assuming Eisenbud is right, and only some kinds of therapists are likely to evoke and observe such phenomena, what distinguishes them from others? We don't know very much about this. Judging from the persons whose accounts I have read or heard firsthand, I can only offer three possible generalizations. One is that all of them seemed to be themselves very interested in psi. The other is that they were all unusually open and creative, and frequently artistic, people themselves. The third is that they tend to be unusually undefensive themselves, or at least they are very committed to face their own emotional issues when they might arise in the context of treatment and interfere with its progress. Of course, all of these characteristics would accord with the predictions of First Sight theory.

SHOULD THERAPISTS MENTION PSI TO THEIR PATIENTS?

The welfare of the patient is the predominate concern in the therapeutic situation. The therapist must not harm and must try to help above all else. If a therapist is certain that ESP does not exist, he or she may still sometimes trust more intuitive processes if they seem useful, believing that implicit knowledge comes from "somewhere normal." But while this therapist may be kind and tolerant about a patient's belief in paranormal knowledge, it will never occur to him or her to bring up the possibility of ESP in discussion with a patient. If a therapist does believe that ESP occurs and understands that it may be expressed in the psychotherapeutic process itself, the situation is not so simple. Is it dangerous to mention psi to patients? Would it be irresponsible?

Actually, I have come to believe that there are very few black-and-white rules that tell us what positions and behaviors will be beneficial or harmful to all patients. What is helpful or not is a matter entirely to do with the meaning of the behaviors at the moment to the patient, in light of his or her understanding and unconscious issues.

John Weiss (1993) and his colleagues at Mt. Zion Hospital in San Francisco have developed a neopsychoanalytic position called Control/Mastery Theory that is very useful in helping therapists to form useful understandings of their patients' unconscious issues and to construct their own responses accordingly. To put it very briefly, we all form in the course of early childhood experience numerous basic beliefs about the world, other people, and ourselves. Because these are preverbal, they remain largely unconscious, but they guide us very deeply as we develop our lives (this idea is certainly consistent with First Sight). The child who has especially difficult experiences to cope with early is likely to form *pathogenic beliefs* that certain important wishes or needs or behaviors of her own must not be pursued, else some kind of harm or shame will come to herself or important others. A child who is beaten brutally may conclude that it was his own dependent behavior that led to the abuse and tend to be unable thereafter to depend upon others. A girl whose depressed mother cries frequently and withdraws may decide that she must stay close to her mother to watch out for her and later have difficulty in being independent. If we have important pathogenic beliefs, we wish to disprove them and move beyond them to greater happiness and fulfillment, and we may enlist a therapist to help us do this.

This theory assumes that whenever a patient enters psychotherapy it is with the unconscious wish that a relationship might be found in which pathogenic beliefs can be invalidated and moved beyond. The patient begins by structuring this relationship with some sort of test by which he may unconsciously know whether or not this is likely to be a helpful relationship. The therapist's reaction will constitute a response to the test, and it will either pass to some degree or fail. If it passes well, the patient will experience a decrease in anxiety, move forward in the relationship, and unconsciously begin to plan the next test. If the response partly passes, the patient will withdraw a bit and pose the test in some other form. If the therapist fails decisively, the patient will become more anxious and more defended, show more disturbed behavior, and perhaps end the relationship. *Whether or not a response is adequate to pass a test can never be securely determined a priori but only assessed in light of the patient's response to it.*

Suppose a new patient begins an initial therapeutic contact by asserting that he possesses psychic abilities. A test is occurring, but what exactly does it mean? We can only make the crudest guesses at first. Perhaps he is feeling panicked, desperately out of control and confused, but he carries the unconscious pathogenic belief that he must never presume that any powerful person will take an active, decisive interest in him and actually try to relieve his distress. This person might be vastly relieved if the therapist gently but firmly asserts that psychic powers really do not plague people the way the patient is assuming, but that sometimes a disease process overcomes even the best of people, and it must be helped with the best available medication and careful, personal attention. To this man, a prescription for Abilify or Zyprexa may feel like a heaven-sent blessing in his pocket, and coupling the medicine with a quiet hospital with attentive nurses might be even better. A close, but not identical, belief might be that the patient must never presume that he is too intelligent or that anyone might find him worthy of guidance and instruction. In this case a good response might be to begin a process of tactfully deconstructing the patient's false beliefs, with lots of ideas about how beliefs are formed, in the manner of Garety, Fowler, and Kuipers (2000) or Hagen et al. (2010).

Consider a woman who begins her therapy with the same assertion but is acting from a different existential position. She may be a chronically lonely person who lives a very diminished life, with an unconscious pathogenic belief that she must never assert anything special about herself or it will shame and diminish others whom she loves. This woman may move back a step or two emotionally if the therapist reaches too quickly for the prescription pad, or begins, however gently, to question the validity of her ideas. She may decide unconsciously that she has once again threatened someone on whom she might wish to depend and should either diminish her self-presentation or end the relationship. A better way to pass her test might be to respond: "I know that those experiences do occur to people sometimes, and I'm interested in that. Tell me more about it." Continuing to respond with unthreatened interest throughout a session in which the patient elaborates her experiences may then get the treatment off to a secure start. The therapist must remember, though, that successfully passing a test is always rewarded by another test.

Suppose the woman begins the next session by making a more extravagant assertion that the therapist is very dubious about: perhaps she wonders if she sometimes levitates in her sleep. The correct response can still not be determined with certainty a priori. Suppose the unconscious issue is still the doubt about specialness being acceptable. In this case, continuing a posture of tolerant interest would keep the treatment moving along. On the other hand, suppose a different pathogenic belief is being tested: that if people pretend interest in her, it is probably only a disguised wish to get something from her for their own needs. In this case the more extravagant claim is implicitly asking if the therapist merely has a voyeuristic interest in exotic phenomena, and any apparent concern for her more prosaic problems was only a deception. If this is so, interest that seems too eager would tend to fail the test. Simply saying, "Tell me more about it," or reflecting the patient's feelings might pass the test well enough. It might be even better, though, to say something like: "You know, I certainly wouldn't say that things like that couldn't happen, but I wonder if that's really the main thing that is bothering you now."

This contextual approach is not a reassuring one for the therapist who longs for ironclad rules to guide therapeutic behavior that can be reliably trotted out for all patients, or perhaps for all members of certain diagnostic categories. However, I believe it is a marvelously accurate and helpful description of how therapeutic relationships actually work. There is much more to the theory than I can summarize here.

Besides being clinically useful, the theory also has a nicely developing research base.[14] According to this point of view, the therapist must also maintain a scientifically empirical attitude within each therapeutic venture. Since there are no rigid rules and presumptions that can be assumed, each response of the therapist, and the hypothesis behind it, can only be evaluated in the cold light of the data—the response of the patient.

I can think of many examples in my own experience when it has seemed best to me to either explicitly bring up the psi hypothesis in a treatment situation, or, more often, to decline to do so, and I acted accordingly. Generally it has seemed to work out well enough, although I can also remember a few mistakes I made. My name has often been given to persons calling the Rhine Research Center in search of help for distress that they think of in terms of psychic ability, so I may have had to deal with the issue more frequently than most therapists. In my experience, an open-minded tolerance for the experiences that people describe has never seemed to hurt the treatment, and *in no single instance did those experiences remain the focus of attention for long.* In Weiss's terms, the issue was mostly an initial test for our relationship, and deeper, more personal matters quickly came to the fore.

If apparently paranormal information comes to light in the course of treatment, should the therapist consider that it might be genuine and reflect privately on its meaning? I don't see why not, and empirical results such as the ones discussed throughout this book make this seem more reasonable. Of course, the possible information should be treated as only hypothetical. The research literature in parapsychology has taught me, and First Sight emphasizes especially, that psychic information, even when genuine, is almost always quite partial and metaphorical in nature. It is not a good basis for making important decisions if more certain knowledge is available instead. There may be times, however, when the therapist is being alerted to something important that he or she couldn't know about otherwise, and to ignore it would be unwise or possibly even disastrous. Judith Orloff (1997) is a psychiatrist who tells of one situation in which she ignored a strong hunch about danger to a patient because of the defensiveness she had built up in medical school about her own history of psychic experiences. The patient attempted suicide and almost died. On one occasion I acted on a similarly irrational hunch about a patient of my own whom I barely knew, and I averted a suicide that was certain to have happened and that certainly would have been fatal. Such behavior was very unusual for me, and I would be very hesitant to do it again, but I am glad that I acted on the hunch in that case.

FIRST SIGHT AND PSYCHOTHERAPY

First Sight theory is hardly a theory for all of psychotherapy, but combined with whatever points of view a therapist finds most useful it can provide a framework for thinking of apparent instances of psi-conditioned behavior when they occur in psychotherapy. Sometimes clinically useful material may be obtained that would otherwise have never been credited or used. And for those therapists who are interested in the psi question and are otherwise psi conducive as therapists, it can provide a framework within which to collect observations that can be tested more formally in the laboratory.

NOTES

1. Contemporary psychiatry is tending to forget this dimension of meaning and often attempts to reduce such inscrutable suffering to hypothetical biochemical disease processes. This approach can be practically useful in that it has led to pharmaceuticals that reduce suffering, but the psychological approach is also useful. In fact, most studies that have compared them have found them about equally useful in the short run, with psychological treatment being superior in terms of gains lasting after treatment ceases (e.g., Antonuccio, 1996; Wexler and Cicchetti, 1992). More to the point, though, is the fact that unconscious meaning is implicit in this sort of suffering, even though it also has a biological substrate (as does all experience). Recognizing the implicit meanings can be healing as well as correct (Shedler, 2010).

2. Freud, 1965, and Myers, 1961 [1903].

3. Rausch, 1969.

4. Jones was very vexed with Freud's fascination with paranormal phenomena, which he thought was dangerous and embarrassing. At one point he characterized Freud's attitude as an "exquisite oscillation between skepticism and credulity" (Jones, 1957).

5. Schilder, 1955.

6. Ullman and Krippner, 1974.

7. Reik, 1964, p. 260.

8. Hann-Kende, in Devereux, 1953.

9. Schwarz, 1971.

10. Van de Castle, 1989.

11. Alberti, 1974.

12. Greyson, 1977; Zorab, 1957.

13. Pilkington, 2010, p. 13.

14. Gassner, Sampson, Weiss, and Brumer, 1982; Silberschatz, Fretter, and Curtis, 1986; Edelstein, 1992.

Section VI

PROSPECTS FOR
PARAPSYCHOLOGY

[T]his systematic denial on science's part of personality as a condition of events, this rigorous belief that in its own essential and innermost nature our world is a strictly impersonal world, may, conceivably, as the whirligig of time goes round, prove to be the very defect that our descendants will be most surprised at in our own boasted science, the omission that to their eyes will most tend to make it look perspectiveless and short.

—William James

22

Recent Research
Pertinent to First Sight

*Our life is composed greatly from dreams, from the unconscious, and they must
be brought into connection with action. They must be woven together.*

—Anais Nin

As the Nin quote says, much of us is made of unconscious stuff, and its
dreams and other contents are woven together into action. Research should
shed light on the warp and woof of this weaving. A First Sight perspective
calls us to study the unconscious mind, its intentions and personal processes
(PUPPs), with an eye to understanding how psi participates in the ongoing
construction of our experiences and actions. As it happens, such research is
already well underway in several quarters. It has not waited for First Sight or
any overarching theoretical perspective to lead the way, although much ingenious theorizing is being done within smaller domains. More inclusive theory
can help us consolidate what is being done and consciously guide it further.

In this chapter I will cite some examples of recent research that is congruent with First Sight. They are illustrative, not exhaustive. First, we will look
at the study of normal sensory processes, as done by some cognitive, social,
and clinical psychologists; and then at parapsychology.

STUDIES ON UNCONSCIOUS PSYCHOLOGICAL
PROCESSES NOT INVOLVING PSI

Unconscious Goals Guide Our Behavior

Henk Aarts, Kirsten Ruys, and their colleagues at Utrecht University are
carrying out fascinating research on the nonconscious activation of goals,

369

and the impact of this upon a wide range of behaviors and perceptions, from social evaluations to consumer choices.[1] In tune with First Sight, they find that unconsciously active goals are generally more powerful than conscious ones in guiding what we actually do, and these scientists are productive and inventive in helping us understand how such goals operate. This approach has been picked up and developed by many others.

Negative (Inhibitory) Priming Can Affect Various Preconscious Processes

Stephen Tipper of Bangor University in the United Kingdom is one among several psychologists whose work has shed new light on the function of negative subliminal priming: cases in which exposure to a stimulus is followed by a diminished tendency to express that stimulus in a response. From a First Sight perspective, negative priming is closely related to psi-missing as observed by parapsychologists. One example of Tipper's work (2001) suggests that a kind of inhibition of response is responsible for many effects observed. Others contributing to this study of negative priming include Juan Ortells and his colleagues at the University of Almeria in Spain and Christopher Ball at the College of William and Mary in Virginia. Ortells (Ortells and Tudela, 1996) has shown, for example, that recovery of semantic memories, like the formation of visual percepts, can be influenced negatively by merely asking participants to ignore a subliminal prime, and Ball (Ball and Hennessey, 2009) has extended this effect to autobiographical memories.

Unconscious Ideas about the Self Organize Personality

Robert Bornstein is a research clinical psychologist at Adelphi University who studies, among other things, latently held schemas involving the self and shows how they interact with subliminal primes to influence a wide range of personal outcomes, from single decisions to longstanding personality patterns.[2] For example, persons with a dependent self-schema tend to respond to subliminal primes that have dependency-relevant connotations by becoming particularly alert at an unconscious level of functioning to other issues of power, helplessness, and dependency. He has also shown how psychoanalytic ideas have a continuing relevance for research on unconscious processes.[3]

Unconscious Thought Does Some Things Very Well

Ap Dijksterhuis is another Dutch cognitive/social psychologist who has made important contributions to theory and research on unconscious psychological processes. In his theory of unconscious thought (2004), he moves more boldly than most toward thinking in personal, nonmechanistic constructs. He and his students and colleagues have found, among other things, that unconscious thought is often actually better than conscious thought at solving complex problems and that we tend to become conscious of our goals only when they become difficult to achieve.

Deeply Unconscious Information and Marginally Unconscious Information Work Differently

Howard Shevrin and colleagues at the University of Michigan have studied preconscious perceptual processes and related them to unconscious physiological responses (for example, event-related potential responses). They have found, among other things, that an individual's "repressiveness" (tendency to not experience things associated with emotional conflict and trauma) affects their conscious processing much more than it does unconscious cognitive processing.[4] Along with his colleague Michael Snodgrass, he has also distinguished between the processing of information that is deeply subliminal (presentation so brief and/or faint that even knowing that an event of any sort has occurred is rendered impossible) and information that is meager enough that its content cannot be distinguished but the event of a flicker of light could be noted. Processing shows distinctly different patterns at these two levels of "subliminality."[5] One thing that appears when a prime is so brief that its occurrence cannot be detected is quite reminiscent of the findings of parapsychologists: effects become bidirectional, in some cases facilitating a response and in other cases suppressing it, and while meaningful patterns determine which occurs, they are outside of the conscious control of the participant.

While all the groups just mentioned are important, they are only illustrative. There are a large number of researchers currently studying many aspects of the unconscious level of perception, emotion, and action. This work is currently accelerating. It seems that most issues of any major journal in cognitive psychology, social psychology, personality and clinical psychology, and neuropsychology will be found today to contain something to do with subliminal priming or unconscious thought or implicit processes. One line of work that is especially interesting to me is one that is showing how much of our interpersonal life is guided by our implicit prehensions of one another.[6]

RECENT STUDIES ON UNCONSCIOUS PSYCHOLOGICAL PROCESSES INVOLVING PSI

A new generation of research has been developing in parapsychology in the last ten years or so that is implicitly congruent with the basic assumption of First Sight theory—that psi engagement with extended reality is going on all the time and contributing constantly to experiences and decisions and even extrapersonal events. This research does not try to test an individual's psi "ability" by a challenge to demonstrate; it tries to reveal the ongoing activity of psi by isolating variables in such a way that it can become visible.

Psi Information Implicitly Guides Social Behavior

For me, First Sight research began in earnest with a study I conceived to determine whether or not psi functioned like subliminal perception in its contribution to our moods and associations and patterns of social inter-action.[7] The approach was somewhat like the ganzfeld studies discussed earlier, in that a picture was to be randomly selected for each of a number of sessions, and participants would try to discern the target picture out of a field of decoys. Unlike the ganzfeld, however, testing was not to be car-ried by an isolated individual, but rather by an active group of people that would engage in an unstructured session for an hour or ninety minutes and carry "in the backs of their minds" the implicit hope that the contents of the target picture would somehow become expressed by the events that developed in the session—by the feelings, the themes that were spontane-ously chosen for discussion, the conflicts or rapprochements or silliness, or whatever else might happen. This group began in 1986 and met weekly for several years, with some breaks and some changes of membership. I participated myself throughout. The members were usually mostly psycho-therapists who were accustomed to group therapy, so the sessions might sometimes be unusually revealing and intense.

Generally, the issue of the targets seemed to be genuinely forgotten dur-ing the session as we became absorbed in our own process. Then at the end of the meeting, we conducted a ritual of calling colleagues in another town for a number identifying a packet containing four pictures (there were one hundred such packets available). These were spread out for all to see, and each person silently rated each picture in terms of how much it matched or mismatched the session that had just transpired. After these ratings were collected, a second call was made, and we learned which of the four had been the true target. Our colleagues in the other town did not look at the target or know its contents; they were only passing along numbers picked randomly by a laboratory computer.

Overall, we did quite well at identifying the correct targets. Our results were highly significant. We showed that psi does contribute to our experi-ence and behavior and the ongoing flow of our interactions, and its influ-ence can be discerned in retrospect.

We also rated the quality of each session right after it ended and before any pictures were seen. We rated things like how engaging the time had been, how anxiety provoking, how deeply revealing. The relationship of these ratings to our success was instructive. Sessions that were rated as relatively lighthearted and not too intense produced especially high scoring. Sessions that were very intense, with heavy emotional work, produced negative scoring. Does this mean that psi stopped working in those meetings? I think not, since it was my strong impression that during meetings of great seriousness and emotional intensity the intuitive and caring people in the group expressed their psi *on each other* and on the issues at hand and avoided the distracting ESP target. They certainly displayed their characteristically high levels of intuitive understanding, from whatever sources it was being drawn. When the focus was intensely upon one another the target scores did not drop to chance, they became negative, expressing an avoidance of the target material. During sessions that were more playful and less focused we showed a marked openness to the target and in different ways inadvertently acted out its contents. Had First Sight theory been developed then to the point it is today, this result would have been expected.

Psi Information Helps Us Anticipate Emotional Events

Dean Radin of the Institute for Noetic Sciences and Dick Biermann of the University of Amsterdam and some others have developed a line of research that shows that persons are always reacting at an unconscious, physiological level to events that are shortly to occur in the future and will show this by marked patterns of response when those events will be emotionally significant.[8] This has been called *presentiment* or *prestimulus response,* and it has already been discussed in previous chapters. Events that will be alarming or fearful seem to be especially selected by the unconscious mind for this kind of response. It is expressed by subtle, anticipatory doses of the kinds of response that people make to a full-out, consciously perceived threat (changes in electrodermal response, heart rate, etc.), but at such a slight level as to not be consciously perceptible.

Psi Information Helps Us See Patterns in Things

John Palmer is a psychologist at the Rhine Research Center who has been studying how the mind makes use of future events cognitively, rather than emotionally and physiologically. He has adapted a protocol used by cognitive psychologists to study implicit learning. In his studies, participants observe a sequence of numbers proceeding one by one across a computer monitor. Their task is to try to discern any pattern in the numbers (perhaps an odd number follows each occurrence of "2," and these numbers decrease each time by one—or really any pattern the experimenter has chosen). Before each number appears they must guess what it will be. When their guesses become more accurate than chance would predict, the experimenter can see that learning has occurred. The learning is often implicit in that participants usually demonstrate it before they can explain it.

Palmer wondered if such implicit learning might use cues not only from the series being viewed but also from the future. He presented participants with a series of truly random numbers while telling them that there was some underlying pattern and they should try to predict it with their choices. After that series of numbers was finished, he then presented them with a second series of numbers, and this time there was a hidden order. He found evidence here for implicit learning, but of more interest parapsychologically, he also found that participants had patterned their guesses in the first (random) series in ways that accorded with the pattern that would only come later. It is as if they were implicitly learning, but unconsciously finding no meaningful pattern in the current series—they were precognitively reaching ahead to the next one for some guidance. He has repeated this finding and elaborated it. True to the First Sight hypothesis of *functional equivalence*, he has demonstrated that psi prehensions will be drawn upon along with other implicit information in forming responses.

Psi Information Helps Us Learn, Gravitate to Things That Will Be Familiar, and Respond Quickly When Something New Happens

Daryl Bem (2005, 2011) has also shown that people use psi information about the future in implicitly forming responses to events much as they use other unconscious information. He has demonstrated this in several series of clever experiments. These have also been discussed elsewhere in this book, but in this context, it is important to note that he took normal, well-studied psychological protocols and altered them in such a way that participants could be seen to be implicitly making use of psi information just as they would information acquired in real-time, sensory experience. Do people use subliminal information in such a way as to come to prefer it on later exposure? They do, and use extrasensory information the same way. Do they remember information that they have practiced, and call upon those memories when they have to deal with those things later? Of course they do, and they use precognitive "memories" as well in exactly the same way. Do they respond more quickly to something when a subliminal prime has alerted them to it, as if it matters and may be forthcoming? Yes they do, and they use extrasensory primes in the same way to anticipate experience-to-come. In all these cases, it was participants who were highest on the extraverted trait of stimulus seeking that sought out the future most strongly.

While these studies are similar to others just listed in showing the continuous, implicit use of psi, they are also distinctive in their impact. This is because Bem is such a prominent psychologist, and his studies are so well done, and he has reported them so prominently (in the prestigious *Journal of Personality and Social Psychology*, the journal psychologists most widely read). As the goings-on of minority ghetto dwellers may be unknown to a larger majority society, the work of parapsychologists has been largely invisible for mainstream scientists. Bem's work brings it out of the closet again. A storm of interest and controversy has erupted among psychologists over this research on a scale that has not been seen since the days of J. B. Rhine. Stay tuned to see what becomes of it.

Our Shared Meanings Are Implicitly Expressed by an Increase of Orderliness in the World

Roger Nelson, Dean Radin, and Dick Biermann and their colleagues have carried out bold and fascinating research on psychokinetic effects using random event generators that moves beyond thinking of PK as an ability that is expressed on demand to helping us see how it is an ongoing, implicit aspect of our interaction with the physical world.

PK research has typically been thought of as demonstrating that one's explicit intention can be expressed in physical events, such as the rolls of dice or the digital productions of electronic randomizing devices. These researchers have moved beyond that to show that PK functions implicitly. I believe they also show that unconscious intentions seem to affect physical processes all the time (although they don't use precisely that language).

Very briefly, this work began by placing binary random event generators in settings in which different amounts of implicit group consensus of intention and attention might be expected. Situations characterized by high levels of such consensus, such as ritual observances, intense working groups, and highly engaging conferences somehow had the effect of increasing the order displayed by the randomizing devices (they produced a greater density of either ones or zeros per unit time than would be expected by chance). Other situations with low levels of such consensus, such as lunch breaks at gatherings or academic meetings, did not show this effect.

These workers have gone on to develop a network of random event generators around the planet that run constantly. Normally, their behavior is satisfyingly random. However, when certain events of high "global consciousness" occur, they tend to display a tendency to become orderly again. Over sixty such devices are scattered about in every continent, and the network has collected data for several years. The times of events expected to be of high general interest (for example, the attacks on the World Trade Center, the death of Princess Diana, the nomination of Barak Obama) are compared to control periods without such events. The events are always picked before any data are examined. To date, over 350 such events have been studied, and the degree of coherence displayed by the devices at those times is enormously unlikely to be due to chance (odds of about a billion to one).

It appears that our psychokinetic engagement with the world is ongoing. However, we share the world with others, and normally our intentions are quite various so to accommodate us all effects generally would need to appear cheerfully random. But there are also moments when to some extent our intentions arise in unison. During these periods of unified intention, the machines become more orderly. Specifically, the deviations of their scores from chance become larger. In the words of our theory, their performance becomes more extreme. The effect has been generally attributed to coherence in *attention* rather then *intention*, whereas First Sight theory would predict that it is intention that is the critical thing. It seems noteworthy to me that some events that attracted high levels of attention but not unified intention, such as World Series or World Cup games, did not tend to show the effect as reliably as ones in which both intention and attention would be expected to be consensual. Many people follow World Cup matches, but they want different things.

Just as one person's PK scores are expected to be more extreme when individual intention becomes more stable and unified, First Sight would expect that PK effects at large should become more extreme as intentions across people are more stable and unified. Kierkegaard said, "Purity of heart is to will one thing." This seems to be true among us as much as within us.

THE STATE OF THINGS WITH RESEARCH ON PERSONAL UNCONSCIOUS PSYCHOLOGICAL PROCESSES

John Bargh, a prominent researcher in the field of subliminal primes, reflected recently on where that field has come to after twenty-five years of productive work and startling discoveries.[9] We now know that ". . . such effects are ubiquitous and pervasive across the major forms of psychological phenomena: appraisal and evaluation, motivation and goal pursuit, social perception and judgement, and social behavior. This research has been impressive in demonstrating the wide scope and reach of nonconsciously instigated influences on our daily lives."[10] In Bargh's opinion, this work's childhood is over, and a period of harder, more complex, more integrative questions must be addressed. For example, how do these implicit processes interact with conscious ones, and to what extent are they consciously controllable? Given that the effects occur in parallel, how do they interact with one another? Which ones emerge as most determinative of experience and behavior in natural complex environments?

We must add that psi prehensions also take their part in this unconscious mix and must be understood as well. How does the mind manage all of this? What are the principles? And how do we do all of this together with one another, socially and psychically permeable beings that we are for one another? With our conscious minds we are seeking to map our unconscious minds. Not since Freud has all this seemed so interesting.

Clearly, in addition to accretion of more and more single findings there is a need for new psychological theories of the mind to guide us in constructing an account of these complex, integrative principles. Bargh favors models that focus more upon the action potentials of meaning as opposed to its logical structures and would have us make room for the interpersonal context of all perceiving and doing. First Sight, coming from parapsychology, is congruent with these emphases and offers one step in the path of integrative work.

Like the research featured in this chapter, First Sight emphasizes that unconscious psychological processes are at work in silent and exquisitely complex ways all the time. Psi is not a rare ability to be inherited by a few or attained by a few. It is not a trait, greater in some and lesser in others. It is not best seen by conscious efforts to call it up and make it explicit. It is unconscious, it works for us every moment with remarkable delicacy, and it is as perpetual for us as the air we breathe and the ground we walk on. Research should not aim to capture it as much as reveal it. In this it is like all of our unconscious processes.

As we come to work more together with other scientists of the mind, parapsychology will offer its piece to understanding our unconscious depths and include the reality of psi in the bargain.

NOTES

1. See, for example, Aarts, Custers, and Marien, 2008.
2. Bornstein et al., 2008.
3. Bornstein and Masling, 1998.
4. Shevrin, 2001.
5. Snodgrass and Shevrin, 2006.
6. Chartrand and Bargh, 1999; Chartrand, Dalton, and Fitzsimons, 2007.
7. Carpenter, 2002.
8. Bierman, 2000a; Bierman and Radin, 1997, 1998; Radin, 1997, 1998, 2004a.
9. Bargh, 2006.
10. Bargh, 2006, p. 148.

23

Applications of First Sight

If you're so smart, why ain't you rich?

—Proverbial insult

Any sufficiently advanced technology is indistinguishable from magic.

—Arthur C. Clarke

First Sight theory is a way of trying to understand more about how unconscious psi processes work contextually in the creation of experience and behavior and extrasomatic events. We are trying to penetrate these unconscious activities consciously. As this effort advances and we come to know more about the underlying principles that guide the expression of psi, the issue of applying this knowledge will naturally arise. We will want to not only know the principles but also to use them.

We may first think of a kind of personal use, as in the approaches to self-development discussed in chapter 20. However, as exciting as this is, it falls short of the kind of technological possibilities that are normally opened up by scientific understanding. These have vastly expanded our capacities beyond what is possible for any single person. To rest with self-development would be like trying to solve the problem of human flight by training to be a better high jumper. A few more inches and seconds perhaps, but nothing like the vast extensions of human capacity that have emerged from scientific understanding: for example, our understanding of fluid dynamics and materials science and so on that have produced the modern aircraft.

As the science of psi develops we will better understand the principles that guide the unconscious use of psi prehensions, their weighting, signing, and unconscious expression and suppression. Perhaps these processes that we use naturally to implicitly inform experience can be made more explicit by our conscious understanding of the processes and then rendered into something explicitly useful in itself.

We can think of analogies that make this possibility seem less far-fetched. As I stand outside on a sunny day and look up at the sky in which, say, Saturn is overhead, a few photons from Saturn will reach my retina. However, so many other photons bombard my retina that my mind naturally selects the dominant ones for my experience, and I have no hint of that far-off planet. At night it is a bit better. I may discern a spot of light in the sky and know it to be Saturn. But suppose I wish to see the *rings* of Saturn.

As far as I know, no amount of vision training can permit us to see the rings of Saturn. However, once Galileo constructed the basic equations of refraction he could build a telescope. A science of optics was born, and along with it a new technology of optical enhancement. Point a good telescope at Saturn on a clear, dark night and you can see its rings. Not one photon of light has been added to the situation. It is simply our understanding of refraction and the properties of lenses that now easily permits us to optimize the photons that are flowing toward us and see the rings if we wish to.

And psi? As we come to understand the principles by which we access and express the extrasomatic world inadvertently, can we develop ways to amplify these expressions deliberately when we wish to, beyond what is normally possible for even the most skilled individual?

This is an exciting question, and even with our currently crude understanding of psi, some beginning steps toward answering it have been reported.

EFFORTS TO APPLY PSI

Attempts to apply psi surely began in our dim and unrecorded past, long before anyone dreamed of a science of psi. Prophets, fortune-tellers, and seers have always been called upon at times when no better source of information was available to answer some pressing question.

In ancient Greece, according to Herodotus (1890), the oracle of Delphi passed a very early ESP test administered by Croesus, the king of Lydia, who wanted to determine the finest psychic of the day. Several oracles were asked to tell him what he was doing at a certain time, and she replied, "I count the grains of sand on the beach and measure the sea; I understand the speech of the dumb and hear the voiceless. The smell has come to my sense of a hard shelled tortoise boiling and bubbling with a lamb's flesh in a bronze pot: the cauldron underneath it is of bronze, and bronze is the lid." This was said to literally match his actions at the time.

Croesus then asked the oracle if he should make war with the Persians. She replied that if he did a great empire would be destroyed. Perhaps sensing a certain ambiguity in her response, he paid a handsome sum and then asked if his monarchy would last long. She replied: *Whenever a mule shall become sovereign king of the Medians then, Lydian Delicate-Foot, flee by the stone-strewn Hermus, flee, and think not to stand fast, nor shame to be chicken-hearted.*

Croesus decided that since a mule could never be king of the Medians, there was no need for chicken-heartedness, and he made war. Unfortunately, he lost the war and his empire was destroyed. He seems to have forgotten that Cyrus, the victor, was half Mede and half Persian, and thus would be considered a "mule."

We can zoom forward to contemporary times to find efforts still being made to find (or train) the very best psychics and use them to help answer important questions. During the Cold War, U.S. Army Intelligence, in cooperation with scientists at the Stanford Research Institute, carried out an arduous training program of remote viewing and used a selected group who performed reliably well to help gather intelligence information about Soviet activities and other issues of national concern.[1] The program was called Stargate. They tried to gain information about real-world targets, not symbols on cards or photos that would be flashed on computer monitors. Much of the work is still classified, and contrasting assessments of its value have been given. Many remarkably successful anecdotes have been reported from it, though, fully as accurate as any of those of the ancient oracle.

Stargate has not been the only effort to use ESP through remote viewing for practical purposes. Almost all of these have appeared in popularly oriented books and periodicals and not in peer-reviewed journals, and details have tended to be scanty. Still, results have often appeared to be impressive, and they have ranged broadly in subject matter, including gathering military intelligence,[2] assisting police in solving crimes,[3] predicting silver futures,[4] finding good real-estate opportunities,[5] and discovering lost archeological sites.[6] Perhaps because of the dramatic nature of the claimed results and the paucity of details, these reports have sometimes spawned considerable controversy.[7]

Is this work an application of science? Surely the Stargate project and earlier SRI work at least was, in that the training program was scientifically tested, with good controls, careful measurements, and objective evaluation. Hypotheses were tested, refined, and retested in many studies that were assiduously carried out. The viewers that successfully emerged from it had demonstrated a capacity to gather real knowledge that could not have been obtained normally, to a degree that was strongly extrachance. But we must remember that no psi-training program has been proven to work in general terms. Those on the inside at Stargate, for example, clearly believe that the program identified talent much more than created it.[8] Remote viewing is far from an infallibly psi-conducive procedure. It is probably best seen as a disciplined protocol that is very useful in objectively assessing psi expressions when they occur, not in evoking them.

We must say that all of the applications of remote viewing that have been reported rely, in the last analysis, upon special people. The best results show them working on their best days. They capture miracles. In this sense they are like the legendary feats of the oracle, or the remarkable telepathic bulletins to come from the best mediums of the heyday of psychical research.[9] This work does not exploit an understanding of psi of the sort that First Sight assumes—that it is going on for everyone all the time and might potentially be reliably captured and used with any of us the way a telescope uses the photons beaming down from the rings of Saturn.

Some efforts have been made to increase the reliability of nonspecial, unselected participants and move us toward a time when better understanding can lead to application. The first two explore ideas that I would call "bootstrap methods," in that they try to exploit features of a participant's guessing performance to render it more reliable. These are called *majority vote* and *index sampling*. The third is also a kind of bootstrap if used by itself, since it tries to use a person's ESP performance as a means to predict something beyond itself. This is *associative linkage*. The fourth approach is like the first two attempts to enhance reliability, but it is not a bootstrap method. We could call this *independent prediction*, and it means just that—predicting performance by some independent criterion that we have reason to believe will be reliably associated with scoring.

REPEATED GUESSING

In this approach, participants make several guesses at the same targets and the results are averaged in the hope of obtaining more reliable results. The idea of combining judgments of imperfect reliability in order to improve the correctness of the averaged judgments is a commonplace that is used to ensure accurate information transfer between computers and is used routinely in psychology and other disciplines whenever measurements with imperfect reliability must be used.[10] A single trial in an ESP test certainly represents a situation of imperfect reliability, even with the most talented performers on their best days. In parapsychology this technique has been referred to as the "repeated guessing technique,"[11] the "majority vote technique,"[12] and "redundancy."[13]

Those who have attempted to apply this intuitively appealing idea to increasing the reliability of ESP performance have not always understood that it will only work if overall scoring in the study is positive. Fisk and

West (1956) applied the approach almost as an afterthought in a study involving clock targets and mood ratings and got very encouraging results. Two more applications, however, resulted in null results[14] and in significant psi-missing.[15] More recent applications of the basic approach with positive results have been reported by Brier and Tyminski (1970a, 1970b), Puthoff (1985), Puthoff, May, and Thompson (1986), and Radin (1991).

Unsuccessful applications that have been reported (and probably not reported) have foundered on the pitiless logic of arithmetic.[16] Averaged repeated trials will only enhance whatever scoring tendency is in the collection of individual trials to begin with. If there is overall negative scoring, then averaged calls will score at a more strongly negative rate. If the data set has an overall chance level of scoring, averages will be robustly at chance. This bootstrap offers no panacea unless high scoring can be independently predicted. Averaging can help, but we are still at the mercy of the presence or absence of the oracle.

INDEX SAMPLING

This is a method designed to predict whether a participant is scoring above or below chance. If it works, it can permit a majority vote method to work (when performance is predicted to be negative, the calls can be reversed to the targets not called and added into a majority-vote analysis). To use it, the experimenter must know the identity of some of the targets that are being called, but not others. After some calling is done, the scores on the known targets are tallied. These serve as an *index* for the remaining trials in the set. If scoring on the index is above chance, above-chance scoring on the remainder is predicted. The opposite prediction is made when index trials score negatively.

This technique was first used in a somewhat intuitive way by Cadoret (1955) and rendered more mathematically precise by Taetzsch (1958, 1962). Brier and Tyminski (1970b), already cited, used not only repeated calls but also index sampling in their application of ESP predictions to the real world of casino gambling. Results were significantly positive and apparently lucrative. Dean and Taetzsch (1970) reported a suggestively significant replication of the approach.

The fact that casinos are still in business and little more research of this sort has been reported suggest that this bootstrap technique often fails as well—and reason says that it should. Index sampling by itself requires that another key assumption be met by the data to be sampled. This is the requirement that the sets of ESP data (like the runs in standard forced-choice testing) be internally consistent in scoring direction. As Schmeidler (1960) pointed out, and many others have observed, this assumption generally does not hold true for ESP data. Early attempts to find internal consistency, such as split-half reliability with ESP runs, usually failed. Because of this, the scoring directions of index samples and remaining data are as often opposite as they are the same.

There is a situation in which index sampling can be made to work as intended. Just as the overall mean direction of a sample must be predicted for majority votes to be useful, another parameter of performance must be reliably predicted for index sampling to be useful. This is the variance of the performance around chance expectation. If the deviation of a given set of guesses is relatively large, then the scoring directions of any two parts of the whole set will tend to be the same. On the other hand, if the scoring deviation of the whole set is very small, at or very close to chance expectation, then the scoring directions of any two parts of the whole set will tend to be opposite.

There is no magical bootstrap with index sampling, either; but with the assurance of large deviations from chance (extreme scoring) or the ability to know when deviations will be large or small, then it can be quite useful.

LINKING TARGETS TO THINGS
OUTSIDE THE LABORATORY

The forced-choice targets used in much laboratory work do not simply translate into usable information. We do not often need to discern a star from a circle, or a one from a zero. Even the richer targets of free-response testing, such as the film clips of the ganzfeld or the distant locations of remote viewing, do not exhaust all the things we need to know in practical affairs. In addition to this, it is generally accepted that even remote viewers who do particularly well do best with visual, nonverbal information and not so well with words and numbers. The viewers searching for the kidnapped General Dozier, for example, could give compellingly accurate drawings of buildings and nearby geographical features but failed completely at the name of a city or street or the number of an address or telephone.[17] This is not surprising in terms of First Sight theory, since verbal information automatically calls up cognitive work, and this is expected to turn unconscious thought away from psi prehensions. Unexpected or not, however, it is a severe limitation in questions of application.

An approach that has been taken is to take the kinds of targets that participants are discriminating well with and link them associatively to other kinds of information that is desired. An early version of this was carried out in séance rooms with "spirits" who could make raps on walls and tables but could not usually produce human speech out of thin air. If the "spirit" would accept that one knock meant YES and two meant NO, then many questions could be answered.

Milan Ryzl worked with the remarkable Pavel Stepanek, who was good at guessing which side of a card was uppermost (green or white) when it was handed to him sealed inside an opaque envelope. Ryzl worked out a code by which strings of random numbers were associated with strings of binary numbers. These binary numbers were yoked to the two colors, and thereby decile information was "transmitted" to Stepanek by way of his binary choices.[18]

Remote viewing targets, such as physical locations, have also been treated in this way, and then the approach has been called *associative remote viewing* (or simply ARV, for its many enthusiasts). For example, Puthoff (1984) associated certain target pictures with "market up" and others with "market down" and attempted to predict the rise or fall of certain stocks with the help of a group of participants who were highly motivated to earn money for a charitable cause, and Harary and Targ (1985) attempted to predict silver futures in a similar way.

Of course, this technique predicts real-world events only as well as the participants are predicting their associative targets. "Spirits" were known to rap out many falsehoods as well as startling truths, and investments based on ARV have been known to both succeed and fail. Simple associative linkage is one step toward permitting application, but it hardly guarantees it.

PREDICTIONS OF SCORING DIRECTION
(OR SIZE OF DEVIATION) BY INDEPENDENT CRITERIA

Simple attempts to bootstrap parapsychological data to somehow predict itself or automatically predict something beyond itself will inevitably fail as often as they will succeed, since the expression of psi is normally invisible and attempts to simply coax it to be explicitly present will generally not succeed for long. However, we do know more about psi than we used to, and according to the argument of this book, we actually have good evidence for patterns of performance that make sense and that are in accord with findings in other areas of science. These patterns can be used as predictors. Indeed, this is one way of looking at most parapsychological research. To the extent that the predictors successfully predict scoring direction or scoring extremity, they can be used along with techniques such as majority vote and index sampling and render them truly effective. Perhaps surprisingly, relatively little work of this sort has been attempted.

APPLICATIONS BASED UPON PREDICTING THAT
PREVIOUS HIGH SCORERS WILL CONTINUE TO PERFORM

The simplest form of independent prediction, based upon the crudest kind of understanding, is that of identifying a strong and positive scorer by his or her previous performance and hoping that it will remain good. As simple as this is, when it works it makes all of the above methods work well, too.

For Ryzl and Stepanek, it worked remarkably well. Stepanek continued to guess *green* and *white* much more correctly than chance expectation in five series of repeated guesses at ten-item target lists that were associated with long, random numbers. Stepanek's calls were averaged and majorities were used as the final calls at the target items. All five lists were "transmitted" with perfect accuracy, so the associated numbers could be identified correctly in each case.[19] Puthoff's (1984) highly motivated participants also scored above chance. When their guesses were averaged, the majority calls predicted market behavior well enough that their charity ended up $25,000 richer for their efforts. In their initial effort, Harary and Targ[20] reportedly enjoyed good performance from their band of experienced SRI psychics and cashed in on silver futures (although their second try was said to have lost money). As Puthoff put it, such findings have a "bottom line" statistic.

APPLICATIONS BASED UPON INDEPENDENT PREDICTIONS OF PERFORMANCE

As far as I know, my own research is the only work of this sort to date. I began it with a wish to learn more about scoring extremity in ESP tests. Some studies had shown that extreme scoring that was uncontrolled in direction tended to be associated with certain states of mind and to decline as a person worked at an ESP test.[21] To try to assess these shifting states, I began a series of studies in which participants would fill out mood adjective checklists right before they carried out their forced-choice ESP guessing. After accumulating a decent body of data, I used multiple regression to construct a list of mood items that showed promise at predicting when scores would be extreme and when they would be tight. A little later after still more data was at hand, I also used the same method to define a set that could predict direction as well.

Midway in this project I began to use single, randomly determined target lists for all the runs carried out in a given study. This was in order to try out these data as a vehicle for the amplification of effects using a variation of the majority vote procedure. In runs when mood scores predicted high scoring, all calls for each target were tallied. When mood scales predicted below-chance scoring, all calls were reversed (I used binary targets, usually + and O) and the reversed calls were added to the tally. Then, all calls were averaged for a "best guess" at that target. The way of using the mood scale for scoring extremity was somewhat more complicated and used index sampling in addition to averaging.

Over several studies the mood scales performed significantly well, and as they did, the averaged calls always showed a nice boost over the scoring rate of the single calls.[22] Then I decided to try something more ambitious. I would try to use the method to "send" a coded word to my undergraduate participants using this method. I gathered all data I had on hand for a fresh regression analysis to secure the best mood predictors for scoring direction and extremity (responses to the sheep-goat question were included as well). In those Cold War days, I decided that the word *PEACE* would be a good one to use, and translated it to twelve dots and dashes of Morse code. Then I decided that *dot* would be represented by +, and *dash* by O. These coded targets were mixed with thirteen other randomly determined ones for a final target list. I sealed this list in an envelope and placed it under a clutter of papers in a drawer and told no one about it.

Forty-six students volunteered to take part. I used only persons low in authoritarian tendencies, since they had been found to give more valid mood reports.[23] Each carried out four self-testing sessions at home. Each session required a mood scale and five ESP runs guessing +'s and O's. They were not told that they were guessing the same list over and over, nor that an attempt was being made to transmit a word.

I scored data by hand then (and double-checked it all), and it was a laborious process. I still remember the moment when the last majority for + (dot) fell out of the data, and I could see that the word *PEACE* had been retrieved perfectly.[24]

I then decided to carry out a replication with a different word. This time I selected the abbreviation *INFO* as a target word and sealed it in two envelopes. One I hid away as before, and the other I mailed to K. R. Rao, the director of the Foundation for Research on the Nature of Man, who agreed to not open it until after all my new data had been collected and analyzed. Forty-two low-authoritarian participants went through the same drill. Again, they were not told of the repeated use of the same targets nor of the attempt to send verbal information. This time results were good but not perfect. Thirteen Morse code bits were required for the word, and the majority on the last bit was incorrect. The word that emerged was *INFG*. The mood scales did significantly predict performance on the raw data, and the majority votes were quite significant.

The next study in the series also repeated the basic procedure, but with some modifications. I collected data as before, but the target list was picked by Richard Broughton at the FRNM and not told to me or anyone else until the study was analyzed. Broughton wrote a software program to analyze the information. Now a computer randomly shuffled the target order within each run while keeping track of the identity of each item. The program also scored runs and mood scales, made appropriate predictions for each run, tallied votes, and averaged them for each target item. The target chosen by

Broughton was a four-digit octal number, each made up of three binary bits. Only thirty-two participants contributed runs this time, so the results were not expected to be as robust.

Again, the mood scales discriminated data significantly, but votes were distributed quite unevenly across the bits and fewer majorities were successful. Seven of the binary bits were correct, four were wrong, and one was a tie, permitting no decision. When these bits were combined into the octal digits, two of the four were retrieved successfully, one was wrong, and one call could not be determined because of the indeterminate bit.

The last two studies were done several years later and were carried out mostly as demonstration projects for lectures.[25] Since even fewer participants were involved (twenty-five and twenty-two, respectively), less stable results were expected.

The first one attempted to use the same basic procedure (as analyzed by Broughton's program) to predict the rises and falls of twelve financial market entities over a one-week period in the future. I asked Broughton and K. R. Rao to pick the target list and keep it secret. The date of my planned lecture was used as the end point, Broughton agreed to take a *Wall Street Journal* one week before that and note the values that day of the target items, and then do the same thing one week later, noting which had risen and which fallen. This time, a majority vote for + would make a prediction for a rise and a majority for O would predict a fall.

As targets, Broughton and Rao picked a set of market values and industry group comparisons. Six were simple comparisons (the price of West Texas crude either rose or fell), but the other six were relative comparisons across pairs of items. This was to guard against any distortion that might have resulted from the possibility of a general drift in the market that would make the behavior of many things highly correlated. For example, building materials were compared to railroads at week one and then again at week two. If the relative value of one over the other was maintained in direction over the week, the trial was called +. If the advantage between them switched over the week, the target was O.

The analysis of majority votes was rather successful. Eleven items were correctly predicted, and one was wrong. An investor trading in weekly options would have done well if guided by these predictions.

I carried out the same study one year later and again asked Broughton to pick targets. There were two major differences: I decided to focus on more creative participants and I asked a colleague, Kathy Dalton, to collect data. Dalton, already mentioned in chapter 17, has demonstrated a track record of eliciting strong psi performances from her participants. Participants were drawn from university theater and creative writing classes.

In this study the mood scales did not discriminate data significantly well, and the success of the majorities was weaker. Seven were predicted correctly, five incorrectly. However, it seemed worth noting that this study, unlike all the others that had preceded it, yielded overall significantly above-chance scoring. Other studies used participants not selected for any particular qualities (except low authoritarianism), and my approach as an experimenter had been like that of most academic psychologists, one of studied neutrality. Normally one wishes for the experimenter to not be an important variable in a study, so his or her participation is kept very standardized and minimal. Dalton, while she tried to follow my guidelines, also added an irrepressible wish to motivate and inspire her participants. At any rate, while the mood items did not predict so well, a simple majority vote analysis of all guessing done (as if high scoring had been predicted) would have done much better.

These six studies show that a repeated-guessing approach to transmitting or predicting real information is possible using independent variables that are designed to predict scoring patterns. Excepting the last study (which was the least successful), no special participants were used and no testing was done in conditions expected to be "psi conducive." Overall scoring in the data sets was well within chance expectation. However, the mood scales did discriminate performance to some extent, and the majority analyses did distill it to stronger levels.

Altogether, these participants contributed 64,746 votes to their respective analyses, of which 33,427 were correct. This boost above chance, although just shy of only 2 percent, could scarcely have occurred by chance—the odds against that are about a quadrillion to one. These votes were used to try to predict fifty-nine different binary targets. Forty-nine predictions were correct, nine incorrect, and one was a tie. The odds against this result being due to chance are also enormous.

These studies show that even relatively weak prediction of psi performance, if reliable, can potentially be put to practical use in communicating information and in predicting unknown future events. The scales of mood items and attitude items used here have shown modest reliability over a number of studies. However, it is important to note that such mood items are not the only predictors that could be used in such a way, and they are probably far from the strongest that we might find to use. I continued with them only because I began with them and wished to assemble a meaningful body of data with one technique. Stronger and more straightforward predictors might be determined. For example, as implied by the serendipitous findings of the last study, a simple prediction of positive scoring from creative participants working with a charismatic experimenter might be quite successful. Probably work by Targ, Puthoff, Schwarz, and others has already informally exploited it. If such variables can be reliably, objectively, and independently assessed (not just inferred after the fact from good performances) and can prove themselves by repeated confirmation, then a good predictive package could be built.

Any means at all of independently predicting scoring direction or extremity could be put to work in a majority-vote paradigm. The targets given to participants can be yoked to some "real-world" event that we wish to discern. The yoking seems to present no obstacle to persons demonstrating their psi prehensions as they normally do, all in the context of our predictors.

BACK TO THEORY

These studies were carried out before I had formulated First Sight theory. The mood scales were developed empirically, not from any theoretical base. However, like almost all of the research discussed in this book, these scales can be examined to see how well they accord with what the theory would expect. I carried out a factor analysis of the mood items[26] and found that items predicting hitting tended to represent factors of detached relaxation and inward focus (for example, "drifting"), strong intention and freedom from self-doubt and cognitive analysis (for example, "masterful" and "forceful"), and freedom from anxiety—all things that theory would predict. Items predicting extremity represented factors that implied a nonanalytical and holistic state of mind (for example, "carefree") along with a freedom from distraction and cognitive work (for example, "task-involved" scored negatively). This pattern is congruent, too, as we can see from reexamining the hypotheses spelled out within the Intention and Switching corollaries in chapter 2.

As we gain more of a grasp of how psi works unconsciously and what factors influence the manner of its expression, this understanding can be turned into predictions that can in turn permit an amplification of effects. We will be on our way to developing a technology of psi.

EVEN IF WE CAN, SHOULD WE?

If this should happen, would it be good or bad? This is a serious question. I conducted the PEACE study in 1975 and delayed reporting it in written form for sixteen years mainly because of my own ambivalence about this.

This question arises in regard to any potentially powerful development of knowledge. We generally desire new knowledge and fear it at once. More knowledge is more power, and we wonder if our wisdom and humanity will be equal to the challenges of more power. In any case, I have come to think that our scientific understanding of psi will continue to grow and that it will probably be put to work. We may delay that day, but we will not prevent it.

Ideas like "psychic development" and "psychic application" currently tend to be left mostly to practitioners who sell advice on 800 numbers or teach self-development techniques in "mind control" or "remote viewing," with dubious results. Almost all of what one finds in wandering the Internet in search of psi application is nonsense. If it has any value at all, it is entertainment value.

On the other hand, scientific work on psi is developing, and First Sight theory suggests that it can become more programmatic and successful. Scientific understanding has given us our modern world with its vast expansion of human powers, and it will be scientific work that eventually leads to the reliable application of psi.

NOTES

1. McMoneagle, 2002; Smith, 2005.
2. McMoneagle, 2002; Targ and Puthoff, 1977.
3. Lyons and Truzzi, 1991.
4. Harary and Targ, 1985; Targ, 1988.
5. Kasian, 2004.
6. Schwartz, 2001.
7. Harary, 1992; Marks, 2002; May, 1998; Puthoff and Targ, 1976; Utts, 1996; Wiseman & Milton, 1998.
8. McMoneagle, personal communication.
9. James, 1898.
10. See, for example, Schultheiss, Liening, and Schad, 2008, in the area of measuring implicit motives, or Granhag, 1997, in regard to the reliability of forensic testimony.
11. Thouless, 1960.
12. Fisk and West, 1957.
13. Kennedy, 1979.
14. Michie and West, 1957.
15. Fisk and West, 1957.
16. This approach is a straightforward application of the Law of Large Numbers (Feller, 1968).
17. McMoneagle, 2002.
18. Ryzl, 1966.
19. Ryzl, 1966.
20. Larson, 1984.
21. Carpenter, 1966; Rogers and Carpenter, 1966.
22. Carpenter, 1968; 1969.
23. Thayer, 1971.
24. Carpenter, 1975.
25. Carpenter, 2010.
26. Carpenter, 1991.

24

Suggested Directions for Future Research

It is wise in looking at the problem of conducting a psi test properly to keep in mind that it is a purely psychological function that is being tested and to allow it every possible psychological consideration.

—J. B. Rhine

If psi is always going on, if it unconsciously stands behind all of our experience and behavior, then research should consciously work toward elucidating those unconscious processes by which it works. Our theorizing and hypothesizing and operationalizing should all be relevant to the central program of working around our own unconsciousness and bringing these processes into the light where they can be better understood. Such knowledge could be applied. The processes of our digestion are largely unconscious, as is the circulation of our blood, but we now know a great deal about these things by studying them. The same is true of the mind. As Freud and others since him have shown, the unconscious mind can be studied consciously.

Various features of this model suggest particular slants for study to take. The following are examples.

STUDY THE INADVERTENT EXPRESSION OF PSI PROCESSES IN SITUATIONS NOT UNDERSTOOD AS PARAPSYCHOLOGICAL EXPERIMENTS

Since psi processes are presumed to be active all the time, and their typical expression is in the form of inadvertencies, more study should be done to elucidate the functioning of psi in situations in which persons are carrying on "normal" activities and not attempting to express some paranormal effect. This suggestion has been made before by Stanford (1974), and I wish to second it here. Schachter (1997) has summarized research that has looked for unconscious extrasensory effects in such situations as academic tests, and Carpenter (2002), Ehrenwald (1948), and Eisenbud (1969, 1970) have examined the expressions of ESP in psychotherapy. Psi effects in what would otherwise appear to be "normal" experiments on psychological phenomena have been reported also, such as Klintman's (1984) study of reaction times to the presentations of colors and Bem's (2004) examination of relative preference between matched pairs of pictures. Such work suggests directions that we may take, but, assuming that psi functions ubiquitously, we can extend such investigation into almost any behavioral context.

ANALYZE SCORING DIRECTION AND SCORING EXTREMITY SEPARATELY AND ROUTINELY

This model emphasizes that these two parameters of performance are expected to be influenced by different factors and that both are important and continuous aspects of ongoing psi process. Both aspects of performance should be analyzed regularly in studies of ESP and PK performance, with attention paid to variables that affect each of them. It is important to avoid any analyses such as the use of the "direct hit" in ganzfeld research that confound the two parameters, since this creates unnecessary confusion. The rank of number one represents both the most extreme score of psi-hitting and one of the higher values of scoring extremity. Any correlations between some other variable and this binary psi variable (one versus all other ranks) thus confound these two basic parameters of psi process and cannot be clearly interpreted. Palmer (1997) has also addressed this problem. In assessing relevant patterns of performance in rank-order data, the methods of Solfvin, Kelly, and Burdick (1978) are particularly helpful.

FOCUS ON INADVERTENT ASPECTS OF RESPONSE THAT ARE ESPECIALLY LIKELY TO BE SENSITIVE EXPRESSIONS OF PSI

Since psi functioning is intrinsically preconscious, it is reasonable to operationalize it by examining inadvertent expressions of its orienting action, rather than asking subjects to try to generate an approximation of conscious knowledge. Aspects of response that are generally known to reflect preconscious processes are likely to yield fruitful results. Examples of this useful approach are already available, such as the use of unconscious physiological responses,[1] spontaneous social behavior,[2] perceptual judgments,[3] involuntary pupillary fixations,[4] word associations,[5] and affective reactions.[6]

USE IMPLICIT MEASURES OF PSYCHOLOGICAL INDEPENDENT VARIABLES

Since the variables effecting psi functioning (directional orientation and directional switching) act on an unconscious level, it will probably be more useful to study them with implicit or behavioral methods such as projective techniques than with self-report measures such as questionnaires. Such implicit measures tend to be more valid indicators of preconscious processes. As McClelland, Koestner, and Weinberger (1989) point out, self-report measures appear to be most effective at predicting future self-conscious self-representation, as in the responses to future questionnaires. Projective measures on the other hand, or other implicit measures that sample behaviors presumed to implicitly express the unconscious issues being studied, are superior in predicting behavior in future situations in which the behavior is not self-conscious (that is, most of the time, and probably always in regard to psi functioning).[7] Another sort of measure that would be expected to be more valid is the sampling of clear behavioral indications of the variable being assessed, as in those studies that defined as "creative" those persons who successfully do creative work, and in Stanford and Schroeter's (1978) assessment of the subjects' defensiveness by the latter's choice of carrying out a task in a chair that was either fully or partially reclined. Since unconscious intentions and goals are presumed by theory to be particularly important in how psi is expressed, parapsychologists should work on developing contributions in this kind of assessment. Variations on approaches such as the Implicit Associations Test[8] or the Implicit Relational Assessment Procedure[9] may be particularly useful.

STUDY THE ACTION OF PSI PROCESSES IN THE CONTEXT OF OTHER PRECONSCIOUS PHENOMENA

In carrying out parapsychological studies it would be wise to borrow aggressively from mainstream psychologists who are working with preconscious phenomena and collaborate with them as well. Psychologists have been ingenious in recent decades at developing methods for gaining experimental access to some unconscious and preconscious mental processes. Perception-without-awareness, implicit memory, implicit social perception, perceptual defensiveness, and subliminal psychodynamic activation are examples of the fertile work being done. Psi phenomena do not represent disguised knowledge, but the functioning of preknowledge—preperceptual apprehensive mental processes at a point beyond the physical impingement of a stimulus upon the organism. In consciously collaborative work, parapsychologists will have new contributions from their own tradition. For example, although there is some notice of the phenomenon of significant missing in the perception-without-awareness literature,[10] they have paid less systematic attention to this matter than parapsychologists have.

Two studies from the laboratory of the Rhine Research Center demonstrate one form such integrative work might take. In one,[11] our research team examined the effect of an attempted suboptimal manipulation of the subjects' merger motivation, mood of security, and cognitive approach on their ESP performance in the ganzfeld. We hoped to evoke heightened levels of scoring in the condition intended to facilitate a sense of secure merger and a nonintellectual approach to the task. We also examined the effects of the manipulation by analyzing the transcripts of the sessions and the post-session state reports of the percipients. Our results were instructive about ways to best implicitly guide a mood of openness and also showed that the participant's extraversion and relationship with the agent were important conditions, as we expected.

In another series of studies,[12] a first experiment carried out an elaboration of the mere exposure effect described earlier, in that our participants were first exposed to subliminal exposures of some pictures and completely blocked exposures to others, as ESP targets (had they been shown at full exposure they would only be seen as black, opaque rectangles). Participants were then shown the exposed material along with unexposed pictures matched for desirability. We wished to examine how subliminal and extrasensory primes might be used unconsciously to form a sense of attractiveness when they are presented in the same situation. We also exposed half our participants to subliminal primes intended to influence a mood of openness and well-being and the other half to primes arousing mild anxiety. Finally, we administered a number of psychological instruments that have been found to moderate extrasensory and subliminal effects (for example, openness to fantasy for ESP and boredom proneness for subliminal effects). Response to both extrasensory and subliminal exposures was implicit, assessed by preference scores of the exposed material versus unexposed. A number of interesting findings emerged, including the successful prediction of both extrasensory and subliminal effects by almost all of the measures intended to predict them. We further found that these predictions were much stronger in the condition in which a positive mood had been evoked. A second study successfully replicated the predictive relationships with ESP that had been found in the first study, again most strongly in the condition of a positive mood. Interestingly, in the second study subliminal effects were not predicted as well as extrasensory ones!

This research takes some steps in a planned program of study in which we hope to shed new light on how the unconscious mind acts upon extrasensory and subliminal-sensory information at the same time and how these actions might be most reliably predicted.

A THEORY-GUIDED PROGRAM OF RESEARCH

Parapsychological research has largely developed without useful guidance from explicit theory. As a consequence, its findings have seemed less coherent or cumulative than they might have. A theoretical approach that assumes that psi is continuously ongoing as an integral part of the matrix of personal unconscious preconscious processes (PUPPs) should help us to better understand how psi fits in with other processes in the formation of experience and action. Programmatic and integrative work generally proves to be more useful than work that is piecemeal and isolated.

NOTES

1. Braud, 2003; Dean, 1962; Radin, 2004a; Radin, Taylor, and Braud, 1995; Spottiswood and May, 2003.

2. Carpenter, 2002.

3. Kreitler and Kreitler, 1972, 1973.

4. Palmer, 1994.

5. Stanford, 1973.

6. Bem, 2003.

7. See Dauber, 1984, and Weinberger, Kelner, and McClelland, 1997.

8. Greenwald, McGhee, and Schwartz, 1998.

9. Barnes-Holmes et al., 2006.

10. Bonnano and Stillings, 1986; Grosz and Zimmerman, 1965; Merikle and Reingold, 1991.

11. Carpenter, 2006.

12. Carpenter and Simmonds-Moore, 2009a, 2009b.

25

First Sight, Parapsychology, and Other Branches of Science

Is the universe friendly?

—F. W. H. Myers

The First Sight model offers a view of psychological functioning that includes a sensible place for psi processes. It shows how the errant anomalies described by parapsychologists may actually represent tirelessly active and normally unconscious capacities used in our ongoing adjustments to the circumstances of our lives. This model does not prove that psi processes actually occur. However, it is hoped that developing a picture of the mind in which psi can fit together with the other facts of psychological process will make it easier for scientists of other disciplines to attend with more interest to all of the research that does prove that psi phenomena are genuine occurrences. First Sight theory goes some way toward meeting the objection sometimes raised by other scientists that parapsychology has no theory. It does.

At least two other things are necessary, however, before many scientists will take seriously the possibility of the reality of psi. They want from parapsychologists a replicable phenomenon, and they want a mechanism for how a mind may interact with distant matter or with other minds.

THE PROBLEM OF REPLICATION

For some parapsychologists this problem has already been solved. The replicability of an effect is a matter of degree, and many parapsychological hypotheses in broad terms have been shown by meta-analysis to be reliable enough, and free enough of apparent error, to be considered real.[1] Still, no parapsychological phenomenon is perfectly reliable, and no parapsychologist, no matter how many successful studies he or she may have conducted, presently is able to toss a coin into the air and either will or predict with absolute accuracy the face on which it will land. Can this model and theory hasten the day in which such reliability is achieved? They may, since they suggest a direction for understanding not only the sporadic anomalies of apparent psi but also the countless moments of apparent absence of psychic process, all in the same terms. Understanding the true scope of a phenomenon, in its implicit as well as its explicit expressions, will provide a firmer basis for comprehension and prediction. Even if this model should prove to be basically wrong, the research disproving it should lead us in the direction of greater understanding, and as the understanding of psi phenomena improves, the replicability of operations demonstrating it will as well.

A PHYSICAL MECHANISM FOR PSI

I have presented the ideas in this book in the context of a phenomenological approach to the basic ontological and metaphysical problems that appear to beset the psi hypothesis. In a phenomenological approach, a dualistic split between the subjective and objective aspects of experience is eschewed, and the need for providing some sort of physical mechanism linking mind to world or present to future event is avoided. The facts as observed are left to speak for themselves. I believe that this is a sufficient basis for grounding meaningful psychological scientific work. This will not seem satisfying, however, to scientists who are deeply committed to a physicalist conception of the mind. Most scientists probably assume that all mental events are ultimately reducible to physical events, the "promissory materialism" described by Popper and Eccles (1977, 96). As stated earlier, this derivative and reductionistic idea of the mind also leads to the assumption that mere consciousness should have no reach beyond the physical body, and mere intention should have no immediate grip of its own upon physical events. For many scientists, such assumptions are so deeply held as to seem to be given realities. From such a base, psi phenomena will always seem unreal because they will feel impossible.

Developments during the last century in basic theoretical physics call into question this structure of assumptions. Einstein, in his theory of special relativity, proved that the perspective of the observer is an essential part of an adequate account of nature, and in that sense he affirmed the primary reality of consciousness. Current research in physics is heavily involved with the study of what David Bohm (1993) calls "quantum interconnectedness." The theorem of J. S. Bell (1964) specified this expectation of nonlocal correlation between separated quanta of light under certain circumstances. The theorem has been empirically proven.[2] While it cannot be said that a mechanism for psychic connections between mental events and distant physical events has been established by these means, several physicists have argued that these and other aspects of quantum mechanics have opened a door that may lead in that direction.[3] I quote Whiteman (1977) on these matters:

> Modern physics has reached the stage where the clear outlines of a new world-view and methodology are visible, and these provide an "integral understanding" of the world and its psychological and mystical background. With the wider acceptance of such world-view and methodology, new fields of research may be expected to open out, and parapsychology may be considered to have become an established science.

Serious work is underway on many fronts toward developing an expanded understanding of consciousness that is consonant with theoretical physics. Those of us who are not physicists will watch their progress with interest. It may be that some kind of rapprochement of physical science with the science of consciousness that is not merely reductive will ultimately be developed. If it does, the psychological understanding of psi developed in this book should be ultimately congruent with such an expanded conception of the mind.

What about a "psychophysiology of psi"? Preconscious processes are often studied today in terms of the neurophysiological processes that are associated with them. Indeed, this is now what the popular culture identifies with the scientific study of the basis of psychological processes. This work is successful and growing quickly. We know so much now about things like the functioning of the prefrontal lobes in acts of short-term memory and the occipital cortex in visual perception. There is widespread acceptance of the idea that the mind is a set of functions of the brain—it is the subjective side of what the brain does. Such is the current flowering of the neurological explanation of the mind that started with the eighteenth-century model of the human as a reflex machine proposed by La Mettrie and discussed in chapter 6. In light of this, it seems a striking omission that reference to these processes is so absent from this book.

There are several reasons for this omission, none of which imply any lack of appreciation for the importance of this kind of understanding. First, meaningful scientific work on preconscious processes that is more psychological than neurophysiological is also ongoing and growing in a healthy way. It is worth focusing upon in its own right. Second, little research has been done on neurophysiology and psi, so not much is known yet. And third, the very phenomena adduced by parapsychologists seem to involve, by their nature, connections between person and world (prehensions) that cannot be reduced to the psychophysiological functions of a brain. If we do not assume a reductionistic substrate to psi, it seems less imperative to study it primarily in physiological terms.

Even if a scientist is not a reductionist in regard to mental processes, he or she may reasonably want an account of psi phenomena that is elaborated in terms of known psychophysiological processes. First Sight is a psychological model and not a neurophysiological one. But it could certainly be congruent with such neurophysiological accounts as these continue to develop and are specifically applied to psi phenomena. We humans are embodied creatures, and the psychophysiological system must be intimately involved in the psi level of transaction with the world and one another. Many contributions in this area have been made already.[4] The First Sight model of psi, as it is developed further, may provide a useful structure to which accounts of relevant nervous system activity can be related. Analogously, work is already being done that relates preconscious sensory processes with various aspects of psychophysiological activity.[5]

A DIFFERENT SLANT ON FAMILIAR
PSYCHOLOGICAL PROCESSES

Since some of the premises of First Sight theory are different from the premises that are most widely held today, even when psychophysiological processes are being described, different language is needed to be internally consistent. This is true in regard to well-known psychological processes as well. We may read without thinking about it a statement such as: *The condition of threat aroused an anticipatory response.* The wording of this statement does not simply describe a relationship. It houses within itself a certain set of assumptions about the basis of human experience and activity. From the First Sight perspective, we might say: *The unconscious mind treats the threatening thing as something to be anticipated.* This kind of wording may seem odd and somehow too full of extra assumptions. Yet to assume that the mind acts purposefully and unconsciously on things is no more an assumption than to assume that things physically cause human behavior to do one thing or another. It has been a great sin in science to be too anthromorphic and teleological, to assume that certain things, at base, happen because a human intends them to. But if this primary efficacy of intention is ruled out of court, what becomes of all the facts that have been so persistently dug up by parapsychologists? They show sheer human intention at work beyond the reach of any physical impingement and also enter into the workings of extrapersonal human events (like random event generators, or rolling dice). Such facts come to seem confusing or even seditious. This is why parapsychologists have had to do their work largely outside the sanctions of established science.

To draw another example from parapsychology, a summary statement in a paper previously cited by Daryl Bem (2011) reads as follows: "Precognition itself is a special case of a more general phenomenon: the anomalous retroactive influence of some future event on an individual's current responses, whether those responses are conscious or nonconscious, cognitive or affective." The specific content of some of these words are certainly shocking to some who do not imagine precognition to occur, but the metalinguistic, epistemological assumptions embedded in the language are very comfortable. Worded in a way that would be consistent with the teleological assumptions of First Sight, we might say: "Precognition is itself a special case of a more general phenomenon: the apparently anomalous tendency of the unconscious mind to make reference to certain future events in constructing its responses, whether those responses are conscious or nonconscious, cognitive or affective."

Unconscious minds, unconscious intentions, unconscious goals—such constructs are at the core of First Sight. The use of language that implies that these things must function mechanically on a passive organism seems unnecessarily awkward and self-contradictory, no matter how odd or even offensive it may seem to do without it. We are intentional beings, and our goals give us structure. Our language should permit us to think clearly about human agency.

NOTES

1. Utts, 1996.
2. Freedman and Clauser, 1972.
3. Bohm, 1990; Josephson and Pallikari-Viras, 1991; Targ, 2004; Walker, 1975.
4. Broughton, 2002; Ehrenwald, 1976, 1977; Kelly, 2007.
5. Shevrin, 1988; Shevrin, Bond, Brakel, Hertel, and Williams, 1996.

26

Psi and a New
Science of the Mind

*It must be frankly confessed that in no fundamental sense do we know where our
successive fields of consciousness come from, or why they have the precise inner
constitution which they do have.*

—William James

How does consciousness take the form that it does? This book's theory
provides a context within which answers to this perennial, psychological
question might be sought. In such a light what have been considered psychic phenomena actually represent continuously ongoing and normally
unconscious processes that contribute to the construction of experience
and action. Since with psi, the mind is presumed to make access to events
beyond those and before those that are available to sensation, psi may fairly
be referred to as First Sight. The theory also suggests basic ways in which
the mind may use its presensory prehensions in the context of developing
sensory experience and in ways in which its anticipatory effects may be
surmised indirectly.

The model is intended to be useful in several different ways. It develops
an understanding of psi functioning that places it in the context of accepted
preconscious psychological processes. It suggests that the mind uses psi
prehensions in the anticipation and construction of its experiences and actions, much as it uses subliminal, or suboptimal, perceptual information.
Curiously, some researchers in the field of suboptimal perception have
attributed little utility to their phenomena in everyday life. To the contrary, this model proposes that the mind continually uses suboptimal and
extrasensory information in anticipating, constructing, and understanding
its own developing experience and in constructing its countless adaptive

behaviors that occur outside of consciousness. If psi processes function in everyday experience in a continuously active, if normally implicit way, then they cannot be omitted by any psychologist attempting to understand the basic problem of the field: how experience and behavior come to be what they are.

Besides offering a normalization of parapsychology by embedding it in the context of other psychological processes, the model also offers a rubric in terms of which past research may be understood and future research conceived. It even offers a parapsychological way of understanding the ordinary absence of paranormal experience.

The various findings of parapsychology sometimes have been thought to be so contradictory and disorderly that they must represent an unwitting exercise in self-deception[1] or else be a futile attempt to pin down some phenomena that are intrinsically elusive.[2] It seems likely that parapsychological findings are not meaningless but are still inchoate. If psi exists, it must be almost thoroughly unconscious in its functioning. If so, we are like blind persons studying sight. Small wonder that our findings are inductive and groping. We can advance if we can imagine models and theories that tie together what we know and guide it forward. It is in this spirit that First Sight is proposed.

The anomalous observations of parapsychology now lie about our cultural landscape like so many odd, disparate stones. Yet they suggest an implicit coherence that cries out for understanding. Great lurches forward in the history of science have come from deeply questioning similar anomalies. For centuries people puzzled at unusual phenomena in which the inert material of the natural world seemed oddly and transiently active. What was the lightning in the sky? Why did lodestone have the power to attract certain metals? Why did shards of magnetized metal point always to the same invisible point in space? How could a rod of amber, rubbed on velvet, draw to itself feathers and scraps of paper? Most such anomalies were passing curiosities, of little practical concern for everyday life. Then in the nineteenth century the musings of many lifetimes culminated in the work of Hertz and Faraday and Maxwell and their colleagues, and electromagnetic energies were understood to be all-pervasive forces in nature, even constitutive of matter itself. Today our understanding of these forces has yielded a very different world than one that anyone could have dreamed of before.

Understanding the mind itself is the next great task of science. The findings of parapsychology are crucial to the development of an adequate understanding. It is a propitious time. Serious parapsychological work has proceeded for over one hundred years, and findings are now numerous enough and secure enough that implicit patterns are more clearly emerging.

Meanwhile, psychology, after its long focus on the publicly behavioral, has rediscovered consciousness, and at the same time has found a very

fruitful field in the preconscious processes that contextualize consciousness. Efforts to reduce the mind to cybernetic or biological processes have,
in the opinion of many prominent scientists, foundered conceptually and
empirically.[3] The mind must be understood in its own terms, including its
unconscious and extrasomatic dimensions. It is time to think scientifically
of all these things at once. An understanding of psychological reality cannot
be adequate without the anomalies of parapsychology.

If this model, or some other one with similar intentions, helps us in these
purposes, our understanding of the psychological universe may be greatly
enhanced. Our powers of action may be increased as well. Observations
of the soaring of birds' wings, or simply feeling the lift of a hand held at a
certain angle while running, point the way to understanding the processes
of fluids in motion. Once those principles were grasped, human flight became a reality. An understanding of the principles of optics similarly led to
the vast extension of human sight through lenses into the very small and
the very far away.

It seems reasonable to assume that we all normally and unconsciously
participate in an extended universe larger than our skins and our senses. As
Walt Whitman (1900) proclaimed, "I . . . am not contain'd between my hat
and boots." The findings of parapsychology imply that this statement is literally true. As with an understanding of aerodynamics and optics, it seems
inevitable that scientifically understanding our larger selves will lead us to
larger possibilities of knowledge and action.

NOTES

1. Blackmore, 1987.
2. Kennedy, 2001.
3. Kelly, 2007.

Acknowledgments

Many people have helped me in different ways to conceive and bring forth this book. I cannot name them all. However, some stand out and must be acknowledged. I will list them in clusters.

My early interest in the scientific study of the "paranormal" was fostered generously by several mentors, including J. B. Rhine, Gaither Pratt, Kay Banham, John Freeman, Winnie Nielsen, Wadih Saleh, and Harold McCurdy. Gratefully, some of these went on to become dear friends.

My early involvement in this field was firmly cemented by a cluster of deep and lasting friendships with young colleagues (we were all young then) formed at a critical point in our developing professional and personal identities and then sustained over the years. This band included Dave Rogers, Rex Stanford, B. K. Kanthamani, John Palmer, and the late Chuck Honorton and Bob Morris.

For several years I was involved in a group that carried out a long and unusual research project together and at the same time explored the personal experience of extrasensory influence. This shifted me personally from being someone who only studied others to a person who also dared to explore and inhabit this implicit domain firsthand. They helped me define the First Sight model and experience its validity. Without their support and mutual involvement I could not have tolerated and consolidated such a change in worldview. At different points this group included Vicki Barbera, Judy Barnett, Sally Drucker, Sally Feather, Jo Ann Hundley, Judy Moscovitz, Jeff Munson, John Palmer, David Rogers, Bill Roll, Tomiko Smith, Sandy Troth, Linda Vann, Jim Wells, Buddy Wynn, and the late Carol Sanks.

In my work as a clinical psychologist I have had the remarkable opportunity to work in depth with several people who were unusually given to the kinds of experiences we consider psychic. They shared these experiences generously with me. This always became a rich and fascinating dimension in our therapeutic relationship and work together and taught me more than any number of books or courses or experiments. If I had not guessed before that psi is woven into each moment of life, involvement with them would not let me escape the fact. The rules do not allow me to name them, but they understand who they are.

During their tenures as directors of the Rhine Research Center, Richard Broughton and Sally Rhine Feather extended all the facilities at their disposal to help with my scholarship and research and also collaborated personally with many aspects of my studies.

Generous support from the Bial Foundation of Porto, Portugal, allowed me to carry out a series of research projects that were crucial in developing and testing key parts of the First Sight model.

My research collaborators Christine Simmonds-Moore and Steve Moore have helped me define First Sight questions and subject them to test.

Many friends and colleagues have helped to clarify the ideas in this model and sharpen this presentation of them. While I could elaborate my gratitude for their different contributions, I will make do with an alphabetical list: John Ballard, Daryl Bem, Susan Gaylord, Bill Joines, Brian Josephson, Ed Kelly, Emily Williams Kelly, John Palmer, Karl Pribram, Dave Roberts, Dave Rogers, Gary Schwartz, Fiona Steinkamp, and the late Gertrude Schmeidler. Members of my writing group: Barbara Ensrud, Mike Jones, Steve Moore, Ruth Moose, and Valerie Yow helped with my presentation of key parts. Gary Schwartz deserves particular thanks for giving me the name of my model. On hearing the core ideas of it in an intensive work group one day, he thought for a moment and then blurted out: "Wow. So ESP isn't second sight, it's first sight!"

My editor at Rowman & Littlefield, Suzanne Staszak-Silva, has been helpful with her encouragement and (to say it tactfully) structure. Production editor Elaine McGarraugh and assistant editor Evan Wiig have also provided patient and careful assistance.

Without the advice of Sandra Martin I cannot imagine how I would have begun to negotiate the strange new territory of book publishing. Stacy Horn's advice and encouragement have also been helpful in this regard.

My children, Ferrell, Barnaby, and Jordan, have sustained me throughout the long odyssey leading to this book. Their unfailing love and support have shored up the floor beneath me, and they have all helped with this book by discussing concepts and critiquing text, as has my daughter-in-law, Ariel Nazryan, who donated many ideas both creative and practical. Ferrell has also conducted research in the model and reported findings at an international conference. Barnaby and Jordan have worked as trained raters on thousands of utterances of participants in various studies pertinent to the model. Also, Barnaby has acted as a study participant in research focused on creative persons, and Jordan has advised me on experimental design and statistical analysis.

My greatest debt of gratitude is to my wife, Jo. She has tolerated my odd obsession and the countless hours it has absorbed and has helped me in every aspect of my work. She has worked through every word of this text, sharpening the ideas, correcting the grammar, questioning me sternly when something didn't make sense, and celebrating with me when some new finding made something important newly clear. Without ever deserving such a loving partner, I marvel that I have had one.

References

Aarts, H., Chartrand, T., Custers, R., Danner, U., Dik, G., Jefferis, V. E., and Cheng, C. M. (2005). Social stereotypes and automatic goal pursuit. *Social Cognition* 23, 465–90.

Aarts, H., Custers, R., and Marien, H. (2008). Preparing and motivating behavior outside of awareness. *Science* 319, 1639.

Alberti, G. (1974). Psychopathology and parapsychology: Some possible contacts. In A. Angoff and B. Shapin (Eds.), *Parapsychology and the Sciences*, pp. 225–33. New York: Parapsychology Foundation.

Alexander, C. H., and Broughton, R. S. (2001). Cerebral hemisphere dominance and ESP performance in the autoganzfeld. *Journal of Parapsychology* 65, 397–416.

Allison, J. (1963). Cognitive structure and receptivity to low intensity stimulation. *Journal of Abnormal and Social Psychology* 67, 132–38.

Alvarez, F. (2010). Anticipatory alarm behavior in Bengalese finches. *Journal of Scientific Exploration* 24, 599–610.

Amabile, T. M., Goldfard, P., and Brackfield, S. C. (1990). Social influences on creativity: Evaluation, coaction, and surveillance. *Creativity Research Journal* 3, 6–21.

American Psychiatric Association (2004). *Diagnostic and statistical manual of mental disorders*. Washington, DC: American Psychiatric Association.

Anderson, M. (1966). The use of fantasy in testing for extrasensory perception. *Journal of the American Society for Psychical Research* 60, 150–63.

Anderson, M., and Gregory, E. (1959). A two-year program of tests for clairvoyance and precognition with a class of public school pupils. *Journal of Parapsychology* 23, 149–77.

Anderson, M., and White, R. (1956). Teacher-pupil attitudes and clairvoyance test results. *Journal of Parapsychology* 20, 141–67.

Anderson, M., and White, R. (1957). A further investigation of teacher-pupil attitudes and clairvoyance test results. *Journal of Parapsychology* 21, 81–97.

Anderson, M. C., and Green, C. (2001). Suppressing unwanted memories by executive control. *Nature* 410, 366–69.

Andre, E. (1972). Confirmation of PK action on electronic equipment. *Journal of Parapsychology* 36, 283–93.

Andreassi, J. L. (1989). *Psychophysiology: Human behavior and psychological response.* Hillsdale, NJ: Erlbaum Associates.

Angyal, A. (1941). *Foundations for a science of personality.* New York: Commonwealth Fund.

Antonuccio, D. O. (1996). Psychotherapy for depression: No stronger medicine. *American Psychologist* 50, 450–52.

Ashby, F. G., and Gott, R. E. (1988). Decision rules in the perception and categorization of multidimensional stimuli. *Journal of Experimental Psychology: Learning, Memory, and Cognition* 14, 33–53.

Ashton, M. C., Lee, K., and Paunonen, S. V. (2002). What is the central feature of extraversion?: Social attention versus reward sensitivity. *Journal of Personality and Social Psychology* 83, 245–51.

Aström, J. (1965). GESP and the MPI measures. *Journal of Parapsychology* 29, 292–93.

Autumn, K., Sitti, M., Liang, Y., Peattie, A., Hansen, W., Sponberg, S., Kenny, T., Fearing, R., Israelachvili, J., and Full, R. (2002). Evidence for van der Waals adhesion in gecko setae. *Proceedings of the National Academy of Sciences,* published online, doi:10.1073/pnas.192252799.

Avant, L. L. (1965). Vision in the ganzfeld. *Psychological Bulletin* 64, 246–58.

Baars, B. J. (1997). *In the theater of consciousness.* New York: Oxford University Press.

Baldwin, M. W., Fehr, B., Keedian, E., Seidel, M., and Thomson, D. W. (1993). An exploration of the relational schemata underlying attachment styles: Self–report and lexical decision approaches. *Personality and Social Psychology Bulletin* 19, 746–54.

Ball, C. T., and Hennessey, J. (2009). Subliminal priming of autobiographical memories. *Memory* 17, 311–22.

Ballard, J. A. (1980). Unconscious perception of hidden stimuli enclosed with ESP cards. *Journal of Parapsychology* 44, 319–40.

Ballard, J. A. (1991). Rychlakean theory and parapsychology. *Journal of the American Society for Psychical Research* 85, 167–81.

Ballard, J. A., Cohee, J. C., and Eldridge, T. M. (1983). Target affect, anxiety, and belief in ESP in relation to ESP scoring [Abstract]. In W. G. Roll, J. Beloff, and R. A. White (Eds.), *Research in parapsychology 1982* (pp. 105–96). Metuchen, NJ: Scarecrow Press.

Banham, K. M. (1966). Temporary high scoring by a child subject. *Journal of Parapsychology* 30, 106–13.

Banse, R. (1999). Automatic evaluation of self and significant others: Affective priming in close relationships. *Journal of Social and Personal Relationships* 16, 803–21.

Bargh, J. A. (1989). Conditional automaticity: Varieties of automatic influence in social perception and cognition. In J. Uleman and J. Bargh (Eds.), *Unintended thought* (pp. 3–51). New York: The Guilford Press.

Bargh, J. A. (1992). Does subliminality matter to social psychology? Awareness of the stimulus vs. awareness of its influence. In R. F. Bornstein and T. S. Pittman (Eds.), *Perception without awareness.* New York: The Guilford Press.

Bargh, J. A. (2006). Agenda 2006: What have we been priming all these years? On the development, mechanisms, and ecology of nonconscious social behavior. *European Journal of Social Psychology* 36, 147–68.

Bargh, J. A., Chen, M., and Burrows, L. (1996). Automaticity of social behavior: Direct effects of trait construct and stereotype activation on action. *Journal of Personality and Social Psychology* 71, 230–44.

Bargh, J. A., and Huang, J. Y. (2009). The selfish goal. In G. B. Moskowitz and H. Grant (Eds.), *The psychology of goals.* New York: The Guilford Press.

Bargh, J. A., and Tota, M. E. (1988). Context-dependent automatic processing in depression: Accessibility of negative constructs with regard to self but not others. *Journal of Personality and Social Psychology* 54, 925–39.

Bar-Haim, Y., Lamy, D., Pergamin, L., Bakermans-Kranenburg, M. J., and van IJzendoorn, M. H. (2007). Threat-related attentional bias in anxious and nonanxious individuals: A meta-analytic study. *Psychological Bulletin* 133, 1–24.

Barker, R. G., and Wright, H. F. (1971). *Midwest and its children: The psychological ecology of an American town.* Evanston, IL: Row, Peterson.

Barnes-Holmes, D., Barnes-Holmes, Y., Power, P., Hayden, E., Milne, R., and Stewart, I. (2006). Do you really know what you believe? Developing the Implicit Relational Assessment Procedure (IRAP) as a direct measure of implicit beliefs. *Irish Psychologist* 32, 169–77.

Barnett, L. A., and Klitzing, S. W. (2006). Boredom in free time: Relationships with personality, affect, and motivation for different gender, racial and ethnic student groups. *Leisure Sciences* 28, 223–34.

Barrett, W. (1962). *Irrational man: A study in existential philosophy.* New York: Doubleday Anchor Books.

Barron, F. X. (1958). The psychology of imagination. *Scientific American* 199, 150–56.

Barron, F. X. (1969). *Creative person and creative process.* New York: Holt, Rinehart & Wilson.

Barron, F. X. (1995). *No rootless flowers: An ecology of creative perspectives on creativity research.* New York: Hampton Press.

Barron, F. X., Barron, A., and Morturori, A. (Eds.). (1997). *Creators on creating: Awakening and cultivating the imaginative mind.* New York: Tarcher.

Barron, F. X., and Harrington, D. (1981). Creativity, intelligence and personality. *Annual Review of Psychology* 32, 439–76.

Barron, F. X., and Mordkoff, A. M. (1968). An attempt to relate creativity to possible extrasensory empathy as measured by physiological arousal in identical twins. *Journal of the American Society for Psychical Research* 62, 73–79.

Barron, F. X., and Welsh, G. S. (1952). Artistic perception as a possible factor in personality style: Its measurement by a figure preference test. *Journal of Psychology: Interdisciplinary and Applied* 33, 193–203.

Batcheldor, K. J. (1979). PK in sitter groups. *Psychoenergetic Systems* 3, 77–93.

Batcheldor, K. J. (1984). Contributions to the theory of PK induction from sitter-group work. *Journal of the Society for Psychical Research* 78, 105–22.

Batthyany, A., Kranz, G., and Erber, A. (2009). Moderating factors in precognitive habituation: The roles of situational vigilance, emotional reactivity and affect regulation. *Journal of the Society for Psychical Research* 73, 65–82.

Baumann, N., and Kuhl, J. (2005). Positive affect and flexibility: Overcoming the precedence of global over local processing. *Motivation and Emotion* 29, 123–34.

Beck, A. T. (1976). *Cognitive therapy and the emotional disorders.* New York: International Universities Press.

Beck, A. T., and Clark, D. A. (1997). An information processing model of anxiety: Automatic and strategic processes. *Behavior Research and Therapy* 35, 49–58.

Beck, E., Burnet, K. L., and Vosper, J. (2006). Birth order effects on facets of extraversion. *Personality and Individual Differences* 40, 953–59.

Bell, Charles. (1948). Idea of a new anatomy of the brain: Submitted for the observation of his friends. In W. Dennis (Ed.), *Readings in the history of psychology* (pp. 113–24). London: Amberg Press.

Bell, J. S. (1964). On the Einstein-Podolsky-Rosen paradox. *Physics I*, 195–200.

Bellis, J., and Morris, R. (1980). Openness, closedness and psi [Abstract]. In W. G. Roll (Ed.), *Research in parapsychology 1979* (pp. 98–99). Metuchen, NJ: Scarecrow Press.

Beloff, J. (1977). Historical overview. In B. B. Wolman (Ed.), *Handbook of parapsychology* (pp. 3–24). New York: Van Nostrand Reinhold Company.

Beloff, J., and Bate, D. (1970). Research report for the year 1968–1969. *Journal of the Society for Psychical Research* 47, 403–20.

Bem, D. J. (2003). Precognitive habituation: Replicable evidence for a process of anomalous cognition. In S. Wilson (Chair), *Proceedings of Presented Papers from the Forty-sixth Annual Convention of the Parapsychological Association, 2003* (pp. 6–20), Vancouver, Canada.

Bem, D. J. (2004). Precognitive avoidance and precognitive déjà vu. *Proceedings of Presented Papers: The Parapsychological Association 47th Annual Convention, 2004* (pp. 430–32), Vienna, Austria.

Bem, D. J. (2005). Precognitive aversion. *Proceedings of Presented Papers: The Parapsychological Association 48th Annual Convention,* (pp. 31–35), Petaluma, CA.

Bem, D. J. (2011). Feeling the future: Experimental evidence for anomalous retroactive influences on cognition and affect. *Journal of Personality and Social Psychology* 100, 407–25.

Bem, D. J., and Honorton, C. (1994). Does psi exist? Replicable evidence for an anomalous process of information transfer. *Psychological Bulletin* 115, 4–18.

Bem, D. J., Palmer, J., and Broughton, R. S. (2001). Updating the ganzfeld database: A victim of its own success? *Journal of Parasychology* 65, 207–18.

Berger, R. E. (1989). A critical examination of the Blackmore psi experiments. *Journal of Parapsychology* 51, 296–309.

Berman, S. (1979). A study of memory retrieval and psi in a nonwestern academic testing situation. *Journal of Parapsychology* 43, 52.

Bevan, J. M. (1947). The relation of attitude to success in ESP scoring. *Journal of the American Society for Psychical Research* 83, 123–44.

Bevan, W. J., and Zener, K. (1952). Some influences of past experience upon the perceptual threshold of visual form. *American Journal of Psychology* 65, 434–42.

Bexton, W. H., Heron, W., and Scott, T. H. (1954). Effects of decreased variation in the sensory environment. *Canadian Journal of Psychology* 8, 70–76.

Bierman, D. (1995). A free response precognition experiment via the World Wide Web. The Parapsychological Association 38th Annual Convention Proceedings of Presented Papers, 38–42.

Bierman, D. (2000a). Anomalous baseline effects in mainstream emotion research using psychophysiological variables. *The Parapsychological Association 43rd Annual Convention Proceedings of Presented Papers*, 34–47.

Bierman, D. (2000b). On the nature of anomalous phenomena: Another reality between the work of subjective consciousness and the objective world of physics? In P. van Loocke (Ed.), *The physical nature of consciousness* (pp. 269–92). New York: Benjamin Publications.

Bierman, D. J., and Radin, D. I. (1997). *Anomalous anticipatory response on randomized future conditions*. Paper presented at Toward a Science of Consciousness, Tucson IV, Tucson, AZ.

Bierman, D. J., and Radin, D. I. (1998). Conscious and anomalous nonconscious emotional processes: A reversal of the arrow of time? In S. R. Hameroff, A. W. Kaszniak, and D. Chalmers (Eds.), *Toward a Science of Consciousness, Tucson III* (pp. 367–86). MIT University Press.

Bierman, D. J., and Scholte, H. S. (2002). Anomalous anticipatory brain activation preceding exposure of emotional and neutral pictures. *Perceptual and Motor Skills* 84, 689–90.

Blackmore, S. J. (1980). Correlations between ESP and memory. *European Journal of Parapsychology* 3, 127–47.

Blackmore, S. J. (1987). The elusive open mind: Ten years of negative research in parapsychology. *Skeptical Inquirer* 11, 244–55.

Blair, I. (2002). The malleability of automatic stereotypes and prejudice. *Personality and Social Psychology Review* 6, 242–61.

Bless, H., and Schwarz, N. (1998). Context effects in political judgment: Assimilation and contrast as a function of categorization processes. *European Journal of Social Psychology* 28, 159–72.

Blum, G. S. (1955). Perceptual defense revisited. *Journal of Abnormal and Social Psychology* 51, 24–29.

Bodner, G. E., and Masson, M. E. J. (2001). Prime validity affects masked repetition priming: Evidence for an episodic resource account of priming. *Journal of Memory and Language* 45, 616–47.

Bohm, D. (1990). A new theory of the relationship of mind and matter. *Philosophical Psychology* 3, 271–86.

Bohm, D., and Hiley, B. (1993). *The undivided universe*. New York: Rutledge.

Bonnano, G. A., and Stillings, N. A. (1986). Preference, familiarity and recognition after repeated brief exposures to random geometric shapes. *American Journal of Psychology* 99, 403–15.

Boring, E. G. (1950). *A History of Experimental Psychology*. New York: Appleton Century Crofts.

Bornstein, R. F. (1989). Exposure and affect: Overview and meta-analysis of research, 1968–1987. *Psychological Bulletin* 106, 265–89.

Bornstein, R. F., Kale, A. R., and Cornell, K. R. (1990). Boredom as a limiting condition of the mere exposure effect. *Journal of Personality and Social Psychology* 58, 791–800.

Bornstein, R. F., and Masling, J. M. (1998). *Empirical perspectives on the psychoanalytic unconscious*. Washington, DC: American Psychological Association.

Bornstein, R. F., Ng, H. M., Gallagher, H. A., Kloss, D. M., and Regier, N. G. (2008). Contrasting effects of self-schema priming on lexical decisions and interpersonal

Stroop task performance: Evidence for a cognitive/interactionist model of interpersonal dependency. *Journal of Personality* 73, 731–61.

Bornstein, R. F., and Pittman, T. S. (Eds.) (1992). *Perception without awareness: Cognitive, clinical and social perspectives.* New York: Guilford Press.

Boss, M. (1958). *Analysis of dreams.* New York: Philosophical Library.

Boss, M. (1977). *I dreamt last night.* New York: Gardner Press, Inc.

Boss, M. (1979). *Existential foundations of medicine and psychology.* New York: Jason Aronson.

Braud, L. W. (1975). Openness vs. closedness and its relationship to psi [Abstract]. In J. D. Morris, W. G. Roll, and R. L. Morris (Eds.), *Research in parapsychology 1975* (pp. 155–59). Metuchen, NJ: Scarecrow Press.

Braud, L. W. (1976). Openness vs. closedness and its relationship to psi [Abstract]. In J. D. Morris, W. G. Roll, and R. L. Morris (Eds.), *Research in parapsychology 1976* (pp. 162–65). Metuchen, NJ: Scarecrow Press.

Braud, L. W. (1980). Openness vs. closedness and its relationship to psi [Abstract]. In W. G. Roll (Ed.), *Research in parapsychology 1979* (pp. 96–98). Metuchen, NJ: Scarecrow Press.

Braud, L. W., and Braud, W. G. (1974). The influence of relaxation and tension on the psi process [Abstract]. In W. G. Roll (Ed.), *Research in parapsychology 1977* (pp. 135–43). Metuchen, NJ: Scarecrow Press.

Braud, L. W., and Braud, W. G. (1978). Psychokinetic effects upon a random event generator under conditions of limited feedback to volunteers and experimenters [Abstract]. In J. D. Morris, W. G. Roll, and R. L. Morris (Eds.), *Research in parapsychology 1973* (pp. 11–13). Metuchen, NJ: Scarecrow Press.

Braud, L. W., and Braud, W. G. (1979). Psychokinetic effects upon a random event generator under conditions of limited feedback to volunteers and experimenters. *Journal of the American Society for Psychical Research* 50, 21–32.

Braud, L. W., and Loewenstern, K. (1982). Creativity and psi [Abstract]. In W. G. Roll, R. L. Morris, and R. A. White (Eds.), *Research in parapsychology 1981* (pp. 111–15). Metuchen, NJ: Scarecrow Press.

Braud, W. G. (1975). Conscious versus unconscious clairvoyance in the context of an academic examination. *Journal of Parapsychology* 39, 277–88.

Braud, W. G. (1976). Psychokinesis in aggressive and nonaggressive fish with mirror presentation feedback for hits: Some preliminary experiments. *Journal of Parapsychology* 40, 296–307.

Braud, W. G. (1983). Prolonged visualization practice and psychokinesis: A pilot study [Abstract]. In W. G. Roll, J. Beloff, and R. A. White (Eds.), *Research in parapsychology 1982* (pp. 187–89). Metuchen, NJ: Scarecrow Press.

Braud, W. G. (2003). *Distant mental influence.* Charlottesville, VA: Hampton Roads Publishing.

Braud, W. G., and Hartgrove, J. (1978). Clairvoyance and psychokinesis in transcendental meditators and matched control subjects: A preliminary study. *European Journal of Parapsychology* 1, 6–36.

Braud, W. G., Shafer, D., and Andrews, S. (1993). Reactions to an unseen gaze (remote attention): A review, with new data on autonomic staring detection. *Journal of Parapsychology* 57, 373–90.

Braud, W. G., Shafer, D., and Mulgrew, D. (1983). Psi functioning and assessed cognitive lability. *Journal of the American Society for Psychical Research 77*, 193–208.

Braud, W. G., Smith, G., Andrew, K., and Willis, S. (1976). Psychokinetic influences on random number generators during evocation of "analytic" vs. "nonanalytic" modes of information processing [Abstract]. In J. D. Morris, W. G. Roll, and R. L. Morris (Eds.), *Research in parapsychology 1975* (pp. 85–88). Metuchen, NJ: Scarecrow Press.

Braud, W. G., Wood, R., and Braud, L. W. (1975). Free-response GESP performance during an experimental hypnagogic state induced by visual and acoustic ganzfeld techniques. A replication and extension. *Journal of the American Society for Psychical Research 69*, 105–13.

Braude, S. (1996). *The Limits of Influence Vol. 1*, (pp. 1–36). Lanham, MD: University Press of America.

Brewer, M. B. (1988). A dual process model of impression formation. In R. S. Wyer Jr. and T. K. Srull (Eds.), *Advances in social cognition Vol. 1*, (pp. 1–36). Hillsdale, NJ: Erlbaum.

Brewin, C. R., and Andrews, B. (2000). Psychological defense mechanisms: The example of repression. *Psychologist 13*, 615–17.

Brier, R. M., and Tyminski, W. V. (1970a). Psi application: Part I. A preliminary attempt. *Journal of Parapsychology 34*, 1–25.

Brier, R. M., and Tyminski, W. V. (1970b). Psi application: Part II. The majority vote technique. *Journal of Parapsychology 34*, 26–36.

Broca, P. (1861). Remarques sur le siege de la faculte du langage articule, suivies d'une observation d'aphemit (Perte de la parole). *Bulletin de la Société Anatomique 6*, 330–57.

Broughton, R. S. (1991). *Parapsychology: The controversial science*. New York: Ballantine Books.

Broughton, R. S. (2002). Telepathy: Revisiting its roots. *Proceedings of the Symposium of the Bial Foundation 4*, 131–46.

Broughton, R. S. (2004). Exploring the reliability of the "presentiment" effect. *Proceedings of the Parapsychology Association 47*, 15–26.

Broughton, R. S., and Alexander, C. H. (1997). Autoganzfeld II: An attempted replication of the PRL ganzfeld research. *Journal of Parapsychology 61*, 209–26.

Broughton, R. S., and Perlstrom, J. R. (1986). PK experiments with a competitive computer game. *Journal of Parapsychology 50*, 193–211.

Broughton, R. S., and Perlstrom, J. R. (1992). PK in a competitive computer game: A replication. *Journal of Parapsychology 56*, 291–306.

Bruchac, J. (1987). *Survival this way: Interviews with American Indian poets*. Scottsdale, AZ: University of Arizona Press.

Brugmans, H. J. F. (1922). Une communication sur des experiences telepathiques au Laboratoire de Psychologie a Groninque faites par M. Heymans. Docteur Weinberg, et Docteur H. J. F. Brugmans. In *Le Compte Rendu Officiel du Premier Congres International des Ressearches Psychiques*. Copenhagen.

Bryant, R. A., and Panasetis, P. (2005). The role of panic in acute dissociative reactions following trauma. *British Journal of Clinical Psychology 44*, 489–94.

Bucci, W. (2007). Dissociation from the perspective of multiple code theory: Part II; The spectrum of dissociative processes in the psychoanalytic relationship. *Contemporary Psychoanalysis* 43, 305–26.

Buckner, J. D., Maner, J. K., and Schmidt, N. B. (2010). Difficulty disengaging attention from social threat in social anxiety. *Cognitive Therapy and Research* 34, 99–105.

Budd, R. J. (1993). *Jung type indicator: The technical manual.* Letchworth, UK: Psytech International Ltd.

Burkhart, R. C., and Bernheim, G. (1963). *Object question test manual.* University Park: The Pennsylvania State University.

Burton, Jean. (1944). *Heyday of a wizard: Daniel Home, the medium.* New York: Alfred A. Knopf.

Cadoret, R. J. (1952). Effect of novelty in test conditions on ESP performance. *Journal of Parapsychology* 16, 192–203.

Cadoret, R. J. (1955). The reliable application of ESP. *Journal of Parapsychology* 19, 203–27.

Calkins, C. C. (1982). *Mysteries of the unexplained.* Pleasantville, NY: Readers Digest Books.

Campbell, L., Simpson, J. A., Stewart, M., and Manning, J. (2003). Putting personality in social context: Extraversion, emergent leadership, and the availability of rewards. *Personality and Social Psychology Bulletin* 29, 1547–59.

Canli, T., Desmond, J. E., Zhao, Z., and Gabrieli, J. D. E. (2002). Sex differences in the neural basis of emotional memories. *Proceedings of the National Academy of Sciences* 99, 10789–94.

Carpenter, J. C. (1965). An exploratory test of ESP in relation to anxiety proneness. In J. B. Rhine (Ed.), *Parapsychology from Duke to FRNM*, Durham, NC: Parapsychology Press.

Carpenter, J. C. (1966). Scoring effects within the run. *Journal of Parapsychology* 30, 73–83.

Carpenter, J. C. (1967). Decline of variability of scoring across a period of effort. *Journal of Parapsychology* 31, 179–91.

Carpenter, J. C. (1968). Two related studies on mood and precognition run-score variance. *Journal of Parapsychology* 32, 75–89.

Carpenter, J. C. (1969). Further study on a mood adjective check list and ESP run-score variance. *Journal of Parapsychology* 33, 48–56.

Carpenter, J. C. (1971). The differential effect and hidden target differences consisting of erotic and neutral stimuli. *Journal of the American Society for Psychical Research* 65, 204–14.

Carpenter, J. C. (1975). Information amplification techniques applied to low but reliable signal levels. Paper presented at the annual conference of the American Association for the Advancement of Science, New York, January 1975.

Carpenter, J. C. (1977). Intrasubject and subject-agent effects in ESP experiments. In B. Wolman (Ed.), *Handbook of parapsychology* (pp. 202–72), New York: Van Nostrand Reinhold.

Carpenter, J. C. (1983). Prediction of forced-choice ESP performance: Part I. A mood-adjective scale for predicting the variance of ESP run scores. *Journal of Parapsychology* 47, 191–216.

Carpenter, J. C. (1988). Parapsychology and the psychotherapy session: Their phenomenological confluence. *Journal of Parapsychology* 52, 213–24.

Carpenter, J. C. (1991). Prediction of forced-choice ESP performance: Part III: Three attempts to retrieve coded information using mood reports and repeated-guessing technique. *Journal of Parapsychology* 55, 227–80.

Carpenter, J. C. (2001). A psychological analysis of ganzfeld protocols. *Journal of Parapsychology* 65, 358–59.

Carpenter, J. C. (2002). The intrusion of anomalous communication in group and individual psychotherapy: Clinical observations and a research project. *Proceedings of the Symposium of the Bial Foundation* 4, 255–74.

Carpenter, J. C. (2003). *Manual for the projective assessment of ganzfeld protocols.* Research document of the Rhine Research Center. Available by request.

Carpenter, J. C. (2004). First Sight: Part one, a model of psi and the mind. *Journal of Parapsychology* 68, 217–54.

Carpenter, J. C. (2005a). Implicit measures of participants' experiences in the ganzfeld: Confirmation of previous relationships in a new sample. Proceedings of Presented Papers: The Parapsychological Association 48th Annual Convention, 36–45.

Carpenter, J. C. (2005b). First Sight: Part two, elaborations of a model of psi and the mind. *Journal of Parapsychology* 69, 63–112.

Carpenter, J.C. (2006). The manipulation of ganzfeld ESP performance by the control of implicit percipient variables. Unpublished report to the Bial Foundation (Available from James Carpenter, Rhine Research Center, Durham, NC).

Carpenter, J. C. (2008). Relations between ESP and memory in light of the first sight model of psi. *Journal of Parapsychology* 72, 47–76.

Carpenter, J. C. (2010). Laboratory psi effects may be put to practical use: Two pilot studies. *Journal of Scientific Exploration* 24, 47–76.

Carpenter, J. C., and Carpenter, J. (1967). Decline of variability of ESP scoring across a period of effort. *Journal of Parapsychology* 31, 179–91.

Carpenter, J. C., and Simmonds-Moore, C. (2009a). ESP contributes to the unconscious formation of a preference. Paper presented at the meeting of the Parapsychological Association, Seattle, August 2009.

Carpenter, J. C., and Simmonds-Moore, C. (2009b). Some tests of a model of psi functioning, examining the effects of stable subject dispositions, the action of target associated psi primes, and the effect of psi information on the expression of the Mere Exposure Effect. Unpublished report to the Bial Foundation (Available from James Carpenter, Rhine Research Center, Durham, NC).

Carrington, H. (2005). *Eusapia Palladino and her phenomena.* Kila, MT: Kessinger Publishing.

Carter, C. (2007). *Parapsychology and the skeptics: A scientific argument for the existence of ESP.* Pittsburgh, PA: Sterlinghouse Press.

Cattell, R. B. (1957). *Personality and motivation: Structure and measurement.* Yonkers-on-Hudson, NY: World Books.

Chaiken, S. (1980). Heuristic versus systematic information processing and the use of source versus message cues in persuasion. *Journal of Personality and Social Psychology* 39, 752–66.

Chartrand, T. L., and Bargh, J. A. (1999). The chameleon effect: The perception-behavior link and social interaction. *Journal of Personality and Social Psychology* 76, 893–910.

Chartrand, T. L., Dalton, A. N., and Fitzsimons, G. J. (2007). Nonconscious relationship reactance: When significant others prime opposing goals. *Journal of Experimental Social Psychology* 43, 719–26.

Chen, M., and Bargh, J. A. (1997). Nonconscious behavioral confirmation processes: The self-fulfilling consequences of automatic stereotype activation. *Journal of Experimental Social Psychology* 33, 541–60.

Child, I. L. (1977). Statistical regression artifact in parapsychology. *Journal of Parapsychology* 41, 10–22.

Child, I. L. (1985). Psychology and anomalous observations: The question of ESP in dreams. *American Psychologist* 40, 1219–30.

Coles, M. G., Gale, A., and Kline, P. (1971). Personality and habituation of the orienting reaction: Tonic and response measures of electrodermal activity. *Psychophysiology* 8, 54–63.

Colley, A., Roberts, N., and Chipps, A. (1985). Sex-role identity, personality and participation in team and individual sports by males and females. *International Journal of Sport Psychology* 16, 103–12.

Collins, A. M., and Loftus, E. F. (1975). A spreading activation theory of semantic processing. *Psychological Review*, 82, 407–28.

Colwell, J., Schroder, S., and Sladen, D. (2000). The ability to detect unseen staring: A literature review and empirical tests. *British Journal of Psychology* 91, 71–85.

Conty, L., Gimmig, D., Belletier, C., George, N. and Huguet, P. (2010). The cost of being watched: Stroop interference increases under concomitant eye contact. *Cognition* 115, 133–39.

Cooper, C., and Taylor, R. (1999). Personality and performance on a complex cognitive task. *Perceptual and Motor Skills* 88, 1384.

Coover, J. E. (1913). "The feeling of being stared at"—Experimental. *The American Journal of Psychology* 24, 570–75.

Costa, P. T., and McCrae, R. R. (1985). *The NEO personality inventory manual.* Odessa, FL: Psychological Assessment Resources.

Costa, P. T., and McCrae, R. R. (2009). The five-factor model and the NEO inventories. In J. N. Butcher (Ed.), *Oxford handbook of personality assessment* (pp. 299–322). New York: Oxford University Press.

Cox, W. E. (1956). Precognition: An analysis, II. *Journal of the American Society for Psychical Research* 50, 99–109.

Crandall, J. E. (1985). Effects of favorable and unfavorable conditions on the psi-missing displacement effect. *Journal of the American Society for Psychical Research* 79, 27–38.

Crandall, J. E. (1998). Effects of extrinsic motivation on PK performance and its relations to state anxiety and extroversion. In N. L. Zingrone, M. J. Schlitz, C. S. Alvarado, and J. Milton (Eds.), *Research in parapsychology, 1993: Abstracts and papers from the thirty-sixth annual convention of the Parapsychological Association, 1993* (pp. 96–101). Lanham, MD: Scarecrow.

Crick, F. (1995). *Astonishing hypothesis: The scientific search for the soul.* New York: Scribner.

Csikszentmihalyi, M. (1988). *Optimal experience: Psychological studies of flow in consciousness.* New York: Cambridge University Press.

Csikszentmihalyi, M. (1990). The domain of creativity. In M. A. Runco and R. A. Albert (Eds.), *Theories of creativity* (pp. 190–212). Newberry Park, CA: Sage.

Csikszentmihalyi, M. (1991). *Flow: The psychology of optimal experience.* New York: Harper and Row.

Custers, R. (2009). How does our unconscious know what we want?: The role of affect in goal representations. In G. B. Moskowitz and H. Grant (Eds.), *The psychology of goals* (pp. 179–202). New York: The Guilford Press.

Daino, A. (1985). Personality traits of adolescent tennis players. *International Journal of Sport Psychology* 16, 120–25.

Dalkvist, J., and Westerlund, J. (1998). Five experiments on telepathic communication of emotions. *Journal of Parapsychology* 62, 219–54.

Dalton, K. (1997a). Exploring the links: Creativity and psi in the ganzfeld. Proceedings of Presented Papers: The Parapsychological Association 40th Annual Convention, 119–34.

Dalton, K. (1997b). *The relationship between creativity and anomalous cognition in the ganzfeld.* Unpublished doctoral dissertation, Edinburgh University, Edinburgh, Scotland.

Dalton, K., Steinkamp, F., and Sherwood, S. J. (1999). A dream GESP experiment using dynamic targets and consensus vote. *Journal of the American Society for Psychical Research* 93(2), 146–66.

Dalton, K., and Utts, J. (1995). Sex pairings, target type, and geomagnetism in the PRL automated ganzfeld series. Proceedings of the 38th Annual Convention of the Parapsychological Association, Durham, NC, 99–112.

Darley, J. M., and Gross, P. H. (1983). A hypothesis-confirming bias in labeling effects. *Journal of Personality and Social Psychology* 44, 20–33.

DaSilva, F. E., Pilato, S., and Hiraoka, R. (2003). Ganzfeld vs. no ganzfeld: An exploratory study of the effect of ganzfeld conditions on ESP. *Journal of Parapsychology* 67, 250–51.

Dauber, R. B. (1984). Subliminal psychodynamic activation in depression: On the role of autonomy in depressed college women. *Journal of Abnormal and Social Psychology* 93, 9–18.

Davis, G. A., Peterson, J. M., and Farley, F. H. (1974). Attitudes, motivation, sensation seeking, and belief in ESP as predictors of real creative behavior. *Journal of Creative Behavior* 81, 31–39.

Dean, E. D. (1962). The plethysmograph as an indicator of ESP. *Journal of the Society for Psychical Research* 41, 351–53.

Dean, E. D., and Taetzsch, R. (1963). An ESP test for speakers using computer scoring. *Journal of Parapsychology* 27, 275–76.

Dean, E. D., and Taetzsch, R. (1970). Psi in the casino: Taetzsch method. In W. G. Roll, R. L. Morris, and J. D. Morris (Eds.), *Proceedings of the Parapsychological Association: Number 7, 1970* (pp. 14–15). Durham, NC: Parapsychological Association.

DeCoster, J., and Claypool, H. M. (2004). A meta-analysis of priming effects on impression formation supporting a general model of information biases. *Personality and Social Psychology Review* 8, 2–27.

Debes, J., and Morris, R. L. (1982). Comparison of striving and non-striving instructional sets in a PK study. *Journal of Parapsychology* 46, 297–312.

De Graaf, T. K., and Houtkooper, J. M. (2004). Anticipatory awareness of emotionally charged targets by individuals with histories of emotional trauma. *Journal of Parapsychology* 68, 93–127.

Dellas, M., and Gaier, E. L. (1970). Sales effectiveness and personality characteristics. *Psychological Research Journal* 7, 59–67.

Dellas, M., and Gaier, E. L. (1983). Identification of creativity: The individual. *Psychological Bulletin* 73, 55–73.

Denissen, J. J. A., and Penke, L. (2008). Motivational individual reaction norms underlying the Five-Factor model of personality: First steps towards a theory-based conceptual framework. *Journal of Research in Personality* 42, 1285–1302.

Devereux, G. (1953). *Psychoanalysis and the occult.* New York: International Universities Press.

Dijksterhuis, A. (2004). Think different: The merits of unconscious thought in preference development and decision making. *Journal of Personality and Social Psychology* 87, 586–98.

Dijksterhuis, A. (2006). A theory of unconscious thought. *Perspectives on Psychological Science* 1, 95–109.

Dijksterhuis, A., Preston, J., Wegner, D. M., and Aarts, H. (2008). Effects of subliminal priming of self and God on self-attribution of authorship for events. *Journal of Experimental Social Psychology* 44, 2–9.

Dijksterhuis, A., and Smith, P. K. (2002). Affective habituation: Subliminal exposure to extreme stimuli decreases their extremity. *Emotion* 2(3), 203–14.

Dillard, A. (1974). *Pilgrim at tinker creek.* New York: Harper Collins.

Dingwall, E. J. (1968). Hypnotism in France 1800 to 1900. In E. J. Dingwall (Ed.), *Abnormal hypnotic phenomena*, Vol. I. New York: Barnes and Noble.

Dixon, N. F. (1981). *Preconscious processing.* Chichester, UK: Wiley.

Dollinger, S. I., and Clancy, S. M. (1993). Identity, self and personality: II. Glimpses through the autophotographic eye. *Journal of Personality and Social Psychology* 64, 1064–71.

Dossey, L. (2009). *The power of premonitions.* Hialeah, FL: Dutton Press.

Dunne, B. J., Dobyns, Y. H., Jahn, R. G., and Thompson, A. (1994). Series position effects in random event generator experiments. *Journal of Scientific Exploration* 8, 197–215.

Dunne, J. W. (1927). *An experiment with time.* New York: Macmillan.

Ebbinghaus, H. (1885 [1964]). *Memory.* Trans. H. A. Ruger and C. E. Bussenius. New York: Dover.

Edelstein, S. (1992). *Insight and psychotherapy outcome.* Unpublished doctoral dissertation, Wright Institute Graduate School of Psychology.

Edge, H. I. (1978). A philosophical justification for the conformance behavior model. *Journal of the American Society of Psychical Research* 72, 215–31.

Edge, H. I., Morris, R. L., Palmer, J., and Rush, J. H. (1986). *Foundations of parapsychology.* Boston: Routledge and Kegan Paul.

Ehrenwald, J. (1942). Telepathy in dreams. *British Journal of Medical Psychology* 19, 313–23.

Ehrenwald, J. (1948). *Telepathy and medical psychology.* New York: Norton.

Ehrenwald, J. (1955). *New dimensions in deep analysis.* New York: Grune and Stratton.

Ehrenwald, J. (1970). *The ESP experience.* New York: Basic Books.

Ehrenwald, J. (1976). Parapsychology and the seven dragons: A neuropsychiatric model of psi phenomena. In G. R. Schmeidler (Ed.), *Parapsychology: Its relation to physics, biology, psychology and psychiatry.* Metuchen, NJ: Scarecrow Press.

Ehrenwald, J. (1977). Psi phenomena and brain research. In B. Wolman et al. (Ed.), *Handbook of parapsychology* (pp. 716–29). New York: Van Nostrand Reinhold.

Eisenberg, H., and Donderi, D. C. (1979). Telepathic transfer of emotional information in humans. *Journal of Psychology* 103, 19–44.

Eisenbud, J. (1946). Telepathy and the problems of psychoanalysis. *Psychoanalytic Quarterly* 15, 32–87. (Also in G. Devereux (Ed.), *Psychoanalysis and the occult.* New York: International Universities Press, 1953.)

Eisenbud, J. (1963). Psi and the nature of things. *International Journal of Parapsychology* 5, 245–73.

Eisenbud, J. (1967). *The world of Ted Serios.* New York: William Morrow.

Eisenbud, J. (1969). Chronologically extraordinary psi correspondences in the psychoanalytic setting. *Psychoanalytic Quarterly* 56, 9–27.

Eisenbud, J. (1970). *Psi and psychoanalysis.* New York: Grune and Stratton.

Ellenberger, H. F. (1970). *The discovery of the unconscious.* New York: Basic Books.

Emmerich, D. (1976). The effects of word associations on psi-memory interaction. *Journal of Parapsychology* 40, 56–57.

Engel, L., and Ferguson, T. (1990). *Imaginary crimes: Why we punish ourselves and how to stop.* Boston: Houghton Mifflin.

Epstein, S. (1990). Cognitive-experiential self-theory. In L. Pervin (Ed.), *Handbook of personality theory and research: Theory and research* (pp. 165–92). New York: Guilford Publications, Inc.

Epstein, S. (1994). Integration of the cognitive and the psychodynamic unconscious. *American Psychologist* 49, 709–24.

Erdelyi, M. H. (1990). Repression, reconstruction and defense. In J. L. Singer (Ed.), *Repression and dissociation.* Chicago: University of Chicago Press.

Erdelyi, M. H. (1988). Hypermnesia and insight. In A. J. Marcel and E. Bisiach (Eds.), *Consciousness in contemporatory science.* Oxford: Clarendon Press.

Etaugh, C. F. (1969). Experimenter and subject variables in verbal conditioning. *Psychological Reports* 25, 575–80.

Evans, L., and Thalbourne, M. (1993). The feeling of being stared at: A parapsychological investigation. *Journal of the American Society for Psychical Research* 93, 309–25.

Eysenck, H. J. (1956). The inheritance of extraversion-introversion. *Acta Psychologica* 12, 95–119.

Eysenck, H. J. (1957). *The dynamics of anxiety and hysteria.* London: Routledge and Kegan Paul.

Eysenck, H. J. (1967). *The biological basis of personality.* Springfield, IL: C. C. Thomas.

Eysenck, H. J. (1970). *The structure of human personality.* New York: Methuen.

Eysenck, H. J. (1995). *Genius: The natural history of creativity.* Cambridge, England: Cambridge University Press.

Eysenck, H. J., and Eysenck, S. B. G. (1975). *Manual of the Eysenck personality questionnaire.* London: Hodder and Stoughton.

Eysenck, M. W., Derakshan, N., Santos, R., and Calvo, M. G. (2007). Anxiety and cognitive performance: Attentional control theory. *Emotion* 7, 336–53.

Faithorn, L., Edison, R., Jenks, S., Tyndall, S., and Isaacs, J. D. (1988). An ethnographic study of the "remote action project": A psychokinesis training program [Abstract]. In D. H. Weiner and R. L. Morris (Eds.), *Research in parapsychology 1987* (pp. 27–31). Metuchen, NJ: Scarecrow Press.

Fazio, R. H., Jackson, J. R., Dunton, B. C., and Williams, C. J. (1995). Variability in automatic activation as an unobstrusive measure of racial attitudes: A bona fide pipeline? *Journal of Personality and Social Psychology* 69, 1013–27.

Fazio, R. H., Powell, M. C., and Herr, P. M. (1983). Toward a process model of the attitude-behavior relation: Accessing one's attitude upon mere observation of the attitude object. *Journal of Personality and Social Psychology* 44, 723–35.

Feather, S. R. (1967). A quantitative comparison of memory and ESP. *Journal of Parapsychology* 31, 93–98.

Feather, S. R., and Schmicker, M. (2005). *The Gift: ESP, the extraordinary experiences of ordinary people.* New York: St. Martin's Press.

Feist, G. J. (1998). A meta-analysis of the impact of personality on scientific and artistic creativity. *Personality and Social Psychology Review* 2, 290–309.

Feist, G. J., and Runco, M. A. (1993). Trends in the creativity literature: An analysis of research in the *Journal of Creative Behavior* (1967–1989). *Creativity Research Journal* 6, 271–86.

Feller, W. (1968). Laws of large numbers, ch. 10, in T*An Introduction to probability theory and its applications, vol. 1, 3rd ed.*T New York: Wiley, pp. 228–47.

Fellini, F. (1997). Miscellany. In F. X. Barron (Ed.), *Creators on creating: Awakening and cultivating the imaginative mind.* New York: Jeremy P. Tarcher/Putnam.

Fenigstein, A. (1979). Self-consciousness, self-attention, and social interaction. *Journal of Personality and Social Psychology* 37, 75–86.

Fisher, C. (1988). Further observations on the Poetzl phenomenon: The effects of subliminal visual stimulation on dreams, images, and hallucinations. *Psychoanalysis and Contemporary Thought* 11, 3–56.

Fisk, G. W., and West, D. J. (1956). ESP and mood: Report of a "mass" experiment. *Journal of the Society for Psychical Research* 38, 1–7.

Fisk, G. W., and West, D. J. (1957). Towards accurate predictions from ESP data. *Journal of the Society for Psychical Research* 39, 157–62.

Flavell, J. H., and Draguns, J. (1957). A microgenetic approach to perception and thought. *Psychological Bulletin* 54, 197–217.

Fleeson, W. (2001). Toward a structure- and process-integrated view of personality: Traits as density distributions of states. *Journal of Personality and Social Psychology* 80, 1011–27.

Fleeson, W. (2007). Situation-based contingencies underlying trait-content manifestation in behavior. *Journal of Personality* 75, 825–61.

Flew, A. (1989). Evidencing the improbable and the impossible. In G. Zollschan, J. F. Schumacher, and G. F. Walsh (Eds.), *Exploring the paranormal: Different perspectives on belief and experience.* Dorsett, England: Prism Press.

Flournoy, T. (1900). *From India to the planet Mars: A study of a case of somnanbulism with glossolalia.* New York: Harper & Bros.

Fodor, N. (1942). Telepathic dreams. *American Imago* 3, 61–83.

Fodor, N. (1949). *The search for the beloved.* New York: Hermitage Press.

Forwald, H. (1954). Chronological decline effect in a PK placement experiment. *Journal of Parapsychology* 18, 32–36.

Fox, E. (1996). Selective processing of threatening words in anxiety: The role of awareness. *Cognition and Emotion* 10, 449–80.

Fox, E., Russo, R., and Georgiou, G. A. (2005). Anxiety modulates the degree of attentive resources required to process emotional faces. *Cognitive, Affective and Behavioral Neuroscience* 5, 396–404.

Freedman, S., and Clauser, J. (1972). Experimental test of local hidden variables theories. *Physical Review Letters* 28, 934–41.

Freeman, J., Butcher, H. J., and Christie, T. (1971). *Creativity: A selective review of research.* London, England: Social Research and Higher Learning.

Freeman, J., and Nielsen, W. (1964). Precognition score deviations as related to anxiety levels. *Journal of Parapsychology* 28, 239–49.

Freud, A. (1937). *The ego and the mechanisms of defence.* Trans. C. Baines. London: Hogarth. (Original work published 1936.)

Freud, S. (1892 [1963]). On the psychical mechanism of hysterical phenomena. In Philip Rief (Ed.), *The collected papers of Sigmund Freud: Early psychoanalytic writings* (pp. 27–34). New York: Collier Books.

Freud, S. (1926). *Hemmung, symptom und angst.* Leipzig-Vienna-Zurich: International Psychoanalytic Verlag; G.W. 14: 111–205; Inhibitions, symptoms, and anxiety. *SE* 20: 77–172.

Freud, S. (1933). *New introductory lectures on psychoanalysis.* New York: W.W. Norton and Company.

Freud, S. (1958a). Recommendations to physicians practicing psycho-analysis. In J. Strachey (Ed. and Trans.), *The standard edition of the complete psychological works of Sigmund Freud*, Vol. 20 (pp. 87–172). London: Hogarth Press. (Original work published 1912.)

Freud, S. (1958b). The psychopathology of everyday life. In J. Strachey (Ed. and Trans.), *The standard edition of the complete psychological works of Sigmund Freud*, Vol. 7. London: Hogarth Press. (Original work published 1912.)

Freud, S. (1965). *The interpretation of dreams.* New York: Basic Books.

Friedman, N. (1967). *The social nature of psychological research: The psychological experiment as a social interaction.* New York: Basic Books.

Fritsch, G. T., and Hitzig, E. (1870 [1960]). On the electrical excitability of the cerebrum. In G. Von Bonin (1960) (Trans.), *Some papers on the cerebral cortex.* Springfield, IL: Charles C. Thomas.

Fulcher, E. P., and Hammerl, M. (2002). When all is revealed: A dissociation between evaluative learning and contingency awareness. *Consciousness and Cognition* 10, 524–49.

Furnham, A., Moutafi, J., and Crump, J. (2003). The relationship between the revised NEO-Personality Inventory and the Myers-Briggs Type Indicator. *Social Behavior and Personality* 31, 577–84.

Gambale, J. (1976). Word frequency and association strength in memory-ESP interaction: A failure to replicate [Abstract]. *Journal of Parapsychology* 40, 339–40.

Gambale, J., Margolis, F., and Cruci, K. (1976). The relationship between ESP and memory—and attempted replication with modifications [Abstract]. *Journal of Parapsychology* 40, 340.

Gange, J. L., Geen, R. G., and Harkins, S. G. (1979). Autonomic differences between extraverts and introverts during vigilance. *Psychophysiology* 4, 392–97.

Garety, P. A., Fowler, D., and Kuipers, E. (2000). Cognitive behavioural therapy for people with psychosis. In B. Martindale, A. Bateman, and F. Margison (Eds.), *Psychosis: Psychological approaches and their effectiveness.* London: Royal College of Psychiatrists.

Garrett, E. J. (2002). *Adventures in the supernormal.* New York: Helix Press. (Originally published in 1949.)

Gasper, K., and Clore, G. L. (2002). Attending to the big picture: Mixed and global vs. local processing of visual information. *Psychological Science* 13, 34–40.

Gassner, S., Sampson, H., Weiss, J., and Brumer, S. (1982). The emergence of warded-off contents. *Psychoanalysis and Contemporary Thought* 5(1), 55–75.

Gauld, A. (1968). *The founders of psychical research.* New York: Schocken.

Gauld, A. (1984). *Mediumship and survival.* Chicago: Academy Psychology Publishers.

Geen, R. G. (1984). Preferred stimulation levels in introverts and extraverts: Effects on arousal and performance. *Journal of Personality and Social Psychology* 46, 1303–12.

Gelade, G., and Harvie, R. (1975). Confidence ratings in an ESP task using affective stimuli. *Journal of the Society for Psychical Research* 48, 209–19.

Gendlin, E. (1997). *Experiencing and the creation of meaning: A philosophical and psychological approach to the subjective.* Chicago: Northwestern University Press.

Gilbert, P., and McGuire, M. T. (1998). Shame, status, and social roles: Psychobiology and evolution. In P. Gilbert and B. Andrews (Eds.), *Shame: Interpersonal behavior, psychopathology, and culture.* New York: Oxford Universities Press.

Gissurarson, L. R. (1989). *Psychokinetic attempts on a random-event based microcomputer test using imagery strategies.* Unpublished PhD dissertation, University of Edinburgh, Scotland.

Gissurarson, L. R. (1992). Studies of methods of enhancing and potentially training psychokinesis: A review. *Journal of the American Society for Psychical Research* 86, 303–46.

Glidden, S. H. (1974). A random-behavior maze test for humans. *Journal of Parapsychology* 38, 324–31.

Goldberg, L. R. (1999). A broad-bandwidth, public-domain, personality inventory measuring the lower-level facets of several five-factor models. In I. Mervielde, I. Deary, F. De Fruyt, and F. Ostendorf (Eds.), *Personality psychology in Europe*, Vol. 7 (pp. 7–28). Tilberg, Netherlands: Tilberg University Press.

Gollwitzer, P. M. (1990). Action phases and mind-sets. In E. T. Higgins and R. M. Sorrentino (Eds.), *Handbook of motivation and cognition*, Vol. 2) (pp. 53–92). New York: Guilford Press.

Gough, H. G. (1979). A creative personality scale for the Adjective Check List. *Journal of Personality and Social Psychology* 37(8), 1398–1405.

Gough, H. G., and Heilbrun, A. B. (1980). *The adjective check list manual.* Palo Alto, CA: Consulting Psychologists Press.

Goulding, A. (2005). Participant variables associated with psi ganzfeld results. *European Journal of Parapsychology* 20, 50–64.

Grad, B. (1961). A telekinetic effect on plant growth. *Cognition* 113, 105–10.

Granhag, P. A. (1997). Realism in eyewitness confidence as a function of type of event witnessed and repeated recall. *Journal of Applied Psychology* 82, 599–613.

Gray, K. L., Adams, W. J., and Garner, M. (2009). The influence of anxiety on the initial selection of emotional faces presented in binocular rivalry. *International Journal of Parapsychology* 3, 5.

Green, C. E. (1965). The effect of birth order and family size on extra-sensory perception. *Journal of the Society for Psychical Research* 43, 181–91.

Green, C. E. (1966). Extrasensory perception and the Maudsley Personality Inventory. *Journal of the Society for Psychical Research* 43, 285–86.

Greenwald, A. (1992). New Look 3: Unconscious cognition reclaimed. *American Psychologist* 47, 766–79.

Greenwald, A. G., McGhee, D. E., and Schwartz, J. L. K. (1998). Measuring individual differences in implicit cognition: The Implicit Association Test. *Journal of Personality and Social Psychology* 74, 1464–80.

Grey, H., and Wheelwright, J. B. (1946). Jung's psychological types; their frequency of occurrence. *Journal of General Psychology* 34, 3–17.

Greyson, B. (1977). Telepathy in mental illness: Deluge or delusion? *Journal of Nervous and Mental Disease* 165, 184–200.

Griffin, M., and McDermott, M. R. (1998). Exploring a tripartite relationship between rebelliousness, openness to experience, and creativity. *Social Behavior and Personality* 26, 347–56.

Grosz, H. J., and Zimmerman, J. A. (1965). Experimental analysis of hysterical blindness: A follow-up report and new experimental data. *Archives of General Psychiatry* 13, 255–60.

Guilford, J. P., Christensen, P. R., Merrifield, P. R., & Wilson, R. C. (1978). *Alternate Uses: Manual of instructions and interpretations*. Orange, CA: Sheridan Psychological Services.

Guilford, J. P., and Guilford, R. P. (1939). Personality factors D, R, T, and A. *Journal of Abnormal and Personality Psychology* 34, 21–36.

Guilford, J. P., Merrifield, P. R., and Cox, A. B. (1961). Creative thinking in children at the junior high school level. *Reports from the Psychological Laboratory*. Los Angeles: University of Southern California.

Gurney, E., Myers, F. W. H., and Podmore, F. (1886). *Phantasms of the living*, Vol. 1). London: Trubner.

Hagen, R., Turkington, D., Berge, T., and Grawe, R. (Eds.) (2010). *CBT for psychosis: A symptom-based approach*. New York: Routledge/Taylor and Francis Group.

Haight, J., Kanthamani, H., and Kennedy, J. E. (1978). Interaction of personality variables and feedback in a computerized ESP test. *Journal of Parapsychology* 42, 51–52.

Hallett, S. J. (1952). A study of the effect of conditioning on multiple-aspect ESP scoring. *Journal of Parapsychology* 16, 204–11.

Hann–Kende, F. (1953). On the role of transference and countertransference in psychoanalysis. In G. Devereux (Ed.), *Psychoanalysis and the occult* (pp. 158–67). New York: International Universities Press.

Haraldsson, E. (1993). Are religiosity and belief in an afterlife better predictors of ESP performance than belief in psychic phenomena? *Journal of Parapsychology* 6, 1–17.

Haraldsson, E., and Gissurarson, L. R. (1985). Perceptual defensiveness: Ganzfeld and the percipient-order effect. *European Journal of Parapsychology* 57, 259–73.

Haraldsson, E., and Houtkooper, J. M. (1992). Effects of perceptual defensiveness, personality and belief on extrasensory perception tasks. *Personality and Individual Differences* 13, 1085–96.

Haraldsson, E., and Houtkooper, J. M. (1995). Meta-analysis of 10 experiments on perceptual defensiveness and ESP: ESP scoring patterns and experimenter and decline effects. *Journal of Parapsychology* 59, 251–71.

Haraldsson, E., Houtkooper, J. M., and Hoeltje, C. (1987). The Defense Mechanism Test as a predictor of ESP performance: Icelandic Study VII and meta-analysis of 13 experiments. *Journal of Parapsychology* 51, 75–90.

Haraldsson, E., Houtkooper, J. M., Schneider, R., and Baeckstroem, M. (2002). Perceptual defensiveness and ESP performance: Reconstructed DMT-ratings and psychological correlates in the first German DMT-ESP experiment. *Journal of Parapsychology* 66, 249–70.

Haraldsson, E., and Johnson, M. (1981). Trait and state factors influencing ESP performance in the ganzfeld. In W. G. Roll and J. Beloff (Ed.), *Research in parapsychology 1980* (pp. 106–7). Metuchen, NJ: Scarecrow Press.

Haraldsson, E., and Johnson, M. (1986). The Defense Mechanism Test (DMT) as a predictor of ESP performance: Icelandic studies VI and VII. In D. H. Weiner and D. I. Radin (Eds.), *Research in parapsychology 1985* (pp. 43–44). Metuchen, NJ: Scarecrow Press.

Harary, K. (1976). A study of psi, memory and expectancy. In J. D. Morris, W. G. Roll, and R. L. Morris (Eds.), *Research in parapsychology 1976* (pp. 121–26). Metuchen, NJ: Scarecrow Press.

Harary, K. (1992). The goose that laid the silver eggs: A criticism of psi and silver futures forecasting. *Journal of the American Society for Psychical Research* 86, 375–410.

Harary, K., and Targ, R. (1985). A new approach to forecasting commodity futures. *Psi Research* 4, 79–88.

Harley, T. A. (1989). Psi missing in a dream clairvoyance experiment. *Journal of the Society for Psychical Research* 56, 1–7.

Harley, T. A., and Sargent, C. L. (1980). Trait and state factors influencing ESP performance in the ganzfeld. In W. G. Roll (Ed.), *Research in parapsychology 1979* (pp. 126–27). Metuchen, NJ: Scarecrow Press.

Hassin, R., Bargh, J. A., Engell, A. D., and McColloch, K. C. (2009). Implicit working memory. *Consciousness and Cognition* 18, 665–78.

Heath, P. R. (2003). *The PK Zone: A cross-cultural review of psychokinesis.* Bloomington, IN: iUniverse.

Heath, P. R. (2011). *Mind-matter interaction: A review of historical reports, theory and research.* Jefferson, NC: McFarland.

Heidegger, M. (1962). *Being and time.* San Francisco: Harper.

Henjum, A. (1982). Introversion: A misunderstood individual difference among students. *Education* 103, 39–43.

Henley, S. H. A., and Dixon, N. F. (1976). Preconscious processing in schizophrenia: An exploratory study. *British Journal of Medical Psychology* 49, 161–66.

Herodotus. (1890). *The Histories: Vol. II.* G. C. Macauley (Trans.). London: Macmillian and Company.

Heseltine, G. L., and Kirk, J. H. (1980). Examination of a majority-vote technique. *Journal of Parapsychology* 44, 167–76.

Heymans, G. (1929). *Inleiding tot de speciale psychologie.* Bonn: Harlem.

Higgins, E. T. (1996). Knowledge activation: Accessibility, applicability, and salience. In E. T. Higgins and A. W. Kruglanski (Eds.), *Social psychology: Handbook of basic principles* (pp. 133–68). New York: Guilford.

Hilgard, E. (1965). *Hypnotic susceptibility.* New York: Harcourt, Brace and World.

Hinterberger, T., Studer, P., Jager, M., Haverty-Stacke, C., and Walach, H. (2007). Can a slide-show presentiment effect be discovered in the brain electrical activity? *Journal of the Society for Psychical Research* 71, 148–66.

Hocevar, D., and Bachelor, P. (1989). A taxonomy and critique of measurements used in the study of creativity. In E. P. Torrance, J. A. Glover, R. R. Ronning, and C. R. Reynolds (Eds.), *Handbook of creativity, assessment, research and theory.* New York: Springer.

Holland, H. C. (1962). The spiral after-effect and extraversion. *Acta Psychologica* 20, 29–35.

Hollander, E., and Simeon, D. (2003). *Concise guide to anxiety disorders.* Washington, DC: American Psychiatric Publishing, Inc.

Hollós, I. (1933). Psychopathologie alltäglicher telepathischer Erscheinungen. *Imago* 19, 529–46.

Holt, N. J. (2006). Research note: Testing for precognitive boredom with a population of visual artists: A pilot study. *Journal of the Society for Psychical Research* 70, 110–20.

Holt, N. J. (2007). Are artistic populations "psi-conducive"?: Testing the relationship between creativity and psi with an experience-sampling protocol. Proceedings of Presented Papers: The Parapsychological Association 50th Annual Convention, 31–47.

Holt, N. J., Delanoy, D., and Roe, C. (2004). Creativity, subjective paranormal experiences and altered state of consciousness. Proceedings of Presented Papers: The Parapsychological Association 47th Annual Convention, 433–36.

Holt, R. R. (1970). Artistic creativity and Rorschach measures of adaptive regression. In B. Klopfer, M. Meyer, F. Brawer, and W. G. Klopfer (Eds.), *Developments in the Rorschach technique, vol. III: Aspects of personality structure.* New York: Harcourt Brace Javonovich.

Honorton, C. H. (1965). The relationship between ESP and manifest anxiety level. *Journal of Parapsychology* 29, 291–92.

Honorton, C. H. (1967). Creativity and precognition scoring level. *Journal of Parapsychology* 31, 29–42.

Honorton, C. H. (1969). A combination of techniques for the separation of high- and low-scoring ESP subjects. *Journal of the American Society for Psychical Research* 63, 69–82.

Honorton, C. H. (1972). Significant factors in hypnotically induced clairvoyant dreams. *Journal of the American Society for Psychical Research* 66, 86–102.

Honorton, C. H. (1977a). Effects of meditation and feedback on psychokinetic performance: A pilot study with an instructor of Transcendental Meditation [abstract]. In W. G. Roll, J. D. Morris, and R. L. Morris (Eds.), *Research in parapsychology 1976* (pp. 95–97). Metuchen, NJ: Scarecrow Press.

Honorton, C. H. (1977b). Psi and internal attention states. In B. B. Wolman (Ed.), *Handbook of parapsychology* (pp. 435–72). New York: Van Nostrand Reinhold.

Honorton, C. H. (1997). The ganzfeld novice: Four predictors of initial ESP performance. *Journal of Parapsychology* 61, 143–58.

Honorton, C. H., Barker, P., and Sondow, N. (1983). Feedback and participant-selection parameters in a computer RNG study [Abstract]. In W. G. Roll, J. Beloff, and R. A. White (Eds.), *Research in parapsychology 1982* (pp. 157–58). Metuchen, NJ: Scarecrow Press.

Honorton, C. H., and Barksdale, W. (1972). PK performance with waking suggestions for muscle tension vs. relaxation. *Journal of the American Society for Psychical Research* 66, 208–14.

Honorton, C. H., Berger, R. E., Varvoglis, M. P., and Quant, M. (1990). Psi communication in the ganzfeld: Experiments with an automated testing system and a comparison with a meta-analysis of earlier studies. *Journal of Parapsychology* 54, 99–139.

Honorton, C. H., Carlson, T., and Tietze, T. (1968). Combined methods in subject selection. In J. B. Rhine and R. Brier (Eds.), *Parapsychology today* (pp. 138–45). New York: Citadel Press.

Honorton, C. H., and Ferrari, D. C. (1989). "Future telling": A meta-analysis of forced-choice precognition experiments, 1935–1987. *Journal of Parapsychology* 53, 281–308.

Honorton, C. H., Ferrari, D. C., and Bem, D. J. (1998). Extraversion and ESP performance: A meta-analysis and a new confirmation. *Journal of Parapsychology* 62, 255–76.

Honorton, C. H., and Harper, S. (1974). Psi-mediated imagery and ideation in an experimental procedure for regulating perceptual input. *Journal of the American Society for Psychical Research* 68, 156–68.

Honorton, C. H., and May, E. (1976). Volitional control in a psychokinetic test with auditory and visual feedback [Abstract]. In W. G. Roll, J. D. Morris, and R. L. Morris (Eds.), *Research in parapsychology 1975* (pp. 90–91). Metuchen, NJ: Scarecrow Press.

Honorton, C. H., Ramsey, M., and Cabibbo, C. (1975). Experimenter effects in extrasensory perception. *Journal of the American Society for Psychical Research* 69, 135–39.

Honorton, C. H., and Stump, J. P. (1969). A preliminary study of hypnotically induced clairvoyant dreams. *Journal of the American Society for Psychical Research* 63, 175–84.

Hoover, T. O. (1978). The hand test: Fifteen years later. *Journal of Personality Assessment* 42, 128–38.

Houtkooper, J. M. (2003). An ESP experiment with natural and simulated sferics: Displacement scores and psychological variables. *European Journal of Parapsychology* 18, 49–63.

Houtkooper, J. M., Schienle, A., Stark, R., and Vaitl, D. (1999). LXXXVIII. Atmospheric electromagnetism: The possible disturbing influence of natural sferics on ESP. *Perceptual and Motor Skills* 89, 1179–92.

Houtz, J. C., and Krug, D. (1995). Assessment of creativity: Resolving a mid-life crisis. *Educational Psychology Review* 7, 269–301.

Howat, S. J. (1994). *Remote staring detection and personality correlates.* (BSc Honors thesis). Retrieved from the Library of the Department of Psychology, University of Edinburgh.

Humphrey, B. M. (1945). An exploratory correlation study of personality measures and ESP scores. *Journal of Parapsychology* 9, 116–23.

Humphrey, B. M. (1946). Success in ESP as related to form of response drawings: I. Clairvoyance experiments. *Journal of Parapsychology* 10, 78–106.

Humphrey, B. M. (1951). Introversion-extraversion ratings in relation to scores in ESP tests. *Journal of Parapsychology* 15, 252–62.

Hutchinson, E. D. (1931). Materials for the study of creative thinking. *Psychological Bulletin* 28, 398–410.

Hutchinson, E. D. (1939). Varieties of insight in humans. *Psychiatry* 2, 323–32.

Hyman, R. (1996). The evidence for psychic functioning: Claims vs. reality. *Skeptical Inquirer* 20.2, 24–26.

Hyman, R. (2010). Consistently inconsistent. In S. K Krippner and H. L. Friedman (Eds.), *Debating psychic experience.* Westport, CN: Praeger Press.

Ionescu, M. (1991). *Hypermnesia for subliminal stimuli.* Unpublished doctoral dissertation, Graduate School of the City University of New York, New York.

Irwin, C. P. (1982). The role of memory in free-response ESP studies: Is target familiarity reflected in the score? *Journal of the American Society for Psychical Research* 76, 1–22.

Irwin, H. J. (1979a). On directional inconsistency in the correlation between ESP and memory. *Journal of Parapsychology* 43, 31–39.

Irwin, H. J. (1979b). *Psi and the mind.* Metuchen, NJ: Scarecrow Press.

Irwin, H. J., and Watt, C. A. (2007). *An introduction to parapsychology (5th edition).* Jefferson, NC: McFarland.

Isaacs, J. (1984). The Batcheldor approach: Some strengths and weaknesses. *Journal of the American Society for Psychical Research* 78, 123–32.

Jackson, M., Franzoi, S., and Schmeidler, G. R. (1977). Effects of feedback on ESP: A curious partial replication. *Journal of the American Society for Psychical Research* 71, 147–55.

Jahn, R. G., and Dunne, B. J. (1987). *Margins of reality: The role of consciousness in the physical world.* San Diego, Harcourt Brace Jovanovich.

James, W. (1890). *The principles of psychology.* New York: Henry Holt and Company.

James, W. (1898). Psychical research. *Psychological Review* 5, 420–24.

James, W. (1903). Review of *Human personality and its survival of bodily death,* by F. W. H. Myers. *Proceedings of the Society for Psychical Research* 18, 22–33.

James, W. (1962). *Psychology: Briefer course.* New York: Collier.

Janet, P. (1889). *L'Automatisme psychologique: Essai de psychologie expérimentale sur les formes inférieures de la vie mentale,* dissertation. Paris: Félix Alcan; reprinted Société Pierre-Janet, 1973.

Janet, P. (1907). *The major symptoms of hysteria.* New York: Macmillan Publishers.

Jaskowski, P., and Skalska, B. (2003). How the self controls its "automatic pilot" when processing subliminal information. *Journal of Cognitive Neuroscience* 15, 911–20.

Jaspers, K. (1964). *General psychopathology.* Chicago: University of Chicago Press.

Jephson, I. (1928). Evidence for clairvoyance in card-guessing. *Proceedings of the Society for Psychical Research* 36, 223–71.

Joesting, J., and Joesting, R. (1969). Torrance's creative motivation inventory and its relationship to several personality variables. *Psychological Reports* 24, 30.

Johnson, M. (1965). An attempt to effect scoring behavior in a group test of precognition by means of manipulation of motivation and by the use of individually assigned emotionally loaded target material. *Research Letter of the Parapsychological Division of the Psychological Laboratory,* University of Utrecht, 15–32.

Johnson, M. (1971). Continuation of psi research at Lund University [Abstract]. *Journal of Parapsychology* 27, 288.

Johnson, M. (1973). A written academic exam as a disguised test of clairvoyance. In W. G. Roll, J. D. Morris, and R. L. Morris (Eds.), *Research in parapsychology 1972* (pp. 28–30). Metuchen, NJ: Scarecrow Press, 28–30.

Johnson, M. (1974). ESP and subliminality. In W. G. Roll, J. D. Morris, and R. L. Morris (Eds.), *Research in parapsychology 1973,* (pp. 22–24). Metuchen, NJ: Scarecrow Press.

Johnson, M. (1977). A blind matching experiment with a selected subject using emotionally loaded targets. In J. D. Morris, W. G. Roll, and R. L. Morris (Eds.), *Research in parapsychology 1976.* Metuchen, NJ: Scarecrow Press, 103–05.

Johnson, M., and Haraldsson, E. (1984). The Defense Mechanism Test as a predictor of ESP scores: Icelandic Studies IV and V. *Journal of Parapsychology* 48, 165–200.

Johnson, M., and Hartwell, J. (1979). Skin potential activity and guessing performance of more and less defensive subjects in a GESP task. *European Journal of Parapsychology* 2, 365–70.

Johnson, M., and Houtkooper, J. M. (1988). The effect of anxiety on scoring and observer effects in a blind-matching test with targets of specific and emotional implications to the subjects. In D. H. Weiner and R. L. Morris (Eds.), *Research in parapsychology 1987* (pp. 56–60). Metuchen, NJ: Scarecrow Press.

Johnson, M., and Kanthamani, B. K. (H.) (1967). The Defense Mechanism Test as a predictor of ESP scoring direction. *Journal of Parapsychology* 31, 99–110.

Johnson, M., and Lubke, C. (1975). At attempt to influence ESP scoring by means of subliminal stimulation in an experiment in which the target is related to a problem-solving task [Abstract]. In J. D. Morris, W. G. Roll, and R. L. Morris (Eds.), *Research in parapsychology 1975* (pp. 130–44). Metuchen, NJ: Scarecrow Press.

Johnson, M., and Nordbeck, B. (1972). Variation of the scoring behavior of a "psychic" subject. *Journal of Parapsychology* 36, 122–32.

Jones, A. (1910). *A psychic autobiography.* New York: Greaves Publishing Company.

Jones, E. (1926). Letter from Ernest Jones to Sigmund Freud, February 25, 1926. In E. Jones, R. A. Paskauskas, and R. Steiner (Eds.), *The Complete Correspondence of Sigmund Freud and Ernest Jones 1908–1939* (pp. 592–93). Boston: Belknap Press.

Jones, E. (1957). *The life and work of Sigmund Freud* (vol. 3). New York: Basic Books, Inc., 375.

Jones, R. A., and Cooper, J. (1971). Mediation of experimenter effects. *Journal of Personality and Social Psychology* 20, 70–74.

Josephson, B. D., and Pallikari-Viras, F. (1991). Biological utilisation of quantum-nonlocality, *Foundations of Physics* 21, 197–207.

Jung, C. G. (1960a). A psychological theory of the types. In *The collected works of C. G. Jung, Volume 6: Psychological types*. New York: Pantheon Books.

Jung, C. G. (1960b). Spirit and life. In *The collected works of C. G. Jung, Volume 8: The structure and dynamics of the psyche*. New York: Pantheon Books.

Jung, C. G. (1960c). Synchronicity: An acausal connecting principle. In *The collected works of C. G. Jung, Volume 8: The structure and dynamics of the psyche*. New York: Pantheon Books, 516–18.

Jung, C. G. (1963). *Memories, dreams, reflections*. Trans. R. Winston and C. Winston. New York: Pantheon Books.

Jung, C. G. (1998). *Jung on synchronicity and the paranormal*. Princeton, NJ: Princeton University Press.

Juniper, Z., and Edlmann, M. (1998). *The relationship between perceptual vigilance/defensiveness and psychophysiological responses to remote staring in the ganzfeld condition*. Honor's thesis. Retrieved from the Psychology Library of the University of Edinburgh (UMI No. 9441031).

Kagan, J. (1994). *Galen's prophecy*. New York: Basic.

Kahn, S. D. (1952). Studies in extrasensory perception: Experiments utilizing an electronic scoring device. *Journal of the Society for Psychical Research* 25, 1–48.

Kaminsky, J., Call, J., and Tomasello, M. (2004). Body orientation and face orientation: Two factors controlling apes' begging behavior from humans. *Animal Cognition* 7, 216–23.

Kanthamani, B. K. (H.) (1965). A study of the differential response in language ESP tests. *Journal of Parapsychology* 29, 27–34.

Kanthamani, H., and Broughton, R. S. (1992). Personality and ESP: The classroom project. In E. W. Cook and D. L. Delanoy (Eds.), *Research in parapsychology 1991*. Metuchen, NJ: Scarecrow Press.

Kanthamani, H., and Broughton, R. S. (1994). An experiment in ganzfeld and dreams: A further confirmation. Proceedings of Presented Papers: The Parapsychological Association 35th Annual Convention, 59–73.

Kanthamani, H., and Kelly, E. F. (1974). Awareness of success in an exceptional subject. *Journal of Parapsychology* 38, 355–82.

Kanthamani, H., and Khilji, A. (1990). An experiment in ganzfeld and dreams: A confirmatory study. Proceedings of Presented Papers: The Parapsychological Association 33rd Annual Convention, 126–37.

Kanthamani, H., and Rao, K. R. (1971). Personality characteristics of ESP subjects: I. Primary personality characteristics and ESP. *Journal of Parapsychology* 36, 190–212.

Kanthamani, H., and Rao, K. R. (1972). Personality characteristics of ESP subjects: III. Extraversion and ESP. *Journal of Parapsychology* 36, 190–212.

Kanthamani, H., and Rao, K. R. (1973). Personality characteristics of ESP subjects: IV. Neuroticism and ESP. *Journal of Parapsychology* 37, 37–50.

Kanthamani, H., and Rao, H. H. (1974). A study of memory-ESP relationships using linguistic forms. *Journal of Parapsychology* 38, 286–300.

Kanthamani, H. and Rao, H. H. (1975). The role of association strength in memory-ESP interaction. *Journal of Parapsychology* 39, 1–11.

Kanthamani, H., and Rao, H. H. (1975). Response tendencies and stimulus structure. In J. D. Morris, W. G. Roll, and R. L. Morris (Eds.), *Research in parapsychology 1974*. Metuchen, NJ: Scarecrow Press, 154–77.

Kasian, S. J. (2004). Remote viewing of real estate: Entrepreneurial explorations. *Journal of Indian Psychology*, 22, 34–43.

Kelly, E. F. (2007). A view from the mainstream: Contemporary cognitive neuroscience and the consciousness debates. In E. F. Kelly and E. W. Kelly (Eds.), *Irreducible mind: Toward a psychology for the 21st century* (pp. 1–46). Lanham, MD: Rowman and Littlefield.

Kelly, E. F., Kanthamani, H., Child, I. L., and Young, F. W. (1975). On the relation between visual and ESP confusion structures in an exceptional ESP subject. *Journal of the American Society for Psychical Research* 69, 1–31.

Kelly, E. F., Kelly, E. W., Crabtree, A., Gauld, A., Grosso, M., and Greyson, B. (2007). *Irreducible mind: Toward a psychology for the 21st century*. Lanham, MD: Rowman and Littlefield.

Kelly, G. A. (1955). *The psychology of personal constructs* (2 Vols.). New York: W. W. Norton and Co.

Kelly, G. A. (1979). *Clinical psychology and personality: Selected papers of George Kelly*. New York: Krieger Publishing.

Kennedy, J. E. (1978). The role of task complexity in PK: A review. *Journal of Parapsychology* 42, 89–122.

Kennedy, J. E. (1979). Redundancy in psi information. *Journal of Parapsychology* 43, 290–314.

Kennedy, J. E. (2001). Why is psi so elusive? A review and proposed model. *Journal of Parapsychology* 65, 219–45.

Kennedy, J. E., and Kanthamani, H. (1995). An exploratory study of the effects of paranormal and spiritual experience on peoples' lives and well-being. *Journal of the Society for Psychical Research* 89, 249–54.

Kennedy, J. E., Kanthamani, H., and Palmer, J. (1994). Psychic and spiritual experiences, health, well-being, and meaning in life. *Journal of Parapsychology* 58, 353–83.

Kier, F., Melancon, J. G., and Thompson, B. (1998). Reliability and validity of scores on the Personal Preferences Self-Description Questionnaire (PPSDQ), *Educational and Psychological Measurement* 58, 612–22.

Kierkegaard, S. (1956). *Purity of heart is to will one thing*. New York; Harper One.

Klintman, H. (1984). Is there a paranormal (precognitive) influence in certain types of perceptual sequences? Part II. *European Journal of Parapsychology* 5, 129–40.

Kohler, W. (1947). *Gestalt psychology: An introduction to new concepts in modern psychology*. New York: Liveright Publishing.

Komarraju, M., Karau, S. J., and Schmeck, R. R. (2009). Role of the big five personality traits in predicting college students' academic motivation and achievement. *Learning and Individual Differences* 19, 47–52.

Kragh, U. (1960a). DM–testet—ett instrument for diagnostik cJch urval. (The Defense Mechanism Test: An instrument for diagnosis and personnel selection.) *Nordisk Psykologi* 12, 235–53.

Kragh, U. (1960b). The Defense Mechanism Test: A new method for diagnosis and personnel selection. *Journal of Applied Psychology* 44, 4.

Kragh, U. (1962). Prediction of success of Danish attack divers by the Defense Mechanism Test (DMT). *Perceptual and Motor Skills* 7, 103–6.

Kragh, U., and Neuman, T. (1982). *DMT manual.* Stockholm: Swedish Psychology. (Also London: Interpersona, n. d.).

Kragh, U, and Smith, G. W. (1970). *Percept-genetic analysis.* Lund, Sweden: Gleerups.

Kreiman, N. (1978). Memoria secundario y ESP. *Cuadernosde Parapsicología* 3, 3–12.

Kreitler, H., and Kreitler, S. (1972). Does extrasensory perception affect psychological experiments? *Journal of Parapsychology* 36, 1–45.

Kreitler, H., and Kreitler, S. (1973). Subliminal perception and extrasensory perception. *Journal of Parapsychology* 37, 163–88.

Kreitler, H., and Kreitler, S. (1982). Psi transmission of anger and its enhancement through meaning. *European Journal of Parapsychology* 4, 199–242.

Krishna, S. R., and Rao, K. R. (1991). Effect of ESP feedback on subjects' responses to a personality questionnaire. *Journal of Parapsychology* 55, 147–58.

Krippner, S. C. (1962–63). Creativity and psychic phenomena. *The Indian Journal of Parapsychology* 4, 1–20.

Krippner, S. C. (1968). Experimentally-induced telepathic effects in hypnosis and non-hypnosis groups. *Journal of the American Society for Psychical Research* 62, 387–98.

Krippner, S. C., and Friedman, H. L. (2010). *Debating psychic experience: Human experience or human illusion.* Santa Barbara, CA: Praeger.

Krippner, S., and Zeichner, S. (1974). Descriptive analysis of art prints telepathically transmitted during sleep. In W. G. Roll, R. L. Morris, and J. D. Morris (Eds.), *Research in parapsychology 1973* (pp. 27–28). Metuchen, NJ: Scarecrow Press.

Kris, E. (1952). *Psychoanalytic explorations in art.* New York: International Universities Press.

Krishna, S. R. & Rao, K. R. (1981). Personality and belief in relation to language ESP scores [abstract]. In W. G. Roll and J. Beloff (Eds.), *Research in parapsychology 1980* (pp. 61–63). Metuchen, NJ: Scarecrow Press.

Kruglanski, A. W. (1989). The psychology of being "right": The problem of accuracy in social perception and cognition. *Psychological Bulletin* 106, 395–409.

Kunst-Wilson, W. R., and Zajonc, R. B. (1980). Conscious and unconscious perception: Experiments on visual masking and word recognition. *Cognitive Psychology* 15, 197–237.

La Mettrie, J. (1748 [1996]). *L'homme machine.* In A. Thomson (Ed.), *Machine man and other writings.* Cambridge: Cambridge University Press.

Laing, R. D. (1961). *The self and others.* London: Tavistock Publications.

Lamont, P. (2006). *The first psychic: The peculiar mystery of a notorious Victorian wizard.* Burlington, MA: Abacus Software.

Lang, P. J., and Greenwald, M. K. (1993). *International affective picture system standardization procedure and results for affective judgments.* Gainesville, FL: University of Florida Center for Research in Psychophysiology.

Larson, E. (1984, October 22). Did psychic powers give firm a killing in the silver market? *Wall Street Journal.*

Lawrence, T. R. (1998). Gathering in the sheep and goats: A meta-analysis of forced-choice sheep-goat studies, 1947–1993. In N. L. Zingrone, M. J. Schlitz,

C. S. Alvarado, and J. Milton (Eds.), *Research in parapsychology 1993*. Lanham, MD: Scarecrow Press, 27–30.

Layton, B. D., and Turnbull, B. (1975). Belief, evaluation, and performance on an ESP task. *Journal of Experimental Social Psychology* 11, 166–79.

Leander, N. P., Moore, S. M., and Chartrand, T. L. (2009). Mystery moods: Their origins and consequences. In G. B. Moskowitz and H. Grant (Eds.), *The psychology of goals*. New York: The Guilford Press, 480–504.

Lefell, D. A. (2010). *Painting the portrait, Lewis*. Sanbornton, NH: Signalar Art Videos.

Lehrer, J. (2010, December 13). The truth wears off. *New Yorker*, 22–27.

Lieberman, R. (1975). Role of varied time interval and association strength in memory-ESP interaction for group and individual testing [abstract]. In J. C. Morris, W. G. Roll, and R. L. Morris (Eds.), *Research in parapsychology 1975* (pp. 126-129). Metuchen, NJ: Scarecrow Press.

LeShan, L. (2009). *A new science of the paranormal: The promise of psychical research*. Wheaton, IL: Quest Books.

Levi, A. (1979). The influence of imagery and feedback on PK effects. *Journal of Parapsychology* 43, 275–89.

Levine, F., and Stowell, J. (1963). The relationship between creativity and clairvoyance. Paper presented at the 6th Annual Convention of the Parapsychological Association, New York, abstract in the *Journal of Parapsychology* 27, 272.

Levine, G. M., Halberstadt, J. B., and Goldstone, R. L. (1996). Reasoning and the weighting of attributes in attitude judgments. *Journal of Personality and Social Psychology* 70, 230–40.

Lewin, K. (1935). *A dynamic theory of personality*. New York: McGraw Hill.

Li-Pang Tang, T. (2001). Effects of Type A personality and experimenter interest in behavior. *Journal of Social Psychology* 127, 619–27.

Loomis, M. (1982). A new perspective for Jung's typology: The Singer-Loomis Inventory of Personality. *Journal of Analytic Psychology* 27, 59–69.

Louwerens, N. G. (1960). ESP experiments with nursery school children in the Netherlands. *Journal of Parapsychology* 24, 75–93.

Lovitts, B. E. (1998). The sheep-goat effect turned upside down. *Journal of Parapsychology* 45, 293–309.

Lowry, R. (1981). Apparent PK effect on computer-generated random digit series. *Journal of the American Society for Psychical Research* 75, 209–20.

Lucas, R. E., Diener, E., Grob, A., Suh, E. M., and Shao, L. (2000). Cross-cultural evidence for the fundamental features of extraversion. *Journal of Personality and Social Psychology* 79, 452–68.

Luke, D. P., Delanoy, D., and Sherwood, S. (2008). Psi may look like luck: Perceived luckiness and beliefs about luck in relation to precognition. *Journal of the Society for Psychical Research* 72, 193–207.

Luke, D. P., Roe, C. A., and Davison, J. (2008). Testing for forced-choice precognition using a hidden task: Two replications. *Journal of Parapsychology* 72, 133–54.

Lyons, A., and Truzzi, M. (1991). *The blue sense: Psychic detectives and crime*. New York: Warner Books.

MacDonnell, R., O'Neill, T., Kline, T., and Hambley, L. (2009). Bringing group-level personality to the electronic realm: A comparison of face-to-face and virtual contexts. *Psychologist-Manager Journal* 12, 1–24.

MacKinnon, D. W. (1965). Personality and the realization of creative potential. *American Psychologist* 20, 273–81.

MacKinnon, D. W. (1978). *In search of human effectiveness*. Buffalo, NY: Bearly Limited with Creative Education Foundation, Inc.

MacLeod, C. (1991). Half a century of research on the Stroop effect: An integrative review. *Psychological Bulletin* 109, 163–203.

MacLeod, C., Matthews, A., and Tata, P. (1986). Attentional bias in emotional disorders. *Journal of Abnormal Psychology* 95, 15–20.

MacLeod, C., and Rutherford, E. M. (1992). Anxiety and the selective processing of emotional information: Mediating roles of awareness, trait and state variables, and personal relevance of stimulus materials. *Behavior Research and Therapy* 30, 479–91.

Macmurray, J. (1991). *The self as agent*. Amherst, NY: Prometheus Books.

Magnussen, S. (2009). Implicit visual working memory. *Scandinavian Journal of Psychology* 50, 535–42.

Mandler, G., Nakamura, Y., and Van Sandt, B. J. S. (1987). Non-specific effects of exposure on stimuli that cannot be recognized. *Journal of Experimental Psychology: Learning, Memory, and Cognition* 13, 646–48.

Marcel, A. J. (1983). Conscious and unconscious perception: An approach to the relations between phenomenal experience and perceptual processes. *Cognitive Psychology* 15, 238–300.

Marcel, A. J., and Bisiach, E. (1988). *Consciousness in contemporary science*. New York: Clarendon Press.

Marks, D. (2002). *The psychology of the psychic*. New York: Prometheus Books.

Martin, A. J., and Jackson, S. A. (2008). Brief approaches to assessing task absorption and enhanced subjective experience: Examining "short" and "core" flow in diverse performance domains. *Motivation and Emotion* 32, 131–57.

Martin, D. R., and Stribic, F. P. (1940). Studies in extrasensory perception: III. A review of all University of Colorado experiments. *Journal of Parapsychology* 4, 159–248.

Martin, L. L., Tesser, A., and McIntosh, W. D. (1993). Wanting but not having: The effects of unattained goals on thoughts and feelings. In D. M. Wegner and J. W. Pennebaker (Eds.), *Handbook of mental control* (pp. 552–72). Englewood Cliffs, NJ: Prentice Hall.

Matas, F., and Pantas, L. (1972). A PK experiment comparing meditating and non-meditating subjects [Abstract]. In J. D. Morris, W. G. Roll, and R. L. Morris (Eds.), *Research in parapsychology 1971* (pp. 12–13). Metuchen, NJ: Scarecrow Press.

Mauskopf, S., and McVaugh, M. (1980). *The elusive science: Origins of experimental psychical research*. Baltimore, MD: Johns Hopkins University Press.

May, E. C. (1998). Response to "Experiment one of the SAIC remote viewing program: A critical re-evaluation." *Journal of Parapsychology* 62, 309–18.

May, E. C., Paulinyi, T., and Vassy, Z. (2005). Anomalous anticipatory skin conductance response to acoustic stimuli: Experimental results and speculation about a mechanism. *Journal of Alternative and Complementary Medicine* 11, 695–702.

Mayer, E. L. (2007). *Extraordinary knowing: Science, skepticism and the extraordinary power of the human mind*. New York: Bantam/Random House.

McClelland, D. C., Koestner, R., and Weinberger, J. (1989). How do self-attributed and implicit motives differ? *Psychological Review* 96, 690–702.

McCrae, R. R., and Costa, P. T. Jr. (1987). Validation of a five-factor model of personality across instruments and observers. *Journal of Personality and Social Psychology* 52, 81–90.

McCrae, R. R., and Costa, P. T. Jr. (1989). Reinterpreting the Myers-Briggs Type Indicator from the perspective of the five-factor model of personality. *Journal of Personality* 57, 17–40.

McCraty, R., Atkinson, M., and Bradley, R. T. (2004a). Electrophysiological evidence of intuition: Part I. The surprising role of the heart. *Journal of Alternative and Complementary Medicine* 10, 133–43.

McCraty, R., Atkinson, M., Bradley, R. T. (2004b). Electrophysiological evidence of intuition: Part 2. A system-wide process? *Journal of Alternative and Complementary Medicine* 10, 325–36.

McCurdy, H. (1961). *The personal world*. New York: Harcourt, Brace and World.

McCurdy, H. (1965). *Personality and science: A search for self-awareness*. New York: Van Nostrand Reinhold.

McDonough, B. E., Don, N. S., and Warren, C. A. (1994). EEG in a ganzfeld psi task. Proceedings of Presented Papers: The Parapsychological Association 37th Annual Convention, 273–83.

McDougall, W. (1929). *Modern materialism and emergent evolution*. Princeton, NJ: D. Van Nostrand.

McElroy, T., Seta, J., and Waring, G. (2007). Reflections of the self: How self-esteem determines decision framing and increases risk taking. *Journal of Behavioral Decision Making* 20, 223–40.

McGuire, K., Percy, E., and Carpenter, J. C. (1974). A multivariate approach to the prediction of ESP performance [Abstract]. In J. D. Morris, W. G. Roll, and R. L. Morris (Eds.), *Research in parapsychology 1975* (pp. 34–35). Metuchen, NJ: Scarecrow Press.

McKeachie, W. J., Lin, Y., Milholland, J., and Isaacson, R. (1966). Student affiliation motives, teacher warmth, and academic achievement. *Journal of Personality and Social Psychology* 4, 437–61.

McMoneagle, J. (1997). *Mind trek*. Charlottesville, VA: Hampton Roads Publishing.

McMoneagle, J. (2000). *Remote viewing secrets: A handbook*. Charlottesville, VA: Hampton Roads Publishing.

McMoneagle, J. (2002). *The Stargate chronicles: Memoirs of a psychic spy*. Charlottesville, VA: Hampton Roads Publishing.

Meerloo, J. A. M. (1949). Telepathy as a form of archaic communication. *Psychiatric Quarterly* 23, 691–704.

Meerloo, J. A. M. (1964). *Hidden communication: Studies in the communication theory of telepathy*. Oxford: Helix Press.

Megargee, E. I. (1972). *The California psychological inventory handbook*. San Francisco: Jossey-Bass.

Merikle, P. M., and Reingold, E. M. (1991). Comparing direct (explicit) and indirect (implicit) measures to study unconscious memory. *Journal of Experimental Psychology: Learning, Memory, and Cognition* 17, 224–33.

Mershon, B., and Gorsuch, R. L. (1988). Number of factors in the personality sphere: Does increase in factors increase predictability of real-life criteria? *Journal of Personality and Social Psychology* 55, 675–80.

Metzger, W. (1930). Optische Untersuchungen am Ganzfeld: II. Zur phanomenologie des homogenen Ganzfelds [Optical investigation of the Ganzfeld: II Toward the phenomenology of the homogeneous ganzfeld]. *Psychologische Forschung* 13, 6–29.

Michie, D., and West, D. J. (1957). A mass ESP test using television. *Journal of the Society for Psychical Research* 39, 113–33.

Mikulincer, M., Hirschberger, G., Nachmias, O., and Gillath, O. (2001). The affective component of the secure base schema: Affective priming with representations of attachment security. *Journal of Personality and Social Psychology* 81, 305–21.

Miller, R. L. (1976). Mere exposure, psychological reactance and attitude change. *Journal of Abnormal and Social Psychology* 59, 1–9.

Miller, S. W., and York, M. S. (1976). Perceptual defensiveness as a performance indicator on a free-response test of clairvoyance. In J. D. Morris, W. G. Roll, and R. L. Morris (Eds.), *Research in parapsychology 1975*. Metuchen, NJ: Scarecrow Press.

Milton, J. (1992). Effects of "paranormal" experiences on people's lives: An unusual survey of spontaneous cases. *Journal of the Society for Psychical Research* 58, 314–23.

Milton, J., and Wiseman, R. (1999). Does psi exist? Lack of replication of an anomalous process of information transfer. *Psychological Bulletin* 125, 387–91.

Mintz, E. (1983). *The psychic thread*. New York: Human Sciences Press.

Mischo, J., and Weis, R. (1973). A pilot study on the relations between PK scores and personality variables. In W. G. Roll, J. D. Morris, and R. L. Morris (Eds.), *Research in parapsychology 1972* (pp. 21–23). Metuchen, NJ: Scarecrow Press.

Mitchell, G. W. (1876). *X + Y = Z; Or the sleeping preacher of north Alabama*. New York: W. C. Smith.

Mogg, K., Bradley, B. P., and Hallowell, N. (1994). Attentional bias to threat: Roles of trait anxiety, stressful events, and awareness. *Quarterly Journal of Experimental Psychology* 47, 841–64.

Moon, M. (1973). *Extrasensory perception and art experience*. (Doctoral dissertation), Pennsylvania State University, 223 pages; AAT 7416047.

Moon, M. (1975). Artists compared with non-artists concerning belief in ESP: A poll. *Journal of the American Society for Psychical Research* 69, 161–66.

Moriarty, A. E., and Murphy, G. (1967). An experimental study of ESP potential and its relationship to creativity. *Journal of the American Society for Psychical Research* 61, 326–38.

Morris, R. L. (1971). Guessing habits and ESP. *Journal of Parapsychology* 35, 335–36.

Morris, R. L. (2000). Parapsychology in the 21st century. *Journal of Parapsychology* 64, 123–37.

Morris, R. L., Cunningham, S., McAlpine, S., and Taylor, R. (1993). Toward replication and extension of autoganzfeld results. Proceedings of Presented Papers: The Parapsychological Association 36th Annual Convention, 177–91.

Morris, R. L., Dalton, K., Delanoy, D., and Watt, C. (1995). Comparison of the sender/ no sender condition in the ganzfeld. Proceedings of presented papers, The Parapsychological Association 38th Annual Convention, Durham, NC, 244–59.

Morris, R. L., and Hornaday, J. (1981). An attempt to employ mental practice to facilitate PK [Abstract]. In W. G. Roll and J. Beloff (Eds.), *Research in parapsychology 1980* (pp. 103–04). Metuchen, NJ: Scarecrow Press.

Morris, R. L., Nanko, M., and Phillips, D. (1979). International observer influence upon measurements of a quantum-mechanical system: A comparison of two imagery strategies [Abstract]. In W. G. Roll (Ed.), *Research in parapsychology 1978* (pp. 146–50). Lanham, MD: Scarecrow Press.

Morris, R. L., and Reilly, V. (1980). A failure to obtain results with goal-oriented imagery PK and a random event generator with varying hit probabilities [Abstract]. In W. G. Roll (Ed.), *Research in parapsychology 1979* (pp. 166–67). Lanham, MD: Scarecrow Press.

Morris, R. W., Summers, J., and Yim, S. (2003). Evidence of anomalous information transfer with a creative population in ganzfeld stimulation [Abstract]. *Journal of Parapsychology* 67, 256–57 .

Moscovitz, G. B., and Gesundheit, Y. (2009). Goal priming. In G. B. Moskowitz and H. Grant (Eds.), *The psychology of goals*. New York: The Guilford Press, 203–33.

Moss, T. (1969). ESP effects in "artists" compared with "non-artists." *Journal of Parapsychology* 33, 57–69.

Moss, T., and Gengerelli, J. A. (1968). ESP effects generated by affective states. *Journal of Parapsychology* 32, 90–100.

Moss, T., Paulson, M. J., Chang, A. F., and Levitt, M. (1970). Hypnosis and ESP: A controlled experiment. *American Journal of Clinical Hypnosis* 13, 46–56.

Moulton, S. T. (2000). *Implicit measures of ganzfeld success: An experimental assessment.* Unpublished Honors Thesis, Harvard University, Cambridge, MA.

Moulton, S. T., and Kosslyn, S. M. (2008). Using neuroimaging to resolve the psi debate. *Journal of Cognitive Neuroscience* 20, 182–92.

Mueller, J. H. (1979). Anxiety and encoding processes in memory. *Personality and Social Psychology Bulletin* 5, 288–94.

Müller, J. (1826). *Zur vergleichenden Physiologie des Gesichtssinnes des Menschen und der Thiere.* Leipzig: K. Knobloch.

Munroe, R. L. (1955). *Schools of psychoanalytic thought.* New York: Holt, Rinehart and Winston, Inc.

Murphy, D. B., and Myers, T. I. (1962). Occurrence, measurement, and experimental manipulation of visual hallucination. *Perceptual and Motor Skills* 15, 47–54.

Murphy, G. (1948). What needs to be done in parapsychology. *Journal of Parapsychology* 12, 15–19.

Murphy, G. (1949). Psychical research and human personality. *Proceedings of the Society for Psychical Research* 48, 1–15.

Murphy, G. (1956). The boundaries between the person and the world. *British Journal of Psychology* 47, 99–94.

Murphy, G. (1963). Creativity and its relation to extrasensory perception. *Journal of the American Society for Psychical Research* 57, 203–14.

Murphy, G. (1966). Research in creativeness: What can it tell us about extrasensory perception? *Journal of the American Society for Psychical Research* 60, 8–22.

Murphy, S. T., Monahan, J. L., and Zajonc, R. B. (1995). Additivity of nonconscious affect: Combined effects of priming and exposure. *Journal of Personality and Social Psychology* 69, 589–602.

Murphy, S. T., and Zajonc, R. B. (1993). Affect, cognition and awareness: Affective priming with optimal and suboptimal stimulus exposures. *Journal of Personality and Social Psychology* 64, 723–39.

Murray, H. A. (1938). *Explorations in personality.* New York: Oxford University Press.

Myers, F. W. H. (1891–92). An alleged movement of objects without contact. Part II. *Proceedings of the Society for Psychical Research* 7, 383–94.

Myers, F. W. H. (1961 [1903]). *Human personality and its survival of bodily death.* New York: University Books.

Myers, I. B., with Myers, P. B. (1980). *Gifts differing.* Palo Alto, CA: Consulting Psychologists Press.

Nakamura, C. Y., and Wright, H. G. (1965). Effects of experimentally induced low drive, response mode, and social cues on word association and response speed. *Journal of Experimental Research in Personality* 1, 122–31.

Nanko, M. (1981). Use of goal-oriented imagery strategy on a psychokinetic task with "selected" subjects. *Journal of the Southern California Society for Psychical Research* 2, 1–5.

Nash, C. B. (1958). Correlation between ESP and religious value. *Journal of Parapsychology* 22, 204–09.

Nash, C. B. (1960). The effect of subject-experimenter attitudes on clairvoyance scores. *Journal of Parapsychology* 24, 189–98.

Nash, C. B. (1963). Relations between ESP scoring level and the MMPI. *Journal of Parapsychology* 27, 274–75.

Nash, C. B. (1986). Comparison of subliminal and extrasensory perception. *Journal of the Society for Psychical Research* 53, 435–53.

Nash, C. B., and Nash, C. S. (1967). Relations between ESP scoring level and the personality traits of the Guilford-Zimmerman Temperament Survey. *Journal of the American Society for Psychical Research* 61, 64–71.

Nash, C. B., and Nash, C. S. (1968). Effect of target selection, field dependence, and body concept on ESP performance. *Journal of Parapsychology* 32, 249–57.

Nelson, L. A., and Schwartz, G. B. (2005). Human biofield and intention detection: Individual differences. *Journal of Alternative and Complementary Medicine* 11, 93–101.

Nelson, M. C. (1964). Psi communication as seen in parallel dreams. *Journal of the American Society for Psychical Research* 58, 280–83.

Nelson, M. C. (1965). Birds of a feather: Psychoanalytyic observations on parapsychological phenomena. *Israeli Annals of Psychiatry and Related Disciplines* 3, 73–87.

Nelson, M. C. (1975). Psi in the family. *Clinical Social Work Journal* 3, 279–85.

Nelson, M. C. (1988). Imagery, self-containment and psi. *Psychotherapy Patient* 4, 345–60.

Neppe, V. (1983). Temporal lobe symptomatology in subjective paranormal experiences. *Journal of the American Society for Psychical Research* 77, 1–30.

Neuberg, S. L., and Newsom, J. T. (1993). Personal need for structure: Individual differences in the desire for simpler structure. *Journal of Personality and Social Psychology* 65, 113–31.

Newell, A., and Rosenbloom, P. S. (1981). Mechanisms of skill acquisition and the law of practice. In J. R. Anderson (Ed.), *Cognitive skills and their acquisition* (pp. 1–55). Hillsdale, NJ: Lawrence Erlbaum Associates, Inc.

Nicholls, J. G. (1972). Creativity in the person who will never produce anything original and useful. *American Psychologist* 27, 717–27.

Nicol, J. F., and Humphrey, B. M. (1953). The exploration of ESP and human personality. *Journal of the American Society for Psychical Research* 47, 133–78.

Nicol, J. F., and Humphrey, B. M. (1955). The repeatability problem in ESP-personality research. *Journal of the American Society for Psychical Research* 49, 125–56.

Nielsen, W. (1970a). Studies in group targets: A social psychology class. *Proceedings of the Parapsychology Association* 7, 55–57.

Nielsen, W. (1970b). Studies in group targets: An unusual high school group. *Proceedings of the Parapsychology Association* 7, 57–58.

Nietzsche, F. (2000). *Basic writings of Nietzsche*. Trans. Walter Kaufman. New York: Modern Library.

Norfolk, C. (1999). Can future emotions be perceived unconsciously? An investigation into the presentiment effect with reference to extraversion. Unpublished manuscript, Department of Psychology, University of Edinburgh.

O'Brien, D. P. (1976). Recall and recognition processes in a memory-ESP paired-associate task. *Journal of Parapsychology* 40, 57–58.

Orloff, J. (1997). *Second sight*. Boston: Warner Books.

Ortells, J. J., and Tudela, P. (1996). Positive and negative sematic priming of attended and unattended parafoveal words in a lexical decision task. *Acta Psychologica* 94, 209–26.

Osis, K. (1952). ESP tests over long and short distances. *Journal of Parapsychology* 20, 81–95.

Osis, K. (1956). A test of the occurrence of a psi effect between man and cat. *Journal of Parapsychology* 16, 233–56.

Osis, K., and Bokert, E. (1976). ESP and changed states of consciousness induced by meditation. *Journal of the American Society for Psychical Research* 65, 17–65.

Owen, I. M., and Sparrow, M. (1976). Conjuring up Philip. Ontario, Canada: Fitzhenry and Whiteside.

Packard, V. (2007). *The hidden persuaders*. Brooklyn: Ig Publishers.

Palmer, J. (1972). Scoring on ESP tests as a function of belief in ESP. Part II. Beyond the sheep-goat effect. *Journal of the American Society for Psychical Research* 66, 1–26.

Palmer, J. (1977). Attitudes and personality traits in experimental ESP research. In B. Wolman (Ed.), *Handbook of parapsychology* (pp. 175–201). New York: Van Nostrand Reinhold.

Palmer, J. (1978). Extrasensory perception: Research findings. In S. Krippner (Ed.), *Advances in parapsychological research 2* (pp. 59–243). New York: Plenum Press.

Palmer, J. (1982). ESP research findings: 1976–1978. In S. Krippner (Ed.), *Advances in parapsychological research 3* (pp. 41–82). New York: Plenum Press.

Palmer, J. (1989a). Confronting the experimenter effect: I. *Parapsychology Review* 20 (4), 1–4.

Palmer, J. (1989b). Confronting the experimenter effect: II. *Parapsychology Review* 20 (5), 1–5.

Palmer, J. (1992). Effect of a threatening subliminal stimulus on the perceptual ESP test: A partial replication. *Journal of Parapsychology* 58, 115–48.

Palmer, J. (1994). Explorations with the perceptual ESP test. *Journal of Parapsychology* 56, 189–204.

Palmer, J. (1995). The effect of subliminal stimulation on perceptual ESP test results with uniform targets. Proceedings of Presented Papers: The Parapsychological Association 38th Annual Convention, 260–69.

Palmer, J. (1996). Further studies with the perceptual ESP test: Feast and famine. Proceedings of Presented Papers: The Parapsychological Association 39th Annual Convention, 375–88.

Palmer, J. (1997). Correlates of ESP magnitude and direction in the PRL and RRC autoganzfeld databases. *Proceedings of the Parapsychological Association, (Number 40)*, 283–98.

Palmer, J. (1998a). Correlates of ESP magnitude and direction in the FRNM manual ganzfeld database. *Proceedings of the Parapsychological Association, (Number 41, 108–23.*

Palmer, J. (1998b). The perceptual ESP test in a religious context. In M. J. Schlitz and N. L. Zingrone (Eds.), *Research in parapsychology 1993.* Lanham, MD: Scarecrow Press, 115–19.

Palmer, J. (2001). Motor automatisms as a vehicle of ESP expression. *Proceedings of the Parapsychological Association (Number 44),* 205–17.

Palmer, J. (2003). ESP in the ganzfeld: Analysis of a debate. *Journal of Consciousness Studies* 10(6–7), 51–68.

Palmer, J. (2006a). Anomalous anticipation of target biases in a computer guessing task. *Proceedings of the Parapsychological Association 2006* 49, 127–40.

Palmer, J. (2006b). Memory and ESP: A review of the experimental literature. *6 Simposio da Fundação Bial: Behind and beyond the brain.* Porto: Casa do Médico.

Palmer, J. (2011). Motor automatisms as a vehicle of ESP expression. *Journal of Parapsychology* 75, 45–60.

Palmer, J., Ader, C., and Mikova, M. (1981). Anxiety and ESP: Anatomy of a reversal. In W. G. Roll, J. Beloff, and J. McAllister (Eds.), *Research in parapsychology 1980.* Metuchen, NJ: Scarecrow Press, 77–81.

Palmer, J., and Carpenter, J. C. (1998). Comments on the extraversion-ESP meta-analysis by Honorton, Ferrari, and Bem. *Journal of Parapsychology* 62, 277–82.

Palmer, J., and Johnson, M. (1991). Defensiveness and brain hemisphere stimulation in a perceptually mediated ESP task. *Journal of Parapsychology* 55, 329–48.

Palmer, J., Khamashta, K., and Israelson, K. (1979). An ESP ganzfeld experiment with transcendental meditators. *Journal of the American Society for Psychical Research* 73, 333–48.

Palmer, J., and Lieberman, R. (1975). The influence of psychological set on ESP and out-of-body experiences. *Journal of the American Society for Psychical Research* 69, 193–213.

Pang, H., and Frost, L. (1967). Relatedness of creativity, values and ESP. *Perceptual and Motor Skills* 24, 650.

Parker, A. (1975a). A pilot study of the influence of experimenter expectancy on ESP scores [abstract]. In J. D. Morris, W. G. Roll, and R. L. Morris (Eds.), *Research in parapsychology 1974.* Metuchen, NJ: Scarecrow Press, 42–44.

Parker, A. (1975b). Some findings relevant to the change in state hypothesis [abstract]. In J. D. Morris, W. G. Roll, and R. L. Morris (Eds.), *Research in parapsychology 1974.* Metuchen, NJ: Scarecrow Press, 40–42.

Parker, A., and Beloff, J. (1970). Hypnotically-induced clairvoyant dreams: A partial replication and attempted confirmation. *Journal of the American Society for Psychical Research* 64, 432–42.

Parker, A., and Sjöden, S. (2010). Do some of us habituate to future emotional events? *Journal of Parapsychology* 74, 99–117.

Parker, K. (1976). A study of immediate memory and ESP. In J. D. Morris, W. G. Roll, and R. L. Morris (Eds.), *Research in parapsychology 1975.* Metuchen, NJ: Scarecrow Press, 130–34.

Parker, K., and Wiklund, N. (1987). The ganzfeld experiments: Towards an assessment. *Journal of the Society for Psychical Research* 54, 261–65.

Parkhomtchouk, D. V., Kotake, J., Zhang, T., Chen, W., Kokubo, H., and Yamamoto, M. (2002). An attempt to reproduce the presentiment EDA response. *Journal of International Society of Life Information Science* 20, 190–94.

Parra, A., and Villanueva, J. (2003). Personality factors and ESP during ganzfeld sessions. *Journal of the Society for Psychical Research* 67, 26–36.

Paterson, R. J., and Neufeld, R. W. J. (1987). Clear danger: Situational determinants of the appraisal of threat. *Psychological Bulletin* 101, 404–16.

Paunonen, S. V., and Ashton, M. C. (2001). Big five factors and facets and the prediction of behavior. *Journal of Personality and Social Psychology* 81, 524–39.

Peirce, C. S., and Jastrow, J. (1884). On small differences in sensation. *Memoirs of the National Academy of Science* 3, 75–83.

Perez-Navarro, J., Lawrence, T., and Hume, I. (2009a). Personality, mental state and procedure in the experimental replication of ESP: A preliminary study of new variables. *Journal of the Society for Psychical Research* 73, 1–16.

Perez-Navarro, J., Lawrence, T., and Hume, I. (2009b). Personality, mental state and procedure in the experimental replication of ESP: A logistic regression analysis of a successful experimental condition. *European Journal of Parapsychology* 24, 68–92.

Perls, F. S. (1970). Four lectures. In J. A. Fagan and I. Shepherd (Eds.), *Gestalt therapy now.* Palo Alto, CA: Science and Behavior Books.

Peters, K. R., and Gawronski, B. (2011). Are we puppets on a string? Comparing the impact of contingency and validity on implicit and explicit evaluations. *Personality and Social Psychology Bulletin* 37, 557–69.

Peterson, D. M. (1978). *Through the looking glass: An investigation of the faculty of extra-sensory detection of being looked at.* Unpublished MA thesis, University of Edinburgh.

Pilkington, R. (1984). The use of fantasy in a children's ESP experiment. Doctoral dissertation, Saybrook Institute. *Dissertation Abstracts International*, 45(3-B), 1049.

Pilkington, R. (2010). *Esprit: Men and women of parapsychology, personal reflections, volume 1.* New York: Anomalist Books.

Pincombe, J. L., Luciano, M., Martin, N. G., and Wright, M. J. (2007). Heritability of NEO PI-R Extraversion facets and their relationship with IQ. *Twin Research and Human Genetics* 10, 462–69.

Poetzl, O. (1917). The relationship between experimentally induced dream images and indirect vision. Monograph No. 7, *Psychological Issues* 2, 41–120.

Polanyi, M. (1958). *Personal knowledge: Towards a post-critical philosophy.* Chicago: University of Chicago Press.

Poortman, J. J. (1959). The feeling of being stared at. *Journal of the Society for Psychical Research* 40, 4–12.

Popper, K. R., and Eccles, J. C. (1977). *The self and its brain.* Berlin: Springer-Verlag.

Pratt, J. G. (1946). Lawfulness of position effects in the Gibson cup PK series. *Journal of Parapsychology* 10, 243–68.

Pratt, J. G. (1973). A decade of research with a selected ESP subject: An overview and reappraisal of the work with Pavel Stepanek. *Proceedings of the American Society for Psychical Research* 30.

Pratt, J. G., Rhine, J. B., Smith, B. M., Stuart, C. E., and Greenwood, J. A. (eds.). *Extrasensory perception after sixty years,* 2nd ed. Boston: Humphries.

Pratt, J. G., and Woodruff, J. L. (1939). Size of stimulus symbols in extrasensory perception. *Journal of Parapsychology* 3, 121–58.

Price, H. H. (1949). Psychical research and human personality. *Hibbert Journal* 47, 105–30. (Reprinted in J. R. Smythies (Ed.), *Science and ESP.* New York: Humanities Press, 1967.)

Prince, W. F. (1928). *Noted witnesses for psychical research.* Oxford, England: Boston Society for Psychical Research.

Puharich, A. (1973). *Beyond telepathy.* New York: Anchor Press.

Puthoff, H. E. (1984). Calculator assisted psi amplification. In R. A. White and J. Solfvin (Eds.), *Research in parapsychology 1984* (pp. 48–51). Metuchen, NJ: Scarecrow Press.

Puthoff, H. E., May, E. C., and Thompson, M. J. (1986). Calculator assisted psi amplification II: Use of the sequential-sampling technique as a variable-length majority-vote code. In D. H. Weiner and D. I. Radin (Eds.), *Research in parapsychology 1985* (pp. 73–77). Metuchen, NJ: Scarecrow Press.

Puthoff, H. E., and Targ, R. (1976). A perceptual channel for information transfer over kilometer distances: Historical perspective and recent research. *Proceedings of the IEEE* 64, 329–44.

Putnam, F. (1989). *Diagnosis and treatment of multiple personality disorder.* New York: Guilford Press.

Putnam, F. (1999). Pierre Janet and modern views of dissociation. In M. J. Horowitz (Ed.), *Essential papers on post traumatic stress disorder.* New York: New York University Press.

Quinn, D. M., Chaudoir, S. R., Kallen, R. W., Calogero, R. M., Tantleff-Dunn, S., and Thompson, J. K. (2011). Performance and flow: A review and integration of self–objectification research. In R. M. Calogero, S. Tantleff-Dunn, and J. K. Thompson (Eds.), *Self-objectification in women: Causes, consequences, and counteractions* (pp. 119–38). Washington, DC: American Psychological Association.

Radin, D. I. (1991). Enhancing effects in psi experiments with sequential analysis: A replication and extension. In L. A. Henkel and G. R. Schmeidler (Eds.), *Research in parapsychology 1990* (pp. 21–25). Metuchen, NJ: Scarecrow Press.

Radin, D. I. (1997). Unconscious perception of future emotions. *Journal of Scientific Exploration* 11, 163–80.

Radin, D. I. (1998). Further investigation of unconscious differential anticipatory responses to future emotions. *Proceedings of the Parapsychological Association* 41, 162–84.

Radin, D. I. (2004a). Electrodermal presentiments of future emotions: An experiment in presentiment. *Journal of Scientific Exploration* 11, 163–80.

Radin, D. I. (2004b). The sense of being stared at: Analysis of previous data and a pilot replication. *Journal of the Society for Psychical Research* 68, 245–53.

Radin, D. I. (2005). The sense of being stared at: A preliminary meta-analysis. *Journal of Consciousness Studies* 12, 95–100.

Radin, D. I. (2006). *Entangled minds: Extrasensory experiences in a quantum reality.* New York: Paraview Pocket Books.

Radin, D. I. (2009). *The conscious universe: The scientific truth of psychic phenomena.* New York: HarperOne.

Radin, D. I., and Borges, A. (2009). Intuition through time: What does the seer see? *Explore* 5, 200–11.

Radin, D. I., and Lobach, E. (2007). Toward understanding the placebo effect: Investigating a possible retrocausal factor. *Journal of Alternative and Complementary Medicine* 13, 1–7.

Radin, D. I., and Nelson, R. D. (1989). Evidence for consciousness-related anomalies in random physical systems. *Foundations of Physics* 19, 1499–1514.

Radin, D. I., Taylor, R. D., and Braud, W. (1995). Remote mental influence of human electrodermal activity: A pilot replication. *European Journal of Parapsychology* 11, 19–34.

Rajamanickam, M., and Gnanaguru, K. (1981). Physiological correlates of personality. *Psychological Studies* 26, 41–43.

Rammohan, V. G. (1990). Psi in the academic context: Two further studies. *Journal of Parapsychology* 54, 229–44.

Randall, J. L. (1974). Card-guessing experiments with schoolboys. *Journal of the Society for Psychical Research* 47, 421–32.

Rao, K. R. (1962). The preferential effect in ESP. *Journal of Parapsychology* 26, 252–59.

Rao, K. R. (1963). Studies in the preferential effect. I. Target preference with types of targets unknown. *Journal of Parapsychology* 27, 23–32.

Rao, K. R. (1964). The differential response in three new situations. *Journal of Parapsychology* 28, 81–92.

Rao, K. R. (1965a). The bidirectionality of psi. *Journal of Parapsychology* 29, 230–50.

Rao, K. R. (1965b). ESP and the Manifest Anxiety Scale. *Journal of Parapsychology* 29, 12–18.

Rao, K. R. (1965c). *Experimental parapsychology: A review and interpretation.* Springfield, IL: Charles Thomas.

Rao, K. R. (1978). Further studies of memory and ESP. *Journal of Parapsychology* 42, 167–78.

Rao, K. R. (1991). Consciousness research and psi. *Journal of Parapsychology* 55, 1–44.

Rao, K. R., and Kanthamani, H. (1990). Exploring normal-paranormal interaction within a memory-ESP testing paradigm. In L. Henkel and J. Palmer (Eds.), *Research in parapsychology 1989.* Metuchen, NJ: Scarecrow Press, 62–66.

Rao, K. R., Kanthamani, H., and Palmer, J. (1990). Exploring normal/paranormal interaction within a memory-ESP testing paradigm. *Journal of Parapsychology* 54, 245–59.

Rao, K. R., Kanthamani, H., and Sailaja, P. (1971). ESP scores before and after a scheduled interview. In W. G. Roll, R. L. Morris, and J. D. Morris (Eds.), *Proceedings of parapsychology association 5* (pp. 57–59). Durham, NC: Parapsychology Association.

Rao, K. R., Morrison, M., and Davis, J. W. (1977). Paired-associates recall and ESP: A study of memory and psi-missing. *Journal of Parapsychology* 41, 165–89.

Rao, K. R., Morrison, M., Davis, J. W., and Freeman, J. A. (1977). The role of association in memory recall and ESP. *Journal of Parapsychology* 41, 190–97.

Rao, K. R., and O'Brien, J. T. (1977). ESP performance in classroom and examination settings. *Journal of Parapsychology* 41, 1–9.

Rao, K. R., Sundari, K. G., Rao, Y. J., and Rao, R. N. (1977). SSP and ESP with a weight discrimination task [Abstract]. In J. D. Morris, W. G. Roll, and R. L. Morris (Eds.), *Research in parapsychology 1975* (pp. 79–81). Metuchen, NJ: Scarecrow Press.

Raush, H. L. (1969). Naturalistic method and the clinical approach. In E. Willems and H. Raush (Eds.), *Naturalistic viewpoints in psychological research*, New York: Holt, Rinehart and Winston.

Rawlings, D., Twomey, F., Burns, E., and Morris, S. (1998). Personality, creativity, and aesthetic preference: Comparing psychoticism, sensation seeking, schizotypy, and openness to experience. *Empirical Studies of the Arts* 16, 153–78.

Rebman, J., Radin, D., and Stevens, P. (1996). A precognition experiment on the World Wide Web. Proceedings of the Parapsychological Association 39th Annual Convention, 207–18.

Reed, K. (1988). An experimental evaluation of a belief in ESP [Abstract]. In D. H. Weiner and R. L. Morris (Eds.), *Research in parapsychology 1987* (pp. 85–87). Metuchen, NJ: Scarecrow Press.

Reik, T. (1964). *Listening with the third ear.* New York: Pyramid Edition.

Rhine, J. B. (1934 [1973]). *Extrasensory perception* (Rev. ed.). Boston: Bruce Humphries.

Rhine, J. B. (1946). Hypnotic suggestion in PK tasks. *Journal of Parapsychology* 10, 126–40.

Rhine, J. B. (1948). Conditions favoring success in psi tests. *Journal of Parapsychology* 12, 58–75.

Rhine, J. B. (1952). The problem of psi-missing. *Journal of Parapsychology* 16, 90–129.

Rhine, J. B. (1953). Psi, psyche and psychology. In *New world of the mind.* New York: William Sloan Associates.

Rhine, J. B. (1957). *Parapsychology: Frontier science of the mind.* New York: Charles C. Thomas.

Rhine, J. B. (1958). On the nature and consequences of the unconsciousness of psi. *Journal of Parapsychology* 22, 175–86.

Rhine, J. B. (1964). Special motivation in some exceptional ESP performances. *Journal of Parapsychology* 28, 42–50.

Rhine, J. B. (1977). The history of experimental studies. In B. B. Wolman (Ed.), *Handbook of parapsychology* (pp. 25–47). New York: Van Nostrand.

Rhine, J. B. (1979). *Reach of the mind.* New York: William Morrow and Co.

Rhine, J. B., and Humphrey, B. M. (1945). Position effects in the six-by-six series of PK tests. *Journal of Parapsychology* 8, 296–302.

Rhine, L. E. (1953). Subjective forms of spontaneous psi experiences. *Journal of Parapsychology* 17, 77–114.

Rhine, L. E. (1962a). Psychological processes in ESP experiences. Part I. Waking experiences. *Journal of Parapsychology* 26, 88–111.

Rhine, L. E. (1962b). Psychological processes in ESP experiences. Part II. Dreams. *Journal of Parapsychology* 26, 172–99.

Rhine, L. E. (1963). Spontaneous physical effects and the psi process. *Journal of Parapsychology* 27, 84–122.

Rhine, L. E. (1964). Factors influencing the range of information in ESP experiences. *Journal of Parapsychology* 28, 176–213.

Rhine, L. E. (1967). *ESP in life and lab: Tracing hidden channels.* Oxford, England: Macmillan.

Rice, G., Williss, D., Lafferty, C., Little, J., and Mauldin, C. H. (1966). Emotional closeness, communication of affect, and ESP. *Journal of Parapsychology* 30, 285–86.

Richards, D. (1991). A study of the correlations between subjective psychic experiences and dissociative experiences. *Dissociation: Progress in the Dissociative Disorders* 4, 83–91.

Richardson, J. T. (1982). Introversion-extraversion and experimenter effects in memory tasks. *Personality and Individual Differences* 3, 327–28.

Rivers, O. B. (1964). An exploratory study of the mental health and intelligence of ESP subjects. *Journal of Parapsychology* 14, 267–77.

Roberts, J. V. (1985). The attitude-memory relationship after 40 years: A meta-analysis of the literature. *Basic and Applied Social Psychology* 6, 221–41.

Robinson, M. D., and Clore, G. L. (2002). Belief and feeling: Evidence for an accessibility model of emotional self-report. *Psychological Bulletin* 128, 934–60.

Roe, C. A., Davey, R., and Stevens, P. (2003). Are ESP and PK aspects of a unitary phenomenon? A preliminary test of the relationship between ESP and PK. *Journal of Parapsychology* 67, 343–66.

Roe, C. A., Henderson, S. J., and Matthews, J. (2008). Extraversion and performance at a forced-choice ESP task with verbal stimuli: Two studies. *Journal of the Society for Psychical Research* 72, 208–21.

Roe, C. A., McKenzie, E. A., and Ali, A. N. (2001). Sender and receiver creativity scores as predictors of performance at a ganzfeld ESP task. *Journal of the Society for Psychical Research* 65, 107–21.

Roe, C. A., Sherwood, S. J., and Holt, N. J. (2004). A further consideration of the sender as a PK agent in ganzfeld ESP tasks. *Journal of Parapsychology* 69, 113–28.

Roe, C. A., Sherwood, S. J., and Holt, N. J. (2005). Interpersonal psi: Exploring the role of the sender in ganzfeld ESP tasks. *Journal of Parapsychology* 68, 361–80.

Roe, C. A., Sherwood, S. J., Luke, D. P., and Farrell, L. M. (2002). An exploratory investigation of dream GESP using consensus judging and dynamic targets. *Journal of the Society for Psychical Research* 66, 225–38.

Rogers, D. P. (1966). Negative and positive affect and ESP run-score variance. *Journal of Parapsychology* 30, 151–59.

Rogers, D. P. (1967). Negative and positive affect and ESP run-score variance. Study II. *Journal of Parapsychology* 31, 290–96.

Rogers, D. P. (1975). Driving subjects crazy. In J. D. Morris, W. G. Roll, and R. L. Morris (Eds.), *Research in parapsychology 1974* (pp. 165–70). Metuchen, NJ: Scarecrow Press.

Rogers, D. P., and Carpenter, J. C. (1966). The decline of variance of ESP scores within a testing session. *Journal of Parapsychology* 30, 141–50.

Rogo, D. S. (1977). The use of short-duration Ganzfeld stimulation to facilitate psi-mediated imagery. *European Journal of Parapsychology* 4, 72.

Roll, W. G. (1966). ESP and memory. *International Journal of Neuropsychiatry* 2, 505–21.

Roll, W. G., and Klein, J. (1972). Further forced-choice ESP experiments with Lalsingh Harribance. *Journal of the American Society for Psychical Research* 66, 103–12.

Roll, W. G., Morris, R. L., Damgaard, J. A., Klein, J., and Roll, M. (1973). Free verbal response experiments with Lalsingh Harribance. *Journal of the American Society for Psychical Research* 67, 197–207.

Rose, R. (1955). A second report on psi experiments with Australian Aborigines. *Journal of Parapsychology* 19, 92–98.

Rosenthal, R. (1966). *Experimenter effects in behavioral research.* New York: Appleton-Century.

Rosenthal, R. (1967). Covert communication in the psychological experiment. *Psychological Bulletin* 67, 356–67.

Rosenthal, R. (1980). Replicability and experimenter influence: Experimenter effects in behavioral research. *Journal of Parapsychology* 50, 315–36.

Rosenthal, R. (1986). Meta-analytic procedures and the nature of replication: The ganzfeld debate. *Parapsychology Review* 11, 5–11.

Ross, A. O., Murphy, G., and Schmeidler, G. R. (1952). The spontaneity factor in extrasensory perception. *Journal of the American Society for Psychical Research* 46, 14–16.

Ross, C. A., and Joshi, S. (1992). Paranormal experiences in the general population. *Journal of Nervous and Mental Disease* 180, 357–61.

Rothermund, K. (2003). Automatic vigilance for task-related information: Perseverance after failure and inhibition after success. *Memory and Cognition* 31, 343–52.

Rubin, I., and Honorton, C. H. (1971). Separating the yins from the yangs: An experiment with the *I Ching. Proceedings of the Parapsychological Association* 8, 6–7.

Rumi, J. A. (1981). *Night and sleep,* C. Barks and R. Bly, trans. Cambridge, MA: Yellow Moon Press.

Rychlak, J. F. (1968). *A philosophy of science for personality theory.* Boston: Houghton Mifflin Co.

Rychlak, J. F. (1973). *Introduction to personality and psychotherapy.* Boston: Houghton Mifflin Co.

Rychlak, J. F. (2003). *The human image in postmodern America.* Washington, DC: American Psychological Association.

Ryzl, M. (1962). Training the psi faculty by hypnosis. *Journal of the Society for Psychical Research* 41, 234–52.

Ryzl, M. (1966). A model of parapsychological communication. *Journal of Parapsychology* 30, 18–30.

Ryzl, M., and Beloff, J. (1965). Loss of stability of ESP performance in a high-scoring subject. *Journal of Parapsychology* 29, 1–11.

Ryzl, M., and Pratt, J. G. (1963). A repeated calling ESP test with sealed cards. *Journal of Parapsychology* 27, 161–74.

Ryzl, M., and Ryzlova, J. (1962). A case of high-scoring ESP performance in the hypnotic state. *Journal of Parapsychology* 26, 153–61.

Saboonchi, F., and Lundh, L. (1999). State perfectionism and its relation to trait perfectionism, type of situation, priming, and being observed. *Scandanivian Journal of Behavior Therapy* 28, 154–66.

Sagan, C. (1986). *The dragons of Eden: Speculations on the origin of human intelligence.* New York: Ballantine Books.

Sailaja, P., and Rao, K. R. (1973). *Experimental studies of the differential effect in life settings (Parapsychological Monographs No. 13).* New York: Parapsychology Foundation.

Sailaja, P., and Rao, K. (1979). Response patterns and psi scoring [Abstract]. In W. G. Roll (Ed.), *Research in parapsychology 1978* (pp. 139–142). Metuchen, NJ: Scarecrow Press.

Sarason, I. G. (1984). Stress, anxiety, and cognitive interference. *Journal of Personality and Social Psychology* 46, 929–38.

Sargent, C. L. (1977). An experiment involving a novel precognition task. *Journal of Parapsychology* 41, 275–93.

Sargent, C. L. (1978). Hypnosis as a psi-conducive state: A controlled replication study. In W. G. Roll (Ed.), *Research in parapsychology 1978* (pp. 101–104). Metuchen, NJ: Scarecrow Press.

Sargent, C. L. (1980). *Exploring psi in the ganzfeld.* New York: Parapsychology Foundation.

Sargent, C. L. (1981). Extraversion and performance in extrasensory perception tasks. *Personality and Individual Differences* 2, 137–43.

Sargent, C. L. (1982). An unusually powerful response-bias effect. *Parapsychology Review* 13, 8–10.

Sargent, C. L, Bartlett, H., and Moss, S. (1981). Response structure and temporal incline in ganzfeld free-response GESP testing. In R. L. Morris (Ed.), *Research in parapsychology 1981* (pp. 79–81). Metuchen, NJ: Scarecrow Press.

Sargent, C. L., and Harley, T. A. (1981). Ganzfeld GESP performance with variable-duration testing. [Abstract]. In W. G. Roll, J. Beloff, and R. A. White (Eds.), *Research in parapsychology 1981* (pp. 159–60). Metuchen, NJ: Scarecrow Press.

Sargent, C. L., Harley, T. A., Lane, J., and Radcliffe, K. (1981). Ganzfeld psi optimization in relation to session duration. [Abstract]. In W. G. Roll and J. Beloff (Eds.), *Research in parapsychology 1980* (pp. 82–84). Metuchen, NJ: Scarecrow Press.

Sargent, C. L., and Matthews, G. (1981). Three studies using a psi-predictive trait variable questionnaire. *Journal of Parapsychology* 45, 199–214.

Satchidananda, S. S. (1990). *The yoga sutras of Patanjali.* New York: Integral Yoga Publications.

Savva, L., Child, R., and Smith, M. D. (2004). The precognitive habituation effect: An adaptation using spider stimuli. *Proceedings of Presented Papers: The Parapsychological Association 47th Annual Convention*, 223–29.

Savva, L., and French, C. C. (2002). Is there time-reversed interference in Stroop-based tasks. The Parapsychological Association 45th Annual Convention, Proceedings of the Presented Papers, 194–205.

Schacter, D. L. (1997). *Searching for memory: The brain, the mind, and the past.* New York: Basic Books.

Schechter, E. I. (1977). Nonintentional ESP: A review and replication. *Journal of the American Society for Psychical Research* 71, 337–74.

Schechter, E. I. (1984). Hypnotic induction vs. control conditions: Illustrating an approach to the evaluation of replicability in parapsychological data. *Journal of the American Society for Psychical Research* 78, 1–27.

Scherer, W. B. (1948). Spontaneity as a factor in ESP. *Journal of Parapsychology* 12, 126–47.

Schilder, P. (1942). *Mind: Perception and thought in their constructive aspects.* New York: Columbia University Press.

Schilder, P. (1955). Psychopathology of everyday telepathic phenomena. In G. Devereux (Ed.), *Psychoanalysis and the occult* (pp. 204–09). New York: International Universities Press.

Schlitz, M. J., and Braud, W. (1997). Distant intentionality and healing: Assessing the evidence. *Alternative Therapies* 3, 62–73.

Schlitz, M. J., and Honorton, C. (1992). Ganzfeld ESP performance within an artistically gifted population. *Journal of the American Society for Psychical Research* 86, 83–98.

Schlitz, M. J., and LaBerge, S. (1994). Autonomic detection of remote observation: Two conceptual replications. Proceedings of Presented Papers, 37th Annual Parapsychological Association Convention. Amsterdam, the Netherlands: Parapsychological Association: 352–60.

Schlitz, M., Wiseman, R., Radin, D., and Watt, C. (2005, August 11–15). *Of two minds: Skeptic-proponent collaboration within parapsychology.* Paper presented at the 48th Annual Convention of the Parapsychological Association, Institute of Noetic Sciences, Petaluma, CA.

Schmeidler, G. R. (1945). Separating the sheep from the goats. *Journal of the American Society for Psychical Research* 39, 47–49.

Schmeidler, G. R. (1952). Rorschachs and ESP scores of patients suffering from cerebral concussion. *Journal of Parapsychology* 16, 80–89.

Schmeidler, G. R. (1960). The accuracy of parapsychological information. *Indian Journal of Parapsychology* 2, 169–73.

Schmeidler, G. R. (1963). Tests of creative thinking and ESP scores. *Indian Journal of Parapsychology* 4, 51–57.

Schmeidler, G. R. (1964a). An experiment on precognitive clairvoyance: Part II. The reliability of the scores. *Journal of Parapsychology* 28, 15–27.

Schmeidler, G. R. (1964b). An experiment on precognitive clairvoyance: Part IV: Precognition scores related to creativity. *Journal of Parapsychology* 28, 102–08.

Schmeidler, G. R. (1968). A search for feedback in ESP: Part I. Session salience and stimulus preference. *Journal of the American Society for Psychical Research* 62, 130–41.

Schmeidler, G. R. (1980). Does ESP influence the recall of partially learned words? In W. G. Roll (Ed.), *Research in parapsychology 1979* (pp. 54–57). Metuchen, NJ: Scarecrow Press.

Schmeidler, G. R. (1981). ESP and memory: Support for Kreiman's summary hypothesis [Abstract]. In W. G. Roll (Ed.), *Research in parapsychology 1980* (pp. 118–20). Metuchen, NJ: Scarecrow Press.

Schmeidler, G. R. (1982). A possible commonality among gifted psychics. *Journal of the American Society for Psychical Research* 76, 53–58.

Schmeidler, G. R. (1983). ESP and memory: Some limiting conditions. *Parapsychological Journal of South Africa* 4, 51–69.

Schmeidler, G. R. (1986). Subliminal perception and ESP: Order in diversity? *Journal of the American Society for Psychical Research* 80, 241–64.

Schmeidler, G. R. (1988). *Parapsychology and psychology: Matches and mismatches*. Jefferson, NC: McFarland.

Schmeidler, G. R., and Maher (1981). Judges' responses to the nonverbal behavior of psi-conducive and psi-inhibitory experimenters *Journal of the American Society for Psychical Research* 75, 241–57.

Schmeidler, G. R., and McConnell, R. A. (1958). *ESP and personality patterns*. New Haven: Yale University Press.

Schmeidler, G. S., Mitchell, J., and Sondow, N. (1975). Further investigations of PK with temperature records [Abstract]. In J. D. Morris, W. G. Roll, and R. L. Morris (Eds.), *Research in parapsychology 1974* (pp. 71–73). Metuchen, NJ: Scarecrow Press.

Schmidt, H. (1970a). A quantum mechanical random number generator for psi tests. *Journal of Parapsychology* 34, 219–24.

Schmidt, H. (1970b). PK experiments with animals as subjects. *Journal of Parapsychology* 34, 255–61.

Schmidt, H., and Pantas, L. (1972a). PK tests with internally different machines. *Journal of Parapsychology* 36, 222–42.

Schmidt, H., and Pantas, L. (1972b). PK tests with psychologically equivalent conditions and internally different machines. In W. G. Roll, R. L. Morris, and J. D. Morris (Eds.), *Proceedings of the parapsychology association 1971*, 49–51.

Schmidt, S., and Schlitz, M. (1989). A large-scale pilot PK experiment with pre-recorded random events. In L. A. Henkel and R. E. Berger (Eds.), *Research in parapsychology 1988* (pp. 6–10). Metuchen, NJ: Scarecrow Press.

Schmidt, S., Schneider, R., Utts, J., and Walach H. (2004). Distant intentionality and the feeling of being stared at: Two meta-analyses. *British Journal of Psychology* 95, 235–47.

Schneider, R., Binder, M., and Walach, H. (2000). Examining the role of neutral versus personal experimenter-participant interactions: An EDA-DMILS experiment. *Journal of Parapsychology* 64, 181–94.

Schouten, S. A. (2002). Beyond the enchanted boundary. *Journal of the American Society for Psychical Research* 96, 164–71.

Schultheiss, O. C., Liening, S. H., and Schad, D. (2008). The reliability of a Picture Story Exercise measure of implicit motives: Estimates of internal consistency, re-test reliability, and ipsative stability. *Journal of Research in Personality* 42, 1560–71.

Schwartz, G. E., and Simon, W. (2003). *The afterlife experiments: Breakthrough scientific evidence of life after death*. New York: Atria Books.

Schwartz, S. (2001). *The Alexandria project*. Bloomington, IN: iUniverse.

Schwarz, B. E. (1965). *Psychic-dynamics*. New York: Pageant Press.

Schwarz, B. E. (1967). Possible telesomatic reactions. *Journal of the Medical Society of New Jersey* 64, 600–603.

Schwarz, B. E. (1971). *Parent-child telepathy.* New York: Garrett Publications.

Schwarz, N., and Bless, H. (1992). Constructing reality and its alternatives: An inclusion/exclusion model of assimilation and contrast effects in social judgments. In L. L. Martin and A. Tesser (Eds.), *The construction of social judgments* (pp. 217–45). Hillsdale, NJ: Lawrence Erlbaum Associates, Inc.

Sendak, M. (1988). *Caldecott and co.: Notes on books and pictures.* Gordonsville, VA: Farrar, Straus and Giroux, Inc.

Servadio, E. (1935). Psychoanalysis and telepathy. *Imago* 21, 489–97. (Also in G. Devereux (Ed.), *Psychoanalysis and the occult.* New York: International Universities Press, 1953.)

Servadio, E. (1955). A presumptively telepathic-precognitive dream during analysis. *International Journal of Psychoanalysis* 36, 27–30.

Sheargold, R. K. (1972). An experiment in precognition. *Journal of the Society for Psychical Research* 46, 201–208.

Shedler, J. (2010). The efficacy of psychodynamic psychotherapy. *American Psychologist* 65, 98–109.

Sheldrake, R. (1998). The sense of being stared at: Experiments in schools. *Journal of the Society for Psychical Research* 62, 311–23.

Sheldrake, R. (1999). The "sense of being stared at" confirmed by simple experiments. *Biology Forum* 92, 53–76.

Sheldrake, R. (2000). The "sense of being stared at" does not depend on known sensory clues. *Biology Forum* 93, 209–24.

Sheldrake, R. (2001a). Experiments on the sense of being stared at: The elimination of possible artifacts. *Journal of the Society for Psychical Research* 65, 122–37.

Sheldrake, R. (2001b). Research on the sense of being stared at. *Skeptical Inquirer,* March/April, 58–61.

Sheldrake, R. (2002). The sense of being stared at: An experiment at Holma College. *Gränsoverskridaren* 10, 21–23.

Sheldrake, R. (2003). *The sense of being stared at, and other aspects of the extended mind.* London: Hutchinson.

Sheldrake, R. (2005). The sense of being stared at part 1: Is it real or illusory? *Journal of Consciousness Studies* 12, 10–31.

Sherwood, S. J., Dalton, K., Steinkamp, F., and Watt, C. (2000). Dream clairvoyance study II using dynamic video-clips: Investigation of consensus voting judging procedures and target emotionality. *Dreaming* 10, 221–36.

Sherwood, S. J., and Roe, C. (2003). A review of dream ESP studies conducted since the Maimonides dream ESP studies. *Journal of Consciousness Studies* 10, 85–109.

Sherwood, S. J., Roe, C., Simmonds, C. A., and Biles, C. (2002). An exploratory investigation of dream precognition using consensus judging and static targets. *Journal of the Society for Psychical Research* 66, 22–28.

Shevrin, H. (1988). Unconscious conflict: A convergent psychodynamic and electrophysiological approach. In M. Horowitz (Ed.), *Psychodynamics and cognition* (pp. 117–67). Chicago: University of Chicago Press.

Shevrin, H. (2001). Event-related markers of unconscious processes. *International Journal of Psychophysiology* 42, 209–18.

Shevrin, H., Bond, J. A., Brakel, L. A., Hertel, R. K., and Williams, W. J. (1996). *Conscious and unconscious processes.* New York: Guilford Press.

Shrager, E. F. (1978). The effect of sender-receiver relationship and associated personality variables on ESP scoring in young children. *Journal of the American Society for Psychical Research* 72, 35–47.

Siegel, P., and Weinberger, J. (1998). Capturing the "mommy and I are one" merger fantasy: The oneness motive. In R. F. Bornstein and J. M. Masling (Ed.), *Empirical perspectives on the psychoanalytic unconscious*. Washington, DC: American Psychological Association.

Sigstedt, C. O. (1952). *The Swedenborg epic: The life and works of Emanuel Swedenborg*. New York: Bookman Associates.

Silberschatz, G., Fretter, P., and Curtis, J. (1986). How do interpretations influence the process of psychotherapy? *Journal of Consulting and Clinical Psychology* 54(5), 646–52.

Silverman, L. H. (1976). Psychoanalytic theory: The reports of my death are greatly exaggerated. *American Psychologist* 31, 621–37.

Silverman, L. H. (1983). The subliminal psychodynamic activation method: Overview and comprehensive listing of studies. In J. Masling (Ed.), *Empirical studies of psychoanalytic theories* (pp. 69–100). Hillsdale, NJ: Lawrence Erlbaum Associates.

Silverman, L. H., Lachman, F. M., and Milich, R. H. (1982). *The search for oneness*. New York: International Universities Press.

Simonton, D. K. (1999). Creativity and genius. In L. A. Pervin and O. P. John (Eds.), *Handbook of personality theory and research* (pp. 629–52). New York: Guilford Press.

Simonton, D. K. (1999). Creativity and genius. In E. F. Borgatta and W. W. Lambert (Eds.), *Handbook of personality theory and research* (pp. 900–42). New York: Guilford Press.

Sinclair, U. (1930). *Mental radio*. London: T. Werner Laurie.

Singer, J. L. (1995). *Repression and dissociation: Implications for personality theory, psychopathology, and health*. Chicago: University of Chicago Press.

Singer, J. L., and Bonanno, G. A. (1990). Personality and private experience: Individual variations in consciousness and in attention to subjective phenomena. In L. A. Pervin (Ed.), *Handbook of personality theory and research* (pp. 419–44). New York: Guilford Press.

Skibinsky, M. (1950). A comparison of names and symbols in a distance ESP test. *Journal of Parapsychology* 14, 140–56.

Sloman, S. A. (1996). The empirical case for two systems of reasoning. *Psychological Bulletin* 119, 3–22.

Smith, B. M., and Humphrey, B. M. (1946). Some personality characteristics related to ESP performance. *Journal of Parapsychology* 10, 269–89.

Smith, E. R., and DeCoster, J. (1999). Associative and rule-based processing: A connectionist interpretation of dual-process models. In S. Chaiken and Y. Trope (Eds.), *Dual process theories in social psychology*. New York: Guilford.

Smith, E. T. (1969). *Psychic people*. New York: Bantam Books.

Smith, P. (2005). *Reading the enemy's mind: Inside star gate: America's psychic espionage program*. New York: Forge Books.

Smythies, J. (2000). The theoretical basis of psi. *Journal of the Society for Psychical Research* 64, 242–44.

Snodgrass, M., Bernat, E., and Shevrin, H. (2004). Unconscious perception at the objective threshold exists. *Perception and Psychophysics* 66, 888–95.

Snodgrass, M., and Shevrin, H. (2006). Unconscious inhibition and facilitation at the objective detection threshold: Replicable and qualitatively different unconscious perceptual effects. *Cognition* 101, 43–79.

Snodgrass, M., Shevrin, H., and Kopka, M. (1993a). The mediation of intentional judgments by unconscious perceptions: The influences of task strategy, task preference, word meaning, and motivation. *Consciousness and Cognition* 2, 169–93.

Sohlberg, S., Billinghurst, A., and Nylen, S. (1998). Moderation of mood change after subliminal symbiotic stimulation: Four experiments contributing to the further demystification of Silverman's "mommy and I are one" findings. *Journal of Research in Personality* 32, 33–54.

Sohlberg, S., Samuelberg, P., Siden, Y., and Thorn, C. (1998). Let the healer beware: Two experiments suggesting conditions when the effects of Silverman's mommy and I are one phrase are negative. *Psychoanalytic Psychology* 15, 93–114.

Soldz, S., and Vaillant, G. E. (1999). The big five personality traits and the life course: A 45-year longitudinal study. *Journal of Research in Personality* 33, 208–32.

Solfvin, G. F., Kelly, E. F., and Burdick, D. S. (1978). Some new methods of analysis for preferential-ranking data. *Journal of the American Society for Psychical Research* 72, 93–110.

Solley, C. M., and Murphy, G. (1960). *Development of the perceptual world.* New York: Basic Books.

Sondow, N. (1979). Effects of associations and feedback on psi in the ganzfeld: Is there more than meets the judge's eye? *Journal of the American Society for Psychical Research* 73, 123–50.

Sondow, N. (1986a). The relationship between hypnotizability, creativity and psi in the ganzfeld. Unpublished doctoral dissertation, City College of the City University of New York.

Sondow, N. (1986b). Exploring hypnotizability, creativity, and psi: Conscious and unconscious components to psi success in the ganzfeld. In *Research in Parapsychology 1986: Abstracts and papers from the 29th Annual Convention of the Parapsychological Association.* Metuchen, NJ, and London: The Scarecrow Press, Inc.

Sondow, N. (1989). The decline of precognized events with the passage of time: Evidence from spontaneous dreams. *Journal of the American Society for Psychical Research* 82, 33–51.

Sondow, N., Braud, L., and Barker, P. (1981). Target qualities and affect measures in an exploratory psi ganzfeld. *Proceedings of the 24th Annual Convention of the Parapsychological Association.*

Spottiswood, S. J., and May, E. C. (2003). Skin conductance prestimulus response: Analyses, artifacts and a pilot study. *Journal of Scientific Exploration* 17(4), 617–41.

Srull, T. K., and Wyer, R. S. Jr. (1980). Category accessibility and social perception: Some implications for the study of person memory and interpersonal judgments. *Journal of Personality and Social Psychology* 38, 841–56.

Stafford, W. (1998). *Crossing unmarked snow: Further views on the writer's vocation.* Ann Arbor: University of Michigan Press.

Stanford, R. G. (1966a). The effect of restriction of calling upon run-score variance. *Journal of Parapsychology* 30, 161–71.

Stanford, R. G. (1966b). A study of the cause of low run-score variance. *Journal of Parapsychology* 30, 236–42.

Stanford, R. G. (1967). Response bias and the correctness of ESP responses. *Journal of Parapsychology* 31, 236–42.

Stanford, R. G. (1968). An effect of restricted spontaneity on ESP run scores. In J. B. Rhine and R. Brier (Eds.), *Parapsychology Today*. New York: Citadel.

Stanford, R. G. (1970). Extrasensory effects upon "memory." *Journal of the American Society for Psychical Research* 64, 161–86.

Stanford, R. G. (1973). Extrasensory effects upon associative processes in a directed free-response task. *Journal of the American Society for Psychical Research* 67, 147–90.

Stanford, R. G. (1974a). An experimentally testable model for spontaneous psi events. I. Extrasensory events. *Journal of the American Society for Psychical Research* 68, 34–57.

Stanford, R. G. (1974b). An experimentally testable model for spontaneous psi events. II. Psychokinetic events. *Journal of the American Society for Psychical Research* 68, 321–56.

Stanford, R. G. (1975). Response factors in extrasensory performance. *Journal of Communication* 25, 153–62.

Stanford, R. G. (1977). Conceptual frameworks of contemporary psi research. In B. B. Wolman (Ed.), *Handbook of parapsychology*. New York: Van Nostrand Reinhold.

Stanford, R. G. (1978). Toward reinterpreting psi events. *Journal of the American Society for Psychical Research* 72, 197–214.

Stanford, R. G. (1981). "Associative activation of the unconscious" vs. "visualization" as methods for influencing the PK target: A second study. *Journal of the American Society for Psychical Research* 75, 229–40.

Stanford, R. G. (1991). An experimentally testable model for spontaneous psi events: A review of related evidence and concepts from parapsychology and other sciences. In S. Krippner (Ed.), *Advances in parapsychological research, volume 6*. Jefferson, NC: McFarland and Co., Publishers.

Stanford, R. G. (1992). The experimental hypnosis-ESP literature: A review from the hypothesis-testing perspective. *Journal of Parapsychology* 56, 39–56.

Stanford, R. G., Frank, S., Kass, G., and Skoll, S. (1989). Ganzfeld as an ESP-favorable setting: I. Assessment of spontaneity, arousal and internal attention state through verbal transcript analysis. *Journal of Parapsychology*, 53, 1–42.

Stanford, R. G., and Kottoor, T. M. (1986). Disruption of attention and PK test performance [Abstract]. In D. W. Weiner and D. I. Radin (Eds.), *Research in parapsychology 1985* (pp. 21–24). Metuchen, NJ: Scarecrow Press.

Stanford, R. G., and Rust, P. (1977). Psi-mediated helping behavior: Experimental paradigm and initial results [Abstract]. In J. D. Morris, W. G. Roll, and R. L. Morris (Eds.), *Research in parapsychology 1976* (pp. 109–10). Metuchen, NJ: Scarecrow Press.

Stanford, R. G., and Schroeter, W. (1978). Extrasensory effects upon associative processes in a directed free-response task: An attempted replication and extension. In W. G. Roll (Ed.), *Research in parapsychology 1977*. Metuchen, NJ: Scarecrow Press, 52–64.

Stanford, R. G., and Stein, A. G. (1994). A meta-analysis of ESP studies contrasting hypnosis and a comparison condition. *Journal of Parapsychology* 58, 235–70.

Stanford, R. G., and Stio, A. (1976). A study of associated mediation in psi-mediated instrumental response. *Journal of the American Society for Psychical Research* 70, 55–64.

Stanford, R. G., Stio, A., O'Rourke, D., Barile, F., Wolyniec, J., Bianco, J., and Rumore, C. (1976). A study of motivational arousal and self–concept in psi–mediated instrumental response. *Journal of the American Society for Psychical Research* 70, 167–78.

Stanford, R. G., Zenhausern, R., Taylor, A., and Dwyer, M. A. (1975). Psychokinesis as psi-mediated instrumental response. *Journal of the American Society for Psychical Research* 69, 27–133.

Steilberg, B. J. (1975). "Conscious concentration" vs. "visualization" in PK tests. *Journal of Parapsychology* 39, 12–20.

Stein, M. (1968). Creativity. In R. J. Sternberg (Ed.), *Handbook of creativity* (pp. 3–15). Chicago: Rand McNally.

Steinkamp, M. (2005). Does precognition foresee the future? Series 4: A postal replication. *Journal of Parapsychology* 69, 341–51.

Sternberg, R. J., and Lubart, T. I. (1999). The concept of creativity: Prospects and paradigms. In R. J. Sternberg (Ed.), *Handbook of creativity* (pp. 3–15). Chicago: Rand McNally.

Stevenson, I. (1970). *Telepathic impressions.* Charlottesville: University of Virginia Press.

Storm, L., Tressoldi, P. E., and Di Risio, L. (2010). Meta-analysis of free-response studies, 1992–2008: Assessing the noise reduction model in parapsychology. *Psychological Bulletin* 136, 471–85.

Stormark, K. M., Nordby, H., and Hugdahl, K. (1995). Attentional shifts to emotionally charged cues: Behavioral and ERP data. *Cognition and Emotion* 9, 507–23.

Stravinsky, I. (1942). *The poetics of music.* Cambridge, MA: Harvard University Press.

Stroop, J. R. (1935). Studies of interference in serial verbal reactions. *Journal of Experimental Psychology* 18, 643–62.

Stuart, C. E. (1946). GESP experiments with the free-response method. *Journal of Parapsychology* 10, 21–35.

Suls, J., and Wheeler, L. (2007). Psychological magnetism: A brief history of assimilation and contrast in psychology. In D. L. Stapel and J. Suls (Eds.), *Assimilation and contrast in social psychology* (pp. 9–44). New York: Psychology Press.

Sumner, P., Tsai, P-C., Yu, K. Nachev, P., and Purves, D. (2006). Attentional modulation of sensorimotor processes in the absence of perceptual awareness, *PNAS Proceedings of the National Academy of Sciences of the United States of America* 103, 10520–25.

Suslow, T., Konrad, C., Kugel, H., Rumstadt, D., Zwitserlood, P., Schöning, S., Ohrmann, P., Bauer, J., Pyka, M., Kersting, A., Arolt, V., Heindel, W., and Dannlowski, U. (2010). Automatic mood-congruent amygdala responses to masked facial expressions in major depression, *Biological Psychiatry* 67, 155–60.

Swann, I. (2000). *Everybody's guide to natural ESP: Unlocking the extrasensory power of your mind.* New York: Tarcher.

Swets, J. A., Tanner, W. P. Jr., and Birdsall, T. G. (1964). Decision processes in perception. In *Signal detection and recognition in human observers.* New York: Wiley.

Szczygielski, D., and Schmeidler, G. R. (1975). ESP and two measures of introversion [Abstract]. In J. D. Morris, W. G. Roll, and R. L. Morris (Eds.), *Research in parapsychology 1974* (pp. 15–17). Metuchen, NJ: Scarecrow Press.

Taddonio, J. L. (1976). The relationship of experimenter expectancy to performance on ESP tasks. *Journal of Parapsychology* 40, 107–14.

Taetzsch, R. (1958). Application of statistical quality control techniques to statistical psi control problems [Abstract]. *Journal of Parapsychology* 22, 304.

Taetzsch, R. (1962). Design of a psi communication system. *International Journal of Parapsychology* 4, 35–70.

Talbot, N., Duberstein, P., and Scott, P. (1991). Subliminal psychodynamic activation, food consumption and self-confidence. *Journal of Clinical Psychology* 47, 813–23.

Tanous, A. and Ardman, H. (1976). *Beyond coincidence.* New York: Doubleday.

Targ, R. E. (1988). ESP on Wall Street. *Explorer* 4(2), 1–2.

Targ, R. E. (1993). A decade of remote–viewing research. In B. Kane, J. Millay, and D. H. Brown (Eds.), *Silver threads: 25 years of parapsychology research.* Westport, CT: Praeger Publishers.

Targ, R. E. (2004). *Limitless mind.* Novato, CA: New World Library.

Targ, R. E., and Puthoff, H. (1977). *Mind reach: Scientists look at psychic abilities.* New York: Delacourt.

Tart, C. T. (1963). Physiological correlates of psi cognition. *International Journal of Parapsychology* 5, 375–86.

Tart, C. T. (1976). *Learning to use extrasensory perception.* Chicago: University of Chicago Press.

Tart, C. T. (1984). Acknowledging and dealing with the fear of psi. *Journal of the American Society for Psychical Research* 78, 133–43.

Tart, C. T. (2007). "The decline effect in spontaneous and experimental psychical research": Comment. *Journal of the Society for Psychical Research* 71, 114–17.

Tart, C. T., and Boisen, M. (1972). Some studies of psychokinesis with a spinning silver coin. *Journal of the Society for Psychical Research* 46, 143–53.

Tart, C. T., and LaBore, C. M. (1986). Attitudes toward strongly functioning psi: A preliminary study. *Journal of the American Society for Psychical Research* 80, 163–73.

Tchaikovsky, P. I. (1906). *Life and letters of Peter Ilich Tchaikovsky* (Ed. R. Newmarch). London: John Lane.

Tenhaeff, W. H. C. (1953). *Telepathy and clairvoyance: Views of some little investigated capabilities of man.* New York: Charles Thomas.

Terry, J. C., and Honorton, C. (1967). Psi information retrieval in the ganzfeld: Two confirmatory studies. *Journal of the American Society for Psychical Research* 70, 207–17.

Thalbourne, M. A., and Jungkuntz, J. H. (1983). Extraverted sheep vs. introverted goats: Experiments VII and VIII. *Journal of Parapsychology* 47, 49–51.

Thayer, R. E. (1971). Personality and discrepancies between verbal reports and physiological measures of private emotional experiences. *Journal of Personality* 39, 57–69.

Thorne, A. (1987). The press of personality: A study of conversations between introverts and extraverts. *Journal of Personality and Social Psychology* 53, 718–26.

Thorne, A., and Gough, H. (1991). *Portraits of type: An MBTI research compendium.* Palo Alto, CA: Consulting Psychologists Press.

Thouless, R. H. (1945). Some experiments on PK effects in coin spinning. *Proceedings of the Society for Psychical Research* 47, 277–81.

Thouless, R. H. (1949). A comparative study of performance in three psi tasks. *Journal of Parapsychology* 13, 263–73.

Thouless, R. H. (1949–1952). A report on an experiment in psychokinesis with dice and a discussion of psychological factors favoring success. *Proceedings of the Society for Psychical Research* 49, 107–30.

Thouless, R. H. (1951). A report on an experiment in psycho-kinesis with dice, and a discussion on psychological factors favouring success. *Proceedings of the Society for Psychical Research* 49, 107–30.

Thouless, R. H. (1960). The repeated guessing technique. *International Journal of Parapsychology* 2, 21–36.

Thouless, R. H. (1972). *From anecdote to experiment in psychical research.* London: Routledge and Kegan Paul.

Thouless, R. H. and Wiesner, B. P. (1946). On the nature of psi phenomena. *Journal of Parapsychology* 10, 107–19.

Tipper, S. P. (2001). Does negative priming reflect inhibitory mechanisms? A review and integration of conflicting views. *Quarterly Journal of Experimental Psychology A: Human Experimental Psychology* 54A, 321–43.

Titchener, E. B. (1898). The feeling of being stared at. *Science* (New Series) 308, 895–97.

Tornatore, R. P. (1984). The use of fantasy in a children's ESP experiment [Abstract]. In R. A. White and R. S. Broughton (Eds.), *Research in parapsychology 1983* (pp. 102–03). Metuchen, NJ: Scarecrow Press.

Torrance, E. P. (1962). *Guiding creative talent.* Englewood Cliffs, NJ: Prentice.

Torrance, E. P. (1972). Some validity studies of two brief screening devices for studying the creative personality. *Journal of Creative Behavior* 5, 94–103.

Torrance, E. P. (1972). Creativity testing in education. *Creative Child and Adult Quarterly*, 1, 136–48.

Trapmann, S., Hell, B., Hirn, J. W., and Schuler, H. (2007). Meta-analysis of the relationship between the Big Five and academic success at university. *Zeitschrift für Psychologie/Journal of Psychology* 215, 132–51.

Treffinger, D. J. (1985). Research on creativity assessment. In S. Isaksen (Ed.), *Frontiers of creativity research: Beyond the basics* (pp. 103–19). Buffalo, NY: Bearly Limited.

Tressoldi, P. E., Martinelli, M., Zaccaria, E., and Massaccesi, S. (2009). Implicit intuition: How heart rate can contribute to prediction of future events. *Journal of the Society for Psychical Research* 73, 1–16.

Tsu, Lao (1996). *Tao Te Ching.* J. H. McDonald, trans. West Valley City, UT: Waking Lion Press.

Tversky, A., and Kahneman, D. (1974, September). Judgment under uncertainty: Heuristics and biases. *Science* 185, 1124–30.

Uleman, J. S., and Bargh, J. A. (Eds.). (1989). *Unintended thought.* New York: Guilford Press.

Ullman, M. (1949). The nature of psi processes. *Journal of Parapsychology* 13, 59–62.

Ullman, M. (1959). On the occurrence of telepathic dreams. *Journal of the American Society for Psychical Research* 53, 50–61.

Ullman, M. (1975). Parapsychology and psychiatry. In A. M. Freeman, H. I. Kaplan, and B. J. Saddock (Eds.), *Comprehensive textbook of psychiatry, 2nd ed.,* Vol. 2, pp. 2552–61. Baltimore: Williams and Wilkins.

Ullman, M., and Krippner, S. (1974). *Dream telepathy.* Baltimore: Penguin.

Utts, J. M. (1996). An assessment of the evidence for psychic functioning. *Journal of Scientific Exploration* 10, 3–30.

van Busschbach, J. G. (1959). An investigation of ESP in the first and second grades of Dutch schools. *Journal of Parapsychology* 23, 227–37.

Van de Castle, R. L. (1977). Sleep and dreams. In B. B. Wolman (Ed.), *Handbook of parapsychology* (pp. 473–99). Jefferson, NC: McFarland.

Van de Castle, R. L. (1989). Psi manifestations in multiple personality disorder. In L. Coly and J. McMahon (Eds.), *Psi and clinical practice.* New York: Parapsychology Foundation, Inc.

Vaughn, A. (1973). *Patterns of prophecy.* New York: Hawthorne Press.

Verney, S. P., Granholm, E., and Marshall, S. P. (2003). Pupillary responses on the visual backward masking task reflect general cognitive ability. *International Journal of Psychophysiology* 52, 23–36.

von Franz, M. L. (1980). *On divination and synchronicity: The psychology of meaningful chance.* Toronto, Canada: Inner City Books.

von Lucadou, W. (1995). The model of pragmatic information (MPI). *European Journal of Parapsychology* 11, 58–75.

von Lucadou, W. (2000). Hans in luck: The currency of evidence in parapsychology. *Journal of Parapsychology* 65, 3–16.

von Lucadou, W., Römer, H., and Walach, M. (2007). Synchronistic phenomena as entanglement correlations in generalized quantum theory. *Journal of Consciousness Studies* 14, 15–74.

Walach, M., Schmidt, S., Schneider, R., Seiter, C., and Boesch, H. (2002). Melting boundaries: Subjectivity and intersubjectivity in the light of parapsychological data. *European Journal of Parapsychology* 17, 72–96.

Walker, E. H. (1975). Foundations of parapsychological phenomena. In L. Oteri (Ed.), *Quantum physics and parapsychology.* New York: Parapsychology Foundation.

Wallach, M., & Kogan, N. (1965). Modes of thinking in young children. New York: Holt, Rinehart, & Winston.

Wallas, G. (1926). *The art of thought.* New York: Harcourt, Brace and Co.

Walter, C., Hilsenroth, M., Arsenault, L., Sloan, P., and Harvill, L. (1998). Use of the Hand Test in the assessment of combat-related stress. *Journal of Personality Assessment* 70, 315–23.

Watkins, G. K., Watkins, A. M., and Wells, R. A. (1973). Further studies on the resuscitation of anesthetized mice. In W. G. Roll, R. L. Morris, and J. D. Morris (Eds.), *Research in parapsychology 1972* (pp. 157–59). Metuchen, NJ: Scarecrow Press.

Watson, D., and Friend, R. (1969). Measurement of social-evaluative anxiety, *Journal of Consulting and Clinical Psychology* 33, 448–57.

Watt, C. A. (1991). Meta-analysis of DMT-ESP studies and an experimental investigation of perceptual defence/vigilance and extrasensory perception. In Proceedings of Presented Papers, 34th Annual Convention of the Parapsychological Association, Petaluma, CA. Parapsychological Association, Heidelberg, 8–11.

Watt, C. A. (1993). Perceptual defense/vigilance and extrasensory perception: A successful replication study and a comparison of explicit and implicit measures. In Proceedings of Presented Papers, 36th Annual Convention of the Parapsychological Association, Petaluma, CA. Parapsychological Association, Toronto, 15–19.

Watt, C. A. (1996). Knowing the unknown: Participants' insight in three forced-choice ESP studies. *Journal of the American Society for Psychical Research* 90, 97–114.

Watt, C. A. (2007). A peek in the file–drawer: Review of 96 undergraduate student projects at the Koestler Parapsychology Unit. In Proceedings of Presented Papers, 50th Annual Convention of the Parapsychological Association, Petaluma, CA. Parapsychological Association, Columbus, OH, 133–42.

Watt, C. A., and Baker, I. S. (2002). Remote facilitation of attention focusing with psi-supportive versus psi-unsupportive experimenter suggestions. *Journal of Parapsychology* 66, 151–68.

Watt, C. A., and Brady, C. (2002). Experimenter effects and the remote facilitation of attention focusing: Two studies and the discovery of an artifact. *Journal of Parapsychology* 66, 49–71.

Watt, C. A., and Morris, R. L. (1995). The relationships among performance on a prototype indicator of perceptual defence/vigilance, personality and extrasensory perception. *Personality and Individual Differences* 19, 635–48.

Watt, C. A., and Ramakers, P. (2003). Experimenter effects with a remote facilitation of attention focusing task: A study with multiple believer and disbeliever experimenters. *Journal of Parapsychology* 67, 99–116.

Watt, C. A., and Ravenscroft, J. (1999). Defensiveness, neuroticism and extrasensory perception. *Journal of the American Society for Psychical Research* 93, 341–54.

Watt, C. A., and Ravenscroft, J. (2000). A study of non-intentional psi in a helping task. *Journal of Parapsychology* 64, 19–32.

Weber, E. H. (1834 [1978]). De subtilitate tactus. In H. E. Ross and D. J. Murray, (Trans.). *E. H. Weber: The sense of touch.* London: Academic Press.

Wegener, D. T., and Petty, R. E. (1995). Flexible correction processes in social judgment: The role of naive theories in corrections for perceived bias. *Journal of Personality and Social Psychology* 68, 36–51.

Weinberger, J. (2000). William James and the unconscious: Redressing a century-old misunderstanding. *Psychological Science* 11, 439.

Weinberger, J., and Hardaway, R. (1990). Separating science from myth in subliminal psychodynamic activation. *Clinical Psychology Review* 10, 727–56.

Weinberger, J., Kelner, S., and McClelland, D. (1997). The effects of subliminal symbiotic stimulation on free-response and self-report mood. *Journal of Nervous and Mental Disease* 185, 599–605.

Weinberger, J., Siegel, P., and Decamello, A. (2000). On integrating psychoanalysis and cognitive science. *Psychoanalysis and Contemporary Thought* 23, 147–75.

Weinberger, J., and Westen, D. (2008). RATS, we should have used Clinton: Subliminal priming in political campaigns. *Political Psychology* 29, 631–51.

Weiner, D. H. (1986). Stalking the variable subject: A test of some predictions of scoring magnitude. In D. H. Weiner and D. I. Radin (Eds.), *Research in parapsychology 1985* (pp. 54–58). Metuchen, NJ: Scarecrow Press.

Weiner, D. H., and Haight, J. (1980). Psi within a test of memory: A partial replication. In W. G. Roll (Ed.), *Research in parapsychology 1979* (pp. 52–53). Metuchen, NJ: Scarecrow Press.

Weiss, J. (1993). *How psychotherapy works.* New York: The Guilford Press.

Welsh, G. H. (1981). Personality assessment with origence/intellectence scales. *Academic Psychology Bulletin* 3, 299–307.

Welsh, G. H. (1987). *Manual for the Barron-Welsh art scale.* Redwood City, CA: Mindgarden.

Werner, H. (1935). Studies in contour. *American Journal of Psychology* 64, 40–64.

Werner, H. (1956). Microgenesis and aphasia. *Journal of Abnormal and Social Psychology* 52, 347–53.

Wexler, B. E., and Cicchetti, D. V. (1992). The outpatient treatment of depression: Implications of outcome research for clinical practice. *Journal of Nervous and Mental Disease* 180(5), 277–86.

White, R. A. (1964). A comparison of old and new methods of response to targets in ESP experiments. *Journal of the American Society for Psychical Research* 58, 21–56.

White, R. A. (1997). Dissociation, narrative, and exceptional human experiences. In S. Krippner and S. P. Powers (Eds.), *Broken images, broken selves: Dissociative narratives in clinical practice.* Philadelphia: Bruner/Mazel.

White, R. A. (2002). The narrative is the thing: The story of "necessary spirit" and psi. *Journal of the American Society for Psychical Research* 96, 121–42.

Whiteman, J. H. M. (1977). Parapsychology and physics. In B. Wolman (Ed.), *Handbook of parapsychology* (pp. 730–56). New York: Van Nostrand Reinhold.

Whitman, W. (1900). *Leaves of grass.* Philadelphia: David McKay.

Whittlesey, J. R. B. (1960). Some curious ESP results in terms of variance. *Journal of Parapsychology* 24, 220–22.

Wiggins, J. S. (1989). Review of the Myers-Briggs Type Indicator. In J. C. Conoley and J. J. Kramer (Eds.). *The tenth mental measurements yearbook.* (pp. 537–38). Lincoln, NB: The University of Nebraska Press.

Wildey, C. (2001). *Impulse response of biological systems.* Master's thesis, Department of Electrical Engineering, University of Texas at Arlington.

William, C. T. (2003). *Mere exposure effects for affectively valenced stimuli.* Ann Arbor: Dissertation Abstracts International.

Williams, J. M. G., Watts, F. N., MacLeod, C., and Matthews, A. (1997). *Cognitive psychology and emotional disorders.* Chichester, England: Wiley.

Williams, L. (1983). Minimal cue perception of the regard of others: The feeling of being stared at. *Journal of Parapsychology* 47, 59–60.

Williams, L. B., and Duke, D. M. (1980). Qualities of free-response targets and their relationship to psi performance. In W. G. Roll (Ed.), *Research in parapsychology 1979* (pp. 74–77). Metuchen, NJ: Scarecrow Press.

Wilson, T. D., Lisle, D., Schooler, J. W., Hodges, S. D., Klaaren, K. J., and LaFleur, S. J. (1993). Introspecting about reasons can reduce post-choice satisfaction. *Personality and Social Psychology Bulletin* 19, 331–39.

Wiseman, R., and Milton, J. (1998). Experiment one of the SAIC remote viewing program: A critical re-evaluation. *Journal of Parapsychology* 62, 297–308.

Wiseman, R., and Schlitz, M. (1997). Experimenter effects and the remote detection of staring. *Journal of Parapsychology* 61, 197–207.

Wiseman, R., and Schlitz, M. (1999, August 4–8). Replication of experimenter effect and the remote detection of staring. Paper presented at the 43rd Annual Convention of the Parapsychological Association, Palo Alto, CA.

Wiseman, R., and Smith, M. (1994). A further look at the detection of unseen gaze. Proceedings of Presented Papers, 37th Annual Parapsychological Association Convention. Amsterdam, the Netherlands: Parapsychological Association, 465–78.

Wiseman, R., Smith, M., Freedman, D., Wasserman, T., and Hurst, C. (1995). Examining the remote staring effect: Two further experiments. Proceedings of Presented Papers, 38th Annual Parapsychological Association Convention. Durham, NC: Parapsychological Association, 480–90.

Woolf, V. (1987). *The letters of Virginia Wolf, Vol. V.* N. Nicholson and J. Troutman, eds. New York: Mariner Books.

Wright, J. C., and Mischel, W. (1987). A conditional approach to dispositional constructs: The local predictability of social behavior. *Journal of Personality and Social Psychology* 53, 1159–77.

Young, S. G., and Claypool, H. M. (2010). Mere exposure has differential effects on attention allocation to threatening and neutral stimuli. *Journal of Experimental Social Psychology* 46, 424–27.

Zajonc, R. B. (1968). Attitudinal effects of mere exposure. *Journal of Personality and Social Psychology* 9, Monograph supplement No. 2, Part 2.

Zajonc, R. B. (2008). Feeling and thinking: Preferences need no inferences. In R. H. Fazio and R. E. Petty (Eds.), *Attitudes: Their structure, function, and consequences* (pp. 143–68). New York: Psychology Press.

Zakay, D., Lomranz, J., and Kaziniz, M. (1984). Extraversion–introversion and time perception. *Personality and Individual Differences* 5, 237–39.

Zeigarnik, B. (1927 [1967]). On finished and unfinished tasks. In W. D. Ellis (Ed.), *A sourcebook of Gestalt psychology* (pp. 300–14). New York: Humanities Press. (Originally published as *Das Behalten erledigter und unerledigter Handlungen*, Psychologische Forschung 9, 1–85.)

Zingrone, N. L. (1994). Images of women as mediums: Power, pathology and passivity in the writings of Frederic Marvin and Cesare Lombroso. In L. Coly and R. A. White (Ed.), *Women and parapsychology* (pp. 90–121). New York: Parapsychology Foundation.

Zingrone, N. L., Alvarado, C. S., and Dalton, K. (1998–1999). Psi experiences and the big five: Relating the NEO-PI-R to the experience claims of experimental subjects. *European Journal of Parapsychology* 14, 31–51.

Zorab, G. (1957). ESP experiments with psychotics. *Journal of the American Society for Psychical Research* 39, 162–64.

Index

Aarts, Henk, 369–70
activation: cortical, or introverts and
    extraverts, 253; of affective responses
    by weighting, 51; of amygdale,
    27; of apprehensive network, 51;
    of goals, 369–70; spreading, 160;
    subliminal psychodynamic, 395–40;
    unconscious, 15, 60
Adjective Check List, 170
adventurousness: importance of, 318
afferent extrasomatic prehension (A-
    ESP), 90, 287. *See also* psychokinesis
afferent psi, 178, 89–90, 287
agency, 44, 114, 100, 158, 403
Alexander, Cheryl, 284
Alternate Uses test, 175
Alvarez, F., 200
Anderson, Margaret, 180, 183, 284,
    291–92 Angyal, Andras, 7
anticipation corollary, 20–21
Antonuccio, D. O., 365n1
anxiety: and cognitive work, 213;
    and extraversion, 255–56, 273;
    at psi success and failure, 297,
    299–300; build up over success,
    299; conscious and psi, 218–22;
    defenses against, 198, 213,
    230–41; disorders, 190; effect of

experimenter upon, 290; effects on
    memory, 144; effects on psi, 65–66,
    316–17; effects on subliminal
    perception, 191–96; *freedom* from,
    118; function of situation, 197,
    223–24, 242, 263–64, 344; implicit
    measurement of, 220, 253n53;
    moderating relation between
    creativity and psi, 179, 184; mood
    measurement of freedom from, 390;
    need to avoid danger and awareness,
    190–242; optimal level of, 169; over
    success, 297, 299; personal fear of
    psi, 338; relation to inhibition of
    memory, 144; subliminal reduction
    of, 128–29; vulnerability to, 201–2,
    204, 224–29, 318. *See* fear
Ashton, M. L., 256–57
assimilation and contrast: basic
    expectation of First Sight in regard
    to, 138–39; effects of motivation
    to be original, 177; function of
    intention, 24–27, 256; guided by
    congruence with closure, 27; in
    person perception, 280; origin of
    concern in parapsychology with
    scoring extremity, 72n3; relation
    of turning toward or away from,

467

About the Author

Dr. Jim Carpenter is both a clinical psychologist and a research parapsychologist. He is a diplomate in clinical psychology, American Board of Professional Psychology; a fellow in the American Academy of Clinical Psychology; and a clinical associate professor in the Department of Psychiatry of the University of North Carolina School of Medicine. He served two terms on the board of directors of the American Academy of Clinical Psychology and carries on an active private practice

Dr. Carpenter has been active in parapsychological research since he came to Duke University as an undergraduate in order to meet and work with Dr. J. B. Rhine who founded the Parapysychology Laboratory there. His research has continued since then, with over one hundred research articles, book chapters, and other articles. He has been president of the Board of the Rhine Research Center and has served on the Board of Directors of the Parapsychology Association. For many years he has also provided pro bono clinical consultation for persons who approach the Rhine Center for help with unpleasant experiences that they think of as psychic.